This Book is   the Property of

John H. MacGregor

THE BEST PLAYS OF 1950–1951

EDITED BY

BURNS MANTLE

THE BEST PLAYS OF 1899-1909
(*With Garrison P. Sherwood*)
THE BEST PLAYS OF 1909-19
(*With Garrison P. Sherwood*)
THE BEST PLAYS OF 1919-20
THE BEST PLAYS OF 1920-21
THE BEST PLAYS OF 1921-22
THE BEST PLAYS OF 1922-23
THE BEST PLAYS OF 1923-24
THE BEST PLAYS OF 1924-25
THE BEST PLAYS OF 1925-26
THE BEST PLAYS OF 1926-27
THE BEST PLAYS OF 1927-28
THE BEST PLAYS OF 1928-29
THE BEST PLAYS OF 1929-30
THE BEST PLAYS OF 1930-31
THE BEST PLAYS OF 1931-32
THE BEST PLAYS OF 1932-33
THE BEST PLAYS OF 1933-34
THE BEST PLAYS OF 1934-35
THE BEST PLAYS OF 1935-36
THE BEST PLAYS OF 1936-37
THE BEST PLAYS OF 1937-38
THE BEST PLAYS OF 1938-39
THE BEST PLAYS OF 1939-40
THE BEST PLAYS OF 1940-41
THE BEST PLAYS OF 1941-42
THE BEST PLAYS OF 1942-43
THE BEST PLAYS OF 1943-44
THE BEST PLAYS OF 1944-45
THE BEST PLAYS OF 1945-46
THE BEST PLAYS OF 1946-47
CONTEMPORARY AMERICAN PLAYWRIGHTS (1938)

EDITED BY

JOHN CHAPMAN

THE BURNS MANTLE BEST PLAYS OF 1947-48
THE BURNS MANTLE BEST PLAYS OF 1948-49
THE BURNS MANTLE BEST PLAYS OF 1949-50
THE BEST PLAYS OF 1950-51

INDEX TO THE BEST PLAYS SERIES, 1899-1950

THE BEST PLAYS
OF 1950–1951

AND THE
YEAR BOOK OF THE DRAMA
IN AMERICA

EDITED BY
JOHN CHAPMAN

With Illustrations

DODD, MEAD AND COMPANY
NEW YORK   -   -   -   TORONTO
1951

INTRODUCTION

THIS volume, thirty-fourth in the series of New York theatrical records begun by Burns Mantle, is the record of the first year in the second half of the Twentieth Century. One cannot even speculate, let alone predict, what will have happened between now and the season of 1999-2000. The only prediction I can make with safety is that I won't be here when 'Ninety-Nine–Two Thousand rolls around. Some other editor will be maintaining the record for this book.

What great plays are in store for us? What great dramatists? What actors and actresses? What changes of method, of approach, of technique will the theatre make? For, be assured, there *will* be a theatre, since play-acting and play-going are instinctive with human beings. If the next forty-nine years are as good to us as were the preceding fifty-one, we will see exciting changes. The American theatre had only begun to grow in 1900, and it has grown to a position of world eminence, while the once-dominant European theatre has suffered a decline. But we must not look toward the future with any great amount of confidence, for the American theatre, too, has been in a decline during all the recent years. This decline has been both economic and artistic. Inflation has caused the economic decline, and few people in the nation can afford to be regular theatregoers any more. Artistically, the last decade has been less exciting than the period of 1920-1930, which found and developed the most important group of American dramatists we have yet known. In these days good new dramatists are hard to come by—an Arthur Miller one year, a Tennessee Williams the next, and that's about all. It is the veterans who are keeping the stage as alive as it may be. These veterans would, I think, like to turn the stage over to younger men and women—but where are the young ones capable of taking the job? A few years ago I thought the young ones would be emerging from the colleges, for hundreds of colleges and universities now have theatre departments of one kind or other. But, so far, the colleges have missed the boat; they seem to be teaching scenepainting, directing and acting at a furious rate, but if they are also teaching playwriting it is not noticeable on Broadway. Apparently there are no George Pierce Bakers, no Brander Matthewses, on today's college teaching staffs.

v

Sooner or later the wheel will come full circle and we shall have another exciting, creative decade or two on Broadway. Perhaps it will start this year, or next—but perhaps not. I wish it would start soon, for I'd like to be in on it. At the moment we are doing as well as anybody else—but we should be doing better.

JOHN CHAPMAN

Westport, Connecticut, July, 1951

CONTENTS

	PAGE
INTRODUCTION	V
THE SEASON IN NEW YORK	3
THE SEASON IN BOSTON	13
THE SEASON IN PHILADELPHIA	26
THE SEASON IN CHICAGO	31
THE SEASON IN SAN FRANCISCO	34
THE SEASON IN SOUTHERN CALIFORNIA	38
GUYS AND DOLLS, BY DAMON RUNYON	45
DARKNESS AT NOON, BY SIDNEY KINGSLEY	72
BILLY BUDD, BY LOUIS O. COXE AND ROBERT CHAPMAN	100
THE AUTUMN GARDEN, BY LILLIAN HELLMAN	125
BELL, BOOK AND CANDLE, BY JOHN VAN DRUTEN	155
THE COUNTRY GIRL, BY CLIFFORD ODETS	178
THE ROSE TATTOO, BY TENNESSEE WILLIAMS	210
SEASON IN THE SUN, BY WOLCOTT GIBBS	237
AFFAIRS OF STATE, BY LOUIS VERNEUIL	259
SECOND THRESHOLD, BY PHILIP BARRY	283
THE PLAYS AND THEIR AUTHORS	304
PLAYS PRODUCED IN NEW YORK	308
OFF BROADWAY	373
STATISTICAL SUMMARY	376
LONG RUNS ON BROADWAY	377
NEW YORK DRAMA CRITICS CIRCLE AWARDS	379

PAGE

PULITZER PRIZE WINNERS 380

PREVIOUS VOLUMES OF BEST PLAYS 382

WHERE AND WHEN THEY WERE BORN 394

NECROLOGY 402

THE DECADES' TOLL 410

INDEX OF AUTHORS 413

INDEX OF PLAYS AND CASTS 418

INDEX OF PRODUCERS, DIRECTORS AND DESIGNERS . . . 425

ILLUSTRATIONS

Following page 86

GUYS AND DOLLS
DARKNESS AT NOON
BILLY BUDD
THE AUTUMN GARDEN
BELL, BOOK AND CANDLE
THE COUNTRY GIRL
THE ROSE TATTOO
SEASON IN THE SUN
AFFAIRS OF STATE
SECOND THRESHOLD

THE BEST PLAYS OF 1950–1951

THE BEST PLAYS OF 1950–1951

THE SEASON IN NEW YORK

THE year 1950-1951 on Broadway, running from June to June, was a good one so far as averages went, but it is not likely to distinguish itself in theatrical histories as anything in particular—unless it becomes known as the Year of Adaptations. There were more productions than there had been the previous year, and there was the usual quota of great hits which sold out for six months or more ahead. The highs were not as high as, say, "Death of a Salesman" or "The Glass Menagerie," and not nearly as high as "The Iceman Cometh." The lows were as low as possible, but happily there were few of them—and these were merely inept and stupid, not foul. The average was generally good, so that an editor bent upon choosing the Ten Best Plays could name his ten with a clear conscience and have a few deserving candidates left over.

There were eighty-seven professional commercial productions—thirty-nine new plays, fourteen new musicals, twenty-six play revivals and eight musical revivals. But, as the season progressed, it struck me that nearly everything was based on something else. The Critics Circle voted Sidney Kingsley's "Darkness at Noon" the best play of the season—and it was based on a novel by Arthur Koestler. The Circle voted "Guys and Dolls" the best musical—and this engaging entertainment, although it sparkled with the originality of its writers, was based on one short story and several short story characters created by the late Damon Runyon. Even as original and individual a writer as Arthur Miller wasted his time making an adaptation of Ibsen's "An Enemy of the People." Five of the principal new musicals of the season were based on the work of some other original writer, including an ancient Greek, and six of the new plays were adaptations. Statistically, this score does not look alarming, but it becomes alarming when some of the theatre's best original writers use somebody else's work as a crutch. Rodgers and Hammerstein adapt "Anna and the King of Siam" into one of the season's great hits, "The King and I"; George Abbott, with the help of the original author, adapts "A Tree Grows in Brooklyn" for another musical hit; Paul Green messes around with Ibsen's "Peer Gynt"; Preston Sturges, noted for his mad originality in

3

Hollywood, makes a pointless revision of an old Molnar comedy, "The Good Fairy," for the book of a musical, "Make a Wish." Theatrical business men explain that an adaptation of an old success, such as a best-selling novel, is insurance, particularly in the case of musicals. It is easier to get money from backers if the proposed show is based on something that has already proved itself a hit. The business of borrowing from a success usually is successful; indeed, it has resulted in some of our best dramas and entertainments; but it is a confession of weakness on the part of the theatre itself and is thus a source of worry to many observers, including myself.

The season was somewhat distinguished by the formation of the Council of the Living Theatre, headed by Robert E. Sherwood, and by the acquisition of the old Guild Theatre by the American National Theatre and Academy, where this high-minded organization of torchbearers presented a series of ten productions of erratic artistic merit. In January, 1751, one is told, the first commercial playhouse in New York was made from a couple of warehouses in Nassau St.; so it was deemed opportune to dedicate the year 1951 as the bicentennial of the New York stage—and, by implication, the American theatre. The League of New York Theatres made available a fund for this celebration and the Council of the Living Theatre dedicated itself to arousing national interest in round actors. By June, no great results were noticeable; as you will note in reports from other cities in this volume, the country at large may have been interested in the living theatre but it wasn't getting much of it.

Also concerned over the wellbeing of the stage—and quite properly, because their own wellbeing is directly involved—the Association of Theatrical Press Agents and Managers named a committee to draw up a report on the state of the stage in the union, with recommendations. The report led off with the direful statement that fewer than two percent of the people in the United States attend legitimate theatre performances, and fewer than one percent of these are under 25 years of age. The recommendations of the committee, though many and detailed, boil down to the simple exhortation, "Let's persuade more people to go to the theatre." Amen! My own alarm at the ATPAM statistics grows from the statement that so few of our youth attend the theatre. I do not think it is from lack of interest, but from lack of funds. The true stage addict should be caught and trained in his formative years, but with ticket prices as high as they are the youngster can't afford to go to a play very often, if ever. Youthful interest in the living stage is enormous and intelligent—and if you have ever been to a performance at the New York City Center of Music and Drama you will know the truth of this statement. The City Center, which offers good productions—and some great ones—at the lowest prices in town, has an enormous audience of teen-agers and men and women in their early twenties; and this audience is, I think, the best in New York.

In spite of statistics, the theatre keeps going. The 1950-1951 season began in June with a revival of "The Madwoman of Chaillot" at the City Center and had its first excitement with the opening of Michael Todd's "Peep Show" in July. Mr. Todd, self-confessed showman, had been pondering the state of the stage and had come to the conclusion that musicals have become too serious and artistic. He determined to turn back the clock a quarter century and offer, for bald-heads, conventioneers and other valued customers an old-fashioned revue with nothing in it but dames and jokes. The day after "Peep Show" opened the city commissioner of licenses invited Mr. Todd down town for a chat and suggested that some of the jokes be purified and that some of the dames be persuaded to be less feminine. Mr. Todd cheerfully complied, and "Peep Show" had a pretty good run of 278 performances—but not enough to pay for the producer's $300,000 experiment in turning back the clock. People kept right on going to "South Pacific," which is decorous and rather serious.

The season's first disappointment occurred in mid-August when Garson Kanin, whose "Born Yesterday" was so admirably written and staged, offered his newest work, "The Live Wire," under the auspices of Mr. Todd. This comedy, about some hungry actors living in a Quonset hut, was considerably below Mr. Kanin's reputation and ability.

In mid-September the first of several British importations, "Daphne Laureola," arrived for only 56 performances. This comedy had a fine and amusing performance by Dame Edith Evans, but even Dame Edith was not strong enough to carry the show for long. The first big hit, Louis Verneuil's "Affairs of State," arrived on September 25. With engaging performances by Celeste Holm and Reginald Owen, it was a nice combination of Washington intrigue and nicely naughty French sex comedy. Late in the month another English star, Flora Robson, came over in another English play, Miss Lesley Storm's "Black Chiffon," and both had a moderate success. This was a psychoanalytical drama about a well-bred woman who turned shoplifter because she subconsciously wanted to prevent her son's marriage. Had it not been for Miss Robson's illness, it

might have had more than 109 performances. In the final offering
of September, a drama critic dared all by submitting a play he wrote
for the consideration of his colleagues. The critic, Wolcott Gibbs,
of *The New Yorker;* the play, based on a series of magazine sketches
about life on Fire Island, "Season in the Sun."   Some playgoers felt
that this comedy was too naughty or too loosely built, and accused
Gibbs' fellow critics of being too kind to him in their very good
notices. But the public in general agreed with the paid playgoers,
and "Season in the Sun" was still running at season's end.

The indefatigable but not entirely indestructible Ole Olsen and
Chic Johnson came to town in October with another revue, "Pardon
Our French," which they said would be different from their usual
boisterous entertainment because it was partly from the Folies
Bergère in Paris. It wasn't any different, except that a fine French
sample of exterior decoration, Denise Darcel, was on display. Mr.
Olsen was unable to participate in the show because of a broken
ankle, but partner Johnson succeeded in firing enough guns for both.
The boys withdrew after 100 performances. The next October event
was Aldous Huxley's interesting suspense play, "The Gioconda
Smile," with a bravura performance by Valerie Taylor. But it has
become evident during the last few seasons that New Yorkers no
longer will go along with the patient, careful, polite type of English
thriller, and "Smile" soon faded. James Gow and Arnaud d'Usseau,
whose first success was the worthy "Tomorrow the World," were
responsible for an unworthy comedy, "Legend of Sarah." Then,
on October 12, Russel Crouse and Howard Lindsay presented their
long-heralded "Call Me Madam," with music by Irving Berlin and
singing by Ethel Merman. This, at least, was an original work,
inasmuch as the authors denied that it was based on Mrs. Perle
Mesta, the party-giving diplomat. It was coincidence that Miss
Merman also was an ambassador and a great party-thrower. Some
of us, hoping for a musical satire as good as "Of Thee I Sing," were
disappointed in the fairly obvious plotting and gagging of "Call
Me Madam," but the musical was an enormous hit. John Steinbeck
was hurt rather badly, I think, by the critical reception of his odd
drama, "Burning Bright."   He had sought to make it a poetic
allegory, in which the same actors as three different sets of characters—circus folk, farmers and seafarers—went through three
versions of the same plot in which the leading man was sterile. Mr.
Steinbeck's intentions were artistic and honorable, but his drama
could not be taken as seriously as it should have been.

During the season David Heilweil and Derrick Lynn-Thomas
continued to operate New York's only theatre-in-the-round, the

Arena, in a ground-floor ballroom of a hotel. They had done quite well with "Julius Caesar" and very well with a revival of "The Medium" and "The Telephone," and now in October they tried Shaw's "Arms and the Man" and had a gratifying run of 110 performances. Later they were to come an expensive cropper and give up their project when they produced a small review, "Razzle Dazzle." None of the other October plays was a success, or artistically important.

Samson Raphaelson, who had not been heard from in some seasons, came up with a quite admirable woman's drama, "Hilda Crane," on the first evening of November. It offered a problem not uncommon to women—whether to marry for security or to live in sin for love. When Hilda Crane reached the conclusion that she had made the wrong choice she committed suicide—which may have militated against the longevity of a well-made and well-acted play; the run was only 70 performances. Next came the season's first failure of anything with uncommon artistic pretensions—an operatic adaptation of Langston Hughes' drama, "Mulatto," with a libretto by Mr. Hughes and music by Jan Meyerowitz. "The Barrier," as it was called, could manage no more than four performances even with such singers as Lawrence Tibbett and Muriel Rahn. Next— on November 8—came Christopher Fry's comedy in verse, "The Lady's Not for Burning," with a beautiful physical production by Oliver Messel and some interesting acting by John Gielgud, Pamela Brown, Esme Percy and others. This gaudy fable about a witch who didn't want to be burned and an adventurer who wanted to be hanged, set in the Fifteenth Century and embellished by an extraordinary output of words by the author, was a great success among the intellectuals, having a run of 151 performances and winning the Critics Circle citation as the year's best foreign play. A dissenter in the Circle's voting was the editor of this yearbook, who felt that the play was more literary pretentiousness than literature. The season's next success was "The Country Girl," an interesting drama about an alcoholic actor and his realistic wife, by Clifford Odets. Here Odets was his old self, writing directly and pungently and forgetting the verbiage and breast-beating of his last failure, "The Big Knife." "The Country Girl" ran out the season. Next came another play which ran out the season, John van Druten's comedy about a witch on Murray Hill, "Bell, Book and Candle." The comedy was running to capacity when it was forced to close June 2 by the departure of its stars, Rex Harrison and Lilli Palmer, to fulfill movie commitments. It was planned to reopen the play within a few weeks or months with an entirely new cast. Mr. Harrison and Miss Palmer were not the only stars to desert successes during the season.

Several plays of modest value followed "Bell, Book and Candle," and then, on November 22, came a production of John Vanbrugh's Restoration farce, "The Relapse, or Virtue in Danger." Some, including myself, thought it engaging and hilarious, with a remarkable performance of Lord Foppington by Cyril Ritchard. Others thought "The Relapse" was less remarkable, and unhappily they were in the majority; so the production had only 30 performances. Then came another play which stirred the carriage-trade intellectuals, Christopher Fry's translation—not in verse—of Jean Anouilh's "Ring Round the Moon." I found it a muddled fantasy about an actor who plays twin brothers, although its setting, by Georges Wakhevitch, was one of the year's treasures. It had 68 performances. Next came "Guys and Dolls," concerning which there will be more farther along in this book.

The American National Theatre and Academy, which boasts that it is the only theatrical organization chartered by Congress and whose aim is to improve the stage any way it can, had acquired the old Guild Theatre for a showcase and workshop and inaugurated its first season there on November 26 by presenting Judith Anderson in a distinguished, supercharged performance of Clytemnestra in Robinson Jeffers' poetic version of various works by Aeschylus, titled "The Tower Beyond Tragedy." ANTA had got off to a good start, and had succeeded even in making the drama critics pay cash for their season tickets. This led to published expressions of irritation by some of the reviewers and drama editors, who felt that a free ride was necessary to the job. But, having started well, ANTA blundered badly in December by presenting an amateurish production of an amateur play, "The Cellar and the Well."

The season's first regrettable failure had four performances beginning December 13. It was "Let's Make an Opera," a musical novelty with a libretto by Eric Crozier and music by Benjamin Britten. Conducted by an engaging maestro, Norman Del Mar, this was the manufacture from scratch of a children's operetta, in which the audience was invited to join. New Yorkers did not want to sing and evidently thought the whole project a bit silly, so "Let's Make an Opera" failed to achieve the popularity it has had in England. A full-scale failure of the month was "Bless You All," a revue. It had a few bright songs and sketches, but not enough. Next came a musical comedy based on the Amphitryon legend, "Out of This World," which served to bring long-legged Charlotte Greenwood back to the stage. Critics agreed that one of the stars of this production was Lemuel Ayers, who designed the out-of-this-world settings. Christmas Eve brought José Ferrer and Gloria Swanson in a revival of the Hecht-MacArthur farce, "Twentieth Century," under the auspices of ANTA. This was a rather odd choice for an organization dedicated to fostering new theatrical talent, but it was a thumping commercial success—at least until Mr. Ferrer abandoned it for movie commitments in June.

Christmas night brought the most regrettable failure of the entire season, a production of "King Lear" with Louis Calhern in the title role. This play had been done by only five actors since 1900; Calhern, the sixth, gave what this editor carefully calls a memorable performance. But not all the notices were ecstatic and "King Lear" languished until its closing was announced; then a box-office landslide occurred, but it was too late. The National Theatre had been pledged to another management and "Lear" had to vacate in spite of the astonishing momentum it had acquired. The end of December was signalized by an odd, interesting and unsuccessful adaptation by Arthur Miller of Ibsen's "An Enemy of the People." Mr. Miller saw in the drama a very modern protest against suppression and oppression, and so did Fredric March and Florence Eldridge, its chief players.

The new year began with a production of the late Philip Barry's last play, "Second Threshold." This perceptive and skillful examination of the relationship between a father and his daughter was in practically playable shape at the time Mr. Barry died; his old friend, Robert E. Sherwood, attended to the customary touching-up before and during rehearsals and tryout. The New York City Center, which had begun its play-revival season with "Captain Brassbound's Conversion" in December, next essayed a revival of the Kaufman-Ferber success, "The Royal Family." It had an ill-fated première. John Emery, impersonating the volatile John Barrymore in this theatrical comedy, stumbled down a stair in the second act, tearing ligaments in his ankle. There was a long intermission during which he was being bandaged and soothed, and the veteran Ethel Griffies filled in the time by telling stories. Mr. Emery managed to finish the third act, but that was the end of his engagement and a replacement carried on for the rest of the scheduled fortnight.

The first really bad play of the season arrived on January 17 and departed, quite properly, on January 18. This was a comedy by Joseph Kesselring, author of "Arsenic and Old Lace," titled "Four Twelves Are 48." It had something to do with Indians who could multiply, genetically speaking. Another January entry, "Angel in

the Pawnshop," proved once more that the present economy and
state of mind of Broadway do not allow for nice, pleasant, little
plays.   There was nothing terribly wrong with "Angel"; it just
wasn't a wow. For two weeks beginning January 24 the City Center
had a distinguished production and performance—the Margaret
Webster-Maurice Evans "King Richard II." Three more revivals
came in before the month's end—"The Mikado," as done by the
D'Oyly Carte Company; Ibsen's "Peer Gynt," as revised by Paul
Green and played with great muscle by John Garfield, and Ray
Bolger's always-popular "Where's Charley?" The D'Oyly Carte
Company had put the cart before the horse by having spent most of
its time on the road with only moderate success and therefore being
limited to only four weeks in New York. Capacity audiences would
have warranted a much longer stay.

February's first important entry was Tennessee Williams' lusty
and lustful comedy, "The Rose Tattoo," in which the playwright
definitely and pointedly abandoned his customary theme of female
frustration. The next noteworthy event was a comedy production
which all but started a shooting war between Canada and the peace-
loving state of New York. The play was "Ti-Coq," by and with an
immensely popular French-Canadian entertainer who calls himself
Fridolin and whose real name is Gratien Gélinas. "Ti-Coq" got a
cynical reception from the reviewers and lasted only three performances, a disaster which aroused the anger of innumerable citizens of the Province of Quebec. Fridolin's one great mistake was
to try to present an essentially French character comedy in English.
He could talk English fairly well and so could his leading lady, but
the rest of his company were simply dismayed by the language and
New Yorkers never did find out what made "Ti-Coq" so popular
in Quebec and Montreal.

It is an axiom that, in these days, a play must be a hit or a flop,
with no comfortable room in between. In February a drama which
was a flop to start with refused to give up and had a nice little run.
It was the adaptation of Herman Melville's short novel, "Billy
Budd." This well-made, well-acted play would have closed, just as
"King Lear" did, very soon after its opening, had it not been for
the enthusiasm of a few individuals and the financial sacrifices of
the cast. When "Billy Budd" was announced to close, Herman
Shumlin, a highly regarded play producer who had no interest in
the production, bought advertising space in a morning newspaper in
which to express his enthusiasm. This generously donated ad was
a turning point of sorts, for "Billy Budd" went on for a total of 105
performances and came within two votes of winning the Critics

Circle scroll as the best play of the season.

In years past, Elmer Rice has become so irritated at drama critics as to berate them personally and to announce his retirement from the theatre; but this season he appears to have mellowed. A comedy he wrote several years previously, "Not for Children," was produced in mid-February by the Playwrights' Company, to the great puzzlement of the reviewers. It lasted only seven performances, but Mr. Rice kept private whatever denunciations he may have had in mind. Next came a many-scened, lavishly produced comedy drama about a mother, "The Small Hours," by George S. Kaufman and his new wife, Leueen MacGrath. It could do no better than 20 performances. Ironically, this was the play which had been booked into the National Theatre, where "King Lear" had gained momentum too late. In the latter half of February three or four minor dramatic events took place, and then, on the 26th, there arrived "Springtime Folly," which probably was one of the two worst plays of the season. It was a comedy about a manufacturer of maternity dresses who forgot to allow for expansion in his garments.

March began with an admirable revival of Barrie's "Mary Rose," sponsored by Helen Hayes for ANTA, of which she is president. Lillian Hellman followed with her perceptive, admirable comedy, "The Autumn Garden," which had the best large cast of the year. And, when March was only eight days old, Barbara Bel Geddes captured the city with her performance in a very slight but very adroit comedy by F. Hugh Herbert, "The Moon Is Blue." Another Hollywoodian, Olivia de Havilland, fared less happily in a scenically stunning "Romeo and Juliet." Undaunted after only 49 performances, Miss de Havilland prepared to invade the Summer theatre circuit with Shaw's "Candida." A third Hollywoodian, Edward Everett Horton, braved Broadway with Benn W. Levy's comedy, "Springtime for Henry," which Mr. Horton had used as a touring vehicle more or less continuously since 1932. Broadway won, and Mr. Horton announced that he was putting the play aside for good.

As regrettable as the closing of "King Lear" was the 44-performance failure of a full-scale revival of Marc Connelly's "The Green Pastures." No amount of enthusiasm on the part of individuals, including this editor, could make this American miracle play stick. Modern Broadway was just not interested in de Lawd, Gabriel and the fish-loving angels. "Pastures" arrived March 15 and departed April 21. On March 18 ANTA had one of its most interesting productions—the Louis Jouvet company of Paris in Molière's "L'Ecole des Femmes." In spite of the language handi-

cap, New Yorkers besieged the limited run. The month ended with
another smash hit by Richard Rodgers and Oscar Hammerstein
2d, "The King and I," based on Margaret Landon's novel, "Anna
and the King of Siam." Here were sentiment and pageantry in
liberal amounts, and the St. James Theatre box office looked forward
to several seasons of business.

Mid-April brought another very bad little play, "Angels Kiss
Me." Its intentions were good and honorable, but in writing and
performance it was nowhere near the Broadway standard. Another
mid-April entry was a handsome musical based on Molnar's comedy,
"The Good Fairy," titled "Make a Wish." Preston Sturges had
made the original adaptation—if any adaptation can be called original—and Abe Burrows, the new play-doctor who rose to fame with
his work on "Guys and Dolls," was called in for last-minute re-
pairs. His patchwork was not entirely successful, but "Make a
Wish" continued into the next season. One evening later a solid
musical success opened—"A Tree Grows in Brooklyn"—another
adaptation, of course, from Betty Smith's novel. Shirley Booth,
who was praised last for her performance in "Come Back, Little
Sheba," won new critical and popular honors for her playing of
Cissy, the Brooklynite who couldn't say No. The most interesting
entry for the remainder of April was ANTA's production of Edmund
Wilson's drama, "The Little Blue Light." Here was a play which
had, perhaps, more intelligence and intellect than anything else of
the season—but it never managed to make a play. Mr. Wilson's
thoughts on the political and social future of the United States
were less stimulating on the stage than they should have been, and
the makings of a fine play went for little.

The final month of the theatrical year, May, had a few revivals
and two interesting new productions. The first of the new ones was
"Stalag 17," a farcical comedy about—of all places—a German
prison camp inhabited by irrepressible U. S. airmen. The second
novelty was one of the few original musicals of the season—no
adaptation. It was "Flahooley," by E. Y. Harburg, Fred Saidy
and Sammy Fain. It was a fantasy about the invention of a laughing doll whose humor was dampened by serious consideration of such
problems as the law of supply and demand—a law that the Democrats have not quite licked yet. The season of 1950-1951 ended
happily with a spirited revival of the first of the Rodgers-Hammerstein musicals, "Oklahoma!" During the year a few stars were
born but many more died; no new playwrights emerged, but the
old ones kept working—even if they had to make adaptations.

THE SEASON IN BOSTON

By Elliot Norton

Drama Critic of the *Boston Post*

THE Boston drama season of 1950-51 presents something of a paradox to a keeper of the records. It ended gloomily, offering only two plays in the entire month of April and a lone musical in May. It found few attractions for some of the best playhouses of the city, as, for instance, the Wilbur, which was open for only six weeks, and the Plymouth, where nine attractions were exhibited for a total of 18 weeks of the 52.

No play was presented at the Copley Theatre, on Huntington Avenue, for the Messrs. Shubert turned it over to pictures during this year. The Majestic, also Shubert-owned, had two plays, each for two weeks, then turned also to the movies.

On the other hand, the statistics prove that there were four more plays and musicals offered in the city's regular downtown theatres in the season than in the previous 12 months.

More important, a reasonably high percentage of these productions were first rate.

To deal further in seeming paradox: the theatre managers had a gloomy year, with too few attractions and some of these failing to win a properly large public, yet the average playgoer was able—except in April and May—to see as many fine plays and musicals as most average playgoers are likely to be able to afford in a season.

The record also shows that Boston continues to be a tryout center. Of the 43 productions seen during the year, 21 plays or musicals were being prepared here for a Broadway engagement. The year before there had been 20.

Here are some of the principal statistics for the Boston drama season of 1950-51:

Number of Plays and Musicals Presented in the Regular Downtown Theatres of Boston Between June 1, 1950, and May 31, 1951, incl. 43
Number of Plays and Musicals in Previous Season 39
Number of Musicals, 1950-51 15
Number of Tryouts, 1950-51 21

13

Number of Tryouts, 1949-50. 20
Number of Tryouts of 1950-51 Season which were subse-
    quently rated as commercially successful in N. Y.   7
Longest run, 1950-51 . . . . "Mister Roberts"; 21 weeks
    (Note that part of the "Roberts" run accrued in the pre-
    vious season. The engagement straddled two seasons. The
    play opened March 6, 1951, and continued through July
    29, 1951.)
Number of plays presented during the season by the Boston
    Summer Theatre, which offers professional stock, in New
    England Mutual Hall, each attraction playing for one
    week only. 10

The record of the tryouts is pretty good. As the figures indicate,
one in every three new plays or musicals presented here in prepara-
tion was subsequently adjudged a hit on Broadway. These seven
were: John van Druten's "Bell, Book and Candle"; Wolcott Gibbs'
"Season in the Sun"; Rodgers' and Hammerstein's "The King and
I"; Lindsay's and Crouse's "Call Me Madam"; Christopher Fry's
"The Lady's Not for Burning"; F. Hugh Herbert's "The Moon Is
Blue," and Clifford Odets' "The Country Girl."

One other Boston tryout, "Black Chiffon," was rated a failure in
New York, but apparently only because its star, Flora Robson,
was taken ill.

Two others, "Courtin' Time" and "Seventeen," didn't get to New
York until after the new season had begun. If one or another of
those should prove to be successful, the record of success would be
swelled by that much.

It needs to be pointed out, for what interest it may have, that this
is a reasonably high record of success for tryouts. It is also important
to spread this fact on the record: that of all the seven attractions
which went from a Boston beginning to New York acclaim, only one,
"The Country Girl," was not successful in Boston. This despite the
fact that all of them, except the English import "The Lady's Not for
Burning," were more or less drastically repaired here, and even the
English play was handicapped by failure of its players, with the
exception of John Gielgud, to speak loudly enough at the opening
performance.

The reason for emphasizing these facts, which producers and
playwrights can readily check at the box offices, is that during the
last two seasons a rumor has prevailed in the underworld of Show
Business that many plays do poor business in Boston tryouts.
Though there are exceptions like "The Country Girl," this is

generally untrue, and even in the case of "The Country Girl" there is usually a reason which the rumor-mongers do not know, or else refuse to hear. "The Country Girl," for instance, had two good acts and one very bad one—the third—when it opened here. That third act was rewritten twice and eventually, in New York, became scene two of act three.

This canard that Boston does not support good attractions has been spread spitefully by producers and others, who have brought poor plays here and had them fail, or by similar showmen who stumbled in here with plays or musicals which got a bad reception and which were then drastically overhauled and which, *because of the overhauling*, were able to make the grade in New York. Such producers resent Boston because they can't fool Boston, and they take out their resentment by spreading spiteful rumors for gullible people who don't bother to consult the figures.

Getting back on the main line of this record: the season opened on June 1 with "Mister Roberts" flourishing at the Colonial Theatre in a production which featured John Forsythe in the name part, with Jackie Cooper as Ensign Pulver, James Rennie as the Captain, and Robert Burton as the Doctor. It had begun its engagement at the same playhouse on March 6.

Because he wanted him to stay with the company at the expiration of his contractual year, Producer Leland Hayward elevated Mr. Forsythe to stardom on June 1. This is the first time in memory that any player has become a star during a Boston engagement.

While "Roberts" flourished at the Colonial, the national company of "Kiss Me, Kate" brought that merry, melodic and kinetic Cole Porter musical comedy to Boston for the first time. Fighting against hot weather in the Shubert Theatre, the show stayed for eight good weeks, beginning Monday, June 19. Featured were Frances McCann and Robert Wright, in the leads, with Benny Baker, Marc Platt and Betty George heading the support.

In July, the Boston Summer Theatre, operated by Lee Falk, who is a successful comic strip artist during the cool weather, and Al Capp, creator of Li'l Abner, whom Mr. Falk describes as his "silent and invisible" partner, began a successful 10 weeks' season at New England Mutual Hall with the following plays and stars:

Week of July 3, Franchot Tone in "The Second Man"; week of July 10, Laraine Day in "Angel Street"; week of July 17, Cole Porter's "The Gay Divorce," with Jack Whiting, Carol Stone and Lenore Lonergan; week of July 24, Edward Arnold, in "The Apple of His Eye"; week of July 31, Nancy Walker, in "On the Town";

week of August 7, Eve Arden, in "Over Twenty-one"; week of August 14, Brian Aherne, in "Dear Brutus"; week of August 21, Zachary Scott in "Blind Alley"; week of August 28, Edward Everett Horton in "My French Wife," and week of September 4, "Finian's Rainbow."

"Mister Roberts" ended its Boston career on Saturday, July 29. "Kiss Me, Kate" stayed until August 12. After that, there were no openings in the city except at the Summer Theatre until Monday, September 4, when Olsen and Johnson came down, like wolves on the fold, with a revue entitled "Pardon Our French." This was not the best revue they had ever presented, though they seem to think it was. It did poor business during four weeks at the Boston Opera House, then went on to New York to disaster.

A week after Ole and Chic had arrived, the English melodrama "Black Chiffon" was first presented here at the Plymouth Theatre. This revealed Flora Robson giving an extraordinarily artful and moving performance in a company whose other players were almost equally impressive. To one playgoer, the fundamental premise of the play seemed preposterous. That any department store would prosecute for theft a woman of good family, with a large charge account, for stealing a chiffon nightgown which she didn't even get out of the store seemed wildly at variance with the truth. Other Boston playgoers loved it, however, and "Black Chiffon" stayed two weeks at the Plymouth Theatre.

A play by a drama critic, Wolcott Gibbs of *The New Yorker,* was next to arrive, on September 12. "Season in the Sun" had two good weeks at the Wilbur Theatre. Bostonians liked it. All but one.

Ethel Merman arrived at the Shubert Theatre in "Call Me Madam" on Tuesday evening, September 19, in an uproar of happy anticipation. Needless to say, Miss Merman let nobody down, nor did Irving Berlin. However, tinkering and tailoring were required for the show itself, which had begun in the minds of Lindsay and Crouse as a sharp political satire and had to be toned down because of the Korean war.

Some sharply effective surgery made "Madam" a far better show during three weeks at the Shubert Theatre. One song number was eliminated entirely from the second act, and a brand new one was written by Irving Berlin. For the new tune a new dance production number was created and rehearsed, though the dancers were working through it in their street clothes and the new scenery had not yet been finished when they left town. To strengthen the weak second act further, the biggest of the Berlin hits, "You're Not Sick, You're Just in Love" was transferred from act one.

Give Leland Hayward and George Abbott credit for making that one over. Give Ethel Merman credit for just being in it.

John Patrick's "The Curious Savage," another tryout, opened at the Wilbur on Monday, September 25. Escorted by the Theatre Guild, this new comedy had been tried during the previous week in Wilmington and there, on Saturday night, had lost its leading lady, Patricia Collinge. For Boston, her understudy, Marie Carroll, took over. But the Guild rushed Lillian Gish here to replace Miss Carroll during the second week of the engagement.

The evening of September 25 was a good deal more notable for the arrival at the Colonial Theatre of "Oklahoma!" making its sixth Boston visit for a happy three weeks with a cast which had been playing and singing it on the road.

October proved to be the busiest and generally the best month of the year, with thirteen productions, among them five tryouts, of which three would be hits.

John Steinbeck's "Burning Bright" came in first, opening October 2, for two weeks at the Plymouth Theatre. Though it afterwards proved a failure in New York and although it was by no means entirely successful, this seemed one of the stimulating and challenging dramas of the season, curious and arresting in its form, affirmative in its philosophy of life, beautifully enacted by Barbara Bel Geddes, Kent Smith, Howard DaSilva and Brooks Martin. Here it was respectfully, if not altogether enthusiastically received. Being experimental in form and daring in its philosophy, it could only be an eventual success if the New York reviewers should acclaim it. They, however, did not support it.

Neither experimental nor successful was Frederick Lonsdale's comedy "The Day After Tomorrow," which opened at the Shubert Theatre on Monday evening, October 9. The droll acting of Melville Cooper gave this strangely dated drawing room comedy a faint flavor of fun, but it was obviously not long for this world.

Following the Steinbeck drama at the Plymouth came S. N. Behrman's "I Know My Love," in a return engagement of two successful weeks beginning October 16. This comedy drama of Cold Roast Boston was well admired here and the acting of Alfred Lunt and Lynn Fontanne stirred everyone to proper enthusiasm.

For the first time since the war, the D'Oyly Carte Opera Company of London came to Boston in October, opening a three weeks' season at the Opera House, Monday evening, October 16, with a joint bill, "Cox and Box" and "The Pirates of Penzance." Subsequently, they sang "Trial by Jury," "Pinafore," "The Mikado," "Iolanthe," "The Gondoliers" and "Patience."

Though they sang them wonderfully well, and won universal commendation, the D'Oyly Carters were not financially successful in Boston. For this woeful fact, various explanations were offered, of which two would seem reasonable: their prices were too high and the Boston Opera House is not the best theatre in town for their kind of attraction.

The last week of October produced three of the year's new hits.

Imported from London with English players headed by John Gielgud and Pamela Brown, "The Lady's Not for Burning" gave Boston its first work by the poet Christopher Fry. Audience response was complicated somewhat by failure of all the cast, except Mr. Gielgud, to speak loudly enough during the first act on the first night and even later. The play was welcomed, nonetheless, for its wit and charm and melody, and because it was played with distinction for two weeks beginning October 23, at the Shubert Theatre.

As recorded above, Clifford Odets' "The Country Girl" was not well received here, though it won some critical enthusiasm. Brilliantly acted by Paul Kelly and Uta Hagen and the rest of its players, this drama seemed powerful indeed for two acts and pretty unconvincing in its third. Mr. Odets did some drastic rewriting and some adroit rearrangement, to reclaim it for Broadway. It played here at the Majestic Theatre for two weeks beginning October 23.

John van Druten's pleasant comedy "Bell, Book and Candle" was a hit here during its two weeks' engagement. Opening Monday, October 30, it exhibited Rex Harrison and Lilli Palmer playing with easy elegance a comedy which might not have been easy to take without them.

Signe Hasso was starred in the next entry, an English mystery melodrama called "Edwina," by William Dinner and William Morum. It is pleasant to look at Miss Hasso, but her play wasn't much and not very many people went to the Majestic Theatre during the engagement which began there on November 6 and extended for two weeks, prior to Broadway.

Also opening on the giddy evening of November 6 were "The Consul," the opera by Gian-Carlo Menotti, at the Shubert Theatre, and "Ring Round the Moon," adapted from the French of Jean Anouilh by Christopher Fry, and enacted by English actors at the Colonial Theatre.

For some reason, "The Consul" failed to win much public interest in the beginning, though it was universally acclaimed by the Boston press in a brilliant production, with Patricia Neway singing magnificently in the leading role. Before the end of the engagement, however, Bostonians awoke and the last few performances were sold out.

The Anouilh play had a measure of elegance and style rare in the contemporary theatre but proved a little too fragile and elusive for our audiences.

"A Streetcar Named Desire" made its third Boston appearance for two weeks beginning November 13, with a company headed now by Louise Pratt. Not many people were waiting for a "Streetcar" this time, but it managed to get by at the Plymouth Theatre, whence reports of its quality proved too discouraging for one reviewer who admired the play immensely when it was presented by other actors.

The final week of November provided two attractions: the English novelty, "Let's Make an Opera," which seemed pretty desperately cute, and Cole Porter's "Out of This World," which was scenically beautiful, but not so much otherwise. The first show opened at the Wilbur Theatre on the 27th for two weeks, but stayed only one for lack of public interest. The other remained at the Shubert for three weeks and was well attended, especially after the city "censor" ordered some lines out and some clothes on.

December brought Arthur Miller's great drama, "Death of a Salesman," to Boston, with Thomas Mitchell giving a most impressive performance as Willy Loman. This play had a curious engagement here. For three weeks, beginning December 4, at the Colonial Theatre, it did excellent business. In the two final weeks, it was not successful, though everyone who saw it had been impressed.

"Second Threshold," a literate posthumous drama by Philip Barry, which his friend Robert E. Sherwood had revised with loving care, opened here on December 18. As the middle-aged career man who was planning to terminate a life that had gone flat and stale, Clive Brook acted in this with eminent distinction. At the opening performance, however, Margaret Phillips seemed a little mechanical. Boston liked "Second Threshold" with reservations. It played for two weeks at the Plymouth Theatre and there Mr. Sherwood made further revisions before moving it on to New York.

Our Christmas present was "Where's Charley," the musical comedy made by George Abbott from that ancient wheeze, "Charley's Aunt." Ray Bolger had determined to restore it to the stage for a brief new engagement in New York and for other subsequent runs in Los Angeles and San Francisco before making the movie version in England. Having by-passed his home town in the original tryout, he brought it here on Christmas night, 1950, and kept it here for five happy weeks. Business was fine, Bolger was fine, Everything was fine.

Also opening on Christmas, at the Opera House: "Blossom Time," for two weeks, an annual revival which finds its own following. Although this cannot, unfortunately, be proved with statistics, it would appear to be true that "Blossom Time" and other such operettas attract an audience whose members do not patronize the theatre for anything else.

Our New Year began innocently with "The Innocents," in a production which offered Sylvia Sidney in the role of the governess which Beatrice Straight had originated during the previous season in New York. Miss Sidney looked as handsome as usual, but this was not her best performance. In Boston, during two weeks beginning New Year's Day at the Plymouth Theatre, "The Innocents" languished.

The first new Irish play in many years occupied Bostonians beginning January 29th, also at the Plymouth Theatre. "The King of Friday's Men," as New Yorkers came subsequently to discover, had a certain amount of Celtic eloquence but its story was not particularly persuasive. The acting in it of Walter Macken, actorauthor, had all the force and imagination we expect from an Abbey Theatre actor, but what could one man do against so many?

With Jean Arthur flying lightly across the stage as Peter and Boris Karloff acting gravely both Mr. Darling and wicked Captain Hook, "Peter Pan" arrived at the Opera House on Tuesday evening, January 30, and remained for two pleasant weeks.

No play but a ballet company dominated the theatre in January. The Sadler's Wells Ballet of London spent one week at the Opera House beginning January 8, and with Margot Fonteyn as its star to dazzle and delight audiences who had been contending for tickets since the previous May when a canny management first began to peddle them. Miss Fonteyn seemed to some of us the greatest ballerina we had ever seen.

The first entry of February was the revival of "The Green Pastures," with William Marshall as de Lawd. Although it was injured by mechanical difficulties at the first performance this was a joyful theatrical occasion and the eventual failure of "The Green Pastures" is one of the most bewildering and disheartening facts of the season.

Booked into Boston on only nine days' notice, after having previously canceled because of the sudden death of the producer, Dwight Deere Wiman, "The Green Pastures" was handicapped commercially by this short notice. Except for musical comedies, Bostonians don't ordinarily buy theatre tickets far in advance.

The first week's business was fair, the second week's fifty percent greater. In the opinion of the Colonial Theatre's manager, Saul Kaplan, if it had been possible to keep the play here for an additional two weeks, Bostonians by that time would have been fighting to get in. Booking commitments in Philadelphia, however, had to be kept. "The Green Pastures" went on to Philadelphia and dreadful business there. That it also failed in New York is part of another record.

It needs to be set down as a matter of fact that all the Boston reviewers accepted this revival with great enthusiasm and that those playgoers who saw it were equally pleased.

With Olivia de Havilland starred, a new production of Shakespeare's "Romeo and Juliet" opened at the Shubert Theatre on Tuesday evening, February 13, one night after "The Green Pastures" had got under way at the Colonial. Much heralded, this revival proved meritorious in some ways yet disappointing, because Miss de Havilland's Juliet was mechanical and labored, where it should have been flushed with lyric spontaneity. It did only moderate business here, as—according to report—in other tryout centers. Some observers had anticipated that Miss de Havilland's eminence in the cinema would bring out her followers by legions, but this proved not to be so. Is it possible that picture stars no longer have the magnetic appeal which they once possessed?

The final entry of February proved to be one of the season's few comedy hits. "The Moon Is Blue," by F. Hugh Herbert, came to Boston Monday, February 19, for two weeks, during which it was altered a good deal: a brand new third act was written and eventually inserted and this involved the total elimination of one character.

The major event of March and perhaps of the entire season was the arrival of Rodgers' and Hammerstein's "The King and I," which came to the Shubert Theatre on Tuesday evening, March 6, and played here for a total of three weeks, less one day.

In a previous week of tryout at New Haven, "The King and I" had been cut a good deal. Here it was further tightened and acquired three new songs, all of them created at the Ritz Carlton Hotel, which would seem to be the greatest incubator in the world of show music.

The new songs were "Getting to Know You," which Gertrude Lawrence sings in the schoolroom scene, "Funny Western People," which opens the second act, and "I Have Dreamed."

It may be of interest to record the fact that "Getting to Know You" has a melody which Richard Rodgers originally wrote for "South Pacific," but which he discarded in favor of "Younger Than Springtime." It came to his mind here when he cast about for a bright new song to lighten the tone of "The King and I." He turned it over to Oscar Hammerstein, who "lashed himself to a bedpost" in the Ritz and produced a brand new lyric for it.

For two evenings in March, the 15th and 16th, at the Colonial

Theatre, Bostonians got to see and hear the great French star, Louis Jouvet, and his company from the Théâtre de l'Athénee, Paris, in their first American performances of the Molière classic "L'Ecole des Femmes." ANTA sent Jouvet to Boston, and a local committee of enthusiasts, headed by the French consul general, Albert Chambon, and Dr. Marston Balch of Tufts College, saw to it that every available ticket for the two performances was sold long in advance.

With Ethel Waters, Julie Harris and Brandon DeWilde featured, as they had been during the New York engagement, "The Member of the Wedding" arrived at the Colonial Theatre for four weeks beginning Monday, March 26. Some members of the cast—not Ethel Waters!—had difficulty pitching their voices high enough to be heard in the Colonial Theatre after 15 previous months in the smaller New York Empire, but this engagement was one of the Boston season's happiest in all ways.

April produced only two new plays. John Cecil Holm's "Gramercy Ghost" came to the Plymouth Theatre Monday, April 9, for two weeks. On the same evening, the Shubert drew "Courtin' Time," a musical comedy adaptation by William Roos of an English play, "The Farmer's Wife." Laid now in Maine, though it had no hint of real Maine color, the musical had Lloyd Nolan of the movies playing a farmer who would like to take a wife. In a subsequent engagement in Philadelphia, Mr. Nolan would withdraw and later Joe E. Brown would succeed to the part.

"Courtin' Time" remained at the Shubert for three weeks and was succeeded after an interval by "Seventeen," the only legitimate theatre entry of May, 1951. Written by Sally Benson from the Booth Tarkington original, with lyrics by Kim Gannon and music by Walter Kent, "Seventeen" began its Boston engagement of three weeks on Monday, September 28, the final show of the theatrical year.

When it opened, all other Boston playhouses were dark and had been for a month, and would, apparently, stay dark until September. The managers were gloomy indeed.

Technically, the Brattle Theatre does not belong in the Boston record, because it is located in Cambridge rather than Boston. But Cambridge is immediately adjacent to Boston, so this two-year-old company is really part of the Boston picture, and an important part.

The Brattle record for the year from June 1, 1950, to May 31, 1951, divides into two periods. In July and August, the company presented more or less conventional Summer stock on a week-to-week basis, with stars. In the Fall, the "regular" policy was resumed, with visiting stars appearing for three or four weeks each in plays of classic or semi-classic quality.

The Brattle Theatre is, in effect, a stock company under Equity regulations, employing guest stars and presenting, for the most part, the better plays of the drama's past centuries rather than the conventional comedies and melodramas of the usual stock company.

On June 1, 1950, the Brattle actors were presenting Wycherley's "The Country Wife," with Cyril Ritchard and Madge Elliott featured. This production had opened on May 11 and would continue for seven weeks, through June 25.

From that time, for the rest of the Summer, the company followed its Summer theatre policy, playing the following attractions for one week each:

Opening June 27, Shaw's "Arms and the Man" with Helmut Dantine and Beatrice Pearson; opening July 4, Shakespeare's "Julius Caesar," starring John Carradine; opening July 11, Nigel Bruce in "Yes, M'Lord"; opening July 18, Zero Mostel in "The Imaginary Invalid," by Molière; opening July 25, Ruth Ford in "No Exit," by Jean-Paul Sartre; opening August 1, Ernest Truex in "Androcles and the Lion"; opening August 8, Estelle Winwood in "Hay Fever"; August 15-26 (two weeks) Jessica Tandy and Hume Cronyn in the world première of "The Little Blue Light" by Edmund Wilson; August 29, Festival Productions' presentation of "Crimes and Crimes" with Sam Wanamaker, Valerie Bettis, Blanche Yurka and Helmut Dantine; September 4, Ann Corio in "Rain."

As a side venture, the Brattle Company also presented an eight weeks' Summer season at nearby Cohasset, using plays and players from Cambridge, as follows: week of July 3, "Arms and the Man"; week of July 10, "Julius Caesar"; week of July 17, "Yes, M'Lord"; week of July 24, "The Imaginary Invalid"; week of July 31, "Misalliance"; week of August 7, "Androcles and the Lion"; week of August 14, "Hay Fever"; week of August 21, "Rain."

The regular season at Cambridge began for the Brattle Theatre on October 3, with Joseph Schildkraut and Ruth Ford in Pirandello's "Six Characters in Search of an Author," an interesting production, which ran for four weeks.

The remaining productions, with opening dates and length of runs, are as follows:

November 1, three weeks, Arthur Treacher in "The Magistrate," by Arthur Wing Pinero; November 22, four weeks, Eva LeGallienne and Margaret Webster in "The Three Sisters," by Chekov; January 23, 1951, three weeks, Sam Jaffe in "Tartuffe," by Molière; February 14, four weeks, resident company in "Henry IV, Part II";

March 14, four weeks, Hermione Gingold in a musical revue tryout, "It's About Time," produced by Mary Hunter and the Brattle Theatre Company (American debut of the comedienne in a revue including some sketches from her English revues, "Sweet and Low," "Sweeter and Lower," "Sweetest and Lowest"; April 11, three weeks, "The Kidders," a new play tryout, by Donald Ogden Stewart, produced by Robert Whitehead, with Jocelyn Brando and others; May 2, three weeks, Nancy Walker in "The Roaring Girl" (Walker replaced in final week by Jenny Lou Law); May 23 (to continue through June 24, 1951), "Love's Labour's Lost" with Ian Keith and Hurd Hatfield.

The Brattle Theatre Company also, during the 1950-51 season, participated in two shows on Broadway and tour: "The Relapse," presented by the Theatre Guild, in which 10 members of the resident company appeared, and for which costumes, scenery, assistant director, etc., were provided by Brattle (6-week tour—4 weeks on Broadway), and "The Little Blue Light" presented at the ANTA Playhouse (2 weeks on Broadway).

The semi-professional Tributary Theatre of Boston, playing in New England Mutual Hall under the general direction of David Tutaev, presented the following attractions:

October 11, "The Alchemist," by Ben Jonson (4 performances); November 1, "Julius Caesar," by William Shakespeare (5 performances); November 10 (Norwood High School, Norwood, Mass.); November 29, "The Marriage Proposal," by Anton Chekov, also "My Heart's in the Highlands," by William Saroyan (4 performances); January 3, "Three Men on a Horse," by George Abbott and John Cecil Holm, April 3 (General Electric, Lynn, Mass.) (5 performances); January 31, "Morra: Game of Chance" (ballet), by Giglio Dante; February 17 (Arlington, Mass.), "Pygmalion," by George Bernard Shaw (5 performances); February 21, "St. Joan," by George Bernard Shaw (4 performances); March 16, "The Emperor Jones," by Eugene O'Neill (2 performances); April 13, "The Emperor Jones," by Eugene O'Neill (2 performances); May 2, "The Beggar's Opera," by John Gay, starring Claudia Pinza, at Boston Conservatory Auditorium.

The Tributary Children's Theatre presented eight attractions of its own during the season, most of them at Saturday matinees, as follows:

October 7, "Aladdin," November 17 (Arlington, Mass., under sponsorship of Community Council); December 26 (played American Theatre Corporation suburban movie houses during Christmas vacation, under the sponsorship of the ATC movie chain)—total performances, 10; October 28, November 4, 11, "The Patchwork Girl of Oz" (3 performances); November 25, December 2, 9, "Little Women" (3 performances; December 16, 23, "Christmas Carol," Charles Dickens (2 performances); January 20, 27, February 3, 10, "Snow White and the Seven Dwarfs" (4 performances); February 17, 24, "Penrod" (2 performances); March 10, 17, 24, "Jack and the Beanstalk," April 7 (Malden, Mass., under sponsorship of Teachers' Association) (4 performances); March 31, April 14, 21, 28, "Toby Tyler and the Circus" (4 performances) at John Hancock Hall. (All performances not otherwise indicated were given at New England Mutual Hall.)

Boston got opera during 1950-51 from three companies, the local New England Opera Theatre of Boris Goldovsky, the visiting San Carlo Opera Company and the great Metropolitan, all of them at the Boston Opera House.

Their schedules were as follows:

New England Opera Theatre: October 29, "The Marriage of Figaro"; December 10, "Violanta's Revenge" (Mozart); January 7, "Don Giovanni"; February 11, "Eugene Onegin." All these for one performance only.

The San Carlo Opera Company in eight days beginning Sunday, November 5, 1950, presented "La Bohême," "La Traviata," "Carmen," "Aïda," "Butterfly," "Rigoletto," "Faust," "Trovatore," "Cavalleria Rusticana," "Pagliacci" and "Tosca."

The "Met," making its first local visit under the direction of Rudolph Bing, opened on Monday evening, April 9, with "La Traviata," and gave the following operas at successive performances: "The Magic Flute," "La Bohême," "Il Barbiere di Siviglia," "Die Fledermaus," "Don Carlo" (first Boston performance), "Madama Butterfly," "Faust" and "Tristan und Isolde."

The Ballet Russe de Monte Carlo also danced here for one week, beginning Monday, April 23, with Frederic Franklin, Alexandra Danilova, Nina Novak and Leon Danielian among the leading dancers.

The Boston Dance Theatre, a local organization which imports concert dance attractions, presented during the season at the Boston Conservatory Auditorium, among others, Jean Leon Destine, December 7-8, Charles Weidman and his dancers, January 18-19, and May O'Donnell and her group, March 1-2.

A special attraction outside the regular run of theatrical attractions but worth putting into the record was a single performance by Eddie Cantor at Boston Symphony Hall on the evening of September 28. For two hours Mr. Cantor recalled the tunes and topics that have made Eddie Cantor celebrated. A large audience enthused.

THE SEASON IN PHILADELPHIA

By Arthur B. Waters

Drama Critic of the Philadelphia *Gazette-Democrat*

NO matter how else the 1950-51 legitimate theatrical season in Philadelphia may be described or—eventually—remembered, it will be characterized by many local critics, students of the "drayma" and casual playgoers as the "year of the big musicals."

Not in many moons—certainly not since the lush days of the Turbulent Twenties when Dillingham opened all his musicals at the old Forrest and the Garrick (both defunct) and Ziegfeld and Vinton Freedley and Schwab and Mandel and Max Gordon and Lew Fields were equally partial to our Quaker City as a testing ground for new tune pieces—has Philadelphia played host to such an array of musical tryouts.

No fewer than eight musicals, supposedly being readied for Broadway assignments, were tried out "for size" on local audiences. One of them—"The Lady from Paris"—was a revamp of an earlier show, "Melody in My Heart," and proved more disastrous than the original. The others, chronologically listed, were "Guys and Dolls," "Out of This World," "Bless You All," "Make a Wish," "A Tree Grows in Brooklyn," "Flahooley" and "Courtin' Time." Of these seven, "Guys and Dolls," "Out of This World" and "Make a Wish" were what *Variety* succinctly catalogues as "world preems." The others came here after brief tuning-up spells elsewhere, usually New Haven.

"Guys and Dolls" and "A Tree Grows in Brooklyn" went on to become solid New York hits; "Bless You All" was a medium-lived Gotham resident; "Out of This World" ran six months and took in a million and a quarter or so, but actually according to reports lost around $160,000. "Make a Wish" and "Flahooley" (which was acclaimed here by critics and playgoers alike as the best of the lot and the most distinguished musical in years) have not, at present writing, played long enough in New York to allow their status to be determined, and "Courtin' Time," also as of current writing, hasn't as yet reached Manhattan.

At all events, those local first nights of big, elaborate musicals like "Guys and Dolls," "Out of This World," "A Tree Grows in

26

Brooklyn," "Make a Wish" and "Flahooley" provided about the only excitement that the 1950-51 season afforded. Certainly it was noteworthy for an abysmal lack of interesting new dramas. Non-musical tryouts included only "Darkness at Noon," "The Man That Corrupted Hadleyburg" and "The Autumn Garden" (premières) and "Billy Budd," "Let Me Hear the Melody," "Affairs of State" and a couple of others that would be best unmentioned and, if possible, completely forgotten.

Statistically, our 1950-51 season compared closely to its predecessor. There were 41 attractions in all, as against 42 in 1949-50, but these 100 active "lighted" weeks divided between five legitimate playhouses as compared to 83 last year. This, I imagine, is to be accounted for by the fact that the 1950-51 season got under way on Labor Day (Philadelphia's old, traditional "tee-off" time) whereas 1949-50 wasn't launched until the very end of September.

In figuring the total number of attractions, I am omitting "Two on the Aisle," a new farce which doesn't open here until June 18, just as last year I left out Mike Todd's "Peep Show," another June entry.

Once again there were surprisingly few productions offered this season that came here with Broadway reputations. In fact, I figure just six of them, "As You Like It," "The Innocents," "Come Back, Little Sheba," "I Know My Love," "Peter Pan" and "The Lady's Not for Burning." Among the frequent return engagements must be listed "Mister Roberts," "Kiss Me, Kate," "Streetcar Named Desire," "The Consul," "Death of a Salesman" and "Oklahoma!" "Blossom Time" came back again, and we had four delightful (but not too profitable) weeks of the D'Oyly Carte Company in Gilbert and Sullivan. New productions of old favorites were "The Green Pastures," "The Guardsman," and "Springtime for Henry" and special bookings included Maurice Schwartz and "The Borscht Capades."

Non-musicals that paused here en route to New York included "Affairs of State," "The Legend of Sarah," "The Relapse," "Hilda Crane," "Edwina Black," "The Golden State," "Darkness at Noon," "Billy Budd," "The Autumn Garden," "Let Me Hear the Melody," "Gramercy Ghost," "Angels Kiss Me" and "The Man That Corrupted Hadleyburg." That's a total of thirteen with "Darkness at Noon," "The Autumn Garden," "Angels Kiss Me" and "The Man That Corrupted Hadleyburg" being the "world preems."

The 1950-51 season got off to a promising start on Labor Day night when "Affairs of State," with Celeste Holm, made its bow at the Locust after a brief warm-up elsewhere. It was received in a friendly if not vociferous fashion. "Kiss Me, Kate," with a different company, returned to the Shubert the same night and on Tuesday the Forrest re-lighted with another welcome returning visitor, "Mister Roberts," which had the distinction of remaining seven weeks, which was the season's "high."

Then, after two inactive weeks as far as openings were concerned, there was an unhappy conflict on September 25 when a tryout nonmusical, "Legend of Sarah" at the Locust, opened against the Theatre Guild's fine revival of "As You Like It" at the Shubert. Local critics, following an old tradition here, covered the new show and weren't any too happy about it. On Tuesday of that week the aforementioned "Lady from Paris" reopened the Erlanger as an independent house, directed by Lawrence Shubert Lawrence and William Goldman. The Erlanger had been dark for several seasons and attendance for the two weeks of "The Lady from Paris" and its successor "Streetcar Named Desire" on October 9 was distinctly not encouraging.

"The Relapse" re-lighted the Walnut on October 9 and was given credit for artistry and charm. Then on the 14th (first Saturday opening in some time here) "Guys and Dolls" bowed at the Shubert. It was a sellout from the start, received rave notices and after three weeks at the Shubert moved to the Erlanger for three more capacity weeks. There didn't seem to be any doubt in anybody's mind about this one.

On October 16, "Hilda Crane" began a two weeks' tryout at the Locust with complimentary notices and fairly good business. Later it was one of those "almosts" in New York. "The Late Edwina Black" (as the English thriller was known here) did two disastrous weeks at the Forrest beginning October 23 and then, on November 4, the season's second big musical first night occurred at the Shubert when "Out of This World" had its première. The advance sale was terrific, probably on the strength of Cole Porter's name and "Kiss Me, Kate's" experience of two seasons back. The notices were generally complimentary but not overwhelmingly so and when it became known that the big musical fantasy stood in need of considerable doctoring, the sale eased off. However, it was a big hit in its three weeks here and there was talk of moving it to the Erlanger, but Boston was finally chosen instead.

On November 6 Samuel Spewack's "The Golden State" had its première at the Walnut and proved a distressing disappointment. Much the same can be said of the revue, "Bless You All," which arrived at the Forrest on Tuesday, April 21, after a week's break-in up in New Haven. "Death of a Salesman" also began a return visit at the Locust on November 20.

Following that, although attendance had been on the goodish side all Fall and had indeed been very big for deserving attractions, Philadelphia experienced a drought of legitimate fare for a period of roughly two and a half months. The D'Oyly Carte Company, which arrived at the Shubert on November 27 and remained there four weeks, was the only legitimate offering in the city until Christmas, when "The Consul" opened at the Shubert for a short return. "Darkness at Noon" had its première at the Forrest (26th) and Maurice Schwartz came to the Walnut (24th). It was freely noted that the holiday bills here this year were of a heavy and sordid nature.

After that the only activity for a period of a month or more was a nightmarish comedy tryout, "Four Twelves Are 48," at the Locust on January 1; the perennial "Blossom Time" at the Shubert on January 8 and "The Innocents" at the Erlanger on January 15.

Over the period just noted there was the unprecedented number of twenty-six dark weeks divided between the five houses.

January 29 saw another embarrassing conflict—that of "Billy Budd" (Forrest) and "Come Back, Little Sheba" (Walnut), the critics choosing the former as being the novelty and a tryout. On February 12, the Lunts paid Philadelphia their first visit in many moons with "I Know My Love," which enjoyed two capacity weeks at the Walnut. On Tuesday (the 13th) "Peter Pan," as revived with Jean Arthur, began a successful three weeks' run at the Shubert.

"The Autumn Garden" had its "world preem" at the Locust on Wednesday, the 21st, and received mixed notices. "The Green Pastures," in a stirring revival, came to the Forrest on the 27th, received good reviews but did only fairly well. "Springtime for Henry," with a new production but Edward Everett Horton still in his old, familiar role, arrived at the Locust on March 1. These were all, by the way, save when otherwise noted, all two-week engagements.

"Make a Wish" had its première at the Shubert the week of March 12, with a tremendous advance sale racked up. Adverse notices and word-of-mouth, however, put a damper on the business and although the show added an extra week here while the "fixing" was done by Abe Burrows and others, attendance wasn't very good after the opening full week.

"Let Me Hear the Melody" was another opening the week of March 12 and got high praise from the second-string critics who covered it at the Walnut and from the first-stringers in subsequent Sunday columns. Its closing here came as a complete surprise, although later partially explained by the statement that the show will reopen next season.

"Gramercy Ghost," a mildly amusing comedy, opened a tryout at the Locust March 19 and its star, Sarah Churchill, received glowing notices as she later did in New York. Another big musical came this way (from New Haven) on March 26 when "A Tree Grows in Brooklyn" began a three weeks' stay at the Forrest, with enthusiastic notices and fine attendance. Still another nasty conflict came on April 2 when "Angels Kiss Me," a comedy, had its première at the Walnut against "The Lady's Not for Burning" at the Locust. This time, however, the critics chose the Broadway success and accorded it "super-raves." "Angels Kiss Me" was an immediate and deserving flop.

On the disappointing side, too, was "The Man That Corrupted Hadleyburg" which "preemed" at the Erlanger on Saturday, April 14. This was produced by Lawrence Shubert Lawrence, who had seen and liked it very much as presented at the Hedgerow Theatre in Rose Valley near here last fall. Some of the critics had admired it there too.

"The Guardsman," as revived by Jeanette MacDonald, with a musical interlude, arrived at the Forrest on April 16 and although the critics weren't much impressed, the star's film following helped a lot at the box office. Then on Tuesday, the 17th, "Flahooley" opened a three weeks' engagement at the Shubert to uniformly enthusiastic notices. Indeed a greater set of "raves" has seldom been seen here and the audience reaction, right from the start, was equally laudatory. The show built to capacity half-way through the run and was a sensational sellout all the last week. Local reaction to New York's tepid and generally unfavorable reception was one of amazement and even disgust.

"Courtin' Time," still another new musical with plenty "on the ball," came to the Forrest from a week's tryout in New Haven on April 20 and was also very well liked. The illness of Lloyd Nolan, the star, necessitated substitution of Alfred Drake, the director, for a number of performances. It stayed here two weeks, as did "Borscht Capades," the Yiddish-English revue which opened at the Locust on the same date. "Oklahoma!," paying us its fourth visit, came to the Forrest for a fortnight on the 14th and did nicely.

The season of 1950-51 was by no means as disappointing as that of 1949-50, but the only thing that saved the day for it was the abundance of rousing big new musicals.

THE SEASON IN CHICAGO

By Claudia Cassidy

Drama Critic of the *Chicago Tribune*

IT was not our season in the sun. The encroaching shade of our theatrical decline spread wider, so that the least selective count could scarcely dig up more than 23 shows and 152 weeks of 1950-51 playgoing. Most of our theater was from one to two seasons old, or was likely to arrive by default or inadvertence.

Eddie Dowling did what he could to alleviate our ennui by calling on us first in "Angel in the Pawnshop," and Fridolin arrived, and as hastily departed, in "Ti-Coq." We were under the impression that "The Rose Tattoo" tried out here, until the august *Herald Tribune* explained that the show played "four weeks of rehearsals in Chicago which the public was permitted to attend."

It would be nice, if we could, to consult other oracles. To discover why, for instance, neither "The Cocktail Party" nor "The Lady's Not for Burning" came our way. Why "Guys and Dolls," in duplicate, will arrive in its second season, by way of California. Why "The Member of the Wedding" bypassed us on spring tour in order to bolster Theatre Guild subscription in 1951-52, with the hazards of an altered cast. Why the only show all season smart enough to duplicate itself for its and our immediate benefit was "The Moon Is Blue."

Patience is an enervating virtue and a good many Chicagoans have shrugged off the possibility of doing much serious playgoing in Chicago. Still, we do pretty well by shows of less than pristine vintage, having a taste for theatre and not much choice in satisfying it. When "South Pacific" finally arrived after 19 months of managerial cogitation resulting in a less than inspired cast, we poured $550,000 into the Shubert's coffers in ecstatic advance, and patronized it royally for the 29 weeks clicked off at season's end, when it was hard to believe that it was really Irene Bordoni waiting in the wings to play Bloody Mary.

The fact that Chicago's playgoing plight is neither new nor unique doesn't make it more palatable. Nor has it turned up a solution. Tennessee Williams is all for a decentralized theatre, with each city giving fresh, fully professional production to plays otherwise subject to incalculable delay and deterioration if, indeed, they ever arrive at all. This would at least reassure playgoers affronted by the managerial assumption that they should be content with a more or less rancid approximation of a production's original flavor. At the moment, integrity and imagination are our life savers. It was an imaginative coup that put piquant Maggie McNamara in the Barbara Bel Geddes role and made an overnight hit of Chicago's "The Moon Is Blue." It was integrity that kept the Lunts gallant if weary in "I Know My Love," a "vehicle" they had to carry when it should have given them a ride—and that had a first night apologist for Lynn Fontanne's injured arm saying that Miss Fontanne hoped we would "pay no attention to the cast."

But if Oscar Hammerstein 2d says his favorite scene in "South Pacific" is the first meeting of Nellie and her planter friend, and I see his point, how can he be happy about a Chicago company in which that meeting is all wrong? If a world of care is lavished on the fragile illusion of "The Innocents," why turn it over to less scrupulous producers whose insensitive approximation of the original deprived it of the more delicate turns of the screw? Is it to tour such a cut-down version that Theatre Guild subscription was born?

"Come Back, Little Sheba" restored some waning Guild prestige, for Shirley Booth and Sidney Blackmer kept it a deeply disturbing, agonizingly absorbing performance of what in the end was a wistful rather than a powerful play. "Lost in the Stars" almost turned into a controversy—lack of money closed it where a campaign might have saved it—and some of us regretted being forced to say that where the book was magnificent, the musical was earnest, that a great cry of anguish had been muted to a stylized moan. Still, it was a cut above the average show, and it gave us what it had without stinting.

Several shows left us with fulminations and manifestoes, on their way, they said, to Broadway and true connoisseurs. One was "Springboard to Nowhere," apt only in title, being a pseudo-surrealist piece by Alexander Lidor, pretentiously staged by Eddie Dowling with Julie Haydon, Romney Brent and a femme fatale named Cara Williams. "Mike McCauley," a paratrooper piece with spies, was played by Don De Fore, Isa Miranda and others, with all the stops out and all the camera angles in. "Red, White and Blue," a gargantuan flop sponsored by the ill-advised American Legion, expired with a sigh said to have cost $600,000.

Even Mae West seemed a little tired of the joke when "Diamond Lil" limped into town, and it was compounding a felony to put Kenny Delmar in "Texas, Li'l Darlin'." Katharine Hepburn was duly christened Fair Rosalimb, but the Shakespearean champagne was pretty flat. The D'Oyly Cartes did a landoffice business and regretted cutting a three-week booking to two. "Peter Pan" told a bedtime story in the huge Civic Opera House, and rang up $149,600 in 24 performances. At the last playing Joan McCracken stepped in for Jean Arthur, and her Peter was lyrical, mischievous and delightful.

"It's a Great Day" was a brave attempt by war veterans in wheel chairs to stage a revue. "Borscht Capades of 1951"—well, how would you like to be confronted with that, even to keep a theatre out of mothballs? How would you like a bedraggled return engagement of "A Streetcar Named Desire," hauled in by truck to a managerial shrug, "Well, the boobs seem to like it."?

As an indication that the booby trap may be on the other foot when producers so rashly miscalculate Chicago, the local gross for 17 performances of the Sadler's Wells Ballet was $232,380. Even the Metropolitan Opera in less than its most luxurious estate piled up more than $96,000 in four performances, though $35,000 of that went to a benefit audacious enough to ask $18 for "Fledermaus."

In any case, for the record, the 1950-51 listing, compiled as of June 2:

Harris: 37 weeks—"Two Blind Mice," 14 weeks' holdover, 18 in all; "The Innocents," 9; "Ti-Coq," 2½; "Mike McCauley," 4 performances; "A Streetcar Named Desire," 6 weeks' return engagement; "The Moon Is Blue," 5 weeks to date.

Shubert: 29 weeks—"South Pacific's" record to date.

Blackstone: 25 weeks—"Diamond Lil," 16 weeks in revival; D'Oyly Carte Opera Company, 2 weeks of Gilbert and Sullivan repertory; "It's a Great Day," 5; "Borscht Capades of 1951," 2.

Great Northern: 20 weeks—"Lend an Ear," 15 weeks' holdover, 25 in all; "Texas, Li'l Darlin'," 3; "Lost in the Stars," 2.

Erlanger: 19 weeks—"Oklahoma!", 7 weeks' return engagement holdover, 13 in all; "Mister Roberts," 5 weeks' return engagement; "As You Like It," 3; "The Rose Tattoo," 4.

Selwyn: 16 weeks—"Springboard to Nowhere," 2; "Angel in the Pawnshop," 10; "I Know My Love," 4.

Civic Opera House: 6 weeks—"Red, White and Blue," 3; "Peter Pan," 3.

THE SEASON IN SAN FRANCISCO

By Fred Johnson

Drama Editor, *The Call-Bulletin*

AS the season ended, San Francisco was winning some distinction, however dubious, as a showman's experimental ground. The field, it was true, had appeared wide open, with no more than twenty bona fide attractions as the theatrical year's total, evenly divided between touring and Coast-originated shows. In 1947 there had been at least ten more.

The Eastern road companies had no part in the experimentation. They had to be assured of their welcome and a profitable stay in what has long been known as "a good show town," but one sharing with some other centers in a loss of such prestige. No musical of size would risk the long jaunt westward unless sponsored by the San Francisco and Los Angeles Light Opera Associations and the certainty of profitable engagements in both cities. But there was no less temerity on the part of certain dramatic road attractions as well.

Retrospect of the past season's slim theatrical pickings might well spur San Francisco showmen to more effective bidding for the road companies. Rather than developing an isolationist attitude and the independent resolve to create their own theatre in the "Coast Defender" style of some old-time actors, there is seen a need of banding together the entire Coast theatrical forces for a circuit that would insure the traveling attractions a profitable playing time.

The latch has long been out, in a way, from San Diego to Seattle on the Coastwise front, with Salt Lake City and Denver in equally flirtatious mood. But still lacking is the co-operative action that would lead to more comfortable theatres, a unified subscription plan —and a necessary awakening from slumber.

Since the Civic Light Opera Associations named have guaranteed the Coast visits of several Broadway hit musicals, with original casts or duplicated national companies, opportunity is seen for the extension of a Western circuit beyond San Francisco and Los Angeles for the backing of non-musical attractions as well. The Theatre Guild offerings have been all too infrequent, with a continuing uncertainty as to their scheduled number and dates.

A boon to the San Francisco theatre from Spring until Summer's

34

end has long been the light opera season. Among its 1950 successes were the original company in "Lost in the Stars" and the touring cast in "South Pacific," the latter tenanting the War Memorial Opera House of United Nations Conference memory. Preceding these had come revivals of "The Chocolate Soldier" and "Rose Marie." All played to capacity business, with "South Pacific" continuing for six weeks. Following this regular series was "Gentlemen Prefer Blondes," starring Gertrude Niesen, in a transfer from the Los Angeles Greek Theatre in which Gene Mann annually offers a summer musical season. The same producer had 1951 plans to alternate his attractions between the two cities, with San Francisco's opera house under seasonal lease.

Since the experiments mentioned were inevitable, it was a case of "try anything once." If the field were to be called a proving ground there was the risk of proving only that there might be better luck next time. So there were Coast-incubated revues that were virtually vaudeville, new comedy and drama feelers and a repertory company that aimed to be local, professional and permanent, with the added intention of doing off-beat plays. That one ended with a brief and futile switch to popular comedy, which in turn gave way to a Hollywood-grown revue.

The repertory experiment, of more rosy hue in last season's report, was the venture of Robert T. Eley, a Californian of Old Vic and Cherry Lane (New York) experience. He had established in a remodeled church the San Francisco Repertory Company and introduced such seldom-played items as "The Adding Machine," "Trio," "No Exit" and "Duet with Two Hands." The experiment faded out, with Eley in search of a Hollywood "name" to head the cast of a popular comedy. Failing in his quest, a movieland revue titled "Strictly Informal" moved in at the close of this summary. Whether or not the engagement was to end as a dry run was yet to be determined.

To ascertain whether San Francisco would like a comedy called "The Square Needle" to the extent that patrons did in its stay at Hollywood's Las Palmas Theatre (original home of "Lend an Ear"), the adaptation of a Samuel W. Taylor novel was brought to the Downtown Theatre—a former musical and vaudeville house—heralded as a "very warm for May" importation. Impresario Edward G. Maley presented Victor Jory, Wayne Morris and Carol Thurston in the charade about officers and men in a London public relations office of the U. S. Air Force. A badly built play, it still proved laugh-worthy.

In a city boasting of its music-loving clientele—and ably supporting grand opera, symphony and ballet—"The Medium" and "The Telephone" were badly neglected for three weeks, despite the excellence of casts headed by Mary Davenport in a Coast production by James A. Doolittle. But "Les Ballets de Paris" set the town agog for the same period later on. "Kiss Me, Kate," in a return engagement with Frances McCann and Robert Wright, did a month's capacity business.

The year's outstanding dramatic event, as expected, was "Death of a Salesman," with Thomas Mitchell and June Walker, rewarded with a seven weeks' run but with patronage slightly off in the final stanzas. "Summer and Smoke," teaming Dorothy McGuire and John Ireland, had a profitable three weeks, as did Maurice Evans in "The Devil's Disciple," though short of the expected capacity houses. A Coast revival of "Strictly Dishonorable," starring Cesar Romero, was not to the public's taste, even though it had not been locally presented within the last two decades. But "Come Back, Little Sheba," with Sidney Blackmer and Shirley Booth, might have run longer than its allotted two weeks. This also was an "event."

A casualty of Coast origination was "Mike McCauley," a tragi-comedy of the late war's Italian fighting, co-starring Don De Fore and Isa Miranda of the films. Its end came within a fortnight, after poor support, to be given shorter shrift in Chicago, with authors Fred F. Finklehoffe and Leo Liberman continuing their revisions. "The Innocents," with Sylvia Sidney, survived two weeks, but to small profit.

By far the year's most melancholy disaster was Frank Fay's "If You Please" revue, branded the worst offering of 1950, in any category, by the San Francisco Critics' Council. This would have been the aisle observers' verdict aside from their panning by the comedian after each nightly performance through his single week's stay. Besides supplying music, lyrics, scenes and dialogue, the late star of "Harvey" had also undertaken too much as an almost continuous performer. Completing the disaster, he had overly invested in the production—a less than noble experiment.

Katharine Hepburn in "As You Like It," with support by William Prince and Aubrey Mather, received the town's acclaim for three excellent weeks. But so did Mae West for the same period in "Diamond Lil," which she had first played in San Francisco some twenty years before. It remained for Henry Fonda to enter the season's longest local run—eight weeks—as this chronicle closed.

"Where's Charley," with Ray Bolger, launched the 1951 Civic Light Opera season, playing five weeks to capacity, followed by General Director Edwin Lester's revival of "The Merry Widow," starring Jane Pickens and Hollywood's Paul Henreid in a four weeks' engagement. The latter was to be replaced in Los Angeles by Carl Brisson. The light opera season was to be completed with the national company of "Guys and Dolls" and an original production of "Three Wishes for Jamie," based on James O'Neal's prize-winning novel, "The Three Wishes of Jamie McRuin."

An event of extraordinary interest was San Francisco Town Hall's western première of The Drama Quartet in George Bernard Shaw's "Don Juan in Hell," from "Man and Superman." Co-starred were Charles Boyer as Don Juan, Charles Laughton as The Devil, Agnes Moorehead as Donna Anna and Sir Cedric Hardwicke as The Statue. With a return engagement promised, the company was scheduled for later performances in this country and perhaps in London.

Summer theatre festivals were held concurrently at Stanford University and at the Palo Alto Community Playhouse, where peninsula groups were included. At Stanford "Orestia" was the 1951 season's highlight production.

THE SEASON IN SOUTHERN CALIFORNIA

By Edwin Schallert

Drama Critic of the *Los Angeles Times*

BESET by television and economic change, the theatre fought a losing battle in its attempt to maintain anything like a consistent hold on the public during the 1950-51 season in Southern California. The stage was not the lone sufferer. It had a commiserating associate in the films. Pictures didn't draw any more readily than live shows by and large. Both had to face the issue of an elusive audience bent on shopping for only the best of the best.

Encouragement for new effort in the footlight world was thus at its lowest ebb. Only a brave adventurer or two—notably Harold J. Kennedy—had the courage to essay producing plays in Los Angeles. Kennedy's effort was particularly noteworthy in such a bad season, because successively at two different theatres he attained class in his presentations, and wasn't deterred even by poor financial results. He helped to inaugurate Harout's Ivar Theatre as a new showhouse, and proffered a very distinguished production of "The Madwoman of Chaillot" among other smart showmanship exploits.

Notwithstanding very fitful support up to the end of the season when he was preparing to stage "Detective Story," Kennedy was firm in the belief that rewards were still lurking for his enterprise. He had joined forces then with Herman D. Hover, the night club proprietor, and former associate of Earl Carroll, who had taken over the theatre. He had signed a five-year contract to take full charge of production, directing, casting, etc., a deal made with movie-like options.

While Kennedy's determination to proceed met with praise from the thin and apparently wavering line of stage devotees, they still were speculating on how it would all come out. The grip of television on the Southern California public is peculiarly strong. This is understandable in a huge sprawling community like Los Angeles, where traffic and parking complexities have grown greater day by day. No rapid transit system helps the situation, and the automobile is relied on by the majority of theatregoers who have to reach widely scattered destinations.

The habit of going to shows has been lost. It is so much simpler to stay at home and watch something on a screen in the living room. Besides, money that might have been used for the theatre has been invested in installment buying of television sets.

It is hoped, of course, that when television sets are paid for and the novelty of this form of entertainment has worn off people will seek entertainment away from home once again. Just when that upturn would occur nobody was quite sure about on June 1, 1951.

Stage show prices are a problem, Kennedy himself felt, in estimating the future. A $3.60 top is imperative at a theatre of less than 400 capacity like the Ivar. Kennedy opined that a theatre with about 800 capacity that would charge $2.40 top might fare better.

Yet during the season a theatre of somewhat greater capacity than 800, which had had a number of major successes, including the famous "Ken Murray's Blackouts," the El Capitan, was turned over to NBC for television. The old Music Box on Hollywood Boulevard, which subsequently was operated as a film theatre, also was taken over by the new medium under the CBS aegis. A similar fate happened to the Century Theatre, which was launched during 1949-50. Other playhouses will unquestionably be making a like transition.

Through all these changes light opera still holds its large audiences. "Where's Charley?" with Ray Bolger and a company including Allyn McLerie, coming directly from New York, pleased the patrons of the Los Angeles Civic Light Opera Association for five weeks. They felt that the show was mainly Bolger, but that didn't lessen their enjoyment.

As the season closed "The Merry Widow," Coast produced, with Carl Brisson as Prince Danilo, and Jane Pickens in the title part, became the second event of the 1951 season. Brisson had replaced Paul Henreid during the final performances of the San Francisco engagement. It was an admirably staged revival, with Brisson appearing in a role he has played many times since 1923 in England. For Miss Pickens it was a new venture following her light opera debut in "Regina." It might be called a stylized presentation of a semi-classic.

The Civic Light Opera Association in 1950 closed impressively with "Lost in the Stars," brought to the Coast and presented under the guidance of Rouben Mamoulian, who had originally staged it, with Todd Duncan as the star. Previously "Rose Marie" had been given following the long run of "South Pacific" with Patrice Munsel, Wally Cassel, Jack Goode, Clarissa and others in the featured cast.

The Greek Theatre season (outdoors) under the management of Gene Mann had reached high points of success with "Finian's Rainbow," starring Ella Logan and David Wayne, with Albert Sharpe, and "Gentlemen Prefer Blondes" with Gertrude Niesen. "Miss Liberty" was interesting because of Mary McCarty's presence, and Kenny Baker and Beverly Tyler singing the romantic leads. "The Desert Song" with Brian Sullivan, Helen Bliss and Sterling Holloway, and "Rio Rita" with John Raitt, Marina Koshetz and Pinky Lee were the other productions.

While the theatre was dark much of the time during the latter half of the season, the Biltmore had a fair succession of touring attractions past the turn of the year. "Death of a Salesman," early in the season, was pre-eminent with Thomas Mitchell, later replaced by Albert Dekker, June Walker and Paul Langton heading the cast during a six weeks' engagement.

Maurice Evans, warmly received in his Shakespeare and "Man and Superman," did not find a very responsive audience for "The Devil's Disciple," by George Bernard Shaw. "Summer and Smoke," by Tennessee Williams, which started at La Jolla and then went on tour through the Southwest, had more appeal, with Dorothy McGuire, John Ireland and Una Merkel in leading roles. High in quality were the visits of "Come Back, Little Sheba," with Shirley Booth and Sidney Blackmer, and of "As You Like It," with Katharine Hepburn, William Prince, Vanessa Brown and Milton Parsons. This brought 1950 to approximately its close, except for the arrival of "Les Ballets de Paris" at the Biltmore December 25.

In 1951 the succession of attractions included the return of "Kiss Me, Kate," with Frances McGann, Robert Wright, Benny Baker, Marc Platt and Betty George; "Apple of His Eye," starring Edward Arnold; "Diamond Lil," with Mae West; "The Innocents," with Sylvia Sidney, aided by David Cole, Patsy Bruder and Regina Wallace. Things were quiet for touring companies from mid-April on.

First of the Kennedy productions, staged at Las Palmas Theatre, was a revival of "Strictly Dishonorable," with Cesar Romero, Marilyn Erskine, Kennedy himself, and Fred Clark in leading parts. He followed that with "The Winslow Boy," acted by Vincent Price, Jane Wyatt, John Hoyt, Rose Hobart and young Robin Camp. After this came "Horace," starring Nancy Walker, which Kennedy wrote himself, and which turned out less happily. Lynn Bari, Marjorie Riordan and Peter Adams were in the cast.

Kennedy then changed locations to the Ivar Theatre, where he presented "The Barretts of Wimpole Street," with Susan Peters and Philip Reed; "Joan of Lorraine," starring Luise Rainer, and "The Madwoman of Chaillot," starring Aline MacMahon, which played for five weeks. After that the theatre was taken over briefly for the production of "Tartuffe" in the Miles Malleson adaptation of Molière, with Sam Jaffe in the title role, and Albert Band producing in association with the Actors' Album, Kennedy's organization. Jaffe had previously done this at the Brattle Theatre at Cambridge, Mass.

Peter Adams and Frances Austin were associated with Kennedy at Harout's Ivar Theatre, and indicative of his ability to assemble unusual casts was the presence of Clarence Derwent, Cora Witherspoon, Eve McVeagh, Fay Roope, John E. Wengraf and others.

Here and there through the season were other events worth noting. For a single night the greatest thrill was provided by the First Drama Quartet in their interpretation of "Don Juan in Hell." Charles Boyer, Charles Laughton, Agnes Moorehead and Cedric Hardwicke appeared in this following their tour managed by Paul Gregory, who has sponsored Laughton's solo stint of readings from the Bible, Shakespeare, Dickens, and other celebrated literature. Crowds literally stormed the auditorium to applaud the remarkable Bernard Shaw presentation.

Laughton much earlier in the season was associated with Eugenie Leontovich in a revival of "The Cherry Orchard" at Miss Leontovich's State Theatre. Hardwicke in turn was identified as the director and actor in that far less happy experiment of ANTA, Shaw's "Getting Married," which closed in Los Angeles. It had a remarkable cast including Mady Christians, Dennis King, Judith Evelyn, Arthur Treacher, Ralph Forbes, John Buckmaster, Colin Keith-Johnston and Margaret Bannerman, but failed to lure audiences to the Biltmore.

"The Square Needle," a post-war comedy by Samuel W. Taylor, seemed to justify itself with a 10 weeks' run, though revisions were proceeding as it played. Donald Woods, Marjorie Lord, Alan Hale, Jr., James Flavin and Frank Cady appeared. The play subsequently went on tour with a somewhat different cast.

"Twelfth Night" was sponsored by the Circle Players at the Century Theatre, with John Abbott as an excellent Malvolio, Alan Reed as Sir Toby Belch, and Gus Schilling as Sir Andrew Aguecheek. The comedians fared best in this production directed by Constance Collier with Marjorie Steele (Mrs. Huntington Hartford) whom she schooled for the role as Viola, though good performances were also offered by Don Kreger as the Clown, Eve Halpern as Maria, and Ricki Soma. It was a nicely staged and embellished presentation.

Along classic lines Oliver Goldsmith's "She Stoops to Conquer" was offered by the Hollywood Actors Company at the New Globe Theatre with Miss Soma and Douglas Wood as featured members of the cast. Fred Stone starred in "You Can't Take It with You" as a more modern revival. William Bendix and Marie McDonald appeared under Gene Mann's management in "Born Yesterday." John Dall and Gladys George acted in "The Man." Albert Dekker and Dolores Costello were seen in an inferior affair, "The Great Man." Sized up for their impact scarcely any of these merit more than passing mention.

Others to note for the record were the American Legion revue, "Red, White and Blue," presented by LeRoy Prinz and Owen Crump, with George Jessel as its star in Los Angeles only; "Little Boy Blue," musical produced by Paula Stone and Mike Sloane, which failed; "Ballet Ballads," a very clever song, dance and pantomime affair; "Mr. Big Shot," which might have had some possibilities with revision, by Robert Abel; "The Second Man," with Edward Ashley, and "High and Dry," with Skeets Gallagher.

Effort was made to relight Earl Carroll's Restaurant Theatre with the "New York Latin Quarter Revue," with Frank Libuse as principal comedian. James A. Doolittle brought "The Medium" and "The Telephone" to town, and also staged "The Vagabond King" at the Hollywood Bowl, with Nadine Conner, Leif Erickson, Lucille Norman and Don Wilson as principals. A great triumph was scored by the Sadler's Wells Ballet at the huge Shrine Auditorium, but that was apart from the regular theatre routine.

Theatre-in-the-round gloried in two events—the staging of the musical show "I Love Lydia," by Philip G. and Julius J. Epstein, with music and lyrics by Ray Evans and Jay Livingston of "Buttons and Bows" fame, and "The School for Scandal," with Marie Wilson. An oddity that linked the two shows, one at the Ring, the other at the Circle, was that the Epsteins attempted a modern version of Richard Brinsley Sheridan's "The Rivals" in their musical, Sheridan also being the author of "The School for Scandal." Miss Wilson's surrounding cast included William Schallert as Sir Peter Teazle, John O'Malley as Joseph Surface, and John Goldsworthy.

"I Love Lydia" had a run of 15 weeks, and "The School for Scandal" closed to capacity business after 10 weeks to make way for a very good production of "What Every Woman Knows," with Ruth Conte and Sydney Chaplin. The Ring did "The Corn Is Green" with Doris Lloyd in the Ethel Barrymore role, and "Once in a Lifetime" and "Payment Deferred," directed by Dudley Nichols, during its season. The Circle changed management about the end of the year, and the first play was the rather provocative "Wind without Rain" by Ivan Tors. George Boroff was the prime mover in the new operation. Preston Sturges might be noted as an entrant in the novelty theatre field with his playroom, a restaurant theatre, which presented one-acters. It is a beautifully appointed small establishment.

Pasadena Playhouse in wonted fashion proved anew its broad horizon, including a variety of plays from Shakespeare to modern French and contemporary American, several of which were premièred, though not with any great glory. The 1950 Summer festival dealt with modern playwrights, comprising Noel Coward, Moss Hart, Tennessee Williams, Lillian Helman, Herman Wouk, Harold Brighouse, William Walden and Irving Phillips. Out of the Summer group, "One Foot in Heaven," by Phillips, was held over for four weeks. Hart's "Light up the Sky" was also held over.

Premièred were "Bottom of the Pile," by Ernest Vajda and Clement Scott Gilbert; "Little Scandal," by Florence Ryerson and Alice D. G. Miller; "Pagan in the Parlor," by Franklin Lacey, with James Whale directing; "Heaven Help the Angels," by Lynn Root. "The Enchanted," by Jean Giraudoux, "Anne of the Thousand Days," "Present Laughter," "Much Ado About Nothing," "The Live Wire," "Born Yesterday," "The Man," "The Pied Piper of Hamelin," a Christmastime offering; "Harvey," which was held over; "Kitty Doone," "The Silver Whistle" and "See How They Run," Philip King comedy were in the repertoire.

La Jolla Playhouse, Inc., headed by Gregory Peck, Dorothy McGuire and Mel Ferrer, flourished among Summer theatre enterprises, with a fine advance sale and profit. Hollywood film stars are more ready to work at this theatre than almost any other. The 1950 plays included "Born Yesterday," "Claudia," "Summer and Smoke," which subsequently toured; "Arsenic and Old Lace," "Front Page," "Our Town," "The Silver Whistle" in a noteworthy engagement with José Ferrer; "Clutterbuck" and "Goodbye Again."

Such players as Wendell Corey, Robert Ryan, Don De Fore, Richard Carlson, Michael O'Shea, Teresa Wright, Audrey Totter, Joan Caulfield, Marie McDonald, Florence Bates, Helen Westcott, Beulah Bondi, Leon Ames, Ellen Corby and numerous others were identified with the casts. It is quite the thing to appear at La Jolla.

It might be noted in view of the proximity of La Jolla to San Diego that the latter city has been assuming new importance as a center, with some 21 community type theatres, and a Summer Shakespearean festival. Interest is very keen in the stage in that area.

Laguna Beach had plays for a portion of the 1950 Summer season, given by the Graham Players, in addition to its all-year-round community project. Donald Cook, Brenda Joyce, Roddy McDowall, Jeff Donnell, Mabel Albertson, Skeets Gallagher, Douglas Dick and

Ellen Corby were among those appearing. The Eighteen Actors, Inc., largely professional, is an interesting group in Pasadena, playing during the Winter and Spring. They offered "Autumn Fire," Irish play by T. C. Murray, very interestingly. The Callboard continues its production activities, and still pursuing their way are the Bliss-Hayden, Geller Workshop, Westwood Village Players and various others. The Orchard Gables group also did some effective work during the season. "The Drunkard" is in its 18th year, the Turnabout in its 10th, while the Padua Hills Players are similarly an institution. While attempts to revive "The Mission Play" have not prospered, the Pilgrimage Play is evidently assured each Summer, as is the outdoor "Ramona" in the Spring at Hemet. Turnabout was even briefly blessed with a Junior Turnabout during the season, aimed at entertaining children.

The Theatre remains as sprawling in Southern California as the civic geography of its center, Los Angeles.

GUYS AND DOLLS *

A Musical Fable of Broadway in Two Acts

BASED ON A STORY AND CHARACTERS BY DAMON RUNYON

MUSIC AND LYRICS BY FRANK LOESSER; BOOK BY JO SWERLING AND ABE BURROWS

THE history of "Guys and Dolls" could be one of success from the start, but it isn't. When this "musical fable of Broadway" began its tryout in Philadelphia it was an immediate hit. It looked good enough for Broadway and in less careful hands it would have been brought in in two or three weeks. But everybody concerned with the show wanted to make it as good as possible and circumstances favored a delay. Most musicals and plays lose money on their try-outs, but this one didn't; so "Guys and Dolls" was kept out of town for several additional weeks of experimentation and polishing. Under the direction of George S. Kaufman, the polishing was exceptionally brisk and bright, with the result that the first New York performance was memorable for its perfection. The company had no star box-office names and the writers were not well known—in fact, one of them, Abe Burrows, had never before written for the theatre. The one real box-office name connected with the musical was that of the late Damon Runyon, one of whose stories and many of whose characters were the basis for the libretto. Yet "Guys and Dolls" is the editor's choice to lead off this year's selection of the Ten Best Plays, because of its originality and its avoidance of the usual musical comedy pattern, which is heavily romantic. Far from being romantic, this musical is cynical, looking with Runyon's cool amusement at a weird and fanciful assortment of seamy characters; yet it is not tough and is notably free from dirt. The book, by Jo Swerling and Mr. Burrows, can stand by itself as a skillfully made play. The lyrics, by Frank Loesser, are part and parcel of the book, their main purpose being to reveal character and fit or advance the story. I wish that, somehow, the reader could hear Mr. Loesser's music just by opening these pages, but publishers have not yet got around to this improvement. Still, one can hear the music at the theatre, on the radio or on phonograph records—and, hearing it, can realize that the score, too, is in character.

It is music which begins "Guys and Dolls"—Broadway dance music which illustrates a pantomime played on Broadway itself. Two men who can be described only as shady characters are loitering and watching the passing parade. One of them is snapping his fingers and the other is flipping a coin. A policeman strolls by. Here come two chorus girls, wearing slacks; then two very animated bobby-soxers. Two well-dressed street walkers pause near the two shady characters. The one with the coin flips his coin again and he and his partner take the two chorus girls by the arm and walk on. The parade is constantly changing—an old lady selling fruit, flowers and pretzels; a sightseeing Texan with wife; a sidewalk photographer who snaps the Texans, offers an order blank, gets money— and crumples the blank and throws it away when the visitors have gone on. Here are an actor and an actress—they must be, for she is elegantly dressed and he is wearing a tuxedo. The bobby soxers plead for autographs, but desist in disgust when the man's shirt front lights up and spells "Pessimo Cigars." A paper doll vendor and his lady assistant have a trick sales vehicle which can be quickly converted into a baby buggy; when they see the policeman they stop selling their jumping paper dolls, convert the keister into a pram and nod graciously at the cop as they pass him. A heavyweight prize fighter, with a manager tagging along giving instructions, makes his passage by skipping rope. A sightseeing guide has several tourists in tow, including the Texans. A pickpocket approaches the Texan, points to a tall building and, when the rubberneck stretches his neck to look, lifts his watch and chain. The street walkers flirt with the pickpocket, deftly relieve him of watch and chain and stroll on with him. The Texan has missed his timepiece and sets off in pursuit. Broadway is a street of constant movement, and soon it seems that everybody is chasing somebody.

Benny Southstreet, a little fellow, has come along and he is intently reading a scratch sheet. The prize fighter, coming back, is now shadow boxing. He runs into Benny accidentally and is knocked down by the force of Benny's head against his solar plexus; this frightens him and he runs, followed by manager. Benny, unconcerned, joins a very round man named Nicely-Nicely Johnson, who has just bought a scratch sheet at the newsstand. A third horse-

follower, Rusty Charlie, appears with his own sheet, and the trio
sing, in fugue fashion, *A Fugue for Tinhorns.*
Sings Nicely:

> I got the horse right here
> The name is Paul Revere. . . .

Sings Benny:

> I'm pickin' Valentine, 'cause on the morning line
> The guy has got him figured at five to nine. . . .

Sings Rusty Charlie:

> But look at Epitaph. He wins it by a half
> According to this here in the Telegraph. . . .

Each sings the praises of his favorite. "Can do, can do," Nicely
opines; "Has chance, has chance," asserts Benny, while Rusty advises, "Big threat, big threat." It is indeed a fugue for tinhorns,
and it is musically and lyrically ingenious.
A different kind of music is heard from a different source as a
Mission band appears—Sister Sarah with a tambourine, a woman
playing a trombone, a man playing a cornet, the venerable Arvide
Abernathy playing bass drum and cymbals, and another woman just
carrying a box for Sarah to stand on. Sarah, a very pretty girl even
in her severe Mission uniform, mounts the box and begins to sing
while various wayfarers stop to listen. She exhorts:

> Follow the fold and stray no more,
> Stray no more, stray no more;
> Put down the bottle and we'll say no more—
> Follow, follow the fold.

When the song is ended Sarah goes into prose, pleading, "Brothers
and sisters, resist the Devil and he will flee from you. And that is
why I am standing here, in the Devil's own city, on the Devil's own
street. Hear me, you gamblers"—and she points to Nicely, Benny
and Rusty, who move uneasily. Sarah is a dauntless girl, but sometimes she falters as members of her audience walk out on her. "Just
around the corner," she cries, "is our little Mission where you are
always welcome to seek refuge from this jungle of sin. Come there
and talk to me. Do not think of me as Sergeant Sarah Brown, but
as Sarah Brown, your sister. . . . Remember, friends, it is the Save-
a-Soul Mission. . . ." But by now the audience has drifted away,
all but Benny and Nicely, who are still reading their sheets. The

band disconsolately picks up and moves on, and Nicely comments, "Poor Miss Sarah! I wonder why a refined doll like her is mixed up in the Mission dodge."

"Maybe she owns a piece of the Mission," Benny ventures.

Harry the Horse, a rough-looking character, joins the other two. He wants news about Nathan Detroit: "Is he got a place for his crap game? I'm loaded and looking for action. I just acquired five thousand potatoes."

Nicely inquires in awe, "Where did you acquire it?"

"I collected the reward on my father." Harry departs when he is told that the heat is on and Nathan Detroit is still looking for a place for his game. At the newsstand appears one Brannigan to buy a paper, and with great cordiality Nicely greets him, "Why, Lieutenant Brannigan!" This stops Benny from talking about the crap game. Charmingly, Nicely says, "Mr. Southstreet, it is Lieutenant Brannigan of the New York Police Department."

Brannigan is looking for Nathan Detroit, who has been running a floating crap game and getting away with it by moving it to a different spot every night. He tells Benny and Nicely to warn Nathan that he might as well stop looking for a spot, because everybody knows Brannigan is breathing down his neck. Just as the detective starts away Nathan himself heaves into sight—a slim, nervous, alert man in sharp clothes. Not seeing the officer, he begins, "I'm having terrible trouble. Everybody's scared on account of that lousy Brannigan—"

Brannigan turns back and inquires, icily, "Something wrong, Mr. Detroit?"

Nathan manages a sickly grin and says, "I hope you don't think I was talking about you. There are other lousy Brannigans."

When the detective has gone Nathan's friends eagerly inquire if he has found a place yet. He hasn't. The back of the cigar store and the funeral parlor are out—but he might get the Biltmore Garage, only Joey Biltmore wants a thousand bucks—in cash. Nathan is bitter that Joey won't take his marker, for to him a marker—an I O U—is something sacred, and to welsh on one would be like not saluting the flag. So the garage is out, for Nathan admits he is so broke he couldn't even buy Adelaide a present today, for their fourteenth anniversary. "We been engaged fourteen years," he explains.

More crapshooters begin to drift in, looking for action. Benny exhorts Nathan to do something, for the town is full of high players; even the Greek is here. "But where can I have the game?" Nathan wails, and his companions begin to sing:

NICELY—
The Biltmore Garage wants a grand
BENNY—
But we ain't got a grand on hand
NATHAN—
And they now have a lock on the door
To the gym at P. S. Eighty-Four.
NICELY—
There's the stock room behind McClosky's bar
BENNY—
But Missus McClosky ain't a good scout
NATHAN—
And things bein' how they are
The back of the police station's out.
NICELY—
So the Biltmore Garage is the spot
ALL—
But the one thousand bucks we ain't got.

Crapshooters, as they drift in, take up a chorus:

Why, it's good old reliable Nathan, Nathan Nathan Detroit!
If you're lookin' for action he'll furnish the spot;
Even when the heat is on it's never too hot—
Not for good old reliable Nathan, for it's always just a short walk
To the oldest established permanent floating crap game in New York.

The crowd exhort Nathan, "Where's the action, where's the game?" and Detroit assures them he will find a place and his boys will let them know. The players filter away, and Nathan and his two helpers are joined by Angie-the-Ox, who has some exciting news. Sky Masterson is in town—the highest player of them all. Nathan remembers that once Sky refused to take penicillin when he was sick because he had bet his temperature would go to 104. "He's so lucky it went to 106. Good old Sky!"

It is suggested that Nathan borrow a thousand from Masterson, and Nathan objects, "With him that kind of money ain't lending money—it's betting money." An idea strikes him. "So why don't I bet him? . . . I am perfectly willing to take the risk, providing I can figure out a bet on which there is no chance of losing. He likes crazy bets, like which lump of sugar will a fly sit on, or how far can you kick a piece of cheesecake."

Nathan's idea is developing. He dispatches Benny and Nicely

to Mindy's restaurant to find out how many pieces of cheesecake and how many pieces of strudel Mindy sold yesterday. "Beat it," he urges. "Here comes Adelaide. If she hears I am running the crap game she will never set foot on me again."

Adelaide, a chipper blonde, is on her way to lunch with three other girls from the Hot Box. She tells the girls to run on and order for her while she talks with Nathan a minute. She is carrying a small box. "How's your cold?" Nathan asks.

"Oh, it's much better, thank you. . . . Nathan! Happy anniversary!" Adelaide gives her fiancé the box, which he opens. It contains a belt and a card, which he reads: "Sugar is sweet and so is jelly, so put this belt around your belly."

Nathan feels awkward that he hasn't got a present for her, but Adelaide comforts him, "I kinda like it when you forget to give me presents. It makes me feel like we're married." He assures her that one of these days he'll be in the money and she'll have more mink than a mink. Adelaide tells him she can do without anything just so long as he doesn't run that crap game again.

"What an absurd thought!" exclaims the pious Nathan.

Nicely and Benny return with statistics from Mindy's—twelve hundred cheesecake and fifteen hundred strudel. The puzzled Adelaide tries to find out what this means, but Nathan, growing nervous, gets rid of her by suggesting that his friends escort her to the drug store. He warns, "It's across the street and there're a lot of open manholes around."

Sky Masterson himself comes by, looking healthy and being wealthy from two weeks in Nevada, where he won fifty G's at blackjack. Tomorrow he's flying to Havana, where there is a lot of action.

Nathan carefully and elaborately leads up to his bet by suggesting going over to Mindy's for a piece of cheesecake or strudel, while Sky inquires about Adelaide, saying, "I suppose one of these days you'll be getting married."

"We all got to go some time."

Sky doesn't see it that way. "Guys like us, Nathan," he says, "we got to remember that pleasant as a doll's company may be, she must always take second place to aces back to back."

Offhandedly, Nathan asks Sky to guess what Mindy sells more of—strudel or cheesecake, and when Masterson guesses cheesecake he bets a thousand on strudel. The amused Masterson counters by telling of the warning his father once gave him: "One of these days in your travels a guy is going to come to you and show you a nice brand-new deck of cards on which the seal is not yet broken, and this guy is going to offer to bet you that he can make the Jack of

Spades jump out of the deck and squirt cider in your ear. But son, do not bet this man, for as sure as you stand there you are going to wind up with an earful of cider."

Masterson counters with another bet. Clapping his hand across Nathan's necktie, he bets a thousand Nathan does not know the color of the tie. Nathan is a picture of woe as he tries in vain to remember the color, and finally he says, "No bet."

Benny and Nicely return and Nicely reports, "We took Adelaide to the drug store, and she says for you to be sure to pick her up at the Hot Box after the show and *Don't Be Late.*"

NATHAN—Yes, dear. I mean yes. . . .

SKY—"Yes, dear." That is husband talk if I ever heard it. Nathan, you are trapped. In Adelaide you have the kind of a girl that is most difficult to unload.

NATHAN—I don't want to unload her. I love Adelaide. And a guy without a doll— Well, if a guy does not have a doll—who would holler at him? A doll is a necessity.

SKY—Nathan, I am not putting the rap on dolls. I just say a guy should have them around when he wants them, and they are easy to find.

NATHAN—Not dolls like Adelaide!

SKY—Nathan, figuring weight for age, all dolls are the same.

NATHAN—Oh, yeh?

SKY—Yeah!

NATHAN—Then how come you ain't got a doll? How come your going to Havana alone without one?

SKY—I like to travel light, but if I wish to take a doll to Havana there is a large assortment available. (*The Mission group is heard singing offstage.*)

NATHAN—Not real high-class dolls!

SKY—Any doll! You name her!

NATHAN—Any doll? And I name her! Will you bet on that? You will bet a thousand dollars that if I name a doll you will take her to Havana tomorrow?

SKY—You got a bet! (*The Mission band enters, singing, headed* by SARAH. *Two spectators follow them on.* SARAH *stops.* NATHAN *points to her.*)

NATHAN—I name her!

SKY (*puts his hand to his ear, then withdraws it*)—Her! Cider!

The stage blacks out.

SCENE II

The setting is the interior of the Mission—a drab room with some rows of chairs. A painted sign reads, "There is no peace unto the wicked.—Proverbs 23, 9." The band files in, drops its paraphernalia. "Someday," exclaims Sarah, "I'm going to take a pickax and rip up Broadway from end to end!" The old drummer chuckles, "They do that every day."

In a moment a stranger enters. He is a handsome man, very conservatively dressed, wearing a dark suit, dark blue shirt and a white necktie. He is Sky Masterson, who inquires, "Do you take sinners here?" He claims his heart is heavy with sin. He sinks to a chair and confesses he has wasted his life in gambling and evil betting—but suddenly he has realized the terrible things that betting can lead to.

There is something familiar about him and Sarah inquires, "Didn't I see you a little while ago on Broadway?"

Arvide, the drummer, exults, "I'm glad you found us," and Masterson replies, "The Bible says, 'Seek and ye shall find.'" Arvide sighs, "I wish we could reach more sinners like you. We are out every day, trying." Masterson suggests that they try the night time, for the best time to find sinners is between midnight and dawn. The new sinner is provided with coffee, and the other Mission workers leave him to Sarah, who begins to ply him with pamphlets.

While she is making her campaign, Sky begins his. He thinks Sarah is wonderful, sacrificing herself for this Mission—but hasn't she ever gone any place else? Traveled or something? The discouraged Mission doll exclaims that she'd like to go to Africa, but Sky considers this a little far. "But," he says, "there are a lot of wonderful places just a few hours from New York by plane." Then, "I need private lessons. Why don't we have dinner or something?" The girl coolly turns him down.

Sky, wandering around the room, spots the sign with the quotation and says, "That's not Proverbs—it's Isaiah."

When the disbelieving girl looks it up, she finds to her discomfiture that he is right. He explains his knowledge by saying, "There are two things been in every hotel room in the country—Sky Masterson and the Gideon Bible."

Sarah has not entirely fallen for his claim of being a repentant sinner, but he insists he is a sinner. "If you get me," he urges, "it's eight to five the others'll follow. You need sinners, don't you? Let's be honest. The Mission is laying an egg. I'll bet I can fill this place with sinners."

Sarah remains distant, but Sky offers a proposition. The Mission has a big meeting set for Thursday, and he will guarantee to fill it with one dozen genuine sinners, and will guarantee that they will sit still and listen.

"And what's my end of the bargain?" Sarah inquires cautiously.

"Have dinner with me." He thrusts into her hand his marker— an I O U for one dozen sinners. "I'll pick you up at noon tomorrow, for dinner." He explains it will take some time to get to his favorite restaurant because it is El Café Cubana in Havana.

Sarah exclaims, "Havana!"

"Why not? The plane gets us there in five hours and back the same night."

Sarah is furious, and insulted. When she does go out with a man, it will *not* be with a gambler. Sky wonders what the man will be like, and they sing about it:

SARAH—
    I've imagined every bit of him
    From his strong moral fiber
    To the wisdom in his head
    To the homey aroma of his pipe. . . .
SKY—
    You have wished yourself a Scarsdale Galahad—
    The breakfast-eating, Brooks Brothers type.

The girl insists, as her song continues, "I'll know when my love comes along," but Sky tells her she has it all wrong if she's talking about love. "What are you picking, a guy or a horse? Would you like to hear how a gambler feels about the big heart throb?" She wouldn't, but he sings it to her anyway:

    Suddenly I'll know, when my love comes along,
    I'll know, then and there.
    I'll know, at the sight of her face
    How I care, how I care, how I care—
    And I'll stop and I'll stare
    And I'll know long before we can speak;
    I'll know in my heart,
    I'll know. And I won't even ask,
    Am I right? Am I wise? Am I smart?
    But I'll stop and I'll stare at that face in the throng—
    Yes, I'll know when my love comes along.

Sky kisses the girl; he knows he has made a dent in her defenses. He puts his arms around her and kisses her tenderly; she submits but doesn't respond. Releasing her, he picks up his hat and starts for the door, and Sarah stands, seemingly entranced. She walks toward him, floating on air, and he pauses, confidently anticipating another clinch. But when she reaches him she hits him in the face— hard! Rubbing his cheek, Sky departs, saying, "I'll drop in again in case you want to take a crack at the other cheek." Sarah takes from the desk his marker, throws it into the waste basket, and sings:

> I won't take a chance.
> My love will be just what I need—
> Not some fly-by-night Broadway romance. . . .

The lights dim out.

SCENE III

Nathan Detroit is in a phone booth talking to Joey Biltmore, and Joey's replies can be heard. They are cold replies. Nathan can have his crap game when he puts up a thousand dollars—not before. Joey won't even extend credit when he is told about Nathan's sure-thing bet with Sky Masterson.

The lights black out.

SCENE IV

The scene is a night club, the Hot Box. It is well crowded. A master of ceremonies is introducing the grand finale of the revue— Miss Adelaide and the Hot Box Farmerettes. Adelaide and the dancing girls, in rustic costumes, sing:

ADELAIDE—
> I love you a bushel and a peck
> A bushel and a peck and a hug around the neck
> A hug around the neck and a barrel and a heap
> A barrel and a heap and I'm talkin' in my sleep
> About you—

GIRLS—
> About you

ADELAIDE—
> About you . . .

Nathan has come in and taken a small ringside table during the singing of the number. When the song is over and Adelaide and the girls have exited, the crowd departs, leaving Nathan alone, humming "Bushel and a Peck" over a cup of coffee. A waiter begins sweeping up as Nathan sings, "I love you a bushel and a peck—that lousy Joey Biltmore!" Adelaide, in a dressing gown, comes in bearing a book and a box labeled "Sally's Wedding Shop." Putting the box on a table, she rushes into Nathan's arms. He is curious about the book, and she explains the doctor gave it to her on account of her cold. When she told the doctor she has had the cold a long time he said it might be due to psychology, and he gave her this book.

Adelaide has other things than books on her mind. She is getting a raise next week, and she suggests maybe she and Nathan could finally get married.

NATHAN (*loosening his collar as he feels the strain*)—Well, of course we're going to, sooner or later.

ADELAIDE—I know, Nathan (*Sneeze.*), but I'm starting to worry about Mother.

NATHAN—Your mother? What about your mother?

ADELAIDE—Well, Nathan, this is something I never told you before, but my mother, back in Rhode Island—she thinks we're married already.

NATHAN—Why would she think a thing like that?

ADELAIDE—I couldn't be engaged for fourteen years, could I? People don't do that in Rhode Island. They all get married.

NATHAN—Then why is it such a small State?

ADELAIDE—Anyway—I wrote her I was married.

NATHAN (*standing*)—You did, huh?

ADELAIDE (*each word coming through pain*)—Then, after about two years— (*She comes to a halt.*)

NATHAN—*What* about after two years?

ADELAIDE (*in a very small voice*)—We had a baby.

NATHAN—You told your mother we had a baby?

ADELAIDE—I had to, Nathan. Mother wouldn't understand if we hadn't.

NATHAN—What type baby was it?

ADELAIDE—It was a boy. I named it after· *you,* Nathan.

NATHAN—Thank you.

ADELAIDE—You're welcome.

NATHAN—And—uh—where is Nathan Jr. supposed to be *now?*

ADELAIDE—He's in boarding school. I wrote Mother he won the football game last Saturday.

NATHAN—I wish I had a bet on it.

ADELAIDE—But—(*She turns away.*)—that's not all, Nathan.

NATHAN—Don't tell me he has a little sister.

ADELAIDE—All those years, Nathan! Mother believes in big families.

NATHAN (*puts hands to ears*)—Just give me the grand total.

ADELAIDE (*hardly able to get the word out*)—Five.

NATHAN—Your mother must be a glutton for punishment.

ADELAIDE—Anyway, now we're getting married and it won't be a lie any more.

NATHAN (*a high moral tone*)—Adelaide, how could you do such a thing? To a nice old broad like your mother!

ADELAIDE—But you don't even know my mother!

NATHAN—But I'll be meeting her soon, and what'll I tell her? What'll I tell her I did with the five kids? What are we going to do?

ADELAIDE—We could get married.

The yearning blonde has it all fixed. In the box she brought she has a wedding veil, which she has had for three years. All they need now is a blood test. Nathan incautiously mutters, "First they close my crap game, then they open my veins," and Adelaide, catching him, remonstrates, "You're not planning to run your crap game again?"

Nathan swears he isn't. He loves Adelaide and wants them to be the happiest married couple in the world. But Mimi, one of the dancing girls, has come out to look for an earring she dropped on the stage and, spotting Nathan, accuses, "You! I'm all dated up tomorrow with Society Max and he breaks it on account of your dopey crap game! Honestly, Adelaide, I pity you. . . ."

Adelaide is crushed, angry and sneezing, and deaf to Nathan's protestations of love. He is in a hurry to get away, and when he does, the girl begins to sing a lament:

It says here (*Reading her book, then singing.*)
The average unmarried female, basically insecure
Due to some long frustration, may react
With psychosomatic symptoms, difficult to endure,
Affecting the upper respiratory tract. (*Looks up from book.*)
In other words, just from waiting around
For that plain little band of gold,

A person . . . can develop a cold.
You can spray her wherever you figure the streptococci lurk;

You can give her a shot for whatever she's got, but it just won't work.
If she's tired of getting the fish-eye from the hotel clerk,
A person . . . can develop a cold.

The girl, sniffling and coughing, continues her lament, ending,

From a lack of community property and a feeling she's getting too
old,
A person . . . can develop a bad, bad cold!

The lights black out.

SCENE V

The backdrop depicts a side street of the Broadway area. The
Mission is campaigning again, with the band playing "Follow the
Fold." One of the women is carrying the sign Sky Masterson spotted—with Masterson's Biblical correction. Sarah is patently annoyed, for Sky is doggedly following the band . . . and sneaking
after him are Nicely and Benny. As the band marches on, Benny
calls and asks Nicely what he is looking at, and that happy gentleman reports that Sky was following Sarah and that Sarah was
snooting him. "She gave him a look that would have cooled off a
moose at mating time."
"Great!" Benny agrees. "Just so he don't take her to Havana."
The men wonder where Nathan is, for the game ought to be lining
up. Nicely ventures that it's Adelaide, always taking Nathan's mind
off honest work. Benny agrees. Both agree, in song:

NICELY—
What's playing at the Roxy?
I'll tell you what's playing at the Roxy:
A picture about a Minnesota man, so in love with a Mississippi
girl
That he sacrifices everything and moves all the way to Biloxi—
That's what's playing at the Roxy!
BENNY—
What's in the *Daily News?*
I'll tell you what's in the *Daily News:*
Story about a guy who bought his wife a small ruby
With what otherwise would have been his union dues—
That's what's in the *Daily News!*

The men continue to relate the plight of men with maids. . . .

BENNY—
   When you see a sport and his cash has run short,
   Make a bet that he's banking it with some doll.
NICELY—
   When a guy wears tails with the front gleaming white,
   Who the hell do you think he's tickling pink on Saturday night?
BENNY—
   When a lazy slob takes a good steady job,
   And he smells from Vitalis and Barbasol . . .
BOTH—
   Call it dumb, call it clever, ah, but you can give odds forever
   That the guy's only doing it
   For some doll, some doll, some doll—
   The guy's only doing it for some doll!

   The lights fade.

SCENE VI

   The scene is the exterior of the Mission, and the band is filing disconsolately toward the door. Sarah looks behind to see if Sky is
still following, but he isn't. She is deeply despondent and feels
she should never have volunteered for this job; she just can't make
a start toward converting Broadway.

   Marching briskly and grimly toward the Mission is Matilda B.
Cartwright in a uniform which proclaims who she is—General Cartwright, head of the Save-a-Soul Mission. They all give the General
respectful good-mornings, but the lady is in no good mood. Sarah
has fallen down on the job, and Headquarters has decided to close
this branch of the Mission. Agatha, one of the missionaries, protests that a big meeting has been announced for tomorrow night,
and the General sniffs, "But will anyone be here?"

   Coming up on this conversation is Sky Masterson, who introduces
himself to the General with quiet dignity. "I couldn't help over-
hearing," he says. "I'm Sky Masterson, former sinner. I wish to
protest the closing of this Mission. I believe Miss Sarah can be a
big success here." He notices that his marker is in the trash basket
at the curb, pick it up surreptitiously and suggests to the General,
"Why don't you come to the meeting tomorrow night and find out
for yourself?" He drops his marker into Sarah's tambourine. "I
personally guarantee you one dozen genuine sinners."

   "Hallelujah!" cries the General. "Hallelujah!" says Sky.

   The lights black out.

Scene VII

There is a gathering of crapshooters on a street off Broadway, all waiting to find out where the game is going to be. They wear red carnations for identification. Nathan hasn't the money for the Biltmore Garage yet, but he has left Nicely at his hotel to wait for the money from Sky. Harry the Horse, tough man from Brooklyn, becomes threatening, warning Nathan, "If you do not have no place for your game, tell us, and we will seek elsewhere for entertainment. I happen to be entertaining a very prominent guest tonight." He points to a big, tough-looking guy next to him. "I would like you to meet Big Jule from Chicago.

Big Jule is a man of few words, all of which he growls in a deep rasp. "I came here to shoot crap. Let's shoot crap." Harry reminds Nathan that Big Jule does not like to be displeased. The group is joined by Brannigan, who jovially surveys them. "The cream of society! Angie-the-Ox . . . Society Max . . . Liver Lip Louie . . ." He ticks them off. He stops at Big Jule and says, "I'm bad on names but your face looks familiar. Mind telling me where you're from?"

"East Cicero, Illinois."

"Oh. What do you do there?"

"I'm a Scoutmaster."

Brannigan hasn't missed the red carnations and he wants to know what they're for. "A party," flounders Benny. Just then he sees Adelaide coming and inspiration strikes him. "A bachelor dinner. Nathan's getting married." The crapshooters enthusiastically begin to sing "For he's a jolly good fellow." Adelaide is thrilled, exclaiming, "Just think—after fourteen years I'm going to become Mrs. Nathan Detroit. Time certainly does fly."

Brannigan isn't exactly fooled. He wants to know the wedding date, and when Nathan is vague he suggests that the affianced couple could elope to Maryland and get married right away. Extending congratulations, the detective moves on. Adelaide, aflutter with plans for eloping, flutters off, but Nathan has other things on his mind as Big Jule prods, "Let's shoot crap." The money hasn't come yet.

"Maybe," ventures Benny, "he took the doll to Havana."

"He couldn't have," wails the desperate Nathan.

They hear the music of the Mission band approaching, and Nathan galvanizes to attention. The band marches by and Nathan counts them. They all are there—except Sarah. Nathan collapses on Benny's shoulder.

The lights black out.

SCENE VIII

Sarah has gone to Havana with Sky, all right. He tries to take her to a dance dive, but she flees; so he takes her to the restaurant at the Hotel Nacionale for a ham sandwich. Then, with guidebook in hand, she leads him on a wearying tour of the sights, including the grave of Columbus. They pause at a cheap street café and Sarah orders a milk shake. Holding up two fingers, Sky orders from the shoddy waiter, "Dulce de Leche." The waiter returns with two drinks in cocoanut shells, and Sarah finds hers delicious. "What's in it besides milk?" she inquires.

"Oh, sugar and—sort of a native flavoring."

"What's the name of the flavoring?"

"Bacardi."

"It's very good," says Sarah. "I think I'll have another one." The lights dim for a moment and when they come up a stack of empty cocoanut shells indicates that some time has passed. Sarah, a little woozy, inquires if there isn't alcohol in Bacardi and Sky answers, "Only enough to act as a preservative."

"You know," the Mission doll decides, "this would be a wonderful way to get children to drink milk."

Sarah now is ready for action. They go to the dive Sky wanted to take her to in the first place, and all is wonderful until a Cuban man tries dancing with Sarah and a Cuban girl tries same with Sky. There is a chair-breaking, hair-pulling brawl, but Masterson finally manages to pick up Sarah and carry her out bodily. She is in her shirtwaist, and they don't bother to go back for her uniform jacket. On the street Sky sets her down and asks, "Are you all right?" She carols happily, "Am I all right! Ask me how do I feel," and sings:

> Ask me, now that we're cozy and clinging—
> Well, sir, all I can say is
> If I were a bell I'd be ringing!
> From the moment we kissed tonight
> That's the way I've just got to behave;
> Boy, if I were a lamp I'd light
> And if I were a banner I'd wave!

Ask me how do I feel—
Little me with my quiet upbringing—
Well, sir, all I can say is
If I were a gate I'd be swinging;
And if I were a watch I'd start popping my spring,
Or if I were a bell I'd go
Ding, dong, ding, dong, ding!

Sarah is so high she wants to stay in Havana a few days more—
and now it is Sky who is being stuffy. She must go home now. He
confesses that he's no good for her—that he merely took her here
to win a bet. He picks up the struggling girl once more and heads
for the airport as she cries, "Oh, you talk just like a missionary!"

The lights black out.

Scene IX

It is four A.M. by the time Sky deposits Sarah in front of the
Mission. She is coatless and hatless and he is hatless. Sarah is
contrite. Down the street comes Adelaide, draped with assorted
kitchen utensils and followed by four girls carrying more utensils.
The girls have given Adelaide a shower. Adelaide breaks the news
to Sky that she and Nathan are eloping tomorrow night right after
the Bot Hox show is over. The girls go on. Sarah, asking what
time it is and being told it is about four, says to Sky, "This is your
time of day, isn't it?" He answers in song:

My time of day is the dark time,
A couple of deals before dawn,
When the street belongs to the cop
And the janitor with the mop
And the grocery clerks are all gone;
When the smell of the rain-washed pavement
Comes up clean and fresh and cold,
And the street lamp light fills the gutter with gold—
That's my time of day,
My time of day—
And you're the only doll I've ever wanted to share it with me.

"Obadiah," Sky says suddenly. "Obadiah Masterson. That's
my real name." It is obvious that this is a profound personal revelation.
The two lovers sing, "I've never been in love before, now all at

once it's you." They are standing in the street, having a long kiss, when Arvide and the rest of the band return from their all-night campaign. The clanging bell of an approaching police patrol wagon is heard. A man runs to the door of the Mission, sticks his head in and whistles shrilly. There is pandemonium as men scurry from the Mission, putting on their coats as they run. The coats have red carnations. Sky spots the fleeing Nathan and hollers, "Hey, what is this?" "Canasta," Nathan shouts over his shoulder.

Brannigan and two cops arrive—but too late. The detective surveys the establishment and says, "I've seen a lot of things in my time, but this is the first time I ever see a floating crap game going full blast in a Mission."

Sarah is stunned. This wouldn't have happened if she'd been here. This is why Sky took her to Havana—and he can't make her believe he had nothing to do with it. The romance has gone from her as she says, "It's no good, Sky."

"Why not? What the hell kind of a doll are you, anyway?"

"I'm a Mission doll!" she exclaims with spirit. She and the band go into the Mission, leaving Masterson.

The curtain falls.

ACT II

The Hot Box night club is hot—well filled, and the show going on. The number at the moment is Miss Adelaide and her Debutantes. Adelaide's eight dancing girls walk with exaggerated gracefulness; they carry long gold cigarette holders with cigarettes and are wearing golden gowns, shoes, hats, pearl necklaces and mink stoles.

Adelaide begins:

He bought me the fur things five Winters ago,
The gown the following Fall—
The hat, the gloves, the shoes and the bag, that was late forty-eight,
    I recall;
Then last night in his apartment
He tried to remove them all,
And I said as I ran down the hall—

Take back your mink,
Take back your pearls—
What made you think that I was one of those girls?
Take back the gown, the shoes and the hat;
I may be down, but I'm not flat as all that!

I thought that each expensive gift
Was a token of your esteem,
But now when I think of what you want in exchange
It all seems a horrible dream—

As Adelaide continues, the girls join in the second chorus—and as they sing they remove mink, pearls, gowns and hats, until, down to dancing scanties, they go into a dance. As the number ends Sky comes in, unshaven and a bit crumpled, looking for Nathan. A waiter says Mr. Detroit hasn't been in all evening. Sky takes a small table and orders a drink. Soon Nicely appears, looking for Adelaide. He tells Sky he brings a message from Nathan for her— "Nathan's aunt in Pittsburgh was suddenly taken ill with—er—" Sky suggests "a rare tropical disease. . . . Where *is* Nathan?" Nicely says the game is still going on—since last night! Big Jule is a large loser and does not wish the game to terminate, so they find another place and the game goes on. Would Sky like some action? Sky is leaving town tonight, but he would like to talk to some of the guys. He explains vaguely that he gave someone a marker and he'd like to clean it up before going. Adelaide approaches and Nicely blurts, "Miss Adelaide, Nathan is in Pittsburgh with a rare tropical aunt. Good-by." He skitters out. Adelaide has a hunch that it's the crap game again—and on the night they were supposed to elope.

"You know Nathan," Sky says gently. "Why does it surprise you?"

"But he promised to change."

"Change, change. Why is it that the minute you dolls get a guy that you like, you take him right in for alterations?"

Adelaide counters vigorously, "What about you men? Why can't you marry like other people do and live like normal people? Have a home with—wallpaper, and bookends?"

Sky shakes his head sadly. It's no good when dolls get mixed up with guys like him and Nathan. He says good-by.

"Will you see Nathan before you go?"

"Maybe."

"Tell him I never want to talk to him again and have him call me here." When Masterson has gone, Adelaide, sniffling again, resumes her song of lament—"In other words, just from sitting alone at a table reserved for two, a person can develop the flu. . . ."

The lights black out.

Scene II

A street scene. A rail is guarding an open manhole and a light-company repair wagon stands by, its warning lights blinking red. Not far away is an empty box. Sarah hurries along the street, followed by a panting Arvide, carrying his drum. He asks for a breather. They talk about the meeting scheduled for tonight and wonder if anybody will come looking for salvation. Sarah doubts it; the only time sinners came to the Mission was to shoot craps. Arvide chuckles, remembering Masterson, and says, "I didn't know you were going to get stuck on him."

"I'll get over it."

But why should she want to get over it, he asks. What he wants is for her to be happy. He sings it, as she sits on the box:

> Velvet I can wish you
> For the collar of your coat,
> And fortune smiling all along your way;
> But more I cannot wish you
> Than to wish you find your love—
> Your own true love this day. . . .

It is a gentle, sentimental song, sung by a gentle, sentimental man who has loved Sarah always—for he is her grandfather. Nicely comes by, with Sky in tow. Sky gives Sarah a good evening, talks to Brother Abernathy about the big meeting tonight. Arvide frankly doesn't think anybody will come. "Miss Sarah," says Sky, "you've forgotten something, but being a gambler I never forget things like this. You hold my marker for twelve sinners tonight." Sarah, cold, would like to forget about it. Last night's visit of his friends was enough. She marches off haughtily, and Arvide, following, says privately to Masterson, "If you don't pay off that marker I'll tell the whole town you're a dirty welcher."

"Where's the crap game?" Sky demands of Nicely.

"About ten minutes from here. . . . This way." And Nicely vanishes down the manhole.

The lights black out.

Scene III

The resourceful Nathan has moved his game to a sewer. There is a ladder leading down to a platform with a vaulted ceiling, and on the platform are the gamblers. The opening scene is a crapshooters' ballet. (A remarkably fine ballet, staged by Michael Kidd.—Ed.) When the dance is finished the crapshooters begin putting on coats and ties, getting ready to leave the game. "Wait a minute," Big Jule bellows. "I came here to shoot crap." Nathan pleads that the boys are tired, having been shooting for nearly twenty-four hours, but Big Jule, being 25 G's loser, is firm. He pats his shoulder holster threateningly, and the weary game is resumed. At each play, Nathan removes his "take" from the money bet. After a while Big Jule sighs, "Well, that cleans me," and everybody is relieved. "But I ain't through yet," Big Jule adds. "I will now play on credit." He decides he will play with Nathan, who must have quite a bundle by now. "If I lose, I will give you my marker."

NATHAN—And if I lose?

HARRY THE HORSE—You will give him cash.

NATHAN—Let me hear from Big Jule.

JULE—You will give me cash.

NATHAN—Now I heard it.

JULE—Here is my marker. (NATHAN *looks at it, then at* BIG JULE.) Put up your dough. Is anything wrong?

NATHAN—No—no. "I O U one thousand dollars." Signed X! How is it you can write one thousand, but you cannot write your signature?

JULE—I was good in arithmetic, but I stunk in English.

NATHAN (*puts his money down*)—Here! This will put you through Harvard.

JULE—I'm rolling a thousand. And to change my luck I will use my own dice.

NATHAN (*horrified*)—Your own dice!

JULE—I had them made for me especially in Chicago.

NATHAN—Big Jule, you cannot interpolate Chicago dice in a New York crap game.

BENNY—That is a breach of etiquette.

HARRY—Show me where it says that in Emily Post.

NATHAN—Not that I wish to seem petty, but could I look at these dice? (*All men crowd around looking at dice as* BIG JULE *gives them to* NATHAN.) But these—these dice ain't got no spots on 'em. They're blank!

JULE—I had the spots taken off for luck. But I remember where the spots formerly were.

NATHAN—You are going to roll blank dice and call 'em from remembering where the spots formerly was?

JULE (*threateningly*)—Why not? (*Pulls* NATHAN *up by coat.*)
NATHAN (*wipes perspiration from forehead*)—I see no reason.
JULE (*rolls*)—A five—and a five. Ten. My point is ten.
NATHAN—Well, I still got a chance.
JULE (*shaking dice*)—Tensy, tensy, come againsy!
NATHAN—I wish he'd fall down on his endsy.
JULE—Hah! A ten! I win!
NATHAN—A ten?
JULE (*pointing*)—A six and a four.
NATHAN (*looking*)—Which is the six and which is the four?
JULE—Either way. (*Picks up dice.*) Now I'm shooting two thousand.
NATHAN (*looking at watch*)—I just remembered. I'm eloping tonight. Adelaide is waiting for me. (*Starts to exit.* BIG JULE *grabs him and pulls him back.*)

Nathan is caught. Big Jule cleans him out of six thousand dollars and refuses Nathan's offer to play with his own marker as security. Jule is about to start on the other shooters again when Sky arrives. Sky ignores Jule's challenge to a game, for he wants to talk to the others about Sarah Brown's Mission. Jule elbows in, saying Sky is slowing up the action, and Sky smoothly offers him a bet—"Am I right handed or left handed?" Jule wouldn't know. "I'll give you a clue," Sky offers, and knocks the gangster down with a right. Big Jule staggers up, reaches groggily for his shoulder gun—but Masterson gets it first and tosses it to Nathan, who gingerly passes it on to Benny.

Sky has everybody's attention now, and he tells the crowd that a midnight prayer meeting is being held in Sarah's Mission. He promised her some sinners, and he wants them to come. To a man they demur and Masterson turns to go, but is stopped by Nathan. "About that Havana business," he says, "I regret I temporarily do not have the one thousand to pay you."

"You don't have to pay me," says Sky, pulling out a bill. "You won." With new money, Nathan is back in the game again with Big Jule, and this time, he announces, he will play with his own dice. Harry the Horse is on his feet with an objection. "With those dice he cannot make a pass to save his soul."

That phrase, save his soul, gives Masterson an inspiration. He offers to play each man for a thousand cash each against their markers for their souls. If a man wins, he gets the thousand; if he loses he must show up at what Harry the Horse calls the Mission doll's cabaret. It's a tempting gamble, and soon all the players are putting up their markers. With so much riding on a roll of the dice—not just money, but Sarah herself, Sky hesitates, nervously tossing the dice as he sings:

> Luck, be a lady tonight,
> Luck, be a lady tonight,
> Luck, if you've ever been a lady to begin with,
> Luck, be a lady tonight. . . .

The song rises in excitement and volume as the men join in. At last Sky rolls, and together he and the players exclaim, "Right! Huh!"

The lights black out.

SCENE IV

Out on the street again, crapshooters go grumbling toward the Mission. Big Jule growls, "If it ever gets back to Chicago that I went to a prayer meeting no decent person will talk to me." Adelaide has been sauntering along, hiding behind a newspaper and looking for Nathan—and when she catches him she upstages him. Resisting Nathan's embrace, she says, "Please! Let us not have a vulgar scene. After all, we are civilized people—we do not have to conduct ourselves like a slob." Nathan, worried, begins to plead, and Adelaide, breaking down with a sneeze, falls into his arms. She insists that they must be married soon, for she has had a letter from Mother and Mother has put in a letter to Nathan. She gives it to him and he reads it aloud. It is Mother's first letter to her "Dear Son Nathan" but she knows him from her daughter's letters. It must be a great responsibility to be the assistant manager of an A & P. He breaks off reading and demands of Adelaide, "I'm not even manager?" "I was going to promote you for Christmas," she replies. Nathan goes on with the letter, which says Mother is proud to have him for a son-in-law. He wilts, saying, "I feel like a heel." Okay, he says, he will elope with Adelaide right now—but Benny and Nicely, passing by, remind him he can't elope just now. "I got to go to a prayer meeting," he explains to Adelaide.

This is another last straw for Adelaide—the biggest lie yet. In song she berates him, and in song he defends himself, saying, "Call a lawyer and sue me, sue me—what can you do me? I love you. Give a holler and hate me, hate me, go ahead and hate me. I love

you." But Adelaide's warm heart has turned to stone, and all
Nathan's mournful warbling goes for nothing. She walks out on him
as he is still pleading, "Sue me, sue me, shoot bullets through
me. . . ."

The lights dim out.

SCENE V

In the Mission, all the Missionaries are waiting expectantly—including the still-skeptical General. It is several minutes past midnight and nobody has come. Sarah takes the blame on herself and
is about to ask to be drummed out of the Mission when the gamblers
shuffle in, herded by Sky. Nathan makes a late entrance and Sky
says, "Miss Sarah, here you are. One dozen or more assorted
sinners." He commands his prisoners, "Sit down, all of you!" Sky
announces he hasn't time to stay, but appoints Nathan major domo
in his place and warns the mob they must not indulge in any un-
pleasantness. He leaves, and Nathan, turning ceremoniously to
Arvide, says, "Brother Abernathy, your dice." Abernathy turns the
meeting over to the greatly impressed General, who calls for the first
volunteer to give testimony.

"Benny, give testimony," Nathan commands.

"I ain't no stool pigeon," Benny objects—but nevertheless he has
to testify and he gets it over quickly. He was a gambler but he
ain't going to do it no more. At command, Big Jule rises and de-
poses: "Well, I used to be bad when I was a kid, but ever since then
I have gone straight as I can prove by my record—thirty-three ar-
rests and no convictions."

Harry's confession accidentally reveals to Sarah what has happened when he talks about when Sky was rolling them for their
souls. She explains to the General that the men are here because
Sky won them in a dice game and the befuddled General thinks this
is wonderful.

In crashes Detective Brannigan, ready for a big gambling pinch,
but Major Domo Nathan removes Brannigan's hat, motions him to
be silent and continues the testimony. It's Nicely-Nicely's turn, and
he makes his confession in the form of song. It is a narrative song,
in the form of a revival meeting number, about Nicely's dream of
shooting craps on the boat to Heaven and the passengers crying,
"Sit down, sit down, you're rockin' the boat!" It is a rousing number, and as it progresses everybody takes part—Missionaries, bums,
even the detective.

When it's over Brannigan turns cop again. When Nathan asks
him if he'd like to testify, he announces he will do it in court. He
will testify that he saw them all here running a crap game last night.
"Miss Sarah," he says, "you saw them."

Sarah looks the men over, very slowly, then announces, "I never
saw them before in my life." From the rear of the Mission Big Jule
booms, "There's a right broad!" Brannigan leaves, defeated. Now
Nathan himself confesses—confesses that he made a bet with a certain guy that he could not take a certain doll with him on a trip.
This he should not have done, although he won the bet.

"You won the bet?" Sarah asks, with an odd look. "Hallelujah!"
cries the General. The band strikes up "Follow the Fold" and while
all are singing Sarah quietly picks up her cape and slips out the door.

The lights dim out.

SCENE VI

A side street. Two roped bundles of tabloid newspapers are on
the sidewalk. Adelaide, walking disconsolately, sits on one of the
bundles, sneezes, sings her lament to herself. Sarah, not noticing
Adelaide, sits on the bundle and also sings to herself—"I've never
really been in love before. . . ."

Suddenly the girls notice and recognize each other. Soon they are
exchanging miseries and talking about their men. Can't men like
them ever change? Adelaide shakes her head. "I've sat and pic-
tured him by the hour. Nathan—my Nathan—in a little place in
the country . . . happy . . ." As she dreams her dream again,
lights go up behind a transparent New York backdrop, revealing
Nathan, in overalls and a farmer's hat, treating a trellis of roses
with a spray gun.

Sarah, too, has her dream. "If only Sky—" she sighs. And as
the vision of Nathan vanishes a vision of Masterson appears, in a
back yard somewhere, in an apron, hanging up the wash.

"But they just can't change," Adelaide decides. Sarah isn't so
sure, remembering, "A little while ago at our prayer meeting there
were a lot of gamblers who acted as though maybe they could
change." The blonde does a double-take. Prayer meeting? Was
Nathan Detroit there? A darling little fellow with a cute mustache?
Sarah thinks he was, and Adelaide explodes, "How do you like that
rat! Just when he should have been lying he's telling the truth!"

But it's no go. Both girls realize they can't escape their men, so
they lay plans for managing the future—in song:

ADELAIDE—
   At Wanamaker's and Saks' and Klein's
   A lesson I've been taught—
   You can't get alterations on a dress you haven't bought.
SARAH—
   At any vegetable market from Borneo to Nome,
   You mustn't squeeze a melon till you get it home.
ADELAIDE—
   You've simply got to gamble—
SARAH—
   You get no guarantee. . . .
ADELAIDE—
   Now doesn't that kind of apply to you and I?
SARAH—
   You and me.
ADELAIDE—
   Why not?
SARAH—
   Why not what?
ADELAIDE—
   Marry the man today,
   Trouble though he may be—
   Much as he loves to play
   Crazy and wild and free
SARAH AND ADELAIDE—
   Marry the man today,
   Rather than sigh and sorrow;
ADELAIDE—
   Marry the man today—
   And change his ways tomorrow!

The Mission doll and the night club blonde have got hold of a
fine idea. They keep on developing it, until—

The lights fade.

SCENE VII

It is the same Broadway scene we encountered before, and the
same people are there—the two shady Broadway characters, the
street walkers, the prize fighter, the sightseers. And the crapshooters
all are there, too, cleaned up and wearing gardenias. Brannigan goes
to the newsstand. Adelaide arrives, in a wedding outfit, carrying a
bouquet, and her dancing girls are the bridesmaids. Adelaide calls,

"Nathan! We're waiting for you." Brannigan, at the stand, says, "Gimme a late paper." The man running the stand is Nathan! He is wearing a red turtle-neck sweater, and he sticks his head out and bawls, "Just a minute! I'm waiting on the lieutenant." The purchase made, Nathan closes his stand by pulling down a shade lettered, Nathan Detroit's News Stand. In a moment the man himself emerges—resplendent in cutaway, top hat and cane, and complaining that Adelaide has picked the busiest time of day.

"Let's go," urges Harry the Horse. "Where's the wedding?"

Disaster smites Nathan. He confesses, "I didn't get a place for the wedding." Nicely suggests the Biltmore Garage. And now the Mission band marches in with the same personnel as always—except that Arvide now has an assistant to carry and beat the drum for him. The assistant, looking splendid in a Mission uniform and singing "Follow the Fold" loudly, is Sky Masterson.

"Brothers and sisters," cries Sky, "life is one big crap game, and the Devil is playing with loaded dice!"

Big Jule's ears prick up. "Where's the crap game?"

Nathan taps the drum with his cane and asks of Brother Masterson, "Can we get married in your Mission—Adelaide and I?"

Arvide cuts in, "Certainly. I married Brother Masterson and Sister Sarah. Glad to do the same for you." Sky offers his congratulations, adding a bet of eight to five they'll be very happy.

"Thank you very much," says Adelaide. "I *know* we're going to be happy. We're going to have a little place in the country, and Nathan will be sitting there, beside me, every single night."

Nathan explodes an enormous sneeze.

Adelaide's blissful expression changes as she realizes its implications.

CURTAIN

DARKNESS AT NOON *

A Play in Three Acts

By Sidney Kingsley

Based on the Novel by Arthur Koestler

THE Critics Circle award for 1950-1951 went to "Darkness at Noon," an adaptation of a novel by Arthur Koestler. A strong runner-up in the voting was "Billy Budd," adapted from a short novel by Herman Melville. The previous season, the critics gave their prize to "The Member of the Wedding," an adaptation of a novel (but in this case the adaptation was made by the original author). The trend of the last few seasons toward making use of other material has led many followers of the stage to express concern, for they feel that the theatre is as good a medium as any other for original thought and expression. But others believe that the stage should make use of anything that suits its purpose—and certainly "Darkness at Noon," as made into a play by Sidney Kingsley, was a strong and striking drama.

In the published version of the play and in the theatre programs, it is stated that "Darkness at Noon" is "based on" Arthur Koestler's novel. The phrase "adapted from" is purposely avoided. Kingsley, who heretofore had written originally and directly for the stage, was strongly attracted to the novel. He believed that its analysis of the Communist mind and methods was of immediate importance, and that the book could somehow be made into a potent stage piece. In making arrangements with the author, he stipulated that he could make changes if he felt they were necessary—that, in other words, he could use his creative function as a dramatist and add to or subtract from, as the case might be. One instance of a change is one of the strongest scenes in the play—the meeting of the sailors in Marseille. In the novel this incident occurred in another country, but Kingsley shifted the locale for reasons of logic and convenience.

The novel presented a great technical challenge to Kingsley both as dramatist and as director—as does any stage treatment of a more leisurely and farther-reaching novel. The fictioneer, like the movie camera, can wander at will, but the dramatist is confined to the space of a stage and the time of a performance. Early in his plotting of "Darkness at Noon," Kingsley began devising a stage setting which would allow for many quick-changing scenes without the use of cumbersome, time-consuming turntables. He made cardboard models and maneuvered them for many weeks. When "Darkness at Noon" was ready for production, several scene designers were approached, and they expressed doubt that the scheme would work— a scheme that would include many rooms of a prison and locations ranging from Berlin to Marseille in what was to be essentially a single setting. Finally the stage artist Frederick Fox agreed that Kingsley's notion might be made to work. Fox did make it work, and his settings were among the best of a stage season that was scenically notable.

The main scene, out of which the drama moves and to which it always returns, is granite and iron—a deep underground part of a Russian prison; a timeless dank grave for a living corpse, where there is no night, no day. There is a corridor, and a steep flight of stone steps leading upward; there is a stone cell, whose heavy door has an eye-level peephole, and to the right of this cell is a tier of other cells which, now, are enclosed in an ominous column of sweating granite. A guard in the corridor halts his pacing as an officer brings a prisoner to the cell and bolts him in. The prisoner is N. S. Rubashov, a short, stocky, smooth-shaven, bespectacled man in his early fifties. He has a large head with a wide forehead; his erect carriage bespeaks fierce authority. After he has surveyed his cell, which has only an iron bed and a straw mattress, he reaches into his pocket for cigarettes and then remembers what happened. Going to the peephole in the door, he calls, "Comrade guard! They've taken away my cigarettes, too. Can you get me a cigarette? I've been dragged out of a sick-bed. I have a fever. I need some cigarettes."

The guard makes a harsh refusal. Rubashov, rubbing an inflamed cheek, painfully takes off his overcoat, throws it on the cot and murmurs to himself, "So it's come. You're to die, Rubashov. Well, the old guard is gone!" He lies down, staring grimly at the ceiling. Suddenly he hears an odd, measured ticking. Three ticks . . . pause . . . three more ticks. It seems to come from a wall. He taps three times on this wall with his spectacles—and now he is in communication with the man in the next cell. It does not take him long to learn the prison telegraph code.

"Who?" the man in the next cell wants to know. The granite walls of this cell dissolve as the lights within it come up, revealing a verminous, filthy man in the remaining rags of a Tsarist uniform. Somehow, this long-buried human wreck maintains an air; he has kept his monocle and some of his swagger. As he taps his queries, he speaks them, unconsciously, and Rubashov speaks his replies aloud; but he won't say who he is at first. ﹅

"What day?" asks the prisoner in Cell 402.

"Tuesday."

"Month?"

"March."

"Year?"

"1937."

"The weather?"

"Snowing."

Again, "Who are you?"   Rubashov, shrugging, figures he may as well tell.   "Nicolai Semonovitch Rubashov."   Bursting into wild, ugly laughter, 402 taps, "The wolves are devouring each other!" No. 402 has news for the prison; he taps it to the prisoner in the cell above, who is, as the lights come up in his cubicle and the wall vanishes, a young, thin man whose face is white, bruised and burned. The new prisoner, the boy in 302 learns, is Rubashov, ex-Commissar of the People, ex-Member of the Central Committee, ex-General of the Red Army, Bearer of the Order of the Red Banner.   "Pass it along," 402 orders; but the boy, stunned, cries out, "Oh, Father, Father, what have I done?"   Then 302 passes the word to 202, a peasant with insane eyes, and 202 taps the news along to someone else.   Soon the whole prison will know.   The cell tier vanishes, but one can hear the whisperings of the prison: "N. S. Rubashov arrested!   Rubashov!   Rubashov!"   The voices grow into the roar of a mighty throng as Rubashov, in his cell, remembers another time. Now, young and triumphant, he is addressing a great crowd—soldiers and sailors of the Revolution.   "The great, terrible and joyful day has arrived!"   The Romanovs have been deposed, and dead, too, is the bourgeois democratic Provisional Government.   "Power to the Soviets!" he exults.   "Land to the peasants!   Bread to the hungry!   Peace to all the peoples!"

Rubashov's dream vanishes, interrupted by more tapping from 402.   Although he can only tap, 402 is shouting, too—"Long live His Majesty, the Tsar!"   He reviles Rubashov, exults in his imprisonment.   Rubashov begins pacing his cell, remembering other times,

other faces. Comrade Luigi . . . Pablo . . . And Luba. "My
debt will be paid," he says, as if to her—and of a sudden the cell
becomes the office of the Commissar of the Iron Works. Huge
graphs hang on the walls, and through the window are chimneys
and the skeletons of new buildings. Luba, the secretary, is bent
over her notebook, taking dictation as Rubashov paces. "To meet
the Five Year Plan we must step up our tempo," he orders. "Lag-
gards will be deprived of their food cards. We must be guided by
one rule, dash, the end justifies the means, period."

Suddenly he notices the stenographer, grumpily notices her ear-
rings and high heels, demands her name. "Luba Loshenko," replies
the girl in a low, hoarse but gentle voice. The Commissar is rather
surprised that this pretty girl, who has been working for him for
three weeks but whom he has just now noticed, is not afraid of him.
Most people are. He resumes his dictation . . . but now his memory fades and he is back in his cell, repeating, "Yes, Luba, I will pay.
I will pay my debt to you, above all."

The man in 402 taps that he is sending tobacco—but when he
asks a guard to take it, even offering a bribe, the guard refuses.
"You are in for it," 402 taps to Rubashov. On a sudden impulse,
Rubashov bangs on his cell door, crying for his guard and demanding that he speak to the Commandant at once. Roughly the guard
tells him, "You're Number 400, in solitary, and you're probably
going to be taken down in the cellar and shot. Now don't give me
any more trouble." The other prisoners nearby can hear this exchange through the judas-holes in their doors. Now they are tapping again. 302 relays a message to Rubashov through 402—just
his greetings. Just an old friend who was tortured last week. Won't
give his name. Tortured for political divergencies.

"Your kind?" Rubashov asks of the old Tsarist.

"No," says 402. "Your kind. I'm extinct. Ha! Ha!" The
Tsarist exults that there are thousands of prisoners here—Rubashov's kind. Rubashov throws himself on his cot, but is aroused
soon by the arrival of a huge young man in an officer's uniform;
with his shaven skull he looks like a death's head. Behind him, outside the cell door, stand the guard and the officer who arrested
Rubashov and brought him here. The newcomer is named Gletkin;
he has come to put a stop to Rubashov's banging on the door. Gletkin demands how long the prisoner has been here, and when he is
told it has been ten minutes, Gletkin reprimands the officer. "His
arrest was ordered for three A.M. sharp. What happened?" He is
told the car broke down.

RUBASHOV—It's not his fault. It wasn't sabotage.

GLETKIN (*writes, without glancing up*)—How do you know it wasn't?

RUBASHOV—Make allowances.

GLETKIN—For what?

RUBASHOV—Our roads.

GLETKIN (*puts away the note-book and measures* RUBASHOV *impersonally*)—What's the matter with our roads?

RUBASHOV—They're primitive cow paths.

GLETKIN—Very critical, aren't we? I suppose the roads in the bourgeois countries are better?

RUBASHOV (*looks at* GLETKIN, *smiles cynically*)—Young man, have you ever been outside of our country?

GLETKIN—No. I don't have to . . . to know. And I don't want to hear any fairy tales.

RUBASHOV—Fairy tales? (*Sits up.*) Have you read any of my books or articles?

GLETKIN—In the Komsomol Youth I read your political-education pamphlets. In their time I found them useful.

RUBASHOV—How flattering! And did you find any fairy tales in them?

GLETKIN—That was fifteen years ago. (*Pause.*) Don't think that gives you any privileges now! (*The* GUARD *appears, flapping a dirty rag.* GLETKIN *takes it, throws it at* RUBASHOV's *feet.*) When the morning bugle blows, you will clean up your cell. You know the rules. You've been in prison before?

RUBASHOV—Yes. Many of them. But this is my first experience under my own people. (*He rubs his inflamed jaw.*)

GLETKIN—Do you wish to go on sick call?

RUBASHOV—No, thanks. I know prison doctors.

GLETKIN—Then you're not really sick?

RUBASHOV—I have an abscess. It'll burst itself.

GLETKIN (*without irony*)—Have you any more requests?

RUBASHOV—Tell your superior officer I want to talk to him and stop wasting my time!

GLETKIN—Your time has run out, Rubashov! (*He starts to go, pulling the door behind him.*)

RUBASHOV (*murmurs in French*)—Plus un singe monte . . .

GLETKIN (*re-enters quickly*)—Speak in your own tongue! Are you so gone you can't even think any longer except in a filthy, foreign language?

RUBASHOV (*sharply, with military authority*)—Young man, there's nothing wrong with the French language as such. Now, tell them I'm here and let's have a little Bolshevik discipline! (GLETKIN *stiffens, studies* RUBASHOV *coldly, turns and goes, slamming the iron door. The jangle of the key in the lock; his footsteps as he marches off down the corridor. Suddenly* RUBASHOV *bounds to the door. He shouts through the judas-hole.*) And get me some cigarettes! Damn you! (*Rubs his inflamed cheek, ruefully. To himself.*) Now, why did you do that, Rubashov? What does this young man think of you? "Worn-out old intellectual! Self-appointed Messiah! Dares to question the party line! Ripe for liquidation . . ." There you go again, Rubashov—the old disease. (*Paces.*) Revolutionaries shouldn't see through other people's eyes. Or should they? How can you change the world if you identify yourself with everybody? How else can you change it? (*Paces. He pauses, frowning, searching his memory.*) What is it about this young man? Something? (*Paces.*) Why do I recall a religious painting? A Pietà, a dead Christ in Mary's arms? Of course—Germany. The Museum, Leipzig, 1933.

Slowly the prison becomes a museum in Germany. An S.S. officer, black-uniformed, wearing the swastika arm band, is staring at the Pietà painting. He does not resemble Gletkin but he has the same cold, fanatical expression. Rubashov, museum catalogue in hand, walks slowly down an invisible row of paintings, pauses to study the Pietà. Soon the officer departs and another visitor appears. He is middle-aged, with a sensitive face. He, too, has a catalogue, from which he is reading to himself the description of a Titian. The man inquires of Rubashov, "What page is it in your catalogue, please?" It's a password. Rubashov hands over his catalogue, the man glances quickly at it, hands it back and whispers hoarsely, "Be very careful. They're everywhere."

"Give me your report," Rubashov orders. The man informs him that since the Reichstag fire the Party has been massacred. Two days ago the Storm Troopers took the man's own wife. The man is frightened and shaken—but not Rubashov; he sees clearly and he sees ahead. Right now, he disapproves of this man, Comrade Richard. Comrade Richard's pamphlets have been off the Party line, too sympathetic toward the Liberals and the Social Democrats. He is playing into the enemies' hands. Suddenly, warningly, Rubashov drops his voice, as a young Storm Trooper enters with a girl; they, too, have catalogues and are studying them and the paintings. Comrade Richard quickly resumes his own book and begins reading aloud to himself. When the Trooper and his girl have moved on, Richard continues sternly, "You must give your promise to write only according to the line laid down by the Comintern." Rubashov tries to make clear to this Party leader that he writes what he believes and feels—it's the only way he can arrive at the truth; but Rubashov cuts him off, saying, "We have already arrived at the truth. . . . You know what's expected of you. Keep on the line. We will send you further instructions."

But Comrade Richard is still a man, still an individual. He can't do what is against his conscience, and boldly he says he doesn't believe in "their" policy. Rubashov, threatening to turn the agent over to the Nazis, says without emotion, "Those who are not with us are against us." He is not moved by Richard's soft but intensely voiced outburst, "Who can say what your Revolution once meant to me? The end of all injustice. And my Truda now lies bleeding in some S.S. cellar." "There's nothing more to be said," Rubashov states flatly as he walks off, and Comrade Richard, alone, groans, "Christ!" He knows this implacable man, knows that he is in disfavor and therefore doomed.

Rubashov is back in his cell as the museum vanishes, and the odd old Tsarist in 402 is tapping eagerly again. This time the fellow wants to know how long it has been since Rubashov slept with a woman. What was it like? What were her breasts like? Her thighs? Rubashov, to satisfy the entombed prisoner, improvises answers: Three weeks ago . . . Breasts snowy, fitting into champagne glasses. Soon he has had enough and he taps, "You idiot—I'm teasing you." But this conversation by prison telegraph has aroused another memory, and Rubashov, lying on his cot, hears soft music, which swells into Beethoven's Sonata Appassionata. The cell has become Luba Loshenko's bedroom, and he and Luba are listening to a small gramophone on a table. She, clad only in a chemise, is sitting at the edge of the bed, smoking dreamily. "So tomorrow," she says, "I'll have a new boss."

Rubashov is going away—for how long he does not know. On this last day, and with this music, Luba has become sentimental. Rubashov, kissing her throat, remarks, "This music is dangerous."

LUBA—When I was a little girl in the Pioneer Youth I would start crying at the most unexpected moments.

RUBASHOV—You? In the Pioneer Youth? You, Luba?

LUBA—You're surprised? I wasn't in very long. I wasn't good material. (RUBASHOV *smiles*.) I would cry suddenly for no reason at all.

RUBASHOV—But there was a reason?

LUBA—I don't know. (*She smokes for a moment.*) Yes, I do. Our primer books made little Pavelik such a hero. All of us children wanted to turn our mothers and fathers over to the G.P.U. to be shot.

RUBASHOV—Was there anything to turn them in for?

LUBA (*laughs gently*)—No. Nothing. But I would picture myself doing it anyway and becoming a great national hero like Pavelik. Then I would burst out crying. I loved my parents very much. Of course no one knew why I was crying. So I was expelled, and my political career ended at the age of nine! (RUBASHOV *smiles.* LUBA *hums the melody.*) My father loved this. He and mother used to play it over and over and over.

RUBASHOV—Where are they now?

LUBA—They died in the famine after the Revolution. My father was a doctor.

RUBASHOV—Have you any family left?

LUBA—One brother. He's a doctor too. He's married. My sister-in-law is very nice. She's a Polish woman . . . an artist. (LUBA *picks up a small painting, crosses to* RUBASHOV, *kneels at his side.*) She painted this picture. It's their baby. A little boy. Two years old. Isn't he fat?

RUBASHOV (*studies it*)—Yes, he is fat. (*He puts it aside, looks at* LUBA.) Why don't you get married, Luba, and have some fat babies of your own? Isn't there a young man at the office . . . ?

LUBA—Yes.

RUBASHOV—I thought so. And he wants to marry you?

LUBA (*rests her cheek on his knee, lovingly caresses his hand*)— Yes, he does.

RUBASHOV—Well . . . ?

LUBA—No!

RUBASHOV—Why not?

LUBA—I don't love him.

RUBASHOV—Mm, I see, I see. (*A pause.*)

LUBA (*suddenly*)—You can do anything you wish with me.

RUBASHOV (*studies her*)—Why did you say that? (LUBA *shrugs her shoulders.*) You don't reproach me?

LUBA—Oh, no, no, no! Why should I? (*The music swells and fills the room.*)

RUBASHOV—This music is dangerous. When you listen to this and you realize human beings can create such beauty, you want to pat them on the head. That's bad. They'll only bite your hand off.

LUBA (*takes his hand and kisses it*)—Like this?

RUBASHOV (*gently*)—Luba, you know, with us, there can never be anything more.

LUBA—I don't expect anything more. Did I give you the impression I expected anything more?

RUBASHOV—No. You've been very kind, Luba, and sweet. (*Pause.*) I may be gone a long time. I may never see you again.

LUBA—Where are you going?

RUBASHOV (*hands her the painting*)—Wherever the Party sends me.

LUBA (*rises*)—I understand. I'm not asking anything. Only, wherever you go, I'll be thinking of you. I'll be with you in my mind always!

RUBASHOV (*snuffs out cigarette*)—But this is exactly what I don't want.

Rubashov's reverie is broken by the jangling of keys at his cell door, and a guard brusquely orders him to get up and come along. The man in cell 402 taps to 302, "They've taken him up. . . . Pass it on." The taps echo and re-echo through the prison: "Rubashov taken up." "Up" is an office in the prison; a barred window reveals dawn and snow falling. Outside the window a guard, bayonet fixed on his rifle, paces like a metronome. On a wall over the desk can be dimly seen a portrait of the Leader, and seated at the desk, smoking a long Kremlin cigarette, is a middle-aged man in officer's uniform. Perhaps he once was handsome; now he looks dissipated and cynical. When Rubashov is brought in he greets the prisoner with a nickname, "Kolya!" This man, named Ivanoff, is an old friend. He presses cigarettes on Rubashov, and the prisoner notices, remembering, that Ivanoff limps when he goes to the door to close and lock the judas-hole. Ivanoff genially recalls the last time he saw Rubashov—three years ago, in Moscow, after he had escaped from a German prison. Rubashov was speaking, and Ivanoff remembers, "I was proud of my old General." The men begin a cat-and-mouse game, starting with peasant personalities; then Ivanoff shoots a question, "When did you cut yourself off from the Party?" Rubashov does not deign to answer the query. "I'm tired, and I'm sick, and I don't care to play any games with you. Why have I been arrested?" "Supposing *you* tell *me* why," Ivanoff cynically suggests. As they talk, Rubashov reveals something of his mind in spite of his self-control. The necessary bloodiness of the Revolution is now being used, he says heatedly, to strangulate the Revolution; the Terror has been turned *against* the people.

"Damn it, Kolya, I'd hate to see you shot," Ivanoff ruminates over a cigarette.

RUBASHOV (*polishing his glasses, smiles sarcastically*)—Very touching of you. And exactly why do you people wish to shoot me?

IVANOFF (*flares up*)—"You people!" Again. What the hell's happened to you? It used to be "we."

RUBASHOV (*on his feet again*)—Yes, it used to be. But who is the "we" today? (*He points to the picture on the wall.*) The Boss? The Iron Man and his machine? Who is the "we"? Tell me.

IVANOFF—The people, the masses . . .

RUBASHOV—Leave the masses out. You don't understand them any more. Probably I don't either. Once we worked with them. We knew them. We made history with them. We were part of them. For one little minute we started them on what promised to be a new run of dignity for man. But that's gone! Dead! And buried. There they are. (*He indicates the faded patches of wall-paper.*) Faded patches on the wall. The old guard. Our old comrades. Where are they? Slaughtered! Your pock-marked leader has picked us off one by one till no one's left except a few broken-down men like myself, and a few careerist prostitutes like you!

IVANOFF—And when did you arrive at this morbid conclusion?

RUBASHOV—I didn't arrive at it. It was thrust on me.

IVANOFF—When? On what occasion would you say?

RUBASHOV—On the occasion when I came back from the Nazi slaughterhouse, when I looked about for my old friends, when all I could find of them were those—(*Again he waves his spectacles at the tell-tale patches.*)—faded patches on every wall in every house in the land.

IVANOFF (*nods his head, murmurs reasonably*)—Mm, hm! I see. That's logical. And that, of course, was when you . . . (*The telephone rings.* IVANOFF *picks up the receiver, barks:* I'm busy, *and hangs up.*) . . . when you joined the organized opposition . . .

RUBASHOV (*slowly, deliberately*)—You know as well as I do, I never joined the organized opposition.

IVANOFF—Kolya! Please! We both grew up in the tradition.

RUBASHOV (*sharply*)—I never joined the opposition.

IVANOFF—Why not? You mean you sat by with your arms folded? You thought we were leading the Revolution to destruction and you did nothing? (*Shakes his head.*)

RUBASHOV—Perhaps I was too old and used up.

IVANOFF (*sits back again, clucks with good-natured disbelief*)—
Ekh, ekh, ekh!

RUBASHOV (*shrugging his shoulders*)—Believe what you will.

IVANOFF—In any event, we have all the proofs.

RUBASHOV—Proofs of what? Sabotage?

IVANOFF—That, of course.

RUBASHOV—Of course.

IVANOFF—If that were all.

RUBASHOV—There's more?

IVANOFF (*nods*)—And worse. (*Rises.*) Attempted murder.

RUBASHOV—Ah! And who am I supposed to have attempted to murder?

IVANOFF—Not personally. You instigated the act. Naturally.

RUBASHOV—Naturally.

IVANOFF—I told you we have proofs. (*Picks up a sheaf of typewritten pages and waves them under his nose.*)

RUBASHOV—For instance?

IVANOFF—Confessions.

RUBASHOV—Whose?

IVANOFF—For one, the man who was to do the killing.

RUBASHOV—Congratulations. And who was it I instigated to murder whom?

IVANOFF—Indiscreet question.

RUBASHOV—May I read the confession? (RUBASHOV *reaches out for the papers.* IVANOFF *smiles, draws them out of his reach.*) May I be confronted with the man? (IVANOFF *smiles again, shakes his head.*) Who the hell would I want to murder?

IVANOFF—You've been sitting there for ten minutes telling me. (*He opens a drawer, drops in the sheaf of papers.*) The man you tried to murder is the Leader. (*He slams the drawer shut.*) Our Leader.

RUBASHOV (*takes off his glasses, leans forward, speaks deliberately, between his teeth*)—Do you really believe this nonsense? (*He studies* IVANOFF.) Or are you only pretending to be an idiot? (*He suddenly laughs knowingly.*) You don't believe it.

IVANOFF (*sits slowly, adjusting his prosthetic leg*)—Put yourself in my place. Our positions could very easily be reversed. Ask yourself that question—and you have the answer. (IVANOFF *rubs his thigh at the amputation line, stares moodily at the false leg.*) I was always so proud of my body. Then to wake, to find a stump in a wire cage. I can smell that hospital room. I can see it as if it were happening now: you sitting there by my bed, soothing, reasoning, scolding, and I crying because they had just amputated my leg.

(*He turns to* RUBASHOV.) Remember how I begged you to lend me your pistol? Remember how you argued with me for three hours, till you persuaded me that suicide was petty bourgeois romanticism? (*He rises, his voice suddenly harsh.*) Today the positions are reversed. Now it's you who want to throw yourself into the abyss. Well, I'm not going to let you. Then we'll be quits.

RUBASHOV (*putting on his glasses, studies* IVANOFF *for a second, with an ironic smile*)—You want to save me? You've a damned curious way of doing it. I am unimpressed by your bogus sentimentality. You've already tricked me into talking my head off my shoulders. Let it go at that!

IVANOFF (*beams*)—I had to make you explode now, or you'd have exploded at the wrong time. Haven't you even noticed? (*Gestures about the room.*) No stenographer! (*He crosses back to his desk, opens a drawer.*) You're behaving like an infant. A romantic infant. Now you know what we're going to do? (*Extracts a dossier out of the drawer.*)

RUBASHOV (*grimly*)—No, what are we going to do?

IVANOFF—We are going to concoct a nice little confession.

RUBASHOV—Ah!

IVANOFF—For the public trial.

Ivanoff's plan is a clever one; he is as sure of it as he is of himself. His old friend will admit developing a deviation and joining an opposing bloc. He will give their names, and this will make no difference because they all have been shot already. He will say that, when he learned of their terroristic plans, he broke off with them. The murder charge is refuted; Rubashov will get, perhaps, twenty years, but in two or three he will be reprieved and back in the ring again.

The prisoner flatly refuses to go along with such a plan, even when Ivanoff warns him that the alternative is a secret trial and shooting. The once-great leader will just vanish, and his followers will be unable to make a demonstration because they don't know what happened; for all they will know, Rubashov will be off on some mission. A phone call interrupts Ivanoff, and after he has taken it Ivanoff chuckles, "Oh, you old fox!" On the phone again, he summons Gletkin, and when this officer appears he charges him with bungling the Rubashov arrest. It was to have been done quietly—but it wasn't. Gletkin's men had to shoot the lock off Rubashov's door and were forced to carry their man bodily from his home. The whole neighborhood heard and saw the arrest. Ivanoff now dismisses the chastened officer after instructing him that Rubashov is to be treated with care and given cigarettes and medical attention. When Gletkin has gone, the investigator tells the prisoner that he will be given pencil and paper, too . . . in case he should like to begin writing his confession.

"Many thanks, but it won't work," Rubashov replies. "Kindly have me taken to my cell." Ivanoff has lost the first round, but he is sure that he will win in the end. He calls for a guard, who takes Rubashov back, and then he summons Gletkin and gives him a harsh dressing-down. No more bungling; this is no ordinary prisoner; his trial will be of great political and historical importance, and they simply must have his confession.

"Then why not turn him over to me?" suggests Gletkin. "I'll bring you his confession in three days." But Ivanoff knows by what brutal means, and he orders different tactics. Rubashov is to be left in peace and have all he wants. This will bring about the confession. Boldly, Gletkin disagrees with such kid-glove methods; he is very sure, very zealous and very fierce. He knows from experience that the human nervous system can stand only so much —even the system of so stout a man as Rubashov. Ivanoff laughs softly, "I'd hate to fall into your hands."

Gletkin is not awed by Ivanoff's position, although it may be that he must obey orders. He observes, "You older men always talk as if only the past were glorious . . . or some distant future. But we're far ahead of any other country, here and now! As for the past, we have to crush it. The quicker, the better."

"Well," says Ivanoff, "that may be. As for Rubashov, my instructions remain. He's to have time for reflection. He's to be left alone, and he will become his own torturer."

Rubashov is back in his cell, and once again the prison telegraph is clacking. Cell 402 messages, "Prisoners ask Rubashov not to confess. Die in silence."

"How was 302 tortured?" Rubashov taps.

"Steam."

The prisoner grimly puffs his cigarette into a glowing coal and deliberately pushes it into the back of his hand, holding it there, without flinching.

"You'll die in silence?" comes the query.

"I will. Tell them. I will."

The curtain falls.

ACT II

Rubashov has been in his cell five weeks. He is sleeping feverishly, dreaming fitfully. Voices out of other times come to his ears.

Suddenly, in his sleep, he cries, "Death is no mystery to us. . . .
It's the logical solution to political divergencies." There is the
sound of Gletkin's heels outside—a Gletkin who is coming up from
the execution cellar. He and a young fellow officer are moving
toward Rubashov's cell when Ivanoff, descending from above, catches
them and halts Gletkin sharply. "Have you been at my prisoner?"
he demands. Gletkin says he has not seen the prisoner for five
weeks, but has been informed that his fever is worse. He suggests
the prison doctor be sent, but Ivanoff vetoes the suggestion. "My
orders still stand," he declares—and as he turns to go he blows
cigarette smoke in Gletkin's face, which leads the young officer to
comment to Gletkin that Ivanoff's nerves are wearing thin.

"Tonight," says Gletkin to his young companion, "I'll break this
prisoner. Not against orders. I won't so much as go near his
cell. But inside an hour he'll be ready to confess. . . . It'll be
very interesting."

The officers vanish as the lights of the cell tier come up. Rubashov has awakened with a start; the other prisoners are pacing
nervously, for they sense that something has happened and they
don't know what. One of them asks another, "Who is Mischa
Bogrov?" Something has happened about a Bogrov. Rubashov
remembers this Bogrov, and as he remembers a men's chorus is
heard. They are soldiers and marines of the Revolution, warming
their hands at a fire. General Rubashov is there. A big marine
sings a Revolutionary song, and as he finishes the crowd applauds,
"Bravo, Mischa Bogrov!" Mischa, laughing and glowing, approaches his general and offers Rubashov a curved, silver-handled
dagger. "The Civil War is over," he exults. "No more killing.
Now we go home. We build a new life." General Rubashov accepts the gift and in turn makes a gift to Bogrov by informing
him that, tomorrow, he will become a member of the Party. The
young marine seems overcome by the honor, and promises he will
be faithful until death. . . .

The memory fades as the man in 402 interrupts with more tapping. He wants to be assured again that Rubashov will die in silence. Then the old fellow gets off on his obsession about women
and becomes irritated at Rubashov's disinterested replies. Wasn't
Rubashov ever in love? "No. Never." Rubashov sighs, frowns,
thinks heavily. Now he is at his desk, the Commissar of the Iron
Works. A timid, gray-haired employee, Hrutsch, is at the desk
with some charts, and nearby is the secretary, Luba Loshenko.
Rubashov, leaning heavily on a cane, steps up to greet her, and she
bids him welcome back home. From the charts Rubashov notes

that the quotas of iron and steel have not been filled, and old Hrutsch, whose heart trouble makes breathing hard, alibis that sabotage is a problem. Adroitly he changes the subject by talking admiringly of Rubashov: Those Nazis! What they did to him! Yet he escapes and comes home, right to work! Rubashov dismisses him and turns again to Luba, who says, "I wondered if I'd ever see you again. . . . My prayers were answered. I prayed for you."

"To which god?" He observes that she is the same little bourgeoise. He affects surprise that she is not yet married, has no babies.

Luba answers simply, "I thought you were dead and I didn't want to go on living." He puts his arms around her and kisses her; then, again becoming the Commissar, orders the girl to prepare for dictation and to call in Hrutsch, declaring, "I'm afraid we're going to have to get rid of that milksop."

The memory fades and Rubashov resumes his pacing. His fever is bad, yet he feels a chill and pulls his overcoat close about him. Suppose, he muses, the Leader is right and he is wrong; well, he must be logical and work things out to their final conclusion as he always has. A memory of such a conclusion strikes him and the figures of some dock workers materialize. They are sitting at an iron table in a *bistro* on the Marseille waterfront. There is a big man in a sailor's sweater and stocking cap; also a little hunchback, and a third man. Rubashov, accompanied by a young French intellectual named Albert, joins the trio, and Albert introduces the hunchback as Comrade Luigi, head of the dockworkers' union. Rubashov is on a mission from Moscow itself. The big dockworker, Pablo, is the business manager of the union; he is proud of the union's strength and of its determination to strangle Mussolini. The workers now are on strike against Italian ships because of the rape of Ethiopia. As the men talk Luigi, the hunchback, reveals much of himself. He escaped from Italy three years ago without a passport, was promptly deported to Belgium by the French police. Six times he came back to France, only to be rejected again, until finally Pablo fixed him up with a passport and got him a job with the union.

Rubashov throws a bombshell into the group, telling them that the strike must be called off, on orders from Moscow. The Italians are building three warships for Russia and have threatened to stop the work unless the Communist dock strike is called off. André and Luigi take it hard; they cannot understand an order in favor of the Fascist enemy. "There are principles," Luigi expostulates,

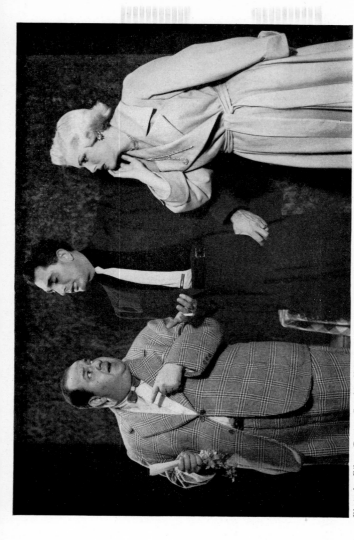

Photo by Eileen Darby, Graphic House, Inc., New York.

"GUYS AND DOLLS"

"Miss Adelaide," says Nicely-Nicely Johnson to Adelaide, "Nathan is in Pittsburgh with a rare tropical aunt. Good-by."

(Stubby Kaye, Robert Alda and Vivian Blaine)

"DARKNESS AT NOON"

Rubashov assures Luba, "There are no charges against you. Nothing's going to happen!"

(Claude Rains and Kim Hunter)

"BILLY BUDD"

The First Officer reads the sentence of death to Billy Budd.

(Dennis King, Winston Ross, Guy Spaull, Preston Hanson, Lee Marvin, Charles Nolte and Bill Froelich)

"THE AUTUMN GARDEN"

Nick says, "Champagne's always been a lousy drink for me. How did I get down here?"

(Fredric March)

"BELL, BOOK AND CANDLE"

The unwitting Shep gives the bewitching Gillian a family heirloom.

(Rex Harrison and Lilli Palmer)

"THE COUNTRY GIRL"

Bernie Dodd demands of Frank Elgin, "Do you know it's laced with twenty-two per cent alcohol?"

(*Uta Hagen, Paul Kelly and Steven Hill*)

"THE ROSE TATTOO"

"Si, si, una rosa," says Alvaro to the astonished Serafina.

(*Eli Wallach and Maureen Stapleton*)

Photo by Talbot-Giles, New York.

"SEASON IN THE SUN"

Says Emily to George, "Just look at that lovely, lovely ocean. I wouldn't be surprised if this was just about the best place in the world."

(Nancy Kelly and Richard Whorf)

"AFFAIRS OF STATE"

Constance Russell thanks Irene Elliott for being such a good "wife" to her lover, while the Secretary of State looks on.

(*Celeste Holm, Barbara O'Neil and Harry Bannister*)

"SECOND THRESHOLD"

Says Josiah Bolton to his daughter, "I'm leaving here shortly. Figuring on a little trip."

(*Clive Brook and Margaret Phillips*)

and as he does so he coughs blood. His two companions vote with him to continue the strike, but Rubashov warns them that he is in authority here now. There is a job to be done and it will be done.

ALBERT—In spite of agents provocateurs. (PABLO *reaches over, grabs* ALBERT *by the lapels of his coat, and shakes him.*)

LUIGI (*rises*)—No, Pablo, stop that! Stop! (PABLO *releases* ALBERT. LUIGI *addresses* ALBERT.) Provocateurs? For who, in God's name?

ALBERT (*furious, his voice shrill*)—For the Fascists.

PABLO—Because we won't load their ships? You hear, Comrades. That's a joke—a rotten joke, isn't it?

LUIGI (*softly*)—No, it's not a joke, Pablo; it's rotten, but it's not a joke. (*He looks up at the caricature of Mussolini.*) The joke is Benito brought me into socialism, me and my two brothers. We lived in Forli, 1911. Italy was starting a war with Tripoli. There was a big anti-war meeting, banners, posters. Benito took the platform. Benito, the humble socialist, in a dirty black suit and a bow tie. (*He imitates the crowd.*) "Bravo, Benito!" (*He mimics the gestures and facial expressions of Mussolini.*) "Fellow workers, militarism is our enemy! We hate war!" (*He becomes the crowd.*) "Bravo, Benito!" (*Again he is Mussolini.*) "We don't want iron discipline, we don't want colonial adventures! We want bread and schools and freedom." "Bravo, Benito!" (*He angrily admonishes the invisible crowd.*) "Don't applaud me! Don't follow me. I hate fetishism. Follow my words!" (*Softly, nodding to himself.*) Benito. (*He leans on the table; to* RUBASHOV.) We followed his words, my two brothers and I. Ten years later he gives my brothers the castor-oil treatment. To some that sounds like a joke, too. You know what happens when a quart of castor oil is poured down your throat? It tears your intestines to pieces, like you put them in a butcher's grinder, to little pieces. Two brothers I had. Not like me. Well-formed, beautiful, like Michelangelo carved them out of Carrara marble—one a David and one a Moses. I, the ugly one, I escaped. (*Softly, tenderly.*) Two brothers I had . . . and now—(*Fiercely.*)—Mother of God, I'm a Fascist! (*He coughs convulsively into his handkerchief.*) Back where I started with Benito. (*He spits at the caricature of Mussolini.*)

PABLO (*fervently*)—I swear to God it's all true.

ANDRÉ—Luigi's not a Fascist!

ALBERT (*rises, gesticulating with the long slender hands*)—Now, Comrades, you're thinking mechanistically. Dialectically, the fact is that, whoever does not serve the long-distance aims of the Party

is an enemy of the Party and therefore, even though he may think
himself subjectively an anti-Fascist, he is in fact objectively a
Fascist . . .

PABLO (*ironically seizes some dishes, tosses them into the air,
juggles them, catches them, then proffers them to* ALBERT *with an
ironic bow*)—Here! You do it better than I.

RUBASHOV (*rising*)—The ships are to be unloaded tomorrow.

LUIGI—Over my dead body.

PABLO—And mine.

ANDRÉ—And mine.

RUBASHOV—You can tear up your cards! (*Silence.*) The meeting is adjourned. (*Indicating the phone.*) Albert. (ALBERT *nods,
crosses to the phone, picks it up.*)

LUIGI (*to the others*)—Come. (*The three men leave,* LUIGI
coughing as he does.)

ALBERT (*at phone*)—André, Pablo, Luigi. Yes. Publish their
pictures in tomorrow's press. Front page. Agents provocateurs.
Any Party member who even talks to them will be dismissed at once.

RUBASHOV—Their passports!

ALBERT—Ah, of course. (*On phone.*) Also notify the French
police their papers here are forged. Arrange for their immediate
arrest and deportation. (*He hangs up, grins smugly.*) That'll
do it! Now little Luigi is really a man without a country!

RUBASHOV (*stonily*)—Yes. (ALBERT *laughs.* RUBASHOV *turns
a withering look of revulsion on him, and then, unable to endure
it, shouts at him.*) What the hell are you laughing at? What's
so funny? (ALBERT'S *laughter dies in his throat. He looks pained
and puzzled. With an exclamation of disgust* RUBASHOV *walks
away.*)

As the memory ends, Rubashov paces his cell and considers
what he has remembered; he has destroyed people he was fond of
—but History put him in that position and what else could he do?
The prison grapevine begins its clatter; 402 has information that
some executions are to take place soon, but he doesn't know who.
This reminds Rubashov that he, too, may be executed, but he still
can save himself with a "confession." The first doubt of his own
fortitude strikes him as he thinks, "Isn't the important thing to go
on?" He remembers another time—a bright Sunday afternoon in
Luba's room, with the gramophone playing Beethoven and the girl
humming as she prepares a vase of apple blossoms. She senses
that Rubashov has something on his mind. "Troubles," he says;
then he comes out with it and tells the girl, "Orders came in yes-

terday. You'll have to report back to Moscow. You're to leave tonight." Terror mounts in the girl and questions pour from her, but Rubashov gives only vague answers. He doesn't know how long she will be gone and he does say her work has been excellent. But "they" are investigating the files and production records of the Iron Works. He would like to intercede for Luba, but it would look bad for her if he did. She must go. Luba is now hysterically frightened, and Rubashov tries to convince her that nothing will happen to her—that she will not be arrested. He gives her her train ticket and travel warrant.

Lights reveal the other cells, with the prisoners, ears to the wall, listening for news on the telegraphic relay. They hear that a death sentence has been read. That the victim is being brought in, screaming and hitting. "Who is he?" Rubashov demands, and the answer comes, "Mischa Bogrov." The news makes Rubashov feel faint. The prison becomes vibrant with subdued drumming as the tapping of the men in their cells takes on the sound of muffled drums. Rubashov fancies he sees two uniformed figures dragging a third. They pass his cell door and he sees the third man is Bogrov. One of the officers is Gletkin, grim as usual. As they pass Cell 302 Bogrov cries Rubashov's name in anguish. Suddenly there is silence in the prison and Rubashov collapses on his cot. He does not know how long he has been thus, in a daze, but when he recovers his wits he sees Ivanoff standing beside him, holding a bottle of brandy and a glass. Rubashov takes a drink, then avidly asks for a cigarette. "How long have I been here?"

"Five weeks tomorrow." Ivanoff offers more brandy, but now the prisoner's mental faculties have returned and he spurns it, exclaiming, "You pimp!" He continues to berate his prison-keeper, but Ivanoff remains smiling and unperturbed. He informs his old general that Bogrov has been shot, after several days of torture at the hands of Gletkin. Ivanoff personally disapproves of Gletkin's methods—but Gletkin has even been urging the use of the same methods on Rubashov! The prisoner grimly declares torturing will bring no results, and the smiling Ivanoff asks, cynically, "Won't it?" The prison official makes an earnest plea for a confession.

RUBASHOV—Why was Bogrov tortured?

IVANOFF—He was stubborn like you.

RUBASHOV—Did you hear him whimpering?

IVANOFF—No. I didn't hear it. But I've heard and seen others. (*He wheels on* RUBASHOV, *stabbing an accusing finger at him.*) And so have you! And so have you, my General! (*He hobbles*

to RUBASHOV, *face thrust forward, accusingly.*) What of it? A
conscience is as unsuited to a revolutionary as a double chin. Since
when did N. S. Rubashov develop this bourgeois conscience? Hm?
When? (*Pause.*) Shall I tell you? The day, the hour, the minute? Nine months, two weeks ago—at 3:10 A.M.—when your little
secretary, Luba Loshenko, was shot! (*He sits next to* RUBASHOV.)
You were sleeping with her, weren't you? Now she's dead. So
you're making the world a metaphysical brothel for your emotions.
What have the shape of Luba Loshenko's breasts or Bogrov's whim-
perings to do with the new world we're creating?

RUBASHOV—Bogrov's dead, she's dead. You can afford a little
pity.

IVANOFF—I have many vices:—I drink; for a time, as you know,
I took drugs; but so far I've avoided the vice of pity. One drop
of that and a revolutionary's lost. (*He fills his glass.*) The great
temptation! To renounce violence, to make peace with ourselves . . . Hm? (*He drinks.*) I prefer my synthetic ecstasy in
a glass. You get over it in the morning.

RUBASHOV (*after a long silence, shakes his head, murmurs sadly*)
—Our golden dream! (*Then savagely.*) What a stinking mess
we've made of it.

IVANOFF (*setting down the glass, articulates carefully*)—Have
we? (*He lights a fresh cigarette.*) We've taken the land from
the landlords. (*He blows a smoke ring.*) We've freed them from
industrial exploitation. (*He blows another.*) For the first time
in history a revolution is functional.

RUBASHOV—Functional? (*He jumps to his feet, furious.*) So
functional in taking the land, in one year, we let five million
farmers and their families die of starvation! Deliberately. So
functional—(*He begins to pace up and down.*)—in freeing the people
from industrial exploitation we sent ten million of them to forced
labor under worse conditions than galley slaves. (*He plucks off his
spectacles nervously and waves them at* IVANOFF.) So functional,
to settle a difference of opinion, the omnipotent Leader knows only
one argument—Death!—whether it's a matter of submarines, ma-
nure, or the party-line in Indo-China. Death! (*He replaces his
spectacles and glares at* IVANOFF.)

IVANOFF (*rises, belligerently*)—That woman has really given
you softening of the brain! What of the millions who die of
starvation in China and India, of tuberculosis in rice fields, cotton
plantations . . . ?

RUBASHOV—In negatives we agree. Where has it led us?

IVANOFF—Well, where?

RUBASHOV—Our standard of living is lower than the most backward country in Europe. Labor conditions are harder; discipline's more inhuman. Our country is run by the police. (*Again he plucks off the glasses for emphasis.*) We've torn the living skin off our people and left them standing with bare tissues, muscles and nerves quivering.

IVANOFF—Well, and what of it? (*With warmth and conviction.*) Don't you find that wonderful? Has anything more wonderful ever happened in history? We're tearing the old skin off mankind and giving it a new one! That's not an occupation for people with weak nerves, but there was a time it filled you with enthusiasm.

RUBASHOV—I know.

IVANOFF—Look at the pamphlets put out by the anti-vivisectionists. When you read how some poor cur who has just had his liver cut out, whines and licks his tormentor's hand, it breaks your heart. But if we listened to these sentimentalists we'd have no cures for typhus, cholera, diphtheria . . .

RUBASHOV—I know, I know, I know. (*He turns away, sits, moodily.*)

IVANOFF (*following him, persistently*)—Of course you do. Better than I. And you still insist on being a martyr? (*He waits for an answer. Finally he throws up his hands and growls in disgust.*) All right. Have it your way. (*He picks up the bottle and glass.*) If you must throw yourself into the dust-bin of history, I can't stop you. Go. Let Gletkin have you. You're his. (*He turns to the door, pauses, turns back. His voice becomes soft.*) Only tell me, why? Why are you so in love with death? It stinks! Why do you want to die?

RUBASHOV (*hoarsely*)—I don't want to die. No one does.

IVANOFF—You act as if you do.

RUBASHOV—It's a fake. (*He clutches his throat.*) From here up, I'm resigned. From here down, I'm frightened.

IVANOFF—Yet I offer you your life.

RUBASHOV—On what terms?

IVANOFF—The only terms that matter. To go on being useful. (*He places the bottle on the floor and fumbles in his pocket.*)

RUBASHOV—To act the fool in public trial? No, thanks. The terms are too high.

IVANOFF (*taking out an official communication, pushes it under* RUBASHOV's *nose*)—Here's a confidential report I received today. (RUBASHOV *takes it, glances at it.*) Read between the lines.

RUBASHOV (*dryly*)—I need no instructions, thank you. (*Studies the document.*)

IVANOFF—What do you see?

RUBASHOV—War! It's coming.

IVANOFF—How soon?

RUBASHOV—Depends on how we play our cards. Perhaps years, perhaps months.

IVANOFF—The last war gave us Russia, Kolya; the next gives us the world. Or does it?

RUBASHOV—It could, if . . .

IVANOFF—If . . . ? Good! (*He sits next to him.*) There's a breach in the Party, in the whole country; the people are restless, dissatisfied; our economy is in pieces. The breach must be mended first; and you, and those who think like you, must mend it!

RUBASHOV—Hence the trials! (*Hands him back the document, contemptuously.*) They're better than the opera or the theatre.

IVANOFF—The goal, Kolya. It's coming. Nearer. Listen. You can hear it on the wind. And when that day comes . . .

RUBASHOV—The Gletkins take over.

IVANOFF—They're brutes. They don't count.

RUBASHOV (*plucking off his spectacles and glaring at* IVANOFF)— Who made them brutes? We did! Their Byzantine leader worship is frightening. Their cultivated ignorance is disgusting.

IVANOFF—Would they have been any use to us any other way?

RUBASHOV—You'd trust our revolution to them?

IVANOFF—Why do you think I'm risking my neck to save you? It's your brain I want to save. When the day comes, your brain will be needed. We'll get rid of them. You'll be needed more than ever!

Ivanoff's arguments have begun to make an impression and Rubashov, beginning to soften, wearily says, "I'll think it over." Ivanoff departs, well pleased with himself. In the corridor he encounters Gletkin, and, contemptuously blowing smoke in the man's face, announces, "He'll confess." Gletkin stares stonily.

The curtain falls.

ACT III

The days go by, and now Rubashov, seated on his cot with his shoes off and his coat across his shoulders, has a pad of paper on his knee and is writing intently. From the stack of pages beside him it is evident he has been writing for some time. He tries to ignore the insistent tapping of Cell 402, but finally gives in and taps an answer. He stuns the man by declaring, "I am confessing." "Have you no honor? You're pure son of a bitch," says 402. An officer comes for Rubashov and the prisoner says, "Well, it's about time! I've been waiting on Commissar Ivanoff for several days." As Rubashov is led away the cells clatter with the news of the confession. The boy in Cell 302 taps, "Oh, my God! Pray for me."

In Ivanoff's office a man in uniform is at Ivanoff's desk—but it isn't Ivanoff; it is Gletkin! Rubashov's smile vanishes as Gletkin regards him, stony-faced. "You will make your confession to me," he orders. A grim-lipped female secretary sits with pencil poised, and a fierce white light strikes Rubashov full in the eyes. Rubashov removes his glasses and tries to avoid the glare. Gletkin orders him to a chair full in the light, and Gletkin, in a monotone, begins reading a formal charge: Counter-revolutionary . . . in the pay of hostile foreign governments . . . inciting an attempt to assassinate the Leader. . . . "You plead guilty?" he demands.

Rubashov, shielding his eyes with a hand, makes a plea of guilt —but his own. He pleads guilty of bourgeois sentimentality, of having wanted an extension of freedom to the masses. But he categorically denies the charges Gletkin has just read. Gletkin strikes his face with a thick sheaf of paper, exclaiming, "Lies! Lies!" Pushing a button, he summons a guard with the prisoner from Cell 302—the boy, who now looks like a helpless child. He moves and talks like a sleepwalker. Under Gletkin's questioning, 302 makes astonishing statements. "Citizen Rubashov instigated me to murder the Leader of the Party by poison." The details are pat and glib: He was with Citizen Rubashov in Brussels, in his apartment, on the seventeenth anniversary of the Revolution. . . .

Rubashov, eyeing again the mangled, ghost-like face of the other prisoner, finally recognizes him as Joseph Kieffer, son of an old friend, Professor Kieffer. The boy continues an account of how he and his father went to Rubashov's apartment, and the two men drank and talked.

Gletkin reminds the boy, "That was three months before the discovery of your father's counter-revolutionary crimes and his execution." Haltingly, under prodding, the youth continues his recital, saying that on the night of that meeting Rubashov had said that "the Boss" had made the Party bureaucracy his puppets, and that he could only be removed by force.

"By this," Rubashov interrupts, "I meant political action."

The boy haltingly proceeds with testimony that is a strange and sinister twisting of the circumstances under which Rubashov and Professor Kieffer had talked that night in Brussels. At last a guard leads 302 out, and for an instant Rubashov meets the lad's imploring glance. When the boy is gone he exclaims, "Poor devil! What have you done to him?"

"What can be done to you," Gletkin bellows savagely.

All Rubashov's pent-up feelings explode as he shouts, "You ignorant young ass! What do you know about the Revolution? When you were peeing in your diapers we were working and fighting and studying one thing: Revolution! . . . We rotted away in every prison in Europe; we knew poverty, we knew persecution . . . but every living second we dreamed and built the Revolution. . . . Are you insane? Do you really believe that we have all suddenly become venal and corrupt?"

Gletkin's anger is almost apoplectic as he denounces Rubashov as a washed-out, disgusting, rotten old man. "You didn't make the Revolution—the Revolution made you!" he cries. But, he says, the likes of Rubashov never fooled the Leader; the Leader knew what they were, but used them because they were needed for a while. And now a new generation is at the helm and the day of the Rubashovs is over. "You are going to die!" he shouts.

Something does die within Rubashov; the will and the spirit go out of him and he suddenly looks what he is—a tired, sick old man. Gletkin buzzes for another witness. . . .

Time passes. A new secretary is making notes and a new interogator has replaced Gletkin, and the weary Rubashov is fighting his last fight . . . and losing it. The questions, the demands of "Yes or no," hammer at him. Bone-weary, he is made to stand—and to stand at attention as he answers his inquisitor. After a while, Gletkin and his secretary come in, fresh and rested, to take over. The questioning has been going on for ten hours. "Admit your crimes and get it over with," commands Gletkin—and Gletkin has brought with him a new weapon of torture: Rubashov's own books, Rubashov's own words, which now are thrown at him. "The objective result is everything." . . . "For the masses, what is right must be gilded, what is wrong must be black as pitch." . . . "The consequences of our thinking will be felt unto the seventh generation. Hence a wrong thought from us is more criminal than a wrong deed from others." As the questioning and quotations go on, Rubashov's mind wanders in the past—to Comrade Richard, to Luigi and Pablo and Albert. . . .

It is Gletkin who brings up Luba. She was tried and shot for sabotage. She was an ordinary young woman, but infatuated—Rubashov's disciple. "You taught her to hate us," Gletkin accuses. Rubashov denies this, but admits he did nothing to save the girl, in order that he, himself, could go on working. "I was one of her interrogators," the officer informs the prisoner. "I have here a transcript . . ." As he reads—

(LUBA'S *image appears in space, bowed, drenched with pain. She shakes her head slowly, moving her lips silently at first, then her trembling voice becomes barely audible, grows stronger, finally topping and supplanting* GLETKIN'S *voice.* GLETKIN *continues to read from the transcript.*)

LUBA—No one's. I've told you a hundred times there were no orders.

GLETKIN—Stop lying.

LUBA—No matter what I say you don't believe me. Oh, God! I'm so tired.

GLETKIN—I want the truth.

LUBA—I've told you the truth, over and over and over and over. I'm so tired, I can't . . .

GLETKIN—Who gave you these instructions?

LUBA—No one.

GLETKIN—You sabotaged without instructions?

LUBA—No, no, no. You're twisting my words.

GLETKIN—That's what you said.

LUBA—I didn't say that! I said I didn't do these things and no one asked me to.

GLETKIN—We've all the proofs.

LUBA—What are you trying to make me say?

GLETKIN—Stop shielding Rubashov!

LUBA—I'm not shielding anyone.

GLETKIN—You're shielding Rubashov.

LUBA—A man like that doesn't need shielding. A man like that . . .

GLETKIN—You were sleeping with him, weren't you?

LUBA—I loved him.

GLETKIN—You loved him?

LUBA—Yes.

GLETKIN—You'd do anything he asked you?

LUBA—He wouldn't ask me to commit crimes.

GLETKIN—Idiot! This man has used you.

LUBA—No!

GLETKIN—He's made a fool of you.

LUBA—No!

GLETKIN—And now when you need him, where is he? Where is he?

LUBA—Oh, God, God, make them leave me alone!

GLETKIN—God is dead, Luba Loshenko!   God is dead.

LUBA—What do you want of me?

GLETKIN—Rubashov's making you responsible for his guilt.

LUBA—He's not.

GLETKIN—Use your head!   He's refused to testify for you.

LUBA—I don't believe that.

GLETKIN—Here are the proofs!   Look, look!

LUBA—I don't want to look.

GLETKIN—He was asked to testify and he's refused.

LUBA—I don't believe that.   I don't believe you . . . I don't believe you . . .

RUBASHOV (*staring into space, murmurs*)—I had no choice, Luba. Don't you see?   I had no choice.   I couldn't have saved you.   It was only a trap to destroy my usefulness. (*The* SECRETARY *rises, leans forward to catch* RUBASHOV's *words and writes them down.*)   I tried!   I went everywhere—to my friends in high places.   They said no, nothing will help.

GLETKIN (*reads on*)—Save yourself!   This is your last chance, Luba Loshenko!   You admit these acts of sabotage.

LUBA—I can't admit them because there weren't any.   There was no sabotage.   There were only tired men and sick men and frightened men.

GLETKIN (*slaps his hand as he reads*)—You stupid bitch! (LUBA's *image recoils as if she'd been struck.*)   All right!   Then you'll be shot in the back of your neck!

LUBA—What are you doing to us?   What are you doing to us? We're not stones, we're not machines!   We're human beings.   We feel, we think, we see, we dream, we're a part of God.   Why have you done this to us?   You say God is dead, but you've made your own god out of darkness, out of misery and lies and pain!   Why? Why are you doing this to us?

RUBASHOV (*stands up unsteadily, staring into space, calls out*)— This was not the way it was to be.

Back in the terrible reality of the inquisition office, Rubashov has had enough.   Saying, quietly, "I'm going to faint," he slides to the floor.   Smelling salts are brought, and when he regains consciousness he murmurs, "Sleep.   I must sleep."   Gletkin insists, "You understand what the Party expects of you. . . . This is the last service you can perform. . . ."   Rubashov nods exhausted assent, and Gletkin orders him taken back to his cell.   Then, to his relief man, he says, "In exactly twenty minutes bring him back here.   I'll interrogate him till midnight, you take him till five A.M.,

and I'll take him again at five. This Loshenko thing—that's the
lever. Work it around in his belly."

Rubashov, in his cell, is remembering something else in his past—
but this is his very recent past. He is before the Supreme Court of
the U.S.S.R.—a President and six judges. The prosecution has
ended its case, and now Comrade Rubashov is being permitted to
make his last plea. A portable microphone is put in his hand, and
Rubashov begins, in a dead voice:

"Citizen judges. Covered with shame, trampled in the dust,
about to die—let me serve my final purpose. Let my horrible
story demonstrate how the slightest deflection from the Party line
must inevitably drag one down into counter-revolutionary banditry.
If I ask myself today: "For what am I dying?" I am confronted
by absolute nothingness. Therefore, on the threshold of my final
hour, I bend my knees to my country and to my people. The
political masquerade is over. We were dead long before the Public
Prosecutor demanded our heads. With this my task is ended.
I have paid my debts. To ask for mercy would be derision. You
must hate me, and you must kill me! I have nothing more to say."

PRESIDENT—I will announce the sentence of the Military Collegium of the Supreme Court. (*He reads.*) "The Sentence. The
Military Collegium of the Supreme Court of the U.S.S.R. sentences
N. S. Rubashov to the supreme penalty—to be shot, with the con-
fiscation of all his personal property . . ."

(*His voice trails off. The lights fade. The court vanishes. Only*
RUBASHOV *remains, sitting in his cell, wrapped in meditation, his
head between his hands, his brow furrowed, his face old and gray as
if all the blood had been drained out of him. An insistent tapping.*
402 *comes into view, tapping three times, waiting, and gently repeating the code.*)

RUBASHOV (*coming out of his reverie, rises feebly, crosses unsteadily to the wall, taps*)—Yes?

402 (*taps*)—I thought 302 behaved quite well. He went like a
brave man.

RUBASHOV (*taps*)—Yes.

402 (*taps*)—You still have about ten minutes. What are you
doing?

RUBASHOV (*taps*)—I'm thinking.

402 (*taps*)—Thinking's bad. You won't show the white feather!
We know you're a man. A man. (*Pause.*) Do you still remember
"Breasts fit champagne glasses!" Ha! Ha! What a man you are!
(RUBASHOV *listens for a sound from the corridor.* 402 *senses his*

thoughts.)   Don't listen.   I'll tell you in time when they are coming.
(*Pause.*)   What would you do if you were pardoned?

RUBASHOV (*thinks, taps*)—I'd study astronomy.

402 (*taps*)—Ha! Ha! Me too, perhaps. But they say other stars are perhaps also inhabited. That would spoil it. (*Pause.*) May I give you some advice?

RUBASHOV (*taps*)—Yes.

402 (*taps*)—But don't take it wrong. Technical suggestion of an old soldier. Empty your bladder. Is always better in such case. The spirit is willing but the flesh is weak. Ha! Ha!

RUBASHOV (*smiles, taps*)—Thanks. (*Pause.*)

402 (*taps*)—Why astronomy?

RUBASHOV (*taps*)—As a boy I loved to watch the stars. I wanted to solve the riddle of the universe.

402 (*taps*)—Why? Talk to me.

RUBASHOV (*to himself*)—Recently I read they have discovered the Universe is finite. Forty years pass and I read that. If the Public Prosecutor had asked, "Defendant Rubashov, what about the Infinite?", I would not have been able to answer. Perhaps there is my real guilt.

402 (*taps*)—It's too late to worry about guilt.

RUBASHOV (*taps*)—How can I die till I find out what I'm dying for? (*Pause, taps.*) Sorry! Tell me, what are your prospects?

402 (*taps slowly*)—Eighteen years more. Not quite. Only six thousand five hundred thirty days. (*Pause.*) Think of it. Another six thousand five hundred thirty days without a woman. I envy you really. My brain is turning to water. I have returned to the habits of my childhood. I loathe myself!

RUBASHOV (*to the wall*)—Oh, you poor, poor devil! (*To the entire prison, to all Russia.*) All of you! My hundred and eighty million fellow prisoners, what have I done to you? What have I created? If History is all calculation, Rubashov, give me the sum of a hundred and eighty million nightmares. Quickly calculate me the pressure of a hundred and eighty million cravings. Where in your mathematics, Rubashov, is the human soul? At the very beginning you forgot what you were searching for? (*Footsteps ring out in the corridor.*)

402 (*taps*)—They're coming. (*The footsteps grow louder.*) What a shame. We were having such a pleasant talk.

RUBASHOV (*taps*)—You've helped me a lot. Thanks.

402 (*taps*)—Farewell. I envy you, I envy you. (*The door of RUBASHOV's cell is thrown open with a clang. GLETKIN enters.*)

GLETKIN—Enemy of the People Nicolai Semonovitch Rubashov, before you are executed, have you any last wish? (*A long pause.*)

RUBASHOV—One. (*He tries to catch* GLETKIN's *eyes.*) If I could only make you understand where in the very beginning we failed.

GLETKIN—These are your last words. Don't waste them.

RUBASHOV (*passionately*)—You don't build a Paradise out of concrete. My son . . .

GLETKIN (*quickly, distastefully*)—I am not your son.

RUBASHOV (*after a long pause, sadly*)—Yes, you are. That's the horror. (*He shakes his head, bitterly.*) The means have become the end; and darkness has come over the land.

GLETKIN—Have you any last wish?

RUBASHOV—To die.

(GLETKIN *motions him to walk.* RUBASHOV *moves slowly out of the cell;* GLETKIN *takes out his pistol, cocks it and follows. The* GUARD *opens the gate to the cellar, a shaft of light coming up catches them.* 402 *begins to drum on the door. From all over the prison comes the hollow muffled drumming, which mounts higher and higher as* RUBASHOV *and* GLETKIN *descend, and the iron gate clangs behind them. The drumming reaches a climax as* . . .

THE CURTAIN FALLS

BILLY BUDD *

Play in Three Acts

By Louis O. Coxe and Robert Chapman

Based on the Short Novel by Herman Melville

WHEN "Billy Budd" opened on Broadway, it did not have quite enough enthusiasts—although it had some—among the reviewers to make it the overnight success which is so important and so necessary these days. So the play had to fight, and it fought a long, game fight. Not long after it opened, the closing was announced; whereupon Herman Shumlin, a theatrical manager having no connection with the play, wrote and paid for of his own volition a display advertisement in *The New York Times,* expressing his admiration and enthusiasm for the drama and its production. This provided enough of a spurt at the box office to prevent the closing. The actors in "Billy Budd," similarly enthusiastic, volunteered to take drastic wage cuts, and the producers, Chandler Cowles and Anthony Brady Farrell, poured in more funds than they had been committed for. The result of all this spiritual and fiscal enthusiasm was a satisfactory run in number of performances, if not in profit made. When it came time for the Critics Circle to make its annual award, the favorite play among the dopesters was "Darkness at Noon," which won; among other plays considered to be likely contenders, "Billy Budd" was far down the list. Yet, when the critics' ballots were counted, it was revealed that "Billy" came close to winning. "Darkness at Noon" polled ten votes and "Billy Budd" won a surprising eight.

This play was first produced January 29, 1949, by the Experimental Theatre, for seven performances. But the production now under consideration is not a revival, but a different work. The authors tell about it in notes appended to the published version of the play (Princeton University Press). "The version presented here

is that of the final Broadway production. The play in this form
has passed through several stages. The original version (titled
"Uniform of Flesh") was in stricter poetic form and was more
austere in tone and structure; much of it seemed to us too bald and
expository. We have tried to thicken the texture of the play with
much added dramatic incident, contrapuntal conflict, and realistic
speech. There is, of course, some danger that we have fallen between two stools: what we have done may not please either the
average theatregoer or the Melville scholar. But for our part we
have done! Our original faith in the novel remains and supports
our faith in our own work."

The authors' faith in the novel was this: they saw in it a morality
play—"a story of good, evil and the way of the world." They saw
in the characters of the Melville novel—which was very short—
symbols, "certain permanent attitudes, qualities, moral images."

But the images are visual as the curtain rises. It is a fine morning in early August, 1798, and the man-o'-war *H.M.S. Indomitable*
is at sea. In spite of the sunlight spilling down the companionway
into the between-decks compartment of the crew's quarters, it is dark
and shadowy except where the sun strikes directly. A smoking-lamp
burns feebly over a wooden mess table flanked by two benches.
Jenkins sits at the table, mending a piece of clothing, and in the
shadow the Dansker sits on a low sea chest, smoking a pipe. Neither
man is talking. Jenkins is captain of the maintop and the Dansker
(the Dane) is a mainmastman. Jackson, a maintopman, lurches
down the companionway into the compartment, doubled with pain,
and topside one hears the cold voice of Claggart calling, "You there!
Jackson!" Claggart is Master-at-Arms, and is feared for his person
as well as for his position. Jackson, cowering, groans, "He'll send
me aloft again, sure, and I can't hang on."

Claggart follows Jackson into the quarters and orders him topside, ignoring the sailor's protests that he is so sick he nearly fell off
the mainmast—and ignoring, too, the humanitarian protests of
Jenkins. "This ship needs all hands," says Claggart. "You'll have
to go aloft." Jackson, starting up the ladder, cries, "God, sir, I
can't, I can't stand it! It'll be my death, sure!" But he goes topside, with Claggart after him. When the Master-at-Arms has vanished Jenkins mutters, "God damn your bloody heart! I'll stick
him one day before long!"

Three other crewmen, Butler, Talbot and Kincaid, come in from
the next compartment of the crew's quarters. They are hungry and
they call for the messboy, who brings an iron pot of food. They are
joined by O'Daniel and Payne, maintopmen. As they eat they gos-

sip, and they wonder if their group will be getting the new man—the one who was 'pressed this morning off a merchantman. One of the group, however, is too upset to eat—Jenkins, who is still boiling at the way Claggart forced the ailing Jackson back aloft. "Plain murder, by God," he exclaims. He predicts that Jackson will fall, for sure. One of the group reminds Jenkins that Claggart wouldn't be doing such things without the backing of "Captain Starry Vere and that red snapper Seymour and them other bloody officers." Another crewman speaks up in favor of Captain Vere, who is a saint in heaven compared to some other high officers he has known. This man, O'Daniel, was in the naval rebellion at Spithead and he recalls how fine it was, with the officers quaking in their cabins. The two most quick-tempered men in the group, Talbot and Jenkins, get into a violent argument over who would be the braver in case of an attack upon officers, and in an instant they are at each other with drawn knives. They fight silently, thrashing around the compartment, upsetting benches and food, while the others look on unmoved. Finally Jenkins throws Talbot on the deck and holds his knife against his throat; then, suddenly, he lets the man up, offers a handshake and reminds his recent enemy, "I'm leading seaman in this compartment." Talbot hits the proffered hand and goes off angrily.

Down the companionway come Squeak, Billy and Gardiner. Squeak is well named; he is the Man Friday of the Master-at-Arms. Gardiner is a junior officer—very junior: a midshipman who feels important far beyond his youth. Billy is Billy Budd, the new sailor who has been impressed from the merchantman. His face is open, innocent and handsome and his body is large, well-formed and strong. Gardiner and Squeak are simply delivering Billy to his section of the crew. Squeak explains to the newcomer that this is the larboard section of the maintop and the captain of the watch is Jenkins. Jenkins complains, "What's a green hand dumped in here for?"

When Squeak and the midshipman have gone topside, Billy offers his new mates a friendly countenance and introduces himself: "My name is Budd. Billy, if you like." Kincaid is the first to respond, by offering his own name, and he shows the youngster where he should swing his hammock. Then Kincaid points out the others around—O'Daniel, Payne, Butler, the Dansker—and Jenkins, captain of the watch.

"How long you been going to sea, baby?" The question from Jenkins is patronizing, belittling.

"About ten years, but in the merchant service. . . . I know I'm new at Navy work, and probably there are some things I'll need help with."

Jenkins sneers, "No doubt, little boy," and Billy eagerly replies, "I'll learn fast, never fear." The men seem fascinated by Billy Budd, for with his open countenance and forthright answers he is something new. To O'Daniel he says, "You're Irish, aren't you? I like the Irish. There was an Irishman on the *Rights of Man*, with big red whiskers. . . . When I came away he gave me a silver knife. This is it."

Jenkins invites, "Tell us about home and mother, Baby Budd."

"There's not much to tell," the boy replies simply. "I've got no home, and never had a family to remember." He tells the men what it was like aboard the merchantman *Rights of Man*. Most of the sailors had no other home—not even the skipper. The skipper was a kind old bloke who looked fierce. Used to keep a bird in a cage in his cabin, and would let Billy feed it. At the mention of food, Kincaid offers some of the warship's fare, saying, "We don't know what it is, but we been eating it for a long time." Billy accepts some and laughs, "I could eat anything right now. Even this."

"What's the Captain like?" the boy inquires. "On the *Rights of Man* the captain . . ."

Jenkins cuts him off with a snarling, "You going to jaw some more about that rocking horse? I suppose *you* was at Spithead, too?"

Billy doesn't know what Spithead means, and is informed it was a mutiny the Navy had a year ago. The lad asks, "Why did they mutiny?" Jenkins replies, "Jimmy-Legs is ten good goddam reasons for it, himself."

Billy pursues, "Who is Jimmy-Legs?" He is told this is the name for the Master-at-Arms, the devil himself between decks.

JENKINS—How old are you, kid? Sixteen?

BILLY—I don't know, maybe . . . twenty.

JENKINS—He don't even know how old he is! My guess is, too young to know what his parts are for.

O'DANIEL—Is it anybody is that young?

KINCAID—Stow it, Jenkins. Come on, don't pay no attention to him. He's feeling ugly today.

JENKINS—Well now, ain't you getting holier than a bloody bishop. Let him talk up for himself, if he don't like it.

KINCAID—Stow it, I say. You got no reason to crawl over Bill. Let him be.

BILLY—That's all right, Tom. I don't mind a joke. Black's the white of me eye, mates! (*All laugh except* JENKINS.)

JENKINS—Mama taught you pretty manners, huh? Oh! Ain't got no mama, you say? Well now, think what that makes you! (*Laughs.*)

BILLY—Tell me what you mean, Mister Jenkins.

PAYNE—What's gnawing your arse, Jenkins? Can't you see the boy's trying to be friendly?

JENKINS—You forgetting who's leading seaman here? Come on, Baby, talk back, why don't you? Scared?

BILLY—N-no. Why do you think I'd be scared, M-M-Mister Jenkins?

JENKINS—He stammers! What do you know! The little bastard's so scared he's stammering.

BILLY—Don't call me that again.

JENKINS—Sounds good, ha? Sounds fine. I like the way it rolls out your mouth. Bastard Baby Budd . . .

(BILLY *strikes him.* JENKINS *staggers and falls, pulls a knife and gets up, lunging at* BILLY. PAYNE, BUTLER *and* KINCAID *get up and stand close to* BILLY, *silently protecting him.*)

JENKINS—Get away, God damn you! He's got to find out who gives orders here.

KINCAID—Not this time, Jenkins. Lay off.

O'DANIEL—Belay it. You're wearing me out, the pair of yous.

BUTLER—Put away the knife. (JENKINS *sees their determination and relaxes a little, uncertain what to do.*)

BILLY—Will you shake hands? Or would you rather fight?

JENKINS—You little bas . . . (*Lunges forward.* BILLY *catches his arm and bends it, holding* JENKINS *cursing and powerless.*)

BILLY—That's enough, mate. Pipe down and let us be.

O'DANIEL—Good lad! Save the great strength is in you, Jenkins, for fighting the devil is after your soul.

JENKINS—All right, all right. You can let me go now.

O'DANIEL—Leave him go, lad. I won't hurt him at all.

BILLY—You're like Red Whiskers on the *Rights,* he liked to fight too. (*Freeing him.*) Will you shake hands, mate?

JENKINS (*momentarily uncertain what to do*)—Shake hands, is it? . . . Well, you beat me fair. You got guts, which is more than I give you credit for. (*They shake hands.*)

KINCAID—You're a hell of a peacemaker, Bill.

PAYNE—That's the only time I ever hear Jenkins eating his own words.

O'DANIEL—Ah, that's a terrible diet, would make any man puke.

JENKINS—Don't you be getting any wrong ideas. I'm still a match for you!

KINCAID—Better belay your mess gear, Bill.

JENKINS—Where you come from, Baby?

PAYNE—Stow it! Jimmy-Legs! (BILLY *goes on talking as* CLAGGART *enters.*)

BILLY—I don't know, I guess from Portsmouth. I never lived ashore, that I can remember. Where do you come from? (*Drops a pot on deck.* CLAGGART *stands over him.*)

CLAGGART—Handsomely done, young fellow, handsomely done. And handsome is as handsome did it, too. You can wipe that up, Jenkins. (*To* BILLY.) What is your name?

BILLY—Budd, sir. William Budd, ship *Rights of Man.*

CLAGGART—Your ship is *H.M.S. Indomitable* now.

BILLY—Aye, sir.

CLAGGART—You look sturdy. What was your station aboard the merchantman?

BILLY—M-m-mizzentopman, sir.

CLAGGART—You like that station?

BILLY—Aye, sir, well enough.

CLAGGART—How long have you been at sea?

BILLY—Ten years, sir, near as I can tell.

CLAGGART—Education?

BILLY—None, sir.

CLAGGART—So. You come aboard with nothing but your face to recommend you. Well, while beauty is always welcome, that alone may not avail us much against the French. There are other requirements in the service.

BILLY—I'll learn quickly, sir.

CLAGGART—The sea's a taskmaster, young fellow. It salts the sweetness out of boyish faces. You cannot tell what motion lies asleep in that flat water. Down where the manta drifts, and the shark and ray, storms wait for a wind while all the surface dazzles.

BILLY—I am a seaman, sir. I love the sea. I've hardly lived ashore.

CLAGGART—Then let the wind and sea have license to plunder at their will. As of today, a new maintopman swings between sky and water. (*He turns toward the ladder and notices the mess on deck.*) I thought I asked you to wipe that up, Jenkins.

JENKINS—That's the messboy's job.

CLAGGART—Clean up, Jenkins. (JENKINS *hesitates.*) That is an order. Turn to.

BILLY—I'll give you a hand, Jenkins. Come on.

CLAGGART—Ah, there. See how helpful Billy is. Why can't you take a leaf from this innocent young David's book, Jenkins? (*Turns*

away.   JENKINS *accidentally brushes against him and receives a
savage cut from* CLAGGART'S *rattan across his face.*)   Watch what
you're doing, man!
    JENKINS—I swear . . . !

On deck there is a loud scream and a crash.   Then running footsteps and shouts for the Surgeon.   The men surge toward the ladder
but are halted by Claggart.   Jenkins shouts, "It's Jackson!   I knew
it, by God, I told you so!"
    And it *is* Jackson.   Several sailors carry him down the companion-
way and carry him off to the sick-bay, the Surgeon directing them.
Jenkins' rage is beyond control.   He points at Claggart and cries,
"Killed him, he did!   We'll have a showdown now!   After him,
mates!"   The men move toward the Master-at-Arms in a rush, cursing, with drawn knives—and are halted by the appearance of Captain Vere in the companionway.   Captain Vere is an immaculate,
almost dandified, Naval officer, but his voice is a voice of command
as he orders, "Stand fast!   Master-at-Arms, what is the matter
here?"
    "The dogs are out of temper, sir."
    Vere addresses the men: "This is a wartime cruise, and this vessel
sails under the Articles of War.   Volunteer or 'pressed man, veteran
seaman or recruit, you are no longer citizens, but sailors; a crew
that I shall work into a weapon. . . . You have but two duties: to
fight and to obey, and I will bend each contumacious spirit, each
stiff-necked prideful soul of you, or crush the spirit in you if I
must. . . ."
    But it isn't the attack upon Claggart that has brought the Captain.
He has come to find out about the sailor who fell from the yardarm.
How did it happen?   Claggart says he does not know.   Nor does
Butler.   Nor does Jenkins—and as he questions this man the Captain notices the cut across his face.   In explanation of the wound
Jenkins falters, "I fell."   As he turns to go topside the Captain notes
a new face—Billy Budd's.   Claggart identifies him as the maintopman 'pressed from the *Rights of Man* this morning.
    "Let him speak for himself," says Captain Vere.   Billy tries to
talk but can only stammer incoherently until the Captain soothes
him with a gentle, "Take your time."   Then Billy speaks up: "I saw
a man go aloft, sir, as I came on board just a while ago.   He looked
sick, sir, he did.   This officer was there, too—he can tell you."   And
to Claggart he says, "Don't you remember, sir?"
    Claggart stiffly denies that he sent a sick man aloft.   The Surgeon
enters from sick-bay and reports that Jackson is dead, and after a

pause Captain Vere orders, "Carry on, Master-at-Arms." He goes up the companionway, followed by the Surgeon. Claggart, venomous, says to Billy, "You've made a good impression on the Captain." And as he goes topside he strikes Jenkins viciously on the arm with his rattan.

The men are astir with excitement. One of them speaks admiringly of the way Billy spoke up to the Captain. Another warns the boy that Jimmy-Legs is already down on him, to which Billy replies, "Why, he's friendly to me."

"Poor bastard," says Jenkins, "I pity him, I do."

"He's dead, ain't he? Better off than us," argues Butler.

"Not Jackson," says Jenkins. "I mean the baby here, Billy."

The curtain falls.

Scene II

In the early evening of this day the off-duty sections of the crew are mustered aft on the maindeck for Jackson's funeral. On the forward break of the quarterdeck above them stands Captain Vere, uncovered, reading the Committal Prayer. The sky is fading from yellow to red to darkness. As the Captain finishes the prayer there is a slow drum roll, and the muffled splash of Jackson's body. Officers and petty officers spring into action and voice, dismissing sections, until all who remain at the rail are Butler, Jenkins, Payne, Kincaid and Billy—all thinking of the sailor who has just gone to rest in the sea. Jenkins observes that Jackson, at least, isn't worrying. "I like to live," says Billy. "Even when it seems bad, there's a lot that's good in it."

"Maybe for you, Bill," Jenkins agrees. "You wouldn't know trouble if it come up and spit in your eye." The men go below—all but Jenkins and Billy. Jenkins warns, "Stay clear of Jimmy-Legs" —and he, too, goes down the hatchway. Billy remains staring over the side, and Claggart, not noticing his presence, comes near the quarterdeck ladder and stares seaward, too. In a moment Billy sees him and speaks, "Good evening, sir." The Master-at-Arms returns his greeting with subtle sarcasm.

The fact that Billy seems at ease amazes and interests Claggart, who asks, "How have you stomach to stand here and talk to me? . . . You know my reputation. . . . Have you not intelligence enough to be afraid of me? To hate me as all the others do?"

"Why should I be afraid of you, sir? You speak to me friendly when we meet."

"You're a fool, fellow. In time you'll learn to fear me like the rest."

Billy disagrees most pleasantly. The men are wrong. Billy was just noticing the way he was looking off to leeward, kind of sad. "Have you no heart for terror, fellow?" demands Claggart. "You've seen this stick in use. Have you not got sense and spleen and liver to be scared, even to be cowardly?"

BILLY—No, sir, I guess not. I like talking to you, sir. But please, sir, tell me something.

CLAGGART—I wonder if I can. Well, ask it.

BILLY—Why do you want us to believe you're cruel, and not really like everybody else?

CLAGGART—I think you are the only child alive who wouldn't understand if I explained; or else you'd not believe it.

BILLY—Oh, I'd believe you, sir. There's much I could learn from you: I never knew a man like you before.

CLAGGART (slowly)—Do you—like me, Billy Budd?

BILLY—You've always been most pleasant with me, sir.

CLAGGART—Have I?

BILLY—Yes, sir. In the mess, the day I came aboard? And almost every day you have a pleasant word.

CLAGGART—And what I have said tonight, are these pleasant words?

BILLY—Yes, sir. I was wondering . . . could I talk to you between watches, when you've nothing else to do?

CLAGGART—You're a plausible boy, Billy. Aye, the nights are long, and talking serves to pass them.

BILLY—Thank you, sir. That would mean a lot to me.

CLAGGART—Perhaps to me as well. (Drops his rattan. BILLY picks it up and hands it back to him. CLAGGART stares at it a moment, then at BILLY.) No. No! Charm me, too, would you! Get away!

BILLY (surprised and puzzled)—Aye, sir. (He exits down the hatchway. After a pause in which CLAGGART recovers his self-control SQUEAK appears.)

CLAGGART (without turning)—Come here. I thought I told you to put that new seaman Budd on report. Why was it not done?

SQUEAK—I tried, Mister Claggart, sir. I couldn't find nothing out of place. Gear all stowed perfect.

CLAGGART—Then disarrange it. You know the practice. I want him on report.

SQUEAK—Two of his messmates is ones nearly caught me at it before.

CLAGGART—Then be more careful. Now get along and see you make out something.

The Captain has stepped out on the quarterdeck and he asks what Squeak was doing above decks. Claggart smoothly explains that he was the ship's corporal making a routine report. "There is nothing in this ship," warns Vere, "of so routine a nature that I do not concern myself in it. Remember that."

The Master-at-Arms, with an "Aye, aye, sir," leaves, and in a moment the Captain is joined on the quarterdeck by his first officer, Philip Michael Seymour, who comments that it is a fine evening—however, the glass is falling and he expects they'll toss a little before morning. Seymour is about to return to his cabin to inspect the deck logs, but Vere asks him to remain and talk; for in the days and nights to come they may not have another such opportunity.

"Aye, sir. I expect the French will put us to our stations any hour now."

Vere is depressed, he confesses. Somehow, the death of the man Jackson seems a melancholy prologue to the voyage—an omen. An accident, his first officer assures him.

"It was more than an accident, Seymour. The man was sent aloft sick, by the Master-at-Arms, contrary to my standing order. Budd, the new seaman, implied as much, and the maintop watch confirmed it. The Master-at-Arms lied to me."

But the Captain is not going to do anything about it for the present. A court-martial could do no more than strip Claggart of his rank for misconduct. "I will let him have his head until some act puts him squarely counter to the law, then let the law consume him."

Seymour argues that Claggart is a valuable man, and needed, as things are now. Why not let things be? Vere exclaims, "Must a man always shrug, let things alone and drift? Would to God I could take this power of mine and break him now—smash all the laws to powder and be a man again!"

"We must serve the law, sir," says Seymour, "or give up the right and privilege of service. It's how we live."

The Captain knows Seymour is right—that they must keep an order they cannot understand. "The world demands it: demands that at the back of every peacemaker there be the gun, the gallows and the gaol. I talk of justice, and would turn the law gentle for those who serve here; but a Claggart stands in my shadow, for I need him. So the world goes, wanting not justice, but order . . . to be let alone to hug its own iniquities. Let a man work to windward of that law and he'll be hove down. No hope for him, none."

Wyatt, the sailing master, comes to the quarterdeck with his eight o'clock report. Ship inspected and all in order. The Captain looks down to the hatch, then slowly upward at the sails.

The curtain falls.

SCENE III

On the maindeck several nights later four bells is struck. Claggart stands by the larboard rail. A sailor climbs wearily down the ratlines, drops to the deck and goes below. Billy, coming up from below decks, says "Hello, sir," to Claggart. Without answering, the Master-at-Arms moves forward. The Dansker follows Billy up from below, and Billy finishes some conversation that started between decks: "Well, that's all there is to tell, Dansker. I always lash my hammock just so, and stow my gear same as all the others. They don't get in trouble."

"Mister Claggart is down upon you, Billy," says the Dansker.

Billy can't see it that way. Claggart almost always has a pleasant word; he is a friend. Billy climbs aloft, up the ratlines, and the Dansker watches him go. When Claggart reappears the Dansker ignores him and goes aft. As Jenkins comes into view, climbing down the ratlines, Claggart makes a motioning gesture and then fades into a shadowy corner. As Jenkins drops to the deck, Claggart's man, Squeak, appears, and seeks to make conversation with the maintop captain. Jenkins, showing distaste, would rather not stop, but the oily little cockney detains him with a mysterious hint about Billy Budd. He says he overheard Billy talking, and it might surprise Jenkins to know the things Billy said about Jenkins and his messmates. "He don't fancy us! Not like his feather boys aboard the merchantman." Jenkins denounces Squeak as a lying cutthroat who will need some other way to get Bill into trouble. Seizing and shaking the man, he exclaims, "Get back to Jimmy-Legs. And stay out of my way!"

The maintop captain goes below and Claggart emerges from the shadow. "You lack subtlety," he comments to Squeak. "Improve your style, or you stand tomorrow forenoon at the gratings! Keep Budd in petty troubles—that you can do. Unlash his hammock. Keep him on report. In time I'll let you know what plans I have for him. Get aft!"

Squeak is glad to get aft. The Dansker comes by, and Claggart invites him to stop and have a pipe. "I have the watch," says the imperturbable Dansker, and he turns to go, but Claggart stops him. "You move away from me as though I were some kind of stalking beast. . . . You are a hand older than most, and older in your hatred, I have no doubt. But why, man? You at least should see me as I am, a man who knows how the world's made: made as I am."

The Dansker surprises Claggart by saying that he, Claggart, reminds him of Billy Budd; then he explains: "You have half the truth and Billy Budd the other. He can't see there's evil in the world, and you won't see the good."

It is obvious that these two men have known each other for a long time, else they would not talk so frankly. The Dansker continues, "You recognize the hatred of your shipmates as an honor paid to a soul they cannot understand. Your fine contempt for human love is nothing but regret." Claggart interrupts him, saying he knows the rest of this by heart—but nothing the Dansker says does more than clatter in his belly.

"You don't believe in anything besides yourself, eh, John?"

Claggart answers, "I've said what I have said. I know myself, and look to that. You should try it. Go to your post, old man, and your everlasting duties."

Billy scrambles excitedly down the ratlines, crying, "Quarterdeck ho! Strange sail one mile off the larboard beam!" On the quarterdeck, John Ratcliffe, first lieutenant, begins a swift and efficient series of orders: Midshipman Gardiner to report to the Captain; Payne to the wheel; a man to the mast to relay lookout's reports; Claggart to inspect battle stations and report when they are fully manned. The Captain and his first lieutenant come on the quarterdeck as a drummer sounds beat-to-quarters. From the mast comes a shout that the vessel is a French frigate, and the Captain orders that they make chase. Even though the Frenchman is a faster ship, they are bound to try. His lieutenant asks, "May we try a shot at her now?" The Captain orders, "Commence firing," and there is a roar of guns.

The curtain falls.

ACT II

A few minutes before 8 the next morning, with the quarterdeck and part of the maindeck visible. On the quarterdeck are Lieutenant Wyatt, Midshipman Rea and the helmsman, Stoll. Their watch is about over, and Midshipman Rea is tired. Wyatt instructs him to make his entry in the log before his relief comes up; then he orders the helmsman to keep the ship as close-hauled as he can, and the next watch can reef sail if they want to. Wyatt's relief, Ratcliffe, appears on time, makes routine inquiries about course and weather. The relief helmsman takes over. The only man missing is the mate of the watch, Midshipman Gardiner, but in a moment he comes on deck with Midshipman Rea, whom he is to replace. Ratcliffe observes that Gardiner looks happy, which means trouble for some poor devil. Gardiner snatches the log out of Rea's hands and bounds up to the quarterdeck.

REA—I've been relieved, sir. Horatio, Lord Gardiner has the watch.

WYATT—Ah, Midshipman Gardiner. The backbone of the British Navy.

RATCLIFFE—The backside, if you ask me.

WYATT—All right, Rea. You can turn in. (REA *exits.*)

RATCLIFFE—Pity we lost that Frenchman last night. A little action would season the monotony of these interminable watches.

WYATT—Did you ever hear of a ship-of-the-line running down a frigate, even with the wind? Ah, it's a magnificent morning! Thickening overcast, heavy ground swell, a fresh levanter breeze, and you, Johnny, are the Pride of the Morning!

RATCLIFFE—Mmm. Has the skipper been on deck yet?

WYATT—Not since sunrise. He came up then and paced the deck and stared off east like a sleepwalker. Then went below again without a word.

RATCLIFFE—He thinks too much.

WYATT—Well, if you ever make captain, your crew won't have that to complain of, anyway. Am I relieved?

RATCLIFFE—Yes, I relieve you. (*Tosses his cap to* WYATT.) Here. Take this below, will you?

WYATT—What? You'll be out of uniform, man. Mister Gardiner wouldn't approve of your standing watch without a hat, would you, Midshipman Gardiner?

GARDINER—Sir, the Articles state that officers on watch . . .

RATCLIFFE—Well, hang it, I lost twelve shillings the last time my hat went over the rail, and this is the only other one I've got. To hell with the Articles.

WYATT—Mind your language! It's downright mutinous. Well, don't expect me to stand your watches if you catch your death of cold. Good morning. (*Exit.*)

GARDINER—Midshipman Rea, sir, I don't like to say it, but his log entries are impossible.

RATCLIFFE—Then enter yourself, Mister Gardiner. So are you.

GARDINER—Yes, sir. But I do think he ought to be told . . .

RATCLIFFE—Go find the Captain and report to him the wind's abeam. Respectfully suggest we ought to take in topsails.

GARDINER—Aye, aye, sir. (*Goes down stairs.*)
RATCLIFFE—And don't forget to tell him I haven't got a hat.
GARDINER—What's that, sir?
RATCLIFFE—Nothing, sir! You got my order. Dump your ballast and shove off!
GARDINER—I thought you spoke to me, sir.
RATCLIFFE—I avoid that whenever possible. Move!
GARDINER—Yes, sir.
RATCLIFFE—Ye gods, what a brat. Nothing off, helmsman. She's well enough thus.
BYREN—Nothing off, sir.
GARDINER (*nearly bumping into* VERE *as he emerges from cabin, followed by* SEYMOUR *and* HALLAM)—Atten-tion!
RATCLIFFE—Good morning, sir.
VERE—Morning, Mister Ratcliffe.
GARDINER (*starting after* VERE, *bumps into* HALLAM)—Damn it, man, watch what you're doing!
VERE—Midshipman Gardiner.
GARDINER—Sir?
VERE—How long, pray, have you been in this ship, or any ship?
GARDINER—This is my first cruise, sir.
VERE—Your first cruise. A wartime cruise as well. And you are a midshipman. A midshipman, Mister Gardiner, let me tell you, is neither fish, flesh, nor fowl, and certainly no seaman. You're a salt-water hermaphrodite, Mister Gardiner. And unless you have a mind to be generally known as Spit-kit Gardiner, I recommend more tolerance toward the men. Now, is that clear?
GARDINER—Aye, aye, sir!
VERE—Very well, you may carry on.
RATCLIFFE—We've a weather helm, sir, and bow seas.
VERE—Take in topsails, if you please, Mister Ratcliffe.
RATCLIFFE—Aye, aye, sir. Mister Duncan!
DUNCAN (*enters*)—Aye, sir?
RATCLIFFE—Douse your topsails and topgallants. Haul in the weather braces.
DUNCAN—Aye, aye, sir. (*Exit.*) Away aloft! Hands by topgallant sheets and halyards!
GARDINER—Aloft there! Keep fast the weather sheets till the yards are down, da . . . if you please!
RATCLIFFE—Get aloft yourself, Mister Gardiner, see they do it right, since you're not satisfied.
GARDINER—Sir, the Articles state that . . .
RATCLIFFE—Did you hear me?

GARDINER—Aye, aye, sir. (*Exits up ratlines.*)

DUNCAN (*off*)—Haul tort!

VERE—You disapprove of Gardiner, Mister Ratcliffe?

RATCLIFFE—He seems to think he's the only midshipman aboard capable of doing anything properly. He's always looking at you as if your hat weren't squared.

VERE—That is an unfortunate simile under the present circumstances.

RATCLIFFE (*caught*)—Oh, I—er— Keep her close to the wind, helmsman. Don't fall away!

DUNCAN (*off*)—Let go topgallant bowlines!

VERE—I think Gardiner has had enough correction for one day. Call him down to our level, Mister Ratcliffe.

RATCLIFFE—Aye, sir. Mister Gardiner! You may come off your perch now! (BILLY *descends rigging and starts offstage.*) What do you think of our new man Budd, Captain?

SEYMOUR—That boy did a smart piece of work for us last night, sir. He's the nimblest man on the tops I've ever watched. Wyatt wants him for captain of the foretop.

VERE—Very well, let Budd take the post. He certainly deserves it for his actions last night during the chase. I'll speak to him myself.

Billy is summoned, and is told by the Captain that he has been recommended for the captaincy of the foretop. When Billy protests that Williams already has this job, Vere explains that the station calls for a younger man. Then he asks how Budd is liking them, now that the awesomeness has worked off a bit. The lad replies that it's a bustling world and he gets lost sometimes, but his mates even lend him a hand. Why, even Jimmy-Legs—begging the Captain's pardon, the Master-at-Arms—is good to him.

Billy is dismissed and Claggart is summoned. While he is waiting for the Master-at-Arms, Vere comments to his first officer, Seymour, "If I had a son, I'd hope for one like Budd." "Fine boy," the officer agrees. "He's a force for order on the ship. I hope his charm's contagious." Drily, the Captain comments, "One such is enough. Men cannot stand very much perfection."

When Claggart appears he is informed that Williams, present captain of the foretop, is assigned to the afterguard, and is replaced with Billy Budd. Claggart acts as though he has not heard aright, asking, "William Budd, sir? You do not mean the so-called Handsome Sailor?"

That is just whom the Captain means. Claggart starts to say,

"You must be aware, sir, that he is—" and then he stops to re-phrase his attack. "I wondered if he were entirely trustworthy. He has been aboard such a brief time."

Vere cuttingly informs the Master-at-Arms that Billy has been aboard long enough to prove himself to the Captain, and to his shipmates, but Claggart insists, "Will there not be some dissatis-faction among the foretopmen who have been aboard much longer than Budd?"

"Master-at-Arms," says Vere in his coldest, most incisive voice, "I concern myself with these matters. They are none of your func-tion. Until such time as the senior topmen formally object to Budd for incapacity, he is captain of the foretop." Vere withdraws from the quarterdeck, Claggart from the maindeck. Ratcliffe spits over the rail.

The curtain falls.

Scene II

Night—eight bells—on the forward part of the deck. A man descends the rigging, goes below. Claggart strolls by, stands by the hatch for a moment, then goes on forward. Billy comes down off watch, drops to the deck and leans over the rail, in shadow. From below, Jenkins comes silently and stealthily. Billy sees him and says, "Jenkins! What are you doing topside?" The maintop captain claps a hand over the boy's mouth and whispers for him to stow the noise. Billy, when the hand is withdrawn, whispers, "You're after Mister Claggart, like you said you would!" Jenkins won't deny it, and Billy warns him, "He knows! He's ready for you!"

Jenkins will not be stopped. He has a knife in his hand and he is in a murderous passion. He advises Billy to get below, but the boy still tries to take the knife from him, warning, "You'll hang yourself!" Jenkins pleads, "Take your hands off! The moon's under. I can do it now. Oh, sweet mother of God, leave me go!" He strikes at Billy; Billy wrests the knife out of his hands and it falls to the deck. Then the boy knocks the man down, just as Claggart appears, demanding to know the cause of the noise.

"I had to hit him, sir," says Billy. "He struck at me."

"Mm. And drew that knife on you, too, no doubt."

"Yes, sir."

Claggart now says something surprising. "I have been waiting forward there, for Jenkins. You intercepted him, I take it. You shouldn't meddle, my fine young friend, in matters that don't con-cern you! I was expecting him." The Dansker comes into view and Claggart orders him to help Jenkins up.

The row has been heard by Wyatt, the sailing master, who calls from a distance to find what's up. Claggart grimly whispers to Jenkins, "That sweet and pleasant fellow saved you. But I reserve you still for my own justice in due time. . . . Say nothing to this officer." When Wyatt appears he is satisfied with Claggart's explanation that two men had been found here, contrary to the Captain's orders, and he was just sending them below. But the Captain himself, and Hallam, have also been aroused, and they, too, want to know what's up. The story about two men on deck sounds lame to Vere, but when nobody will speak up with any other explanation he orders Billy and Jenkins below. Then he notices the knife on the deck and inquires, "Your knife, Master-at-Arms?" Claggart replies, "William Budd's, sir, I believe."

The Captain orders, "Return it to him," and retires with Hallam and Wyatt. Claggart is rapping the rail in vexation with his rattan as Squeak approaches warily. He orders the cockney, "Give Budd just time enough to get to sleep. At four bells wake him. Bring him to the lee forechains." But even Squeak has felt the boy's charm, and he begs, "We done enough to him. He's a good lad, Mister Claggart." But Claggart is firm; he threatens Squeak with the flogging whip. But now Squeak warns that the Dansker is approaching, and the Master-at-Arms orders him to move back, and wait.

Tauntingly, the Dansker says, "Baby saved you, eh? And you are angry."

CLAGGART—Saved me, you say? From what? I've tried to tempt Jenkins to this blow, so as to break his toplofty spirit with his neck; and I am "saved" by that guileless idiot! He'd turn the other cheek to me, in Christian kindness! Well: there's a second pleasure in striking that same face twice. I can destroy him, too, if I choose to do it!

DANSKER—Crazy, crazy!

CLAGGART—All right, old man, call it madness then. Whatever its name, it will plunder the sweetness from that face, or it will kill us both.

DANSKER—You are afraid of him.

CLAGGART—Afraid? Of Budd? What nonsense is that?

DANSKER—He usurps the crew; they turn from hating you to loving him, and leave you impotent.

CLAGGART—That bastard innocent frighten me! That witless kindness that spills from him has neither force nor aim. Stand out from between us, or you founder together, sink in five hundred fathoms with him, if I want it so!

DANSKER—Aye, then, if you take that tack, let it be both of us. You expect me to sit by and watch your deliberate arm seize him and force him under?

CLAGGART—Why not? You have always done that. I thought your practice was to stay outside. What breeds the saintly knight errant in you?

DANSKER—I am old, but I have some manhood left.

CLAGGART—What can you do? You've drifted with the tide too long, old one. You are as involved as I am now.

DANSKER—So you may say. In this ship a man lives as he can, and finds a way to make life tolerable for himself. I did so. That was a fault. But no longer.

CLAGGART—Stand clear. You haven't courage to cross me.

DANSKER—Eh, I'm not afraid of you; I see your scheme.

CLAGGART—Damn your feeble, ineffectual eyes! (*Striking him; the* DANSKER *falls.*) You can see only what I let you see!

DANSKER—Say what you like. I see your scheme; so will Captain if need be.

CLAGGART (*pulling him to his feet*)—Take a warning for yourself, old man. And keep away! You are on watch, eh? Well, go back to sleep again, or I'll report you. (DANSKER *exits.* CLAGGART *watches him go, then violently breaks his rattan and throws the pieces over the side.*)

The curtain falls.

SCENE III

It is four bells, and on the forward part of the main deck Claggart is waiting. When he hears a sound he fades into the shadow. It is Squeak, bent over and running. Billy, sleepily rubbing his eyes, follows, asking what it is Squeak wants.

Deviously, Squeak begins by saying, in a conspiratorial voice, that he has heard Billy is captain of the foretop. Now, he continues, Budd can be of more use to his shipmates than ever before. Billy does not know what the man is driving at. "You was impressed now, weren't you?" Squeak continues. "Well, so was I. We're not the only impressed ones, Billy. There's a gang of us. Could you help . . . at a pinch?"

Still Billy doesn't understand. Squeak holds up two gold guineas as an offering. "Put in with us. Most of the men aboard are only waiting for a word, and they'll follow you. There's more for you where these come from. What d'you say? If you join us, Bill, there's not a man aboard who won't come along! Are you with us? The ship'll be ours when we're ready to take it!"

Billy angrily says he doesn't know what Squeak is driving at, and tells him to go where he belongs. From nearby the Dansker calls, "What's the matter?" He sees Billy and says, "Something must have been the matter, for you stammered." Claggart, severe, joins them and demands Billy's reason for being topside against orders. Billy stammers that he found an afterguardsman here and bid him off where he belongs. Claggart demands the man's name and Billy makes excuse that he couldn't see him clearly. The boy is ordered below.

"I'm glad you saw this mutinous behavior," says Claggart to the Dansker—but the Dansker is not to be fooled, saying, "I stood in the shadows forward while your pander Squeak slipped by me, running from this place. You set him on, on purpose to trap Billy."

"And I will do that, old man," Claggart admits. "But you will say nothing about it; see you don't."

Again the Captain appears, followed by Hallam, a marine. "Well, Master-at-Arms, you stand long watches," he observes. Claggart informs him he has something for his private ear, and the Dansker and Hallam are ordered off. Unctuously, Claggart begins his story: He has found at least one man aboard who is dangerous. Lately he has noticed signs of some movement secretly afoot. He feels the cruel responsibility of reporting a matter involving such serious consequences to the sailor concerned, but the safety of the ship comes first. The sailor is William Budd, a secret, vicious lad . . .

Vere calls to Hallam to find Budd and keep him nearby. Claggart resumes his story: Tonight, discovering Budd's hammock unused, he combs the ship and finds him in conclave with several rebellious growlers. They were collected here, and when Claggart ordered them below, Budd and others threatened to drop him and other officers they hate overboard some misty night. And if corroboration is wanted, it is not far away.

Hallam brings Billy up. "Stand apart," Vere tells Hallam, "and see that we are not disturbed. . . . And now, Master-at-Arms, tell this man to his face what you told me of him."

Coolly, Claggart moves near Billy, looks directly at him, and begins, "I said this man, this William Budd, acting so out of angry resentment against impressment and his officers, against this ship, this Service, and the King, breeds in the crew a spirit of rebellion. . . ." Claggart's denunciation is complete, even to Billy's threatening his officers with murder.

Billy tries to speak, but he can make only incoherent sounds. He seems to be in pain, judging from the contortions of his face and the gurgling which is all he can effect for speech. "Speak, man!" the Captain urges. "Defend yourself!" Remembering the boy's impediment now, he puts a reassuring hand on the boy's shoulder and tells him to take his time. But the kindness seems to increase the boy's agonized dumb gesturing and stammering. Finally he hits Claggart, hard, and the Master-at-Arms falls and lies still.

"It was a lie, then!" cries Vere.

Claggart remains inert. Vere raises him to sitting position, then is forced to lower him. Billy, still unable to speak, is crying and badly frightened. "No need to speak now, Billy," says the Captain. He calls for the marine, orders him to bring the Surgeon and to ask First Officer Seymour to report to his cabin without delay. Then he indicates a stateroom aft and tells Billy to go there and stay until he is sent for. The Surgeon arrives, bends over Claggart, looks up in surprise at the Captain.

"Come," says Vere, "we must dispatch. Go now. I shall presently call a drumhead court to try the man who out of God's own instinct dropped him there." He instructs the Surgeon to tell the officers of the killing, and to warn them to keep the matter to themselves. Then, alone, he muses, "The divine judgment of Ananias! Struck dead by the Angel of God . . . and I must judge the Angel. Have I that choice?"

The curtain falls.

ACT III

Within a quarter hour, Captain Vere and First Officer Seymour have met in Vere's cabin. Seymour simply cannot believe that Budd would beat a man to death, but the Captain explains the boy was tempted to it past endurance. The problem now is, what to do —and its solution is by no means easy. Granted, Claggart was a liar and a vicious dog; but Claggart was an officer—he represented and was, indeed, authority. The tortured Vere hopes Seymour will show him some way out—show him a way around clearly stated law. Billy has killed an officer, and there are laws covering such deeds, even though, as Seymour says, they give victory to the devil himself. Yet, says Vere, without these laws there would be a worse tyranny of anarchy and chaos. "Oh," he exclaims, "if I were a man alone, manhood would declare for Billy."

"Let him go," urges Seymour.

But Vere cannot, although he would give his own life to save the boy's if he could. Billy must be tried. The court convenes in the cabin—Seymour heading it, as senior member; Wyatt and Ratcliffe the other members. Seymour states the case: the foretopman, Budd, has killed the Master-at-Arms, and there is one witness—Vere. Billy, manacled, is brought in, stammering a "T-thank you, sir," when Seymour invites him to sit down. Vere, acting as witness and not speaking as Captain, begins his account of Claggart's charge that Billy was mutinous.

"That's absurd," the sailing master, Wyatt, interrupts, and is bidden by Seymour to be quiet. Seymour also interrupts the Captain's testimony, hoping to find some other witness, by asking if Billy had spoken to anybody in Claggart's hearing. The boy answers that he spoke a little with the Dansker, and the Dansker is sent for. Vere continues his narrative of the events, and when he has finished Billy is asked if the account is accurate. "It is just as Captain Vere says," the boy declares, "but it is not as the Master-at-Arms said. I have eaten the King's bread, and I am true to the King."

Seymour asks if there was any malice between the boy and Claggart and Billy says he bore none. "I did not mean to kill him. If I'd found my tongue, I would not have struck him." "Now," pursues Seymour, "why should he have lied with such obvious malice when you have declared that there was no malice between you?" The boy is at a loss for an answer, and Vere interposes, "Can he rightly answer it? Or anyone else, indeed, unless it be he who lies within there?"

The Dansker is brought in to testify. Is there malice—the choice of "is" is deliberate, for Claggart's death has been kept secret—between the two? "Aye," the Dansker answers—but it was one-sided. The Master-at-Arms hated Billy. He uses the past tense, sensing that Claggart must be dead. "Master-at-Arms made his world in his own image. Pride was his demon, and he kept it strong by others' fear of him. Billy could not imagine such a nature, saw nothing but a lonely man, strange, but a man still, nothing to be feared. So Claggart, lest his reason be proven false, planned Billy's death."

This concludes the testimony, and Billy declares he has nothing further to say for himself. He is removed to the after compartment and the court begins its discussion. Ratcliffe and Wyatt are immediately in favor of acquittal. "We have found a verdict, sir," Seymour announces to the Captain.

"I know that, Seymour," says Vere. "Your verdict sets him

free, and so would I wish to do. But are we free to choose as we would do if we were private citizens? The Admiralty has its code. Do you suppose it cares who Budd is? Who you and I are?" Logic forces Vere to say what he must—that this ship must be kept effective, and in time of war, under the Mutiny Act, even striking an officer calls for the death penalty. The crew on board know this—so what happens if the proper penalty is not adminis- tered? The court's clemency might be put down as an evidence of fear—a shame to the officers and a deadly blow to discipline. They must rule out their hearts. Whether or not Billy had intent to kill makes no difference. "The gold we wear shows that we serve the King, the Law. What does it matter that our acts are fatal to our manhood, if we serve as we are forced to serve? What bitter salt leagues move between our code and God's own judgments! We are conscripts, every one, upright in this uniform of flesh. There is no truce to war born in the womb. We fight at command."

Wyatt and Ratcliffe still fight against Vere's reasoning, looking for some way out. But there is no way out, and the French are closing in. Wyatt, in particular, is vehement and bitter; he will not bear to hang a man he knows is innocent. Vere argues, gently, with Wyatt, "Can't you see you must first strip off the uniform you wear, and after that your flesh, before you can escape the case at issue here? Someone must decide. We are the law; law orders us to act, and shows us how. . . . But do not think me pitiless in thus demanding sentence on a luckless boy. I feel as you do for him. But even more, I think there is a grace of soul within him that shall forgive the law we bind him with, and pity us, stretched on the cross of our choice."

Seymour asks that the court reach a decision. The officers write their verdicts. Seymour reads them and reports to the Captain, "He is condemned, sir. Shall we appoint the dawn?"

The curtain falls.

Scene II

It is four in the morning. Sunrise is at 4:52. The Captain orders Seymour to bring Budd to the cabin. When the prisoner arrives his manacles are removed and the two are left alone.

Billy—I was thinking, locked up below there . . . the Captain knows the rights of all this. He'll save me if it's right. Then you sent for me. Is there hope for me, Captain?

Vere—Billy, what hope is there?

BILLY—Tell me why. I only want to understand.

VERE—How young you still are, Billy! Oh, I can tell you this: nothing is lost of anything that happens. I have given you the judgment of the world . . . deadly constraint . . . a length of hemp and a yard-arm. I have done this to you, no one else.

BILLY—I can't get the rights of all that's happened.

VERE—There's not much right, Billy. Only necessity. You and Claggart broke man's compromise with good and evil, and both of you must pay the penalty.

BILLY—Penalty? What for? Would anyone make laws just to be broken by fellows like me?

VERE—Aye, boy. You have learned this late. Most of us find out early and trim to a middle course.

BILLY—Do you mean . . . it's better to be like that?

VERE—Better as this world goes. When a man is born, he takes a guilt upon him, I can't say how or why. And life takes its revenge on those who hurt its pride with innocence.

BILLY—Do you think Claggart knew it would come to this?

VERE—He knew he would kill you, and he died to gain that end. But if you trust me, he'll not win entirely.

BILLY—How could he hate me like that?

VERE—The world we breathe is love and hatred both, but hatred must not win the victory.

BILLY—Claggart is dead. Now I'm to hang. Doesn't that show the law is wrong, when it can't choose between him and me?

VERE—Yes, it's all wrong, all wrong.

BILLY—I don't know, Captain. I never was a hand to wonder about things, but now I think that maybe there's a kind of cruelty in people that's just as much a part of them as kindness, say, or honesty, or m-m-m . . . I can't find words, I guess, Captain.

VERE—There are no words. We are all prisoners of deadly forms that are made to break us to their measure. Nothing has power to overcome them, except forgiveness . . . Can you forgive what I have done?

BILLY—I *can* trust you, can't I? *Can* you show me it's all right, my being . . .

VERE (*turns away; a long pause*)—It's nearly dawn, lad. In the Spanish villages they're lighting fires.

BILLY—I'm not afraid, sir. (*Steps toward* VERE.) It's getting light.

VERE—There's no time for either of us left. Go, take the morning. God knows you have the right to it. And when you are on the mainyard, think of me, and pray for those who must make choices. Hallam. (*Enter* HALLAM *in doorway.*) Take Budd into your charge. (BILLY *and* HALLAM *go out.*) Time has run out.

The curtain falls.

SCENE III

It is an impressive scene on the maindeck, aft. Wyatt and the two midshipmen, Gardiner and Rea, are supervising the formation of the men in ranks, and there is the noise of orders and reports. "All hands stand by to witness punishment! Stand easy," Wyatt commands. In the ranks, Kincaid wonders aloud where Billy is— and who is being punished, and what for? Jenkins guesses it will be a flogging for somebody, but the Dansker, old and wise, says, "They flog men at noon. The early morning's for hanging." Jenkins devoutly hopes it's Claggart who will be hanged—and then they notice Claggart isn't here, either.

Jenkins describes to others a shipboard hanging. "He goes up them ratlines, out on the yard, they slips a noose around his neck, and then he jumps and hangs himself." O'Daniel remarks they'd have the devil's work getting O'Daniel to jump, and Kincaid points out, "It's jump, or get pushed."

At last the prisoner is brought in, between two sentries, and the crew breaks ranks and sets up an astonished murmur as Billy Budd appears. Wyatt shouts for silence, makes the men re-form. Seymour begins reading the formal document of the trial and condemnation. When he reaches the statement that Billy has killed the Master-at-Arms the men talk excitedly. There are exclamations of "Good lad!" "Serves him proper!" "Hi, Billy! Hurrah!" Again the sailing master quiets them and orders them to strict attention.

Seymour reaches the end. "Therefore, the court sentences the aforementioned William Budd, foretopman, Royal Navy, to die by hanging on the first watch of the day following these proceedings. By authority of His Gracious Majesty George Rex and Alan Napier, Viscount Kelsey, First Sea Lord. Signed, Philip Seymour, Senior Member."

The crew, angry now, has begun to break formation again, and there is a chorus of cries: "No, he don't! Hang the jemmies instead, say I! Not Billy, you swineheads!"

The officious Gardiner commands, "Stand back, you damned clods!" Seymour roars for discipline. Surlily, the men move into irregular but quiet lines. "Prisoner," Seymour addresses the boy, "have you anything to say?" Billy shakes his blond head. "If you have nothing to say, when the drum roll is sounded, you will proceed to carry out the sentence of this court."

The drum begins its roll and Billy starts up the ropes, just as he had before he sighted the enemy vessel. Again the crew cries out, begging Billy to wait. There is a shout of "Rush the deck, mates," but there is no concerted movement—for Billy, on the ratlines, turns and looks at Vere and cries, loud and clear, without the trace of a stammer, "God bless Captain Vere!" Vere is profoundly shaken. The boy disappears aloft, and all men look upward in a deep and breathless quiet.

CURTAIN

THE AUTUMN GARDEN *

A Play in Three Acts

By Lillian Hellman

LILLIAN HELLMAN'S plays, from "The Children's Hour" to the adapted "Montserrat," have been "strong" plays—either dramatic or melodramatic. In "The Autumn Garden" Miss Hellman has taken a different approach, and her play is a comedy—not a comedy in the slapstick or joke sense, but in the Chekhovian sense that it looks rather affectionately upon the sad and funny frailties of the human being. Many observers, including the editor of this book, feel that "The Autumn Garden" is Miss Hellman's best play; and many also agreed that, as it was produced on Broadway, it revealed some of the best and best-integrated acting of the year. The company included Fredric March, Florence Eldridge, Ethel Griffies, Colin Keith-Johnston, Kent Smith and Joan Lorring.

The time is September, 1949, and the place is the Tuckerman house in a Summer resort on the Gulf of Mexico, about a hundred miles from New Orleans. One can see the living room, with its handsome but slightly shabby furniture, and outside it a side porch. Quite a few vacationers have gathered in the living room. One of them is General Griggs, a good-looking, somehow preoccupied man of fifty-three, who is reading a paper. Beside him is his wife, Rose, a soft-looking, once-pretty woman of about forty-three who wears an evening dress that is much too young for her. Rose is chatting with Carrie Ellis, a distinguished-appearing woman of about forty-five. Nearby is Carrie's mother-in-law, Mary Ellis, a woman in her seventies who can be sprightly when she wishes to be, or can act broken and senile whenever there is a purpose in doing so. Then there is Frederick Ellis, about twenty-five, pleasant-looking, who is reading and correcting a manuscript. And, on the porch with his back to the others is Edward Crossman, forty-six, who looks worn and rather ill.

Rose Griggs is a little hard to follow until one gets used to her. She is saying, "Now, where is it? Everything's been so topsy-turvy all evening. If I can't have it immediately after dinner then I just about don't want it. At home you can bet it's right waiting for us when we leave the dining room, isn't it, Ben? Too bad it's Thursday. I'd almost rather go and see him than go to the party. I think it's what keeps you awake, Mrs. Ellis. I mean a little is good for your heart, the doctor told me always to have a little, but my goodness—the amount you have every night!"

Old Mrs. Ellis manages to get all this decoded by asking a few questions. Rose is talking about coffee, of course, and Robert Taylor of the movies. The old woman comments to Rose's husband, "You know, General Griggs, after seven Summers I have come to the conclusion that your wife considers it vulgar to mention anything by name." Rose's attention flits now to her husband; she'd like to have him say something nice about her dress and her looks, and he utters an unenthusiastic "It's nice"; then Rose calls to Edward Crossman and reports that his sister, in New Orleans, says he is getting to be a regular old hermit—and it's dangerous, liking to be alone.

The telephone in the entrance hall rings and Sophie, a plain, shy girl with a hesitant, over-polite manner and a slight European accent, comes to answer it. She has on a party dress, and over it is an apron. To whoever has called she replies that the house does not take transient guests—only permanent guests. Sophie and young Frederick are engaged, but Frederick is a little put out at his mother because she has told some of the other guests about it. Since the plans are not definite, he'd rather not have the engagement talked about. His mother, Carrie Ellis, squirms uncomfortably and pleads that it's only natural for a mother to want to talk about her son. The General speaks up, saying, "Don't you know that women have no honor, Frederick, when it comes to keeping secrets about marriage or cancer?"

Old Mrs. Ellis has taken a look at Frederick's manuscript and comments, "I know I'm too young to be reading Payson's book. Full of the most confused sex. I can't tell who is what." Frederick defends the book, and says Payson is going to be the most important young writer. His mother reminds him he said the same about Payson's first two books, and neither sold very well. The young man is annoyed. His grandmother remarks that his mother has plenty of time to grow moral because she doesn't have the hardship of clipping coupons; it's the old lady who clips the coupons and hands them out. "And then, of course," she says to Frederick, "you who don't even have that much trouble are left at leisure to be moral about those who have to go to the trouble of living on unearned money."

Rose asks her husband, the General, if he won't come to a party that is being given, and he says he won't. For the fifth time she asks him if he likes her dress, and patiently he says again, "It's nice." She chatters on, "I wish the Denerys would come before we leave. . . . Is he absolutely fascinating?" Carrie answers, "I don't know. I haven't seen him in twenty years or more." Rose calls the same question out to Crossman, who grew up with Nicholas Denery, and he replies that he doesn't remember that any of the crowd was fascinating.

Sophie brings in a coffee tray and Frederick helps her with it. Leon, a young colored butler, follows with the coffee. Rose asks to see the girl's dress, and Sophie takes off her apron. The chatter-box comments that it's right nice, but; then she makes the helpless girl sit down while she fusses with her hair. Crossman, coming in from the porch, comments, "Makes her look like everybody else. That's desirable, isn't it?"

Constance Tuckerman, owner of the Tuckerman house, comes through the hall carrying two vases of flowers. She is handsome, about forty-three. When the phone rings again she puts down a vase and answers it; it's Mr. Payson, asking for Frederick. Rose kittenishly asks Constance when the Denerys will arrive, and Con-stance, on her way upstairs, advises her to wait and see them at breakfast. "My," says Rose, "Constance is nervous. Well, I sup-pose I should be if I were seeing an old beau for the first time in—." Nobody listens much. Rose notices that her husband has wandered off to the porch, and in a moment Crossman goes back there, too, carrying coffee and a brandy bottle. She asks, "Now, are you boys just going to sit here and share the bottle—"

Frederick returns to the room after talking on the phone and tells his mother he won't be able to take her to the Carters' party, and he hopes she and Sophie and Grandma will excuse him. Pay-son has said his manuscript proof must be in the mail in the morn-ing, which means Frederick will have to finish with it tonight, together with Payson. Sophie, instead of acting disappointed, forthrightly says she is glad Frederick can't go because she doesn't like parties and now she won't have to go. Carrie is puzzled and disturbed about her son; she says, "Frederick, I want to talk to you." The young man, on his way out, tells his mother in a rather superior voice, "When you use that tone of voice you need two hours. Let's make it in the morning." But Carrie will not be silenced. She asks her son as a favor to her to break his appointment with Payson. And why should the man always be consulting Frederick, anyway? Her son has no sense of obligation, either to her or to Sophie, she says. Further, she is getting tired of Mr. Payson. When he stayed with them last Winter she was led to understand he was a brilliant and gifted writer—but now, when he follows Frederick here—

Frederick, speaking slowly and angrily, declares, "He did not follow me down here and I wouldn't like you to put it that way again. He came here for the Summer and is that your business, Mother?" Old Mrs. Ellis, who seems to have been dozing, has been listening. Now she gets out of her chair to start for bed, and she bids Frederick to kiss his mother good-night and forgive her. "I have nothing to forgive her for, Grandma."

"Of course not. But even when your mother starts out being right she talks and talks until she gets around to being wrong." With that she leaves the room. Carrie, softening, tells her son she is sorry if she spoke unfairly, and suggests that he try to join the party later. She, too, goes out.

Young Sophie confesses to her fiancé that she is puzzled by the argument. Everything in English sounds so important, and she gets a headache from listening. The young man tells her not to take these things too seriously—and, as a matter of fact, his mother was right when she said he was rude and neglectful toward Sophie. He says to the girl, "We're an awkward pair. . . . I like you." Warmly she replies, "I like you, Frederick." He hopes she understands about his going to Europe with his mother in two weeks; it was arranged long before they got—engaged. "Sophie," he goes on, "I think we'll have to sit down soon and talk about ourselves. I don't think we even know how we got engaged."

SOPHIE—Sometimes it is better not to say things. There is time and things will come as they come.

FREDERICK—The day we got engaged, we tried to speak as honestly as we both knew how but we didn't say very much—

SOPHIE—And I think we should not try so hard to talk. Sometimes it is wise to let things grow more roots before one blows them away with many words— (Shyly touches his hand.) It will come better if we give it time.

FREDERICK—We will give it time. And you'll make no decisions and set no dates until you are sure about what you think and feel.

SOPHIE—Oh, I have made the decision for myself. And I am pleased.

FREDERICK (pleased)—And you are quite sure of your decision?

SOPHIE—You know, sometimes I have thought that with rich people—(*Very quickly.*)—with educated people, I mean, decisions are made only in order to speak about changing them. It happens often with Aunt Constance and with your mother, also, I think. And the others.

FREDERICK—Yes. (*Takes her hand.*) We'll get along fine. I want you to know that I feel very lucky—

SOPHIE—Lucky? You will have to be patient with me. I am not a good success here.

FREDERICK—Now, you stop that. I don't want you a good success. And you're to stop thinking it. You're to stop a lot of things: letting Mother boss you about, letting Mrs. Griggs tell you what to wear, or pull your hair—

SOPHIE—Oh, I do not mind. Because I look so bad makes Mrs. Griggs think she looks so good.

FREDERICK (*smiles*)—Good night, my dear.

SOPHIE (*smiles*)—Good night. (*He exits.* SOPHIE *begins to pick up the coffee cups, brandy glasses, etc. After a minute* ROSE GRIGGS *comes down the steps carrying a light summer wrap. She comes in the room.*)

ROSE—Where are the Ellises?

SOPHIE—They went to the party, Mrs. Griggs.

ROSE—No! Without me? I *must* say that's very rude. They can't have done that, Sophie—

Rose wails to her husband, out on the porch, "The Ellises left without me! You'll have to walk me over." The General, coming into the room, points out that it's just across the street—not a very dangerous journey. As he approaches, she declares, "I think it's shocking. In front of other people. God knows what they know or guess this Summer." Then she notices Sophie, who is collecting coffee cups, and says, sharply, "Sophie, don't wait here listening." The General sharply interrupts, "Rose!" His wife puts on the charm and apologizes, but Sophie keeps on going out of the room with a tray.

The General refuses his wife's pleas to pick her up at the party at midnight, or to meet her then at the tavern. She wants to talk to him. "Again?" Griggs says drily. "Tonight? And every night and every day? The same things over and over? We're worn out, Rose." And then, with a touch of kindness, "There is no more to say." She is baffled; after twenty-five years of marriage he suddenly wants a divorce. She just won't take him seriously. He never has given her a good reason. Whenever she asks if there is another woman, he says no, naturally. . . .

GRIGGS—There is no other woman.

ROSE (*giggles*)—You know what I think? I think it's that little blonde at the drugstore, and the minute my back is turned—

GRIGGS—Please, Rose. Please stop that.

ROSE—Never at any time, during this divorce talk, have you mentioned them. You'd think we didn't have sons, and the awful effect on them. Did you write them today?

GRIGGS—I did not write them because you begged me not to.

ROSE—Oh, yes, I forgot. It will break their hearts.

GRIGGS—Their hearts won't be broken. They won't even bother to finish the letter.

ROSE (*softly, shocked*)—You can't love them, to speak that way.

GRIGGS—I don't love them. I did love them but I don't now. They're hard men to love.

ROSE—Oh, I don't believe a word you say. You've always enjoyed shocking me. You've been a wonderful father and you're just as devoted to them as they are to you.

GRIGGS—They aren't the least devoted to me—when they think about me it is to find my name useful and when it isn't useful they disapprove of me.

ROSE (*moving to door*)—Look, Ben. I just can't stay and talk all night. I'm late now. There's no use our saying the same things over and over again— (*He laughs.*) If you won't come to the party what are you going to do?

GRIGGS—I am going down by the water, sit on a bench and study from a Chinese grammar.

ROSE—You'll be lonely.

GRIGGS—Yes, but not for parties.

ROSE—It's very hard to take seriously a man who spends the evening with a Chinese grammar. I'll never forget that winter with the Hebrew phonograph records. (*Pats his arm.*) Now, good night, darling. And don't worry about me: I am going to try to have a good time. We'll talk about all this another day. (*She starts out.*)

GRIGGS (*sharply*)—No. No, we're not going to do that. You're turning it into a pleasure, Rose, something to chatter about on a dull winter night in the years to come. I've told you it isn't going to be that way. (*She is in the hall.*) It isn't going to be that way. When you go back to town next week I'm not going with you. (*He turns to see that she has gone.*)

ROSE'S VOICE (*from the hall*)—Good night, darling.

Crossman, out on the porch, has heard everything. The General, joining him, apologizes, saying, "I don't know why I want to say this, but don't think too badly of my wife. All professional soldiers marry Rose. It's in the Army manual. She is as she always was. It is my fault, not hers." But now the General wants to go away somewhere, alone, and think. He goes out of the house. Constance comes down stairs, notes that the living room seems neat, joins Crossman on the porch, saying, "I'm tired." He suggests a brandy from his bottle, but she declines it. She tells him of the arrangements she's made for the Denerys: Nick will go in Sophie's room, Mrs. Denery in the yellow room, the maid and the chauffeur in the boat house, and Sophie will sleep down here in the living room, on the couch. Constance has made extraordinary preparations as to food and wine—stuffed crabs, for instance. Nick loved them. She remembers he had them twenty-three years ago, the eighteenth of next month, the night he decided to go to Paris and study. And now she will see him again—and his wife. They are rich, she knows, and Constance is a little nervous about meeting the wife. She will have a brandy, after all; so Crossman pours her one and himself another. He notes, amusedly, that she has changed her dress three times since dinner; Constance is somewhat apologetic about her clothes because they are inexpensive. Sophie made this one last Winter—sewing for an old country aunt when she could have been out dancing.

"Ned," she says, "you don't look so well this Summer. I wanted to tell you— Don't you think—"

Pouring himself another brandy, Crossman interrupts, very pleasantly, "Don't I think you should mind your business? Yes, I do."

Sophie brings sheets, a quilt and a pillow to the living room and joins the two on the porch. Constance explains to Ned, "Sophie's mother taught her to sew. You know that Ann-Marie is a modiste?" The girl laughs a denial; her mother is sometimes a home-seamstress, sometimes a factory worker.

A car stops outside and Constance hurries into the house. "Why is Aunt Constance so nervous about the visit of this lady and gentleman?" the girl asks Crossman, who answers, "Because she was once in love with Nicholas Denery, this gentleman." Sophie thinks it's such a long time to stay nervous. When she hears Nick's voice calling, "Constance!" Sophie vanishes off the porch into the yard. Nick comes into the living room, still calling. He is about forty-five, handsome—and a little soft looking. Behind him comes his wife, Nina, about forty, good-looking, chic, tired and delicate. Behind her comes a maid, Hilda, carrying a jewel case, an overnight bag and two coats. In German she asks if she should take the bags

upstairs, and in German Nina replies, "We don't know where upstairs is."

"Oh, I know," says Nick. "I know every foot of this house. It
was *the* great Summer mansion and as kids we were here more than
we were at home." He examines the room and wonders, softly, if
the house has changed—or has he? He urges Nina, who has hung
back in the hallway, to come into the room, but she is reluctant
to do so. It might be pleasanter for Nick to see old friends without
her, and besides, she is very tired. She is tired so much lately, and
she knows this bores Nick.

Nick, wandering about the room, reaches the porch and, seeing
a man there, asks where he can find Miss Tuckerman. "Hello,
Nick," Crossman greets him, and after a second's hesitation the new
arrival exclaims, with extravagantly affectionate enthusiasm, "My
God, Willy! How many years, how many years? . . . Nina, this
may be my oldest and best friend in the world." Crossman shakes
hands with Nina and says, drily, that his name is Edward. His
brother was named Willy. Nick is eager to catch up on the years
that have passed, and Crossman tells how Old Man Tuckerman surprised everybody by dying broke, and how Constance had to sell the
New Orleans house but managed to hang onto this one by turning
it into a Summer guest house. Sam Tuckerman, Constance's brother,
died during the war. He had gone to Europe in the thirties and
married there—and five years ago Constance brought Sam's daughter
here. She is Sophie.

Constance almost trips as she comes nervously into the room.
Nick takes her face in his hands, kisses her, then stands back to have
a look. "You've changed and you've changed well. Do you still
have the portrait, Constance?" She answers, "It's the only important thing that I have got." Nick wants his wife to see it, explaining, "Nina knows a great deal about painting. Sometimes I think
she knows more than I." Constance would like to hear about his art
work, but Nick would rather reminisce—inaccurately—about old
times here. He had thought surely Constance and Ned Crossman
would marry, and he adds, "No wonder you drink too much, Ned"—
a piece of information some tourist from home had given him in
Paris. Nick realizes his blunder, starts to apologize, and Ned says,
edgily, "Ever have syphilis, Nick? Kind of thing one has to know
right off, if you understand me." Bidding Nina good night, Ned
goes up to bed.

At Nick's behest, Constance goes to get the portrait he did of her
those many years ago, and when Nick is alone with his wife he says,
"You haven't been too warm or gracious, Nina."

NINA—What can I do when I don't even know the plot?

NICK—What are you talking about?

NINA—You told me about Constance Tuckerman the first night we met? And about dear Willy or Ned, and I've done quite a little teasing about her all these years?

NICK—I did tell you about her immediately—

NINA—You mentioned her very casually, last week, years after the night you met me and you said that you could hardly remember anything more about her than a rather silly—

NICK (quickly)—Are you going to be bad-tempered for our whole visit here? For years I've looked forward to coming back— (NINA laughs.)

NINA—So you came to do her portrait?

NICK—No, I didn't "come to do her portrait." I thought about it driving down here. If the one I did is as good as I remember, it would be wonderful for the show. The young girl, the woman at forty-five. She's aged. Have we changed that much? I don't think you've changed, darling.

NINA—I've changed a great deal. And I wouldn't want it pointed out to me in a portrait to be hung side by side with a picture of what I used to be. (He doesn't answer her.) That isn't a nice reason for being here and if I had known it—

NICK—We have no "reason" for being here. I just wanted to come back. Nothing mysterious about it—

NINA—You're simply looking for a new area in which to exercise yourself. It has happened many, many times before. But it always happens when we return from Europe and spend a month in New York. It's been too important to you, for many years, that you cannot manage to charm my family. And so, when our visit is finished there, you inevitably look around for— Well, you know. You know what's been and the trouble.

NICK (cheerfully)—I don't know what the hell you're talking about.

NINA—I'm tired of such troubles, Nick—

NICK—Do you know that these sharp moods of yours grow more sharp with time? Now I would like to have a happy visit here. But if something is disturbing you and you'd prefer not to stay, I'll arrange immediately—

NINA (as if she were a little frightened)—I'd only prefer to go to bed. Sorry if I've been churly about your—home-coming. (She starts out, meets CONSTANCE who comes in carrying portrait.) Will you excuse me, Constance? The long drive gave me a headache.

CONSTANCE—I am sorry. Will I bring you a tray upstairs?

NINA—No, thank you. (CONSTANCE *moves as if to show her the way.*)

NICK—Come, I want to see the picture. Nina will find her way. (*He takes the picture from* CONSTANCE.)

CONSTANCE—The yellow room on the left. Your maid is unpacking. I peeked in. What lovely clothes. Can I come and see them tomorrow?

NINA (*going up the stairs*)—Yes, of course. Thank you and good night.

Nick admires his picture, saying, "Damn good work for a boy of eighteen." Constance reminds him he was twenty-two, and when he finished it he had put down his brushes and said damn good work for a boy of twenty-two—and then he asked Constance to marry him. Embarrassed now, she changes the subject by saying that after she dies the painting will go to the Delgado Museum. Nick laughs that he wants to borrow it first, for a retrospective show he is having this Winter in London. And he wants to do a new portrait—Constance as she is now, to exhibit beside it. Womanlike and conscious of passing years, she objects; she doesn't want to see all the changes, or have people standing and talking about them, perhaps laughing at her or pitying her. She is hurt. Nick shrugs it off, saying, "Well, it would have meant a lot to me."

He starts for bed, but in the hall encounters the incoming Carrie Ellis and Rose Griggs. Carrie is holding Rose's arm. Nick delivers another of his warm greetings and is introduced to Rose, who, Carrie explains, isn't feeling well—became a little dizzy dancing. But Rose is still a match for Nick; she turns on the charm and informs him he is a famous gentleman in this town. The volatile painter volunteers to take the ailing stranger upstairs, but Carrie moves in, takes Rose's arm and impatiently pushes her up the stairs. Carrie says, on departing, that she hopes Nick is staying a while and he answers, "I think we'll have to leave tomorrow." This is news to Constance; she feels he must be angry with her, and contritely she says he may do another picture if he wishes—but she will have to pose early, before everybody comes down for breakfast. Casually he says, "Good. We'll start in the morning. Do you make a living out of this place, darling?"

Not much of a living, he learns. Constance brought over Sam's daughter, because she and her mother went through the Occupation and were very poor, and she has tried to send Sophie to the best school. She had been planning a debut for the girl, but now she wants to get married. Sophie's mother didn't want to come here, and neither did Sophie, really. She was thirteen and working in a fish store, and Constance practically demanded that she leave home and come to the United States.

Nick asks Constance why she never married Ned and she won't answer. "Why not?" he persists. "I'd tell you about myself or Nina." Constance sighs, "Oh, it's one thing to talk about lives that have been good and full and happy and quite another— Well, I don't know. We just never did marry." Bored, he is about to start for bed again when Sophie enters the room and is introduced by her aunt. To Constance's puzzlement, he says warmly to the girl, "I've been looking forward to meeting you for many years. You follow in the great tradition of Tuckerman good looks." The shy Sophie doesn't know what to say.

General Griggs comes in and is introduced. Nick knows about him, saying, "We almost met before this. When your boys marched into Paris. I was in France during the German occupation." At this, Sophie turns and gives him a sharp look. Nick goes on to say that the Germans were damn smart about the French, for they acted like gentlemen. Griggs answers pleasantly, "That's a side of them I didn't see," and, looking at the girl, "you didn't either, Sophie?"

Hilda, the maid, appears in the doorway and tells Nick in German that his wife would like to see him before he retires; she has a surprise gift she bought for him in New Orleans. In German he replies, "No. Tell Mrs. Denery I will see her in the morning. Tell her to take a sleeping pill." Constance can't understand the colloquy, but she notices that Sophie is frowning and that General Griggs has turned away. Sophie begins making up her bed on the couch, and Denery goes on up. Constance asks the girl what it was the maid and Nick said; at first the girl remains silent, but when her aunt insists she tells about the gift and Nick's refusal and the suggestion about the sleeping pill. The disturbed Constance asks, "Just like that?" Then she remembers that Rose has returned, feeling ill, and she informs the General. He doesn't move, until she explains that Carrie is upstairs with his wife waiting, and probably would like to return to the party. He goes on up, and Constance, kissing her niece good-night, leaves, too. Sophie goes to fetch a pair of pajamas and Crossman, coming quietly down stairs, crosses the room to the porch, gets his brandy bottle and a glass and starts back. Sophie returns, and he stops to talk to her; his voice and manner are slightly different as he explains to the girl that he needed another book and another bottle. Sophie gives him polite answers until he says, sharply, "You're beginning to talk like an advertisement, which is the very highest form of American talk. It's not *your* language, nor your native land. You don't have to care about it. You shouldn't even understand it."

SOPHIE—Sometimes I understand.

CROSSMAN—That's dangerous to admit, Sophie. You've been so busy cultivating a pseudo-stupidity. Not that you'd ever be a brilliant girl, but at least you used to be normal. Another five years and you won't be *pseudo*-stupid.

SOPHIE (*smiles*)—I will not mind. It will be easier. (*Carefully.*) You notice me too much, Mr. Ned. Please do not feel sorry or notice me so much.

CROSSMAN—You came here a nice little girl who had seen a lot of war and trouble. You had spirit, in a quiet way, and you were gay, in a quiet way, which is the only way women should be gay since they are never really gay at all. Only serious people are ever gay and women are very seldom serious people. They are earnest instead. But earnestness has nothing to do with seriousness. So. (*Suddenly.*) What the hell is this marriage business between you and Fred Ellis?

SOPHIE (*softly*)—It is the marriage business between me and Fred Ellis.

CROSSMAN—But what's the matter with you? Haven't you got sense enough to know—

SOPHIE (*quickly*)—I do the best I can. I do the best I can. And I thank you for worrying about me, but you are an educated man with ideas in English that I am not qualified to understand.

CROSSMAN—Listen to me, Sophie. Sometimes when I've had enough to drink—just exactly enough—I feel as if I were given to understand that which I may not understand again. And sometimes then—but rarely—I have an urge to speak out. Fewer drinks, more drinks, and I'm less certain that I see the truth, or I get bored, and none of my opinions and none of the people and issues involved seem worth the trouble. Right now, I've had just enough: so listen to me, Sophie. I say turn yourself around, girl, and go home. Beat it quick.

SOPHIE—You take many words to say simple things. All of you. And you make the simple things—like going to sleep—so hard, and the hard things—like staying awake—so easy. Go home, shall I? Just like that, you say it. Aunt Constance has used up all her money on me, wasted it, and for why and what? How can I go home?

CROSSMAN—If that's all it is I'll find you the money to go home.

SOPHIE (*wearily*)—Oh, Mr. Ned. We owe money in our village, my mother and I. In my kind of Europe you can't live where you owe money. Go home. Did I ever want to come? I have no place here and I am lost and homesick. I like my mother, I— Every night I plan to go. But it is five years now and there is no plan and no chance to find one. Therefore I will do the best I can. (*Very sharply.*) And I will not cry about it and I will not speak of it again.

CROSSMAN (*softly, as if he were moved*)—The best you can?

SOPHIE—I think so. (*Sweetly.*) Maybe you've never tried to do that, Mr. Ned. Maybe none of you have tried.

CROSSMAN—Sophie, lonely people talking to each other can make each other lonelier. They should be careful because maybe lonely people are the only people who can't afford to cry. I'm sorry. (*He exits through the hall, goes up the stairs as the curtain falls.*)

ACT II

It is before breakfast Sunday morning a week later. Constance, in a most unbecoming house dress, is leaning on the railing against the outside edge of the porch. Her hair is drawn back tight, and she seems to have aged considerably. She is posing for Nick, who is painting. In the living room Sophie finishes folding her bedclothes and is running a carpet sweeper. Leon, the colored butler, comes from the dining room to the porch with a tray of dishes and begins to arrange them. Constance tries to give Leon and Sophie orders about breakfast without moving her head or mouth. Nick is annoyed at all the noise, but is told it can't be helped; breakfast simply must be got ready.

The first one to come down looking for breakfast is old Mrs. Ellis, who pauses to look at Nick's work and declares, "Constance, he's made you look right mean and ten years older." Sophie brings a large urn and some small cups to the living room, and prepares a cup with three spoons of sugar in it for Mrs. Ellis. "Ten years older," the old lady repeats. "When you pay an artist to paint your portrait he makes you ten years younger. I had my portrait done when I was twenty-one, holding my first baby. And the baby looked older than I did." She takes her coffee from Sophie and asks the girl, "Will you come up to town and stay with me for a few weeks while Carrie and Frederick are in Europe?" "I would like that," the girl says. Crossman comes down next, and Mrs. Ellis asks him, "Ned, what shall I give Sophie for her wedding present? My pearls or my mother's diamonds?" Crossman's answer is directed at the girl: "The rich always give something old and precious to their new brides. Something that doesn't cost them new money." He asks Mrs. Ellis why she doesn't give a nice new check, and the reply is, "Only if I have to."

Constance pleads that her neck is breaking and Nick stops work. Sophie gives the two of them coffee and Nick, holding Sophie's hand, says, "You're the girl I want to paint. Change your mind and we'll start today." The girl disengages her hand and declares, "I am not pretty, Mr. Nicholas."

Crossman comes to the porch, stares at Constance and exclaims, "My God, you look awful. What did you get done up like that for? You're poor enough not to have to pretend you are poor." Nick laughs, "Go 'way, Ned. You've got a hangover. I know *I* have." He tells Constance of the get-together he and Ned had last night, like old times, and Ned loosened up and talked—spoke his heart out—sang a juke-box song called Constance. Ned starts to become annoyed, then decides to laugh. He doesn't remember anything of the sort, and he doesn't think he was so drunk he can't remember. Nina has come in, and is close enough to the porch to hear. Ned sees her and says he is sorry she didn't join them last night. She smiles, "I'm never invited to the pouring of a heart."

"Nick said you had a headache."

"Nick always says I have a headache when he doesn't want me to come along—or sees to it that I do have one."

Leon rings the breakfast bell and Mrs. Ellis pops out of her chair, calling for Carrie and Frederick. She hasn't eaten since four this morning and is hungry. Crossman follows her. Before going to the kitchen Constance asks Nick where he got the dress she has on and is surprised and a little hurt to learn that he bought it in a cheap Negro store. Ned must be right, she says—Nick must deliberately want her to look awful.

"Haven't you figured out that Ned is jealous?" the painter asks. "He's in love with you, girl. You're all he talked about last night." Constance won't believe it; Ned never talks about himself—but Nick pours it on thicker than ever, until Constance goes to the kitchen. Nina puts down her coffee in the living room and joins her husband on the porch, where they will have breakfast. She is a knowing woman, wealthy and experienced, and now she demands of her husband, "Why have you done that? To Constance?"

"Look," he argues, "it makes her happy—and if I can get a little sense into her head it will make him happy." They take seats and Leon serves them; Nina laughs at her husband, taunts him for being on a rampage of good will. Then she asks how much longer they must stay and he tells her a few more days. The house officially closes this week; the Ellises are going tomorrow and the Griggses on Tuesday. They'll stay just until Nick finishes the portrait.

Rose Griggs, done up in a hat and dress that are too pretty and too fussy, comes down, puts a small overnight case in the hall and stands at the porch entrance. She motions as though she wants Nick to come to her, but he invites Rose to join him and his wife. "Well," says Rose hesitantly, "I wanted to tell *you* but I don't want to worry Nina." Nina declines to move, so Rose, approaching them, continues, "I called him last night. Just like you advised. And I'm driving right over now. He's the executor of my trust fund, you know. He's very wise; I've got gilt-edged securities."

Nick can't understand or remember whom she is talking about and she has to explain that it's her brother Henry. She will tell him the whole story and he will know what to do. And now she is going to drive to her doctor's. To Nina she explains, "I had a heart murmur. They had to take me out of school for a year."

Nina queries, "Recently?" and Nick chokes back a laugh. Rose asks Nick, "Should I do *just* as you told me yesterday?" Nick doesn't remember what he did tell her but he says, "Sure." His wife puts in, "I think, Mrs. Griggs, you'll have to remind Nick what he told you." Rose reveals that it's about a divorce, and Nick has been so kind—and now what does he think she should do about the boys, telephone them or let Henry? Nina gets up and moves away, trying not to laugh, and Rose seizes the chance to say, softly and secretly to Nick, "And I'm going to just *make* Henry commission the portrait. You remember though that I told you she can't take the braces off her teeth for another six months." She goes to the dining room for her breakfast, but Nina doesn't resume her seat with her husband.

Carrie, coming down, meets Sophie carrying a tray to the dining room and asks if Frederick is in there. He hasn't come down yet, so Carrie goes to the porch and says, "Your maid said you wanted to see me, Nick." Nick pretends hesitation, then comes out with it: Carrie mustn't travel around Europe with the Payson man. He happened to see Frederick and Payson in a travel agency yesterday. After the pair had gone, Nick got some information from the travel agent, an old friend: Frederick had just paid for a third passage on the *Queen Elizabeth* for Payson—and Payson is no good. Last Winter he was in a filthy little scandal in Rome. Nick won't reveal what kind of scandal, though. Carrie, greatly disturbed, thanks him and goes slowly to the dining room. The painter looks around at his wife and shrugs, "What would you have done?" She answers idly, "Have you ever tried leaving things alone?" Nick defends himself; he likes Carrie, and the chances are that she and perhaps the boy, too, don't know what the hell it's all about.

Nina says she wants to leave, now. She can smell trouble coming —a smell that travels ahead of Nick when he becomes so helpful, loving and lovable. "I want to leave," she repeats urgently, and he snaps, "Then leave. I told you we'll go Friday. If you want to go before, then go. But stop talking about it, Nina, or we'll be in for one of your long farewells—and long returns. I don't think I can stand another." He goes to her, puts his arms around her, kisses her, asks her to "gentle down" and leaves the porch. Sophie begins to gather up the dishes and Nina moves in toward the stair. Frederick is coming down, and Nina, after saying good morning, seems about to say something else to the boy; then she thinks better of it and goes on up. Sophie has heard Fred, and, running into the living room, she asks him if he'd like to have breakfast on the porch. He says sure, but why, and the girl stammers, "Your mother—is—er— she has found out that— Come."

Frederick figures that Denery has told his mother of seeing him in the travel agency, but it doesn't worry him; he was going to tell his mother this morning anyhow. Smiling, he asks Sophie if she is sure she feels all right about his going away tomorrow for six months, and she assures him it is all right.

"We will visit your mother," he says—and Sophie quickly cries that they mustn't because she hasn't written about her engagement yet. She offers a faltering excuse that no "date of time" has been set. Kindly the young man tells her, "I don't think you want a date of time, Sophie. And you don't have to be ashamed of wishing you could find another way. But if there isn't any other way for you, then I'll be just as good to you as I know how. And I know you will be to me."

Sophie leaves the room and Frederick calls into the dining room for his mother, who comes out in a moment. He assures her there is nothing to be upset about. They're going to have a companion, that's all—and Payson knows all of Europe. Mrs. Ellis, joining her grandson and daughter-in-law, surprises them by agreeing that they are lucky to get Mr. Payson to come along. But Carrie is too disturbed at the prospect; she announces, "We are not going to Europe."

After a second Frederick says, quietly, "I am." Carrie insists they'll go another time, and Frederick, laughing unpleasantly, says he will be disappointed if his mother doesn't wish to come with him —but he is sailing on the sixteenth. He has never had much fun, and there is so much to do and see. Softening, he adds, "I'll come back, and you can take up my life again." His grandmother puts in, "Perhaps you wouldn't want to come back at all? I wouldn't blame you."

Frederick goes back upstairs. Carrie is furious with her mother-in-law, but is no match for this firm old lady. Mrs. Ellis instructs Carrie to go upstairs and tell her son she is reconciled to his going—but that Frederick must tell his guest that his ten thousand a year ends today and will not begin again. Carrie says she will not cut off Frederick's allowance, and the old lady points out that the allowance comes from her, and *she* will cut it off. "I will simply send him mine," says the defiant mother—but again she is beaten when Mrs. Ellis flatly announces, "Then I won't give you yours. . . . Go up now, and press him hard, and do it straight. . . . I'm off to church now. You can skip church today, Carrie." Carrie moves slowly up the stair as Rose comes in from the dining room and stands waiting at the window.

Soon Rose's husband appears from outside, dressed in riding pants and an old shirt. Rose announces she is going to see Henry and the General tells her to go ahead. But she wants to be talked out of it—or to talk herself out of it. She rambles on about how upset Henry will be if she walks into his happy home and just says Ben wants a divorce but she doesn't know the reason. Pointedly, she speaks of Henry's great influence in Washington, saying it was he who got Ben his last promotion.

Griggs knows she is lying. He suggests a good reason to offer Henry: "Tell him my wife's too young for me. . . . You've done more than stay young; you've stayed a child."

Rose is pitiful as she tries another tack, hinting that quite a few men have found her attractive. He agrees quickly and says that many more will.

Rose—I always knew in the end I would have to tell you although I haven't seen him since you came home. That I promise you. I told him you were a war hero with a glorious record and he said he wouldn't either any longer—

Griggs (*who is at the window*)—Henry's chauffeur is outside, Rose.

Rose—He was very, very, very, very much in love with me while he was at the Pentagon.

Griggs—Good place to be in love. The car is outside, Rose.

Rose—Even after we both knew it, he kept on saying that you didn't make love to a friend's, more than a friend's, wife.

GRIGGS (*gently*)—Rose, don't let's talk this way.

ROSE—Does it hurt you? Well, you've hurt me enough. The third time you went to Europe was when it really began, maybe the second. Because I, too, wanted affection.

GRIGGS (*gently*)—I can understand that.

ROSE—Ask me who it was. Ask me, Ben, and I will tell you. (*No answer.*) Just ask me.

GRIGGS—No, I won't do that, Rose.

ROSE—Remember when the roses came from Teheran, I mean wired from Teheran, last birthday? That's who sent them. You didn't even like Teheran. You said it was filthy and the people downtrodden. But he sent roses.

GRIGGS—He sounds like the right man. Go to him, Rose, the flying time is nothing now.

ROSE (*angrily*)—You just stop being nasty. (*Then:*) And now I am going to tell you who it is.

GRIGGS (*begins to move toward door, as if he were backing away from her*)—Please, Rose. We have had so many years of this— Please. (*As she is closer to him.*) Do I have to tell you that I don't care who it is?

ROSE (*she begins to move on him*)—I'd like to whisper it. I knew if I ever told you I'd have to whisper it. (*He begins now really to back away.*) Ben, you come right here. Ben, stand still. (*He starts to laugh.*) Stop that laughing. (*Very loudly, very close to him.*) It was your cousin, Ralph Sommers. There. (*She turns away.*) There. You won't ever speak with him about it?

GRIGGS—You can be sure of that.

ROSE (*outside an automobile horn is sounded*)—Oh, I'm late. I can't talk any more now, Ben. (*She starts for door, stops.*) What am I going to tell Henry? Anyway, you know Henry isn't going to allow me to give you a divorce. You know that, Ben. (*Carefully.*) And therefore I won't be able to do what you want, and the whole day is just wasted. Please tell me not to go, Ben.

GRIGGS (*as if he has held onto himself long enough*)—Tell Henry that I want a divorce. But in any case I am going away. I am leaving. That is all that matters to me or need matter to you or him. I would prefer a divorce. But I am going, whatever you and Henry decide. Understand that, Rose, the time has come to understand it.

ROSE (*gently, smiling*)—I am going to try, dear. Really I am. It's evidently important to you. (*She exits through hall.* GRIGGS *sits down as if he were very tired.*)

Crossman, coming from the dining room with the Sunday papers, gives the General a front section, takes a chair and starts on the comics. Nina enters, sits down silently; then Constance appears, wearing an old-fashioned flowered hat and carrying a palmetto fan. She is off to church—and she amazes Ned by asking him if he wants to go along. Seeing his look of surprise, she falters, "I just thought— Well, Nick told us that you told him last night—" Becoming conscious of Nina and Griggs, she smiles awkwardly and then with great determination leans over Crossman and kisses him, saying, "Good-by, darling." He is so surprised he gets up, and stands watching her leave the room. Then he sits down again, staring ahead.

Somewhat hesitantly, Nina tells the two men she has a car and a full picnic basket and a cold bottle of wine. Would they—? They would, indeed, and when the General smilingly asks if one bottle is enough on a Sunday, she laughs and declares she will get five or so more. As they follow her out, Sophie clears up the breakfast dishes on the porch and finds a piece of roll and some bacon left, which she thriftily eats.

The curtain falls.

Scene II

It is nine-thirty that Sunday evening. Nick is lying on the couch, an empty champagne glass on the floor near him. A bottle is in a cooler on the table. Constance is at the table playing solitaire and humming to a record playing on the phonograph. On the porch, Sophie is reading to the elder Mrs. Ellis. Nick, bored and irritated, gets up and pours himself some more champagne. He takes the bottle to Constance, but she doesn't want any more. He takes the bottle to the porch.

Mrs. Ellis (*looks up at him*)—For the fourth time, we don't want any. Please go away. We're having a nice time. We're in the part I like best.

Nick—A nice time? Will I think such a time is a nice time when I am your age? I suppose so.

Mrs. Ellis—No, Mr. Denery. If you haven't learned to read at your age, you won't learn at mine.

Nick (*laughs, pats her shoulder*)—Never mind, I like you.

Mrs. Ellis—You must be damn hard up. People seldom like those who don't like them.

Nick (*pleased*)—You haven't forgotten how to flirt. Come on inside and talk to me. My wife disappears, everybody disappears—

(*Stretches.*) I'm bored, I'm bored.

MRS. ELLIS—And that's a state of sin, isn't it?

NICK—Unfortunately, it isn't. I've always said I can stand any pain, any trouble—but not boredom.

MRS. ELLIS—My advice is to try something intellectual for a change. Sit down with your champagne—on which you've been chewing since early afternoon—and try to make a paper hat out of the newspaper or get yourself a nice long piece of string.

NICK (*goes to* SOPHIE)—Sophie, come in and dance with me.

MRS. ELLIS (*calls in*)—Constance, whistle for Mr. Denery, please.

NICK (*to* SOPHIE)—You don't want to sit here and read to Mrs. Ellis.

SOPHIE—Yes, sir, I do. I enjoy the adventures of Odysseus. And the dollar an hour Mrs. Ellis pays me for reading to her.

NICK (*laughs, as* MRS. ELLIS *laughs*)—Give you two dollars an hour to dance with me.

MRS. ELLIS—It's not nearly enough, Sophie.

NICK (*pats* MRS. ELLIS)—You're a corrupter of youth—you steal the best hours.

MRS. ELLIS (*shakes his hand off her shoulder*)—And you're a toucher: you constantly touch people or lean on them. Little moments of sensuality. One should have sensuality whole or not at all. Don't you find pecking at it ungratifying? There are many of you: the touchers and the leaners. All since the depression, is my theory.

NICK (*laughs, pats her again*)—You must have been quite a girl in your day.

MRS. ELLIS—I wasn't. I wasn't at all. (NICK *wanders into the room.* MRS. ELLIS *speaks to* SOPHIE.) I was too good for those who wanted me and not good enough for those I wanted. Like Frederick, Sophie. Life can be hard for such people and they seldom understand why and end bitter and confused.

Nick wanders back to Constance and brings up the subject of Ned again, saying she could have married him instead of dangling him around. Expansively he tells her that last night Ned said he loved her and wanted her and had wasted his life loving and wanting. Then he pains and startles her by adding that Ned said he wasn't coming here any more on his Summer holidays from the bank.

A distracted Carrie comes in; she has been looking for her son since morning and can't find him. She even telephoned Payson. Old Mrs. Ellis is unperturbed, but Carrie thinks she should call the police, for one person had seen Frederick down by the water. Nick, with an energy coming from champagne and boredom, tells Carrie she must go to the police right away, and he will get a boat. But Sophie stops him by rising and saying angrily, in French, "Do not enjoy the excitement so much. Stop being a fool." Then in German she tells him to mind his business—and to Carrie she gently explains that Frederick is in the cove down by the dock; he has wanted to be alone. Nick demands an apology from Sophie, but when the girl won't answer he goes out of the house.

The old lady has come into the room and has decided that now is the time for definite decision. She feels sure Frederick does not now want to go to Europe—so a wedding date should be set. Sophie says she is willing if he is. Carrie and Constance, whose minds are on love, cannot understand the expression "willing"—but Sophie . . . a new Sophie, it seems . . . makes it clear to them. She tells her aunt she has not been happy and cannot continue here. She is grateful to her aunt—but these last years have been a waste for them both. Constance, reaching a new understanding of the girl, gently asks her if she wants to go home, and Sophie says, painfully, no, not now; there are too many debts at home. "Frederick and I will have a nice life," she assures her aunt. "We will make out." Carrie says sharply that Constance need not be disturbed—that she has decided that her son is going to Europe and there will be no interference.

The long-missing Frederick appears and tells his mother he is not going to Europe. Payson made that clear to him this morning— that he wasn't wanted if he couldn't supply the money. "I don't want to see him again," the boy cries. His mother offers to fix things up with Payson, but old Mrs. Ellis exclaims, "Carrie, you're an ass." She advises her grandson not to be bitter; why shouldn't Payson want his money?

Sophie has saved some dinner for Frederick and she takes him to it, hand in hand. Nick reappears, and asks Carrie to go for a sail, but she is too bewildered to do anything but go upstairs. Nick tries to put his arms around Constance, but she pushes him off and advises him to go to bed. Instead, he goes for more champagne. The telephone rings and Constance answers; it is Rose Griggs, who first asks for her husband, who isn't in, and then for Nick. "Tell her I'm busy," says Nick—but then he takes the call. From the words he can get in, it is clear that the portrait has been commissioned— it's to be of Rose's niece—and that Nick will stay with her brother.

Nina, Griggs and Crossman return from their picnic jaunt. They all decline to drink with the artist, who by now is drunk. He seeks a quarrel with Crossman, but Crossman walks out on him. He tries to advise the General not to leave his wife, and Griggs walks out on him. Nick tries to be casual about informing his wife that their next stop will be at Rose's brother's in New Orleans, where he will do a portrait of a daughter for five thousand dollars. Nina angrily says he is crazy and points out that he hasn't finished a portrait in twelve years. What he really is up to is a silly flirtation with Mrs. Griggs. "I'm not going to New Orleans," she declares. "I'm not going to watch it all again." She pleads with him not to go; he must realize that he is an amateur—a gifted amateur. Nick asks why, then, did she pretend to believe in his ability, and she answers, simply, "I loved you."

His dignity has been hurt and he decides, "I think you ought to leave tomorrow, Nina. For good and forever." She agrees softly and starts out of the room, and he follows, advising her to spare herself the return, the begging and the disgusting self-contempt. Constance, coming into the hall, hears his last words. She stands for a moment, then puts out the porch lights and all but one lamp in the living room. Sophie brings in her bedding and Constance helps her make up the couch. The girl is in pajamas and a robe. Her aunt kisses her good-night, and Sophie, taking off her robe and putting it over her shoulders, gets into bed and puts out the light.

Nick comes in, stumbles over a chair, turns on a light, sees Sophie and says, "You're cute." He pours himself a drink and sits down on her bed. He invites her to drive away with him for a few days, and then lies down, his head on her knees. Sophie tells him quietly to take his bottle upstairs, but he insists that she get him a drink. She gets up and pours one, and when she brings it to him he pulls her toward him, spilling the champagne on the bed. The girl, still calm, urges him to go away. He springs up, angry, but sits across the room instead of leaving. Deciding she can't get rid of him, Sophie picks up a book, gets into bed and begins to read. He approaches the bed, talking incoherently about love, and playfully pours a glass of champagne on her blonde hair. He sits beside her and holds her. "Mr. Denery, I am sick of you," Sophie declares. Nick, now self-pitying, promises to go away if she will give him a kiss. Resignedly sighing, she turns a cheek toward him, and he takes her in his arms. She struggles angrily to get away from him and threatens to call his wife, but he just laughs and says he and Nina are getting a divorce. With a final effort the girl manages to free herself and spring away from the bed. He catches her robe, rolls over on it, settles down comfortably, and is deaf to her demands that he leave. At last he passes out, breathing heavily. Sophie tugs at his legs but can't move him, and he murmurs, "I'll go away in a few minutes. Don't be so young. Have a little pity. I am old and sick."

Resignedly, the girl moves slowly to the other side of the room. The curtain falls.

ACT III

It is seven o'clock the next morning and Nick is still asleep on the couch. Sophie is sitting in a chair drinking coffee. Mrs. Ellis comes down, ready for breakfast as usual, and stops, staring at Nick. The girl explains that he became drunk and went to sleep, and she couldn't budge him. Mrs. Ellis says Nick must be got out immediately, and the girl offers to get Leon and the cook to help take him upstairs. The old lady vetoes the scheme, saying, "Rose Griggs may be the president of the gossip club for Summer Anglo-Saxons, but Leon is certainly the president of the Negro chapter." She pulls the blankets off Nick and notices with satisfaction that he is dressed. Telling Sophie to bring coffee, she commands Nick to sit up. He manages to move his head slightly. Sophie holds his head up while the old lady tries to make him drink, but he mutters that they should let him alone. Mrs. Ellis shouts a command that he get up and out immediately; he gives a bewildered look around the room, murmurs "Julie!" and closes his eyes. The old lady keeps shouting at him until he comes to and recognizes her. "I passed out?" he asks. "Did I do anything or say anything?" Grimly Mrs. Ellis tells him how he has compromised a girl in a small, gossipy Southern town. "Get up and get the hell out of here," she shouts.

But it is too late. Rose comes in with her overnight bag and realizes that Nick has been sleeping here. "Well," says Mrs. Ellis cynically to Nick, "that's that. Perhaps you wanted it this way, Mr. Denery." Leon, carrying in the coffee urn, stands in the doorway, very curious. Mrs. Ellis shoos him to the dining room and follows him.

The romantic Rose is hurt. After getting Nick a portrait commission, and after taking his advice and having gone to a doctor (although she'd never have gone if she had known) she finds this. Perhaps there is an explanation, she hopes—but he offers none. Constance comes in, angry. She points out to Nick, through the window, that the Carters have extra guests on their breakfast porch, and next door the Gable sisters seem to be unexpectedly entertaining. The telephone rings; Constance answers, listens a moment, flushes and hangs up. "Please explain to me what happened," she demands of Nick. Sophie steps up and tells what happened, but with no animosity toward Nick. Constance asks Sophie why she stayed in the room and why hadn't she called for help. Constance hasn't noticed Rose yet, but now she does, for Rose comments meaningfully on Sophie's calm appearance as she is folding up the bed things—"like it happened to her every night. You can blame Nick all you like. But you know very well that a nice girl would have screamed."

Constance, furious, suggests that Rose leave today, and Rose, feeling sorry for herself because of what the doctor has told her, asks for breakfast in bed and goes to her room. When Crossman comes in, Constance asks him what can be done, but he is realist enough to know that nothing can be done now. He smiles amusedly at Sophie and asks how she is. Constance turns on Nick, heatedly berating him for dishonoring her house, and the artist is genuinely contrite and willing to say or do anything that might help. He knows what it means to Sophie.

It will be a bad scandal, but with Nick a home town boy and Sophie a foreigner, the girl will get the worst of it. Upstairs, Rose has told Nina of the situation, and soon Nina, preceded by the maid with baggage and accompanied by Rose, comes down. Nick ingratiatingly tries to explain nothing happened, but his wife coldly observes that it is a tasty little story—particularly for a girl who is going to get married. Nina is making the nine-thirty train for New York, and she advises her husband to call one Horace and have him take care of the legal stuff. Life is crowding hard upon Nick, and he passionately begs his wife not to leave him. "We've only had one trouble; you hate yourself for loving me," he argues. "Because you have contempt for me."

NINA—For myself. I have no right—
NICK—No, nobody has. No right at all.
NINA—I wouldn't have married you, Nick, if I had known—
NICK—You would have married me. Or somebody like me. You've needed to look down on me, darling. You've needed to make fun of me. And to be ashamed of yourself for doing it.
NINA (softly)—Am I that sick?
NICK—I don't know about such words. You found the man you deserved. That's all. I am no better and no worse than what you really wanted. You like to—to demean yourself. And so you chose me. You must say I haven't minded much. Because I've always loved you and known we'd last it out. Come back to me, Nina, without shame in wanting to. (He leans down, kisses her neck.) Put up with me a little longer, kid. I'm getting older and I'll soon wear down.

NINA (*she smiles, touched*)—I've never heard you speak of getting old.

NICK (*quickly*)—Yes. (*Then:*) The *Ile* sails next week. Let's get on. We'll have fun. Tell me we're together again and you're happy. Say it, Nina, quick.

NINA—I'm happy. (*He takes her in his arms, kisses her. Then he stands away, looks at her, and smiles shyly.*)

NICK—There'll be no more of what you call my "home-comings." Old friends and all that. They are damn bores, with empty lives.

NINA—Is that so different from us?

NICK—If we could only do something for the kid. Take her with us, get her out of here until they get tired of the gossip—

NINA (*laughs*)—I don't think we will take her with us.

NICK (*laughs*)—Now, now. You know what I mean.

NINA—I know what you mean—and we're not taking her with us.

NICK—I suppose there isn't anything to do. (*Softly, his hand to his head.*) I feel sick, Nina.

NINA—You've got a hangover.

NICK—It's more than that. I've got a sore throat and my back aches. Come on, darling, let's get on the train.

NINA—You go. I'll stay and see if there's anything I can do. That's what you really want. Go on, Nicky. Maybe it's best.

NICK—I couldn't do that.

NINA—Don't waste time, darling. You'll miss the train. I'll bring your clothes with me.

NICK (*laughs, ruefully*)—If you didn't see through me so fast, you wouldn't dislike yourself so much. (*Comes to her.*) You're a wonderful girl. It's wonderful of you to take all this on—

NINA—I've had practice—

NICK (*hurt*)—That's not true. You know this never happened before.

NINA (*smiles*)—Nicky, it always confuses you that the fifth time something happens it varies slightly from the second and fourth. No, it never happened in this house before. Cora had a husband and Sylvia wanted one. And this isn't a hotel in Antibes, and Sophie is not a rich Egyptian. And this time you didn't break your arm on a boat deck and it isn't 1928—

NICK—This is your day, Nina. But pass up the chance to play it too hard, will you? Take me or leave me now but don't—

NINA—You're right. Please go, darling. Your staying won't do any good. Neither will mine, but maybe—

Nick's spirits have revived, and Nina becomes gay, too, as he talks boyishly of returning to France in the bridal suite of the *Ile*. When he has gone, Nina asks for breakfast on the porch and Constance goes to order it. Frederick and his mother come down, and Frederick is laughing and assured. He is not upset about the events of the night and he advises his mother not to be. Carrie has been thinking ahead, and has figured it will be best if Sophie travels home with them right now; but Sophie, too, has been thinking ahead—and differently. If she leaves, it will be running away from scandal; they all must act as though nothing had happened. The Ellises will go home, as planned, and Sophie will remain here. The girl lightly caresses Frederick's face and murmurs, "You are a nice man."

But still another person has been thinking ahead—perhaps the one with the clearest sight of all: Grandma Ellis. When Frederick and Carrie have gone in to breakfast, Mrs. Ellis comes out and speaks plainly with Sophie. She predicts that Carrie will have a change of mind in a week or two and will take Frederick off to Europe, postponing the marriage. The marriage will always be postponed, for Carrie will never want her son to marry, and Frederick will always give in. Sophie instantly understands that the old lady has hit upon the truth, and she instantly reaches a decision. When Constance returns from a household errand the girl tells her aunt, "I will not be going to New Orleans, and there will be no marriage between Frederick and me."

Sophie goes to the porch. Leon has just served Nina and is about to pour coffee. The girl takes the pot from him, dismisses him, pours the coffee and sits down unasked. "Now," she says, "could I speak with you and Mr. Denery?"

Nina uncomfortably explains that Nick has gone, and asks, "What can I do?"

"You can give me five thousand dollars." Demurely, and in a pronounced accent, she seems to be reciting as she says, "I have been subjected to the most degrading experience from which no young girl easily recovers." She says the same thing in French, relishing it, and continues, "I am utterly, utterly miserable, Mrs. Denery. I am ruined." Nina thinks she is joking, but Sophie is serious. The girl wants the five thousand, she explains, so she can go home.

"Then I will be happy to give it to you," Nina announces—but the odd girl says she will not accept it as a gift. "We will call it a loan, come by through blackmail," she stipulates. "One does not have to be grateful for blackmail money. You will give me five thousand dollars because if you do not I will say that Mr. Denery seduced me last night."

Nina laughs at first, then becomes angry as she realizes Sophie is a tough, clear-headed opponent. But Sophie wins. When Crossman appears in the hall the girl calls him to the porch, where Nina asks if he can vouch for her at the bank for a large sum of money. He readily agrees, and she departs. Sophie announces to Crossman, "I will be going home, Mr. Ned." "Good," he says, as he looks at her and then at the departing Nina. He follows Mrs. Denery out.

Rose, hurried and nervous, comes downstairs, asks Sophie why her breakfast has not been brought up to her. The girl goes to see about it just as the General returns from his morning ride. Rose rambles on to him about Nick's affair, and the heat in town, and Athalia's braces, until her husband pins her down by asking what point she has come to about his decision. Softly and agitatedly she starts explaining that, before going to see her brother, she saw Dr. Wills. "I have bad heart trouble, Ben," she reveals. He thinks it is the same old trick until she gives him a letter the doctor, a man of high repute, has written to him about her condition. "I just didn't know it was this bad," she goes on. "Wills says I must lead a—well, a very different life."

She is frightened, badly frightened, and she begins to weep. "Wills says that if I take good care I might be, probably will be, in fine shape at the end of the year. Please," she begs, "stay with me this year, just this year." She pledges solemnly that she will give Ben his divorce at the end of that time. "Help me, please," she pleads. He goes to her, presses her arm and says, gently, "Of course. Of course." Rose goes gratefully back to her room, and Crossman, coming in, stares at Griggs as if he knew something was wrong; then he asks, "Seen Sophie?"

GRIGGS (*as if it were an effort, idly*)—In the kitchen, I guess. Tough break for the kid, isn't it?

CROSSMAN—Perhaps it isn't. I don't know. (*He watches as* GRIGGS *takes out a cigarette and lights it.* GRIGGS's *hands are shaking and as he puts out the match, he stares at them.*)

GRIGGS (*smiles*)—My hands are shaking.

CROSSMAN—What's the matter?

GRIGGS—Worst disease of all. I'm all gone. I've just looked and there's no Benjamin Griggs.

CROSSMAN (*after a second*)—Oh, that. And you've just found that out?

GRIGGS—Just today. Just now.

CROSSMAN—My God, you're young.

GRIGGS (*laughs*)—I guess I was. (*Slowly, carefully.*) So at any given moment you're only the sum of your life up to then. There are no big moments you can reach unless you've a pile of smaller moments to stand on. That big hour of decision, the turning point in your life, the someday you've counted on when you'd suddenly wipe out your past mistakes, do the work you'd never done, think the way you'd never thought, have what you'd never had—it just doesn't come suddenly. You've trained yourself for it while you waited—or you've let it all run past you and frittered yourself away. (*Shakes his head.*) I've frittered myself away, Crossman.

CROSSMAN—Most people like us.

GRIGGS—That's no good to me. Most people like us haven't done anything to themselves; they've let it be done to them. I had no right to let it be done to me, but I let it be done. What consolation can I find in not having made myself any more useless than an Ellis, a Denery, a Tuckerman, a—

CROSSMAN—Say it. I won't mind. Or a Crossman.

GRIGGS—The difference is you've meant to fritter yourself away.

CROSSMAN—And does that make it better?

GRIGGS—Better? Worse? All I know is it makes it different. Rose is a sick woman. But you know I'm not talking only about Rose and me, don't you?

CROSSMAN—I know.

GRIGGS (*very slowly*)—I am not any too sure I didn't partly welcome the medical opinion that made it easier for me to give up. (*Then in a low voice as if to himself:*) And I don't like Rose. And I'll live to like her less.

Constance appears in the hall with Rose's breakfast tray and the General takes it from her and carries it upstairs. Crossman hands Sophie an envelope with Nina's money in it, and the girl, laughing, goes upstairs to help Rose pack and clean her room. Constance, alone with Ned, says, "I feel so lost. . . . Well, what *have* I built my life on? Do you know what I mean?" He quietly assures her he knows, and then, to change the subject, she informs him that Sophie is going home and wants her to come live with Sophie and her mother. Then, approaching something which frightens her, she asks if Ned really did say he wasn't coming back, or was it another of Nick's lies?

He tries to answer lightly. "Hasn't anything to do with you, Con. Just think I'd be better off. You know, it's kind of foolish —two weeks a year—coming back here and living a life that isn't me any more." She tries to conceal her distress by asking where Nick is, and is informed he and Nina have gone. Constance stares at Ned and says, "Exactly the way he left years ago. . . . We had a date for dinner. He didn't come. He just got on the boat." Violently she exclaims, "What a fool! All these years of making a shabby man into the kind of hero who would come back someday all happy and shining—"

Ned brings her out of it by pointing out that Nick had never asked her to make him what he wasn't, or to wait twenty years to find him out.

"I want to say something to you. I can't wait any longer," says Constance earnestly. "Would you forgive me . . . for wasting all these years? . . . Ned, would you have me now?"

After a second's pause he asks, "What did you say?"

"Would you marry me?"

Ned is silent. Sophie passes through the hall, carrying cleaning things and singing a cheerful French song. Constance smiles and observes, "She's happy."

CROSSMAN (*stares at* CONSTANCE, *then slowly, carefully*)—I live in a room and I go to work and I play a game called getting through the day while you wait for night. The night's for me—just me—and I can do anything with it I want. There used to be a lot of things to do with it, good things, but now there's a bar and another bar and the same people in each bar. When I've had enough I go back to my room—or somebody else's room—and that never means much one way or the other. A few years ago I'd have weeks of reading—night after night—just me. But I don't do that much any more. Just read, all night long. You can feel good that way.

CONSTANCE—I never did that. I'm not a reader.

CROSSMAN (*as if he hadn't heard her*)—And a few years ago I'd go on the wagon twice a year. Now I don't do that any more. And I don't care. (*Smiles.*) And all these years I told myself that if you'd loved me everything would have been different. I'd have had a good life, been worth something to myself. I wanted to tell myself that. I wanted to believe it. Griggs was right. I not only wasted myself, but I wanted it that way. All my life, I guess, I wanted it that way.

CONSTANCE—And you're not in love with me, Ned?

CROSSMAN—No, Con. Not now.

CONSTANCE (*gets up, goes to him*)—Let's have a nice dinner together, just you and me, and go to the movies. Could we do that?

CROSSMAN—I've kept myself busy looking into other people's hearts so I wouldn't have to look into my own. (*Softly.*) If I made you think I was still in love, I'm sorry. Sorry I fooled you and sorry I fooled myself. And I've never liked liars—least of all those who lie to themselves.

CONSTANCE—Never mind. Most of us lie to ourselves, darling, most of us.

CURTAIN

BELL, BOOK AND CANDLE *

A Comedy in Three Acts

By John van Druten

THE fate of "Bell, Book and Candle" was a curious and dis-heartening one. The comedy was one of the great hits of the season and was playing to capacity at the end of May, a time when all actors' contracts expire automatically. At this time Rex Harrison and Lilli Palmer, the stars, exercised their right to quit in order that Mr. Harrison might fulfill previously made motion picture contracts. The play closed. For a while, the producer, Irene Mayer Selznick, hoped that within a few weeks she could find two new leading players and if necessary a whole new cast; but later she decided against reopening the comedy with substitute stars, and the run was brought to a definite and premature end.

The history of "Bell, Book and Candle" is told by Mr. van Druten thus: "I wrote it—a first and rather more serious version—over two and a half years ago, and then I rewrote it quite strenuously. At that time Alfred de Liagre, Jr., had the play, but he was never able to cast it. No one wanted to play it. Finally, he gave it up, and I regarded it as dead. Then Irene Selznick read it, fell in love with the idea, and decided she would produce it—and even when I told her what our casting experiences had been, that she would cast it, too. I did some more but lesser rewriting after talks with her. Then Lilli Palmer agreed to play Gillian. The role of Shep was a tougher problem. Actors turned the part down in dozens. It was not until the end of August, 1950 (with rehearsals scheduled for mid-October), that everything suddenly happened right. All of Rex Harrison's other assignments went West, and it was then that he—whom I had always wanted—agreed to play it with his wife.

"The rest you probably know. There was some more work

done, mainly on Act II, to lighten it a little more, while we were in Boston. We had a New York preview the night before we opened, which was wholly dead—not a laugh in the whole evening— which made our opening night experience a very happy one. . . . I don't know what to say about directing. I don't know where I learned to be able to do it—probably sitting beside the late Auriol Lee for many years while she directed a dozen of my plays. I do think you have to know something of theatre and acting, as well as of playwriting, and to be able to transfer yourself from the role of author to that of audience to do the job. It is a sort of dual role experience! I do think, if an author can do it at all, he is the best person to be engaged—he does know what he means! And for the rest, I think directing is very largely a matter of taste and style, and of pleasing those—in oneself, first. I think the director is a kind of critic, first and foremost."

The setting throughout is Gillian Holroyd's apartment in New York—a first-floor apartment in a converted brownstone house in the Murray Hill district in the East Thirties. The living room is interesting and comfortable—a little on the dark side, with good furniture which looks more family than it does modern or antique. There is a swing door to the kitchen and another door to the bedroom. There's a fire going in the fireplace. A windowed alcove looks out on the street. The entrance door to the apartment looks straight into the room. There is a Christmas tree, trimmed and lighted, for it is about 6 P.M. on Christmas Eve. When we first see this room Gillian is in it, alone—small, alert, direct, very attractive, age 27. She is seated, stroking and talking to a cat. She sighs to the cat, "Oh, Pye—Pyewacket—what's the matter with me? Why do I feel this way? It's all such a *rut*. It was just the same in Mexico. You know it was. Were the Mexican cats any different from the ones you know in New York?" Gillian carries the cat up and down the room, continuing, "Why don't you give me something for Christmas? What would I like? I'd like to meet someone *different*. Yes, all right." One gets the idea that somehow Pyewacket is talking, too. "Like the man upstairs then," says Gillian.

There is a knock on the door, so she switches on the lights and opens it. It is the man upstairs. He might be around 35, is masculine and attractive. He is wearing a topcoat, has hat in hand, and is carrying a couple of Christmas packages. Name, Shepherd Henderson—Shep, usually. He has come by because he understands, correctly, that Gillian is his landlady. She invites him in, asks him to take off his coat, offers a drink. He shouldn't take time for a drink; he's been getting some last-minute presents and will be going out soon; anyhow, his call may not be altogether friendly. The lady on the floor above him has been in his apartment a couple of times and he doesn't like it. He understands the lady is Gillian's aunt; he asks, "Did you ever give her a key to my apartment?" Gillian, astonished, answers, "No, of course not. . . . How did she get in?"

Shep doesn't exactly know. ' The aunt says she found the door open; she may have, the first time, but not the second. He called the agents about it, but it hasn't done any good. And she seems rather—er—a peculiar lady. • Could she be studying dramatics? At night he can hear her through the ceiling and, though he doesn't get the words, she seems to be *reciting* something. And her cooking, if that's what it is; it doesn't smell like anything edible.

Gillian tries to explain: "It's not cooking. She—she *makes* things. Perfumes and—lotions, and things."

The tenant has one further complaint—though he can't be sure it is the aunt who does it. Ever since he caught her and complained to the agents his telephone starts ringing at 8 every morning and around midnight, but when he answers there's nobody there. The phone company can't trace anything.

"I promise you," says Gillian, "none of this will happen again." Shep rises but seems unwilling to go. He says he has heard she has been traveling and she replies, Yes, in Mexico; she has a house in Taxco. His interest quickens and he asks, "You didn't, by any chance, run into Redlitch down there, did you? The man who wrote that book on magic, *Magic in Mexico*."

"No," says Gillian, "he'd left by the time I got there." And then, rather searchingly, she asks if Shep is interested in that sort of thing. "Professionally," he explains. "I'm a publisher. I hear that Redlitch has changed publishers and I'd kind of like his next one. I've written to him several times, but I get no answer."

It is odd, how eagerly Gillian volunteers, "If you'd like to meet him—" She doesn't know this best-selling writer on magic, but she knows people who do and could arrange a meeting. "That would be fine," says Shep. "I hear he's a nut and a drunk, but—" His attention is caught by a drawing on the wall and Gillian tells him her brother Nicky did it. The face of a Brazilian girl who used to dance in a night club here, called the Zodiac. Shep wouldn't know the place; it's a sort of a dive, she explains.

There is a knock on the door and Shep prepares to leave as Gillian opens it. The caller is the woman upstairs—Aunt Queenie Holroyd, a vague, fluttery, eccentric-looking woman dressed in a wispy, bitty and endy evening gown with a trailing scarf. Aunt

Queenie has bangles and a long necklace; her voice is high and feathery and her laugh trills. She, also, is carrying gift packages and a cloak. Shep gives Miss Holroyd an amused and friendly hello as he goes out.

Aunt Queenie knows she is going to get a scolding and she tries, without success, to postpone it. Her attempt to look nonchalant fails. "I'm angry," Gillian chides, "*really* angry."

MISS HOLROYD—Why, what have I done?

GILLIAN—You know. Broken into his apartment—played tricks with his telephone . . .

MISS HOLROYD—That was because he reported me to the agents. That was just to pay him out.

GILLIAN—I don't care *what* it was. You *promised* when I let you move in here . . .

MISS HOLROYD—I promised to be careful.

GILLIAN—And do you call that being careful? Getting caught in his apartment? Twice!

MISS HOLROYD—What harm did I do? I didn't *take* anything. Yes, I read his letters, but it's not as if I were going to make *use* of them. Though I'm tempted to now—now that he's told on me—to you.

GILLIAN (*menacingly, and quite frighteningly*)—Auntie, if you do —well, you'll be sorry. And you know I can *make* you sorry, too.

MISS HOLROYD (*defensively*)—He'd never suspect, darling. Not in a million years. No matter *what* I did. Honestly, it's amazing the way people don't. Why, they don't believe there *are* such things. I sit in the subway sometimes, or in busses, and look at the people next me, and I think: What would you say if I told you I was a witch? And I know they'd never believe it. They just wouldn't believe it. And I giggle and giggle to myself.

GILLIAN—Well, you've got to stop giggling here. You've got to swear, swear on the Manual . . .

MISS HOLROYD (*retreating a step*)—Swear what?

GILLIAN—That you'll stop practicing—in this house—ever.

MISS HOLROYD—*You* practice here.

GILLIAN—I can be discreet about it. You can't.

MISS HOLROYD (*very hurt*)—I shall move to a hotel.

GILLIAN—Very well. But if you get into trouble there, don't look to *me* to get you out.

MISS HOLROYD (*huffily*)—I've other people I can turn to.

GILLIAN (*scornfully*)—Mrs. de Pass, I suppose.

Miss Holroyd—Yes, she's done a lot for me.

Gillian—Well, I wouldn't count on Mrs. de Pass, if *I* turn against you. I'm a lot better than *that* old phony. Now . . . (*She gets a large white-bound book from a closet.*)

Miss Holroyd (*really scared*)—Oh, please—not on the Manual.

Gillian (*relentlessly*)—On the Manual. (*She brings it.*) Now, put your hand on it. (Miss Holroyd *does so, terrified.*) Now, then, I swear that I will not practice witchcraft ever in this house again. So help me Tagla, Salamandrae, Brazo and Vesturiel. Say, "I swear."

Miss Holroyd (*after a moment*)—I swear.

Gillian—Good. (*She replaces the book.*)

Miss Holroyd—I think you're very cruel.

Gillian (*returning, somewhat softened*)—Oh, Auntie, if you'd only have a little sense!

Miss Holroyd (*continuing*)—*And* hypocritical. Sometimes I think you're *ashamed* of being what you are.

Gillian—Ashamed? I'm not in the least ashamed. No, it's not a question of that, but . . . (*Suddenly.*) Auntie, don't you ever wish you *weren't*?

Miss Holroyd (*amazed*)—No.

Gillian—That you were like those people you sit next to in the busses?

Miss Holroyd—Ordinary and humdrum? No, I *was*. For years. Before I came into it.

Gillian—Well, you came in late. And, anyway, I don't *mean* humdrum. I just mean unenlightened. And I don't hanker for it all the time. Just sometimes.

Miss Holroyd—Darling, you're depressed. . . .

Gillian—I know. I expect it's Christmas. It's always upset me.

Miss Holroyd—You wait till you get to Zoe's party, and see all your old friends again.

Gillian—I don't *want* to see all my old friends again. I want something different.

Miss Holroyd—Well, come with me to Mrs. de Pass's, then. She's got some very interesting people. Some French people. From the Paris chapter.

Gillian (*laughing*)—I didn't mean *that*, when I said I wanted something different. I think maybe I'd like to spend the evening with some everyday people for a change, instead of *us*.

Miss Holroyd (*archly*)—With Mr. Henderson?

Gillian—I wouldn't mind.

The amazing Auntie says this is no good. What with the telephone and one thing or another, she has accumulated the information that Mr. Henderson is going to be married to a girl named Merle and the engagement will be announced New Year's Eve. Gillian remembers she knew a Merle once—Merle Kittredge, in college. She used to write poison pen letters and Gillian caught Merle writing one about her. "That's why we had all those thunderstorms that Spring. She was terrified of them."

Auntie looks delightedly at her niece and exclaims, "Oh, Gillian, you were *naughty!*"

They speculate further about this Merle Shep Henderson is going to marry. The one Gillian knew became a decorator. "This one's a decorator," volunteers the aunt. Gillian thinks this may be a coincidence, and if Shep's engaged that rules him out. She is not a Southern belle, like Merle Kittredge, so she won't take other women's men. . . . Unless, of course, Shep's Merle *were* Gillian's Merle. Then she would—but a week wouldn't leave her much time to do it.

Auntie protests that no time at all is needed—just a quick little potion, or four words to Pyewacket. . . . But Gillian wants to get Shep the hard, or normal way, just the way other girls do—and she isn't off to a very good start, either, for Henderson was not exactly friendly this afternoon. "Do you think," she muses, "I could do it in a week—without tricks? I'd like to see how good I am, the other way."

Nicky, Gillian's brother, arrives, dinner-jacketed and topcoated, carrying some small Christmas-wrapped packages. While Gillian is in the kitchen making drinks, Nicky—a young, engaging and impertinent chap—is asked by his aunt to do something for her. She writes a number on a pad by the telephone. "This number," she says. "I want you to fix it for me."

"Fix it?"

"*You* know."

"Why, who is it?" Nicky asks.

"Someone I want to—pay back for something."

Nicky protests, "But you can pull that one for yourself. I taught you," and Miss Holroyd explains, "I just had to promise Gillian that I wouldn't in this house any more." So Nicky obliges. Taking the phone off the cradle but holding down the bar he mutters, "Actatus, Catipta, Itapan, Marnutus. Murray Hill 6-4476." Gillian, coming in with the drinks, laughs, "Just a little Christmas present for a friend? No telephone for a week? Oh, Nicky, when will you grow up?"

Brother, sister and aunt, in a chummy Christmas Eve gathering, exchange presents as they drink Merry Christmas toasts. They all begin opening their packages at once. Aunt Queenie has brought duplicate gifts for the two young people—autographed copies of *Magic in Mexico,* by Sidney Redlitch. Miss Holroyd explains that Mrs. de Pass knows Redlitch, and she got the autographs for her. Nicky's gift from Gillian is phonograph records, and he ruefully explains that he doesn't have a phonograph any more. "I think you'll find you have when you get home," says his smiling sister, and she won't tell Nicky whether it was witched or paid for. The records, she explains, were made at a party in Mexico—incantations. Make music come out of your ears, for instance. The man who made them had a mink as his "familiar."

Gillian's present to Aunt Queenie is a lace mantilla. Miss Holroyd is disappointed when she is told it won't do anything except look pretty. Nicky has a present for her which is more down her line—a small bottle of unguent which will enable her to feel colors. And for Gillian he has a small phial. "It's a sort of paint," he explains. "For summoning. You just paint it on an image—or a drawing or a photograph—of anyone you want, and then set light to it. And they have to come." He suggests trying it now—but on whom?

Gillian holds up Redlitch's book and says, "This man. I've promised to introduce him to somebody. I thought I'd find someone who knew him, but this will save a lot of time. It's got his picture on the back." Gillian cuts out the picture, puts it in a big ash tray and asks Nicky to turn out the lights. With the room illuminated only by the fire and light through a window from a street lamp, she smears paint on the picture of Redlitch and touches a match to it. It goes up in blue flame, and Aunt Queenie squeals with delight. There is a knock on the door, and Nicky exclaims, "Not *already?*"

But the caller is not Redlitch; he is Shep Henderson again. He is somewhat mystified by the flames in the ash tray, but Gillian easily explains that it is just some nonsense her brother brought her. Shep has come to ask if he can use the phone. He has changed into a dinner jacket and a dark coat, and he is carrying a carton filled with presents. His phone, he explains, has gone out of order. Gillian shoots a quick look at her aunt and her brother, but both avoid her eyes.

Shep dials a number, gets a busy; Gillian suggests that he call the phone company and report his own number out of order while he is waiting, and he does so. Aunt Queenie remembers suddenly that she must be going, and starts for her cloak. Gillian firmly asks Nicky for the piece of paper she saw him putting in his pocket when she came in with the drinks and heard him making an incantation over the telephone, and reluctantly he hands it to her. Shep gives his number to the telephone repair operator—Murray Hill 6-4476. "I can't get a dialing tone," he complains. Gillian looks at the slip of paper her brother has surrendered to her and notes, grimly, that the numbers coincide. "It was Nicky," her aunt alibis —and gets out as quickly as she can, saying to Shep, "I hope your telephone gets well, soon." Nicky makes his escape with his aunt, and once more Shep tries the number that was busy before. This time he has it.

"Hello. . . . Is Miss Kittredge there? . . . Merle, it's me. I got delayed. . . . What is it? . . . What's your idea? Tonight? Announce it tonight? Well, wonderful. I thought you were so keen on New Year's Eve. Well, that's fine. . . . Yes, darling."

Shep's enthusiasm has been immense, but not so Gillian's. After listening to his end of the conversation a bit she goes to the kitchen and returns, carrying her cat. "Fifteen minutes. I can't wait. Good-by, darling. Darling!" Shep is exclaiming into the phone. After he hangs up he notices that Gillian is carrying the cat and says he has seen it on the stairs lately, watching him come in and out. Its name? Pyewacket. Well, he must go, and have that drink some other time. He is late, he explains, and it's kind of an important night. He puts on his coat and hat, picks up his carton of presents. Gillian just goes on stroking the cat and murmuring, "Pye—Pye—Pyewacket, this is Mr. Henderson. Mr. Shepherd Henderson . . . Reterrem, Salibat, Cratares, Hisaster."

"What was that?" Shep asks, turning after he has put on his coat. Gillian says lightly, "I was talking to Pyewacket. I think he wants to go out." She takes the cat through the swinging door back into the kitchen, and Shep just stands there, staring. In a moment Gillian is back. Shep takes two steps toward her, puts down his carton, throws his hat aside, and moves closer. She takes a step toward him—and they are in each other's arms.

The curtain falls.

Scene II

Well, by now, three hours have gone by. Gillian and Shep are stretched on the couch of the living room; the curtains have been drawn, and Shep's hat, coat and muffler have been thrown aside. Shep's carton of Christmas presents is just where he left it. The door to the bedroom is partly open.

"You know," says Shep, "there's a wonderful, timeless feeling

to this moment, and the two of us like this.   I feel—spellbound."
Gillian would like to let it go at that, but Shep, rising, finally remembers that he must get going.   He is amazed when he looks at
his watch and sees that it is ten o'clock—a good three hours since
he came in.   "Nothing like this ever happened to *me* before," he
confesses.

GILLIAN—Do you mind?

SHEP—I *ought* to mind. . . .

GILLIAN—Why?

SHEP—In the first place, I was on my way to a party.

GILLIAN—And you found something you'd rather do.

SHEP—That, my girl, is an understatement.   I found something
I couldn't resist doing.

GILLIAN (*smiling*)—You don't have to explain to me.

SHEP—It's fantastic.   (*He comes back to the couch, sets down
his drink, sits beside her, taking her hands.*)   Gillian—tell me—
just what has it meant to you?

GILLIAN—Meant?

SHEP—These three hours.

GILLIAN—They've been—enchantment.

SHEP—And that's all?

GILLIAN—What more?

SHEP—I don't know.   I know it doesn't make sense, but somewhere, I've got an idea—that I must be in love with you. . . . Are
you—at all in love with me?

GILLIAN—I like you more than I can say.

SHEP—That wasn't what I asked you.

GILLIAN—Do we have to talk about it?

SHEP—Yes.   I've got to know.

GILLIAN—Why?

SHEP—Because I've got to face a few decisions.

GILLIAN—Now?

SHEP—I should think so.   There are people waiting for me—
wondering where the hell I am.   There's a whole future that's either
got completely shot to hell, or else—well, I've got to do some fast
talking.   Some *very* fast talking.   And I'd like to know where I
stand.   Where *we* stand.

GILLIAN—What do you want to do?

SHEP (*slowly*)—Right at the moment, I want never to stop seeing
you.   (*He stares into her eyes, and then kisses her, deeply, tenderly,
hungrily.*)   Is it possible—that I can—never stop seeing you?

GILLIAN—You can see me all you want.

SHEP—It hasn't hit you as it has me.

GILLIAN—I want you just as much as you want me.

SHEP—You do?

GILLIAN—And I'm happy. Very happy.

SHEP—Look, I haven't asked you, but—I guess you're free and unattached.

GILLIAN—Yes.

SHEP—Well, that makes a difference—for you. You don't have to ask yourself questions. I do. I'm not free. The thing I've got to decide is—am I going to cut free?

Shep knows it is crazy to talk about love so soon, but makes a firm decision that he will cut free. Again he asks to borrow Gillian's telephone, and this time he asks to be left alone. She goes to the bedroom—but they have a long kiss first. On the wire, Shep asks whoever has answered to get Miss Kittredge—and to find her a place where she can sit down for a minute. "This is me," he announces when she comes on the wire. "I can't get there! No, not at all. Never. . . . I can't explain. I don't understand it myself. . . ." When Merle has hung up on him Shep calls to Gillian that she can come out of the bedroom now. He still doesn't know what has happened to him, and he doesn't know much about this new girl, Gillian, either. Why, for instance, did she offer to arrange for him to meet Redlitch? Was it a come-on?

The buzzer from downstairs in the apartment house sounds and Gillian goes to the intercom telephone to answer. A voice says, "This is Sidney Redlitch. You don't know me, but . . ." Gillian assumes an air of astonishment, but Shep wears a real one. Gillian pushes the button to open the downstairs door and soon Redlitch appears. He is in his fifties—shambling, messy and slightly drunk. She introduces Shep and Redlitch remembers that Shep has been writing to him. This man doesn't quite know why or how he has come here; he's been sitting in a bar alone, on Christmas Eve, and he has thumbed through his wallet and has come across Gillian's address. Some people in Mexico had given it to him. He had heard that Gillian had bought a certain long, black mask, with gold eyes, and he would like to photograph it for an article he is doing.

Gillian explains that the mask has not yet arrived—that it is coming up in a trunk by rail. And why, she asks innocently, is Redlitch so interested? The man answers, heavily, "Just one of the most potent witch-masks that I ran across down there."

Nicky drops in. He is amused that his sister has managed to produce Mr. Redlitch so soon, and that Shep is still here. When

Redlitch has been fed a drink, Shep, the business man, the publisher, gets to work. Is Redlitch writing a new book? Yes, he is just getting ready to—another book on witchcraft. But not in Mexico this time; right here.

"Here?" Gillian asks.

"In New York. *Witchcraft Around Us.* What do you think of *that* for a title?" Nicky and Gillian lead Redlitch on, and he tells them what he has learned for his new book. Right here, all around, there's a whole community devoted to just "that." Redlitch has met a couple of people through his Mexican book, and they have let him in on a few things. "You've no idea," he reveals. "They have their regular hangouts—cafés, bars, restaurants. Ever hear of a night club called the Zodiac?"

Shep remembers that Gillian has mentioned this place, and that Nicky has done a drawing of a dancer there. He points out the drawing on the wall, and the knowing Redlitch, after having looked at it, queries to all, "And I suppose it never occurred to you that she was one?" Nicky voices an incredulous "No!"

"Sure," says Redlitch, adding, "Ever look at the proprietor there?"

"Don't tell me he's a witch, too," Nicky scoffs, and the writer replies, "Well, when it's a man they're called warlocks." Nicky amusedly leads the man on, and Redlitch, full of inside information, tells the group what he has learned about local witches. One of their meeting places is in Harlem; another is in Greenwich Village, and sometimes they use a suite of offices in the Woolworth Building. "You'd be amazed what goes on right under your nose," he declares.

Shep asks what "they" look like. "Like anyone else. Like you—or you—or you," Redlitch answers, pointing to each in turn.

Gillian, joining in the game, asks, "You can recognize them?"

"Like a shot. . . . It's a something. A look. A feeling. . . . But if one were to walk in here right now, I'd know." Redlitch darkly declines to reveal the source of all his knowledge and says he won't be mentioning any names in his book. He has protection, but only up to a certain point—a woman, high up in the movement, is on his side. A Mrs. de . . .

"A Mrs. de Pass," Gillian suggests.

"That's the one," Redlitch agrees. "Matter of fact, I'm going up to her house a bit later."

Redlitch can't stop talking about witches. He volunteers, "I'll tell you another couple of things about them. Witches can't cry. Shed tears, I mean. Or blush. . . . And if you throw them in the water, they float. And they almost all have pets. They're called 'familiars.' You know—familiar spirits who have to carry out their master's bidding."

It's getting a little too warm for Gillian and she suggests that she and Shep leave—for Shep, as soon as he had finished the phone call with Merle, had suggested that he and Gillian go out and have some caviar and champagne together. But, first, Shep wants to sew up the new Redlitch book, so he makes a tentative luncheon date with the author. While these two are talking, Gillian has a quiet conference with her brother. She whispers, worriedly, "You know where Aunt Queenie was going tonight. . . . Stop it, can you?" With a nod toward Redlitch and Shep, she says, "I don't think *that's* a good idea."

Redlitch and Nicky leave the apartment together, at Redlitch's suggestion that they go to a place on Third Avenue called The Cloven Hoof. Shep, waiting to take Gillian out, is in a daze. "This has been the most extraordinary evening," he exclaims. "He seemed to think that *I* was one of them! . . . And now, if we're going to have our first meal together . . ."

Gillian goes for her wrap and Shep puts on his coat and muffler. Then he notices the carton of presents he has brought. He picks up a couple of wrapped gifts and looks at them. "What are you going to do with those?" Gillian asks when she returns from the bedroom, wearing an evening cloak. He says, indifferently, that he supposes he will have them sent around in the morning—and adds, "All these presents—and none for you."

"Give me one," she suggests. "Any one. Shut your eyes and dip. Go on."

Shep rootles in the carton with eyes closed, brings up a small package, looks at it, and exclaims, "How extraordinary!"

GILLIAN—Why—what is it? (*He hands it to her, without a word.*) What is it?

SHEP—Open it. It's a locket. Rather a revolting locket, really. I was giving it to someone—it has some significance or other.

GILLIAN (*stopping her unwrapping*)—Do you still want to give it to them?

SHEP—No. (*She unwraps the package. Inside is a small jeweler's box. She opens it and takes out an old-fashioned locket.*)

GILLIAN—It's beautiful. (*She holds it up.*)

SHEP—You think so, too? It belonged to my—damn it, why can't one say "my mother" without sounding sentimental? (*As she starts to open it.*) You can guess what's inside.

GILLIAN—You?

SHEP (*nodding*)—Aged . . . (*He holds his hand at eight-year-old height.*)

GILLIAN (*looking at it*)—I should have met you earlier.

SHEP (*half amused*)—You think so?

GILLIAN—Yes, I do.

SHEP—Shall I put it on for you?

GILLIAN—If you're really sure?

SHEP—I am. (*She turns and he fastens it around her neck.*)

GILLIAN (*with a little satisfied smile*)—Well, then—thank you. *Very* much.

SHEP (*taking her in his arms*)—Merry Christmas, my darling.

GILLIAN—Merry Christmas to you. (*They kiss.*) Shall we go?

SHEP—Sure. (*He goes to the door and opens it.* GILLIAN *turns out the lights in the room. The only light now comes from the hall outside, and from the glow of the fire, silhouetting them as they stand in the doorway.* SHEP *stands, looking back at the room.* GILLIAN *joins him.*)

GILLIAN—What are you looking at?

SHEP—This place. The place you happened to be in. This room.

GILLIAN—It's just an ordinary room.

SHEP—Not by a long shot. It may *look* like one, but . . . (*He shakes his head.*)

GILLIAN—Well, you'll see it again.

SHEP (*forcibly*)—You bet I will. (*She goes out ahead of him. He stands a moment longer, staring at the room. Then he shakes his head and shrugs his shoulders in complete bewilderment and disbelief, and follows her out.*)

The curtain falls.

ACT II

Two weeks have gone by. The Christmas decorations have been taken out of the apartment, but the Mexican mask which Redlitch was interested in is hanging prominently on the back wall. The time is the afternoon, and Gillian and Shep are coming in. Shep takes the latchkey from the door and puts it in his pocket—an obvious enough indication that he knows where he is going. Gillian is carrying a large box of candy and some letters. She puts the candy on the table in front of the sofa and starts looking at the letters, but Shep demands—and gets—a kiss. "You know something? You get better all the time," he assures her. "Two weeks ago tonight we met. And they've been magic weeks." Gillian agrees, "Enchanted!"

Going toward the kitchen to help Gillian make tea, Shep pauses to pick a pin off the rug and put it in his lapel. She examines the lapel and notes that he has four pins there. He lamely confesses it is sheer superstition and offers to throw them in the fire, but, quickly and unguardedly, she cries, "No! I'll take them." She carries her hat and coat to the bedroom, and he, on his way toward the kitchen again, pauses to look at the Mexican mask which is now hanging prominently on a wall. He teases her about professing to be superstitious, yet having this mask around after what Redlitch said about it.

Shep goes to the kitchen just as the telephone rings, and Gillian answers. It is her brother, who seems to want to meet Shepherd Henderson. Gillian puts him off, saying she is busy, but maybe she can arrange for Nicky to meet Shep some time next week. . . . No, she isn't going to Natalie's party tonight. She'd love to, but can't. Shep, bringing in the tea tray, says something and Gillian, hand over the phone, shushes him. "No, no, don't come over," she adjures Nicky, and hangs up. She won't tell Shep who called. He points out that they have spent all their time together and certain things have been neglected—a pile of manuscripts by his bed in his apartment, for instance, and no doubt Gillian has been neglecting lots of people. He suggests that she go to the party tonight, and maybe later he will join her there. Too quickly, she cries, "Oh, no!"

Out of the blue he asks, "When are we going to get married?" She stares at him in astonishment, saying, "I hadn't thought of marriage."

"Darling, that's the *man's* remark—usually." He tells her it is getting pretty bad—he has let everything slide, his business is shot to hell, his partner isn't speaking, his secretary glares at him. "I can't stay in the office for wanting to get to this place, and to you. When I get here, I can't wait to get close to you. And then I can never get close enough." Banteringly, she counters, "And how do you think marriage would cure that?"

She becomes distant, saying vaguely that she isn't cut out for marriage. She is torn by an inner conflict, for marrying would mean giving up her whole way of living. Shep goes back to the kitchen for boiling water and Gillian says to herself, "I wonder if I could. Suppose he found out afterward. That would be bad." And then, giggling, she adds, "And what would all the others say?" She seems to hear an answering chuckle from the mask and she warns it, "Don't look at me like that. I will if I want to."

And she does want to, so when Henderson comes back with the teapot she announces, "Shep, I will." He embraces her hungrily and begins planning. Perhaps he should buy this house and throw all the tenants out—but she would like to start somewhere afresh. He is a bit disturbed, for he never has been able to learn much about Gillian's past. All she will say is, vaguely, "My life's been sort of—raffish—at least, seen through your eyes. And I don't want to talk about it." Shep can't help being jealous of what he doesn't know—her childhood, all the things that have made her what she is; but she won't give. The past is past and now she wants to be different.

The buzzer sounds. It's Nicky calling up from down stairs. He is an unwelcome visitor, but they let him in, and the first thing he notices is the mask. "Is that the one Redlitch was talking about?" Nicky, the lazy playboy, throws a bombshell: he is working! He holds up an envelope, saying, "Sid's new book. Sid Redlitch. We've been at it night and day."

The unbelieving Gillian asks, "Did you say 'we'?"

"Yes, dear. *Witchcraft Around Us,* by Sidney Redlitch and Nicholas Holroyd. With illustrations by N. Holroyd."

Shep interrupts, "But—what do you know about that sort of thing?" Nicky blithely replies, "I know as much as he does."

Shep beamingly breaks the news that he and Gillian are going to get married, and Nicky takes the news lightly, almost casually. Suddenly Gillian declares she must talk to Nicky alone, and Henderson obligingly goes upstairs to his own apartment. Nicky gives him the manuscript of the first chapters of the magic book to read. When brother and sister are alone, brother comments, drily, "Well, well, well! Marriage, no less. . . . Between the two of us, he's going to have quite a time."

Nicky asks his sister for some professional help on the book—the manifestoes, for instance. He must have them right, for Sid is a stickler for accuracy. Gillian, in utter dismay, cries, "Nicky, you're not giving him the truth? . . . You don't mean he knows about *you?*"

"Of course."

In great alarm she asks, "You didn't tell him about *me?*"

"No, darling. I told him it was I who summoned him."

She is angry now as she reminds him it never pays to tell outsiders; but he says it is going to pay very well, for Shep has made a very generous offer for the book. "You can't publish that book," she cries.

"What harm can it do you? There are no names in it."

"Nicky," she pleads, "Shep doesn't know about me. And he's

not going to." Teasingly, he says, "I suppose you're going to tell me you're renouncing, too."

"I *have* renounced."

Now Nicky becomes serious, for evidently this marriage plan is on the level. He thinks it's crazy; she can't be in love. She insists she is, and begs him once again to stop the book. When he refuses, she declares, "Very well, then. I'll have to do something about it."

"You don't mean 'pull one'? I thought you'd retired."

"Yes, I have. But I'll make a farewell appearance, to stop this!"

"We've got people on our side, remember," he warns.

"Mrs. de Pass? Well, I'm better than that old battle-ax." Could be, he agrees, but Mrs. de Pass could take it up higher—could get the whole organization behind her. Gillian won't scare; she demands that Nicky bring her every copy of the manuscript or she will "go to work."

Both are angry now. Gillian flounces to the kitchen, carrying the tea tray. Nicky dials a number, gets a busy signal, is struck by an idea and begins speaking an incantation into the phone. His sister, returning, interrupts him and warns, "Nicky, I wouldn't do that, whatever it is." She is carrying the cat. Taking a chair, she strokes the animal and says, "Pye—Pye—Pyewacket, Eloas, Bejulet, Phidibus. I don't want that book to be published. Do you hear? Not by anyone."

This is war, and the angry Nicky declares, "You asked for it. I'm going to see that your little romance goes on the rocks, my girl. Shep's going to know all about you. And before the day is out, too."

When Shep returns, Gillian takes the cat into the kitchen and comes back. Shep says he has read the manuscript—and it's crazy. How could anybody imagine he'd fall for it? Apparently Aunt Queenie isn't the only practical joker in the family, for Nick must be one, too. "I've just been talking to Redlitch on the phone," Shep says, "and he said that Nicky had convinced him that he was one of them. I think that was going a little far." Shep is contemptuous of the story about the magic paint having summoned Redlitch, disbelieving of references to a Mrs. de Pass as a sort of Head Witch. "You'd better tell Redlitch the whole thing was a gag," he advises Nicky, "or the book will have to find another publisher."

Nicky replies, pointedly, for his sister's benefit, "I don't guess any other publisher would be any good—now." He departs gaily, leaving his sister wondering what he is up to. Gillian screws up her courage and after a couple of false starts blurts out, "Shep— I'm one. . . . I was one." At first he cannot fathom what she is talking about, so she must explain everything slowly and patiently.

She is one of those people Redlitch is writing about. She can work magic; for instance, she stopped the book being published.

Shep scoffs continually; stopping the book was *his* idea, not hers. Doggedly she goes on, explaining that she cast a spell by using Pyewacket, her familiar. She reminds him of the time when he came in just after she had set fire to the magically painted picture of Redlitch—that brought Redlitch, didn't it? And how about his coming here that time to borrow the phone? It was Nicky who put his telephone out of order.

"Coincidence," says Shep of the whole recital, but his disbelief begins to waver when she reminds him of the details of his attempted departure after he had made the phone call—how she was talking to the cat, and he was almost at the door . . . and suddenly she was in his arms. It was her doing, all of it, she insists, and finally Shep genially concedes, "I believe you cast an absolutely wonderful spell on me, and I'm crazy about it." He kisses her. A knock on the door, and Gillian admits Aunt Queenie, who is full of news. She has found a place where she can cook anything she wants —a kind of club. It's just around the corner from Mrs. de Pass.

Shep does a prodigious take at the mention of this name. Does this mean that Miss Holroyd, too, is—? Gillian nods, and explains to her aunt that she has told Shep everything. Pyewacket is yelling in the kitchen and Gillian goes to him; Shep, still the complete skeptic, lightly asks Miss Holroyd if the place she is moving into is a sort of Witches' Hostel. "Yes," the old lady agrees. "They have a communal kitchen we can all use for our brewing!" Aunt Queenie confides that she always knew she had something, but she thought it was artistic temperament and never would have become a witch if her parents had let her go on the stage. Even as a witch she isn't much, she says; Gillian is the one who's really talented.

SHEP—Miss Holroyd, you don't really believe that Gillian has any powers?

MISS HOLROYD—I know she has.

SHEP—Name me one thing she has ever done.

MISS HOLROYD—She's done wonderful things. Those thunderstorms. While she was in college on account of—(*Intimately.*)— you-know-who!

SHEP (*irritable*)—I have no idea who.

MISS HOLROYD—Your friend. Merle Kittredge.

SHEP—Oh, nonsense! Gillian has never heard of Merle Kittredge.

MISS HOLROYD—But, of course she has! I told her myself that you were getting married. That's why she went after you with Pye-wacket.

SHEP (*stopping and staring at her*)—I beg your pardon?

MISS HOLROYD—Oh, but I promise you she wouldn't have used magic, if she'd had time for the usual feminine methods. No matter how great enemies she and Miss Kittredge were.

SHEP—You mean—she went after me because of Merle?

MISS HOLROYD—Well—she thought you very attractive, already. You've no idea how much she likes you. Or, perhaps you have. . . .

SHEP—Miss Holroyd, what are you trying to say?

MISS HOLROYD—Well, Shep—with us, it's like the Saints.

SHEP—Saints?

MISS HOLROYD—Yes, only the other way around! At least, that's what the books say. Saints love everyone. Just everyone. With no thought of themselves. But with us, it's just the contrary.

SHEP—Look, maybe I'd better read some of those books of yours, after all.

MISS HOLROYD—Yes, Shep, then you'll see how impractical—well, how impossible, really—*love* is. Not sex. Sex is allowed. In fact, it's almost encouraged! But, of course, you must know that.

SHEP (*turning, angrily*)—Miss Holroyd . . .

MISS HOLROYD—Oh, no, Shep, can't I be Auntie now?

SHEP—Miss Holroyd, I don't think we had better go on with this.

MISS HOLROYD—Oh, dear, I haven't been too bold, have I? (GILLIAN *returns from the kitchen.*)

GILLIAN—Pyewacket is acting very strangely. I had to coax and coax him.

MISS HOLROYD—I must go, darling. I was late, even when I came. But I couldn't resist it. I just couldn't resist the urge.

GILLIAN (*with a sudden suspicion*)—Auntie, Nicky didn't send you, did he?

MISS HOLROYD (*vaguely and innocently*)—Nicky? No. I just passed Nicky on the street. He waved to me—rather a funny kind of wave, but . . . Darling, I must trot. Good-by. Good-by, Shep —*dear!* (*She goes out.*)

When Gillian returns from the kitchen, Shep is full of serious questions and serious suspicions. He hadn't known that Gillian was acquainted with Merle Kittredge. He wonders if Gillian is really in love with him—if she can *be* in love, even. He is angry and she is unhappy. When she puts a hand to her head he snarls, "And you needn't pretend to cry. Because you can't do that, either, if I remember rightly." He loudly denies that he believes this witchcraft nonsense, and cuttingly he asks, "Can you take off spells that you put on? . . . I'm getting the hell out of here!"

"No, no, you can't."

"Oh, yes, I can! I don't know how one deals with witches, but don't think, because you put a spell on me, that I'm coming back. Because I'm not. Ever."

He slams out of Gillian's apartment. "The spell! He'll have to come back," Gillian assures herself—and in a moment Shep bursts through the door, looking wild and bewildered. Then, after a moment of staring at her, he retreats slowly, as though fighting conflicting forces, crying "No! No!! No!!!" He manages to get out and slam the door again.

The curtain falls.

ACT III

Later in the night Gillian is sitting in the window seat staring into the street. The only light is from the street lamp, but it is enough to show that the Mexican mask is on the floor, broken in two. Nicky enters, silently, and makes his presence known by saying, gaily, "Ah, a dull moment around here!" He knows that Shep has walked out on her, for he has seen the publisher at Sid's place.

Gillian tells her brother she has been fighting the temptation to take the spell off Shep, so he might go back to Merle. That is why she broke the mask. But if she leaves things the way they are, she moans, Shep will still love her—and loathe her for it.

A knock on the door and Nicky opens it—to Shep, who says he has private conversation to make with Gillian. Nicky departs, agreeably, and Shep, most unfriendly, says he has come only because he was told he had to—by Mrs. de Pass. Redlitch has taken him to see this woman, and Shep has asked her to take the spell off—which she has done, with the help of a very dirty old parrot. So now he doesn't feel a thing, he informs Gillian, except goddamned mad. Mad at the whole business, and at himself for getting into it, and for paying Mrs. de Pass a lot of money. "The only reason that I came," he says, "was that she said the thing wouldn't be complete until I'd seen you and told you."

He starts to go, and with an effort Gillian asks, "What about Merle? . . . Are you going back to her?" Henderson announces that the only place he is going is to get a couple of stiff drinks and knock himself out. He bids her a firm and final good-by. Nicky, who has been waiting outside, comes back in and insinuatingly asks his sister if she is going to let Mrs. de Pass get away with this. "Come on back to us, where you belong," he urges. "Come to

Natalie's party with me."

Aunt Queenie taps on the door and is admitted. She says she has Redlitch with her—she met him at Mrs. de Pass'—and Redlitch wants to see Gillian about something important. He is afraid Gillian will blame him for what happened. The writer is allowed in. He is most conciliatory, seeking to explain that all he did was take Shep to Mrs. de Pass.

GILLIAN—And now you're afraid of the consequences.

REDLITCH—Well, only from you. I mean . . .

GILLIAN—Why don't you ask Mrs. de Pass to protect you, if you think so highly of her? I'm sure she wouldn't consider a little thing like rendering me impotent beyond her powers. Or you might go to the local minister and get me exorcised—with Bell, Book and Candle.

REDLITCH—Now listen, don't get mad. I haven't done anything, except what I was asked to do!

GILLIAN—Suppose you'd been asked to commit a murder. Or introduce someone to a murderer, who'd do the job for the sum of . . . Yes, what does she charge for a little chore like this?

MISS HOLROYD—Well, she varies her prices, dear. According to people's means. She asked me about Shep . . .

GILLIAN—And what did you tell her?

MISS HOLROYD—I told her I thought he was quite well off. You see, I'd seen his bank book, and letters from his broker . . .

NICKY—What did that set him back?

MISS HOLROYD—She said she was going to ask five thousand dollars.

GILLIAN—*What?*

MISS HOLROYD—Well, I thought it was a little high, but she did point out that—supposing you and he had been married, it would cost him a lot more than that to get divorced. . . .

GILLIAN—Another pretty comparison.

REDLITCH—Look, Miss Holroyd, I don't want to intrude on you in your—hour of grief, but—put yourself in my place.

GILLIAN—I'd rather not, Mr. Redlitch. But don't worry, I won't do anything to *you.*

REDLITCH—Gee, that's swell of you, Miss Holroyd. Thank you, thank you. And—just one thing more. About the book. Nicky said you'd sort of—put a stopper on it. . . .

GILLIAN—Yes, I did.

REDLITCH—Well, don't you think—I mean, now that Shep's not— don't you think you might—I mean—well, sort of release it?

(*Hastily.*) Oh, I don't mean right now—naturally. But some time when you've nothing else on your mind. . . . If you could just flip that off . . .

GILLIAN (*breaking in*)—Mr. Redlitch, don't you think from now on that you'd better stay clear of this kind of thing? I don't think you've got the temperament for it. Or the nerve, apparently.

REDLITCH—Maybe you're right. I only meant . . .

GILLIAN—Mr. Redlitch—*go away!*

The writer flees. Nicky asks his sister if she feels, now, like coming to Natalie's party and she answers, "Maybe, but I've got a little job to do here first."

"Old Bianca?"

Gillian nods grimly. She is in a vengeful fury. "She's got a lot of valuable Chinese rugs, you once told me. And that mink coat! Well, we'll start with some *moths!*" And Merle won't be getting Shep back, either. Gillian opens the kitchen door and calls for Pyewacket—but the cat isn't in the apartment. Still in a passion of vengeance, Gillian unlocks a closet and sorts over a number of bottles hidden there. She finds what she is looking for and says, musingly, "Now, what have we got of theirs?" Since there doesn't seem to be anything, Gillian decides that merely writing the names of Mrs. de Pass and Merle Kittredge will do. She writes the names on separate sheets of paper, then commands Nicky to turn out the lights. Crumpling the papers in a big ash tray, she sprinkles them with a pinch of herbs from a bottle, muttering, "Zaitux, Aorami, Elastot." She strikes a match to set fire to them, but the match sputters and goes out. A second match does the same. The papers just won't burn—not even when she tosses on a whole lighted book of matches.

Suddenly Gillian switches on the lights and announces that she will not go through with her spell. She has changed her mind. But Nicky senses what has happened: she has been "defrosted." "So it's true, after all?" he declares. "The old wives' tales are true." He goes on to Natalie's party, and Aunt Queenie asks her niece if it *is* true—if she really has lost her powers.

"I guess so," says the dejected Gillian. "I guess I'm through. Through as a witch, anyway." She bursts into tears and her aunt exclaims, "Oh, darling! Tears. Real tears."

"Yes," sobs Gillian. "And to think I've always envied people who *could* cry! It feels horrible!"

The curtain falls.

Scene II

Two months have gone by, and much has changed. All objects savoring of witchcraft have been removed from the apartment. Gillian has found a job, seeing movies and writing reports on them. Nicky and Aunt Queenie are in the apartment, waiting for Gillian to come home. When she arrives, she and her brother have some pleasant, if rather distant, chat. Gillian reveals that Pyewacket has run away and Nicky observes, "Nothing for him to do around here any more? . . . You know, Gill, you *look* different. . . ." When he leaves, Gillian turns to her aunt and, with sudden intensity, says, "Shep's upstairs! I saw him at his window. . . . I'm afraid he may have seen me."

Gillian has been thankful that Shep has not been in the house the last two months, and now, just feeling that he is up there is more than she can stand. There is a knock on the door, and Gillian knows it must be Shep. She begs her aunt not to leave her, and opens the door. Henderson is carrying a suitcase. "Are you busy," he asks, "or could I see you for a moment?" Gillian lets him in— and Aunt Queenie double-crosses her by inventing a dinner engagement and leaving suddenly.

"This isn't a friendly visit," Shep announces. He is leaving for Europe and has come to get some things he needs—because he discovers that the apartment is still his. He has told his secretary to move him out and sublet the place—but there has been no sublet. Obviously, Gillian must have "fixed" it that way—trying to hold him here out of sheer vindictiveness.

Gillian angrily tells him that nothing of the sort has happened. If he'd take the trouble to look at his lease, he would find that the owner of the building specifies that Gillian, the tenant of the house, may not allow any subleases. "I don't want you in this house," she shouts. "I'd rather you were out of it. And I'll make that clear by canceling your lease, if that will suit you!"

It suits Shep fine. He would, if he might, like to use the phone and tell his secretary about the arrangement. He makes the call and explains that the lease is being canceled. Since he won't be in the office in the morning, he would like to have the secretary move him out. He will leave the key with Gillian.

The call over, he says to Gillian that he must owe her some money —three months' rent, anyway; but she won't take it, saying, "I owe you far more than that."

"What do you owe me?"

"Well—well, five thousand dollars, anyway, that Mrs. de Pass charged you. That was outrageous." Gillian asks how Merle is, and his answer is so vague she pursues her inquiry and learns that Shep did go back to Merle, but has left her. Something happened, he says, still vague.

"It wasn't—a letter? An anonymous letter, was it?"

Shep is surprised, for Gillian has hit the nail on the head. When he was going with Gillian, Merle had written a letter to his partner —which was why the partner wasn't speaking. "I'm sorry," says Gillian, genuinely.

Shep says the same thing Nicky did—"You look different. . . . There is something different about this place, too. . . ." Gillian, eager to end the interview, says, "Look, please, you don't have to stay and be polite." He moves to go, then remembers to give her his apartment key. This reminds her of something else: she goes to the bedroom and brings a locket Shep had given her, and he accepts it very reluctantly. "Now I think I'd like you to go," she announces—but he stands looking at her, saying she looks like someone who is completely new and strange instead of the person he has known so intimately. Gillian turns her back and urges, "Do you mind going?"

Shep goes to her, turns her around, looks at her averted face and exclaims, "Gill—you're not blushing!" She struggles to keep her head turned away. "You're crying, too," he notices.

She admits, angrily, "All right, then, I'm crying!"

"But I thought . . ."

"You thought we couldn't—didn't you? Well, you were wrong."

Shep slowly asks, "Are you quite sure of that? Tell me—are you —not one, any more? Is it that? Is it? I've got to know."

Gillian, turning violently toward him, admits she has lost her powers—and now will he please leave her alone? "What's the point in going on at me like this?" she cries.

"Because," he says slowly, "something has been happening since I came into this room. I want to be sure that it's the real thing— this time." She knows what he means, and her face shines with incredulous rapture. He smiles and says, "I *will* go now. And maybe I won't go to Europe—just yet." Teasingly he asks, "I suppose you have got some idea of what I'm talking about?"

"I—think so. It's been happening to me, too—for—such a long time."

"It has?"

In a small voice Gillian declares, "I'm only human." They are in each other's arms.

CURTAIN

THE COUNTRY GIRL *

A Play in Two Acts

By Clifford Odets

WHEN Clifford Odets burst upon the theatrical scene with one long play and two short ones in the season of 1934-1935, he was hailed as a dramatist of vigor and social consciousness. These plays —"Awake and Sing," "Waiting for Lefty" and "Till the Day I Die" —were dramas of protest. So were "Golden Boy" in 1937-1938 and "Rocket to the Moon" in 1938-1939. So was "The Big Knife" in 1948-1949. In these dramas society, or some part of society, was the antagonist. In "Golden Boy" a young man who wanted to become a great musician was forced, because he had to earn a living and he could earn a good one this way, to become a prize fighter. In "The Big Knife" a movie star who wanted to break away from Hollywood was detained by the political and financial power of a studio which used blackmail and blackjack methods with unabashed criminality. In his newest drama, "The Country Girl," Odets has found a new antagonist for his central character—the man himself. This play shows a new depth in the author's work, for he has approached his three principal characters from within themselves; the externals of society—in this case, the society of the theatrical world, which Odets knows intimately—have little to do with the events of the play.

It is a backstage drama and it begins upon a stage—not the glamorous platform of a performance, but a bare and gloomy cavern illuminated only by a pilot light and a strip. Some chairs are strewn about in an order which indicates the demarcation of a set, and at the left there is a work table. The people there include Bernie Dodd, a director; Paul Unger, a playwright; Phil Cook, a producer, and Larry, a stage manager. It is morning; a play has been in rehearsal, and now some kind of crisis has risen. The actors are waiting offstage or in dressing rooms until Bernie Dodd tells Larry to let them go, but to warn them to stand by for a possible

* Copyright 1949, 1951, by Clifford Odets. Published by the Viking Press, Inc., New York. Author's agent, Harold Freedman, 101 Park Avenue, New York City.

178

seven o'clock call for tonight. All but Frank Elgin, that is. The director wants Elgin to come in.

Bernie Dodd is 35; small, wiry and energetic. Normally his manner is friendly, but when he is at work he is given to fretting and prowling. His face is saturnine and impassive—a protective mask he has put on to make himself what a good director should be: objective and impersonal. An actor should be a tool, a piece of machinery—and now Bernie wants to fit Frank Elgin into the machinery. Frank is 50, and seedy; but his seediness does not hide a certain distinction of personality. He is nervous now, but he deports himself like the important actor he used to be.

"Frank," says Bernie, "I want you to do something for me. Not so much for me as for our producer and Mr. Unger, the author. Read the part of Judge Murray for them." Frank realizes what has happened. He is in the company as general understudy, but now, early in rehearsals, the leading actor has left and he is going to be tested for the job. Instead of being eager he is hesitant, and this hesitancy seems to annoy Cook, the producer of the play. Larry hands Frank a script and Bernie, taking another, starts to cue him in on the scene he wants read. Trying to hide his agitation, Frank paces, looking upward for the best reading light.

FRANK—"I didn't ask you to sit down . . . because I don't want a louse on my furniture." That it?

BERNIE—Yes. (*Continuing in the play.*) "I don't think this furniture will be yours much longer, Judge Murray!"

FRANK—"And I think I'll have to ask for an explanation of this big-mouth attitude. You damn Reform Party kids come and go like a ten-cent piece of ice. Now get out before I kick you out! You only got in here because you know Ellen!"

BERNIE—"I resent that!"

FRANK—"Not as much as I—" (*He moves nervously under the lights.*) What is that? I can't make it out. (*Then:*) Oh! "Not as much as I resent you, you little Wop bastard!"

BERNIE—"I'm not letting you put this discussion on any personal plane! There's too much at stake!"

FRANK (*as* BERNIE *begins to read the same line*)—"I represent the collective will of thousands of our best—"

BERNIE—No, that's my line, Frank.

FRANK (*lamely*)—Well, it's in this part. I can't see what I'm reading. I mean the light—I mean—Hertz is got the whole part penciled up.

BERNIE (*urgently*)—Go on, don't stop.

FRANK—I can't. I'm sorry. I'm saying, "Hands, behave!" but they're shaking like a leaf.

BERNIE—Start right from where we left off. (FRANK *looks at* BERNIE *and* COOK *from under his eyebrows, not lifting his head; then he drops his eyes and slowly shakes his head.*) What's the matter?

FRANK—It won't do, Mr. Dodd. I always was a dead buñny when it came to sight reading. Thanks for the chance, but it won't do. (*He walks to a table with bitter dignity and puts the part down.* COOK *enjoys this part of the scene.* BERNIE *is annoyed.*)

BERNIE (*to* UNGER)—Give him a clean script, Paul.

FRANK (*unhappily*)—What's the use? You've been very nice, Dodd. You looked me up before—gave me the general understudy —I appreciate what you did, but—

BERNIE (*abruptly calling offstage*)—Dammit, I want that door shut and stay shut! (*He throws the script to the table and turns.*) I can't be that wrong, Frank—I know an actor when I see one! Let's forget the damn script! Let's improvise the scene! Just the situation—not the author's scene!

FRANK—How do you mean?

BERNIE—Ad lib, just ad lib it. Improvise it. Look at me! I'm a fresh kid—I wanna marry your grandchild and you don't want me to. That's the situation. (*He begins to pace, waving the others aside. Soon he is pacing around* FRANK, *like a bull fighter around a helpless animal, which is the impression* FRANK *gives for the moment. Then, angrily:*) "I don't leave this house until I get your answer. Don't call in any servants or I'll knock them all on their ears!"

FRANK (*slowly*)—"What . . . do you want?"

BERNIE—"I want to marry your grandchild and you don't want me to!"

FRANK—"Why should I let you marry my grandchild?" (*Anxiously.*) Right? (*Then:*) "Who the hell are you to come busting in this house like a hurricane?"

BERNIE—"You don't answer phones, so I'm here in person!" (*They are gradually slipping into a really dramatic scene,* FRANK *standing stock-still until, in a moment, he begins to follow* BERNIE *wherever he moves; shortly they begin banging on the table.*)

FRANK—"I usually make up my own mind when and when not to answer the phone. As far as Ellen's concerned, as far as she's concerned—you can go to hell!"

BERNIE—"You won't talk to me that way again!"

FRANK—"I'll talk to you that way again and again and again!"
Is that what you want? (*Suddenly choleric.*) "Now get out before
I open your head with a poker!"

BERNIE—"We have to have a talk, a long talk, Frank."

FRANK (*dropping his voice*)—"I'll talk, I'll talk to you, son.
Let's see what's really on your mind."

BERNIE (*tauntingly*)—"I don't think you can stop me, Frank!"

FRANK (*scornfully*)—"Oh, I'll stop you! I'll stop you, Dodd, if
it's the last thing I do! Don't underestimate me. I haven't begun
to fight yet. And—"

BERNIE—"I'm sorry for you! By next week you'll be front-
page news!"

FRANK (*angrily*)—"Wait a minute, wait a minute! What the
devil are you talking about? Explain this thing to me!"

BERNIE—"I'm head of the Citizens' Non-Partisan Committee,
too." (FRANK, *really acting now, looks at him incredulously and
then abruptly bursts into laughter. He breaks that up with a fit of
coughing.*)

FRANK—"Did you ever tell that to Ellen?"

BERNIE—"I'm telling her tonight."

FRANK (*chortling*)—"Well, boy, that's just what I want you to
do! God Almighty, I want you to tell her your plans! I want to
be behind a door when you tell her your plans!"

BERNIE (*quickly*)—That's it, Frank! Now change the color.
You've lost everything. Where is Ellen—you haven't seen her for
two days—she's deserted you.

FRANK (*changing to a pensive thoughtfulness*)—"Ellen? Where's
Ellen? Haven't seen her for two days . . ." (*He has seated himself, but now he slowly stands, shakes his head, shows worry and
nervousness for the first time.*) "Is . . . my daughter in the
house?" (*He turns and moves around like an old man.*) "I have
the greatest confidence in her!" (*Scornfully.*) "Now I think I
asked you to get out of here about a long moment ago!" (*The two
men are standing, facing each other. Now, after a pause, BERNIE
drops out of the scene.*)

BERNIE (*admiringly*)—That's it, Frank! That's the way you
used to go! (*But FRANK, as BERNIE glances triumphantly at COOK
and UNGER, continues the scene with strength and bitterness, fling-
ing his overcoat in BERNIE's face.*)

FRANK—"Now get out of here! Don't look at me that way. Nobody wants your pity or your help. It's no satisfaction in a cold
world to have your colder pity! Werba was a great man in his day

—that's what all the loafers are saying. Werba made his millions, but the boy wonder is living with his in-laws now, they say! And now you come here and tell me, 'Mr. Werba, you're going to prison within the month.' Well, let me tell you—Werba won't give up his name and take a number! Werba is still a great man! He tore an empire out of the world before he was thirty and he'll live to do it again! And when that time comes—you listen to this!—I won't forget my enemies or my friends. I will never forget those who dragged me down!" (FRANK *has been talking directly front to* BERNIE, *who has seated himself at the table, his back to the theatre. Now* FRANK *sighs deeply, breaking a strange spell of majesty.*)

BERNIE—That was the last speech of *Werba's Millions,* wasn't it?

FRANK—Yes . . . (*Standing, he rubs his hands and shakes his head, as if he were dizzy. He gives the impression of slowly waking into a colder, shabbier world.*) It came back to me . . .

BERNIE (*glancing briefly at the others, gently to* FRANK)—Frank, would you wait outside for me? Two minutes, in one of the dressing rooms, please.

Bernie, repressing his own satisfaction, asks the others what they think. Unger, the author, has great enthusiasm and speaks of the power and majesty of a seedy-looking guy. But producer Cook is cynical; five minutes of reading don't make an entire performance in a $70,000 play—and he remembers that Frank has been "laying in pickle" for ten years. But Bernie is all for engaging Frank; he remembers other lushes who have made great theatrical comebacks and he is ready to take on this one in the emergency. And it is an emergency. The play is booked to open its tryout in Boston in three weeks and two days, and even Cook admits a postponement is impossible. Cook grudgingly gives in, but insists that Frank Elgin be given only a two weeks' deal and not a run-of-the-play contract. Excited and enthusiastic, the young director calls offstage for the actor he has fought for. But the actor has not waited as he said he would; he has left the theatre.

The curtain falls.

SCENE II

Nor is Frank Elgin home at this moment; only his wife is—and Georgie Elgin is suffering from a toothache and is packing a suitcase to leave home. "Home" is a shabby furnished room west of Eighth Avenue, so badly lighted by a small and viewless window that a lamp is turned on, even though it is noon. The room contains an iron bedstead, a chest, a wardrobe, a chair or two and a small radio, and in a little alcove is a kitchenette.

When she hears a knock on the door, Georgie turns off the radio, stuffs a dress into the suitcase and pushes the case under the bed. Then she opens the door, and it is Bernie Dodd looking for Frank.

"You don't look like one of Frank's friends," says Georgie, and he explains he is the director of the play Frank is working in. He asks, "Does Frank usually come right home?"

"Unless he sits out on the brownstone stoop. . . . Is something wrong?"

Bernie counters by asking if Frank still drinks and she evades the question; Bernie is beginning to annoy her and she says so— but before she says much her husband arrives and uneasily greets the visitor. "I asked you to wait. I'm a busy man," Bernie snaps, and Frank explains to his puzzled wife that Mr. Dodd wants him to play the lead in his play. Briskly and in an annoyed tone, Bernie explains that it is a starring part that needs an actor who can stay sober and learn lines. "Are you that actor or not?" he demands.

Frank has a flare of pride as he exclaims, "I'm an actor! . . . I don't drink on a show."

But Bernie has done some checking. How about that play in 1944? Frank looks at Georgie before answering, "We lost our little daughter . . . that year." His courage ebbs; he couldn't learn his lines in time for the Boston opening. . . .

Bernie will not give up. When he was a kid he saw Frank Elgin give two great performances in two mediocre plays, one of which was "Werba's Millions," and he is confident he can get the same show out of Frank right now—if he lays off the liquor. Georgie is becoming interested in this dynamic stranger; why is he so sure of what he can do with her husband? To her query Bernie replies, "I come from realistic people—I'm Italian. I'm not blind to Frank's condition—he's a bum! But I'm tough, not one of those nice 'humane' people; they hand you a drink and a buck and that's exactly where they stop." And to Frank he says, "I won't hand you a buck, but I'll think about you, if you take this job. I'll commit myself to you—we'll work and worry together—it's a marriage! And I'll make you work. I'll be your will!"

Georgie likes that—being her husband's will. Perhaps Frank should take the job, even if it isn't run-of-the-play; but her husband still is hesitant, not wanting to bite off more than he can chew. Not until Bernie promises that the play can stay on the road after the Boston engagement until Frank is letter-perfect does the actor's enthusiasm begin to rise. With an acute sense of the right moment at which to leave, Bernie departs—and on his way out leaves a $20 bill on the radio. Georgie queries, "Is that boy as talented as he throws himself around?"

FRANK (*moodily*)—Best average in both the leagues.

GEORGIE—He's willful, but he meant what he said.

FRANK (*turning aside*)—I can't do it, can I?

GEORGIE—Doesn't it seem strange for you to ask me that?

FRANK (*unhappily*)—You're my wife.

GEORGIE (*quietly*)—Frank, we've been through all this before, many times before. I'm tired, Frank.

FRANK (*brooding, not looking at her*)—What happened? Where did I get so bolloxed up? I was the best young leading man in this business, not a slouch!

GEORGIE—Scripts didn't come . . .

FRANK—I knew it then—on the coast—I lost my nerve! And then, when we lost the money, in '39, after those lousy Federal Theatre jobs—! (*He pauses and shakes his head.*) This is the face that once turned down radio work. (*He paces.*) Whatever the hell I did, I don't know what! (*Abruptly defiant, he stops behind her.*) But I'm good! I'm still good, baby, because I see what *they think* is good! (*He waits, but she is silent.*) Don't you think I'm good? *I* think I'm good!

GEORGIE (*quietly*)—Then take the part. Make it your own responsibility, not mine. Take the part. (*He looks at her. It is plain that the idea frightens him.*) Don't wiggle and caper, Frank. (*Suddenly.*) Can't you admit to yourself you're a failure? You'd die to save your face, not to fail in public—but I'm your wife: you have no face. Try to be clear about this offer—think.

FRANK—I didn't hear him say he'd star me.

GEORGIE (*with dry weariness*)—I have a message for you, Frank: take the part!

FRANK—Yes, but what will *you* do if I—?

GEORGIE (*firmly*)—Leave me out. Take the part and do your level best. (*She slowly rubs a hand against her aching jaw.*)

FRANK (*uneasily*)—But what about that two weeks' clause? You yourself tried—

GEORGIE—All I tried was to get a better deal. But you won't get perfect terms.

FRANK—You certainly gave him a scrap! (*Abruptly excited and cunning.*) Georgie, I'll tell you! That two weeks' clause—they can give me notice any time, but *I* can give *them* notice, too! (GEORGIE *looks questioning.*) Don't you see? They can let me out, but *I* can walk out any time I want! If I feel I'm breaking my neck—

GEORGIE—You can quit?

FRANK—Yeah, that's sort of what I mean, yeah. (*Bright and shrewd.*) You see? Get it?

GEORGIE (*dubious and waiting*)—Yes . . .

FRANK (*cunningly grand*)—Why, with this two weeks' clause I don't even have to come into New York, do I? (GEORGIE *murmurs a "No" as* FRANK *seats himself, chortling.*) That's the thing, that's it—two can play the same game! (*Delighted at this discovery,* GEORGIE *much less so,* FRANK *abruptly snaps his fingers and lights up even more.*) Wait a minute! Quarter to seven this morning I had a dream! I laughed so hard it woke me up! That's a sign, Georgie, a hunch!

GEORGIE (*puzzled*)—A dream?

FRANK (*seeing it*)—A big sign—now get this—a big banner was stretched across the street: "Frank Elgin in . . ." I couldn't make out in what. Mayor La Guardia was in the dream—lots of people laughing and feeling good. I'm going to take that part, Georgie! You don't have to tell me not to drink—haven't I been a good boy all summer? (*He moves around.*) This morning I got up early—that funny laughing dream. And I was thinking about our lives—everything—and now this chance! Don't you see that all those people in the dream, they wish me luck. I won't fail this time! Because that's what counts—if the world is with you—and your wife! (*He looks at her, earnest, boyish, and questioning, appealing for her support.*)

GEORGIE (*finally, with reluctance*)—I don't have any appointments . . . all winter . . .

FRANK (*excitedly*)—That's what counts! I can't fail this time—I feel like Jack-a-Million! I'll let Dodd know—I'll go up to the office in person. (*He takes the twenty-dollar bill.*) But my first stop is the barbershop—I want the tonsorial works. Anything you want me to bring *you* back?

GEORGIE—No . . .

FRANK—Catch that, dear! (*He throws her an extravagant kiss, really excited, and she catches the gift with an open hand. Alone, thinking, we see how unhappy* GEORGIE *is. Then she remembers her suitcase; she takes it from under the bed, opens it, and unhappily looks down at its contents. Then, murmuring, "My God, my*

God, my God . . ." she takes out a dress, goes back to the ward-
robe, and replaces it on a hanger.)

The curtain falls.

SCENE III

Rehearsals have continued for ten days; now, tonight, Bernie
sits at one side, watching, and Larry, the stage manager, is at the
work table intent upon the script as Frank Elgin rehearses a scene
with the ingenue. The stage seems remote from any other place in
the world—remote, even, from the dimly seen audience seats which
look upon it. The ingenue, Nancy Stoddard, is an interesting girl.
She looks as she should: virginal. She can't be much of an actress
yet, for she is only seventeen; but the talent is there—and she
already is letter-perfect in her lines. This is not so with Frank;
he is working well, as old muscles come slowly to life, but one can
sense in his manner that he is worried about being unable to memo-
rize his lines, and he keeps his part rolled in his hand. In his part
Frank, with an Irish flavor in his voice, is calling Nancy his grand-
daughter and asking her what she likes in some boy she is interested
in. Bernie counsels him, "Play it suspicious." Frank reaches for
his next line, fails to get it and asks the stage manager to throw it
to him. In another moment he forgets another line, and before
Larry can supply it young Nancy does, automatically. She knows
the whole play. Frank, who feels a headache building, continues
in his role, saying to Nancy, "You said when you'd grow big I'd
grow small. Children have that delusion, don't they?" Then, to his
director, "That's tricky . . . What does he mean?"
Bernie counsels, "Show that he's trying to win her over to his
side." "But," Frank objects, "he isn't the kind who would *openly*
ask for sympathy," and Bernie explains, "But this is his only
grandchild—his defenses are down." This is a moment in the
theatre that audiences do not see or know—an actor and a director
trying, through patient, intelligent discussion, to get inside a character and make that character grow into a living being. Timidly,
the girl gets into the discussion. "Do *I* know that he wants sympathy?" she queries. Plays are made like that—at these lonely
rehearsals which are sometimes patient, other times stormy. Bernie,
noting that his wrist watch says it is almost 11 o'clock, decides it is
time to send Nancy home to bed. Over the girl's eager protestations
he rules, "Our little ingenue needs her beauty rest"—and the scene
breaks up. With Nancy gone, Bernie turns his attention to the
stage manager. "Larryola, you don't have to hang around." Larry

does his final bit of housekeeping for the night, dragging out a pilot light—a bare 200-watt bulb on a short iron stand. As he is about to leave, Bernie asks him, "Come back if that little man is outside." To Frank he explains that he is ducking a man with a summons. "My wife wants money." And thus Frank learns that Bernie, who hadn't struck him as the type, has been married, is the father of a little girl, and is divorced. Bernie shows a flash of real loneliness, but briskly pulls himself together and gets back to the character. "How do *you* feel the judge?" he asks Elgin.

The actor becomes intent, seeing and feeling something inwardly. The judge would be a fox . . . nimble and quiet, nothing showing, a concrete slab for a face . . .

"That's power," Bernie prompts.

Frank's own face has narrowed with thought and he begins to illustrate his words; a strut comes into his walk. The character of the judge grows as he thinks and talks. Now Frank knows he can play him, and an exultant power comes upon him. As the judge might do, he sends a chair skimming across the stage with a vicious kick. "That's it!" Bernie exclaims admiringly, and Frank, now in full pursuit of his role, explains, "But I have to like him, Bernie, even when he puts his wife away. Otherwise I can't get inside him."

Bernie is aglow. This is the actor he had banked on—not a technical actor, but one who works from the inside. The two men fall silent, smoke for a moment, then start putting on their coats. It's all for tonight—but, no matter how good it has been, and no matter that Frank has forgotten his headache—those lines still worry Frank and he says so.

BERNIE—Don't answer if you don't want to—how did a man with your talents go so haywire?

FRANK (*evasively*)—That's a bow-wow with a very long tail.

BERNIE—What kind of woman is your wife? Just for chatter's sake . . .

FRANK—Georgie's got a very good mind.

BERNIE—Then why didn't she want you to play this part?

FRANK—Was that your impression?

BERNIE—A yard wide!

FRANK (*evasively*)—I don't know—she's on a hairspring, Georgie. Always has been—a hairspring. (*He leafs nervously through his part.*) Sorry I don't know the words yet, Bernie. I wanted to surprise you tonight, but non compos mentis.

BERNIE—The sooner you get that second act out of your hands, the better. Why on a hairspring?

FRANK (*uneasily*)—It's like the hospital scene in the play. Where they tell the judge his wife is—psychotic? What's the exact meaning of the word?

BERNIE—Insane . . .

FRANK (*looking at his part, his voice low*)—The judge, you see . . . isn't glad to get rid of his wife, the way the author says. It's very complicated. (*He clears his throat.*) You tell an unhappily married man his wife is insane. He may feel relief, but at the same time he hopes it isn't true.

BERNIE (*watching him keenly*)—That makes a richer scene.

FRANK—You can even say it's tender when he gets the news. There's so much to remember of living together—all the Winters and Summers, the times they were poor . . . (*His voice trembles.*) And the fights, snarling and yipping—settling blue murder with an hour in the bed . . .

BERNIE (*keenly*)—Yes, if you played the scene that way . . .

FRANK—I'm not talking about the scene.

BERNIE—You're not?

FRANK (*fingering his part*)—Georgie . . . was "Miss America" in the late '30s, the year I met her. She gave up a big career to marry me.

BERNIE (*delicately*)—Is that according to Luke or Mark? You or her?

FRANK (*turning*)—Don't you believe me?

BERNIE—Sure, but what the hell is "Miss America" past twenty-five or thirty? What career? Marriage doesn't suit women any more—they don't want a home: the only piece of furniture they'll touch is the psychoanalyst's couch!

FRANK (*solemnly*)—It cost me thousands . . .

BERNIE (*bitterly*)—I had it for five years with the former Mrs. Dodd.

FRANK—I bought a fourteen-room house down in Great Neck the year we married. Never knew a better life. Swimming, boating, tennis, dinner at six—at seven she'd kiss me good-by and I'd drive into town for my show. On matinee days she'd come in and we'd stay out late. Little spats and things, but it looked like a dream life to me. And then one night, from way out left field—don't know what hit me—I find her dead drunk across a bed—a kid who never took a real drink in her life! I didn't catch on that year—who could figure *that?* Career versus career—she didn't want me to play! Bernie, she was a hopeless drunkard inside a

year. Then we had a child . . . (*Moved, he pauses.*) After that
. . . every part I play, it's just like I ran off with another woman.
I begin to drink myself. Don't ask me where the money went.
She cuts her wrists, sets fire to a hotel suite—any time I'm on the
stage she needs a nurse to watch her. And then, finally, we lost
the child. You don't say, "Go to hell, good-by!" do you? By
1940, '41—well, when you're in that situation you beat a bottle
hard! (*There is a hushed pause.* BERNIE *pulls at an ear.*)

BERNIE—Does she still drink?

FRANK (*smiling ruefully and standing*)—She stopped when I began. But I know how to handle her now—backwards, like a crab.
About this part—to give you an instance—I had to make believe
I didn't want this part. That leaves it open for *her* to convince
me, her idea, not mine, see? (*Both men are standing.* BERNIE,
with a soft exclamation, gathers up his things on the table.)

BERNIE—I guess you have to bring her up to Boston. I'm not
against it. *My* wife was so twisted, "I hope your next play's a
big flop!" she says. "So the whole world can see I love you even
if you're a failure!" (*He turns.*) As far as the work's concerned,
I'm very pleased.

At this Frank, too, is pleased, almost boyishly so. Then Bernie
shoots a query—can Frank's wife louse him up in this show? Frank,
on top, reassures him. He can handle Georgie—and now he offers
some advice to his director: "You're a hot, gifted guy who got
somewhere in a hurry. But you might be surprised in another ten
years what you'll do for a little companionship."

Bernie flatly asserts, "No one now living, under or over the earth,
will ever again put me on a tether! I go wild when—" He stops
abruptly, looking over Frank's shoulder. Mrs. Elgin has suddenly
appeared . . . and there is no way of telling from her reserved,
pleasant manner how much she may have heard. She may have
been there, near the stage door, for a long time, or she may just
have come. She allows them to believe she has just come from a
movie, was passing by and thought they might be through by now.
Bernie says her timing was perfect. They are sure she didn't intrude? No, they tell her, they were just going; but she persists
that she doesn't like to make herself obtrusive when her husband
is working—unless he needs help, of course.

Bernie has been taking her measure. "No," he says, "we were
just closing up shop and giving it back to the theatre ghosts."
Georgie smiles vaguely, steps to the footlights and looks out at the
house, her faint smile seeming both polite and deprecating. Her air

of breeding never leaves her. Softly she says, "Nothing is quite so mysterious and silent as a dark theatre . . . a night without a star. . . ."

Bernie suggests they go get some coffee and Georgie archly agrees. "I'd like to get to know Mr. Dodd better." "And I'd like to get to know you better," Bernie Dodd admits. They go for their coffee.

The curtain falls.

Scene IV

It is early morning in the Elgins' room, a week later. Frank, in high humor, is dressing, and Georgie, in a wrapper, pours coffee at a little folding table. Frank, as he finishes shaving and shakes out a clean shirt, keeps up a boyish running comment about the good things he's going to have, like shaving lotion. In a lull Georgie says, mostly to herself, "Let's see, where would I be if I were a pair of glasses?" She is very nearsighted and, without her glasses, probably would not be able to find her glasses. Frank spots them, gives them to her and chortles, "See? You couldn't get along without me, Georgiana."

His wife smilingly comments that somebody is feeling pretty good today—and then she stops; she has kicked over two empty beer bottles on the floor. Fending off her serious glance, Frank says, "Didn't hide them, did I? Those two bottles of beer gave me a good night's sleep." He explains he got them after she had gone to sleep, when he went out for the morning papers.

Georgie regards her husband most thoughtfully and asks if he is worried about anything. Not a thing, he assures her—except maybe the lines. Frank is keyed up about the impending Boston opening—ah, those fluffy bath towels in a good hotel, the oysters, the lobsters! The critics, even. Dressed at last, Frank sips his coffee and looks at the baseball news in a paper. Georgie interrupts with an odd query, "Does Bernie Dodd like me?" Over-casually careful, he replies, "Why shouldn't the boy like you?"

"Seems to be a chip on his shoulder." She doesn't mind if Bernie doesn't care for her; she just wants to face it. Frank tries to kid her out of it, but she announces she isn't going to Boston. Her fine, womanly intuition tells her she isn't wanted there.

"But *I* want you!"

Georgie gives in. If he needs her up in Boston, that's most likely where she will be. And now, she announces, they've said enough. She gets her husband's suit coat out of the wardrobe and holds it for him. Querulously he reminds her of a loose button, and deftly

she sews it tight, taunting him, "Spoiling for a fight, aren't you? . . .
You mystify me, Frank, your sense of guilt and insecurity. Take
a lesson from my father, the late Delaney the Great. He didn't
care what people thought of him, no matter what he did. Played
every vaudeville house in the world. Didn't show up at home but
twice a year—and those two times he was down in the cellar per-
fecting new magic tricks."

Frank thinks he divines what is on his wife's mind. "You want
me to beg you to come up to Boston, don't you?" Finally he is
ready to go, with his script in his pocket. His good humor begins
to return. To needle his wife he mentions having seen an old
friend, Susie Lewis, the playwright's aunt. As he goes for his topcoat his wife says, "Say good morning to Bernardo the Great for
me." He chuckles, "You can bet your sweet Fanny Maloney I
won't tell him what you're calling him. Don't you go tangling with
him at the run-through tomorrow night."

This he had let slip. Georgie had not known about a run-
through—and he can't think of an excuse for not having told her.
"Don't you want me to come tomorrow night?" Pinned down but
uneasy, Frank admits he'd rather she did not come; anyhow, it
isn't a dress rehearsal—just a run-through with a few props for the
benefit of the financial backers of the play. Georgie accepts this
easily, saying, "Then I'll see it in Boston with the sets and the
costumes."

" 'At's my girl!" He starts out. "My only real worry is the
lines—they won't stick in the dome!"

"We'll drill some more. I'll cue you. . . . Frank, don't get
secretive. If I go on the road with you, tell me straight out anything that's on your mind. Don't shuffle. . . . I don't often talk
this way any more. . . . We're both of us miles behind. Don't
try to catch up all at once. We both know what's happened in the
past. We'll have to live one day at a time, without resentments and
evasions. We're at the bottom—"

"But we'll be at the top," he insists.

"But one rung at a time, separated by quiet, healthy sleep."

Frank squirms. Dodd is a good man, Georgie continues; he's
young, but good. Frank should talk out all his worries with Bernie.
Lowering his gaze, the actor announces, "I love you, Georgie."
And at the door he throws her a defiant kiss, with advice to catch it.
Then, relenting, he returns to hold her and kiss her. As he departs,
Georgie smiles faintly to herself, begins whistling softly, and re-
moves the coffee things to the sink. Again she sees the beer bottles,

and the rhythm of the whistling slows. She picks up the bottles,
looks at them thoughtfully, puts them under the sink and resumes
whistling.

The curtain falls.

Scene V

In a Boston theatre a first dress rehearsal has just been con-
cluded, and interest in the play now shifts to the dressing room
of its leading actor, Frank Elgin. Larry, the stage manager, looks
in; seeing no one, he is about to leave. Then he changes his mind
and helps himself to a cigarette on the make-up shelf. In a moment
Paul Unger, the author, looks in, a script under his arm, and asks
fretfully where Frank is. Unger has a few more cuts in Scene Four.
"I'll take them later, if you don't mind," says Larry. "I'm trying
to find out what happened in Scene Six. They keep blowing in the
same spot." The two men go out together, and a moment later
Georgie enters, surprised to find the room empty. She is chewing
gum and wearing her glasses, as usual. She begins to tidy up the
room. Soon Bernie arrives—also looking for Frank. To a question
from Georgie he replies that Elgin is not onstage. Then, about to
leave, he counsels her to bear in mind that this was a damn rough
dress rehearsal—but what did she think of the show?

Georgie evades a direct answer by saying she didn't judge—just
sat and listened. She removes her gum. It is evident that each is
trying to get on a good footing with the other. Bernie lights a
cigarette and offers her one . . . but she never uses them. What
did she think of her husband? "He was very tense, poor chick."
And so, she observes aloud, is Bernie—tense as a June bug. Laugh-
ingly he shushes her, saying, "My cast thinks I'm made of steel."

"Frank thinks the sun rises and sets in you, Mr. Dodd."

Bernie makes a very careful reply: "You'd make me very happy
by being careful with Frank. You're his wife—he's probably all
focused on your reaction."

"Is his performance pleasing you?"

"What do *you* think?"

"Don't ask me. I had one long old-fashioned cry out there.
Just a country girl."

Bernie assures her that Elgin will be very good in another week
or two. What if the show *is* opening Wednesday night? They'll
get a show then, but not what they'll get in New York. That is
what tryouts are for—education for actors in public. With a con-
sciously used air of candor and with a vocal bow to Mrs. Elgin's
intelligence, Dodd explains the kind of actor he thinks Frank is.

Most actors don't even need four weeks' rehearsing—they've got it all down, glib and superficial, in a week or two. But Frank has acting talent, and the quality of it is improvisatory. This is a blessing but a burden, for he never knows what he is going to do next. He explores and discovers, opening up the part very slowly. The director's problem is to keep Frank open, keep him going, as long as possible—and New York is five long weeks away. Meanwhile, let him flounder—in his case it's healthy.

Having delivered his lecture, Bernie starts to leave, saying, "Don't mention any of this to Frank. Tell him I'll be right back." His polite charm seems to mask a certain scorn, and Georgie is disturbed by him. When he has gone she turns on a small radio and listens until Frank appears—now an imposing, portly, somewhat romantic political boss with gray hair and a mustache. He is nervous and tired and he slams his part down on the make-up shelf. "I was upstairs running lines with the kid. I blew like a bat all night. I hope this doesn't happen Wednesday when we open. . . . Well, what's the verdict?"

Georgie is very moved as she looks at him, and he seems afraid to hear what she will say. What she says first is that he looks wonderful. "Was it bad?" he insists. "Nothing was bad, dear. It was a bad rehearsal, of course."

Frank, disappointed and glum, insists on knowing the worst, but his wife can tell him no worst. "I think you'll be astonishing in the part." Frank is irritable, mistrustful, finally outraged at his wife's seemingly evasive answers. He begins to remove costume and makeup. Suddenly Georgie bursts out, "Frank, I don't . . . You're magnificent in this part! And the play—I'm deeply surprised that quiet, smiling boy has so much talent!"

Frank feels a little better now—spiritually; but physically he is getting a cold and he sniffs loudly. That's all he needs now—a cold. He rejects her proffered aspirins, begins to remove a shoe and complains, "Why don't they give me a dresser? Don't I deserve it? How can I make those fast changes by myself?" Georgie offers to speak to Phil Cook, the producer, about it, and he complainingly suggests that she speak about salary, too. He has found out that Mabel Beck is getting more than he does—and she stinks up every scene. And that damn understudy, always snooping around in the wings—how is Frank supposed to work with that going on?

The actor is well on the way to a high temper when, after a knock at the door, the young playwright and Mr. Cook come in. Frank's manner instantly changes to a jovial, self-deprecating humor. "Don't

tell me about the show," he cries. "I know—stank on rye bread!"
Unger sincerely disagrees, which pleases Frank, and Cook utters a
gloomy, "Me, too." Now Bernie makes a jaunty entrance, and
there is much high-humored talk about a terrible dress rehearsal.
Unger, who, like all playwrights, still must write his play, takes his
departure.

Larry, the stage manager, taps discreetly at the open door, then
asks Frank if he will come onstage and go over the last scene with
the company—the spot where everyone blew. They can't locate
what happened. Protesting that he had just run over the scene
with "the kid," Frank gets up with a mock groan and, towel still
in hand, follows Larry out. With the star out of the way, producer
Cook can be a little more frank. To Bernie he observes, "If he
spoke one line of the author's script tonight, it never reached my
ears." He has started sulkily for the door when Georgie stops
him with, "Mr. Cook, do you think Frank needs a dresser?" and
he retorts, "No, I don't. But I suppose you do?" Bernie sides
with Georgie, and Cook leaves with the dresser won. When they
are alone Georgie remarks, "I'm glad *we're* getting along, Mr.
Dodd." She then takes up the subject of the understudy, a man
named Lucas, who makes Frank nervous, and Bernie says he will
watch that—but is Frank *that* insecure? He seems to be working
well and is in good humor all the time. . . .

Georgie has become friendly as she asks, "Don't you know he
hides behind that humor? He's not a simple man, Mr. Dodd.
That's why I offer myself as a sort of liaison officer between you
both." Bernie's reply is not friendly: "Is that what you're doing?"
Georgie is taken aback, but still she tries to explain her husband
to the director, and Bernie, questioning and listening, tests her. He
is told that Frank won't say anything that might lose him people's
regard or affection, so she has to do it. For instance, right now
Frank is bothered by Cook's attitude, and by the understudy, and
by his inability to retain his lines, by not having a dresser—and
by salary.

They both are beginning to tighten. Bernie reminds her that
it has been a long time since her husband has had *any* salary. Then
he coldly announces that he happens to have other plans for Frank's
financial participation in the show. If he works out and if the
show runs, Dodd will make him a 5 per cent partner, as a gift.

Hesitantly, Georgie asks, "Would you give him that in writing?"

"No," says Dodd, angrily, jumping up. "I won't give you that
in writing!"

GEORGIE (*pallidly*)—It would help him if you did. Tomorrow—this week, staring probable bad reviews in the face . . .

BERNIE (*eying her*)—You're clever—don't overplay your hand. Let's face it. Frank may go anywhere from here, even to a wealthy movie career. Or he may go right back to the gutter, and you right with him!

GEORGIE—Do you think that was called for?

BERNIE—Just like you, I don't always say and do what's "called for."

GEORGIE (*puzzled, hurt, wary, trying to understand*)—I don't mind you being angry if I know why—

BERNIE (*flaring*)—I have no problems with Frank—don't you make them where they don't exist! (*He swings away.*) I could almost love a woman like you. My motto is "No pity!" too!

GEORGIE—I wonder if you'd be kind enough to give me the code. What're you talking about? (*She has turned, careful and restricted. Invited, as it were, he comes down from the door and stands behind her, almost enjoying this moment.*)

BERNIE—Here's the code. I'm ambitious—I wanna get *my* picture on a green postage stamp, too. There's a difference between us, of course. Way up on the twenty-fourth floor is where I live. And sometimes, late at night, I look out way over the sleeping city and think how I'd like to change the history of the world. I know I won't—the idea is talented but phony. I admit I'm a gifted mountebank. What are you? Do you know? Do you admit it, even to yourself?

GEORGIE—What am I?

BERNIE—Lady, you ride that man like a broom! You're a bitch!

GEORGIE (*after a long moment*)—You have a very lyric and lurid opinion of me.

BERNIE (*rapidly, dropping his voice*)—Now, be careful, Mrs. E. It's a bitter mess for me if Frank fails. But I can hire other actors. I doubt if Frank can hire another director.

GEORGIE—I had no idea you were this tense tonight.

BERNIE—I'd tell you these same things any other night.

GEORGIE (*stronger*)—Yes, you would. You have the bloody eye of a man who smokes too much. Tobacco's a drug—it warps your judgment. I'll have to remember that.

BERNIE (*sardonically*)—I have to go stroke some more of my tender chicks. (GEORGIE *stands there in proud, helpless silence, deeply hurt.* BERNIE *walks to the door.* FRANK, *in an exuberant mood, opens it and bumps into* BERNIE.)

FRANK—Shut my mouth, the traffic's bad tonight! Well, that spot's all cleaned up! Bernie, that line mixup—it was the kid's fault all the time!

BERNIE—Be back in two minutes—have to give Mabel Beck some notes. By the way, Frank, does it bother you to have the understudy hanging around?

FRANK (*heartily*)—Me? Why in hell would a Lucas bother an Elgin? Never even heard of the watch! Ha! Ha! Ha! (BERNIE *cocks a quick smart eye at* GEORGIE, *then goes.* FRANK *ripples on like a happy river, washing and dressing quickly.*) Georgie, that line mixup—it was the kid's fault all the time! We'll get a load of fresh air in our lungs—I'll be dressed in a jiffy. How about a walk right across the Common? (*Humming his happy snatch of tune,* FRANK *does not see, as we do, that* GEORGIE, *who has moved to the trunk across the room, is trying to hold back tears.* FRANK *dresses and chatters on happily.*) Guess what I'm in the mood for? One of those one dozen oyster stews, half and half—just what the doctor ordered! Oh, boy, what that'll do for my stomach! What did that Cook say after I left? (*Unable to speak,* GEORGIE *merely shakes her head.* FRANK *half turns.*) What? Huh?

GEORGIE—You're getting a dresser next week. (*She restrains her tears.*)

FRANK (*practically exultant*)—Really? Georgie, you beat the band! Can't live without me! I'll betcha Bernie was on my side!

GEORGIE—Yes.

FRANK—Look at me, just look at me! I'm winging like a lark!

GEORGIE (*half turning*)—Frank, I wonder if I shouldn't go back to New York soon. You're getting a dresser now, and I think I'll be in the way. They resent me here and—

FRANK—What are you talking about? Are you kidding? Who resents you? (*He starts toward her; the lark is grounded now. Turned away,* GEORGIE *abruptly bursts into tears.* FRANK *stops dead, baffled and frightened. Only slowly does he move toward her with the shuffling gait of guilt.*) Why, darling, what's the matter? What is it, dear? Come on now, tell Poppa. What is it? (*He has turned her and has her in his arms.*)

GEORGIE—I really must . . . get these teeth fixed . . .

FRANK (*relieved, with fond and rough sympathy*)—Honey, why don't you tell me when something's on your mind? We'll get you a good dentist in the morning. (*He starts toward the make-up shelf.*) Here, take some aspirin.

GEORGIE (*stopping him*)—No, I took a few.

FRANK (*comes back again, all sympathy, about to kiss and embrace her*)—Darling, don't you know this is gonna be a honeymoon, up here in Boston?

GEORGIE (*as she pulls away and sits, with a bite of bitterness*)— Yes, we all love each other, don't we?

FRANK—Boy, I'll never understand your moods, and that's the truth! A man can't be right, can he? Two strikes against him before he opens his mouth! (*Sullen and offended, he goes back to his dressing. She sits, stiff, cold, and wordless.*) Now my stomach's all in a whirl again. That's what you wanted, isn't it? (*He sits at the make-up shelf; there is silence and distance between them.*)

GEORGIE—One day soon . . . we'll see what I want . . .

The curtain falls.

ACT II

In the dressing room again, past 1 A.M. several nights later— a cold and depressing time—Georgie is sitting on a chair, knitting, and Paul Unger is pecking at a portable typewriter. Frank is onstage with the rest of the company, for photographs of the production are being made for the publicity department. Georgie and Paul have been waiting a long time and are tired of waiting; their conversation is desultory, but the tedium is somewhat relieved by the soft playing of a radio. Unger is a shy man, but a quizzical and droll one; he liked Georgie and frankly tells her she is "touching." Putting up with Frank's drinking, he means. She tells him, forthrightly, how it began—how Frank, who used to be in the money, wanted to become his own producer, lost $80,000 on two bad shows —and was afraid to tell his wife. A year later they lost their little girl. "It was awesome how he went for the bottle," she recalls.

Paul probes her with another question—she doesn't like Bernie, does she? "Don't let that bluster fool you," he advises. "He's actually a very innocent kid. He's in love with art, for instance, and would make it a felony that you are not." Georgie has a question in turn: What about Paul's Aunt Sue, whom Frank used to know? Attractive? He says she is very decent—and rich.

Frank hurries in. He has a bad head cold and is hiding a gnawing, nervous anxiety with affability and bluffness. There are two scenes left to shoot on the stage and he has come in to change— and for some medicine. "Where's that cough syrup?" he demands —and, finding it on the make-up shelf, takes a quick swig. Georgie gets out his smoking jacket for the next picture scene as Frank asks

the playwright how the new scene is coming. "I won't get to bed until it's finished," he promises. "Bernie wants to put it in tomorrow."
Paul feels now that he should go back to his hotel and work alone,
so he leaves. Frank, highly nervous, lights another of countless
cigarettes and takes another gulp from the syrup bottle. Georgie
doesn't like it and points out that the label says the mixture is 22%
alcohol. "You know Poppa," Frank blusters. "Walks like a
mountain goat. Never slips."

Finally Frank's newest worry comes out—Bernie didn't come
backstage after the performance tonight, and neither did Cook.
"I'll hand in my notice," he threatens. "Why should I care—do
they? Producer and director don't come back the second night of a
show!" His wife announces, quietly, "If you walk off *this* show,
too, you'll never see me again." This seems to frighten him, and
he attempts to regain his good humor. Soon Larry appears, announcing that the photographer is ready for the next scene, and on
his way out Frank tries to slip the medicine bottle into his smoking
jacket pocket, but Georgie has spotted the maneuver and tries to
take the bottle from him. He clings to it, saying, softly but fiercely,
"I need it!" Georgie, alone for a moment, looks sad and lonely,
but brightens up when Nancy, the ingenue, comes in to have a look
at herself in the pier glass. She is a beautiful girl in a beautiful
low dress; she feels very dashing but confesses to Georgie that she
is tired of being called "sweet child" or "Nancykins" by everybody. As if to prove her point, Larry calls, "Hey, you're wanted
onstage, Nancykins," and the despairing lass flurries to the stage.
Georgie is alone again, and the radio is playing a waltz; in a moment she is waltzing alone, as if she hopes she can dance herself
back to a better time. The sardonic Bernie discovers her in this
maneuver and murmurs, "Excuse me, the both of you." He is looking for Frank and is told the actor is onstage. "His cold is getting
worse, Mr. Dodd," she says. "He shouldn't be kept up this late."
Georgie closes the dressing room door, shuts off the radio, and tells
Bernie, firmly and unemotionally, "For your edification, he's headed
for a bender." Dodd won't believe it and mocks at her feminine
intuition, but she will not be daunted. She knows her husband, and
she warns, "If you're not careful, you'll have him full of whisky
tonight.

"Why work so hard at this marriage?" Bernie queries irritably.
"You wear your husband down. You make him tense, uneasy.
You don't stop 'handling' him. You try to 'handle' me, too." She
replies angrily, "And don't think I can't, after handling a cunning drunkard for ten years!"

BERNIE (*quickly up on his feet*)—Who the hell do you think you are? Secretary of State?

GEORGIE (*defiantly*)—I'm a drunkard's wife.

BERNIE (*snorting*)—Girlie, I have to give you credit, but—

GEORGIE (*quickly*)—No compliments, Mr. Dodd!

BERNIE—But I'm going to fight you as hard as I can for this man!

GEORGIE (*smiling faintly*)—Not too hard. I may let you have him.

BERNIE—No, you want him wholly dependent! Now let's not waste words. I—

GEORGIE—Oh, it's much too late for that.

BERNIE—I was married to one like you. Roughly half my weight—ninety-seven pounds. It took her two years—she sewed me up!

GEORGIE (*dryly*)—Love is hell . . .

BERNIE—We'll leave it at that—joke ending. (*He goes to the door and turns.*) What a bitter pity you don't realize the size of your husband's talent!

GEORGIE—What have *you* given up for that talent?

BERNIE (*coming back*)—Then why do you stay?

GEORGIE—Because he's helpless!

BERNIE—I'll help him!

GEORGIE—*You!* You wouldn't know where to begin. Life with him is three-quarters the avoidance of painful scenes. He's taught me to be a fish, to swim in any direction, including up, down, and sideways. Now, disregarding facts, you happen to think I wheedle his life away. You're very—

BERNIE (*unable to contain himself*)—Look, look, look! Half the world's shamed by sentiment. Say "mother" or "babe," "sacrifice," and they drip like axle grease! But you have ruined this man—don't explain it away by sentiment!

GEORGIE (*incredulously*)—How did I so overrate your intellect? You're a boy!

BERNIE—Man or boy, I'm putting on a show—it has to work! We can discuss universals some other day! To be frank, you are slightly grotesque to me, Mrs. Elgin!

GEORGIE (*bitterly*)—And what about yourself? Look at you, fearful of failure, effective and hard-hitting—a machine, without manners or style—self-driven, curt, wary, and worried—pretending to a humanity you never practice!

BERNIE (*contemptuously*)—You called your own husband a cunning drunkard?

GEORGIE (*flatly*)—It is necessary for you to know it! (*A pause. They are murdering each other with their eyes.*) This is getting stupid. Now tell me, in God's name, exactly what you want me to do for Frank. (*She sits down at the make-up shelf.*)

BERNIE (*pointing a finger at her*)—That's fair! I'll believe everything you say. Prove it!

GEORGIE—How?

BERNIE—Get out of town! (*He pauses.*) I've just had a bad fight in the box office with Cook. He's got a first-class replacement for Frank and seventy thousand dollars to protect! Frank will improve every day—I think he will, Cook thinks he won't. Well, he won't, unless *you get out of town!* (GEORGIE *thinks, stops, looks, and listens.*)

GEORGIE—Umm . . . I'll do it. I'll go back to New York. (*She stops him from leaving.*) But only on one condition: let *me* carefully tell Frank, in my own way, at my own time.

BERNIE—As long as you're on the train by tomorrow night, understand?

GEORGIE (*nodding*)—Life is earnest, life is real, and so are investments—I understand. But you may be sorry.

BERNIE—You're as phony to me as an opera soprano! (GEORGIE *abruptly slashes him across the face with her open hand.*)

GEORGIE (*fiercely*)—Did I forget to tell you I'm proud? Someone has to stop you from calling me any name that pops into your little head!

Before the shaken Bernie can reach the door, Frank opens it, and, seeing the director, is instantly jovial. At last the photographing is over, and he begins to change into street clothes after first putting the medicine on the shelf. Bernie, who is planning to put in the new scene tomorrow, looks searchingly at his actor; he senses that there may be some truth in what Georgie has said. But to Bernie's questions Frank gives reassuring answers: his nerves are all right, his cold is under control, nothing is bothering him. Suddenly Georgie steps in. "Did you or did you not tell me, ten minutes ago, right in this room, that you wanted to hand in your notice?" Frank even tries to laugh this off, and throws Bernie a long-suffering look. Now it is Bernie's turn to come up with disturbing information. Deliberately he says, "Your wife says she is thinking of returning to New York." She denies it . . . and then, deciding to take a new tack, says yes, she might go back. Frank, now off balance, reaches for the syrup, but his wife takes it from him and bangs it down on the shelf. Bernie examines the bottle and inquires, "Do you know it's laced with 22 per cent alcohol?" Frank seems very surprised and puzzled; looks at the label and says it is something his wife got for him. "Gee, dear," he chides, "you wanna watch yourself on a thing like that." Georgie curtly tells him to get dressed; she wants to go home and she'll wait outside. She closes the door after her.

Bernie has taken the bottle from Frank and is pouring the contents into the sink. "She's jealous of the show and jealous of me," he declares. "This is how far she'd go—far enough to kick you off the wagon!"

"I want her back in New York," the director continues, harshly. And, opening the door, he curtly calls, "Mrs. Elgin!" When she appears he says, tiredly, "Frank knows exactly how I feel. See you at one tomorrow, Frank." And he leaves. Georgie remains silent and her husband, full of childish guilt, doesn't know where to look. He murmurs an "I'm ashamed of myself" and finishes changing for the street. Suddenly Georgie demands where the other bottle is and he denies that he has one. Grimly she searches the pockets of a garment in the wardrobe, opens a hat box, pulls out the top drawers of the trunk; then, suddenly, she abandons the search. Frustrated and angry, she retrieves her knitting and struggles fiercely into her coat as he pleads, "Don't be mad at me. I know I'm no damn good, but I'm worried to death."

"Tell that to Bernardo!"

He is desperate. He doesn't even know the old lines, and tomorrow there will be new ones to learn for a big new scene. He needs her, and if she goes to New York he just can't go on. But she won't listen; she just wants to go to bed, where perhaps she may dream a happy dream. Suddenly nasty, Elgin demands "Who's in New York? What pair of pants you looking for?" Georgie struggles to keep from hitting him, then says, wearily, "Come on, Frank." But he is obstinate; she can go to bed if she wants to, but he may take a walk and get a baked apple and milk. Fed up, Georgie exclaims, "The hell with it! Do what you want!" She slams out angrily. Frank paces, muttering to himself; then his attitude abruptly changes as he tiptoes to the door to listen and then goes to the trunk. From the bottom drawer he takes a full bottle of cough syrup, uncaps it, takes a swig and throws the cap over his shoulder. "Helpmate! Sweetheart! Country girl," he growls bitterly.

The curtain falls.

Scene II

It is early afternoon the next day. The dressing room is dark, but a sound of snoring can be heard. Then the sound of a voice outside, calling "Mr. Elgin?" The lights of the dressing mirror go on and Frank is revealed, fully clothed even to his topcoat—obviously a man who has been very drunk. The voice outside persists, and knocking at the door. There are other voices. Frank finally realizes where he is and what is happening and moans a frightened "Oh, my God . . ." Clumsily he tries to brush his hair with his shaking hands—but he is beyond quick recovery. He knows he is trapped, and thickly he calls, "Yes, yes . . . What is it?" He hangs up his coat but it falls to the floor; then he unlocks his door and is confronted by Larry, Cook and Unger. The stage manager informs him it's past two o'clock, and there was a call for one for the new scene. To Unger's agitated query as to what happened Frank snarls a reply that he has a cold and had a couple of beers and some food. The angry producer exclaims, "Look at him! Smells like the sovereign state of Kentucky in person! . . . That wife of your can help you start packing!" Georgie, too, has appeared in time to hear the ultimatum. When the three men have gone she asks Frank, "Where were you all night?" He falls to the couch and groans, "Get me some water."

Now Bernie appears, with the producer and the playwright following. The director is seething with anger—but more at Georgie than at Frank. He accuses her of lying when he telephoned the Elgins' room this morning to inquire about Frank, and she had replied that she didn't know where he was—and, as to whether her husband had had a good night's sleep, she had said she hoped so. "Where did you get him a bottle after midnight?" he demands.

Georgie, astounded, emits a strained, strange laugh. To the producer Bernie snaps, "There's only one thing to do, Phil," and Cook knows what he means. "I'm going right out to the box office to do it," the producer grimly announces, and Unger follows along. Still in a rage, Dodd announces, "There is still one person too many in this room," and Georgie, taking the hint, leaves, smiling faintly and closing the door after her. Bernie is alone with his actor, and his actor is hangdog and apologetic. "That wife of yours—she—" Words fail Bernie, but Frank comes to her defense. "She's weak," he ventures, and Bernie grates, "She's driven you to drink for ten years and you call her weak? . . . She goes back to New York on the five-oh-five."

"Bernie, kid, I can't leave her," Frank protests weakly. "Left her once—she cut her wrists. She'd cut her wrists again." But Dodd is unmoved. He goes to the door and calls another crisp "Mrs. Elgin!" When Georgie returns she goes directly to her husband with a fizzy drink, which he takes in his hand but does not drink. Bernie, rocklike in his anger, announces, "Frank stays—you go. Frank may follow you in a day or two—I'm not sure. Just now he's moving in with me."

With a sad smile she moves toward the door, but Dodd blocks her and orders, "Tell Frank he has nothing to worry about. He thinks you may go drastic. It's happened before, I understand."

She doesn't know what he is talking about and he bluntly explains, "Phony suicide attempts." Realization now comes to her and she jolts Bernie by replying, "Suicide attempts are Frank's department." He thinks this over for a moment, then, striding to Frank, demands, "Show me your wrists." Frank is agonized, and when Dodd repeats his challenge he slowly raises his wrists. Bernie looks down for several intense seconds, with a look of sickness growing on his face. Frank begins to sob without control.

Bernie Dodd, the young genius who has the theatre by the tail, must now revise his perspective. Now he knows that Frank has been lying to him, and he needs some new answers from Georgie. "You were Miss America in the late '30s?"

Georgie, too, is reaching new realizations. "He told you that?" she asks. "Did I burn down a house in Great Neck? Or a hotel suite? Did I need a nurse to watch me while he was tending work?"

He nods.

"You didn't recognize any of it, from the play you admired him in, 'Werba's Millions'?"

The heart is completely out of her. Frank has not lifted his face from his hands, and, with her eyes now wet with tears, she talks on. Talks on about her romance . . . a girl of 19, romantic . . . a worldly, competent actor . . . who drank, she realized . . . but she'd help him reform. . . . Back to the present, she curtly advises Bernie, "Send him back to the hotel. He needs some rest." Bernie, also back to the present crisis, calls for Larry and makes arrangements for Lucas, the understudy, to go on tonight. Harshly he orders Larry to take Frank to the hotel and dismiss the company that had been called for the afternoon rehearsal. When the actor and the stage manager have gone, Dodd faces what he must do.

GEORGIE—I'm a real lemon drop. You can begin by not calling me Mrs. Dodd. (*Standing, she flicks him a look and begins buttoning her coat.*)

BERNIE—Have you ever left him?

GEORGIE—Twice left, twice returned.   He's a helpless child.
(*Wryly, lifting her purse.*)   Anyone taking a cab to New York?

BERNIE—But if he's as helpless as you say—

GEORGIE—He's not helpless now—he has you.

BERNIE (*earnestly, his voice quivering*)—Listen, he has to be
watched and handled.   You can do that—no one else.   I didn't know
it before.

GEORGIE (*bitterly*)—Then you've learned something—ripeness is
all!

BERNIE—Listen, Georgie, if—

GEORGIE (*opening up*)—I don't intend to stay!   Even the cat's
dragged me up and down the stairs in this theatre!

BERNIE (*unhappily*)—But the man needs you—he has to be
watched!

GEORGIE (*turns from the door, and now he gets it*)—*You* take on
the job with waving banners and twelve hours later hand it back?
YOU'RE TELLING ME!   (*She throws her purse on the couch and begins circling around him.   Helpless, he makes an attempt here and
there to stop her torrential anger.*)   Yes, he has to be watched—he
has to be nursed, guarded, and coddled!   But not by me, my very
young friend!

BERNIE—Please—

GEORGIE—I'm going back to New York, to the fiesta of a quiet
room.   For the first time in twelve years I won't have to wonder
where he is—he'll be in the strong, sober hands of Mr. Bernie Dodd!

BERNIE (*ineffectually*)—Georgie, listen—

GEORGIE—Can you stand him up on his feet?   Because that's
where all my prayers have gone—to see that one holy hour when he
can stand alone!   (*She avoids him as he tries to grab her.*)   And I
might forgive even *you*, Mr. Dodd, if you can keep him up long
enough for me to get out from under!   All I want is my own name
and a modest job to buy the sugar for my coffee!

BERNIE (*his temper slipping*)—Wait—if you'll listen—!

GEORGIE (*evading him*)—You can't believe that, can you, you
goddam man!   You can't believe a woman's crazy-out-of-her-mind
to live alone!   In one room!   By herself!   (BERNIE *is so aroused
by her that he has grabbed her by one arm.   She pulls away; he
grabs with his other hand, whirls her around.*)

BERNIE—Dammit, listen to me!   You're knocking all the apologies out of my head!   (*He has pulled her in close to him and is holding her by both arms.*)   Now, *listen*, Lady Brilliance: you have to
stay—he doesn't play unless you stay!   It's a time for promotion,

not more execution! But I can't take the chance *if you don't stay!*
(*A quick tense moment follows.* GEORGIE *is frozen in his arms, her
hands against his chest.*)

GEORGIE—Why are you holding me? (*Pushing.*) I said you are
holding me! (*Abruptly, not releasing her, he kisses her fully on the
mouth. Then they both step apart and after a moment he walks to
a chair and sits, turned from her.*)

It is difficult to say which is the more surprised, and it takes some
moments before Bernie can recall himself to the problem of the
moment—which is the play. He needs this much time to rearrange
his thinking—and now he asks, "For Frank's sake, I want you to
stay." Before Georgie can assent or decline, Cook bustles irritably
in. He has Ray Newton on the phone in the box office. Newton is
a good actor, and is available; he can reach Boston from New York
by morning. Bernie must come and talk with him. The young director asks Georgie, pleadingly, "Will you stay?"

After a pause, she replies, "Yes," and he starts out after Cook.
"You kissed me," Georgie continues. "Don't let it give you any
ideas, Mr. Dodd."

Quietly, as he leaves, Bernie answers, "No, Mrs. Elgin." When
she is alone she moves a hand slowly to her face. Her fingers touch
her lips.

The curtain falls.

SCENE III

It is Frank's dressing room again—but not the one in Boston.
This is in a New York theatre. Five weeks have passed and this
is the opening night. The second act is on and Georgie, standing
in the doorway, is listening to it. Ralph, Frank's dresser, brings in
several telegrams. Georgie asks, "How is it going on the other side
of the stage?"

"A big man, Mrs. Elgin," Ralph replies. "It's a positive honor
to be working for him." The dresser leaves for the wings with a
loaded powder puff for his new star, and soon Bernie appears, tense,
nervous, ears cocked to the stage. He has been out front, and he
reports that Frank's first act wasn't bad. Larry, a fierce working-
man in shirt sleeves, makes a harried instant's appearance to demand quiet and firmly closes the dressing room door. They can't
listen now, so they must talk. "Georgie," declares Bernie, "five
weeks ago I kissed a woman, a married woman; and now I love a
woman, a married woman, and don't know where to turn." He takes
her arms, but she gently holds him off until he releases her, smiling

wryly. "Are you leaving him?" His need to know is urgent, but she evades an answer and he sinks on a stool in silence. Frank's lifted voice in a scene can be faintly heard through the door. "I hate to see you this way, troubled, contrite," Georgie offers, sympathetically.

Suddenly Bernie turns his attention to the stage play, straining to hear something. He bounds to the door, opens it and hurries out, with Georgie following. There are sounds of running feet and excited whispers, and beyond it Frank's voice has risen high and angry. Bernie returns, leading an excited, half-hysterical Nancy. The girl sobs, "He began to hit me, Bernie, onstage. I can't bear it! I don't know what he's doing out there—he's even changed the lines!"

Bernie sharply orders the girl to be quiet, orders the hovering Ralph to go back to his job and close the door. Nancy's excitement continues as she describes what happened. Frank's eyes were red and he didn't seem to see her even when he looked right at her. He took her and shook her like a doll. And slapped her!

Bernie sharply reminds Nancy that this was the scene. He commands, "Now stop sulking, Junior Miss—go up and change for your last act." Nancy has got over her fright and is obedient. As she leaves Bernie gives her an unsmiling kiss, and she is happy again. Georgie returns to report that it was a spooky scene—Frank was wild out there. Impatiently Bernie snaps, "I've been waiting forty minutes for that burst! If he can play scenes like that, let him do what he wants."

The curtain out there goes down and the applause is strong. The sounds of swarming stage hands are heard. As Bernie and Georgie step aside, Frank reaches his dressing room, heavy and hoarse, like a man in a perspiring trance. He should begin undressing for a change of costume, but, half sobbing, he waves an embittered fist at the world. "I couldn't hold myself back! Did I hurt the kid? I started to go and I couldn't help it!"

Bernie soothes his actor and Georgie helps him undress. Soon he has recovered composure. He notices there are more telegrams and glances at them—messages of remembrance and good wishes. A nice one from Sue Lewis, saying she is out front and mentioning "renewal of a great career. Much affection." They please him. Bernie, leaving, advises, "Keep going wild and I'll bless you in Macy's window."

Producer Cook now pays a call. His comments are either noncommittal or lukewarm, though he does admit "The reactions in the lobby are pretty good." Uneasily he steers toward something else. "Frank, a lot of things . . . are said in the heat and toil of the day.

I hope you'll accept my apologies. . . ."

"Sure," Frank agrees affably—and then a sudden new thought strikes him, seems to make a new Frank Elgin. He adds coldly, "Of course, you include my wife, too, in your apologies." The flustered Cook readily agrees, and Frank tips him farther off balance by ordering, "Then start by taking your hat off."

The actor knows why the producer has come offering apologies. He states, flatly and correctly, "You want me to sign a run-of-the-play contract before the morning papers are out, for half of what I'm worth." Cook, defeated, slithers out confusedly; Georgie is laughing and admiring her husband. "Don't forget," she advises, "it isn't necessary to be liked by every Tom, Dick and Harry Truman, even if he's President!" Humming a tune, she brings her husband his last-act smoking jacket. The third-act stage has been set, and Larry is ready to take up the curtain when all the audience is seated. His third-act cry is heard as a distant echo.

FRANK (*turning, hesitantly nervous*)—Georgie . . . I can be wrong most of the time . . . but any ideas you have, if you want to leave me—don't. (BERNIE *is about to leave, but* FRANK *stops him by crossing over*.) I'm deliberately talking in front of a third person. Maybe I should do it more often—sometimes it's a big relief to fall on your face in public. (*To* GEORGIE.) Am I wrong, Georgie? Aren't you setting up Sue Lewis to put in your place? Don't leave me, darling. Give me a chance. I love you. . . . (GEORGIE *pauses for her answer; one of her hands creeps up to the lapel of* FRANK'S *coat*.)

GEORGIE—Frank, I certainly didn't want to bring up any of this tonight. But you did—so let's have the whole truth. I married you for happiness, Frank. And, if necessary, I'll leave you for the same reason. Right now I don't know where I stand.

FRANK (*humbly*)—You don't . . . ?

GEORGIE (*drops her hand and steps back a little, carefully picking her way*)—No. Because neither of us has really changed. And yet I'm sure that both our lives are at some sort of turning point. There's some real new element of hope here—I don't know what. But I'm uncertain . . . and you, Frank, have to be strong enough to bear that uncertainty.

FRANK (*hushed*)—I think I know what you mean. (LARRY *looks in just long enough to say, "We're waiting, Frank."* FRANK *speaks nervously*.) They're waiting, dear. I—I don't know how to say this, but no matter what happens, you have saved me, Georgie— you and Bernie. (*He kisses her, then pulls himself together*.) I think I have a chance. (*He turns and exits firmly. After a moment* BERNIE *seems about to say something to* GEORGIE, *but she is moved and withdrawn.*)

BERNIE (*as he slips out, muttering*)—I'd better show my face on stage a moment—rah-rah stuff. (UNGER, *wearing a dinner jacket, enters, almost brushing* BERNIE.)

UNGER (*jubilantly*)—Frank is magnificent! He's really showing me what my play is all about!

GEORGIE (*smiling*)—He's onstage—they're going up.

UNGER—You don't look like a veteran of all the wars tonight! You must be damn proud! I know my aunt is—we're sitting together. She's showing all the proprietary interest of a mother hen.

GEORGIE (*quietly*)—Give your aunt my regards.

UNGER—I will. (*He goes over to her, wanting to kiss her or touch her hands. She attempts the same, but it is clumsy and fizzles out. He goes.* GEORGIE *slowly walks to the door; she is thoughtful and inward as she looks out.* BERNIE *returns, his spirits slightly lifted. The intermission music dies away.* LARRY'S *cautioning voice is heard:* "*Quiet backstage, please, we're going up . . . quiet, please . . .*")

BERNIE—Everything shipshape . . .

GEORGIE—It was sweet of you to send him all those wires.

BERNIE (*impassively*)—Who told you?

GEORGIE—Guessed. How many did you send?

BERNIE—Nine or ten. And you?

GEORGIE—Four or five.

BERNIE—There she goes! (*The curtain goes up.* GEORGIE *and* BERNIE *are looking out. A strained pause is followed by a rumble of applause.* BERNIE *speaks mordantly.*) Applauding a third-act entrance—surprise follows surprise. Well, this is the act where he wraps up the show and walks off with the town. (*He goes to get his topcoat from the hook.*)

GEORGIE (*leaning against the doorjamb, to herself*)—He's handsome tonight . . .

BERNIE (*turning to her*)—I'll go out front and watch. Good night, Georgie.

GEORGIE (*crossing to the make-up shelf*)—He'll come off dripping again . . . (*Humming* FRANK'S *snatch of tune, she is picking up some tissues and a towel; when she turns,* BERNIE *has moved in closer to her, almost forcibly making her aware of his presence.*)

BERNIE—Good night, Georgie. (*They are face to face.*)

GEORGIE (*gently*)—Good night, Bernardo.

BERNIE (*wryly*)—I don't know . . . maybe a magician *does* live in this frail, foolish body, but he certainly can't work wonders for himself! You'll never leave him . . . (*He has been fishing in a pocket; now he jerks his hand out, almost angrily it would seem.*) I keep running out of cigarettes!

GEORGIE—You smoke too much.

BERNIE (*mockingly*)—You are impertinent, Madame! (*Longingly.*) And steadfast. And loyal . . . reliable. I like that in a woman!

GEORGIE (*her hand on his arm*)—Wrestle, Bernie. You may win a blessing. But stay unregenerate. Life knocks the sauciness out of us soon enough. (*Lonely, arch, and rueful, he looks at her a moment before stepping in and kissing her lightly on the lips. Then he turns, throws his folded coat over one shoulder, and slowly leaves the room. For a moment she wears a sad and yearning look; finally a towel in her hand calls her back to reality. She crosses and takes* FRANK'S *robe off the wall and starts for the door. Meanwhile* FRANK'S *stage voice is heard, playing a quiet but powerful scene. A thought makes* GEORGIE *stop. She goes back to the dressing shelf, takes down Sue's telegram, considers it quickly, comes to a decision, crumples it into a ball and throws it into the trash basket. Then, head up, she slowly walks out of the room with* FRANK'S *robe across one arm.*)

THE CURTAIN FALLS

THE ROSE TATTOO *

A Play in Three Acts

By Tennessee Williams

THE season of 1950-1951 was a placid one, outwardly at least, in the relationship between professional theatre people and play critics. No manager or dramatist made public a denunciation of the reviewers as members of the Jukes family or uttered any other notable plaints. The only playwright of standing who had any remarks at all about the critics was Tennessee Williams, who wrote a letter to Irving Hoffman, columnist of the *Hollywood Reporter*. In this letter Mr. Williams made mention of the "exorbitant demands which are made by critics who don't stop to consider the playwright's need for a gradual ripening or development . . . a degree of tolerance and patience in his mentors during this period of transition. Painters have it better. They are allowed to evolve new methods, new styles, by a reasonable gradual process. They are not abused for turning out creative variations on themes already stated. If a certain theme has importance, it may take a number of individual works to explore it fully. . . . It would help enormously if there were professional theatre centers outside of New York, so that the playwright would not always be at the mercy of a single localized group."

This letter was not the plaint of a disappointed author; it came from the writer of "A Streetcar Named Desire" and "The Glass Menagerie," who at the moment was having another critical and box office success in "The Rose Tattoo." Yet the letter was not without motivation; between the first two successes and the most recent one there was a play by Mr. Williams, "Summer and Smoke," which had not received total acclaim. Some reviewers pointed out that this play seemed to be but a variant of the other two—a disquisition upon a frustrated woman. Some wondered if Mr. Williams had nothing but frustrated women, and a morbid outlook, in his script case. The next Williams play, "The Rose Tattoo," was different from the others in many respects, and there is evidence that the author had been reading and pondering his critics. His woman this time may have a few frustrations, chief of which is that she is sorry her husband is dead; but in other aspects she is, for a Williams female, remarkably unfrustrated. Furthermore, the attitude of "The Rose Tattoo" is one of comedy rather than tragedy—a departure if not a development. The reader will note in the copyright credits on the first page of this treatment of "The Rose Tattoo" that it was copyrighted in 1950 and again in 1951 in a "revised and published version." What had happened was that Mr. Williams, unlike most authors of assured successes, was not completely satisfied with his play as it stood on the opening night. He made many changes after the run had begun, and some of these were made after the playwright had pondered his criticisms. Which means that, contrary to popular belief, criticism as it is practiced today can be constructive.

The locale of the play is a village populated mostly by Sicilians somewhere along the Gulf Coast between New Orleans and Mobile. There is a frame cottage in a poor state of repair, with a palm tree leaning dreamily over one end of it and at the other end a flimsy little entrance porch. Around the house, besides palm trees, are tall canes with feathery fronds and a fairly thick growth of pampas grass. Back of the house and above it, but not visible, is a highway; one can hear the cars and trucks on it. The facing wall of the cottage is a transparency which can be made to reveal the interior of the cottage. The interior is as colorful as a carnival booth. There are many religious articles, bright pictures, a brass cage containing a gaudy parrot, a bowl of goldfish, cut glass decanters and vases. "Everything is exclamatory in its brightness, like the projection of a woman's heart passionately in love. There are two main rooms visible—the living room and a smaller one evidently used for sewing. Against the wall between the rooms is a shrine consisting of a *prie-dieu* and a little statue of the Madonna, before which always burns a vigil light in its ruby glass cup. In the sewing room are a number of dressmaker's dummies, and outside the house is a sign, "SEWING."

It is the beginning of dusk and the mothers of the neighborhood are calling their children home to supper. Three of the children being called are reposing outside the house, and inside Serafina delle Rose is waiting for the return of her husband, Rosario. A table is set for supper and there is wine in a silver ice bucket. Serafina looks like a plump little opera singer in the role of Madama Butterfly. Her coal-black hair is done in a high pompadour, and a rose is pinned in it. Her voluptuous figure is sheathed in pale rose silk. On her feet are dainty high-heeled slippers. It is apparent, from the way she sits on the sofa, that she is wearing a tight girdle. Expectancy shines in her eyes. She calls, "Rosa, where are you?" Rosa, her pretty, vivacious, twelve-year-old daughter, is outside nearby, and she answers her mother's call, "Here, Mama."

In a moment an old woman in a gray shawl, carrying a basket of herbs, approaches and enters the house, and Rosa follows her in. The woman is Assunta, a *fattucchiera,* who practices a simple sort of herb medicine. Serafina asks what she is peddling and the old woman answers, "Powder, wonderful white powder. You drop a pinch of it in your husband's coffee."

"What is it good for?"

The old lady cackles, "What is a husband good for! I make it out of the dry blood of a goat."

With a proud smile Serafina declares that her husband needs no kind of powder at all. Outside, the sound of a truck on the highway is heard and Rosa cries joyfully, "Papa's truck!" But the noise of the vehicle dies in the distance; it has gone by. To Assunta, the seller of things magical, Serafina reveals something magical; she tells the old lady, impressively, "I knew that I had conceived on the very night of conception! That night I woke up with a burning pain on me, here, on my left breast! A pain like a needle, quick, quick, quick, hot little stitches! I turned on the light, I uncovered my breast!—On it I saw the rose tattoo of my husband! . . . And when I saw it I knew I had conceived!"

The disbelieving old woman thrusts her basket at Serafina and suggests, *"You* sell the powders." Serafina admits that the rose on her breast didn't last very long; her husband never saw it and he just laughed when she told him about it.

Serafina continues her confidences to the old woman. Her husband is not just a driver of a ten-ton truck of bananas. She almost whispers, "On top of the truck is bananas! But underneath—something else!"

"What else?" Assunta asks in Italian.

"Whatever it is that the Brothers Romano want hauled out of the state, he hauls it for them, underneath the bananas. And money, he gets so much it almost spills from his pockets! Soon I don't have to make dresses!" Tonight, she confides, is the last time he does it, and tomorrow he quits, pays for the truck and begins working for himself. And in the house they will have everything electric—stove, deep-freeze—*tutto!*

Another truck roars up, then passes. Serafina drops her fan. As-

sunta opens a bottle of spumanti with a loud pop, pours a glass for
Serafina and advises, "Calm yourself. Drink this wine and before
the glass is empty he'll be in your arms." The old woman leaves
and Serafina, returning indolently to the sofa, lifts her hands to her
swelling breasts and murmurs, "Oh, it's so wonderful, having *two*
lives in the body. . . ." She picks up a bowl of roses and carries
them to the back bedroom.

To the front of the house comes Estelle Hohengarten, a thin
blonde whose hair has an unnatural gloss. The little girl, Rosa, is
there, and Estelle asks if the lady that does the sewing is in the
house. Rosa takes her into the parlor and calls for her mother.
Estelle looks around the room while waiting for Serafina, notices a
small framed picture on the cupboard and picks it up to look at it.
Serafina, coming in, says sharply, "That is my husband's picture."

Estelle seems in an unusual hurry to get a man's shirt made from
some rose-colored silk which she has brought. She needs it by tomorrow, for she is in love with a man and tomorrow is the anniversary of the day they met. She will pay double—triple—even
twenty-five dollars to get the shirt made on time, and she has brought
the measurements with her. Serafina is stunned, but not stunned
enough to refuse the job.

Outside, a boy calls to Rosa, "The black goat's in your yard!"
Forgetting her visitor, Serafina runs out on the porch and begins to
shout furiously, "Catch him, before he gets at the vines!" Another
old woman, known as the Strega, runs into the yard after the goat—
an outlandish woman with wild gray hair, a black skirt she holds
high during the pursuit, and hairy legs. Serafina warns her small
daughter not to look at the Strega, for she is a witch; she has a white
eye and every finger is crooked. But Rosa is a modern child and
unimpressed; she explains to her mother that the Strega has a
cataract and her fingers are crooked from rheumatism. Her mother
knows better: it's the evil eye, and her fingers are twisted because
the Strega shook hands with the devil. She violently pushes her
daughter into the house just as the Strega, still in pursuit of the goat,
looks back at Serafina and chuckles. The seamstress cries, "Maloc-
chio!" and, holding one hand to her face, makes the sign of the horns
with her other hand to ward off the evil eye.

The curtain falls.

Scene II

It is just before dawn the next day. Father De Leo, a priest, and
several black-shawled women, including Assunta, are standing outside Serafina's house. "I think a woman should tell her," the priest

is saying. "I think Assunta must tell her that Rosario is dead."

The lights reveal the interior of the house, and Serafina standing in a frozen attitude with her hands clutching her throat and her eyes staring fearfully toward the sound of voices outside. "I think," says Assunta, "she already knows what we have come to tell her."

The lights dim out.

Scene III

It is noon of the same day. Assunta is removing a funeral wreath on the door of the house and a doctor and Father De Leo are on the porch. The doctor announces, "She's lost the baby," and gives Assunta a hypodermic and some morphine, with instructions how to use it if Serafina screams or tries to get up again.

Father De Leo has other instructions: The body of Rosario must not be burned. True, the body was burned somewhat when Rosario was shot at the wheel of the truck, because the truck caught fire; but there must be no cremation because this is an abomination in the sight of God.

"But the instructions of a widow have to be carried out," the doctor objects, and the priest asks, "Do you know why she wants the body cremated? So she can keep the ashes here in the house. . . . Pagan idolatry is what I call it!"

Estelle Hohengarten comes to the house, black-veiled and carrying a bunch of roses. Within the house there is an instant hubbub of women mourners, who flock out on the porch and whisper and gesticulate excitedly. The priest says, "You must never come here. The widow knows nothing about you." The women mourners shout angrily at Estelle and finally flog her with her own bouquet of roses. Estelle falls weeping on the walk, begging that she be allowed to see Rosario's body, but she is driven off. Everybody goes inside except Rosa, who picks up Estelle's roses and black veil. She puts the black veil over her head and for the first time begins to weep, violently. A little boy comes by, bouncing a rubber ball, and Rosa screams, "Go home! My papa is dead!"

The lights dim out.

Scene IV

Three years have passed. It is morning. A group of local mothers storms Serafina's house, indignant over her delay in delivering the graduation dresses for their daughters. Many of them, chattering in Sicilian, race around the house, banging doors and shutters. One of the women tells another about how, yesterday, she came here and demanded her graduation dress and Serafina had called from the house, "Tomorrow!" This woman was about to go away when she heard a call, and in the window was the girl, Rosa—naked. "She say, 'Signora, please, you call this numero and ask for Jack and tell Jack my clothes are lock up so I can't get out from the house.' Then Serafina come and she grab-a the girl by the hair and she pull her way from the window and she slam the shutters right in my face!"

Why should Rosa be locked up? A boy, of course. One of the women knows about him—a sailor. The girl met him at the high school dance, and when her mother heard about it she locked up her daughter's clothes. Now Rosa can't go to the high school to take the examinations.

The women keep up their clamor around Serafina's house, and at last Serafina staggers out onto the porch. She has on only a soiled pink slip, and her hair is wild. *"Aiuto! Aiuto!"* she screams at the crowd. Miss Yorke, a spinsterish high school teacher, decides she can handle the situation; she walks directly into the house. In a moment Serafina dashes back onto the porch, seemingly demented, and gasps in a hoarse whisper, "She cut her wrist, my daughter, she cut her wrist!" She runs screaming into the yard, calling for a doctor, and her friend Assunta seizes her and leads her toward the house just as Miss Yorke appears and says, "Mrs. delle Rose, your daughter has not cut her wrist. Now come back into the house. Your daughter's all right. And you ladies please go away!" But the ladies won't go away until they get their dresses.

Inside the house, Miss Yorke calls to Rosa, "Come here and show your mother that you are not bleeding to death." The girl appears, silently and sullenly, clad in an undergarment and with a small white handkerchief tied around one wrist. Seeing the handkerchief, the girl's mother gives an animal cry.

ROSA—Lasciami stare, Mama!—I'm so ashamed I could die. This is the way she goes around all the time. She hasn't put on clothes since my father was killed. For three years she sits at the sewing machine and never puts a dress on or goes out of the house, and now she has locked my clothes up so *I* can't go out. She wants me to be like her, a freak of the neighborhood, the way she is! Next time, next time, I won't cut my wrist but my throat! I don't want to live locked up with a bottle of ashes! (*She points to the shrine.*)

ASSUNTA—Figlia, figlia, figlia, non devi parlare cosí!

MISS YORKE—Mrs. delle Rose, please give me the key to the closet so that your daughter can dress for the graduation!

SERAFINA (*surrendering the key*)—Ecco la—chiave . . . (ROSA *snatches the key and runs back through the curtains.*)

MISS YORKE—Now why did you lock her clothes up, Mrs. delle Rose?

SERAFINA—The wrist is still bleeding!

MISS YORKE—No, the wrist is not bleeding. It's just a skin cut, a scratch. But the child is exhausted from all this excitement and hasn't eaten a thing in two or three days.

ROSA (*running into the dining room*)—Four days! I only asked her one favor. Not to let me go out but to let Jack come to the house so she could meet him!—Then she locked my clothes up!

MISS YORKE—Your daughter missed her final examinations at the high school, but her grades have been so good that she will be allowed to graduate with her class and take the examinations later.— You understand me, Mrs. delle Rose! (ROSA *goes into the back of the house.*)

SERAFINA (*standing at the curtains*)—See the way she looks at me? I've got a wild thing in the house, and her wrist is still bleeding!

MISS YORKE—Let's not have any more outbursts of emotion!

SERAFINA—Outbursts of—you make me sick! Sick! Sick at my stomach you make me! Your school, you make all this trouble! You give-a this dance where she gets mixed up with a sailor.

MISS YORKE—You are talking about the Hunter girl's brother, a sailor named Jack, who attended the dance with his sister?

SERAFINA—"Attended with sister!"—Attended with *sister!*—My daughter, she's nobody's sister! (ROSA *comes out of the back room. She is radiantly beautiful in her graduation gown.*)

ROSA—Don't listen to her, don't pay any attention to her, Miss Yorke.—I'm ready to go to the high school.

Serafina, stunned by her daughter's beauty, begs for a kiss, but the girl rushes out on the porch and her mother's shoulders droop in desolation. Serafina moans in Italian that she is alone in the world, and suddenly she dashes to the porch. Rosa covers her face in shame as her mother heedlessly plunges out into the front yard, crying to Miss Yorke, "You give this dance where she gets mixed up with a sailor. What do you think you want to do at this high school?" While Rosa leans against a tree, weeping tears of mortification, the teacher declares to Serafina, "I don't understand how a woman that acts like you could have such a sweet and refined young girl for a daughter!"

The girl sobs, "I'm so ashamed I could die; I'm so ashamed. Oh,

you don't know, Miss Yorke, the way that we live. She never puts
on a dress; she stays all the time in that dirty old pink slip—and
talks to my father's ashes like he was living!" Serafina begins another outburst, and Rosa rushes down the street in the brilliant
Spring light, crying, "Mama, you look disgusting!" The teacher
hurries after her.

Assunta leads Serafina back into the house, but the women gathered round shout that they will not go away until they get their
dresses. Serafina gives in, telling them to come get the dresses;
the names are pinned on all of them. Soon the women come out,
cradling the white voile dresses in their arms and uttering exclamations of admiration. When they have gone, Serafina stands looking
at herself in a mirror. She repeats her daughter's word: "Disgusting!"

Music, rather than lights, indicates a change of scene.

SCENE V

Turning from the mirror, Serafina snatches a long-neglected
girdle out of a drawer, holds it experimentally about her waist,
shakes her head doubtfully. Dropping the girdle, she snatches a
hat off the millinery dummy, tries it, hastily takes it off and replaces
it on the dummy. She tries a gown draped over another dummy
and it won't fit; then she tries the girdle again, but it's no go. The
high school band has begun playing and Serafina can hear it in the
distance. She becomes panicky in fear that she will miss the graduation ceremonies.

Outside the house appear Flora and Bessie, two women of middle
years and juvenile temperament. They are dressed for a party.
One of them, Flora, bangs at the cottage door, and the other one,
Bessie, complains that she fails to understand why it is so important to pick up a polka-dot blouse when it is likely to make them
miss the twelve o'clock train.

Serafina has managed to find in the bedroom a purple silk dress she
can wear, and, hurrying from the bedroom to the sewing room,
she snatches the hat off the millinery dummy again and claps it on
her head. Now she repeats to herself, "Wrist watch! Wrist watch!
Where'd I put the wrist watch?" When she hears Flora shouting
and banging she runs to the front door, sees who it is and says,
"Don't bother me! I'm late for the graduation of my daughter
and now I can't find her graduation present."

But Flora is not easily put aside; she pushes in, followed by
Bessie, and sees her partly finished blouse on the sewing machine.

"Get started, woman," she cries. "Stitch them bandannas together. If you don't do it, I'm a-gonna report you to the Chamber of Commerce and get your license revoked!" Serafina doesn't know about licenses, never having had any, but it sounds ominous, so she goes to work on the blouse with furious speed. A train whistle is heard and Bessie cries to Flora, "Train's pullin' out! Oh, God, you made us miss it!"

Bessie is in a veritable passion to get to the city, for she has been told it is full of excitement—people dropping paper sacks full of water out of hotel windows. Flora reminds her companion that there will be another train at twelve forty-five, and as Serafina works these two talk excitedly about the big doings in the city— Legionnaires tearing the clothes off girls and sending them home nude in taxis and all kinds of pleasant happenings.

Ominously, Serafina warns the pair to watch how they talk, saying, "This here is a Catholic house. You are sitting in the same room with Our Lady and the blessed ashes of my husband!"

Bessie, at the window, cries, "Some Legionnaires are on the highway!" Flora runs to join her, and both start bobbing their heads out the window. Apparently one man is looking their way, and Flora, leaning out, sings, "Mademoiselle from Armentières, parleyvoo!" Bessie joins in the singing. From outside a man's voice returns the salute, singing, "Hadn't been kissed for forty years." More Legionnaires are heard laughing, and a car horn honks as they drive away. Serafina is in a pure fury; she shouts, "Get out on the streets where you kind a wimmen belong! This is the house of Rosario delle Rose and those are his ashes in that marble urn and I won't have—unproper things going on here or dirty talk, neither!"

Serafina continues her outburst as Flora and Bessie taunt her by saying she is wild with envy of them. The seamstress shouts that when she thinks of men, she thinks only of her husband—and now she is thinking of the happiness of her daughter, who's graduating this morning out of high school. "And now I'm going to be late," she wails. "The band is playing, and I have lost her wrist watch! Her graduation present!"

Flora won't budge until she gets her blouse. The high school band can be heard playing a martial air, but Serafina, her chest heaving violently, seems to forget that she must be going. "I remember," she says, "I remember my husband with a body like a young boy and hair on his head as thick and black as mine is and skin on him smooth and sweet as a yellow rose petal."

Flora sneers, "Oh, a *rose,* was he? . . . Yes, a rose of a Wop!— of a gangster!—shot smuggling dope under a load of bananas!"

Serafina does not seem to hear this. Her husband, she says, was the best—not the third best and not the second best, but the *first* best. So now she stays here and is satisfied to remember. She remembers all the nights she held him in her arms. Each night for twelve years—four thousand, three hundred and eighty nights. "I *knew* what love-making was," she exclaims. "And I'm satisfied just to remember . . ." She is panting heavily now as she cries to Flora and Bessie, "Go on, you do it, you go on the streets and let them drop their dirty sacks of water on you! I'm satisfied to remember the love of a man that was mine—*only mine!* Never touched by the hand of *nobody!* Nobody but me!" Serafina runs out onto the porch, sobbing.

FLORA (*crossing to the open door*)—Never touched by nobody?

SERAFINA (*with fierce pride*)—Never nobody but me!

FLORA—*I* know somebody that could a tale unfold! And not so far from here neither. Not no further than the Square Roof is, that place on Esplanade!

BESSIE—Estelle Hohengarten!

FLORA—Estelle Hohengarten!—the blackjack dealer from Texas!

BESSIE—Get into your blouse and let's go!

FLORA—Everybody's known it but Serafina. I'm just telling the facts that come out at the inquest while she was in bed with her eyes shut tight and the sheet pulled over her head like a female ostrich! Tie this damn thing on me! It was a romance, not just a fly-by-night thing, but a steady affair that went on for more than a year. (SERAFINA *has been standing on the porch with the door open behind her. She is in the full glare of the sun. She appears to have been struck senseless by the words shouted inside. She turns slowly about. We see that her dress is unfastened down the back, the pink slip showing. She reaches out gropingly with one hand and finds the porch column which she clings to while the terrible words strike constantly deeper. The high school band continues as a merciless counterpoint.*)

BESSIE—Leave her in ignorance. Ignorance is bliss.

FLORA—He had a rose tattoo on his chest, the stuck-up thing, and Estelle was so gone on him she went down to Bourbon Street and had one put on her. (SERAFINA *comes onto the porch and* FLORA *turns to her, viciously.*) Yeah, a rose tattoo on her chest same as the Wop's!

SERAFINA (*very softly*)—Liar . . . (*She comes inside; the word seems to give her strength.*)

BESSIE (*nervously*)—Flora, let's go, let's go!

SERAFINA (*in a terrible voice*)—Liar!—*Li-i*-arrrrr! (*She slams the wooden door shut with a violence that shakes the walls.*)

BESSIE (*shocked into terror*)—Let's get outa here, Flora!

FLORA—Let her howl her head off. I don't care. (SERAFINA *has snatched up a broom.*)

BESSIE—What's she up to?

FLORA—I don't care what she's up to!

BESSIE—I'm a-scared of these Wops.

FLORA—I'm not afraid of nobody!

BESSIE—She's gonna hit you.

FLORA—She'd better not hit me! (*But both of the clowns are in retreat to the door.* SERAFINA *suddenly rushes at them with the broom. She flails* FLORA *about the hips and shoulders.* BESSIE *gets out. But* FLORA *is trapped in a corner. A table is turned over.* BESSIE, *outside, screams for the police and cries:* "Murder! Murder!" *The high school band is playing* The Stars and Stripes Forever. FLORA *breaks wildly past the flailing broom and escapes out of the house. She also takes up the cry for help.* SERAFINA *follows them out. She is flailing the brilliant noon air with the broom. The two women run off, screaming.* FLORA *calls back.*) I'm going to have her arrested! Police, police! I'm going to have you arrested!

SERAFINA—*Have* me arrested, *have* me, you dirt, you devil, you liar! Li-i-arrr! (*She comes back inside the house and leans on the work table for a moment, panting heavily. Then she rushes back to the door, slams it and bolts it. Then she rushes to the windows, slams the shutters and fastens them. The house is now dark except for the vigil light in the ruby glass cup before the Madonna, and the delicate beams admitted through the shutter slats.*)

SERAFINA (*in a crazed manner*)—Have me—have me—arrested— dirty slut—bitch—liar! (*She moves about helplessly, not knowing what to do with her big, stricken body. Panting for breath, she repeats the word "liar" monotonously and helplessly as she thrashes about. It is necessary for her, vitally necessary for her, to believe that the woman's story is a malicious invention. But the words of it stick in her mind and she mumbles them aloud as she thrashes crazily around the small confines of the parlor.*) Woman—Estelle —(*The sound of band music is heard.*) Band, band, already— started.—Going to miss—graduation. Oh! (*She retreats toward the Madonna.*) Estelle, Estelle Hohengarten?—"A shirt for a man I'm in love with! This man—is—wild like a gypsy."—Oh, oh, Lady—The—rose-colored—silk. (*She starts toward the dining room, then draws back in terror.*) No, no, no, no, no! I don't remember! It wasn't that name, I don't remember the name! (*The band music grows louder.*) High school—graduation—late! I'll be—late for it.—Oh, Lady, give me a—*sign!* (*She cocks her head toward the statue in a fearful listening attitude.*) Che? Che dice, Signora? *Oh, Lady! Give me a sign!*

The lights dim out.

Scene VI

It is two hours later. The house is dark except for the vigil light, illuminating the starry blue robe of the statue of Our Lady above the ruby glass cup. Serafina's voice is heard, very weakly, in the weak, breathless tone of a person near death, pleading, "Oh, Lady, give me a sign. . . ."

There are gay, laughing voices outside the house—Rosa and Jack shouting to some friends in a car and making plans for a picnic. Rosa races up the porch steps, finds the door locked and tells Jack to get the extra key out of the bird bath in the yard. Jack is a sailor—young, good-looking, with a gold earring in one ear. The young people are carrying roses and gifts. Rosa figures that her mother must be out, because the door is locked and the shutters are closed; so Jack opens the door with the extra key and they go in. He puts down the roses he is carrying. Rosa beckons him to her and begins raining kisses upon him until he forcibly removes her face from his. "Just think," she exclaims, "a week ago Friday I didn't know boys existed! . . . Did you know girls existed before the dance?"

Jack—Yes, I knew they existed . . .

Rosa (*holding him*)—Do you remember what you said to me on the dance floor? "Honey, you're dancing too close?"

Jack—Well, it was—hot in the Gym and the—floor was crowded.

Rosa—When my girl friend was teaching me how to dance, I asked her, "How do you know which way the boy's going to move?" And she said, "You've got to feel how he's going to move with your body!" I said, "How do you feel with your body?" And she said, "By pressing up close!"—That's why I pressed up close! I didn't realize that I was— Ha, ha! Now you're blushing! Don't go *away!*—And a few minutes later you said to me, "Gee, you're beautiful!" I said, "Excuse me," and ran to the ladies' room. Do you know why? To look at myself in the mirror! And I saw that I was! For the first time in my life I was beautiful! You'd made me beautiful when you *said* that I was!

JACK (*humbly*)—You *are* beautiful, Rosa! So much, I . . .

ROSA—*You've* changed, *too.* You've stopped laughing and joking. Why have you gotten so old and serious, Jack?

JACK—Well, honey, you're sort of . . .

ROSA—What am I "sort of"?

JACK (*finding the exact word*)—*Wild!* (*She laughs. He seizes the bandaged wrist.*) I didn't know nothing like this was going to happen.

ROSA—Oh, that, that's nothing! I'll take the handkerchief off and you can forget it.

JACK—How could you do a thing like that over me? I'm— nothing!

ROSA—Everybody is nothing until you love them!

JACK—Give me that handkerchief. I want to show it to my ship-mates. I'll say, "This is the blood of a beautiful girl who cut her wrist with a knife because she loved me!"

ROSA—Don't be so pleased with yourself. It's mostly Mercuro-chrome!

SERAFINA (*violently, from the dark room adjoining*)—*Stai zitta! —Cretina!* (ROSA and JACK *draw abruptly apart.*)

JACK (*fearfully*)—I knew somebody was here!

ROSA (*sweetly and delicately*)—Mama? Are you in there, Mama?

SERAFINA—No, no, no, I'm not, I'm dead and buried!

ROSA—Yes, Mama's in there!

JACK—Well, I—better go and—wait outside for a—while . . .

ROSA—You stay right here!—Mama?—Jack is with me.—Are you dressed up nicely? (*There is no response.*) Why's it so dark in here?—Jack, open the shutters!—I want to introduce you to my mother . . .

JACK—Hadn't I better go and . . .

ROSA—No. Open the shutters! (*The shutters are opened and* ROSA *draws apart the curtains between the two rooms. Sunlight floods the scene.* SERAFINA *is revealed slumped in a chair at her work table in the dining room near the Singer sewing machine. She is grotesquely surrounded by the dummies, as though she had been holding a silent conference with them. Her appearance, in slovenly deshabille, is both comic and shocking.* ROSA, *terribly embarrassed.*) Mama, Mama, you said you were dressed up pretty! Jack, stay out for a minute! What's happened, Mama? (JACK *remains in the parlor.* ROSA *pulls the curtains, snatches a robe and flings it over* SERAFINA. *She brushes* SERAFINA'S *hair back from her sweat-gleaming face, rubs her face with a handkerchief and dusts it with powder.*

SERAFINA *submits to this cosmetic enterprise with a dazed look.*
ROSA *gestures vertically.*) Su, su, su, su, su, su, su, su, su! (SERA-
FINA *sits up slightly in her chair, but she is still looking stupefied.*
ROSA *returns to the parlor and opens the curtains again.*) Come in,
Jack! Mama is ready to meet you!

Rosa trembles with eagerness as Jack advances nervously from
the parlor—but before he can get into the sewing room Serafina has
collapsed again. Rosa cries violently, "This is Jack Hunter!" Jack
offers a pleasant hello and the mother stares indifferently at him.
Jack tries to make conversation about the graduation; his sister
and mother and a whole bunch of cousins were there, and he had
hoped that Mrs. delle Rose would be there, too. He says the right
things, and Rosa tries to help out, too, with bright and happy details
of the graduation and the ensuing dance. Suddenly she remembers
her prize and asks Jack to get it from the parlor, and in the moment he is gone she tries deperately to arouse her mother. Jack
returns with the prize Rosa has won—*The Digest of Knowledge.*
Serafina, rousing a bit, asks, "Diploma, where is it? Didn't you get
no diploma?" Her daughter proudly holds up the diploma—and
is told to put it in the drawer with her father's clothes.

Jack tries manfully again, telling Mrs. delle Rose that she should
be proud of her daughter. "How does it feel to be the mother of
the prettiest girl in the world?" he asks. Rosa bursts into delighted
laughter and her mother, suddenly rousing and suddenly angry, tells
Jack to put the prize book in the parlor and shut the front door.
"There was a policeman come here because of—some trouble—"
she says vaguely. Jack returns from his errand, still singing the
praises of Rosa. "Who are *you?*" Serafina asks, and Rosa cries,
"Mama, I just introduced him; his name is Jack Hunter."

Bitterly Serafina queries, "What are you hunting, Jack? . . .
What are all of 'em hunting? To have a good time . . . I'm sick
of men, I'm almost as sick of men as I am of wimmen.—Rosa, get
out while I talk to this boy!" The girl, fearing the happiest day of
her life will be ruined, goes into the back of the house to change
from her graduation dress. Jack tries to tell the girl's mother all
the details of what has happened: He came home to see his folks
after three months at sea and his sister took him to a high school
dance and he danced with Rosa. Next night, he took Rosa to the
movies and they ate a bag of popcorn, and the night after that they
went roller skating and afterward had a soda.

Serafina has been questioning the boy as sharply as a criminal
prosecutor; now she demands, "You mean that you haven't been

alone with my Rosa?" He assures her he has not—and further assures her that he is as much of a virgin as the girl is. He is in love, he says solemnly—very much.

Rosa comes from the back of the house, dressed for the picnic, and her mother orders her out on the porch. Again alone with Jack, Serafina slams the porch door shut. Rosa runs despairingly around the side of the house to lean, with closed eyes, against a tree trunk, and the Strega creeps into the yard, listening. Serafina shouts to Jack, "I know what men want—not to eat popcorn with girls or to slide on ice!" Rosa runs to the back door and pounds on it for admission; she hears her mother ask if Jack is a Catholic, and Jack's reply that he is. At the window now, Rosa listens despairingly as her mother forces Jack to kneel before the statue of Our Lady and repeat after her a most solemn and holy promise that he will respect Rosa's innocence. It is an ordeal for both the boy and the girl, but when it is ended Serafina declares, "I am satisfied now." Her daughter jumps through the window and rushes to her with outflung arms and cries of joy.

Serafina's mood has changed completely. She goes for some wine glasses, so they may drink a toast, and when she is out of sight Rosa seizes Jack's hand and presses it to her throat, her lips, and then to her breast. He snatches his hand away as Serafina returns with the glasses. Outside, voices begin calling for Rosa, and a car horn is blowing. The mother, remembering her graduation present, crouches before the bureau and removes a fancily wrapped package from the bottom drawer. But Rosa and Jack are on their way out, calling good-by. Alone, Serafina says vaguely, "It's a Bulova wrist watch with seventeen jewels in it. . . ." Holding the present, she goes to the door and cries, "Rosa!" But the car has started off. There is a derisive cackle from the Strega outside. The mother absently opens the package, winds the watch and holds it against her ear. Then she holds it away from her and glares at it fiercely, pounding her chest three times and crying, "Tick—tick—tick!" Facing the Madonna she pleads, "Speak to me, Lady! Oh, Lady, give me a sign!"

The curtain falls.

ACT II

It is two hours later, and Serafina is on the porch, barefoot, wearing a rayon slip which has dark wine stains on it. It is difficult for her to stand, but she cannot sit, and she moans almost continually. She drags a broken chair off the porch into the yard and sinks into it, still pleading for a sign. Father De Leo ap-

proaches the house; Serafina tries to hide in her chair, but the priest
sees her and scolds her severely for the change in her appearance
and behavior since her husband died. He knew it would happen
when she broke the Church law and had Rosario cremated—setting
up a little idolatrous shrine in her house. Now, he continues, she
has become a neighborhood character.

Two women approach the house and she shouts at them that she
does no more sewing and they should not hang around in front of
her house. She knows what they are here for: "They think they
know something that Serafina don't know; they think I got *these*
on my head"—and she holds two fingers like horns on either side
of her head. In spite of the urgings of the priest, she will not go
back into her house; it has a tin roof on it and she can't breathe,
she explains. The Strega has been creeping through a canebrake,
pretending to search for chickens, and Serafina, hearing her, drives
her off. The priest argues gently that, though she seems to have no
friends, she is still a young woman, eligible for loving—and bearing—again. But now she has no companions; women don't mix
with her. And indeed they don't; the neighbors prefer to watch,
and even now some women are watching from the embankment.
Serafina glares at them contemptuously, saying, violently:

"They make the life without glory. Instead of the heart they
got the deep-freeze in the house. The men, they don't feel no
glory, not in the house with them women; they go to the bars, fight
in them, get drunk, get fat, put horns on the women because the
women don't give them the love which is glory.—I did, I give him
the glory. To me the big bed was beautiful like a religion. Now
I lie on it with dreams, with memories only! But it is still beautiful
to me and I don't believe that the man in my heart gave me horns!
(*The women whisper.*) What, what are they saying? Does ev'rybody know something that I don't know?—No, all I want is a sign,
a sign from Our Lady, to tell me the lie is a lie! And then I . . .
(*The women laugh on the embankment.* SERAFINA *starts fiercely
toward them. They scatter.*) Squeak, squeak, squawk, squawk!
Hens—like water thrown on them!" (*There is the sound of mocking
laughter.*)

FATHER DE LEO—People are laughing at you on all the porches.
SERAFINA—I'm laughing, too. Listen to me, I'm laughing! (*She
breaks into loud, false laughter, first from the porch, then from the
foot of the embankment, then crossing in front of the house.*) Ha,
ha, ha, ha, ha, ha, ha! Now ev'rybody is laughing. Ha, ha, ha,
ha, ha, ha!

FATHER DE LEO—Zitta ora!—Think of your daughter.

SERAFINA (*understanding the word "daughter"*)—You, *you* think of my daughter! Today you give out the diplomas, today at the high school you give out the prizes, diplomas! You give to my daughter a set of books call the *Digest of Knowledge!* What does she know? How to be cheap already?—Oh, yes, that is what to learn, how to be cheap and to cheat!—You know what they do at this high school? They ruin the girls there! They give the spring dance because the girls are man-crazy. And there at that dance my daughter goes with a sailor that has in his ear a gold ring! And pants so tight that a woman ought not to look at him! This morning, this morning she cuts with a knife her wrist if I don't let her go!—Now all of them gone to some island, they call it a picnic, all of them, gone in a—boat!

FATHER DE LEO—There *was* a school picnic, chaperoned by the teachers.

SERAFINA—Oh, lo so, lo so! The man-crazy old maid teachers!—They all run wild on the island!

FATHER DE LEO—Serafina delle Rose! (*He picks up the chair by the back and hauls it to the porch when she starts to resume her seat.*)—I *command* you to go in the house.

SERAFINA—Go in the house? I will. I will go in the house if you will answer one question.—Will you answer one question?

FATHER DE LEO—I will if I know the answer.

SERAFINA—Aw, you know the answer!—You used to hear the confessions of my husband. (*She turns to face the priest.*)

FATHER DE LEO—Yes, I heard his confessions . . .

SERAFINA (*with difficulty*)—Did he ever speak to you of a *woman?*

The priest picks up his hat and starts away from the house, saying he cannot break the Church laws. The secrets of the confessional are sacred. Becoming more and more aroused, Serafina pursues him, clutches him, begging that he tell her lest she go mad and go back into the house and smash the urn with the ashes of her husband's body. Neighbor women begin to crowd around, muttering in shocked whispers at Serafina's lack of respect for the priesthood. Father De Leo is getting frightened; there are people watching, and if she doesn't let him go he must call for help. "Tell them all," she challenges, "shout it all to them up and down the whole block! The widow delle Rose is not respectable, she is not even a woman, she is an animal! She is attacking the priest! She will tear the black suit off him unless he tells her the whores in this town are lying to her!"

The priest is an old man—sixty-seven—and the neighbors think it is time to move in and rescue him. While he shouts for a policeman, the neighbor women drag Serafina off and lead him away. Serafina collapses on the porch steps, moaning, "Oh, Lady, Lady, give me a sign." If there is an answer this time, it is a mocking one, for up to the house comes a loudly dressed fat man—a novelty salesman. He begins his long spiel about his great novelty offer and she listens dully. The spiel is interrupted by the sound of a truck stopping and the angry cry of a man on the highway, "Hey! Hey, you road hog!"

Down the embankment from the road comes Alvaro, a dark, good-looking Mediterranean type about twenty-five years old. He is short, but has a massively sculptured torso; his face and manner seem, somehow, clownish. Alvaro isn't clowning, though, when he marches up to the salesman and accuses this worthy of forcing his truck off the highway. The salesman further infuriates him by contemptuously calling Alvaro "Macaroni" and then "Spaghetti." Evidently he has been offering similar taunts, like "Wop" and "Dago," on the road. Alvaro declares that, since he is a human being that drives a truck of bananas, he is going to fight. He knows he will get fired if he fights, but fight he will.

Spectators begin to gather around. Alvaro snatches a cigar from the salesman's mouth—and the salesman suddenly brings up his knee into Alvaro's groin. The young man, bent double and retching with pain, staggers to the porch, and the salesman goes away, shouting that he has Alvaro's license number and that he knows his boss. The truck driver groans, "Lady, lady, I got to go in the house!" Serafina follows him in. He leans on a dressmaker's dummy and sobs heavily. "I always cry after a fight," he explains, "but I don't want people to see me. It's not like a man." In sympathy, Serafina begins to sob, too. After a bit they quiet down and she notices that his jacket—his company jacket—is torn. She says she will sew it up if he will take it off.

Alvaro sobs again when he thinks of getting fired on account of the fight—him, with three dependents! Serafina asks him to stop crying so she can stop crying, and directs him to open the shutters so that she can see to work. As light strikes the room she gasps, "Ohhhh," at the sight of his fine torso beneath a wet, clinging undershirt. To herself she says, "The light on the body was like a man that lived here. . . ."

The truck driver asks where the bathroom is, and while he is gone the seamstress marvels, "My husband's body, with the head of a clown! . . . Oh, Lady," she implores the Madonna, "is it a sign?"

Then, impulsively, she clambers on a chair by the cupboard and reaches a bottle of wine—but she cannot get down. Alvaro, returning, lifts her down. He introduces himself: His last name is Mangiacavallo—a comical name in English, he admits, for it means Eat-a-Horse. Today has been a bad day; first his pay envelope was garnisheed, and then this road hog—and what is it she has in her hand—a bottle of vino?

Proudly Serafina replies, "This is spumanti. It comes from the house of the family of my husband. The delle Rose! A very great family. I was a peasant, but I married a baron!" The young truck driver asks politely where the Baron is and she points gravely to the marble urn. He crosses himself. There is a youthful cry from outside, and the woman says, "There is a wild bunch of boys and girls in this town." Alvaro works the cork out of the bottle with a loud pop, pours two glasses of wine, and they drink. Suddenly he springs to the window, shouting, "Hey, you kids, git down off that truck! Keep your hands off them bananas!"

He drives bananas! Serafina tells him her husband hauled bananas, too, and something else. . . . She tells Alvaro of her husband —of the rose tattoo on his chest, even of her having the tattoo on her breast the night she conceived her son—the little boy that was lost when she lost her husband. Today two people told her an awful lie in front of the ashes—so awful a lie that she would smash the urn and throw away the ashes if she thought the lie was true.

Alvaro is all sympathy—and compliments. It's a cozy little place she's got here.

SERAFINA—Oh, it's—molto modesto.—You got a nice place too?

ALVARO—I got a place with three dependents in it.

SERAFINA—What—dependents?

ALVARO (*counting them on his fingers*)—One old maid sister, one feeble-minded grandmother, one lush of a pop that's not worth the powder it takes to blow him to hell.—They got the parchesi habit. They play the game of parchesi, morning, night, noon. Passing a bucket of beer around the table . . .

SERAFINA—They got the beer habit, too?

ALVARO—Oh, yes. And the numbers habit. This spring the old maid sister gets female trouble—mostly mental, I think—she turns the housekeeping over to the feeble-minded grandmother, a very sweet old lady who don't think it is necessary to pay the grocery bill so long as there's money to play the numbers. She plays the numbers. She has a perfect system except it don't ever work. And the grocery bill goes up, up, up, up, up!—so high you can't even

see it!—Today the Ideal Grocery Company garnishees my wages
. . . There, now! I've told you my life . . . (*The parrot squawks.
He goes over to the cage.*) Hello, Polly, how's tricks?

SERAFINA—The name ain't Polly. It ain't a she; it's a he.

ALVARO—How can you tell with all them tail feathers? (*He
sticks his finger in the cage, pokes at the parrot and gets bitten.*)
Owww!

SERAFINA (*vicariously*)—Ouuu . . . (ALVARO *sticks his injured
finger in his mouth.* SERAFINA *puts her corresponding finger in her
mouth. He crosses to the telephone.*) I told you watch out.—What
are you calling, a doctor?

ALVARO—I am calling my boss in Biloxi to explain why I'm late.

SERAFINA—The call to Biloxi is a ten-cent call.

ALVARO—Don't worry about it.

SERAFINA—I'm not worried about it. You will pay it.

ALVARO—You got a sensible attitude toward life . . . Give me
the Southern Fruit Company in Biloxi—seven-eight-seven!

SERAFINA—You are a bachelor. With three dependents? (*She
glances below his belt.*)

ALVARO—I'll tell you my hopes and dreams!

SERAFINA—Who? Me?

ALVARO—I am hoping to meet some sensible older lady. Maybe
a lady a little bit older than me.—I don't care if she's a little too
plump or not such a stylish dresser! (SERAFINA *self-consciously
pulls up a dangling strap.*) The important thing in a lady is understanding. Good sense. And I want her to have a well-furnished
house and a profitable little business of some kind . . . (*He looks
about him significantly.*)

SERAFINA—And such a lady, with a well-furnished house and
business, what does she want with a man with three dependents
with the parchesi and the beer habit, playing the numbers!

ALVARO—Love and affection!—in a world that is lonely—and
cold!

SERAFINA—It might be lonely but I would not say "cold" on this
particular day!

ALVARO—Love and affection is what I got to offer on hot or cold
days in this lonely old world and is what I am looking for. I got
nothing else. Mangiacavallo has nothing. In fact, he is the grandson of the village idiot of Ribera!

SERAFINA (*uneasily*)—I see you like to make—jokes!

ALVARO—No, no joke!—Davvero!—He chased my grandmother
in a flooded rice field. She slip on a wet rock.—Ecco! Here I am.

Alvaro finally gets his boss on the phone and attempts a jovial approach. It doesn't work; he is fired. This means he doesn't need his company jacket immediately, and Serafina can't see very well to work. She has a suggestion: in the bottom drawer of the bureau he will find a shirt in white tissue paper which he can wear until she gets his own garment fixed. She explains that the shirt was made for somebody who never called for it. He gets out the package and she asks if there is a name on it; there is, and he starts to read it, but she fiercely exclaims, "Don't tell me the name! Throw it away, out the window!" . . . It is a beautiful rose silk shirt.

Alvaro slips voluptuously into the garment, and again there is a distant cry of children. One child cries from the front yard that the black goat is there again. Through the yard comes the Strega, carrying a broken length of rope and calling, "Heyeh, Billy! Heyeh, heyeh." Serafina makes the sign of the cross and explains to her visitor that both the Strega and the goat have the evil eye. The goat got into the yard the night she lost her Rosario and her boy. "Get that goat out of my yard," she begs. Alvaro runs out the front door, joins in the chase, soon captures the animal and turns it over to the Strega. He returns to the house and says he must go now, but before going he offers a bit of advice, or comment, saying, "You have put your heart in the marble urn with the ashes." He calmly announces that he will pass by tonight, for supper, and bring the shirt back.

Serafina is not unwilling—if her daughter hasn't come home from the picnic. She must be careful to set her daughter a perfect example—so, if the shutters are open, he can come in; but if they are closed, he must not.

Alvaro leaves, and the widow can hear him shouting for children to lay off them bananas. Then she hears the truck pulling away. "Rosario," she says, "forgive me! Forgive me for thinking the awful lie could be true!"

The curtain falls.

ACT III

The evening has come; outside the house children are playing, and inside is Serafina, sitting stiffly and formally on the sofa in a gown she has not worn since the death of her husband. From her movements it is obvious that she is wearing an unendurably tight girdle. Hearing a truck approaching on the highway, she rises to an odd, crouching position—but the truck passes on. She decides to take off the girdle and goes behind the sofa to do so. She has got it down as far as her knees when a truck stops with a screeching of brakes. Panicky, she manages to hobble through the curtains separating parlor and sewing room just as Alvaro appears out front, calling gaily. He comes in without asking, carrying a package and a candy box, and she, managing to free herself, returns to the parlor and covers her embarrassment by fixing wine glasses on a tray. He exclaims that he didn't expect to see her looking so pretty, and she notes that he has fixed himself up, too.

"I been to the Ideal Barber's. I got the whole works," he boasts. She notices, with some perturbation, that he has rose oil in his hair. He gives her the box of chocolates, and when she protests that she is too fat for such a gift he pinches the creamy flesh of her upper arm and tells her she is not fat—just pleasing and plump. Alvaro divines, from her nervousness, that he is proceeding too rapidly, so he changes the subject and asks about the daughter. Serafina tells him Rosa has the eyes of her father and his wild, stubborn blood. She tells of the graduation, and of the girl's meeting a sailor with a gold ring in his ear.

Taking Serafina's hand, the truck driver asks, casually, "Did he have a tattoo?" The startled woman demands, "Why do you ask me that?"

"*I* got a tattoo!"

Serafina, greatly disturbed, wants to know what kind of tattoo— a South Sea girl without clothes on, or a big red heart. . . . He takes off his tie, slowly unbuttons his shirt and bares his chest. "No, no, no!" she gasps. *"Not a rose!"*

Suddenly she feels faint and staggers out onto the porch, breathing hoarsely. He follows her, arduously, and, fearing the watchful neighbors, she retreats back to the house. He suggests that they try the candy and gives her a piece, but she just stands holding it, staring blankly. He urges her to eat it, but she cannot; so he asks her to put it in his mouth. When she has done so he seizes her hand and licks the chocolate off her fingers. His ambitions are now so obvious, so pronounced, that she orders him out of the house. "Go to the Square Roof," she suggests—but he keeps trying, pursuing her about the parlor until she threatens to smash the box of chocolates in his face. Suddenly he drops to his knees, sobbing and pounding the floor with his fists as he exclaims, "Everything in my life turns out like this!"

Serafina orders him to get up—there are people watching. She demands her shirt back. It has been a bad day for both of them— on account of two women, she thinks, who told her that her husband "had put on my head the nanny-goat's horns. . . . They told me my husband was having a steady affair with a woman at the Square Roof." Her anger continues to rise as she asks if Alvaro remembers the name on the slip of paper on the shirt.

"I remember the name," he says, "because I know the woman. The name was Estelle Hohengarten." Serafina plunges into the sewing room, snatches a knife out of the sideboard drawer there, thrusts it into her purse and returns to Alvaro, hysterically demanding that he take her to the Square Roof. He sees the knife blade sticking out of her purse, grabs the bag and asks her what she wants with this weapon. "To cut the lying tongue out of a woman's mouth! . . . I cut the heart out of that woman, she cut the heart out of me!"

The truck driver tries to soothe her, brings her a glass of wine. Going to the telephone, he gives a number and explains to Serafina that he will settle this whole problem for her. He will ask Estelle Hohengarten and Estelle, who deals a straight game of blackjack at the Square Roof, won't lie. In a few moments he has Estelle on the wire. "This is Mangiacavallo," he says. "I got a question to ask you which is a personal question . . ."

Estelle's answers can be heard in the receiver of Serafina's telephone. Yes, she remembers Rosario delle Rose. . . . Serafina snatches the telephone from Alvaro and screams, "This is the wife that's speaking! What do you know of my husband, what is the lie?" Estelle's reply is loud and clear: "Don't you remember? I brought you the rose-colored silk to make him a shirt. . . . If you think I am a liar, come here and let me show you his rose tattooed on my chest!"

With a terrible cry the widow hurls the telephone to the floor, and Alvaro, after persuading her to lie down on the sofa, goes out back to get some ice in a towel. Serafina gets up, moves toward the shrine, seizes the marble urn and flings it violently into the furthest corner of the room. Outside, mothers can be heard calling their children home, and the chorus is almost like music. Alvaro returns, but without ice, for he has broken the ice pick. Serafina does not want ice; she is trembling with violence as she declares, "Now I show you how wild and strong like a man a woman can be!" Going to the screen door she opens it and shouts, "Buona notte, Mr. Mangiacavallo!"

"You—you make me go *home,* now?" he expostulates.

She whispers her answer: He is not to go home—just pretend to. He must drive the truck out of sight and then return by the back door. "Arrivederci!" she shouts, and Alvaro, running to the embankment, shouts back, "Arrivederci . . . Buona notte!" Alone,

Serafina blows out the vigil light of the little shrine and stands, panting, at the open window. The night seems to be full of sinister noises. In the back of the house a door opens and Alvaro appears. "You have turn out the light!" he whispers.

"The moon is enough," says the widow. He advances toward her.

The curtain falls.

SCENE II

It is just before daybreak, and Jack and Rosa stop quietly in front of the house—back at last from their picnic. Both are very grave. The girl says this has been the happiest day of her life—and the saddest night. Occasionally they can hear a cry of "Rosario!" from the house, and Rosa explains that it is just her mother dreaming of her husband in her sleep. The nearness of the girl is almost overpowering to the young sailor and he wants to go, but she holds him by threatening to scream. Her willingness to give herself to him is a torturing temptation, but he remembers the oath he has taken—and her tender age.

ROSA—When does your—ship sail?

JACK—Tomorrow.

ROSA—Where to?

JACK—Guatemala.

SERAFINA (*from the house*)—Aahh!

ROSA—Is that a long trip?

JACK—After Guatemala, Buenos Aires. After Buenos Aires, Rio. Then around the Straits of Magellan and back up the west coast of South America, putting in at three ports before we dock at San Francisco.

ROSA—I don't think I will—ever see you again . . .

JACK—The ship won't sink!

ROSA (*faintly and forlornly*)—No, but—I think it could just happen once, and if it don't happen that time, it never can—later . . . (*A rooster crows. They face each other sadly and quietly.*) You don't need to be very old to understand how it works out. One time, one time, only once, it could be—God!—to remember.—Other times? Yes—they'd be something.—But only once, God—to remember . . . (*With a little sigh she crosses to pick up his white cap and hand it gravely to him.*)—I'm sorry to you it didn't—mean—that much . . .

JACK (*taking the cap and hurling it to the ground*)—Look! Look at my knuckles! You see them scabs on my knuckles? You know

how them scabs got there? They got there because I banged my
knuckles that hard on the deck of the sailboat!

Rosa—Because it—didn't quite happen? (JACK *jerks his head
up and down in grotesquely violent assent to her question.* ROSA
picks up his cap and returns it to him again.)—Because of the
promise to Mama! I'll never forgive her . . . (*There is a pause.*)
What time in the afternoon must you be on the boat?

JACK—Why?

ROSA—Just tell me what time.

JACK—Five!—Why?

ROSA—What will you be doing till five?

JACK—Well, I could be a goddam liar and tell you I was going to
—pick me a hatful of daisies in—Audubon Park.—Is that what
you want me to tell you?

ROSA—No, tell me the truth.

JACK—All right, I'll tell you the truth. I'm going to check in
at some flea-bag hotel on North Rampart Street. Then I'm going
to get loaded! And then I'm going to get . . . (*He doesn't complete the sentence but she understands him. She places the hat more
becomingly on his blond head.*)

ROSA—Do me a little favor. (*Her hand slides down to his cheek
and then to his mouth.*) Before you get loaded and before you—
before you—

JACK—Huh?

ROSA—Look in the waiting room at the Greyhound bus station,
please. At twelve o'clock, noon!

JACK—Why?

ROSA—You might find me there, waiting for you . . .

JACK—What—what good would that do?

ROSA—I never been to a hotel but I know they have numbers on
doors and sometimes—numbers are—lucky.—Aren't they?—Sometimes?—Lucky?

JACK—You want to buy me a ten-year stretch in the brig?

ROSA—I want you to give me that little gold ring on your ear to
put on my finger.—I want to give you my heart to keep forever!
And ever! And ever! (*Slowly and with a barely audible sigh she
leans her face against him.*) Look for me! I will be there!

JACK (*breathlessly*)—In all of my life, I never felt nothing so
sweet as the feel of your little warm body in my arms . . . (*He
breaks away and runs toward the road. From the foot of the steps
he glares fiercely back at her like a tiger through the bars of a cage.
She clings to the two porch pillars, her body leaning way out.*)

Rosa—Look for me! I will be there! (Jack *runs away from the house.* Rosa *returns inside.* *Listlessly she removes her dress and falls on the couch in her slip, kicking off her shoes.* *Then she begins to cry, as one cries only once in a lifetime, and the scene dims out.*)

Scene III

Daylight is coming, and Rosa is asleep, in her white slip, on the couch. In the back of the cottage someone is heard coughing and groaning in the way a man does who has drunk very heavily the night before. Alvaro comes stumbling into the sewing room, wearing only his trousers, with his tattooed chest bare and the last bottle of wine in the crook of his arm. He collides with a dressmaker's dummy and begs its pardon with great formality. He backs into a table and caroms off it into the parlor, where he sees Rosa. He whispers in admiration, "Che bella!" He drains the wine bottle, slumps to his knees, crawls to the couch and again admires Rosa, repeating "Che bella, che bella." He manages to climb up on the couch and crouch over the girl in a kind of leap-frog position, still uttering exclamations of childish admiration. This time Rosa wakes up, and she screams and springs from the couch, toppling Alvaro to the floor.

Serafina lunges into the room in a torn and disordered nightgown, and flings herself upon the bewildered Alvaro, who tries to explain that he was dreaming and got turned around in the house. Serafina belabors him with a broom, then picks up the phone and bellows "Police!" Her daughter takes the telephone from her, cautioning, "No! You want everybody to know? . . . Just give him his clothes now, Mama, and let him get out!" The furious Serafina orders him out, and in record time he is in the yard, half clad. A tea kettle sails over his head and the Strega can be heard informing all and sundry, "The Wops are at it again. Had a truck driver in the house all night!"

Rosa dresses feverishly. Her mother, tremulous with fear, shame and apology, tries to pretend that she doesn't know how the man got into the house. Then she tries to invent a story about a truck driver getting into a fight and being chased by a policeman, and seeking shelter. It won't stick with the girl, so the mother at last blurts out that the man was a Sicilian who had rose oil in his hair and a rose tattoo. "In the dark room," she confesses, "I couldn't see his clown face. I closed my eyes and dreamed that he was your father. . . ."

Rosa, still furious, continues hasty preparations to leave. She takes a piggy bank from the table, smashes it on the floor and rakes some coins into her purse. Serafina breathes, "How beautiful is my daughter! Go to the boy!" As Rosa leaves her mother snatches up the little gift box and runs onto the porch, calling, "Rosa, Rosa, the wrist watch!" There is no answer, and she turns back into the house, to see Assunta there. "Assunta," she says, "the urn is broken. The ashes are spilt on the floor and I can't touch them."

Assunta stoops to pick up the pieces of the urn, then says, "There are no ashes. The wind has blown them away," and Serafina meditates, "A man, when he burns, leaves only a handful of ashes. No woman can hold him. The wind must blow him away. . . ."

From the embankment Alvaro is calling, "Rondinella felice!" The neighbor women set up a taunting chorus, calling Serafina "Baronessa" and crying that there is a man on the road without a shirt and a rose tattoo on his chest. Defiantly, Serafina tears open the package containing the silk shirt, holds the garment high on the porch and lets it drop. Amidst shouts and laughter the women toss the shirt from one to the other up the embankment. Assunta comes to the porch with a glass of wine for her friend, and Serafina confides breathlessly, "I'll tell you something that maybe you won't believe. . . . Just now on my breast I felt the burning again of the rose. I know what it means. . . ."

Alvaro calls again, his voice sweetly urgent: "Rondinella felice!"

Serafina shouts back, "Vengo, vengo, amore," and starts up the embankment.

CURTAIN

SEASON IN THE SUN *

A Comedy in Three Acts

By Wolcott Gibbs

FOR years Wolcott Gibbs, drama critic of *The New Yorker,* has spent his Summer holidays on Fire Island, a lonely, sandy islet resort off the seaward coast of Long Island. Now and again he would write a sketch or a short story about various characters and events on the island, and many of these were printed in his magazine. When there were enough they were put into a book. Later, Gibbs began making the sketches into a play; when he had finished one act and outlined another he mentioned the work to Courtney Burr, the producer, and Burr took an option on the script, unseen. It was so unseen, in fact, that Gibbs could not find part of it for several weeks. "Season in the Sun" was a success early in the season, and Gibbs became the first drama critic to brave the wrath of his colleagues by writing a play in a great number of years. He was back on Fire Island in the Summer of 1951, writing a new play—an adaptation of the novel "Zuleika Dobson."

The setting is a Summer bungalow on Fire Island—the front porch, the path to town and the approach to the beach. The house has elaborate scrollwork and over the door is a fancy sign naming the place "Dune 'n' Oot." "The whole place," says the author, "is a throwback to the McKinley administration, or would be if the tenants hadn't desecrated the porch with five or six bright, modern beach chairs, a glass-topped iron table, a colored umbrella and two or three vehement Mexican rugs." The boardwalk in front of the place is dilapidated and runs off behind dunes to right and left. Fancy shells and pieces of bone are scattered around the place for decoration. As the curtain rises a rather hard-boiled-looking boy is pulling a battered, squeaking express wagon, loaded with groceries, along the boardwalk. As he passes, he glances up at the porch and sees Marcia Crane, age seven, and her brother Billy, age eleven. The grocery boy whistles obscenely at Marcia, spits derisively when he catches sight of her brother, and passes on. Marcia is busy pouring sand from one container to another and her brother, with only a towel around his waist, is wandering around the porch, bored. His eye lights on a two-inch pile of manuscript, weighted down with a book on the table. With no great interest he takes up the manuscript and leafs through it, reading a bit aloud:

"'New York is a foreign city,' said Harris. 'We haven't any roots in it—no roots in any real American soil.'" Billy can't figure that this means anything, so he starts to put the manuscript down and then, spotting a fly on the porch railing, uses the script for a swatter. His sister warns him he shouldn't do that with Daddy's book—the book Daddy is writing. "You got dead fly all over it," she points out; so he scrapes the fly off and replaces the manuscript.

Marcia begins a song to the tune of a tuneless chant:

She will do nothing at all.
She will just sit there in the noonday sun.
And when they speak to her, she will not answer them,
Because she does not care to.
Oh, she will stick them with spears and put them in the garbage,
And put the cover on.

Billy is certain his sister is crazy; he taunts her and mocks her until she gets angry and begins throwing sand. The children's father, George Crane, a thin, rather pleasant-looking man of about thirty-five, appears in the doorway. He is wearing a sports shirt, dungarees and moccasins, and he has a telegram in his hand. He warns his daughter to stop throwing sand. He sits in a chair and re-reads the telegram, which seems to annoy him; then, noticing Billy's towel garb, orders the boy to go in and put on some pants because his mother has asked some people for cocktails.

Marcia clambers winningly toward her father and informs him she is worried about the cat. Not Albert, but the new little pussy; she seems to keep thinking she has to climb up over those dunes and marry somebody.

George suggests, "Why don't you just *let* her get married?"

"Daddy, don't be *silly!* She can't just marry any old cat! Goodness, she cost twenty-five dollars." Her father suggests maybe she can marry Albert, who cost $39.50. "No," says Marcia, "I asked Mummy about that and she says Albert is too old to be much innarested in getting married, and anyway he had some kind of operation once, so he can't have any children. I don't quite understand about that, Daddy."

"That's Albert's problem."

"Daddy, when you had *your* operation . . ."

George hastens to say, "No, no, it wasn't like Albert's at all. I can have all the children I want. Dozens of them."

Marcia's mother, a brown, cheerful girl who may be thirty-two but doesn't look it, comes out of the house and shoos Marcia inside to wash her face, explaining that Mr. and Mrs. Anderson are coming in a little while. The child takes her two tin pails and a big, limp doll inside. Emily, the mother, sits beside her husband and exults over the place and the immense ocean view. "Yes," he agrees, "this is a hell of a place all right, Emmy. I don't know what would have happened to me if we hadn't been able to get down here last week." She sympathizes warmly, "Ah, you poor baby. You've had a terrible time, haven't you? First that awful accident and then almost the whole Summer in that hospital. I'll never forget the morning when Dr. Fisher told me they were going to operate. He said it wasn't really dangerous, but I didn't believe that for a minute. I knew you were going to die, and I just wanted to die too."

Emily calls to young Billy and asks him to bring out the cocktail things on the kitchen table; then she asks George if he minds watching other people drink. He doesn't, after five months on the wagon —as long as people don't get soused. She assures him the Andersons are very careful drinkers. Then George asks her something, hesitantly but hopefully: "You don't really care about the magazine, do you? You realize I had to quit some time?" She answers, noncommittally, "I suppose you did." He begins to argue his own case: he is supposed to be a writer, but all he has written is a bunch of paragraphs for a fifteen-cent magazine. She reminds him that the price has gone up to twenty cents—and, also, that everybody says his things have been very good.

Billy hauls out glasses and bottles, asks if he can have a cocktail with the guests, and is refused. His father snorts, "Next year I suppose he'll want to be a dope fiend." Emily, leafing through a copy of George's magazine, comes across one of his paragraphs and reads it aloud. It is a short, graceful, light, humorous editorial, and she says she likes it—it's neat and it's funny. But George apparently has sworn off being neat and funny as completely as he has sworn off drinking alcohol. His wife reminds him that Horace William Dodd likes his work, too, and George says he knows it—he has had a telegram from Dodd. He reads it aloud:

YOUR RESIGNATION DECLINED STOP I GOTTA GET OUT FIFTY-TWO ISSUES A YEAR AND NEED ASSISTANCE YOUR ACTIVE IF VACANT LIT-

TLE MIND STOP UNDERSTAND YOU NOW CONTEMPLATE NOVEL RE
SEX OR SOME SUCH STOP NO FUTURE THIS TOPIC AS LADY WRITERS
GOT IT SEWED UP STOP STRONGLY URGE YOU RETURN WRITING FOR
THIS MAGAZINE WHERE UNNECESSARY WORRY WHO SLEEPS WHO
STOP PLEASE PHONE AT ONCE ON RECEIPT THIS STOP REGARDS YOUR
UNFORTUNATE WIFE STOP SIGNED D STOP.

"I like Dodd," says Emily. "So do I," says George. "Hell, I
love him. I'm just not going to work for him any more. Stop." He
is glad he can't telephone Dodd and that Dodd can't telephone him,
because they have no phone. Brusquely he rejects his wife's suggestion that perhaps he could do both jobs together—the book and
the things for the magazine. It isn't just writing the things, he
explains—it's the background you need for them. The way you
have to live to be able to write like that. The way they've been
living. Emily happens to like the way they've been living, but
George is through with it and its irresponsibility. He thought this
out while he was in the hospital after a friend tried to drive his car
through the side of a house. He is going to put a period to a part
of his life and to the people he used to know, with their drinking
and their damn dreary sleeping around. They are vacant, used-up
people—finished.

"As distinguished from the Andersons?" Emily inquires slyly.
George rises to their defense: Paul can still play a hell of a game of
tennis. George gets back to the subject of the exhausted set: They
weren't always like that. Most of them came to New York, as he
did, full of hope of fine lives and fine deeds—but New York got
them. New York is a foreign city with no roots in any real American soil. The customs, the habits of thought, the inherited morali-
ties, have been lost, and all that such people have learned in their
place is a few cheap tricks for getting ahead without bothering to do
any honest work.

It's quite a speech, says Emily, and she rightly suspects it will
turn up in the book. Now, here, he continues, here on Fire Island,
they are only fifty miles from New York but spiritually there's an
enormous distance. The Andersons, for instance, are fine people.

From a distance comes a hearty call, "Anybody home?" The
Cranes' landlady, Mrs. Jermyn, heaves into sight. Heaves would
be the word; she is about sixty, brown and gnarled, with a face like
the figurehead on a pirate ship, clad in a yachting cap, a sweater,
sneakers and a dress that seems to be a ballroom gown cut off at the
knees. "I heard you was going to have a baby," she announces to
Emily, who answers, "Not that I know of."

"The house all right?" she asks, and Emily says everything is
lovely except that the bathroom door sticks. Mrs. Jermyn says she
will tell the handyman, then reveals that she has heard on the radio
that they might be getting a hurricane. The last one took the stoop
right off this house. But if a hurricane comes all one should do is
just set—"They gonna come, they gonna come."

George, standing at the porch rail, informs Mrs. Jermyn there are
a couple of men with bags at her house—probably looking for rooms.
She takes a look and says, "Oh, *them* kind. You know what I do
with them kind? I take the window screens off so's they can *fly* in
and out." She notes that the handyman is at her house talking
with the visitors and evidently has told them where the proprietress
is, for now they are headed this way. In a moment the two luggage-
laden pilgrims appear at the foot of the porch stairs. One of them
introduces himself to Mrs. Jermyn as Charles Farber and says the
other one is Michael Lindsay. "Of course you got my telegram
about the rooms?" he inquires. She says she didn't get it—or at
least she doesn't *recall* getting it. She says vaguely that things get
lost around here—and anyhow she is full up. "I even got the editor
of *The New York Times* sleeping in the shower. Mr. Tremlyn
Dorkins."

Farber exclaims, "Oh. Well, all I can say is that it's *dreadfully*
disappointing. About the rooms, I mean. I have never been so
cross in my *life*. Come, Michael, there's no room at the inn." The
young men withdraw in melancholy, and soon Mrs. Jermyn goes,
promising to tell Quigley, the handyman, about the bathroom door.
She adds, "I wouldn't count too much on him, though. He claims
a man starts having tools around, the tenants are always wanting
stuff fixed."

Emily comments that the young men were rather striking—and
on a sudden, derisive impulse she detaches a bright red bow from
her waist and places it, unfelt by him, on her husband's head.
"Those matching suits and those lovely manners," she coos, and goes
inside. Farber and Lindsay reappear on the walk, scouting to see
if Mrs. Jermyn is gone. Farber catches sight of the ribbon in
George's hair and exclaims, "You know, I *like* that." George feels
his hair, hastily removes the decoration. Farber asks if he and his
companion can borrow an express wagon to haul their bags down
to the village. Emily reappears just as George is saying, in an exaggerated basso-profundo, that he guesses so. She tells the strangers
where the wagon is and they go to get it, promising to return it.
George turns angrily on his wife and demands, "Emmy, what's the
idea of putting that damn ribbon—" But he cuts short when the

Paul Andersons appear. "Sa-a-ay, who are those *characters?*" Paul inquires, and Emily lightly replies, "Oh, just some friends of George's."

"Seriously, though," declares Paul, "I can't say I like to see those babies around a place like this. Of course I haven't any moral feeling . . ."

"Oh, go on, Paul. You're a one-man vice squad at heart," says Emily—and he may indeed be, for Paul is a stuffy fellow. George tries to get the conversation on safer ground by starting some baseball talk. Virginia Anderson seems about as dull and safe as her husband, though she hasn't said anything yet.

There is a hail from the stairway. It is Deedy Barton, a pretty blonde of twenty-two with a surprising figure covered only by shorts and a halter. With her is a large, rather handsome, untidy man, John Colgate, who is drunker than he looks. Emily cries, "George, it's *Deedy!*" George allows that this is wonderful, performs introductions, and asks Deedy what she's doing down here.

DEEDY—Goodness, I forgot. George, I've got another surprise for you. This man says he knows you, too. John Colgate. I met him on the boat.

GEORGE—Johnny Colgate! I didn't recognize you after all these years. Emily, this is unbelievable. I used to know Johnny in Paris. When, Johnny? 1932?

JOHN—Around then. How are you, George?

GEORGE—I was in the hospital for a while this summer. I'm all right now, though. Paul. Virginia. This is John Colgate. He's a reporter. Reporter, hell, he's a distinguished journalist. He won the Pulitzer Prize last year. For a series about the British elections. Damn fine pieces.

JOHN—Thanks. Glad you liked 'em.

GEORGE (*to* JOHN)—Sit down.

VIRGINIA (*archly*)—Oh, a *celebrity*.

EMILY—Yes, I remember now. I liked them, too.

PAUL—Churchill man myself, of course. This damn Socialist government. Bolshevik government, you ask me.

JOHN (*who has taken an immediate dislike to this man*)—You think so?

PAUL—Oh, yes.

GEORGE (*hastily*)—You haven't told me yet, Deedy. What are you doing out here?

DEEDY—I just got down this morning. I'm staying right next door. At that boardinghouse. That's how I found out you were here. The proprietor told me.

EMILY—Mrs. Jermyn?

DEEDY—Yes. Tell me, is she crazy or something, George?

GEORGE (*drily*)—No—just a character.

DEEDY—I just wondered. Goodness, she certainly *looks* crazy. And that house. It's unbelievable. It looks as if she picked everything right up off the beach.

GEORGE—She did.

DEEDY—Well, I only have the room for a week. I guess I can stand it. Especially now that I know you're here. And Emily. Poor Johnny hasn't got any room at all. It seems he forgot to reserve one. I'm going to try and get him in at Mrs. Jermyn's, too.

GEORGE—I wish you luck. How about a drink?

JOHN—Thanks. Say, what the hell is that you're drinking, George?

GEORGE (*putting his glass down and pouring out the others*)— This? Milk.

JOHN—What's the matter? You got cirrhosis of the liver?

GEORGE—No. Just on the wagon, Johnny. I thought I'd see what it was like.

JOHN—What *is* it like?

GEORGE—Fine. I never felt better.

JOHN (*to the company in general*)—By God, this is a day I never thought I'd see. The number of times I poured this baby in bed in Paris. For that matter, the number of times *he* poured me. We used to have quite a time in those days, didn't we, George? You remember the time you wanted to kidnap Mistinguett? Claimed every man ought to have an older woman in his life. I had a hell of a job trying to get him back to the hotel that night.

GEORGE—That's right, Johnny. I guess I must have been pretty stiff.

JOHN—No stiffer than usual. Or the time we had to lock that Agnes in your bathroom . . .

GEORGE (*anxious to stem these memoirs*)—Excuse me just a minute. Martini, Deedy?

DEEDY—Martini is fine. I don't know about *him,* though. (*She points at* COLGATE.)

JOHN (*indignantly*)—What kind of talk is that? I'm probably as sober as . . . as she is. (*He gestures toward* MRS. ANDERSON *who looks a little startled, and then subsides in a chair where in a moment he seems to be asleep. There is a short silence. This is a queerly mixed party and it looks as if the going might be a little hard.* MRS. ANDERSON, *however, rises to the occasion.*)

VIRGINIA—Emmy, I was just wondering this morning. Have you heard anything about Ed Herlicher lately? How's he getting along?

EMILY—Well, he was getting along beautifully, until he shot that fish.

DEEDY—He did what?

EMILY—He shot a pickerel. With a double-barrelled shot-gun. It was up at Jimmy Bett's place in the Adirondacks. He listened to everyone going on practically all one night about this enormous fish that they kept seeing all the time right off the end of Jimmy's dock. Just lurking there—much too smart for anybody to catch. So Ed got up early the next morning—still tight, I guess—and went down to the dock and threw some stuff on the water and when this fish came up he shot it. They couldn't tell how big it was because he blew it to bits. Well, that was the end of him socially. When he got back to New York, it must have got around "21" and places that he wasn't—well, quite a gentleman, because pretty soon he disappeared. He may have shot himself for all I know. (*She yawns and settles back in her chair.* COLGATE *laughs, but the others just seem rather depressed.*) I guess it *is* a pretty dull story. (*There is quite a silence before* PAUL ANDERSON *takes up the ball.*)

PAUL—Ginnie, Emily's pickerel reminds me of our raccoon.

Paul begins a long, pointless story, but it is hard going because his wife frequently tries to take it over and John, bored, interrupts it with a reporter's sharp questions as to factual details. Paul is exhausted and desperate by the time he reaches the end of his recital. Now John begins another animal story, also long but brightly told, about two rats which stole tennis balls from him. They were very clever rats. One would roll on its back, holding a ball, and the other would haul it out by the tail. John's recital is a deliberate burlesque of Paul's pompous and long-winded style, and the atmosphere is getting a little tense. Virginia decides that she and her husband should start home, so she can get to the market before it closes.

When the Andersons have left, George turns upon John, exclaiming, "Those are friends of mine."

John, not nearly as drunk now as he has seemed, exclaims in return, "Those raccoon fanciers? Good God, no! What makes them so dull, George?" Emily adds, "They are, kind of, you know, George."

George has come to the end of his rope and for the first time in his life he shouts at his wife, "Paul and Virginia may be dull by your standards, but at least they know how decent people behave.

I can't imagine Ginnie allowing a guest to be insulted in her house. . . ." He ends his denunciation by banging his fist on the table, upsetting the bottle of gin. Emily is shocked and embarrassed and Deedy's eyes are practically popping out of her head.

John surveys the upset gin bottle, notes that it is now empty, and asks if George has another. No, this was the last one. John suggests they all go down to the village, but George and Deedy give no sign of having heard. John turns to Emily and asks, "You like to come down town and have a drink?" After a pause she says, "I'd like to very much," and the two of them go down the porch stairs and vanish along the boardwalk. George is lost in brooding, but is recalled to the present when Deedy says she thinks she'd better go, too. He urges her to stay and have a drink; he has more in the house. He just didn't want Johnny—

Deedy won't have a drink, but she *will* sit here for a while if George doesn't mind. She asks what George is doing and he tells her he is trying to write a book—which Deedy thinks is wonderful. "Of course," she says, "I loved your things in the magazine, but I was beginning to wonder—well, if you were *really* happy doing just that." She has become a kindred soul, and George reveals to her what his book is about—New York, no roots, exhausting and finishing young people. . . .

"Like Mr. Colgate," Deedy suggests.

A boy comes along with a telegram and interrupts the tête-a-tête by whistling for attention. George takes the wire, reads it, laughs and reads it aloud to Deedy:

SINCE NO CALL FROM YOU CONCLUDE YOU NOW PROFESSIONAL SEX NOVELIST STOP MUCH AMUSED SINCE YOUR EQUIPMENT THIS SUBJECT WELL KNOWN LAUGHABLE STOP NO LONGER URGE STOP DEMAND YOUR RETURN RATIONAL EMPLOYMENT STOP—

The messenger boy is interested, but he also wants a tip. He interrupts George by snapping his fingers and George tips him. The boy starts to go along, then halts when George resumes reading the telegram:

THIS TIPS YOU BLACK SPOT STOP YOU GOT TWENTY FOUR HOURS PHONE OR WIRE WHEN SHALL HIRE SUCCESSOR UNPREOCCUPIED LADIES PANTS STOP LOVE DODD.

"What would you do, Deedy?" George asks.

The girl takes the telegram from him, tears it in pieces and throws it on the boardwalk while the boy nods approvingly.

"Thanks, Deedy," George breathes. "That's what I was going to do, too." He resumes telling her about his book. . . .

The curtain falls.

ACT II

It is the next late afternoon, and the Cranes, the Andersons, Deedy and the children are on the porch. Virginia is telling about how she and Paul were in Black Point for the last hurricane. Paul, who is very little interested in other people's stories, asks George if he thinks they are going to get this one, which is reported coming up the coast. Suppose it does—what will they do? George explains that Mrs. Jermyn says the Coast Guard will give plenty of warning if they think the island should be evacuated.

Emily and George have patched up their quarrel—just about; there still is an obvious tension between them. She asks why he tore up Dodd's second telegram, which she saw on the boardwalk. All she read of it was a piece with the signature on it. George starts to deny that it was he who tore it up, then, catching Deedy's eye, he stops and says he didn't intend to answer it.

Emily asks the Andersons if they knew George is giving up his job to write a book. Paul approves; George's magazine stuff was funny, of course, and was the first thing he turns to every week— but George has the future to consider. "After all," he announces, "that magazine doesn't offer—well—a very *substantial* career." And while he is on the subject he adds that it seemed to him that George and Emily were getting mixed up with some pretty tacky people. "Oh, clever and—and *sophisticated*, I'll grant you that. But tacky."

George is in complete agreement. Emily continues her opinion poll by asking Deedy. Did George tell her what he was doing? After an almost imperceptible hesitation this girl says, "Yes. Yesterday afternoon. After you were gone." Deedy thinks it's the best thing George could possibly do, and Emily, giving her a long and speculative look and deciding she has found out all she wants to know, says "I see" and abandons the subject.

Emily has another subject to take the place of the old one: Do they know who's down here for the weekend, right over at Mrs. Jermyn's? None other than Molly Burden.

"Who?" queries Virginia Anderson.

"She's a madam," George explains. "Quite well known. I didn't think you knew her personally, though, Emily."

George's wife confesses she doesn't—she just learned about Molly Burden yesterday afternoon from Johnny Colgate. They were in Sweeney's in the village having cocktails and this woman came over.

She and Johnny seemed to be quite old friends—a statement Virginia Anderson is not inclined to dispute. The Crane children have pricked up their ears and their mother shoos them into the house.

Speak of the devil. . . . Here comes Molly Burden now, with Johnny and Mrs. Jermyn. Emily has forgotten she asked them over when Johnny suggested it might be a nice change for George. "For God's sake, Emily!" George expostulates—and Paul seems dismayed that Johnny Colgate is returning. Paul and Virginia think it is high time they are leaving—Paul, perhaps, for a different reason than one suspects—but it is too late. The visitors are upon them, and Johnny performs the introductions.

Molly doesn't look any particular age, and the only distinguishing thing about her face is a look of great amiability. Johnny has introduced her as Mrs. Bender and Molly, in a Russian accent, explains, "It saves the nice Mrs. Jermyn from bloshing." She takes a chair offered by George, looks out on the ocean and sighs pleasurably, "It is a lovely place you got. So cute. So ontrobbled. Maybe some day I start up a little business here." George is aghast—until Molly laughs merrily and adds, "Not *that* business. . . . No. A restaurant. What they need here is some place people can go eat. High class. Chip. I am a hell of a cook, espectially on some Rossian specialties I got. Like borscht." She offers to teach Emily how to make borscht, and as an afterthought includes Deedy, who, to her, looks like a good, serious girl.

Prompted by Emily, Molly tells something of her life story. Born in Rostov. Pretty little girl, but poor. Worse than Chekhov. Like Gorki. When she is standing on a corner in a big storm, freezing, a little officer comes up—and first thing you know Molly is in Petrograd. Lovely place. Caviar, vodka, all kinds of clothes. Then comes the Revolution. Little officer is killed. Everybody is killed. So Molly gets out of there. Somehow to England, and boat to America. Same boat a Mr. Herbert Hoover is coming back on from feeding some Belgiums. Fonny, hah? Later she has to laugh when he is President and she is a success, too.

Emily thinks this is "fonny," all right, but the high-nosed Paul doesn't; it's vilifying one of the finest men who ever occupied the White House. Huffily, Paul drags his wife home to the echo of George's desperate apologies. George sulks in a corner of the porch while Emily tries to lead Molly on some more—but Molly clams up.

John asks for a drink and Emily is about to get it when George announces, grimly, "No." There is not going to be any cocktail party here this afternoon. Emily speaks up in a very tight voice and says it's her house, too, and *she* wants a drink. John thinks it's time for his little party to go, and Molly feels that she is the direct cause of all the tension. To George she says, "You got more raspactable friends you like having around more, hah, Mr. Crane? Like those two who left?"

George doesn't see where the Andersons come into the situation at all, until Molly reveals that she has recognized Paul. "Big charge account customer my clob," she says. "Like Hammacher Schlemmacher. Beautiful name that company got, no? Anyway, big three hundred and fifty dollar bum . . . Come on, Johnny. *Now* we go." Johnny, Mrs. Jermyn and Molly start down the boardwalk.

Emily bursts into helpless laughter, crying, *"Paul Anderson!"* George is uncomfortable—even hostile. Suddenly Emily calls down the walk, "Wait a minute, Johnny. I'm coming with you."

Deedy is left alone with George and she proceeds to become a wonderful straight man, agreeing and sympathizing with him at every turn of his disturbed conversation. When he says that everybody is against him she coos, "I don't think you can say *I've* been against you"—and the realization of this comes as a surprise to him. "Listen to me," she urges. "I was just going to ask you if you couldn't get away from here for a little while."

"Where the hell to? I haven't any money to go anywhere else. And anyway I'm damned if anybody is going to drive me off this beach."

Deedy waits a moment and then says she knows a place. A little house. Belongs to her sister, but her sister is away and Deedy can use it. In Bucks County. A little old gray stone house with two rooms and a tiny kitchen.

"I can't cook," George objects. "Hell, I can't even boil an egg."

Deedy tries to make things as plain as possible. There are wonderful old Pennsylvania Dutch women who'd love to come in and do for him—and, naturally, Deedy would help him move in. And she could run down from time to time, if he needs anything. She seems to feel that this is sufficiently explicit. It sounds tempting to George, but there are objections. For one thing, Deedy is a hell of an attractive girl. She doesn't see what that has to do with it; all that matters is that she happens to think he is a great man.

Deedy is on a good approach, and no telling how far she might get; but her campaign is interrupted by the appearance—just as George has taken her hand—of Will Quigley, Mrs. Jermyn's handyman. Will is about sixty-five, with a face like Punch and a body like Santa Claus; his clothes are antiques discarded by Summer guests, and he wears no shoes. He looks about as dissolute and unpromising as a vacant house, but in reality he is a deep, rewarding character. He is carrying a lumberman's crosscut saw and as usual he has been drinking.

QUIGLEY—Hi, Mr. Crane. Hi, Miss Barton. What's all this about some door?

GEORGE—Oh, the bathroom door. It sticks. What the hell is that thing you got there?

QUIGLEY—This? Saw. Crosscut saw, rip saw, I dunno. I got very little experience with saws.

GEORGE—What you need is a plane.

QUIGLEY—Yeah? I got no plane. Anyway, this ain't a very good time for me to be fixing doors. I got the biggest damn blister you ever saw. Here. Have a look. (*He extends his thumb, and* GEORGE *inspects it politely.*) That Mae Jermyn must have had me chop damn near a cord of wood this morning. And then grateful? You know what she said when she seen this blister?

DEEDY (*very coldly*)—I haven't the faintest idea.

QUIGLEY—I showed it her and she said, "You got a blister all right, Will, but I don't know how *big* I'd say it was. Suppose I was to tell you I'd seen a bigger one in Joplin, Missouri, back in 1927." *That's* what she said. What kind of talk is that?

GEORGE—I sympathize with you, Will, but if you don't think you can fix . . .

QUIGLEY (*settling down for a nice long talk*)—It ain't just this blister. I didn't come here to get in any argument about blisters. It's the principle. I've noticed something about Mae Jermyn for a long time. She's too literal. Sometimes I can't figure what I'm doin' workin' for a woman like that. *I* wouldn't call a man on the size of his blister—hell, it could be as big as this house for all I'd care—but Mae's different. With her, everything has got to be exact. I don't mind anybody coming to my house and pretending to know some subject he doesn't, whether it's blisters or the various Presidents of the United States, but with her, the first thing you know you're worked around to what type blisters they got in Joplin, Missouri. Ah, the hell with it. (*He pulls a bottle out of his hip pocket and extends it to his host.*) You want a little drink, Mr. Crane? Miss Barton?

GEORGE—No, thanks. (DEEDY *simply looks as if he'd offered her an asp.*)

QUIGLEY—Well, I'll just finish this off. Then I got to go down town. (*He empties the flask in one rather impressive swallow.*)

GEORGE (*on a samaritan impulse*)—You don't want to go down town, Will. You better just go home. What the hell is down town?

QUIGLEY—Rita.

GEORGE—Rita?

QUIGLEY (*with a hideous leer*)—Just a little lady I happen to know.

DEEDY (*who has been standing at the rail, tapping her foot*)—Oh!

QUIGLEY—What's the matter with Rita, Miss Barton? I suppose she ain't good enough for you? I suppose you want everybody to be a writer? Like George here.

GEORGE (*hastily*)—I bet she's a *fine woman,* Will. I just don't think you want to go down town.

QUIGLEY—You got no right to keep knocking Rita. Just because she's got diabetes.

GEORGE (*doing his best with this very difficult situation*)—Diabetes. What the hell is diabetes? I never give it a thought.

QUIGLEY—That's what I always say. What the hell is diabetes? You look at Mussolini. He had syphilis.

DEEDY—George! *Really!*

QUIGLEY—Yep. Killed him.

GEORGE (*he is firmly back in the peculiar nightmare the last two days have brought*)—I thought they shot him. Listen, Will, maybe you better . . .

QUIGLEY—Shot him? Who shot him?

GEORGE—Paul Muni. Mr. Paul Muni and his magic bullet. Listen, Will, you'll have to go now. Miss Barton and I have something we want to discuss.

QUIGLEY—Discuss? Go right ahead, discuss. Discuss all night you happen to feel like it. The only point I come here to make is I don't want a lot of people going around knocking Rita.

GEORGE—All right, Will. Here's your saw. (*He gets up and hands it to him.* QUIGLEY *rises, too, and weaves over to the top of the stairway.*)

QUIGLEY—So long, George.

GEORGE—So long, Will.

QUIGLEY—So long, Miss Barton. You go right ahead and discuss. But remember what I said. No knocking people just because they got diabetes. It don't look nice. Particularly with this hurricane coming up. (*He goes down the stairs and out, noisily.*)

The place is getting George down and he vows he *is* going to get away from it. But if he should take this house of Deedy's, Emily would leave him, of course, so there is the money angle to consider. Emily has some income, but not enough to live the way they do now—not enough for her to have twenty-eight pairs of shoes. "You poor dear," Deedy consoles him, "I know how hard it must be to . . ."

Deedy stops right there, for Emily comes up the stairs. She has decided not to go with Johnny, after all. Little Marcia comes from the house, tells her mother she has been sitting alone near the front window. George and Deedy look speculatively at the window, and their apprehension is correct—for Marcia in her sweet innocence spills the beans. She mentions Daddy and Miss Barton talking about Daddy going to live in Pennsylvania, and Deedy, talking fast, says, "I must have been telling George about my sister's old place. . . ." She remembers that she is late for a date in Sweeney's and leaves in some disorder.

Little Marcia continues cooking Daddy's goose, prattling about how Miss Barton has everything all *ready* in Bucks County. "And don't you remember, Daddy? She was coming down herself in case you needed anything? Don't you remember, Daddy? That was when you said she was so pretty? I don't think she's so *terribly* pretty, Mummy. I think she's got kind of a *silly* face. . . . Mummy, have you *really* got twenty-eight pairs of shoes?"

Emily suggests that her little daughter go play with somebody, then turns her attention to her suffering husband. He says he would rather not discuss anything right now, but Emily says this is the only time for discussion—because as soon as it's over she is leaving this house. She figures she will take the children to the hotel tonight, and if anybody wonders about this move she will say she is nervous about the children because of the hurricane. And Johnny Colgate has asked her to drive in to New York with him tomorrow.

"Damn it," George objects, "you can't do that. He's a chaser as well as a souse." He points out that Emily has allied herself with some very raffish friends and she admits it—and says, "But they're *people*. They're funny and they're *alive*. I'm only guessing, but I think you're afraid of them."

"Afraid of them?"

"Because they're real, and this damn world you've made up, this absurd little boy's world—can't exist with real people in it, especially Dodd. I think you're much more afraid of him than the others. You're even afraid to telephone him because he might tell you that you're not really in Heaven, with God and all the little woolly angels."

George is stunned—and angry. "All right," he shouts, "do whatever you want to. Go to town with Colgate!" He stamps into the house, which is a little more than Emily had bargained for. As she

is still standing at the foot of the porch stairs Johnny comes whistling along. She tells him she is going down to the hotel, right
now, before George comes out of the house. Johnny says he will
tag along; he was on his way down town for a drink anyhow, and
he'll buy Emily one.

All is serene on the Crane porch for a moment, because nobody
is there. This serenity vanishes with the arrival of Horace William
Dodd and the grocery boy, who is hauling Dodd's luggage in his
wagon. The luggage consists of a brief case and an umbrella.
Dodd, George's editor, is a dark, untidy man almost continuously
involved in maniacal gestures—sweeping his hand wildly through his
upstanding hair, rattling what must be a gargantuan bunch of keys
in his pants pocket, throwing his arms about to indicate his per-
petual state of derision, amazement and disgust with a world that
seems to him wholly populated by astounding incompetents.
"Crane!" Dodd bawls. "Crane! Where the hell are you?"

George appears in the doorway and Dodd rails, "Say, this is quite
a community you got. No telephones, no taxis, I wouldn't be surprised no interior plumbing. And the names on the houses—Sans-
Souci, Shangri-la, Sandy Beds, The Pines, The Shells, The Gulls.
What have you got? A lot of God-damn gulls out here?"

"What do you think we got? Bison?" George counters. Finally
managing to get his unwanted visitor to take a seat and be quiet,
George says, "I know why you came out here." "Sure," says Dodd.
"Your wife phoned me. She thinks you're nuts. So do I."

"All right, now," says George bleakly, "go back to New York."

"She," the editor continues, "said you had some cockeyed idea
that you could come down here and escape from the world, but that
you were horrified to find that people were almost exactly as dissolute in the suburbs. She said you seemed to feel you were the
victim of some kind of a conspiracy. Something about bums and
half-wits, as I recall it."

Self-pityingly, George describes some of the characters who have
been forced upon him. "Might make a good piece," the magazine
boss allows. "You keep any notes?"

Dodd demands a drink of water—he has ulcers and can't drink
liquor—and while George has gone in to get it his eyes light on
the book manuscript. He reads, " 'New York is a foreign city,'
Harris said." He continues reading aloud with great expression
when George reappears with a glass of water. George snatches the
manuscript from him, exclaiming, "You bastard!" He demands that
his ex-boss go back to New York, but Dodd explains he can't—no
more boats until tomorrow. "All right, stay here," says the desper-

ate George. "I hope you get blown to Portugal." He tells Dodd about the hurricane. He also tells Dodd he can fend for himself, and go down to Sweeney's if he gets hungry; George, himself, simply doesn't want to talk to him.

Dodd is just leaving for Sweeney's when he sees Deedy coming around the rear of the house. He nods darkly and goes on. Deedy has returned to find out if Marcia really spilled the beans and is informed that Marcia did spill, and that Emily has gone to the hotel to spend the night. The girl is glad the break has come, but thinks she must not remain here. George begs her to stay and she agrees—if he promises to go right ahead with his writing.

George gets out a portable typewriter and goes to it, with interruptions from Deedy, and pretty soon the Andersons pass by on the way to the village for dinner. They come on up for a minute, and George tries to finish the page he is working on; but the conversation between the three guests makes it hard going and when Paul falls asleep and snores it's worse. It becomes still worse when Deedy hovers over him, chattering. She suggests that incidents in *her* life might be good in the book—like the time a boy gave her a polo pony. She thinks it is going to be such *fun* for the two of them to be working together. George finally gets up, walks slowly into the house, walks slowly back out carrying a bottle of whiskey and a glass.

"I'm going to have a drink," he announces calmly. Paul, having awakened, admonishes him, "You were hitting it pretty hard for a while back there, old boy. . . . I don't know if I ought to let you . . ." Suddenly George sees Paul for what he is—part of the nightmare. He pours himself a formidable drink, toasts his guests, gets it down, gasps a bit and says, "I wouldn't be surprised if I got pretty drunk tonight. I hope nobody minds." Paul and Virginia look disapproving, but Deedy is far from minding. The new rebel pours himself another big one and quotes, " 'Come fill the cup, and in the fire of Spring the Winter garment of repentance fling.' . . . Deedy, go gather me vine leaves for my hair."

"Yes, George," says the blonde, looking anxiously around for vine leaves.

The curtain falls.

ACT III

It is one A.M. and three characters, two of them weaving, find their way to the porch with the aid of a flashlight. The non-weaver is Dodd; the others are Deedy and George, whom Dodd has been entertaining at Sweeney's. To the editor's infinite boredom, the others insist upon singing songs—loud and inharmonious songs.

Dodd finally goes to bed, after Deedy assures him she will be perfectly capable of getting home when perfectly ready.

Soon the roisterers are joined by another who is in the same condition—Johnny Colgate; and he has brought a bottle. George goes for glasses and Johnny asks Deedy what she does besides sing. She says, "I'm going to help George. With his book." "You are?" he inquires incredulously. "Doing what? Numbering the pages?"

Back with the glasses, George is feeling fine—"drunk beyond the memory of the oldest living inhabitant. But I am only drunk in an inquiring spirit. I wanted to see what it would be like to be one of you lovely bastards again." For a while the drinking bout is a feast of affection between the two men, while Deedy has passed out in a chair. Suddenly George's tone becomes somber and he asks if Johnny has happened to see Emily down town. Johnny *has* seen her, and the children were at the hotel in bed. George darkly demands, "What the hell are you supposed to be up to?" Johnny, irked, says "Nothing," and asks his pal what *he* might be up to with *this* little job, Deedy. George forgets his anger and begins to laugh uncontrollably as he says, "Well, she thought she might have a couple of ideas for my book." Johnny begins to laugh just as hard. George swiftly becomes quiet when, in the starlight, he sees Molly Burden and Mrs. Jermyn coming this way; Deedy must be got out of here—but immediately. The two men haul her upstairs to a second-floor bedroom, for Dodd is in the downstairs bedroom. George begs Johnny to try to get rid of the two women, for they are the damnedest gossips this side of the Rockies.

As Molly and her companion approach the house, Mrs. Jermyn notes the light on upstairs and Molly suggests, "You think a little monkeyshines, maybe?" George and Johnny come down from their hauling job and John asks the women if they'll come up for a drink. They don't drink, but they wouldn't mind setting a while. Mrs. Jermyn comments to George, "We seen you down at Sweeney's earlier in the evening. You and that Barton. Kind of tiddly, wasn't you? Him, too—" pointing to Johnny—"with your wife in the hotel bar." George disappoints his inquisitor by being very casual. The women say they've been in a poker game at the house of a village cop and have done pretty well—Molly wins hundred sixty-two bucks, her friend thirty-five, maybe forty. It's an all night game, and John asks if the women would get him in it. George surreptitiously slips him a wad of bills, and John heads for the village again with the two lady gamblers—leaving George at the house with two sleeping guests, one upstairs and one down.

The curtain falls.

Scene II

It is ten A.M. Dodd is on the porch with Crane's manuscript in his lap and a pencil in hand, listening to a report on the progress of the hurricane from a portable radio. He shows deep interest in the hurricane, as he does in all picturesque happenings, but no alarm. The storm, blowing more than a hundred miles an hour, may strike inland from the sea within the next twelve hours.

Deedy, looking worse than she ever did in her life, appears in the upstairs window and calls, "Good morning, Mr. Dodd." He stares at her with horror as she pathetically explains she doesn't know what she is doing up there—she just seems to *be* there. The editor orders the girl to get out of the house before the whole damn island knows she is here. Does she want to ruin his magazine?—no, he means George's reputation. Deedy barely manages to duck from sight as the Andersons, dressed for the city, come by. Virginia is pulling a heavily loaded express wagon. Paul, surmising that Dodd is George's editor and being informed that George is still sleeping, says he wants to go in and wake him up. "I've come to try to get him off this island. Right now. Before he gets back to where he was a few years ago," Paul continues. "He was associating with a lot of dissolute and worthless people."

Dodd won't let Paul into the house, but Anderson is about to push past him when Molly, Will Quigley and Mrs. Jermyn appear. All of a sudden Paul seems anxious to get away, and he urges Virginia to come along. Molly calls, "Good-by. You don't forgat the address my place, hah?"

Virginia demands, "Why should my husband want to know your address?" and Molly shrugs, "You ask him maybe." Paul asserts to his wife that he hasn't the faintest idea what it is all about. "No?" queries Molly—so pointedly that Virginia gets the idea and with a horrified gasp of "Paul!" hurries off, leaving her unhappy husband to follow.

Mrs. Jermyn introduces herself and companions to Dodd—but Horace already knows Molly. Deedy appears again in the window and Dodd, frantically waving her back, seeks to distract the others by admiring a fishing rod Quigley is carrying. He doesn't know a thing about surf-casting, but he asks if he can try it; so he and the three visitors go down to the beach.

Deedy makes her way to the porch. George sticks his head out of another upstairs window, looking even more disheveled than she does. George groans, "I am prepared to apologize to every living man, woman and child in the United States!" The girl urges him to hurry down—they've got to get away from here as soon as possible. "Why?" he asks.

"Why? *Why?* George, what do you suppose after last *night?*" He can't remember a thing, but supposes the worst must have happened. "I need a drink," he moans. "I'll be right out."

Deedy sits on the porch and tries to fix up her face when Emily comes up the stairs. The blonde is dismayed, for she figured Mrs. Crane would be in New York by now. "Is my husband here?" inquires Emily.

"He's inside. We were having a drink." Emily calls out for George to bring her a drink, too; trapped, and with the situation far beyond him, George at last emerges with a tray of glasses. But he isn't drinking. Emily asks if he has had a nice night, and her husband tells her Dodd came down; he doesn't know where Dodd is now, or where he slept last night, either. "I was drunk," he confesses. Emily asks if he is sure Dodd is coming back.

GEORGE—Hell, of course he's coming back.

EMILY—You don't mind if I wait? (*Since* GEORGE *seems to be speechless, she sits down in one of the chairs.*) You're looking very pretty, Deedy. I love that dress. It's the one you had on yesterday, isn't it? By the way, speaking of wearing things, my shoe size is 4-A and at the moment I have nine pairs of them.

DEEDY—I don't know what you're talking about.

EMILY—You don't? I understood that you and George were discussing my shoes. I just thought I might supply you with the facts. And, oh, yes, in regard to my private income . . .

DEEDY—Emily, there's really no use pretending.

EMILY (*after a pause*)—No. I suppose there isn't. You have something you want to say to me, George?

GEORGE (*this is the lowest point of his life*)—Well . . . I . . .

DEEDY—I think you know he has, Emily.

EMILY—Well, he seems very badly rehearsed. What is it, George?

GEORGE—Damn it, I *am* going to have a drink. (*He slams into the house and the ladies sit together for a moment in silence.*)

EMILY—You stayed here last night, didn't you, Deedy?

DEEDY—I certainly did not. You can ask that Mr. Dodd.

EMILY—Apparently the first thing to do is to *find* Mr. Dodd, assuming that he *is* on Fire Island.

DEEDY—You really think . . .

EMILY—Of course I do. I'm not altogether a fool, Deedy. (*As* DEEDY *is momentarily speechless with indignation:*) Well, say it, whatever it is. What's on your pretty mind?

DEEDY—Nothing. I'm not going to stay here and let you insult me, Emily.

EMILY—No?

DEEDY—No. I'm going.

EMILY—Perhaps you'd better.

DEEDY (*putting her unfinished drink on the table*)—Tell George when he wants me, I'll be at Mrs. Jermyn's.

EMILY—I'll tell him. (*As* DEEDY *starts down the stairs, she meets* DODD *coming up. He is carrying one of the damnedest fish anybody ever saw, and at the sight of it* DEEDY *gives a little scream.*)

Dodd is rather amazed at this fish he caught, but Emily has other things to talk about. She says she is leaving George on account of that Cleveland, Ohio, blonde Delilah. She goes into the house to get her bag—and brushes past George, who is dressed for town and carrying *his* bag.

"What did I do?" George asks mournfully, and his boss informs him he got soused last night with the blonde—but that's as far as Dodd's knowledge goes. Hardly any farther than George's, and George, looking at Deedy's upstairs window, mourns, "I'll never know."

Emily returns, and to keep conversation on a safe level he says, "I was—uh—talking to Dodd about my book." The editor takes the cue. George picks up his manuscript and notes that Dodd, a demon editor, has been all through it making marginal corrections and suggestions—such as "Seems to me George just going out of his way to write a book. . . . Hero talks much like my dentist."

Dodd really goes to work on George and his book. "What you've tried to do, George, is deny everything you know as an experienced man. . . . What you really wanted was to be an old man, in the special sense that that friend of yours, Anderson, class of '31, is an old man—lonely and jealous and maybe just a little corrupt on the side, but safe, out of competition. That's the big fallacy, George. A man like you can never be safe or out of competition. . . . You belong to your time and that means accepting the people who go to make it up, whatever your moral opinion of them may be."

Dodd is so urgent, seems so clear-sighted, that suddenly George tears his manuscript in pieces, throws it on the floor and says, "That's that."

Dodd says, "God, I hope I was right, George. . . . You're coming back to the magazine?"

"If you still want me." George tells his wife he is going to town and can be reached at the Princeton Club. Dodd interrupts to say there is an interesting point he wants to clear up with Emily. "You're wrong, Emily. George and I came home together last night. There been any blondes around, I would have noticed them. I was as sober as a snake. . . . If it's the blonde I think you mean—the one I passed just now—last night when I saw her she was stewed down in the village—mixed up with some lifeguard."

George would rather tell the truth, but, since Dodd has given her a way to keep both George and her dignity, she puts her hand over her husband's mouth, exclaiming, "Then I was wrong! . . . Oh, darling, I'm sorry."

The children come running to the house with big news: the Coast Guard wants everybody off the island by tonight. Emily tells them to go in and get their suitcases, which are all packed. John comes by, on his way to town and pulling a wagon. He tosses a big roll of bills to George and George exclaims, "My God, you didn't *win?*"

"Sure I won. About three hundred and fifty dollars."

Emily laughs, "That's exactly what Paul Anderson owes Molly."

Dodd announces that he is not going back to town; he is curious about the hurricane—a thing a lot of men *never* see. The Cranes go along; Dodd darts into the house and emerges with a volume of the encyclopedia and leafs through it: "Hudson. Huldebrand. Humbold, Max. Who the hell? Here we are—Hurricane. What do you know? 'Sometimes as high as a hundred and forty miles an hour.' . . ."

Molly and Mrs. Jermyn pass by, heaving for the safe haven of the church in town. Deedy, wanting a final try at George, appears, and is told that the Cranes have left. Dodd offers her his fish, which she declines. "George has told me a lot about you," she says to Dodd. "He says you're the greatest editor in America." Dodd allows that his life is the life of a hunted animal.

"Perhaps you ought to get away for a while," the blonde suggests.

"Yeah? Where to? All I have is this damn apartment on Fifty-Fifth Street."

"Well," Deedy hazards, "it's probably a foolish suggestion, but I happen to have a sister. She lives in Bucks County and she has . . ." The rising wind drowns out the rest of the line.

CURTAIN

AFFAIRS OF STATE *

A Comedy in Three Acts

By Louis Verneuil

LOUIS VERNEUIL, once the Owen Davis of Paris with some sixty plays in his native French to his credit—not to mention acting with and managing Sarah Bernhardt, is a prolific dramatist even in his adopted tongue and in his adopted country, which is Southern California. Most writers living in Southern California work for the movies, but Verneuil works for the stage. His only reason for living in Holmby Hills is that he likes the climate. It was fortunate, though, that he was where he was when he wrote "Affa·rs of State," for Celeste Holm was in Hollywood making pictures and this comedy was more or less aimed in her direction. It was easy for author and actress to get together, and, since Verneuil was to direct his comedy, the problem of rehearsals was easily met. "Affairs of State" was rehearsed, mostly, in the author's living room—a method he recommends as being artistically satisfactory and quite inexpensive, since no hall has to be rented. At the end of the season Miss Holm left the cast of "Affairs of State" to make a movie, and was replaced by June Havoc.

The setting is an imposing living room in the home of George Henderson at fashionable Chevy Chase, about ten miles out of Washington, D. C. Large French doors opens onto a terrace, which leads to a garden, and a window also looks out on the garden. A double door within the room leads to the library, dining room and the rest of the house. The room contains a large, rectangular table, a low coffee table, comfortable chairs, a couch, a desk with a telephone, a small folding card table with a chair beside it, and a little bar. It is about 6 P.M. in mid-July, and Philip Russell is sitting in a chair, reading a paper, with a highball beside him. Philip is a very distinguished-looking gentleman of 70, and obviously is very much at home here—so much so that telephone calls have been coming for him and he has had to tell Lawrence, the butler, to accept no more. But Lawrence, using discretion, has accepted one more call and comes to tell Philip about it. It's from the White House;

the President is calling.

It is a chummy, cordial conversation, with Russell calling the President Harry. He explains he and his wife are here, enjoying George Henderson's hospitality while their own house is being done over. He reminds the President who George is—former Minister in Lisbon, and before that on Philip's staff; now Henderson has been appointed by the Governor of Colorado to fill out the unexpired term of a Senator who has died. . . . But, certainly, this isn't what the President called about. What is it? A little reluctantly Philip accepts an appointment for three tomorrow, and, smiling, says, "I seem to recall that you accepted my resignation some five months ago. . . . Why don't you ask my successor's opinion? . . ."

Constance Russell, Philip's wife, a handsome, smartly groomed woman of 40, comes in from the garden and while her husband is still on the wire exclaims, "Philip, you're really the most undependable man in the world!" When the call is finished she reminds him that it is now after six, and he had agreed to meet her at the Barlows' at four. They had invited a man specially to meet him, and she waited until five-thirty. How does he think she felt.

Going quietly to the bar, Philip answers, "Like a woman whose husband has been kept longer than he expected." He had had calls from two college presidents, three U.N. delegates, a governor and the President.

"I thought you had retired," Constance objects, and he says, equably, "So many people think I can be helpful. Can I close my door to them?" She continues, "I had hoped that your resignation might give me back my husband. But I see even less of you than before."

He is surprised by this—and flattered. She is nervous and intense as she speaks of the unimportant part she plays in his life. She closes the garden door for privacy and goes on, "I feel that I've always been an irreproachable wife. . . . But it has never been overflowing with gaiety . . . Your friends were great men in their day—but those who have managed to stay alive can now hardly manage to stay awake. . . . And I realize, with some concern, that all too soon *I* might be growing older. . . . I'd like to—oh— to try to live more completely, more intensely, the few years I still have. Philip, would you give me my freedom?"

Philip has not reached the age of 70 in high political circles for nothing. He takes this request with aplomb and observes that she must be in love with someone else—which she denies with dignity, saying, "As long as I was—as I *am* your wife, I could not think of another man."

Aloud, he reviews their marriage: she was one of his secretaries when he lost his first wife, and some months later he asked her to marry him. He was 54 then, and she 24. "Twenty-three," she corrects him—for now she clings to calling herself 39 and not 40. He knew she could not be madly in love—but his name, his influence and his grandfather's woolen mills made him attractive enough—

"And your intelligence . . . and your character," she interrupts, and then declares, "I have no regrets."

"Now that I am old . . . retired . . . it would not be right for you to abandon me," he decides. He gently insists that she must have some reason, but she continues denying there is a specific reason. He warns her how tongues would start wagging against her, but she shrugs it off. "You must remain my wife," he states. "If you don't do it for me, do it for yourself."

Constance seems to accept his logic and his protestations of affection, and finally agrees, "I won't insist."

With relief Philip opens the French doors and sees George Henderson coming in by way of the garden. George is 40, capable-looking, carrying a large portfolio and some papers, which he deposits on the desk. Constance makes him a drink, and the men talk politics. Philip suggests that George may want to do some fence-mending before the elections in November. He has heard that Jesse Crichton, the national chairman, is taking a vacation in Colorado—an old friend of Philip's, even if he is a Republican. And if Crichton should be for George, George is as good as elected to the Senate for a new term.

The manservant brings a card on a tray to Philip Russell. "Oh, Howard!" he says. "Yes, in the library." And to the others he explains, "Howard wants some advice about getting married. Well, marriage is like a besieged fortress: Those who are out want to get in . . . those who are in would like to get out!" When he has gone, George asks Constance in a lowered voice, "You spoke to him?"

CONSTANCE—Yes.

GEORGE—And he refused? . . .

CONSTANCE—For my own good . . . In my own interest . . . You know how he twists everything around. . . .

GEORGE—I know. . . .

CONSTANCE—A great difference in age is the most terrible thing! . . .

GEORGE—Why doesn't your husband understand that?

CONSTANCE (*a little resentfully*)—He knows it well enough! . . . But since I'm the only one who suffers . . .

GEORGE—He simply doesn't realize what he is denying us.

CONSTANCE—And, of course, I couldn't tell him.

GEORGE (*gently*)—That might have been conclusive. . . .

CONSTANCE (*going to him*)—But much too heartless! . . . I love you, George, and yet . . . you understand . . . I still feel, toward Philip, a gratitude and—well—a tenderness, which will always keep me from doing anything to hurt him.

GEORGE—I could never hold that against you. . . . You know how fond I am of him myself! . . . (CONSTANCE *is now very close to him. He takes her in his arms.*)—Oh, Constance! . . . Since you've been living in this house, I realize so much more. . . . Such a companion! . . . Such a partner! . . . I'd find everything in you! . . .

CONSTANCE—What can we do now?

GEORGE—Wait . . .

CONSTANCE—How long?

GEORGE—As long as we have to. You know I'll never change.

CONSTANCE—Yes, George. I know. . . . (*Feeling that there is someone outside, in the entrance hall,* CONSTANCE *promptly tears herself away from* GEORGE. IRENE *appears up left. She's very modestly dressed, and carries a small portfolio under her arm.*)

IRENE (*coming to up stage center*)—Hello, Constance. Good evening, Senator.

CONSTANCE—How are you, darling? How did you get here?

IRENE—On the bus.

Irene Elliott is a 28-year-old blonde, attractive enough, perhaps, but with so great a lack of sophistication in dress and manner that one could not have guessed that she is the niece of Philip Russell. She is pinch-hitting for his vacationing secretary, and has come out to the Henderson house to bring the old gentleman some papers he phoned for. She doesn't mind helping her uncle out, she explains, because she is in his library all day anyhow.

Constance speaks enthusiastically to George about how remarkable Irene is; here she works ten months a year at a deadly job, teaching school in Minneapolis, and instead of taking a real vacation she comes down here to put Constance's husband's library in order —and won't accept any pay for it! Irene can't see anything remarkable in this; she likes books and is having a marvelous vacation. In reply to a direct question from Constance she admits she never thought of getting married; marriage is a lottery with so few winners, and books and children are more satisfying than husbands.

George invites Irene to stay for dinner. Uncle Philip, coming from the library, gives her an affectionate kiss, saying, "You're my wife's niece, but I love you as if you were my own family." Irene reveals that she broke off work in the library this afternoon long enough to attend a meeting of the Veterans Political League at the Shoreham—and that she heard George make a speech there. A wonderful speech—and the Senator is so likable, too. "I believe he's the only politician who is handsome and distinguished *and* well dressed." This is not in George's hearing, for he has gone to arrange for an extra place at the table—and Constance has left the room, too.

"He's on the verge of a great career," Uncle Philip agrees, and then, thoughtfully, says, "It's strange he's never married. . . ."

Irene knows the answer to that one. At the meeting this afternoon she overheard two men at the next table talking about the Senator, and it seems he is deeply in love with a married woman and must wait until she is free. Philip ponders, "What married woman could it be?" Irene has no idea; the men didn't say.

Philip asks where George is and Irene points out the French door toward the garden, where George is talking with the gardener —and Constance is there, too. To get rid of the girl for a moment, Philip asks her to go ask George for Eleanor Roosevelt's telephone number, and when he is alone he dials a number and asks for Jesse Crichton, the national chairman. To Crichton he says, "Is it true you are backing George Henderson in the primaries? . . . . Well, I'd like to talk it over before you come to any decision." They make a date for the morning, just as Irene returns with the Roosevelt telephone number—which Uncle Philip doesn't seem to need now. He sits in an armchair at a table, begins working on some papers, and Irene sits adoringly near him. She says, "With all your responsibilities, I've never seen you angry, or upset, or even nervous!"

The old statesman pensively replies, "To lose one's temper is to lose the game—always! Believe me, Irene, we can tame life only with gentleness."

The curtain falls.

Scene II

It is about three in the afternoon, ten days later. The sun is bright and the French doors are wide open. Constance is in an armchair, embroidering her own initials on a scarf. George is stand-

ing outside on the terrace, reading a newspaper. Irene is sitting
at the card table, sorting papers. And Philip is in another armchair, furtively watching George. George comes into the room,
throws down his paper, starts packing, and Philip reproaches him,
"You shouldn't be so upset. It isn't worth it!"

George bangs the back of a chair with a fist and exclaims, "What
beats me is the switch Jesse Crichton pulled! Not two weeks ago
he told me I was his candidate!" Instead, the chairman has swung
to an insignificant man, one Jonathan Jayes, whom nobody ever
heard of, and if the party thinks it is going to win with him . . .
This Jayes is only the mayor of a town of four thousand people,
and why hasn't the party backed him before. Philip jolts George
by suggesting that, probably, the party always had some better
candidate before. "I have the highest opinion of you, George," he
goes on smoothly, "but the question is not whether you or Mr.
Jayes is more intelligent, but which one can get more votes." He
enumerates Jayes' qualifications: married forty-one years; wife
chairman of the town's Red Cross and president of a Ladies' Afternoon Society; three daughters, safely and impeccably married. A
voter can't be against the head of such a family. And here is
George—still a bachelor at the age of forty! "In this country, a
man who doesn't get married is abnormal, by definition. . . . By
the way, why *don't* you get married?"

George tries to laugh it off, saying perhaps he hasn't found the
right woman. Philip presses his point: George is out of luck now
so far as this election is concerned, but he will be running for other
offices or seeking appointments—"and," he emphasizes, "nine times
out of *nine* you'll be more successful if there's a satisfactory Mrs.
Henderson." Irene thinks the conversation is getting a little too
personal for the ears of a stranger, and on the pretext of finishing
some work she goes to the library.

"So very tactful," Constance approves. "She realized that her
presence was hardly necessary to this conversation . . . which, I
must confess, *I* also find a bit embarrassing!"

George (*quickly*)—Why?

Philip (*to* Constance)—You and I know George well enough
to . . .

George—Of course! . . .

Constance (*to* Philip)—Still, I feel you're rather indiscreet
. . . which is most unlike you. Even a father would hesitate to
advise his son about something like this, unless he were con-
sulted. . . .

PHILIP (*to* CONSTANCE)—George asked me why they had picked Jonathan Jayes. I gave him my opinion.

CONSTANCE—With such an opinion, you should have said you couldn't guess.

PHILIP—From me, George can always expect sincerity. (*Smiling.*) Besides, there are not so many opportunities to speak the truth that I can afford to miss one!

CONSTANCE (*getting impatient*)—But after all, Philip, a man might have the strongest personal reasons for not getting married.

PHILIP (*to* GEORGE)—Have you taken a vow of chastity?

GEORGE (*reproachfully*)—Philip! . . .

PHILIP (*smiling*)—Yes . . . when a man renounces love, he is usually well past forty, and then not guided entirely by his preferences!

CONSTANCE (*slightly shocked*)—Philip, really! . . .

PHILIP (*thinking it over*)—So, could you have a romantic reason? . . . Come, you can tell me! (*Taking* GEORGE's *arm and walking with him.*) Are you having an affair with some woman you can't marry because, well, why? . . . because she's too young . . . or too old? . . . But that isn't a complete obstacle. . . . (*Suddenly releasing* GEORGE's *arm and walking a little away.*) Then, she might be a married woman? . . . *That* would be a real difficulty.

CONSTANCE (*slightly nervous*)—Philip, you astonish me! . . . With your reputation for diplomacy!

GEORGE (*to* CONSTANCE, *smiling*)—Philip has every right to ask questions . . . as long as he forgives me for not answering.

PHILIP—Well . . . if my guess is right, there's a woman who must be suffering great remorse.

GEORGE (*surprised*)—Why remorse?

PHILIP—Because she stands between you and your career. (*Taking again a paper from the table.*) If it were not for her, you would be married, and the Colorado Republicans would undoubtedly have preferred you to Jonathan Jayes. (*As before, he shows the paper to* GEORGE, *pointing again to a certain article.* GEORGE, *angrier than before, grabs the paper, walks up stage, and throws it on the coffee table.* PHILIP *continues, a bit excited.*) But damn it! She must be in love with you . . . otherwise you wouldn't be so peculiarly faithful to her! . . . So she ought to have your interest at heart. She should help you, instead of hindering you!

CONSTANCE (*calmly*)—It's not her fault if she is not free to marry.

PHILIP (*approving*)—True. (*He sits down on the bench and starts chuckling.*)

CONSTANCE—Why do you laugh?

PHILIP (*smiling*)—Because this reminds me of a French novel I picked up recently. . . . It was about a girl. Some experience, in her childhood, had given her an irrepressible aversion toward men, which caused her mother dreadful sorrow. When the mother died, her will provided that the girl could inherit her fortune only if she were married within six months. The old lady was hoping to bring her daughter back to a more normal life. But she didn't bring her anywhere. The girl hired a man to act as her husband . . . in name only, of course . . . So she got the inheritance, and, three months later, her divorce.

CONSTANCE (*smiling*)—That's very French.

PHILIP—I thought so.

GEORGE (*coming down to* PHILIP, *right of bench*)—But why did you happen to tell that story, Philip? . . . (*Smiling.*) You wouldn't by any chance, suggest that *I* should . . .

PHILIP (*gets up, putting his hand on* GEORGE's *shoulder*)— George, I think precisely this: When being a bachelor is so completely detrimental to a man's professional success, then, no matter how great his obligation not to, he should marry just the same. Or, at least, pretend to, which is sufficient in your case.

George is indignant; he loathes the European "marriage of convenience"—but Philip presses his argument, saying that such an arrangement would even be desirable to the woman he loves, because it would take him out of circulation. "Now," says Philip, "all that's left to do is find a girl who is willing to play that slightly unusual role." He has no candidate, but recommends that she be neither too homely nor too pretty, so that George's "lady friend" would rest easy—although, he says with a smile, he doesn't know who the lady is and he would like very much to know.

George begins an earnest protestation, but Philip cuts him off by heading for the garden. He invites his wife to go along, but Constance pleads she is tired. George doesn't want to go to the garden, either, saying he has a stack of work. When Philip has departed, the lovers begin wondering just how much he knows or suspects, and can reach no conclusion. However, Constance is reaching another conclusion—that maybe her husband's suggestion of a marriage of convenience for George makes sense—and for the reason Philip stated. She explains to George, "It's because I love you that I don't want to lose you. He's right. I'm at the mercy of any attractive or designing woman. . . . Yes, George, until I'm free, I'd like someone in your house to—how should I say it?—to counteract the hazards of your solitude!"

At first George is uproariously amused, and he also says that no such mate could be found for him—a woman without too much money, without romantic attachments, and with complete honesty and discretion.

Constance counters, "You are describing exactly the person I have in mind." It is her niece, Irene, who, Constance says, also fills a qualification George forgot to mention—which is being incapable of attracting him. George doubts if Irene would be interested, and the forthright Constance suggests sounding her out right now. On an intercom phone she calls the girl from the library, and George flees to the terrace.

"How much are you being paid as a teacher?" Constance asks Irene.

"Twenty-five hundred dollars a year."

"And what is the largest salary you might earn, and when?"

"Four thousand dollars, in about fifteen years."

Having got in her opening wedge, Constance keeps hammering away. Irene is already 28, and alone, and living in Minneapolis. Certainly no spectacular future in sight. But Constance knows how Irene's life could be changed, completely and desirably, overnight. "There's a young man . . . about 40 . . . wealthy . . . a bachelor, who might offer you a job."

Irene is mistrustful at the start, but Constance continues after pledging her to secrecy. This man she speaks of is in love with a woman whom he can't at the moment marry—but he should be married for the sake of his career. Irene doesn't catch what her aunt is driving at until Constance flatly proposes, "Your job would be to hold that temporary position . . . in name only, of course. And, when this woman is at last free, then your . . . assignment would come to an end."

After she has got over her surprise, the practical Irene begins to consider the suggestion. It is no trouble for her to guess, after hearing what Uncle Philip said, that George Henderson is the man under consideration—but she is a little puzzled at her aunt's interest in the matter. Irene starts to ask, "By any chance could *you*—" and then she dismisses the question and apologizes for it, saying, "Uncle Philip is a wonderful man, and you make him so happy! That idea should never have entered my head. Forgive me." Constance seeks to explain by saying that, since she is Irene's aunt and since she and her husband are George's most intimate friends, she is the obvious intermediary in the deal. Constance offers to talk about the lady George intends to marry one day, but Irene cuts her off, declaring, "As the Senator's employee, his private life is not my concern."

Constance wigwags George in from the garden and announces that Irene is interested, so far. Now it's up to him to work out the details. She, in turn, goes to the garden and George rather embarrassedly faces his prospective wife-in-name-only. Irene is not embarrassed; she is practical. What, she asks, are the usual duties of such a wife?

George smiles, "Exactly those of a real wife . . . with a minor exception." Irene wants more specific details—a brief summary.

GEORGE (*a little embarrassed*)—Well . . . Won't you sit down? . . . First of all, I'd want you to act as hostess . . . for entertaining . . . dinners . . . to keep track of the servants . . . in a word, to be completely mistress of the house.

IRENE—Good. No office work? . . . Copying, filing, typing?

GEORGE—I have two secretaries.

IRENE—Anyway, I know shorthand. . . . In an emergency . . .

GEORGE—Thank you. (*Continuing.*) Usually, I live here. But I spend a lot of time in Colorado, and I also take other trips. . . .

IRENE—Would I go with you?

GEORGE—Sometimes . . . Depending on where or how long . . . But you might have to. . . .

IRENE (*smiling*)—That's fine. I love to travel. (*Changing tone.*) What attitude should I assume toward you?

GEORGE (*not understanding*)—I beg your pardon?

IRENE—When we are alone, complete deference, naturally. No one has ever criticized my manners. But when you have guests? . . . Do you want me to remain aloof and distant, or would you prefer an affectionate and loving wife?

GEORGE (*slightly taken aback*)—Well . . .

IRENE (*continuing calmly*)—Both techniques have their supporters. That's why I asked. Some people insist that any exhibition of tenderness is vulgar, and that even honeymooners should notice each other only when they are alone. On the other hand, some disagree . . . and many men seem willing, or even proud, to let people know their wives are fond of them. What is your approach to that problem?

GEORGE (*smiling*)—I've never had occasion to consider it! . . . On first thought, and only in a small group . . .

IRENE (*quickly*)—Of course! In public, complete dignity!

GEORGE (*continuing*)—Well, I think that, with intimate friends, it might be judicious for you to display some affection . . . and even admiration. . . .

IRENE—I had planned on the admiration anyway! . . . (*Kindly.*) Which will be little effort.

GEORGE—Thank you. As for me, I think I'll show you unmistakable tenderness . . . if you don't object. . . .

IRENE—I don't. I know you well enough to be sure you'll never exceed the proper limits.

GEORGE—Naturally. (*Changing tone.*) Now, something very important: It must be apparent that you take a great interest in my career, in my business affairs. . . .

IRENE—Will you train me?

GEORGE—Certainly. The public wants a prominent official's wife to stand at his side . . . to share in his struggles as well as his rewards. . . . So, that is the prime impression I want you to make.

Irene assures her future husband that he can depend on her to show deep feeling about him when necessary. She takes a pad and pencil and begins making notes about her duties in the fields of entertainment, travel, business, affection and illness. Suddenly she asks, "What about my days off? I wouldn't ask for every Thursday and every other Sunday, like the regular help. But I've got to have a little rest every week." George doesn't know quite what to answer, but Irene disposes of the problem by asking for five full days off each month, even though it isn't customary for wives. Who knows? Maybe she could be interested in somebody else.

They progress very well with their business arrangement, and Irene has carefully noted everything on her pad. George warns that no one on earth should know the details of their agreement—and most of all to be kept in ignorance is Uncle Philip. And now as to salary: "How about fifteen hundred dollars a month?" asks George, and Irene manages to cover her amazement with an impassive air. "Provided I have a guarantee, of course," she stipulates, and points out that if this arrangement washed out in two months she would have given up her whole secure teaching career for only three thousand dollars. She would like a guarantee of a minimum of three years' work, renewable, if necessary, at his option. She calculates efficiently on her pad and says that, should her job end at any time soon, she must receive in a lump sum all the money that she might have earned for the remainder of the three years.

George is quite rightly impressed by her business ability, and he agrees to her stipulations. "What about my clothes?" she now asks. George suggests that for incidentals she take an allowance of $300 a month, and she makes a note of this. "Well, Senator," she concludes, "that should take care of everything. When do I start work? I mean, when will we have the wedding?"

George calculates that a month from now will do it. This will give time for them to notice each other and take interest in each other, to satisfy the public. Irene declares she will go to work on the preliminaries as of tomorrow, whatever time he calls her. She gives him her telephone number.

The curtain falls.

ACT II

Two months have passed, and it is the end of September, in midafternoon. A luncheon is just ending and Irene, Constance, Philip, George and a man named Byron Winkler file into the living room to have the coffee the manservant has laid out. It has been a very special lunch for this man Winkler's benefit. He, a frank and genial man, seems much interested in Irene's account of her honeymoon with George in Europe.

Irene is the perfect wife. She talks interestingly and perceptively about economic and social conditions in Britain and France. George chimes in by recounting the money, the gaiety and the high prices to be found in France. "Such an individualistic country!" exclaims Irene. "And everyone is so charming."

The bland Philip adds, "The truth is, French charm was invented in America. They didn't know they had it until we told them."

Winkler asks what Europeans think about a real war with Russia and George replies, "They refuse to think about it. It would be too unpleasant." And Irene, the ideal spouse, adds, "Spenser said there are two things man cannot face: the sun and death. He should have added a third—truth." Winkler is very much impressed by this woman's intelligence—and he might also be impressed by her appearance, for she is most smartly and beautifully coiffed and gowned. The mousy little teacher from the Middle West has become a woman of the world . . . and a perfect wife. Winkler, who seems to be a very high statesman—one's guess is that he is Secretary of State—admires her extravagantly; but Constance is getting nervous and worried, and George is uncomfortable at his wife's bride-like kisses and her solicitousness over his health, which impels her to force him to take some medicine he doesn't like or need. Irene also is the perfect hostess, talking seriously or wittily as the right occasion arises, serving coffee and brandy graciously.

George manages to get in some pointed conversation too; he has done some investigating abroad, and he is going to let the American people know the "inconceivable" uses to which American money is being put in Western Europe. Obviously, Winkler's ears are more for Irene—and Philip's eyes are upon his wife. He notes with amusement Constance's growing concern. When Irene gives George a seventh-week-of-marriage anniversary kiss Constance can hardly bear it, but Winkler thinks it is charming. So few marriages are so happy—and he says his own is not one of them. Time has flown; it is three-thirty in the afternoon, and Winkler must get back to work; the Rumanian Ambassador has been recalled and is coming to pay his respects at four. Constance wants to call on the Barlows here in Chevy Chase, so Philip leaves her the car and begs a ride with Winkler into Washington. "Thank you, darling. It was wonderful," says Constance to Irene, and Irene replies eagerly, "I'm so glad *you* were pleased!"

As soon as George and Irene are alone, her attitude changes completely; she is now distant and respectful—the conscientious employee. Did she take the right attitude toward Mr. Winkler? Is the Senator satisfied with her work?

George declares he is satisfied, generally speaking—but perhaps she did talk a little too much . . . and she displayed a little too much affection . . . and her dress, though charming, may have been a little too much off the neck for lunch-time. Irene is downcast at these gentle reproofs, and she reminds him he had told her to try to interest Mr. Winkler.

"To interest him mentally, Miss Elliott," George points out. "It is thanks to my own personal merits, if any, that I hope to get ahead in my career! And not by making use of your charms or any desires you might stir up around town!"

Irene explains by offering a quotation: "It's always with the best intentions that we do the most regrettable things—Schopenhauer."

"You are very well read—for a woman."

"But I'm *not* a woman! A woman is something carefree, gay, weak, frivolous. A woman has romances, weddings, divorces. . . . She has a thousand charms I'll never have and she does a million things I've never done!" For a moment Irene has revealed herself—and now she gets primly back to business. Unless the Senator wants her, she has some errands to do. But the Senator does want her; he has an important speech coming up, and would appreciate her doing some research—a résumé of all the instances when the United States has interfered in European affairs since the beginning of the century.

She amazes George with her offhand grasp of the subject. She recalls when the Kaiser was threatening to occupy Venezuela in 1903 or 1904, and Theodore Roosevelt forced an arbitration. She explains sweetly to the Senator that she teaches history.

Constance returns, having found no one home at the Barlows' and Irene discreetly goes to the library to begin her research. Constance comments that her niece's appearance has improved amazingly, and that Winkler will now be going all over Washington saying how happy George is.

GEORGE—Isn't that exactly what you wanted?

CONSTANCE—It is. . . . But was I right? . . .

GEORGE—What do you mean?

CONSTANCE—George, I fear I've made a mistake.

GEORGE—In what way?

CONSTANCE—By urging you to engage that girl! When that idea first came to me . . . or, more accurately, when Philip slipped it into our heads . . . I saw only its good points, which, for your career, are undeniable! . . . The fear of losing you was an obsession! . . . It kept me from realizing my imprudence. It's only today that I am fully aware of it. . . . A little late!

GEORGE—Your imprudence?

CONSTANCE (*with sudden anger*)—Irene has deceived us! . . . Or, rather, I deceived myself about her! . . . To me, she had always been a retiring person . . . slightly awkward . . . in short, a school teacher! . . . (*She gets up and walks toward the French door, with increasing indignation.*) And suddenly, what do I find but a woman of incisive personality, sure of herself, beguiling your guests, kissing you every five minutes, and ordering your servants around as if she had never done anything else in her life!

GEORGE—But all that is what we hired her to do!

CONSTANCE (*nervously*)—Don't pretend not to understand. No woman could change like that if she were only doing a job! . . . This betrays other ambitions.

GEORGE—Such as? . . .

CONSTANCE—To make you fall in love with her, of course!

GEORGE—Constance, that's ridiculous! . . .

CONSTANCE—No, George! . . . I'm positive Irene has made her plans! . . . After all, you're a wonderful catch . . . one she could never have dreamed of! . . . And, to achieve her ends, the idea that she might be breaking my heart won't stop her for a minute. . . . Quite the contrary! . . . Underneath, she's always been jealous of me . . . which is only natural!

GEORGE (*gently*)—Excuse me. . . . Have you told her that *you* are the person I love?

CONSTANCE—No.

GEORGE—Well, then? . . . (*A pause.*) If she knew it, and still tried to supplant you, her own aunt, yes, that would be rather naughty! . . . But since she does not know! . . .

CONSTANCE—Have you ever discussed me with her?

GEORGE—Very often. . . . Never the slightest hint! . . . No indication that she might suspect . . .

CONSTANCE (*triumphantly*)—All the more reason for her to feel free to act! She'll have no scruples! . . .

GEORGE (*laughing, sitting down on armchair*)—My dear, your logic is invincible! . . . If Irene knows that it is you, that will encourage her to play up to me. . . . And if she doesn't know, that will make her even bolder! . . . Are you quite sure you've made a reasonable analysis of the situation?

CONSTANCE (*helplessly*)—A woman in love is never reasonable.

GEORGE (*smiling*)—You're wonderful! . . . And I'd like to ask you one question.

CONSTANCE—Please do.

GEORGE—If I had wanted a real marriage, do you think it would have been difficult for me to find a girl who would be suitable?

CONSTANCE—Certainly not.

GEORGE—Then, why do you think I got into this . . . intrigue? You must admit the situation is not overpoweringly pleasant . . . putting on this endless performance . . . pretending emotions I don't feel . . . abusing the confidence of my friends. . . . (CONSTANCE *starts to protest.*) Yes, I introduce as my wife someone who isn't . . . that's dishonest! . . . When a man gives you such proof of his love, do you really believe he is capable of looking at anyone else?

CONSTANCE (*after a pause, gently*)—You're right. Forgive me. (*She takes her bag from the table and gets up.*) Would you like to drive into Washington?

He pleads that he must work on a radio speech, offhandedly mentioning the Kaiser and Theodore Roosevelt—and looking a little apprehensively toward the library. Irene enters with some papers in her hand. She has changed to a discreet, high-necked dress. Constance has every intention of leaving, but when Irene orders tea to be served, saying she thought the Senator would enjoy a cup while she is reading her notes, Constance changes her mind. She remains, and in spite of George's protestations, reveals to her niece, "My dear, *I* am the woman you are replacing here!"

Irene stands motionless as she absorbs this news. Constance pleads her own case—being married to a man twice her age and then finding a man her own age who loves and wants to marry her. "Help him," she urges with a charming smile. "You'll do so much better, I'm sure, now that you know you are helping me too!" She leaves. George is embarrassed by Constance's revelation, but Irene puts him at his ease by saying, "I've no opinion, sir. . . . Perhaps I might have preferred not to know. But Constance must have had her reasons for telling me. . . ." Then she gets back to business, reading her historical notes while George slowly drinks his tea. She has done a good job, and he remarks flatteringly that she should set up an information bureau for Senators.

"I'll give it some thought," she says. "When you have discharged me and I'm looking for work again." This starts George thinking of something he hadn't thought of before. Irene goes on with her historical data: Woodrow Wilson once reversed his policy on the Monroe Doctrine. George comments, pensively, "And that isn't limited to statesmen. Any normal human being goes through life changing his mind. . . ."

The curtain falls.

SCENE II

About six o'clock in the evening a week later Uncle Philip comes to call on his niece about something important. Byron Winkler called him up this morning on the pretext of asking Philip if he thought Irene would serve on some committee or other, and then he casually asked if George ever discussed his policies with Irene. "I said, 'Always,' " he relates. Philip is a foxy man, and he has figured that the Administration wants to learn George's position on some matter. Irene now begins to understand why it was Winkler had asked her if he might call at six o'clock this evening, and her uncle counsels, "Whatever Winkler has in his mind, you're the one he'll explain it to, and you're the one who'll tell your husband—which can only make him appreciate you more than ever." He states frankly that Irene should make George fall in love with her and that she should really become his wife. She is thunderstruck. He continues, "You can't imagine how important it is to me. . . ."

"Then you know? You've guessed?"

"Does that surprise you? I don't know why I've always looked so stupid to my own family!" He now asks if Irene has been told who the other woman is, and she realizes that her uncle and she have been thinking of different things. "Certainly not," she lies. And certainly it will be impossible for George to fall in love with her, because he is in love with someone else.

"People change!" he urges. He is, for Philip, becoming wrought up as he asks his niece if she ever thought of the other fellow—the woman's husband. He might be a good man; Irene may think she is being noble now, but possibly her duty lies in giving the woman back to her husband by winning George away from her. "She might be a woman of fine qualities," he urges, "who only needs to be disillusioned about George to be a perfect wife again!"

Irene is very moved, but she conceals it.

Philip must go, for he doesn't want Winkler to find him here. Almost casually he remarks that Winkler's duties have increased lately because Ray Brown, the Under Secretary of State, has been ill and may retire any day.

Winkler appears, highly cordial. He explains that a Washington repertory theatre is being started by some society people. Mrs. Winkler is to be chairman of a committee, and he asks if Irene would be chairman of a sub-committee. She feels highly complimented. This over, Winkler now gets down to the business he has in mind, but what he says is always carefully indirect. He knows that George is going to make a speech against Marshall Plan expenditures. Winkler admits that some money is being wasted, but it is better than withdrawing and letting a certain other power step into Western Europe. If George only knew the real reasons for our policy—but of course he can't, because they are top secret within the State Department and among the Chiefs of Staff. . . .

Irene is no mean diplomat herself. Of course, she muses, if George were back in the State Department, then he—but she stops, saying she shouldn't be talking thus. However, she *has* heard, vaguely, that Ray Brown may have to retire. . . .

Winkler gets her point, quickly thinks it over. "Yes," he says, "George has quite a background. . . . George might be interested in coming back to the Department?"

Irene has no idea, but, she says with pointed flattery, he admires Mr. Winkler so very much—and she herself was thinking just the other day, "If Mr. Winkler is in the White House . . ."

By now the Secretary is practically helpless. He exclaims, "I'd like to have George with us!" George arrives, carrying a stack of papers, and is amazed as he recognizes Winkler. The Secretary explains he has just called to offer Mrs. Henderson a committee job, and he must leave now. However, he would like to have George see him soon—at nine tomorrow morning, say. When he has gone George asks Irene what it all is really about, and she tells him—the

Secretary is upset over George's plan to speak against the Marshall Plan. The Secretary has alluded to the real reasons behind our policy, but, unfortunately, only a few top officials could be informed. So, she relates, she has suggested that George be offered one of those high-ranking jobs!

George is amazed and amused—but even more amazed when Irene tells him that Ray Brown is retiring and Mr. Winkler wants to offer him the job in the morning. Finally he manages to stammer a few words of gratitude to Miss Elliott. She is unbelievable! Irene gets in another lick, observing that it seems to her that Winkler is right in arguing that this is no time for party differences over national policy. It makes her happy that things are taking this turn.

GEORGE (*gently*)—Then, you're ambitious for me?

IRENE—A conscientious person is always ambitious for her employer.

GEORGE (*cooler*)—Oh, it's as an employer that . . .

IRENE (*very naturally*)—Of course! I like it here! . . . (*Crossing down to desk, where she puts papers.*) I enjoy my work. You pay me well. . . . Naturally I have your interest at heart. And, for my salary, I try to do everything I can! . . .

GEORGE—Naturally! . . . (*He drinks and brings his glass back to bar.*)

IRENE—Then, I also take a certain personal pride in it.

GEORGE (*from bar*)—Do you?

IRENE (*dreamily*)—Later on . . . when I'm busy with my information bureau for Senators . . . or married . . . I'll remember my life here. . . . You'll be an important personage then . . . And I'll be able to think I was beside you at the moment of your first great success. . . . It will be a wonderful memory! . . . (*A pause —she turns to him, and, with surprise:*) Why do you look at me like that? . . .

GEORGE—It's preposterous! . . . I just can't believe that . . .

IRENE—What?

GEORGE—That this is only the desire to be worth a salary! . . . Any woman who does for her employer what you have . . . (*He stops.*)

IRENE—Well?

GEORGE—She's taking more than a mere professional interest in him!

IRENE—Do you think so, Senator?

GEORGE—I do.

IRENE (*after a pause*)—You might be right! . . . (*Another pause.*) Yes . . . I was prompted by another feeling, I must admit.

GEORGE (*very pleased, taking a step towards her*)—Really? . . . A personal feeling? . . .

IRENE—Yes.

GEORGE (*another step*)—One which has nothing to do with your work?

IRENE—Nothing.

GEORGE (*another step*)—Which you've only been aware of recently?

IRENE—That's true.

GEORGE (*enchanted*)—I was sure of it! . . . (*Another step.*) About how long have you known?

IRENE—I can say exactly.

GEORGE (*happily—another step*)—Can you?

IRENE—One week.

GEORGE (*another step*)—After we got back from Europe?

IRENE—Four days after.

GEORGE (*surprised, stopping*)—Four days?

IRENE—It was the day Mr. Winkler came for luncheon.

GEORGE—And what precisely made you realize? . . . Tell me, please. . . .

IRENE (*quite naturally*)—Certainly. It was Constance's confession.

GEORGE (*stunned*)—What? . . .

IRENE—Until then, I didn't know whom I was replacing here! . . . Now I know that you're in love with my aunt . . . and that, one day, you'll be . . . well, someday you'll be my uncle! . . . (GEORGE *hardly controls his disappointment.*) I almost feel related to you already! . . . And that makes me all the more devoted to you! . . . Isn't it quite natural?

Irene tries to lead the emotionally tantalized man back to business, but he has other ideas. How about having dinner out to celebrate? She resists all his importunities. She would enjoy going out, even though dinner is ordered for here, but she must not allow herself to enjoy it. "You belong to another woman, whom I love and respect," she exclaims.

George is in a turmoil. He cries, "Don't you realize that you're driving me frantic?"—and she plays innocent. Moved by uncontrollable impulses, he kisses her. When the kiss is over she accuses him of being unfair, but he reminds her that she *is* his wife. That marriage, she announces, was a bargain—and he has just

broken the bargain. He has complicated her job terribly and it will
be difficult for her to continue. She tries to leave the room when
the manservant announces dinner, saying, "Excuse me for not having
dinner with you, sir. I think we'd better not see each other until
tomorrow." But George keeps her there. He suspects she is in love
with somone, and he must know. She admits she is in love, but will
not obey his order to tell who the man is. She makes her escape.
George tells the butler he doesn't want dinner now.

In a moment the servant returns, saying that Philip Russell has
come to call on Mrs. Henderson, but Mrs. Henderson has left the
house. Philip is shown in; he has come to learn what happened between Irene and Winkler this afternoon. George says, but in a preoccupied manner, that he is to see the Secretary in the morning.
He seems to be listening for Irene's return. Philip observes, "She's
so much in love with you!" This, George will not believe; why,
Irene has just told him she is in love with somebody else. Philip is
astounded—it sounds so unlike his niece. Affectionately he says,
"You really love her, eh?"—and when George admits "I'm beginning
to think so," Philip sighs audibly.

The distraught young Senator simply must find out where Irene's
heart lies, and he begs Philip to help him—to question her. Philip
assures him he will do what he can, and George, shaking hands,
earnestly says, "Thank you."

The old statesman, smiling broadly, replies, "But why do you keep
thanking me? I tell you it's my greatest pleasure!"

The curtain falls.

ACT III

Two days have passed, and Philip and Constance have come, sep-
arately, to congratulate George. George has been on a flying trip to
Colorado, and is due to return any moment.

"How did you hear the news?" Philip asks his wife.

"On the radio. I drove right out here."

"Winkler telephoned me. Good old George! This is one appointment nobody will object to!"

Irene has been out of the house since morning, Constance has
learned—and perhaps does not know yet that her husband is Under
Secretary of State. Constance herself is mystified as to how it came
about—for usually George never makes an important decision without consulting . . . "us." Philip answers lightly that things are different now—George is married. His wife shrugs off the possibility
that George has been getting advice from his hired wife.

Since they are alone, Philip takes the opportunity to talk seriously to his wife. He points out that, since she asked for her freedom three months ago, he has imposed on her very little—to see if he could accustom himself to living entirely away from her. He has decided it is not wise to hold a woman against her will. Therefore, he is going to take a trip around the world for a year or longer, and this will help Constance get her separation. At first she can hardly believe her ears. "There must be someone waiting for you," he pursues, "but even his patience must have its limits." He suggests that his wife get a divorce in Nevada.

Irene comes home. She knows about George's good fortune—and she explains that he may not be home directly, because when he left the airport he had to go straight to the White House. "I'd better leave you—I'm so busy these days," Philip says. Irene, surprised, asks if he is going somewhere and he answers, "Yes. Constance will tell you . . . perhaps . . ."

When he has gone, Constance tells Irene her uncle is going around the world; no, she is not going along. She breaks the news that she is going to get a divorce. After a pause, Irene smiles and says, "Then I'm through too."

"Yes," Constance agrees. She suggests that they go to Reno together. Quite evidently, George does not know of this additional good fortune which is befalling him, and Irene guesses that he will be very pleased. "I'll have to congratulate him on a lot of things! And I congratulate you too!" Constance accepts with equanimity and says she is sorry her niece's job must end so soon. But the arrangement with George is satisfactory, isn't it?

IRENE—Generous. In fact, I'm delighted with such a prompt solution.

CONSTANCE—Ah?

IRENE (*smiling*)—For weeks, now, I've felt a little like an understudy! . . . I don't believe it's a very popular job. Actresses do it to get started, to keep busy . . . or to make a living. . . . But, as soon as they can get something better, they give it up very willingly!

CONSTANCE—I know how you feel.

IRENE—And, generally speaking, the star has only disdain for her understudy! . . . (CONSTANCE *makes a gesture of protest.* IRENE *continues quickly.*) Not you, of course! . . . But I learned only a few days ago that you were . . . (*Changing tone, and sitting down, left of table.*) By the way, why did you suddenly decide to let me know?

CONSTANCE (*with a smile*)—I can tell you now.

IRENE—Now?

CONSTANCE—That you are leaving this house.

IRENE—Oh?

CONSTANCE—You worried me.

IRENE—How?

CONSTANCE—The outward change in you. . . . You've become so pretty, Irene. Your intimacy with George! . . . He was telling you things about his work that I didn't know. . . . Well, I was afraid you were trying to make him fall in love with you.

IRENE (*looking at her*)—I see. I couldn't be blamed for taking him away from a stranger. . . . Once I knew it was you, that made a difference! . . .

CONSTANCE—Exactly. I gambled on your loyalty.

IRENE—That was very clever.

CONSTANCE—It was a tribute to your character.

IRENE—Still, you were taking quite a risk. . . .

CONSTANCE—How?

IRENE—Announcing that you were the woman involved . . . was also telling me that it was Uncle Philip you were hoping to get rid of! . . . I might have decided that his interests were closer to my heart than yours!

CONSTANCE—You see he's given up: he's agreed to the divorce.

IRENE (*pensive*)—Yes . . . Which seems to me astounding . . .

CONSTANCE—Why?

IRENE—Knowing the way he feels about you, it's hard to realize that he could let you go. . . . (*She gets up and walks around the armchair, thinking it over.*) And . . . knowing my Uncle Philip . . . I wonder if he might not have some idea in the back of his mind.

CONSTANCE—What idea? . . .

IRENE—With him, you never know!

Since George's return is indefinite, Constance goes off on an errand, saying she will be back for tea. Lawrence, the butler, brings in newspapers carrying the story of George's appointment, and says to Irene that he and his wife are happy and proud. "You brought good fortune to the Senator, Madam."

George, coming in, has heard this, and when Lawrence has taken his hat and coat he smiles and says to Irene, "You'd almost think that he knows—that you did the whole thing."

"I didn't," she denies. "I said I could be of some help only because you were the best man."

He has heard the Russells were here, and Irene confesses she got them to go away by saying he wouldn't be back for a while, because she wants to see him alone first—to congratulate him before any of the others. George apologizes for the way he behaved the other night and she replies, "I'm glad you thought of saying that. Now I can leave on a pleasant memory."

He is astonished—and she breaks to him the good news that Constance is to have her divorce. George seems more disturbed than pleased; it is surprising that Philip would— And certainly Irene can't leave soon. Philip might not go ahead with his decision right away, and besides, divorces take time. Until then George does not see why he should deprive himself of his wife's services. Irene is getting a bit nervous as he speaks of her help, his need for her advice. Controlling herself, she interrupts, "Excuse me, sir, but what about *my* desires and *my* intentions?"

George remembers—she has told him she loves somebody else. It has been preying on his mind. He begs her to tell who it is, and finally she declares, "I'm in love with a man who doesn't exist! I had dreamed an ideal picture of him. . . . I knew he was devoted to another woman, and that only increased my admiration for him. . . . One night I discovered he was not the man I thought he was." She looks straight at him as she continues, "You were supposed to be in love with Constance. How could you treat me like a—casual convenience, when we both trusted you so? . . . It's all finished! I can never see you again!"

George is overwhelmed. He pours out his love for her, assuring, "Believe me, I am no longer in any way the man I was even the day before yesterday—and who I wish I had never been!"

Constance has returned and is in the doorway. She gives George a congratulatory handshake, and she presumes he has been told about the divorce being agreed to by Philip. "Yes," George replies. "See, Constance . . . I told you all along that he knew—that he had seen through everything!" George has swiftly reasoned it all out: After months of refusing, Philip suddenly consents to a divorce —two hours after George has been made Under Secretary of State. Why? To force his resignation, of course. A scandal in his private life would be of national importance. Therefore, George announces, he will see Byron Winkler tonight and tell him he can't take the job.

"It can't be done, George," Constance announces. "A man of your standing doesn't give up his career for a woman. A King of England can do that, but *not* an American Under Secretary of State!"

Constance is gallantly determined to be a good loser. Smiling bravely, she tells Irene she has a clear field—and advises her to stay with her present job. Irene, sincerely touched, says, "You're very generous, Constance . . . and very understanding."

"No!—But under any circumstances, I try to keep both my dignity . . . and a smile." As she wipes away a tear she adds, "Sometimes it isn't easy! Still, it can be done . . ."

Philip bounces in with hearty congratulations for George. "I'm leaving on a trip," he announces. "Very soon . . . very far . . . and all alone."

"No, Philip," Constance says quietly. He wonders if she really means it, and adds, "As for me, I never thought anything could put an end to our marriage."

"And nothing will, I promise you," his wife declares. "Do you think you could get another reservation?"

Smiling, the old fox draws two steamship tickets from his pocket, explaining, "I always hoped that, at the last moment, you would want to come with me. In love, you know, there is no resignation. It's only when you no longer care that you give up!"

Constance is thinking this over when her husband adds, "The only time to leave a man is *after* he's made you suffer. It's much easier to get over a wounded love than a happy memory!" She realizes, now, that he has known all along about herself and George. They leave together, and at the door Philip says to Irene, with emotion, "Thank *you*. . . . You're a wonderful girl!" Constance, too, bids a gallant good-by.

"Now, Irene," George says, gently, "I'd like you to see me as a new man . . . someone you've just met . . . who loves you—and wants to marry you!"

CURTAIN

SECOND THRESHOLD *

A Play in Two Acts

By Philip Barry

With Revisions by Robert E. Sherwood

WHEN Philip Barry died in 1949, he probably had come as close
to completing "Second Threshold" as he ever could, short of getting
it into actual production and then doing the revisions necessary to
bridge the inevitable gap between the typewritten script and the
spoken word. It fell to Robert E. Sherwood to make these last
adjustments. Sherwood, who had known Barry since 1921, had
talked with the dramatist about "Second Threshold" but had not
read the script until after Barry's death; and when he did read it,
it moved and excited him. "The work of revision that I did was
in the nature of carpentry rather than creation," Sherwood reports
in a fascinating foreword to the published version of the play. . . .
"What I have done on this play has been generously described as
'a labor of love.' I venture to protest that, despite my affection for
Phil and Ellen Barry, it was no such thing. I was impelled solely
by a sense of professional obligation. When I read it I knew it
must have a hearing, and, since I was asked to undertake the job,
I could not well refuse. I was often urged to change the title, which
was considered puzzling, and the word 'threshold' difficult to articu-
late. But I couldn't bring myself to change it, for I firmly believed
that it was on a second threshold that Phil Barry was standing
when he died. I believe that had he lived to see this one through,
he would have gained a new confidence, a new understanding of the
qualities that were his, a new ability to employ them all. All of the
American theatre mourns his loss, and the absence of all that he
did not live to write."

Barry, according to Sherwood, worked eleven years, on and off,

on this play, and wrote four complete drafts. He kept copious
notes, the first of which began, "Daughter. The man of 42 at the
end of his soul's rope, recovering from attempt at suicide." In the
pages of the same small pocket notebook was another idea, beginning, "The Family in the process of being studied for a piece in
Fortune. Most Unfortunate." This was the genesis of the very
successful "The Philadelphia Story." Sherwood believes there is
much of Barry in "Second Threshold," recalling that the Barrys'
daughter died in infancy and it was a dreadful blow. "I believe,"
says the collaborator, "that in Phil's fanciful imagination this daughter lived and grew and one may see his concept of her in girls that
he wrote, especially Tracy Lord and Miranda Bolton."

The action of the play takes place in the course of twenty-four
hours in the library of Josiah Bolton's house on West Tenth Street,
New York, late in July. The library is moderately large, and its
second-floor balcony looks over a small back garden. French windows open on the balcony. It is a comfortable, handsome room,
mostly Victorian but with an occasional good English or French
piece of furniture. On a table behind the sofa is a tray containing
a carafe of milk, a glass and a plate of sandwiches. It is a little
after midnight, and Toby Wells, who is in his late twenties and has
a humorous, likable face, is sitting in the room, listening and
waiting.

Soon Malloy, a manservant in dark trousers and black alpaca
coat, comes along the hall from downstairs, carrying two suitcases and a smaller piece of luggage. Seeing Toby in the library,
he enters, saying, "I thought surely you'd left by this time." Toby
asks, "Oh, Malloy, is it Miss Bolton?" It is; she is in the kitchen
talking with Mrs. Malloy. The servant has not told her that Toby
is here.

"Go on up," says Toby. "But quietly. He may be asleep."

Malloy asks, skeptically, "You think that, Doctor?" Toby admits
he is skeptical, too. Miranda Bolton appears, switching on the
chandelier light, and is surprised to find anyone in the room. She
smiles and says, "Why, I think I know you. . . ." He supplies his
name and she exclaims, "You're not Dr. Wells' little boy! But of
course. That Summer on Christmas Cove. You had a crew cut—
you were an absolute darling." This was when he was pushing
twenty-one and Miranda was sixteen.

"You haven't been here much recently," Toby ventures.

"Not much," she admits. "But I always love to come back to it."
She asks what he has been up to all these years and he replies,
"Johns Hopkins—University of Edinburgh—Navy." She realizes

he must be a doctor, too, and becomes worried, but he explains easily that his father is away on vacation and he has been dropping in now and then on friendly visits. Toby knows about Miranda, of course, and congratulates her twice—once for graduating from Bennington, and again upon her forthcoming marriage. "I'm sailing tomorrow night," she informs him. "We're being married soon after I land—July thirtieth."

Miranda has been having sandwiches and milk. Malloy appears and asks if she wants Mrs. Malloy to wait up for her house guest; it isn't necessary, because the guest has a key to the front door. Miranda explains to Toby that she is carting a Bennington freshman with her to England—a darling child named Thankful Mather. She moves toward the door with a "Do drop in at any time."

Toby—Very brisk, aren't you? Where do you think you're going? (*She turns and looks at him. She is now moderately annoyed.*)

Miranda—Now?

Toby—Now.

Miranda—To see my father before I fold for the night.

Toby—Sit down.

Miranda—I beg your pardon?

Toby—The hope is he's asleep.

Miranda—How do you mean the hope?

Toby—He hasn't been getting much lately. Sit down please.

Miranda—Well. All right. (*She sits.*)

Toby—Why have you walked out on your father?

Miranda (*astounded*)—Why have I walked out . . .

Toby—You needn't repeat my question. All you have to do is answer it!

Miranda (*smiles*)—When you were at Medical School, dear Doctor, did they include a course in charm?

Toby—Yes. But I flunked it. Must I ask you again—?

Miranda—No. I did not walk out on my father. He deliberately cut himself off from me—from everybody. That was his own choice —and it's his lookout, isn't it?

Toby—He's got no lookout left. That's the trouble.

Miranda—What's the matter with him?

Toby—Your father's hit a blank spot—a very blank spot—where he pulls up short and says, "Well, here I am. But where the hell am I? Where do I go from here?"

Miranda—Or—what do I settle for, maybe?

Toby—Maybe. And what he settles for is the conclusion that life just isn't worth living.

MIRANDA—I don't believe it.

TOBY—I'm sure it's difficult, for the highly intellectual daughter of an even more highly so father—

MIRANDA—You're trying to tell me that he's cracked up?

TOBY—Not precisely that—but something like it.

MIRANDA—I don't believe it. Not him. A man as big as that.

TOBY—It's the big ones—the ones who've been in the so-called high places—who get smacked the hardest. They know what combat really is. They've been in the ring with the champ.

The doctor informs the young woman that her father doesn't like the idea of her going to marry a man old enough to be her—a man twice her age. Her eyes flash with anger as she declares it is her business. He continues to probe her; speaking of her father he says, "You and he used to be very close to each other—" She advises him to go right back to Johns Hopkins and specialize in osteopathy if he thinks he can find anything Freudian in this family. She and her father were friends—companions. Nothing emotional. She was close to her father because she was the only one he could trust *not* to be emotional. After Mother had got her divorce, and he'd lost hope of making anything out of Miranda's brother, Jock, her father took her with him to the Washington conferences and she was useful to him as secretary, hostess—and mostly as a sounding board. "He could talk to me impersonally about anything. That's the way it always was between us—impersonal."

Miranda excuses her having gone to England—and got engaged —at Christmas time instead of coming home by saying her father didn't mind in the least. He has been making it increasingly clear that he wants to be alone, and even after the accident he insisted she didn't come down from college. The accident happened last March, when her father crashed a little chartered plane—completely wrecked it, but escaped with very minor injuries. She never could figure out how it happened, for her father is a marvelous pilot. Now, she wants to know why her father is sitting here, all alone, in the middle of the Summer. What is he doing? Toby replies, sitting, thinking, reading, eating a little, sleeping a little at odd times; hasn't been out of the house in eight weeks, since he drove down to Amagansett "just for a swim"—and with what results Miranda must know.

But she doesn't, and asks, "Are you trying to scare me?"

"Perhaps 'arouse' is the better word."

Toby explains he isn't visiting here as a doctor, but as a friend;

perhaps Miranda can persuade her father to see a doctor—but Toby can't. Miranda asks what she can do, and immediately plans to stay over a few days and fly to England in time for the wedding. The marriage can't be postponed because Matthew has to go out to the Far East in August. Toby guesses that Miranda's job with her father would take three months, maybe six. Perhaps, she speculates, she can get her father to go to England with her, but Toby doubts it. The young doctor would like to leave, but sounds from above indicate that the father is coming down, and Miranda begs Toby to stay just one minute; she and her father are strangers and she doesn't want to be alone with him straight off.

Josiah Bolton comes in, saying in the friendliest possible tone, "Toby!" You still here? Haven't you a home of your own?" Bolton is built like an athlete and is in good trim. He is a man who has borne many responsibilities, much success and many disappointments without having been bent down by them; but there is about him an air of distance that suggests a deliberate self-removal from future involvements, big or little. He is in a dressing gown. Now, having come further into the room, he sees his daughter, exclaims, "Miranda!" and kisses her lightly on the cheek. In answer to her "How are you?" he says, "Never better." The conversation remains on a light, impersonal plane for some moments—even after Toby has left. Then, in great seriousness, Miranda asks her father to sail with her—or fly with her, if he prefers—to the wedding. After all, he is the one who is supposed to give the bride away.

JOSIAH—That quaint old custom is superfluous in this case. Matthew Atwater needs no donor. He just takes things. Where's he holding the ceremony? Westminster Abbey?

MIRANDA—Some Registry Office, whatever that is. Sordid, probably. Father—do you know that it would make me very happy to have you at my wedding?

JOSIAH—It's very nice of you to say so, Miranda. But you're wrong. I'd be a bit of a skeleton at the feast, and I couldn't pretend to be otherwise.

MIRANDA—Toby told me it would be hopeless to ask you.

JOSIAH—That young fellow shows gleams of intelligence now and then.

MIRANDA—What was it you said to Matthew when he telephoned you?

JOSIAH—When was that?

MIRANDA—Last winter, when we got engaged.

JOSIAH—Oh, of course. Didn't he tell you?

MIRANDA—I gathered it wasn't very agreeable.

JOSIAH—He must have exaggerated. We exchanged the usual compliments and courtesies. "So nice to hear your voice again." "So nice to hear *yours.*" That sort of thing. No heads broken. He was most courtly in the manner in which he spoke for your hand in marriage. He gave me a brief summary of his financial position and prospects.

MIRANDA—But what did *you* say?

JOSIAH—I forget my exact words. As I remember, I congratulated him on being so well off in such times as these. However, I confessed to being familiar with the date of his birth. I felt obliged to tell him that I was not offering my daughter for adoption.

MIRANDA—You can be a real stinker, can't you!

JOSIAH (*amused*)—It has been said of me. Matthew knows that. I'm sure he wasn't in the least surprised—or taken aback.

MIRANDA—You hate him, don't you?

JOSIAH—By no means. I admire him as a vigorous force in public life. He is intelligent, he is urbane, he is immensely successful —and he serves as fine a dinner as the present British law will allow. Finer in fact. But as a son-in-law—

MIRANDA—If you won't go to the wedding, I hope you'll give me just one thing . . .

JOSIAH—I want you to choose your own wedding present—anything—

MIRANDA—I'm not talking about that. I want the parental blessing on my marriage.

JOSIAH—Blessing! My God, Miranda, you certainly *are* getting old-fashioned.

MIRANDA—Marriage is an old-fashioned institution. I should treasure your blessing.

JOSIAH—It is not forthcoming. It is not vouchsafed.

MIRANDA—All right. I guess we've washed up that subject.

But they are not quite washed up. In Josiah's eyes, Miranda's admiring Matthew for his mind, his approach to life, is not enough. He is afraid for his daughter—afraid that she is by way of missing life altogether. She may feel secure in her own strength of mind and character—but, he asks, "What about your heart?" "A stout, muscular organ, useful for pumping blood," she shrugs.

But, for all her professed coolness, Miranda is really solicitous for her father. She thinks he should see a doctor; she forces him to take a sandwich and some milk. She asks, "Do you ever hear from Mother?"

"Oh, a telegram now and then. . . . I gather she's very happy. Evidently her new husband—the semi-retired polo player—is good for her."

And Jock? Did his flunking out of law school hurt her father very much? He replies, "I made impossible demands on the poor kid. One of my many miscalculations. I wanted Jock to be a really great lawyer—an exponent of pure law, as opposed to a shrewd opportunist like me. But he wanted to get into something called 'show business'—he preferred *Variety* to Blackstone as reading matter, and that's the way he went, and wisely, no doubt. Grease paint can be a more honorable disguise than the false faces that are worn by us lawyers."

"And what did you want for me? How have *I* disappointed you?" his daughter asks—and he answers, "I've told you what I wanted for you, Miranda. Love. The kind of wonderful, enveloping love that I'm certain you deserve. The kind that I never deserved—and never got."

Josiah has had enough of questioning, and he has one more thing to tell his daughter. Before she sails she should go to the bank and see old Clifford Evans, who has some papers for her to sign. He has made a formal settlement on his children—in cash. He has got rid of the place in the country, and this house is on the market. . . .

Miranda stares at him and quotes, " 'Putting his house in order'?" He puts it, easily, another way—just a gradual shedding of responsibilities. His daughter declares she will take her share of the gift only when he also gives her his withheld blessing. Aroused now, she reminds him of the night in Washington when he wrote his resignation to the President, and how she stormed and railed at him for being a quitter. She adds, "But I certainly didn't know how completely you *had* quit. . . . It sounds lonely. Lonely!"

Josiah goes to the window, saying, "Whistle in the dark enough, and sometimes you may hear an answering one." He looks down into the garden as if listening and calls, "Pleasant weather down there?" He explains to his astonished daughter that he is talking to a vision—an apparition. Quite an intelligent one. He talks to it often.

Miranda asks, passionately, why it can't be the same again as when they worked together and were close. Harshly he replies, "I would remind you of a passage from the Bible—'If the salt has lost its savour wherewith shall it be salted? It is thenceforth good for nothing but to be cast out and to be trodden under foot of men.'" His daughter is sure now that Josiah thinks he is through. The library door opens and Josiah looks with astonishment upon Thankful Mather. She is nineteen, is wearing an evening dress, is very pretty and possesses one expression—somewhat puzzled intentness. What goes on in her head, no one knows; what she has to say proceeds from elsewhere, as Josiah soon learns after he has been introduced. "I'm really flattened, Miranda," Thankful exclaims. "I'm completely all wore out. Pity me. They dance so differently down here. 'Specially Princeton men."

JOSIAH—How in heaven's name old are you?

THANKFUL—I'll be twenty-one next month. No: I needn't lie about it: who am I fooling? I'll be twenty. Why?

JOSIAH—Just the difficulty of believing you're completely all wore out. It generally comes a little later. (JOSIAH *is looking at* THANKFUL *with amused interest.*) And, may I ask, why are you going to Europe? Are you getting married, too?

THANKFUL—Married? Oh, dear no. At least, not as far as I know. I'm going on account of culture.

JOSIAH—Good! Culture is much better than marriage. It lasts longer.

THANKFUL—Mother gave me a list of cathedrals and museums as long as—as—well, you just ought to *see* it. But I'm taking my portable Victrola and a whole stack of records and I expect I'll see *some* American boys here or there—

JOSIAH—Undoubtedly—so the cathedrals and museums can wait —in fact, they *will* wait, indefinitely. (*To* MIRANDA.) What did you say her name is?

MIRANDA—Thankful Mather.

JOSIAH (*smiles*)—Ah, yes. In that case, good night to you both.

MIRANDA—Good night, Father.

JOSIAH—Good night, daughter. (*Kisses her.*) Sleep well.

MIRANDA—Also you.

JOSIAH—Why not? And you, sweet innocent! (THANKFUL *starts slightly.*)

THANKFUL—Me? Oh, I always! (JOSIAH *moves toward the hall.*)

JOSIAH—May heaven's brightest angels watch over thee.

THANKFUL—Thee too. (*At the door he stops and turns to* THANKFUL.)

JOSIAH—Descended from the Reverend Cotton Mather, by any chance?

THANKFUL—Shouldn't be surprised.

JOSIAH—I think *he* would be. (*He goes out.* THANKFUL *takes a deep breath.*)

The girl exclaims how *attractive* Miranda's father is—and then she notices Miranda, whose eyes look funny and starey, sort of. Suddenly Miranda asks, "What would you do if someone—if suddenly you discovered that someone who—who was terribly dear to you, was in terrible danger?" Thankful boxes around with this for a bit and at last suggests, "There's always *people*. That's the nice thing about people. So at least I'd try to, you know, form a rescue party or something. You know: like when you're skiing or something and someone gets lost?"

Thankful is not a fool, and she divines that Miranda is talking about her father, but she can't imagine what the danger might be. Miranda, picking up the phone, calls a Southampton number, and asks that Jock Bolton be waked up and put on the phone. "Jock, you've got to get up here tomorrow morning," she urges. "It's about Father. . . . He's in bad shape. . . . I don't care if you do have a rehearsal. . . . Thank you, Jock, Good night, Jock."

Miranda's head sinks and her shoulders begin to shake as she sobs to herself, "Oh, God, dear God—how I hate the ones who blubber!"

The curtain falls.

SCENE II

It's a little after noon the next day, and Jock has arrived. From the balcony he sees his father working in the garden and the sight amazes him. Thankful trips in, and the two young people have a pleasant encounter. She explains that she is on her way out to buy some Kleenex to take to Europe, and he explains he is an actor. As an actor, he says, he has learned how to handle women, and he might just decide to handle her.

"Kind of crazy, aren't you?" Thankful laughs.

"Kind of. And how about you?"

"I work at it sometimes." He tells the girl she will find a drug store on Sixth Avenue, just by walking left from the front door. He adds that if she comes to a big, wide river, with ferry boats on it, she has overshot her mark. She laughs again and goes on her way.

When Miranda comes in Jock can see that she is in a sober mood. She tells her brother they have run into something desperately serious about their father. Jock won't believe it; his father looks all right. He won't believe it when his sister says flatly, "There's every sign that he intends to kill himself." Jock scoffs, "What—did you find a gun in the desk drawer with one silver bullet in it?"

Miranda shows Jock the legal papers—the settlement of all their father's money upon the two of them. Jock cynically suspects it is some kind of tax dodge, and says he will be glad to co-operate to help the old man out. With great urgency, Miranda insists, rather than asks, "You love him, don't you."

JOCK (*levelly*)—No—I don't think I do. And why should I? Do you love somebody who's never given you anything but contempt?

MIRANDA—Plus a big allowance.

JOCK—Too big, if you ask me. It was conscience money. (*He brandishes one of the papers.*) This is conscience money! (*He tosses the papers on the desk.*) He had a God complex—thought he could create me in *his* image. Well, it didn't work. I failed him, because I happened to have a heart of my own and it just wasn't in the legal profession. Now, I guess, he's begun to suspect that maybe he isn't God, after all, and he's trying to square accounts in the only way he knows how to.

MIRANDA—I'd call you an ungrateful louse, Jock—if I didn't happen to know you aren't a louse. You're just terribly wrong. Last night he talked about you. He said he was the failure, not you—

JOCK (*unimpressed*)—He said that, did he?

MIRANDA—And there was none of that God complex—creating you in his image. He said you'd done the wise thing in choosing to live your own life.

JOCK—Oh, hell, Sis—I hate it—I hate not being fond of him the way I used to be, when we were kids. He never had time to pay much attention to us, and Mother was always all over us, but I never had any respect for her and I had real respect for him. When he did have time for us, he could do nice little human things, like letting me hold the fish pole if there was only one, and the day he bought some Indian arrowheads from an antique shop and planted them in the garden for us to dig up and think we'd discovered them, and he was sore as hell at Mother for telling us the truth. If he'd only done one little human thing since I grew up and disappointed him. Why—last winter I had a terrific part with the Top Hat Players on West 79th Street. I asked Father if he'd like to see it. He said he was sorry, he couldn't get off any evening that week, when I knew he wasn't doing a thing and he knew I knew it. He didn't even send me a telegram saying kindest regards and best wishes.

MIRANDA—He's lost the knack for doing human things, including living.

JOCK (*turns to her*)—Have you figured out how he proposes to knock himself off? (*He is being deliberately hard-boiled to mask a sense of growing alarm.*)

MIRANDA—It will be an "accident"—

Jock is not greatly disturbed, even when his sister tells him she called their mother last night in Santa Barbara, and Mother understood. "She said she always knew that if Josiah Bolton ever lost interest in his chosen mission of reforming the world—he'd be dead. She promised to call him up today."

Jock is not insensible; he realizes there may be something in what his sister says, and that the only doctor who can perform a cure must be someone who loves their father. But he says he is out as a doctor; this may be horrible, but it's true. It is up to Miranda—her problem exclusively. "All he cares about in this world is you," he argues. "It's like an obsession."

Toby comes in and eases the tension by saying to Miranda, "I brought you a handsome wedding present, Mandy—a bucket of clams. Malloy's opening them."

Josiah comes up from the garden and greets his son with, "To what do we owe—and so forth?" Jock tries to break through his father's defenses, but Josiah's guard is well up. If it is money the boy is worried about, all he has to do is go to the bank and talk to old Clifford about it. The young man pleads, "Why don't you get away from here—get out into the fresh air?"

Why not? Josiah agrees pleasantly. As a matter of fact, he tells them he is leaving shortly to go hunting in Arizona. All he is waiting for is a telegram from an old mountain guide out there. Thankful breezes in, with a breathless tale: "It was the darnedest thing. I got the Kleenex and tooth powder and—and things I needed and it made a vast package and the man handed it to me and there I was, all bright-eyed and a bushy tail, when a boy came up to me—he had a corduroy coat on—and said, 'Here, you're too little to h'ist all that,' and he took it away from me. And while we were walking around the block we got to talking and it seems he is an oil painter and I'd be very surprised if he's any good although he is kind of cunning. Well, when we got to the door here he said he'd like to paint *me*. Did you ever *hear* of such a thing?"

Josiah exclaims an amused, "Never!" Malloy announces lunch

has been served on the garden terrace. Josiah leaves them; he doesn't want lunch. Jock turns to his sister and, after closing the library door, says, "You're right to be scared. That hunting trip— all by himself in those mountains—it's murder. . . ."

Jock takes Thankful down to lunch, and Miranda faces Toby somewhat defiantly, stating, "I'm much clearer in my mind now. . . . You said this was a matter of three months—six months. We haven't that time. Father may leave tomorrow. . . . I'm going to find a way to face it out with him now—today—honestly— openly. That's the only kind of treatment he'll ever respond to."

"Shock treatment?" Toby asks.

"If you want to call it that. It's persuading him that he's wanted. . . ."

Toby accuses Miranda of planning this just so she can get off on schedule to Europe, and she blazes at him, "You're a peculiarly loathsome specimen, aren't you?" Pointedly she asks if he doesn't have an appointment someplace—and he says yes, here, for lunch. In a quick motion he takes her face in his hands and kisses her. She stands off from him and demands, "If I'm not being too personal, just what the hell did *that* mean?"

Toby grins an answer, "Only my way of expressing furtive admiration."

Miranda stands still, her mind working fast. "Thank you, Dr. Wells. It's a thought. . . . It's an idea," she says.

The young doctor suggests they go down and swallow some clams.

The curtain falls.

ACT II

It is a little before six in the afternoon. Josiah reads a two-page telegram, smiles slightly, goes to the window, looks down and listens for a moment. Then he says, to whatever is down there, "Of course I do. It's all very touching—all very transparent. And quite natural. They think it's suicide. That's an ugly word, isn't it? Whereas, if the old man were to die a nice, quiet, natural death—now, how do you suppose they'd feel about that, eh?—I agree. They would feel sorry—a little. . . . Oh, you're going? . . . Well, so am I. But we'll meet again." He waves pleasantly toward the garden, then goes toward his gun cabinet.

If Josiah has had any purpose in going to the cabinet, he is halted in it by the appearance of Malloy. Mr. Bolton is wanted on the telephone by Washington. He chats cordially with the caller, then

says, "Oh, no, I couldn't even consider it. Honored and all that . . ."
He is cynical about the call, for Malloy has told him his daughter
put in a call for Washington today, and this is the only explanation
for Washington having found out what his new number is. He
sits in a chair and starts to read a copy of *The Economist*. Thankful tiptoes in behind his chair, puts her hands lightly over his eyes
and says, "Guess who—I mean whom."

Josiah guesses "Sophie Tucker? . . . Louisa May Alcott? . . .
Princess Margaret, you get right back to the palace!" Thankful
laughs and gives him the full treatment, moving closer every time
he uncomfortably suggests that she go sit on the sofa. Josiah asks,
"Just what and what *is* this apparently mad current rush of young
girls toward—I shall put it mercifully—toward somewhat older
men?"

THANKFUL—You think there's one on—a rush, I mean?

JOSIAH—I've observed it in various quarters, even in my own
family. Of course, I've also observed that the men are usually
either well-off or well-known. Not that I qualify in any such—

THANKFUL—Well, don't you think either one's more attractive
than having curly hair or a seven-handicap at golf?

JOSIAH—I am merely asking for information, merely seeking
enlightenment. (*She gets up, circles above chair.*)

THANKFUL—Don't you admit it's being a little more advanced on
girls' parts than on men's, who just keep on always being attracted
to pretty girls just because they're pretty?

JOSIAH—Yes—yes, if pressed, I'm bound to say I do.

THANKFUL—Anyhow, *I* don't *like* curly hair or golf either.

JOSIAH—Flash the news to the Associated Press.

THANKFUL—What does that mean?

JOSIAH—It's known as a quip. Forgive it.

THANKFUL (*moves to the chair*)—Anyhow, you do think I'm
pretty—(*Sits on left arm.*)—don't you?

JOSIAH—Why, yes. Extravagantly. Do you mind?

THANKFUL—Not a bit.—And therefore kind of—irresistible?

JOSIAH—That, my dear child, is none of your business.

THANKFUL (*rising*)—Anyhow, I just want you to get it into your
thick skull that the world's just full of girls like me and for all you
know there might any number of them be ready to be just crazy
about you—and it's fun—within—(*She giggles.*)—certain limits,
of course—and so why don't you do something about it? That is,
unless you're dead on your feet, which would be silly at your age,

don't you think?   (JOSIAH *rises, steps to left of chair and gazes at her, appalled.*)

JOSIAH—Will you kindly inform me who or what on earth put you up to—?

THANKFUL (*steps close to him*)—I made a simple suggestion. (*She raises her face.*)

JOSIAH (*pinned against chair*)—I—if you don't mind, I—I'm afraid I'll (*He puts his hands on her shoulders.*) —I'll tell you what—some rainy Sunday?

THANKFUL (*steps back*)—So long as you don't miss the bus entirely. I'm not necessarily referring to myself.

JOSIAH—I hope not. (*He leans over, takes her face in his hands and kisses her on the top of her head.* MIRANDA *comes in.*)

Thankful leaves, caroling, "Don't forget that rainy Sunday." Miranda's air seems odd—different—to her father. She says she has been out with Toby, sitting on the terrace of the Brevoort, and it was heavenly. She wonders, dreamily, if there's time for a last fling before she gets married-up for life—for isn't it just as natural for a girl to want one as a man?

Josiah advises his daughter against trying any such—not on that young man; not if she wants her hair left on her head. Then, smiling shrewdly at Miranda, he tells her she is her own master, or mistress, and to go ahead. He is thinking of his dear old friend Matthew: Matthew would understand and even approve; it would amuse him. Miranda is not enthusiastic about this turn in the conversation. She asks, "Then you think it is all right—for me, and Toby?"

"For Toby."

"You've given me up, haven't you," she tells her father. "As a bad job. . . . Because we've given you up. We've run out on you."

"On the contrary," Josiah says, looking at his daughter levelly. He points out that he has just had a long telegram from his former wife, asking him to come and stay with her and her new husband in Santa Barbara. Now, whatever could have inspired this wire? Again, there was the telephone call from Washington. Can Miranda imagine such a coincidence? And then Thankful—delicious little Thankful! Some rainy Sunday! And even Jock insisting on having a talk with him. Miranda works up a reasonable reason for each of these circumstances and incidents which does not involve her.

Josiah tells his daughter that his children have no obligations toward him—and there are no obligations on his side, either. She insists that there *are* some on his side, to himself—and he can't escape them by dying. "Dying?" he asks. "Who's dying?" "You are."

Josiah is aroused; he is sick and tired of all the moral regeneration that's going on around here—even with Jock. He informs Miranda that Jock has been wondering if he shouldn't quit the stage and go back to law school. He chortles, "I made short work of *that* ridiculous idea. I told him you could find no higher mission in life than to be an entertainer. . . . I gave him some good advice. . . . You see, I know something about the theatre. I once wrote the book of a Hasty Pudding show and I starred in it. I had a number that knocked 'em dead."

To his daughter's amazement, he begins a dance step and a song together. The song runs,

> Though I'm rarely in the money
> It is really rather funny
> How I always seem to land upon my feet. . . .

Toby comes in. Josiah tells him to sit down and goes on dancing and singing,

> When out strolling with my honey
> On a day that's bright and sunny
> I invariably tell her she's a treat!

He ends his dance with a resounding slap on each buttock. Miranda looks scared and Toby has not sat down. Josiah tells them he has had a telegram from the Arizona guide and will be leaving in the morning after Miranda gets on that ship tonight. He goes to the gun cabinet and takes out a big .30-30 rifle. Miranda, jumping up, cries, "Father! Put it away!" He blandly pays no heed to her as he speculates on tracking mountain lions. It would make no difference if he never got one, because all his life he has been hunting unsuccessfully—for the hidden motive. With the gun he pantomimes the slaying of a motive, even to pulling the trigger and saying "Bang." Finally heeding his daughter's violent protests, he puts the gun away.

Toby suggests that Josiah postpone his trip for a day because Toby's father is returning tonight, and he'd like to have his father authorize so rugged a trip. "Don't worry, my boy," says Josiah blandly. "I absolve him of responsibility. I absolve you. I absolve your whole family."

Miranda has a sense of complete defeat and she confesses to her father, "I thought I could do something for you. Shock therapy! So I'm the one who gets the shock."

"But you *have* done something for me," he counters. "Can't you see the magical change you've wrought? I feel marvelous! And I owe it all to you. You've shaken me out of this—you've put the old spirit of adventure back into me. And just for that—I'm going to take everybody out to dinner. Someplace where there's music—dancing—*noise!*" He spies Thankful in the hall and captures her, exclaiming, "Thankful—we're going out on the town. You and I are going to dance!" And to prove to the lass that he can dance he breaks into his Hasty Pudding routine again.

Miranda, bursting into tears, cries, "Father! Don't!"—and runs out of the room. Toby starts to follow her, but Josiah, speaking quietly and with deep emotion, commands, "No! Leave her alone. Leave her alone."

The curtain falls.

SCENE II

Miranda is asleep on the couch, but she wakes up when Toby comes in. It is ten-thirty that night. Toby says he left the party an hour ago, and she should have been there to see her father and Thankful; Josiah was acting like a buyer from Council Bluffs. Miranda tells Toby she is not sailing tonight; she can get a plane on Friday, and has put in a call to London to tell Matthew so. Thankful can have the steamer cabin to herself.

Miranda confesses she is still scared about her father, and Toby suggests that maybe Josiah would let him go to Arizona with him. "And you would do that?" she asks, looking at him, hard.

"I'd do anything for him. But—it's an empty gesture. He'd never agree to it."

She exults, "There *are* some good people left, after all." She invites him to sit beside her on the couch and says, "I don't believe you are any great shakes as a doctor, Toby. But you can be powerful comforting. And—oh, how I need comforting." Suddenly she puts her head against his chest—just friendly-wise, she warns. She is so tired . . .

Toby leans back into a corner of the sofa and draws her head down upon his shoulder. "Feet up," he commands. She wriggles into a comfortable position, murmuring drowsily, "You *are* a good friend, Toby." Sleepier and sleepier, she mumbles that she is going to marry Matthew if it's the last thing she does. Settling deeper into his shoulder she suggests, "Tell me a story, Toby. Just a story. You're an animal—tell me—an animal story—" He begins reciting the clinical details of an exciting new cure for Rocky Mountain spotted fever, but she doesn't hear much of it because she has fallen asleep.

Thankful bursts in, sees the pair on the sofa and exclaims, "Well, for *heaven's* sake—" This wakes Miranda, who asks where her father is. He is in the pantry, getting some champagne, and some food for Thankful. Malloy announces that the London call has come through and Miranda goes to take it on the downstairs wire. Toby explains to Thankful, "She's breaking the news to the venerable boy friend that she isn't sailing tonight." The girl is slightly fearful at the prospect of sailing alone, but Toby assures her she can take care of herself. "You know how to say No?" he asks.

"No."

"*That's* right! Nothing to worry about. Miranda will be there almost as soon as you—flying."

The young lady falls to wondering if Miranda really loves this Englishman. Personally, she thinks Miranda has a "thing" for Toby. He doesn't think so; so, cheerfully saying, "Well, as long as Miranda doesn't want you—" she playfully lets her hair fall over her face, practically into his, and inquires, "Want to feel some silk?" At this moment Josiah comes in, carrying a tray holding champagne, glasses, sandwiches and milk. Without the flicker of an eye he comments, "Isn't that always the way. You fall madly, wildly in love with an entrancing creature. She gives you some reason to believe that your passion is not entirely unreciprocated. And then—the moment you let her out of your sight—off she goes with a younger man."

Josiah is in a fine mood. He gives Thankful the plate of sandwiches and some milk, and she falls to. He and Toby have wine. Josiah watches the girl with pleasure as she eats and drinks, saying he feels like her beau at commencement day spread. He continues, "We have just heard the commencement day address by an important alumnus. He is a successful bookmaker, who has just been made honorary doctor of laws because he donated a million dollars to the college endowment fund. He has told the graduating class, 'My young friends—you are standing on the threshold of life.' How true that is! And then the years go by—'The years like great, black oxen tread the world—and God, the herdsman, goads them on behind'—and we come to another commencement and a grim orator saying, 'My aged friends—you are standing on the second threshold—a doorstep into the final anteroom that separates life from death. Maybe it is an enormous room, the end of which cannot be seen, maybe it is a stuffy little alcove.' So, let us reject this horrid thought."

When Miranda returns from the telephone her father says he inadvertently heard her say to Matthew that she is not sailing. He seems pleased about this, but dashed when he learns she plans to fly next Friday. Suddenly he seems to want air and moves to open the balcony curtains. He gives the cord a yank and it breaks and dangles in his hand. In something of a frenzy he picks up a pair of long scissors from the desk, looks at them reflectively, snips the brass weight off the cord—and jauntily begins a joint monologue and knot-tying demonstration. As he ties and unties various elaborate knots he tells about a friend, Andy Farren. Best flier he ever saw. Shot down twenty-two Germans in the first World War. But after the Armistice he couldn't stand the prospect of going "back to normalcy"—so he just headed his plane out to sea and vanished. "And now," says Josiah, "I know why I felt so oddly relieved when I knew he was dead. . . . One must belong to his times: live them, write them, paint them, be of them. . . . All he could do was dwell in the past, enraged at the present, full of fear for the future. . . ."

Josiah, toying with his audience, fashions another knot which, Toby guesses, must be a hangman's noose. But it isn't, it's a trick. Josiah breaks the knot with a flick and throws the cord on the desk. Now his gaiety returns, and he astounds everybody—most of all Thankful—by announcing that the hermit has emerged from his cave, the monk from his cell. "In brief, and to wit, I have found a girl—living, breathing, laughing, loving—and my own." He reaches for Thankful's hands and draws her beside him. Thankful seems grateful, if bewildered—but now she must go and throw a few things into a bag.

When the girl has gone, Josiah taunts his daughter, banteringly. Surely Miranda can't be thinking there's a disparity in their ages? And surely she wouldn't deny him this one last fling? His daughter accuses him of being crude and amateurish, and leaves the room. Alone with Toby, Josiah asks if Miranda's decision to postpone her trip might be because she has found a new interest—Toby, he hopes. "You're way off the beam," says Toby. "She's going to marry Matthew Atwater if it's the last thing she does. Those were her very words."

It is plain that Josiah is now inwardly acknowledging total defeat as he says, slowly, "Then—I say—let her go."

"And yourself with her?" Toby prods. Josiah replies, "Why not?" He is becoming bitter and angry.

TOBY—And why are you trying to drag Miranda down with you? (JOSIAH *looks at him, sharply.*) You can't bear to let go of her, can you! So you're poisoning her with your own despair.

JOSIAH—What are you talking about?

TOBY—I'm talking about your daughter, and the health of her heart and mind. Whatever you do to yourself is your business, I'm sorry to say. But what you do to Miranda—

JOSIAH—And is that *your* business?

TOBY—I wish it were. Then I could really do something about it.

JOSIAH—What would you do, Toby?

TOBY—I'd marry her tonight. I'd prove to her that she can be loved for herself—and not merely as a sort of subdivision of Josiah Bolton. You're asserting your domination more violently than ever. You're giving her something terrible to remember you by. You're making the attachment all the stronger, all the more strangling.

JOSIAH—Attachment?

TOBY—That's the word. You're cooking up real tragedy for Miranda, permanent tragedy. She was trying to escape from it. Maybe she didn't choose the wisest means of escape. But she was trying. And she deserved your sympathy, your help, your pity. Instead of which—you're very skillfully fixing it so that there can be no escape for her, by any means, ever.

JOSIAH (*quietly, coldly*)—Perhaps I'm out of date—but—is this the modern concept of correct professional behavior for a doctor?

TOBY—Luckily, I am not here on a professional basis.

JOSIAH—So you can say what you please—and so, by your leave, can I. My daughter is miserable because she is full of illusions about me. I have sought to shatter them by letting her see me as I really am—ruthless, callous. And that may give her a clearer view of Matthew Atwater.

TOBY—All very fine—very slick. But what you're *really* doing is shifting to her the responsibility for your own failure. (MIRANDA *has come in on that last sentence.*)

MIRANDA—Toby! What are you saying!

TOBY—I'm talking out of turn. But I've got to do it! The air's got to be cleared. It's suffocating! (*To* JOSIAH.) Of all the low-down advantages to take of your own child, the threat you're making is the lowest I ever heard of.

MIRANDA—Have you gone crazy?

TOBY—No! Sane! I'm no psychiatrist—nor ever will be. I

don't like the brain as a study. I prefer the digestive tract. It's
much 'more orderly and efficient than the brain, and also much
cleaner. But I'm a doctor and I've looked the gray rat in the eye
quite a number of times, and always I've been given a fair chance
to fight him off. But this is the most humiliating experience of my
career so far—and the most contemptible—and I have to say so—
and the hell with the ethics of my profession, the hell with the Hippo-
cratic oath! (JOSIAH *laughs*.)

MIRANDA—That's brave talk, Toby—but you won't get anywhere with it. (*However, there is a note of tender admiration in
her tone*.)

Josiah remarks, "I don't know—he just might." Toby's outburst has given him a new view of himself—Toby's view. In the
light of this revelation he re-examines himself out loud and finds a
benevolent despot. He declares, "If Josiah Bolton had not been
in his daughter's life what he was, there'd have been no Matthew
Atwater."

Miranda cannot bear to hear her father denounce himself this
way, and she cries, "Liar—liar—"

So let Josiah Bolton rot, her father continues. "Go on—clear
out now, both of you. Leave me alone."

"On whose doorstep are you planning to leave the body?" Toby
inquires, and Miranda furiously demands how he dares talk to her
father like that. "Father," she says, "you can do what you like with
your life. . . . But I'm telling you now: you do *that* with it and
I'll do the same with my own, and straight off! And that's a promise! . . . I love living, I love it—and—oh, if only *you* would again
—because I love you too—and I couldn't stand to see you go that
way, and me not having been able to—and I'm so crazy about Toby
that I don't know where I'm at and—"

She stops suddenly, not quite able to believe she has heard what
she has just said.

Thankful bursts in, ready to leave for the boat and burbling with
thanks. Miranda declares she is going with her. She turns to
Toby and says, "You realize—you must—that I have to go over
and explain it myself? That no letters, cables, telephones will do?"

Josiah goes to his daughter and says, "I'm glad about what's
happened today. . . . I discovered my daughter doesn't want her
father to die." She looks gratefully at him and he gives her a
brusque little kiss—then says, "Now—get the hell out of here. Go
on. Don't keep the Cunard Line waiting."

Miranda, happy, departs. Toby has gone on ahead with Thankful. Malloy comes in to pick up the tray, and says good night. Alone at the window, Josiah looks down at the garden, listening. Suddenly he speaks:

"Yes—I hear you all right. And I have to tell you that I'm not interested. So go away. I don't want you around here. Go away. Beat it. Get out!"

CURTAIN

THE PLAYS AND THEIR AUTHORS

GUYS AND DOLLS, by Jo Swerling, Abe Burrows and Frank Loesser

Frank Loesser was born in Manhattan of a musical family. Here he went to public school and Townsend Harris High School. He was admitted to City College when he was fifteen and flunked out a term later. Between then and the time he wrote his first Broadway show, "Where's Charley?", he managed to work as errand boy and publicity man, got in a few licks at newspaper work and finally connected in the song-writing business by doing lyrics for composers such as Hoagy Carmichael.

His father was a piano teacher; one brother, Arthur, is a concert pianist; a second is music editor of a major newspaper chain and Frank, himself, is a skillful pianist. He and William Howard Schuman, now president of New York's famed Juilliard School of Music, collaborated on his first published song, "In Love with the Memory of You." Loesser provided the lyrics. He kept working with a succession of writers and finally, twelve years ago, attracted attention with his songs for an annual revue staged by a New York artists' group. The show ran only four days, but it sent Loesser to Hollywood. He has become the "Number One Call" out there, writing songs for about seventy-five movies including "Destry Rides Again," "Happy Go Lucky," "Thank Your Lucky Stars," and "Let's Dance." He is the current holder of the Academy Award for his song, "Baby, It's Cold Outside."

His first Broadway show—he wrote music and lyrics for all the songs—was a pet project of his for two years before it was finally produced. Some of his songs like "Praise the Lord and Pass the Ammunition" and "Rodger Young," have become part of the national tradition.

Abe Burrows was born in New York. He attended City College and N.Y.U., studied accounting and worked as a bank-runner, accountant and salesman of maple syrup, wallpaper and woven labels for garment manufacturers. In 1938, he collaborated with Frank Gaylen on a radio script for Eddie Garr, who was guesting on the Rudy Vallee show. The team of Burrows and Gaylen aided and abetted Ed Gardner with a program for which the character of Archie was created and Burrows became head writer for the subsequent "Duffy's Tavern." In 1939 Abe exposed himself to Hollywood, where he wrote some more radio programs and worked as a scenarist for Paramount.

It was Frank Loesser who encouraged Burrows to do take-offs on popular song writing, an idiom in which Abe produced such classics as "The Girl with the Three Blue Eyes," "Morning Becomes Electra, but You Look Better at Night," "I've Got a Girl in Calico Who's Dying for a Mink," and "Oh, How We Danced on the Night We Were Wed, I Needed a Wife Like a Hole in the Head." He is variously referred to as "wit, satirist, singer, lyricist, Latin scholar, student of etymology" and because of these accomplishments is one of television's most sought-after personalities for guest appearances. He has had his own radio and television shows. "Guys and Dolls" is his first work for the Broadway stage.

Jo Swerling has had one previous Broadway production to his credit—"Kibitzer," which was produced in 1929 with Edward G. Robinson in the title role. That led to a Hollywood contract, and Swerling has remained West ever since, writing screenplays. He was born in New York and began as a reporter and feature writer for the *American Magazine, The Nation* and *The New Yorker*. He also worked for a number of Chicago and New York newspapers, and it was on the *New York American* that he became acquainted with Damon Runyon.

Darkness at Noon, by Sidney Kingsley

Sidney Kingsley, a New Yorker, went to Townsend Harris High School and was a classmate of Frank Loesser, the "Guys and Dolls" composer. Once, in a school competition, each won a prize—Kingsley for public speaking, Loesser for art work. "Darkness at Noon," adapted from Arthur Koestler's novel, marks the second time Kingsley has used another source for a play. His dramas include "Men in White," which won the Pulitzer prize in 1934; "Dead End," "Ten Million Ghosts," "The World We Make," "The Patriots" and "Detective Story." "The Patriots" won him his first Critics Circle award, "Darkness at Noon" his second. His "The World We Make" was based on Millen Brand's novel, "The Outward Room."

Billy Budd, by Louis O. Coxe and Robert Chapman

Louis O. Coxe and Robert Chapman got the urge to make a play of Herman Melville's novel, "Billy Budd," when they were studying at Princeton under Prof. Willard Thorp, a noted Melville enthusiast. Coxe and Chapman may not have known naval warfare as it was in the Eighteenth Century, but they found out about it when they were in the U. S. Navy in World War II. Coxe is now a teacher of creative writing at the University of Minnesota, and Chapman is an instructor in playwriting and dramatic literature at Harvard.

The Autumn Garden, by Lillian Hellman

Lillian Hellman, New Orleans-born and New York-educated, chose the South for the locale of her newest play—and with it made her first venture into comedy. Before she turned to playwriting she was a book reviewer, a publicist and a play reader. Her first drama, "The Children's Hour," ran for a year and a half, beginning in 1935. Her theatre works include "Days to Come," "The Little Foxes," "Watch on the Rhine," "The Searching Wind," "Another Part of the Forest" and an adaptation of Emmanuel Roblès' "Montserrat." Miss Hellman won the Critics Circle award for "Watch on the Rhine."

Bell, Book and Candle, by John van Druten

John van Druten was born in London in 1901, of a Dutch father and an English mother. He was a lawyer and a college professor before he took up playwriting in 1925 with "Young Woodley." Prior to "Bell, Book and Candle," van Druten's greatest success was "The Voice of the Turtle." His plays include "There's Always Juliet," "The Distaff Side," "The Damask Cheek," "Old Acquaintance," "I Remember Mama" and "The Druid Circle."

The Country Girl, by Clifford Odets

Clifford Odets was born in Philadelphia in 1906, and began his career as an actor in stock companies. In New York he acted with the Theatre Guild and later for the Guild's young offshoot, the Group Theatre. For the Group he wrote "Awake and Sing," "Waiting for Lefty" and "Golden Boy," among other dramas. His most recent Broadway play, prior to "The Country Girl," was "The Big Knife," a Hollywood drama which starred John Garfield.

The Rose Tattoo, by Tennessee Williams

For the third time, Tennessee Williams is represented by a play in the Best Plays series, the other two having been "The Glass Menagerie" and "A Streetcar Named Desire." He was born in

Columbus, Mississippi, and graduated from Iowa State University. As does Lillian Hellman in "The Autumn Garden," Mr. Williams departs from his customary frame of mind and essays comedy, or at least comedy relief, in "The Rose Tattoo." Mr. Williams has two Critics Circle awards and one Pulitzer prize to his credit.

SEASON IN THE SUN, by Wolcott Gibbs

Wolcott Gibbs was born in New York in 1902. He became a newspaper reporter, then joined the staff of *The New Yorker,* where his career has ranged from copy reader to managing editor. On this magazine he is associate editor, as well as drama critic. A devotee of Fire Island for Summer holidays, Gibbs wrote a number of sketches for his magazine about the island and its characters. These stories later were published in a book, "Season in the Sun," and from them Gibbs adapted his own play.

AFFAIRS OF STATE, by Louis Verneuil

Louis Verneuil was born in Paris in 1893, and his early career included journalism and almost anything connected with the theatre, including scene designing. Beginning with "La Verve Folle" in 1910, he wrote some sixty plays for the Parisian theatre, and acted the leads in some of them. He was manager of one of Sarah Bernhardt's tours of the U. S. In New York, his earlier plays were adapted from the French—such as "Jealousy," which Eugene Walter adapted. He now writes his plays in English.

SECOND THRESHOLD, by Philip Barry, with revisions by Robert E. Sherwood

Philip Barry died in 1949, after having worked something like eleven years, off and on, on the play whose final title was "Second Threshold." The drama was almost completed, and Robert E. Sherwood did what he modestly calls a carpentry job—and not as a labor of love, but as a professional obligation to make sure that this last of Barry's plays would reach the stage. Barry was born in Rochester, N. Y., attended Yale and Harvard and was a student of George Pierce Baker. Prof. Baker's Workshop produced the first Barry play, "A Punch for Judy," for two performances on Broadway in 1921. The Barry play list includes "White Wings," "Paris Bound," "Holiday," "Hotel Universe," "Here Come the Clowns," "The Philadelphia Story" and "Without Love."

PLAYS PRODUCED IN NEW YORK

June 1, 1950—May 31, 1951

(Plays marked "continued" were still running on June 1, 1951)

THE MADWOMAN OF CHAILLOT

(17 performances)

Comedy in two acts by the late Jean Giraudoux, adapted by Maurice Valency; produced by Alfred de Liagre, Jr., at the New York City Center of Music and Drama, June 13, 1950.

Cast of characters—

The Waiter	Ralph Smiley
The Little Man	Harold Grau
The Prospector	Jonathan Harris
The President	Louis Sorin
The Baron	Paul Byron
Therese	Frances Hammond
The Street Singer	Claibourne Bryson
The Flower Girl	Millicent Brower
The Ragpicker	John Carradine
Paulette	Barbara Pond
The Deaf Mute	Martin Kosleck
Irma	Roberta Haynes
The Shoe-Lace Peddler	Maurice Brenner
The Broker	Fay Roope
The Street Juggler	John Beahan
Dr. Jadin	Sandro Giglio
Countess Aurelia, The Madwoman of Chaillot	Martita Hunt
The Doorman	Christopher Drake
The Policeman	James Ramsey
Pierre	Alan Shayne
The Sergeant	Tom Emlyn Williams
The Sewer-Man	Jacques Aubuchon
Mme. Constance, The Madwoman of Passy	Estelle Winwood
Mlle. Gabrielle, The Madwoman of St. Sulpice	Nydia Westman
Mme. Josephine, The Madwoman of La Concorde	Eleanora Mendelssohn
The Presidents	Louis Sorin, Fay Roope, Paul Byron
The Prospectors	Jonathan Harris, Harold Grau, Maurice Brenner
The Press Agents	Christopher Drake, James Ramsey, Jacques Aubuchon
The Ladies	Frances Hammond, Barbara Pond, Millicent Brower
The Adolphe Bertauts	Christopher Drake, Paul Byron, James Ramsey

This was a return engagement of one of the successes of the 1948-1949 season. The comedy had been on tour for twenty weeks, and ended its tour by playing at popular prices at the City Center.

(Closed June 25, 1950)

JULIUS CAESAR

(31 performances)

The Shakespeare play, presented as theatre-in-the-round by David Heilweil and Derrick Lynn-Thomas at the Arena, in the Hotel Edison, June 20, 1950.

Cast of characters—

Cassius	Basil Rathbone
Metellus Cimber	Winston Ross
Artemidorus	Alan Dreeben
Pindarus	Richard Wilder
Messala	Milton Selzer
Julius Caesar	Horace Braham
Calpurnia	Sarah Burton
Antony	Alfred Ryder
Casca	Berry Kroeger
Brutus	Joseph Holland
Cinna, The Conspirator	Herbert Ratner
Lucius	Martin Newman
Decius	Tony Dowling
Trebonius	John Glendinning
Portia	Emily Lawrence
Servant to Antony	Charles Vocalis
Octavius	Kurt Richards

Roman Citizens: Jerry Harvey, Michael Occhipinti, Moses Moses, Michael Davis, Roy Kauffmann, Michael Thorne, Larry Berry, Rafael Arguelles, John Garrison, Marshall Flaum, William Newey, Stephen Joyce, Allan Lewis, Ralph Habberstad, James McLaughlin and Nishan Parlakian.

Staged by Dan Levin; designed by Ralph Alswang; costumes supervised by Beulah Frankel; incidental music and songs by Hall Overton; production stage manager, Morgan O'Brien James.

This theatre-in-the-round production struck the public fancy well enough to go beyond its originally scheduled run of two weeks. It is interesting to note that Joseph Holland, who played Brutus, was the Caesar in Orson Welles' favorably remembered modern-dress version of the drama. Mr. Welles chose Mr. Holland for this role because of his striking resemblance to the late Benito Mussolini.

(Closed July 15, 1950)

MICHAEL TODD'S PEEP SHOW

(278 performances)

Revue in two acts, presented by Michael Todd at the Winter Garden, June 28, 1950. Sketches by Bobby Clark, H. I. Phillips, William Roos and Billy K. Wells; music by Bhumibol & Chakraband (Bhumibol being the nom de plume of the King of Thailand), Sammy Fain & Herb Magidson, Harold Rome, Raymond Scott, Sammy Stept & Dan Shapiro, Jule Styne & Bob Hilliard.

Principal musical and sketch numbers—

ACT I
"STREET SCENE"

"Red" Marshall   Dick "Gabby" Dana
"Hi Wilberforce" Conley   June Allen
"Peanuts" Mann   Shannon Dean
"Bozo" Snyder   Linda Bishop

"YOU'VE NEVER BEEN LOVED"
Words by Dan Shapiro, music by Sammy Stept
Sung by Lina Romay
Peiro Brothers
Ladies and Gentlemen of the ensemble

"FRIENDLY NEIGHORS"
By Billy K. Wells

First Wife ....Lina Romay
First Husband ...."Peanuts" Mann
Second Wife ....Shannon Dean
Second Husband ...."Red" Marshall
Policeman ....Dick "Gabby" Dana

"MINNIE"

Wife ....Christine Moll
Husband ...."Hi Wilberforce" Conley
Second Husband ....Dick "Gabby" Dana
Detective ...."Spike" Hamilton

"DESIRE"
By Raymond Scott

The Cat Girl ....Lilly Christine
Ladies of the ensemble

CLIFFORD GUEST AND LESTER

"MIDWAY"

Barker ....Dick "Gabby" Dana
1st Rube ...."Red" Marshall
2nd Rube ...."Bozo" Snyder
Slicker ...."Peanuts" Mann
3rd Rube ...."Hi Wilberforce" Conley
Passerby ....Shannon Dean
Joseph Paige ...."Spike" Hamilton
Valarie Wallace, Bettina Edwards, Gary Fleming, James Brock,
Frank Reynolds

"I HATE A PARADE"
By Harold Rome

"Hi Wilberforce" Conley   "Peanuts" Mann
"Red" Marshall   Dick "Gabby" Dana
"Bozo" Snyder   Jesus Moll

"BLUE NIGHT"
Words by Chakraband, music by Bhumibol
The Idols ....Myrtill and Pacaud
Sung by Art Carroll
Ladies and Gentlemen of the ensemble

ACT II
"STAY WITH THE HAPPY PEOPLE"
Words by Bob Hilliard, music by Jule Styne
Ensemble
Sung by Lina Romay

"Love Nest"

Proprietor .... Dick "Gabby" Dana
Wilbur Winterbottom .... "Hi Wilberforce" Conley
Mlle. Dagmar Pepper .... Lina Romay
Banker .... "Red" Marshall
Butler .... "Spike" Hamilton

"Violins from Nowhere"
Sung by Art Carroll
Words by Herb Magidson, music by Sammy Fain
Corrine and Tito Valdez and ensemble

"Pocketful of Dreams"
By Harold Rome

"Red" Marshall   "Bozo" Snyder
"Peanuts" Mann   "Hi Wilberforce" Conley

"Cocktails at Five"

Mrs. Irvington Irving .... Shannon Dean
Beechum .... "Peanuts" Mann
First Paperhanger .... "Spike" Hamilton
Second Paperhanger .... "Bozo" Snyder
Mr. Irvington Irving .... Dick "Gabby" Dana
Waldo Bromley .... "Hi Wilberforce" Conley
Lydia Fitz-Hugh .... Linda Bishop
Dr. C. C. Chedder .... "Red" Marshall
Guest .... Clifford Guest

"Gimmie the Shimmy"
By Harold Rome

The Charleston: Gary Fleming, Ralph Linn, James Brock, Frank
Reynolds, Gloria Danyl, Christina Frerichs, Fran Whitney, Lynn
Bernay

The Shimmy: Lilly Christine
Sung by Lina Romay

Staged by Hassard Short; sketches staged by Bobby Clark; dances
by James Starbuck; scenery by Howard Bay; costumes by Irene
Sharaff; musical director, Clay Warnick; stage manager, Ted Hammerstein.

After the opening performance of "Peep Show," producer Michael
Todd was invited to a conference with New York City's Commissioner of Licenses. As a result of this conference, Mr. Todd agreed
to modify certain sketches, strip-tease numbers and other elements
of old-style burlesque.

(Closed February 25, 1951)

THE MEDIUM and THE TELEPHONE

(110 performances)

One-act operas by Gian-Carlo Menotti, revived by David Heilweil and Derrick Lynn-Thomas, in association with Chandler
Cowles, at the Arena in the Hotel Edison, July 19, 1950.

Cast of "The Telephone"—

Lucy .... Edith Gordon
Ben .... Paul King

Cast of "The Medium"—

Monica ....Evelyn Keller
Toby, a mute ....Leo Coleman
Madame Flora (Baba) ....Zelma George
Mrs. Gobineau ....Derna de Lys
Mr. Gobineau ....Paul King
Mrs. Nolan ....Dorothy Staiger
    Staged by Gian-Carlo Menotti; sets by William Riva; William
McDermott, musical director.

The revival of Mr. Menotti's one-acters was the third theatre-in-the-round production at the Arena. The offerings played directly across the street from Mr. Menotti's newer success, "The Consul."

(Closed October 14, 1950)

PARISIENNE

(16 performances)

Comedy in three acts by Ashley Dukes, from the French of Henri Becque; produced by the Festival Theatre (Sam Wanamaker and Terese Hayden) in association with Harriet Ames at the Fulton Theatre, July 24, 1950.

Cast of characters—

Lafont ....Francis Lederer
Clotilde ....Faye Emerson
Adolphe ....Romney Brent
Adele ....Sydna Scott
Simpson ....Helmut Dantine
    The action passes in the drawing room of the Dumesnils' Paris
apartment. The period is 1880-1885. Act I.—Late on a Spring
afternoon. Act II.—Early evening a few days later. Act III.—
Early afternoon three months later.
    Staged by Sam Wanamaker; setting by Howard Bay; costumes by
Paul du Pont; stage managers, George Habib and William Sater, Jr.

(Closed August 5, 1950)

THE LADY FROM THE SEA

(16 performances)

Play in three acts by Henrik Ibsen, produced by the Festival Theatre (Sam Wanamaker and Terese Hayden) in association with Harriet Ames at the Fulton Theatre, August 7, 1950.

Cast of characters—

Ballested ....William Saunders
Lyngstrand ....Steven Hill
Hilda ....Anne Jackson
Boletta ....Joan Chandler
Dr. Wangel ....Herbert Berghof
Arnholm ....Theodore Newton
Ellida ....Luise Rainer
Friman-Johnston ....Jeff Morrow

Staged by Sam Wanamaker; Howard Bay, art director; settings by May Callas; costumes by Paul du Pont; stage managers, George Habib and William Sater, Jr.

This revival signalized the appearance of Luise Rainer, former film actress who began a notable career in Max Reinhardt's company.

(Closed August 19, 1950)

THE LIVE WIRE

(28 performances)

Comedy in three acts by Garson Kanin, produced by Michael Todd at the Playhouse, August 17, 1950.

Cast of characters—

John Tobey, Jr.	Peter Turgeon
Ursula Poe	Sheila Bond
Mr. Finch	Douglas Chandler
Leo Mack	Scott McKay
Horace Lundquist	Rex Williams
Mitchell Mack	Ned Wertimer
Granny Schenk	Elliott Reid
Ev Brogan	Chester Stratton
Rip Hulett	John Drew Colt
Sam Crocker	Joseph G. Sullivan
Sol Margolis	Jack Gilford
Mike Shannon	Pat Harrington
Dorothy Parrish	Elspeth Eric
Liz Fargo	Peggy Cass
Brian Freer	Murvyn Vye
Harry Holland	Heywood Hale Broun

The setting is the interior of a Quonset hut somewhere in New York City; the time is late Summer, 1949, and the action is continuous.

Staged by Garson Kanin; setting by Donald Oenslager; costumes by Forrest Thayer; production under the supervision of Kip Good; production stage manager, David Perdoll.

A group of young male actors, mostly unemployed, share their troubles and small earnings in a Quonset hut. They are happy until they take into their midst Leo Mack, who is a ruthless, ambitious heel. When two girls from *Life Magazine* appear to make a picture layout on the boys, Leo hogs all the scenes and as a result lands a Hollywood contract with the help of a brash agent, Brian Freer.

(Closed September 9, 1950)

BORNED IN TEXAS

(8 performances)

A "tall tale" in three acts by Lynn Riggs, produced by the Festival Theatre (Sam Wanamaker and Terese Hayden) in association with Harriet Ames at the Fulton Theatre, August 21, 1950.

Cast of characters—

```
Pop  Radar  ..................................Frank  Tweddell
Buzzy  Hale  ...............................Clifford  Carpenter
Hannie  .........................................Marsha  Hunt
Red  Ike  .....................................Martin  Newman
Black  Ike  ......................................Wright  King
Texas  ........................................Anthony  Quinn
Marshall  ......................................Joseph  Boland
Neb  ...........................................Dudley  Sadler
Judge  ...........................................Daniel  Reed
Mrs.  Foster  ....................................Jane  Hoffman
```
Act I.—By the side of a road through the woods in Oklahoma Territory early in the Century; sundown of a day in June. Act II.—Scene 1—The same; dawn the next morning. Scene 2—Courtroom near Verdigree Switch; an hour later. Act III.—Same as Act I; an hour later.

Staged by Sam Wanamaker; art director, Howard Bay; settings by May Callas; costumes by Paul du Pont; stage manager, John Stix.

"Borned in Texas" was the third of four productions planned by the Festival Theatre—and, unhappily for the sponsors, the last. The run of Mr. Riggs' play was shortened to a week and production of "Crimes and Crimes" was abandoned.

(Closed August 26, 1950)

DAPHNE LAUREOLA

(56 performances)

Comedy in three acts by James Bridie, produced by Leland Hayward and Herman Shumlin at the Music Box, September 18, 1950.

Cast of characters—

```
Maisie  MacArthur  ................................Joyce  Linden
Bill  Wishforth  ...................................Robin  Lloyd
Helen  Willis  ...................................Eileen  O'Hara
Bob  Kentish  ................................Alexander  Harris
George  .........................................Martin  Miller
Lady  Pitts  ......................................Edith  Evans
Ernest  Piaste  ..............................John  Van Dreelen
A  Bored  Woman  ...........................Elizabeth  Ashley
A  Bored  Man  .................................Ireland  Wood
Mr.  Gooch  .......................................Ernest  Jay
Mr.  Watson  .....................................Mark  Stone
Vincent  .......................................Peter  Williams
Sir  Joseph  Pitts  ...............................Cecil  Parker
The  Manager of  Le  Toit aux  Porcs ...............Terence  Owen
```
Act I.—Le Toit aux Porcs, a London restaurant. Evening. Act II.—Scene 1—A summerhouse in Hampstead. Scene 2—The same, a week later. Act III.—Le Toit aux Porcs, six months later.

Staged by Murray Macdonald; settings by Roger Furse and Roger Ramsdell; stage manager, Terence Owen.

Fiftyish Lady Pitts, wife of eightyish Sir Joseph Pitts, is one who goes on occasional solitary binges. On one such occasion, in a Soho restaurant, she invites all present to tea at her home. One guest, a Polish youth named Ernest Piaste, falls violently and poetically in love with her, but will worship her from afar. When

Sir Henry dies, Lady Pitts marries her butler, which so upsets Ernest that he faints.

(Closed November 4, 1950)

AFFAIRS OF STATE

(288 performances)

(Continued)

Comedy in three acts by Louis Verneuil, produced by Richard W. Krakeur and Fred F. Finklehoffe at the Royale Theatre, September 25, 1950.

Cast of characters—

Philip Russell	Reginald Owen
Constance Russell	Barbara O'Neil
George Henderson	Shepperd Strudwick
Lawrence	Elmer Brown
Irene Elliott	Celeste Holm
Byron Winkler	Harry Bannister

The action takes place in George Henderson's home in a suburb of Washington, D. C. Time, the present. Act I.—Scene 1—Mid-July, late afternoon. Scene 2—Ten days later, 3 P.M. Act II.—Scene 1—Late September, 2:30 P.M. Scene 2—Early October—6 P.M. Act III.—Two days later, afternoon.

Staged by Louis Verneuil; setting by Paul Morrison; costumes by Dorothy Jenkins; production associate, John Haggott; stage manager, Elmer Brown.

See page 259.

SOUTHERN EXPOSURE

(23 performances)

Comedy in three acts by Owen Crump, produced by Margo Jones, Tad Adoue and Manning Gurian at the Biltmore Theatre, September 26, 1950.

Cast of characters—

Miss Penelope Mayweather	Betty Greene Little
Australia	Evelyn Davis
Mary Belle Tucker	Mary Finney
Avery Randall	Victor Sutherland
John Salguod	Cameron Mitchell
Carol Randall	Pat Crowley
Emmeline Randall	Dorothy Elder
Benjamin Carter	Alan Manson

Tourists: Mady Correll, Marion Randolph, Fay Sappington, Isobel Robins, Courteen McVey, Leslie Paul, Ruth Chandler, Adele Fortin, Bruce Hall, Ben Yaffee, John Denney, Clint Anderson, Edwin Gifford, Lois Holmes, Wilhelmina Blake, Vincent Rourke.

The upstairs sitting room of Mayweather Hall, Natchez, Mississippi. Act I.—Scene 1—The present. Noon of an early Spring day. Scene 2—Nine o'clock that evening. Act II.—Scene 1—Next morning. Scene 2—Nine o'clock that evening. Act III.—Eight o'clock next morning.

Staged by Margo Jones; setting by Frederick Fox; costumes by
Kenn Barr; general stage manager, Spencer James.

Penelope Mayweather is the penniless spinster chatelaine of the
finest house in Natchez. Her only income is from tourist fees during the annual sightseeing Pilgrimage to Natchez. "John Salguod,"
a young writer from Vermont, persuades Penelope to rent him a
room. John finds romance with a Southern belle and rescues
Penelope from her genteel poverty.

(Closed October 14, 1950)

BLACK CHIFFON

(109 performances)

Play in three acts by Miss Lesley Storm, produced by John Wildberg at the Forty-eighth Street Theatre, September 27, 1950.

Cast of characters—

Roy Christie .... Richard Gale
Louise .... Patricia Hicks
Thea .... Patricia Marmont
Nannie .... Janet Barrow
Alicia Christie .... Flora Robson
Robert Christie .... Raymond Huntley
Dr. Bennett Hawkins .... Anthony Ireland
    The action takes place in the drawing room of the Christies' house
on Chelsea Embankment, London. Time, the present—November.
Act I.—Scene 1—Afternoon. Scene 2—Three hours later. Act II.—
Scene 1—The following afternoon. Scene 2—Five minutes later.
Act III.—Scene 1—Next morning. Scene 2—A few hours later.
    Staged by Charles Hickman; setting by Larry Eggleston; costumes
by Natalie Barth Walker; stage manager, Philippa Hastings.

On the eve of the marriage of her son, Roy, to a girl named
Louise, Alicia Christie, a woman of good character in decent middle circumstances, unaccountably steals a black chiffon nightdress
from a store and is arrested. A psychiatrist is called in to aid the
defense, and he comes to the conclusion that Mrs. Christie, having
without knowing it an unnatural attachment for her son, has committed the theft in order to spoil the marriage. Rather than have
this bared in court, Alicia pleads guilty and is sentenced to three
months in prison.

(Closed October 7, 1950; reopened October 23; closed January 13,
1951)

SEASON IN THE SUN

(284 performances)

(Continued)

Comedy in three acts by Wolcott Gibbs, produced by Courtney Burr and Malcolm Pearson at the Cort Theatre, September 28, 1950.

Cast of characters—

Billy Crane	Eugene Steiner
Marcia Crane	Kathy Chapman
George Crane	Richard Whorf
Emily Crane	Nancy Kelly
Mae Jermyn	Grace Valentine
Charles Farber	George Ives
Michael Lindsey	Jack Weston
Paul Anderson	Eddie Mayehoff
Virginia Anderson	Doreen Lang
Deedy Barton	Joan Diener
John Colgate	King Calder
Molly Burden	Paula Laurence
Arthur Dodd	Anthony Ross
Will Quigley	Charles Thompson
Messenger Boy	Stanley Martin
An Unidentified Woman	Maggie Gould

The action takes place on the front porch of a Summer bungalow on Fire Island, N. Y. The time is the present. Act I.—An afternoon in early September. Act II.—Late the following afternoon. Act III.—Scene 1—About one o'clock the following morning. Scene 2—About ten o'clock that morning.

See page 237.

PARDON OUR FRENCH

(100 performances)

Revue in two acts, produced by Olsen and Johnson at the Broadway Theatre, October 5, 1950. Music by Victor Young; lyrics by Edward Heyman; sketches by Olsen and Johnson.

The principals—

Denise Darcel	J. C. Olsen
Marty May	George Zoritch
June Johnson	Lubov Roudenko
Bill Shirley	Fay DeWitt
Helene Stanley	Nina Varela
Patricia Denise	"Les huit Chanteuses"

Settings by Albert Johnson; costumes by Jack Mosser; musical director, Harry Sukman; stage manager, Dennis Murray.

Principal songs—

"There's No Man Like a Snow Man," sung and danced by Helene Stanley.

"I Ought to Know More About You," sung by Fay DeWitt, Bill Shirley and "Les huit Chanteuses."

"I'm Gonna Make a Fool Out of April," sung by Bill Shirley and Helene Stanley.

"Dolly from the Folies Bergère," sung by Denise Darcel.   (Music by Harry Sukman, lyrics by Olsen and Johnson.)

Sketches include "No. 96 rue Blondel," "An Evening with Marie Antoinette," "Venezia and Her Three Lovers" (a ballet by Ernest Matray), "A Face in the Crowd" and "A Night on the Ile de France."

(Closed January 6, 1951)

THE GIOCONDA SMILE

(41 performances)

Play in three acts by Aldous Huxley, produced by Shepard Traube at the Lyceum Theatre, October 7, 1950.

Cast of characters—

Henry Hutton	Basil Rathbone
Janet Spence	Valerie Taylor
Nurse Braddock	Mercia Swinburne
Clara	Margaretta Warwick
Doris Mead	Marian Russell
Dr. Libbard	George Relph
General Spence	Charles Francis
Maid	Emily Lawrence
Warder	Charles Gerrard

Time, the present; Spring.   Act I.—Scene 1—The living room in the Huttons' country house, England.   Scene 2—The same; midnight the same day.   Act II.—Scene 1—The same; about two months later.   Scene 2—One month later.   Act III.—Time, late Autumn. Scene 1—General Spence's drawing room.   Scene 2—Prison cell. Scene 3—General Spence's drawing room; late at night.

Staged by Shepard Traube; settings by Feder; stage manager, Bill Ross.

When Henry Hutton's invalid wife dies, he marries Doris Mead, 21, and much younger than he is.   Tongues wag.   An investigation shows the wife was poisoned, and Hutton is convicted and sentenced to hang.   His second marriage has been a shock to Janet Spence, who long has loved Hutton.   Just in time to save him from the gallows, she confesses the murder to Dr. Libbard.

(Closed November 11, 1950)

LEGEND OF SARAH

(29 performances)

Play in three acts by James Gow and Arnaud d'Usseau, produced by Kermit Bloomgarden at the Fulton Theatre, October 11, 1950.

Cast of characters—

Minerva Pinney	Marsha Hunt
Adam Harwick	Tom Helmore
Clementine Pinney	Ethel Griffies
Wanda Mankiewicz	Judith Parrish
P. Walter Landis	Philip Coolidge
Edgar Cameron	Edmon Ryan
Mr. Angus	Joseph Sweeney

Prologue—A small apartment in Greenwich Village. Act I.—
The living room of the Pinney home in Pinneyfield; two years later.
Act II.—The same; that evening. Act III.—Scene 1—The same;
several hours later. Scene 2—The same; the next morning.

Staged by Benn W. Levy; settings by Ralph Alswang; costumes by
Ben Edwards; production stage manager, Leonard Patrick.

After a quarrel with her lover, Adam Harwick, Minerva Pinney
returns to her mother and her ancestral home. Two years later
Adam comes looking for her and finds her immersed in a project
whereby a cultural foundation is to buy the whole town and restore
it to the time of the Revolution. The project is in honor of Minerva's ancestor, Sarah Pinney. When the girl discovers in an old
diary that Sarah was a wanton who even slept with General Howe,
she forces abandonment of the project and withdraws her abandonment of Adam.

(Closed November 4, 1950)

CALL ME MADAM

(267 performances)
(Continued)

Musical comedy in two acts, produced by Leland Hayward at the
Imperial Theatre, October 12, 1950. Music and lyrics by Irving
Berlin; book by Howard Lindsay and Russel Crouse.

Cast of characters—

Mrs. Sally Adams	Ethel Merman
The Secretary of State	Geoffrey Lumb
Supreme Court Justice	Owen Coll
Congressman Wilkins	Pat Harrington
Henry Gibson	William David
Kenneth Gibson	Russell Nype
Senator Gallagher	Ralph Chambers
Secretary to Mrs. Adams	Jeanne Bal
Butler	William Hail
Senator Brockbank	Jay Velie
Cosmo Constantine	Paul Lukas
Pemberton Maxwell	Alan Hewitt
Clerk	Stowe Phelps
Hugo Tantinnin	E. A. Krumschmidt
Sebastian Sebastian	Henry Lascoe
Princess Maria	Galina Talva
Court Chamberlain	William David
A maid	Lily Paget
Grand Duchess Sophie	Lilia Skala
Grand Duke Otto	Owen Coll

Principal dancers: Tommy Rall, Muriel Bentley, Arthur Partington, Norma Kaiser.

The "Potato Bugs": Ollie Engebretson, Richard Fjellman.

Singers: Rae Abruzzo, Jeanne Bal, Trudy DeLuz, Lydia Fredericks, Estelle Gardner, Ruth McVayne, Lily Paget, Noella Peloquin, Helene Whitney, Aristide Bartis, Nathaniel Frey, William Hail, Albert Linville, Robert Penn, Tom Reider, John Sheehan, Stanley Simmonds, Ray Stephens.

Dancers: Shellie Farrell, Nina Frenkin, Patricia Hammerlee, Barbara Heath, Norma Kaiser, Virginia LeRoy, Kirsten Valbor, Fred Hearn, Allan Knolls, Kenneth LeRoy, Ralph Linn, Douglas Moppert, Arthur Partington, Bobby Tucker, William Weslow.

"The play," says the program, "is laid in two mythical countries. One is called Lichtenburg, the other the United States of America." Act I.—The scenes include the office of the Secretary of State, Sally's living room in Washington, the public square in Lichtenburg and two rooms in the American Embassy. Act II.—The scenes include the public square, the Embassy garden, and Sally's rooms in Lichtenburg and Washington.

Staged by George Abbott; dances and musical numbers staged by Jerome Robbins; scenery and costumes by Raoul Pène du Bois; Miss Merman's dresses by Main Bocher; musical director, Jay Blackton; orchestrations by Don Walker; dance music arrangements by Genevieve Pitot and Jesse Meeker; production stage manager, Robert Griffith.

Principal song numbers—

ACT I

The Hostess with the Mostes' on the Ball .... Ethel Merman
Washington Square Dance .... Ethel Merman and Company
Lichtenburg .... Paul Lukas and Singers
Can You Use Any Money Today? .... Ethel Merman
Marrying for Love .... Paul Lukas and Ethel Merman
The Ocarina
    Galina Talva, Bobby Tucker, Potato Bugs and Company
It's a Lovely Day Today .... Russell Nype and Galina Talva
The Best Thing for You Would Be Me
    Ethel Merman and Paul Lukas

ACT II

Something to Dance About .... Ethel Merman, Tommy Rall, Muriel Bentley, Norma Kaiser, Arthur Partington and Company
Once upon a Time Today .... Russell Nype
They Like Ike .... Pat Harrington, Ralph Chambers and Jay Velie
You're Just in Love .... Ethel Merman, Russell Nype

BURNING BRIGHT

(13 performances)

Play in three acts by John Steinbeck, produced by Rodgers and Hammerstein at the Broadhurst Theatre, October 18, 1950.

Cast of characters—

Joe Saul .... Kent Smith
Friend Ed .... Howard Da Silva
Mordeen .... Barbara Bel Geddes
Victor .... Martin Brooks
Act I.—The circus. Act II.—The farm. Act III.—Scene 1—The sea. Scene 2—Hospital room.

Staged by Guthrie McClintic; sets by Jo Mielziner; costumes by Aline Bernstein; stage manager, Windsor Lewis.

The four characters of this drama have three separate existences as circus folk, farmers and seafarers—representing people with long tradition and blood background behind them. Joe Saul and Mordeen are married and much in love—but Joe Saul, who has great pride in his family lineage, is sterile. Out of great love for her husband, Mordeen gives herself to Victor and conceives a child. Joe Saul finally comes to the realization that it is the human race which is important, not himself, and he accepts the child as his.

Like "Of Mice and Men," Mr. Steinbeck wrote "Burning Bright" simultaneously as a novel and as a play, the play being the dialogue from the novel.

(Closed October 28, 1950)

ARMS AND THE MAN

(110 performances)

Comedy in three acts by Bernard Shaw, revived by David Heilweil and Derrick Lynn-Thomas at the Arena, October 19, 1950.

Cast of characters—

Catherine Petkoff	Josephine Brown
Raina Petkoff	Lee Grant
Louka	Anne Jackson
Captain Bluntschli	Francis Lederer
Russian officer	Milton Selzer
Nicola	Fred Stewart
Major Paul Petkoff	Will Kuluva
Major Sergius Saranoff	Sam Wanamaker

Staged by Richard Barr; designed and lighted by Paul Morrison; stage manager, Clinton King.

(Closed January 21, 1951)

THE CURIOUS SAVAGE

(31 performances)

Comedy in three acts by John Patrick, produced by the Theatre Guild and Lewis & Young at the Martin Beck Theatre, October 24, 1950.

Cast of characters—

The Guests:

Florence	Isobel Elsom
Hannibal	Robert Emhardt
Fairy May	Lois Hall
Jeffrey	Hugh Reilly
Mrs. Paddy	Gladys Henson

The Family:

Titus	Brandon Peters
Samuel	Howard Wendell
Lily Belle	Marta Linden
Ethel	Lillian Gish

The Staff:
Miss Wilhelmina ....Flora Campbell
Dr. Emmett ....Sydney Smith
The scene is the living room of "The Cloisters." Act I.—Scene
1—Night. Scene 2—The next morning. Act II.—Scene 1—That
night, after dinner. Scene 2—A few nights later. Act III.—A
few minutes later.
Staged by Peter Glenville; production designed by George Jenkins;
costumes by Anna Hill Johnstone; stage manager, Hardy William
Smith.

Having inherited $10,000,000 from her late husband, Ethel Savage has been using the money as a memorial to him in a curious fashion: She gives it to people who want to indulge their foolish fancies. So three stepchildren have Ethel committed to a genteel retreat for the insane. Here she finds that people are kinder and happier than those in the outside world. She defeats her stepchildren, maintaining her money and her claim to sanity, but is loath to leave her newfound friends.

(Closed November 18, 1950)

THE DAY AFTER TOMORROW

(12 performances)

Comedy in three acts by Frederick Lonsdale, produced by Lee and J. J. Shubert at the Booth Theatre, October 26, 1950.

Cast of characters—

Gerard ....Ralph Michael
Charles, Lord Crayne ....Melville Cooper
The Bishop ....Noel Leslie
Venetia, Lady Crayne ....Madeleine Clive
Helen ....Monica Lang
Ernest ....John Merivale
John ....Jack Watling
Anne ....Valerie Cossart
George, the Duke of Bristol ....Bramwell Fletcher
Mary Flemin ....Beatrice Pearson
Robert Flemin ....Richard Gordon
Dr. Shaw ....George Mitchell
Tinne ....Ralph Sumpter
An Old Lady ....Eva Leonard-Boyne
Time, the present. Act I.—Sitting room at the home of the Duke
of Bristol. Act II.—Four weeks later. Act III.—Scene 1—A room
in a small cottage, the same night. Scene 2—The same as Act I,
the next day.
Staged by Frederick Lonsdale; settings by Edward Gilbert; stage
manager, Edward McHugh.

The Duke of Bristol and all his family are dead broke. To their home come Robert Flemin, an American millionaire, and Mary, his daughter. Mary falls in love with one of the Duke's brothers, Gerard, and offers herself and her fortune. But Gerard is a man of scruples; he will have Mary only on his own terms, which is without fortune. He gets his way, and she prepares for a life of helping him run the estate as a working farm.

(Closed November 4, 1950)

HILDA CRANE

(70 performances)

Play in three acts by Samson Raphaelson, produced by Arthur Schwartz at the Coronet Theatre, November 1, 1950.

Cast of characters—

Clara	Ann Sullivan
Henry Ottwell	John Alexander
Mrs. Crane	Beulah Bondi
Hilda Crane	Jessica Tandy
Mrs. Ottwell	Evelyn Varden
Prof. Charles Jensen	Frank Sundstrom
Nell Bromley	Eileen Heckart
Dink Bromley	Richard McMurray
Mrs. Nordlinger	Madeline King
Mr. Nordlinger	Watson White
Miss Keavney	Frieda Altman

Act I.—Scene 1—Mrs. Crane's living room, Winona, Illinois; mid-afternoon in April. Scene 2—Later that afternoon. Act II.—Scene 1—Two months later; 8:30 in the evening. Scene 2—The following afternoon. Act III.—Scene 1—The Ottwells' living room; a Sunday afternoon in June, two years later. Scene 2—Late that night.

Staged by Hume Cronyn; production designed by Howard Bay; gowns supervised by Harriet Ames; production associate, Victor Samrock; production stage manager, Paul A. Foley.

Hilda Crane, twice divorced and defeated by business life in New York, returns to her mother in a small Illinois town. Here she has two suitors. One of them, an intellectual named Charles Jensen, interests her emotionally but wants her without benefit of marriage. The other, Henry Ottwell, is upright, loving and dull, but he offers financial and marital security. She chooses Henry and commits suicide when she discovers her mistake.

(Closed December 31, 1950)

THE BARRIER

(4 performances)

Musical drama with book and lyrics by Langston Hughes and music by Jan Meyerowitz, produced by Michael Myerberg and Joel Spector at the Broadhurst Theatre, November 2, 1950.

Cast of characters—

William, a son of Col. Tom and Cora	Lorenzo Herrera
Sally, a daughter of Col. Tom and Cora	Charlotte Holloman
Livonia, servant at Albamar	Dolores Bowman

```
Maid ............................................Reri  Grist
Houseman ........................................John  Diggs
Sam, the butler at Albamar ....................Laurence Watson
Talbot, overseer at Albamar Plantation ...........Victor Thorley
Colonel Thomas Norwood .....................Lawrence Tibbett
Cora Lewis, his housekeeper ....................Muriel  Rahn
Fred Higgins, a friend of Norwood .............Richard Dennis
Bert, younger son of Col. Tom and Cora ...........Wilton Clary
Plantation Storekeeper ......................Robert Tankersley
Undertaker .......................................Jesse Jacobs
Assistant to the Undertaker ......................Stuart Hodes
```

CHARACTERS IN THE DANCE SEQUENCE

Young Norwood .... { Sung by Lawrence Tibbett / Danced by Marc Breaux

Young Cora .... { Sung by Charlotte Holloman / Danced by Josephine Keene

The Bride ....Helene Ellis

The action takes place in a rural Georgia community between noon and night of a hot Summer day. Act I.—The living room at Albamar, Thomas Norwood's plantation; noon. Act II.—Scene 1—The same; late afternoon. Scene 2—That night.

Staged by Doris Humphrey; dances by Charles Weidman and Doris Humphrey; setting by H. A. Condell; musical director, Herbert Zipper; stage manager, John Paul.

"The Barrier" was an opera based on Langston Hughes' successful play, "Mulatto." In it Colonel Thomas Norwood has begotten mulatto children by Cora Lewis, his housekeeper. One of these children, Bert, insists on acting his "white half" rather than his black. This infuriates Colonel Tom, and the young son strangles him. When a lynch mob catches up with him, Bert shoots himself.

(Closed November 4, 1950)

THE LADY'S NOT FOR BURNING

(151 performances)

A romantic comedy in verse, in three acts, by Christopher Fry, produced by Atlantis Productions (the Theatre Guild, Tennent Productions Ltd. and John C. Wilson) at the Royale Theatre, November 8, 1950.

Cast of characters—

```
Richard .......................................Richard Burton
Thomas Mendip ...............................John Gielgud
Alizon Eliot ...............................Penelope Munday
Nicholas Devise ..............................David Evans
Margaret Devise .............................Nora Nicholson
Humphrey Devise .............................Richard Leech
Hebble Tyson ..................................George Howe
Jennet Jourdemayne ...........................Pamela Brown
The Chaplain .................................Eliot Makeham
Edward Tappercoom ...............................Peter Bull
Matthew Skipps ..................................Esme Percy
```

A room in the house of Hebble Tyson, mayor of the small market town of Cool Clary; time, "the Fifteenth Century, more or less exactly." Act I.—An afternoon in April. Act II.—An hour later. Act III.—Later the same night.

Staged by John Gielgud; decor by Oliver Messel; stage manager, Alison Colvil.

Jennet Jourdemayne is brought to the mayor's house charged with practicing witchcraft, penalty for which is burning. Thomas Mendip, an adventuring discharged soldier, seeks to take the minds of the authorities off the girl by claiming he has committed murder and demanding to be executed—but his supposed victim turns up. Tappercoom, a soft-hearted justice with a sense of the romantic, permits Jennet to slip away with Thomas, since the pair have fallen in love.

(Closed March 17, 1951)

THE COUNTRY GIRL

(235 performances)

Play in two acts by Clifford Odets, produced by Dwight Deere Wiman at the Lyceum Theatre, November 10, 1950.

Cast of characters—

Bernie Dodd	Steven Hill
Larry	Peter Kass
Phil Cook	Louis Veda Quince
Paul Unger	Joseph Sullivan
Nancy Stoddard	Phyllis Love
Frank Elgin	Paul Kelly
Georgie Elgin	Uta Hagen
Ralph	Tony Albert

Act I.—Scene 1—The stage of a New York theatre. Scene 2— A furnished room, later the same day. Scene 3—The stage, ten days later. Scene 4—The furnished room, a week later. Scene 5— A dressing room in a Boston theatre, after midnight, a week later. Act II.—Scene 1—The Boston dressing room, a few nights later. Scene 2—The same, the next day. Scene 3—A dressing room in a New York theatre, evening, some weeks later.

Staged by Clifford Odets; sets by Boris Aronson; costumes by Anna Hill Johnstone; stage manager, John E. Sola.

See page 178.

(Closed June 2, 1951)

BELL, BOOK AND CANDLE

(233 performances)

Comedy in three acts by John van Druten, produced by Irene Mayer Selznick at the Ethel Barrymore Theatre, November 14, 1950.

Cast of characters—

Gillian Holroyd	Lilli Palmer
Shepherd Henderson	Rex Harrison
Miss Holroyd	Jean Adair
Nicky Holroyd	Scott McKay
Sidney Redlitch	Larry Gates

The scene is Gillian Holroyd's apartment in the Murray Hill district of New York City; time, the present. Act I.—Scene 1—Christmas Eve. Scene 2—About three hours later. Act II.—Two weeks later. Act III.—Scene 1—Four hours later. Scene 2—Two months later.

Staged by John van Druten; setting by George Jenkins; Miss Palmer's costumes by Valentina; other costumes by Anna Hill Johnstone; production stage manager, José Vega.

See page 155.

(Closed June 2, 1951)

A STORY FOR A SUNDAY EVENING

(11 performances)

Play in one act by Paul Crabtree, produced by Trio Productions and Milo Thomas, 1st, at the Playhouse, November 17, 1950.

Cast of characters—

Stage manager .... Henry Jones
David .... Paul Crabtree
Evelyn .... Cloris Leachman
Beatrice .... Nan Martin
Electrician .... Thomas J. King
The setting is a bare stage, with a few props used to indicate the stage itself or two apartments.
Staged by Paul Crabtree; set by Theodore Cooper; costumes by Patricia Montgomery; incidental music by Leighton Tiffault; production stage manager, Buford Armitage.

David is the author and principal actor of a play he is trying to put on before a friendly Sunday night audience. He apologizes for the play not being in shape—and it does not take shape the way he wants it to, for the personalities of his cast keep upsetting it. One is his wife, Evelyn; the other is an actress, Beatrice, who makes a play for him.

(Closed November 25, 1950)

PRIDE'S CROSSING

(8 performances)

Drama in two acts by Victor Wolfson, produced by T. Edward Hambleton at the Biltmore Theatre, November 20, 1950.

Cast of characters—

Bobby .... Robin Michael
Allan .... Donny Harris
Mrs. Bayard Goodale .... Mildred Dunnock
Zilla .... Tamara Geva
Lathrop Goodale .... John Baragrey
Selena Merrill .... Katharine Bard
The action takes place in the small drawing room of the Goodale home at Pride's Crossing, Mass. Act I.—Scene 1—Evening. Scene 2—An hour later. Scene 3—A few days later; late afternoon. Scene 4—A week later; morning. Act II.—Scene 1—The same day; late

afternoon. Scene 2—The following afternoon before dinner. Scene 3—Several hours later.
Staged by Martin Manulis; setting by Ralph Alswang; costumes by Mildred Sutherland; production stage manager, Philip Barry, Jr.

The home of Mrs. Bayard Goodale seethes with conflict and complications. Zilla, her supposed servant, is the arrogant ex-mistress of the late Mr. Goodale and co-owner of the house. Mrs. Goodale's son, Lathrop, who isn't home much, is worried about the health of his small son, Bobby, who has a weak heart. Zilla prompts her own small son, Allan, to play boisterously with Bobby, hoping he will become fatally ill—for then her boy, illegitimate offspring of the late Mr. Goodale, will inherit the house. But Selena Merrill, a newly hired governess, foils the plot.

(Closed November 25, 1950)

EDWINA BLACK

(15 performances)

Drama in three acts by William Dinner and William Morum, produced by Donald Flamm by arrangement with Peter Daubney Productions, Ltd., at the Booth Theatre, November 21, 1950.

Cast of characters—

Ellen ....Marjorie Rhodes
Henry Martin ....Michael Shepley
Gregory Black ....Robert Harris
Elizabeth Graham ....Signe Hasso
The scene is set in the main room of Amberwood House, in a suburb near London. Act I.—Scene 1—An autumn evening in 1895. Scene 2—Morning, a week later. Act II.—The same evening. Act III.—The next morning.
Original London production staged by Chloe Gibson; set by Leo Kerz; costumes by Elfi von Kantzow; stage manager, Hugh Rennie.

Gregory Black's wife, Edwina, dies after long invalidism, and it is a relief to Gregory and his wife's companion, Elizabeth Graham—for these two are in love. The housekeeper, Ellen, is suspicious of them, and because someone has thrown out dark hints, Inspector Henry Martin comes from Scotland Yard to investigate. It turns out that Edwina Black was poisoned. Before the case is solved, suspicion falls on all three members of the household and the love affair is broken up.

(Closed December 2, 1950)

THE RELAPSE, or VIRTUE IN DANGER

(30 performances)

Comedy in three acts by Sir John Vanbrugh, produced by the Theatre Guild at the Morosco Theatre, November 22, 1950.

Cast of characters—

Loveless, Husband to Amanda ....John Emery
Amanda, Wife to Loveless ....Ruth Matteson
Lory, Servant to Young Fashion ....Bryant Haliday
Young Fashion, Brother to Lord Foppington ......Robert Fletcher
Tugg, a Waterman ....Monford Trull
Lord Foppington, Newly-created Peer ....Cyril Ritchard
Page ....Kenneth Scott
La Varole, Valet to Lord Foppington ....Albert Marre
Mendlegs, a Hosier ....George Drew
Mrs. Calicoe, a Seamstress ....Jeanne Tufts
Shoemaker, for Lord Foppington ....Carl Don
Taylor, to Lord Foppington ....Donald Stevens
Coupler, a Matchmaker ....Jerry Kilty
Berinthia, Cousin to Amanda, a Widow ....Madge Elliott
Syringe, a Surgeon ....Earl Montgomery
Worthy, a Gentleman of the Town ....Murray Matheson
Abigail, Maid to Amanda ....Priscilla Morrill
Sir Tunbelly Clumsey, a Country Gentleman ....Thayer David
Miss Hoyden, a Great Fortune, Daughter to Sir Tunbelly
                                           Jan Farrand
Nurse, to Miss Hoyden ....Philippa Bevans
Bull, Chaplain to Sir Tunbelly ....Earl Montgomery
Jermy ....Carl Don
Sir John Friendly, Neighbor of Sir Tunbelly ......Donald Stevens
    Chairmen, Servants to Sir Tunbelly, Wedding Guests, etc. etc.
    Act I.—Scene 1—Loveless' country garden. Scene 2—A street
in London. Scene 3—Lord Foppington's dressing room. Scene 4—
Loveless' lodging in London. Act II.—Scene 1—Lord Foppington's
dressing room. Scene 2—Loveless' garden in London. Scene 3—
The gate outside Sir Tunbelly's manor. Scene 4—Berinthia's cham-
ber. Act III.—Scene 1—Interior of Sir Tunbelly's manor. Scene
2—Berinthia's chamber. Scene 3—A street in London. Scene 4—
Loveless' lodging in London.
    Staged by Cyril Ritchard, with acknowledgment to Anthony Quayle,
who directed the London revival in 1948; associate director, Albert
Marre; sets and costumes by Robert O'Hearn; technical supervisor,
Miles Morgan; music by Leslie Bridgewater; lyrics by Clifford Bax;
musical director, Thomas Phillips; general stage manager, Burry
Frederick.

Sir John Vanbrugh wrote "The Relapse, or Virtue in Danger," as a sequel to Colley Cibber's comedy, "The Last Shift," in which a gay blade, Loveless, married and settled down to a suburban life. Sir John wondered what would happen if Loveless were exposed to the old temptations of London and of such erstwhile companions as Fashion, who has bought himself the title of Lord Foppington. Cibber played the role of Foppington in the first production, in 1695 or 1696. According to the record books, the Theatre Guild's revival of "The Relapse" is the first professional production the comedy ever had in New York. In the production the Guild was materially aided in personnel by the Brattle Theatre Company of Cambridge, Mass.

(Closed December 16, 1950)

RING ROUND THE MOON

(68 performances)

"A charade with music" in two acts, translated from the French of Jean Anouilh by Christopher Fry, produced by Gilbert Miller at the Martin Beck Theatre, November 23, 1950.

Cast of characters—

Joshua	Francis Compton
Hugo	Denholm Elliott
Frederic	Denholm Elliott
Diana Messerschmann	Neva Patterson
Lady India	Georgina Cookson
Patrice Bombelles	Michael Evans
Madame Desmermortes	Lucile Watson
Capulat	Cynthia Latham
Messerschmann	Oscar Karlweis
Romainville	Philip Tonge
Isabelle	Stella Andrew
Her Mother	Brenda Forbes
A General	Marcel Dill
Footmen	William Allyn, Bennett Martin

The play takes place in the winter garden of Mme. Desmermortes' château in Auvergne, France, in the Spring of 1912. Act I.—Scene 1—Morning. Scene 2—Before the ball. Scene 3—The ball. Act II.—Scene 1—After supper. Scene 2—Dawn.

Staged by Gilbert Miller; set designed by Georges Wakhevitch and executed by Raymond Sovey; curtains by Raoul Dufy; music by Francis Poulenc; costumes by Castillo; choreography by Ted Cappy; production stage manager, B. D. Kranz.

This fantasy involves twin brothers (played by one actor); Diana Messerschmann, fiancée of one of them; Isabelle, a ballet dancer who has been engaged by the other brother to appear at a ball being given by their aunt, Mme. Desmermortes; and a number of other guests at the ball.

(Closed January 13, 1951)

GUYS AND DOLLS

(219 performances)
(Continued)

Musical comedy in two acts, based on a story and characters by Damon Runyon, produced by Feuer and Martin at the Forty-sixth Street Theatre, November 24, 1950. Music and lyrics by Frank Loesser; book by Jo Swerling and Abe Burrows.

Cast of characters—

Nicely-Nicely Johnson .... Stubby Kaye
Benny Southstreet .... Johnny Silver
Rusty Charlie .... Douglas Deane
Sarah Brown .... Isabel Bigley
Arvide Abernathy .... Pat Rooney, Sr.
Calvin .... Paul Migan
Agatha .... Margery Oldroyd
Priscilla .... Christine Matsios
Harry The Horse .... Tom Pedi
Lt. Brannigan .... Paul Reed
Nathan Detroit .... Sam Levene
Angie The Ox .... Tony Gardell
Miss Adelaide .... Vivian Blaine
Sky Masterson .... Robert Alda
Joey Biltmore .... Bern Hoffman
Mimi .... Beverly Tassoni
General Matilda B. Carstairs .... Netta Packer
Big Jule .... B. S. Pully
Drunk .... Eddie Phillips
Waiter .... Joe Milan
    Dancers: Wana Allison, Geraldine Delaney, Barbara Ferguson, Lee
Joyce, Marcia Maier, Beverly Tassoni, Ruth Vernon, Onna White,
Forrest Bonshire, Peter Gennaro, Joe Milan, Eddie Phillips, Harry
Lee Rogers, Bud Schwab, Merritt Thompson.
    Singers: Beverly Lawrence, Christine Matsios, Charles Drake,
Tony Gardell, Bern Hoffman, Carl Nicholas, Don Russell, Hal Saun-
ders, Earle Styres.
    Act I.—Scenes include Broadway, the interior of the Save-a-Soul
Mission, the Hot Box (a night club), the exterior of the Mission and
a Havana, Cuba, café.   Act II.—Scenes include the Hot Box, the
West Forties, a subterranean crap game, the interior of the Mission
and Broadway again.
    Staged by George S. Kaufman; dances and musical numbers staged
by Michael Kidd; sets by Jo Mielziner; costumes by Alvin Colt;
orchestral ararngements by George Bassman and Ted Royal; vocal
arrangements by Herbert Greene; musical director, Irving Actman;
production stage manager, Henri Caubisens.

Principal musical numbers—

ACT I

"Fugue for Tinhorns" .... Nicely-Nicely, Benny,
                                                      Rusty Charlie
"Follow the Fold" .... Sarah, Arvide, Calvin,
                                                    Agatha, Priscilla
"The Oldest Established" .... Nathan, Nicely-Nicely, Benny,
                                                            Ensemble
"I'll Know" .... Sarah and Sky
"A Bushel and a Peck" .... Adelaide and Hot Box Girls
"Adelaide's Lament" .... Adelaide
"Guys and Dolls" .... Nicely-Nicely and Benny
"Havana" .... Onna White and Ensemble
"If I Were a Bell" .... Sarah
"My Time of Day" .... Sky
"I've Never Been in Love Before" .... Sky and Sarah

ACT II

"Take Back Your Mink" .... Adelaide and Hot Box Girls
"More I Cannot Wish You" .... Arvide
"Lucky Be a Lady" .... Sky and Crap Shooters
"The Crap Game Dance" .... Ensemble
"Sue Me" .... Nathan and Adelaide
"Sit Down, You're Rockin' the Boat" .... Nicely-Nicely and
                                                            Ensemble
"Marry the Man Today .... Adelaide and Sarah

See page 45.

THE GOLDEN STATE

(25 performances)

Comedy in three acts by Samuel Spewack, produced by Bella Spewack at the Fulton Theatre, November 25, 1950.

Cast of characters—

Betty Williamson	Jocelyn Brando
Mrs. Morenas	Josephine Hull
Sophie Kressner	Polly Rowles
Mr. Jansen	Frank Tweddell
A Young Man	Henry Beckman
Tim White	Ernest Truex
Jesse Weir	Ben Lackland
Joe Williamson	John Randolph
Bob Kressner	Lou Polan
Hubert Clay	John Hudson
Mr. Burns	Robert Pike

The patio and living room of Mrs. Morenas' house in Los Angles. Act I.—Late afternoon. Act II.—Scene 1—Early evening next day. Scene 2—Several days later. Act III.—Two days later.

Staged by Samuel Spewack; setting by Lester Polakov; costumes by Grace Houston; stage manager, William Chambers.

Mrs. Morenas, who holds the not uncommon belief that she is the rightful heir to all of Beverly Hills through a Spanish ancestor, takes in roomers to help herself out. One of her guests is Tim White, a bibulous prospector. When some of Tim's desert ore is accidentally buried in Mrs. Morenas' back yard, he thinks he has found another gold mine. Everybody lives on high hopes—for a while.

(Closed December 16, 1950)

THE TOWER BEYOND TRAGEDY

(32 performances)

Poetic drama by Robinson Jeffers, based on the works of Aeschylus, produced by the American National Theatre and Academy, Cheryl Crawford and Robert Breen, general directors, at the ANTA Playhouse, November 26, 1950.

Cast of characters—

Aeschylus	Robert Harrison
Agamemnon	Frederic Tozere
Clytemnestra	Judith Anderson
Leucippe	Ludie Claire
Corinna	Martha Downs
Cassandra	Thelma Schnee
King's Guard	Victor Thorley
A Townswoman	Ruth Manning
A Townsman	David Elliott
A Captain	John Straub
The Porter	Don McHenry
Queen's Guard	Eric Fleming

Aegisthus .... Philip Huston
Electra .... Marian Seldes
Aegisthus' Attendant .... Michael Thorne
Orestes .... Alfred Ryder
The Queen's Slaves .... Dion Allen, Charles Carruth,
Jack Clay
The Queen's Guard .... Richard Farmer, Dale Parkhill,
Byron Meyer
The King's Guard .... Berger Carlson, Harvey Korman,
Arthur Gorton
Townspeople: Joan DeMarrais, Alta McKay, Rosemary Murphy,
Bette Ramey, Robert Delano, Lee Henry, Dan Lincoln, Dan Rubinate.
Captives: Ted Behr, Bill Froelich, Sidney Kay, William Portrude,
Clay Sanford, Allen Windsor.
Act I.—Agamemnon's homecoming. Act II.—Scene 1—Eight years
later. Scene 2—Evening.
Staged by Robert Ross; scenery by Wolfgang Roth; lighting by
Feder; costumes by Castillo.

This production of Robinson Jeffers' poem about Clytemnestra, Cassandra, Aegisthus, Electra and Orestes was the first of ten new productions planned by ANTA for its newly acquired Playhouse, the former Guild Theatre. The play had first been staged nine years previously by Judith Anderson in California.

(Closed December 22, 1950)

THE CELLAR AND THE WELL

(9 performances)

Drama in three acts by Philip Pruneau, sponsored by the American National Theatre and Academy and produced by George Freedley and R. L. Stevens at the ANTA Playhouse, December 10, 1950.

Cast of characters—

Maureen Mayo .... Ann Dearing
Grandma Mayo .... Eda Heinemann
Theona Pringle .... Helen Harrelson
Maud Mayo .... Dorothy Sands
Howie .... Edgar Grower
Miss Triumph .... Mary Finney
Mr. Hubble .... Henderson Forsythe
Robert Francis Mayo .... Eric Mattson
Mrs. Farley .... Florence Beresford
Mrs. Dennis .... Kathleen Bolton
Mrs. Lofab .... Hannah Toback
A Young Woman .... Alice Winston
Her Husband .... Gerry Walberg
Mrs. Flynn .... Susan Steell
Mrs. Haggerty .... Fay Sappington
Mr. Haggerty .... Frank Rowan
The action takes place in the kitchen and on the back porch of a
second-story flat on the South Side of Chicago. Act I.—Scene 1—A
Summer night in 1949. Scene 2—The same. Act II.—Several
hours later. Act III.—Three nights later.
Staged by Henderson Forsythe; set by Paul Morrison; costumes by
Ruth Morley.

"The Cellar and the Well" was first produced at the Erie, Pa., Civic Theatre, December 13, 1949, where the author was Resident

Playwright. It was the second offering of ANTA's ten-play series. Following the scheme to get fullest use out of the organization's Playhouse, this drama played matinees while "The Tower Beyond Tragedy" played nights. The drama concerned the loves and frustrations of a poor but quarrelsome Irish family in South Chicago.

(Closed December 17, 1951)

LET'S MAKE AN OPERA

(5 performances)

Musical novelty in two acts with book and lyrics by Eric Crozier and music by Benjamin Britten, produced by Peter Lawrence and the Show-of-the-Month Club at the John Golden Theatre, December 13, 1950.

Cast of characters—

THE PLAY

Rosalind Nadell
Paul Carter
Claire Richard
Jo Sullivan
Angela Adamides
Frank Catal .... Played by Themselves
Arlyne Frank
Randolph Symonette
Mario Santamaria
Lawrence Young
Rawn Spearman
Norman Del Mar

THE OPERA

Big Bob	Randolph Symonette
Clem	Rawn Spearman
Sammy	Lawrence Young
Mrs. Baggott	Rosalind Nadell
Rowan	Arlyne Frank
Juliet	Jo Sullivan
Gay	Frank Catal
Sophie	Claire Richard
Tina	Angela Adamides
Hughie	Paul Carter
Johnny	Mario Santamaria
Tom	Randolph Symonette
Alfred	Rawn Spearman

Act I.—The play. Scene 1—Rosalind's home; an Autumn evening. Scene 2—Stage of the school auditorium before dress rehearsal. Act II.—The opera. Scene 1—Nursery at Iken Hall, England, 1810; a January morning. Scene 2—A few minutes later. Scene 3—The following morning.

Staged by Marc Blitzstein; musical director and conductor, Norman Del Mar; sets by Ralph Alswang; costumes by Aline Bernstein; production stage manager, Mortimer Halpern.

Some teachers and children set about creating their own opera, about a little chimney-sweep who gets stuck in a chimney and is rescued by some other children and hidden from his wicked masters. At the urging of the musical conductor, the audience itself joins in singing some of the songs.

(Closed December 16, 1950)

BLESS YOU ALL

(84 performances)

Revue in two acts, produced by Herman Levin and Oliver Smith at the Mark Hellinger Theatre, December 14, 1950. Music and lyrics by Harold Rome; sketches by Arnold Auerbach.

Principal players—

Jules Munshin
Mary McCarty
Pearl Bailey
Jane Harvey
Garry Davis
Gene Barry
Byron Palmer

Charlene Harris
Lee Barnett
Robert Chisholm
Donald Saddler
Noel Gordon
Valerie Bettis

Show girls—

Blanche Grady
Jill Melford
Kris Nodland
Gloria Olson

Dell Parker
Madelyn Remini
Gwenna Lee Smith
Jeane Williams

Dancers—

Eleanor Boleyn
Carlene Carroll
Dorothy Etheridge
Sage Fuller
Elmira Jones-Bey
Billie Kirpich
Vera Lee
Ilona Murai
Emy St. Just
Helen Wenzel

Richard D'Arcy
Joseph Gifford
Donald McKayle
Joe Nash
Philip Nasta
Bertram Ross
Richard Reed
John Sandal
Swen Swenson
Parker Wilson

Singers—

Jane Carlyle
Geraldine Hamburg
Betsy Holland
Dorothy Richards
Irene Riley
Eileen Turner
Grace Varik
Margaret Wright

Fred Bryan
Clive Dill
Gordon Edwards
Noel Gordon
Ray Morrissey
Kenny Smith
William Sutherland
Norval Tormsen

Staged by John C. Wilson; dances staged by Helen Tamiris; sets by Oliver Smith; costumes by Miles White; musical direction by Lehman Engel; orchestrations by Don Walker; general stage manager, Frank Coletti.

Principal song numbers and sketches—

ACT I

SOUTHERN FRIED CHEKHOV
Colonel Jasper Oglethorpe ....Garry Davis
Emmaline, his wife ....Charlene Harris

Marmaduke, his son ....Gordon Edwards
Marybelle, his daughter ....Mary McCarty
The Publisher ....Gene Barry
"Don't Wanna Write About the South" ....sung by Marybelle,
                              the Colonel, Emmaline and Marmaduke
"I Can Hear It Now" ....sung by Jane Harvey
The Poor Girl ....Dorothy Etheridge
The Poor Boy ....Dick Reed
The Rich Girl ....Eleanor Boleyn
The Rich Boy ....Donald Saddler
"When" ....sung by Pearl Bailey
A Boy ....Joe Nash
A Girl ....Elmira Jones-Bey
BACK TO NAPOLI
Benson ....Robert Chisholm
Miss Kane ....Charlene Harris
Jaroslav ....Garry Davis
Laszlo ....Gene Barry
The Ladies ....Gwenna Lee Smith, Dell Parker, Jill Melford,
                                                Jeane Williams
Enrico Bonzo ....Jules Munshin
The Children ....Lee Barnett, Billie Kirpich, Clive Dill,
                                   Irene Riley, Betsy Holland,
                                                Ray Morrissey
"Little Things Meant So Much to Me" ......sung by Mary McCarty
TV OVER THE WHITE HOUSE
Announcer ....Gene Barry
Joseph Gabriel Blow ....Jules Munshin
Jane Blow ....Mary McCarty
Their Son ....Lee Barnett
a—"Love That Man" ....Joe and Ensemble
b—Breakfast with Joe and Jane ⎱
c—"Just a Little White House" ⎰ ....Joe, Jane and Son
d—Somewhere Up There ⎰
George Washington ....Noel Gordon
Abe Lincoln ....Garry Davis
Teddy Roosevelt ....Robert Chisholm
e—"Voting Blues" ....sung by Valerie Bettis
f—Stop the Politics! ....Joe and Jane
Miss Strong Constitution ....Dell Parker
Miss Natural Resources ....Jeane Williams
Miss International Peace ....Kris Nodland
Miss Federal Water Power ....Gwenna Lee Smith

ACT II

THE COLD WAR
Bill Slade ....Jules Munshin
The Druggist ....Garry Davis
"Take Off the Coat" ....sung by Jane Harvey
THE DESERT FLAME
Music composed by Don Walker
Desert Flame ....Valerie Bettis
Monsieur le Commandant ....Parker Wilson
Gendarmes ....Joe Gifford, Donald McKayle, Joe Nash,
                            Philip Nasta, Dick Reed, Bertram Ross
Pepe Le Koko ....Richard D'Arcy
Houris ....Eleanor Boleyn, Dorothy Etheridge, Billie Kirpich,
                          Vera Lee, Ilona Murai, Emy St. Just,
                                                Helen Wenzel
The Texan ....Donald Saddler
Native Drummers ....Joe Comadore, Osborne Smith
The Torturers ....John Sandal, Swen Swenson
Singing Houris ....Eileen Turner, Grace Varik,
                                                Margaret Wright
PETER AND THE P.T.A.
Mrs. Weatherby (Peter) ....Mary McCarty
Mr. Fothergill ....Garry Davis

Wendy ....Lee Barnett
Captain Hook ....Robert Chisholm
"You Never Know What Hit You When It's Love"
                                            sung by Pearl Bailey

(Closed February 24, 1951)

OUT OF THIS WORLD

(157 performances)

Musical comedy in two acts, produced by Saint Subber and Lemuel Ayers at the New Century Theatre, December 21, 1950. Book by Dwight Taylor and Reginald Lawrence; music and lyrics by Cole Porter.

Cast of characters—

Mercury ....William Redfield
Jupiter ....George Jongeyans
Helen ....Priscilla Gillette
Waiter ....Frank Milton
Art O'Malley ....William Eythe
Night ....Janet Collins
Vulcania ....Peggy Rea
Juno ....Charlotte Greenwood
Chloe ....Barbara Ashley
Niki Skolianos ....David Burns
Strephon ....Ray Harrison

Singing Ensemble: Barbara Weaver, Shirley Prior, Enid Hall, Nola Fairbanks, B. J. Keating, Lois Monroe, John Schickling, John Schmidt, Richard Curry, Ken Ayers, Orrin Hill, Robert Baird, Joe Hill, Leo Kayworth, Michael Kingsley.

Dancing Ensemble: Gisella Svetlik, Virginia Bosler, Eleanor Fairchild, Joan Engel, Joan Kruger, Jacqueline Sager, Glen Tetley, David Nillo, Stanley Simmons, Paul Lyday, Eric Kristen, Barton Mumaw, Jan Kovac, Doria Avila.

Act I.—The scenes include Jupiter's portico, the New York Bar, the great hall on Mt. Olympus, the road to Athens, Arcadia Inn and an inn tavern. Act II.—Mt. Olympus, a bedroom, a mountain shrine and Heaven.

Staged by Agnes de Mille; dances staged by Hanya Holm; additional direction by George Abbott; sets and costumes by Lemuel Ayers; orchestrations by Robert Russell Bennett; dance and incidental music by Genevieve Pitot and Trudi Rittman; musical director, Pembroke Davenport; production stage manager, Ward Bishop.

Principal musical numbers—

ACT I

"I Jupiter, I Rex" ....sung by Jupiter and Ensemble
"Use Your Imagination" ....sung by Mercury and Helen
"I Got Beauty" ....sung by Juno and Ensemble
"I Am Loved" ....sung by Helen
"What Do You Think About Men?" ....sung by Helen, Chloe, and Juno
"I Sleep Easier Now" ....Sung by Juno

ACT II

"Climb Up the Mountain" ....sung by Juno, Niki, and Company
"No Lover for Me" ....sung by Helen
"Hark to the Song of the Night" ....sung by Jupiter
"Nobody's Chasing Me" ....sung by Juno

(Closed May 5, 1951)

TWENTIETH CENTURY

(181 performances)

(Continued)

Comedy in three acts by Ben Hecht and Charles MacArthur, based on a play by Bruce Milholland, revived by the American National Theatre and Academy at the ANTA Playhouse, December 24, 1950.

Cast of characters—

Dr. Johnson	Paula Bauersmith
Train Secretary	Robinson Stone
Porter	P. Jay Sidney
Grover Lockwood	Ralph Bunker
Anita Highland	Betty Bartley
Owen O'Malley	Robert Strauss
Conductor	Burton Mallory
Oliver Webb	Donald Foster
Flannagan	John Glendinning
Pullman Conductor	Edward Platt
Matthew Clark	William Lynn
First Beard (Cristus)	Werner Klemperer
Second Beard (Judas)	Leon Askin
Oscar Jaffe	José Ferrer
Waiter	Van Prince
Sadie	Eva Leonard-Boyne
Lily Garland	Gloria Swanson
George Smith	Robert Carroll
First Detective	Paul Lilly
Second Detective	Charles Salez
Max Jacobs	Henry Sherwood
Red Caps	Vincent Donahue, Edward Platt

The action of the play takes place in a car of the Twentieth Century Limited, en route from Chicago to New York.

Staged by José Ferrer; associate producer, Richard Condon; set by Wolfgang Roth; stage manager, Buford Armitage.

After a two-week run at the ANTA Playhouse, this revival was moved, under the production sponsorship of José Ferrer, to the Fulton Theatre. At the end of the theatrical year the stars, Mr. Ferrer and Gloria Swanson, left the company.

KING LEAR

(48 performances)

Shakespeare's tragedy, arranged in three acts, produced by Robert L. Joseph and Alexander H. Cohen at the National Theatre, December 25, 1950.

Cast of characters—

Earl of Kent	Martin Gabel
Duke of Gloucester	Arnold Moss
Edmund	Joseph Wiseman
King Lear	Louis Calhern

```
Duke of Cornwall ..............................Nehemiah Persoff
Duke of Albany .................................Richard Malek
Goneril ........................................Edith Atwater
Regan ..........................................Jo Van Fleet
Cordelia .......................................Nina Foch
King of France .................................Martin Waldron
Duke of Burgundy ..............................Fredric Warriner
Edgar ..........................................Wesley Addy
Lear's Fool ....................................Norman Lloyd
Curan ..........................................Mitchell Agruss
Oswald .........................................Kurt Richards
Loyal Knight ...................................Guy Arbury
Gentleman of the Court .........................E. J. Ballantine
A Knight .......................................Guy Arbury
Servants to Cornwall .............Jack Bittner, McGregor Gibb,
                                                Bernard Pollock
Herald .........................................Thomas Poston
```
Knights and Servants: Ted Baden, Michael Bay, Sam Gilman, Jack Ramsey, Earl F. Simmons, Keith Taylor, Henry Leonard.

Staged by John Houseman; incidental music and songs by Marc Blitzstein; sets by Ralph Alswang; costumes by Dorothy Jeakins; general stage manager, Edward McHugh.

"King Lear" is the least frequently done of Shakespeare's great plays. Only six actors, including Robert B. Mantell, Fritz Leiber and Donald Wolfit, have presented it professionally on Broadway since 1900—and the sixth, Louis Calhern, had a longer run than any of the others.

(Closed February 3, 1951)

CAPTAIN BRASSBOUND'S CONVERSION

(15 performances)

Comedy in three acts by Bernard Shaw, revived by the New York City Theatre Company at the City Center of Music and Drama, December 27, 1950.

Cast of characters—

```
Rankin .........................................Noel Leslie
Drinkwater .....................................Ian Martin
Hassan .........................................Walt Witcover
First Krooboy ..................................Alfred Ruscio
Second Krooboy ................................Paul Steiner
Sir Howard Hallam .............................Clay Clement
Lady Cicely ...................................Edna Best
Muley ..........................................Alan Cahn
Marzo ..........................................Robert Carricart
Brassbound .....................................John Archer
Redbook ........................................Hugh Green
Johnson ........................................Chris Gampel
First Brassbound man ...........................Robert van Hooton
Second Brassbound man .........................Jack Horn
Third Brassbound man ..........................Walt Witcover
Osman ..........................................Wendell Whitten
Sidi El Assif ..................................Bruce Gordon
Cadi of Kintafi ...............................Douglas M. H. Chandler
Bluejacket .....................................Dean Whitmore
Capt. Hamlin Kearney ..........................Loring Smith
```
Sailors, Officers and Arabs: William Ablin, Andrew Bernard, Mario Alcalde, Ted Atwood, William Bush, William Becker, Robert Burns, Alan Cahn, Edwin Christie, George Hoxie, Harvey Korman,

William Leonard, Bill O'Brien, Robert O'Flaherty, Ted Sheraton, Richard Woods, Jackson Young.

Act I.—Late afternoon in Leslie Rankin's garden on the heights overlooking the harbor of Mogador, Morocco.   Act II.—Midday; a room in a Moorish castle.   Act III.—The following afternoon; Rankin's garden.

Staged by Morton DaCosta; settings by Ben Edwards; George Schaefer, executive producer; stage manager, Thelma Chandler.

This revival of "Captain Brassbound's Conversion" opened the 1950-1951 season of the New York City Theatre Company under the artistic supervision of Maurice Evans.

(Closed January 7, 1951)

AN ENEMY OF THE PEOPLE

(36 performances)

Play in three acts by Henrik Ibsen, adapted by Arthur Miller, produced by Lars Nordenson at the Broadhurst Theatre, December 28, 1950.

Cast of characters—

Morten Kiil	Art Smith
Billing	Michael Strong
Mrs. Stockmann	Florence Eldridge
Peter Stockmann	Morris Carnovsky
Hovstad	Martin Brooks
Dr. Stockmann	Fredric March
Morten	Ralph Robertson
Ejlif	Richard Trask
Captain Horster	Ralph Dunn
Petra	Anna Minot
Aslaksen	Fred Stewart
The Drunk	Lou Gilbert

Townspeople: Lulla Adler, Barbara Ames, Edith Case, Paul Fitzpatrick, James Karen, Michael Lewin, Salem Ludwig, Gene Lyons, John Marley, J. Berry Nathan, Charles Park, Richard Purcell, Arthur Row, Arnold Schulman, Robert Simon, Carl Specht, Rod Steiger.

Act I.—Scene 1—Dr. Stockmann's living room in a Norwegian town. Scene 2—The same; the following morning. Act II.—Scene 1—The editorial office of The People's Daily Messenger; afternoon. Scene 2—A room in Capt. Horster's house; evening, two days later. Act III.—Dr. Stockmann's living room; the following morning.

Staged by Robert Lewis; sets and costumes by Aline Bernstein; production stage manager, Robert F. Simon.

(Closed January 27, 1951)

SECOND THRESHOLD

(126 performances)

Comedy in two acts by Philip Barry, with revisions by Robert E. Sherwood, produced by Alfred de Liagre, Jr., at the Morosco Theatre, January 2, 1951.

Cast of characters—

Toby Wells .... Hugh Reilly
Malloy .... Gordon Richard
Miranda Bolton .... Margaret Phillips
Josiah Bolton .... Clive Brook
Thankful Mather .... Betsy von Furstenberg
Jock Bolton .... Frederick Bradlee
The action takes place in the library of Josiah Bolton's house on West Tenth St., New York, in the course of 24 hours late last July. Act I.—Scene 1—Friday night. Scene 2—Saturday noon. Act II.—Scene 1—Saturday evening. Scene 2—Later that night.
Staged by Alfred de Liagre, Jr.; set by Donald Oenslager; production associate, Philip Barry, Jr.

When Philip Barry died, December 2, 1949, he left an almost-completed script of "Second Threshold." Revisions depended mostly upon the casting of the play. Barry's friend, Robert E. Sherwood, made these revisions.

See page 283.

(Closed April 21, 1951)

THE HOUSE OF BERNARDA ALBA

(17 performances)

Play in three acts by Federico Garcia Lorca, translated from the Spanish by James Graham Lujan and Richard L. O'Connell, produced by Stewart Chaney, Boris Tumarin and Lily Turner at the ANTA Playhouse, January 7, 1951.

Cast of characters—

Servant .... Marian Copp
Poncia .... Ruth Saville
Beggar woman .... Betty Morrow
Beggar child .... Jada Rowland
Bernarda .... Katina Paxinou
Angustias .... Helen Craig
Magdalena .... Sarah Cunningham
Amelia .... Mary Welch
Martirio .... Ruth Ford
Adela .... Kin Stanley
Little girl .... Florence Luriea
Maria Josefa .... Tamara Daykarhanova
Prudencia .... Zelda Benjamin
The action of the play takes place in the house of Bernarda Alba in southern Spain, at the turn of the century.
Staged by Boris Tumarin; set and costumes by Stewart Chaney.

Bernarda Alba keeps her five daughters locked in her house, away from men. But one of the daughters manages a clandestine love affair, and when the mother discovers it she takes a shot at the man. She misses—but the daughter, thinking her lover has been killed, commits suicide.

(Closed January 20, 1951)

THE ROYAL FAMILY

(15 performances)

Comedy in three acts by George S. Kaufman and Edna Ferber, revived by the New York City Theatre Company at the City Center of Music and Drama, January 10, 1951.

Cast of characters—

Della	Evelyn Ellis
Jo	Ossie Davis
Hallboy	Wendell Whitten
McDermott	Morris Miller
Herbert Dean	Bernard Nadell
Kitty Dean	Olive Blakeney
Gwen	Peggy Ann Garner
Perry Stewart	Robert Webber
Fanny Cavendish	Ethel Griffies
Oscar Wolfe	J. Edward Bromberg
Julie Cavendish	Ruth Hussey
Anthony Cavendish	John Emery
Another hallboy	Walt Wittcover
Gilbert Marshall	Theodore Newton
Gunga	Chris Gampel
Miss Peake	Marjorie Redmond
Chauffeur	Tom Hughes Sand

The action passes in the duplex apartment of the Cavendishes in the East Fifties, New York. Act I.—A Friday in November; early afternoon. Act II.—Saturday; between matinee and night. Act III.—A year later.

Staged by Richard Whorf; set by Ben Edwards; costume director, Emeline Roche; George Schaefer, executive producer; stage manager, William Johnson.

"The Royal Family" was first produced by Jed Harris December 28, 1927. For the revival the authors brought topical references in the script up to date. On the opening night John Emery stumbled coming down a stair, tore ligaments in his ankle and played the last two acts gallantly and in pain. On the second night he was replaced by John Baragrey.

(Closed January 21, 1951)

DARKNESS AT NOON

(163 performances)
(Continued)

Play in three acts by Sidney Kingsley, based on the novel by Arthur Koestler, produced by the Playwrights' Company at the Alvin Theatre, January 13, 1951.

Cast of characters—

Rubashov	Claude Rains
Guard	Robert Keith, Jr.

```
402 ............................................... Philip Coolidge
302 ............................................... Richard Seff
202 ............................................... Allan Rich
Luba ............................................... Kim Hunter
Gletkin ............................................ Walter J. Palance
1st Storm Trooper ............................. Adams MacDonald
Richard ........................................... Herbert Ratner
Young Girl ........................................ Virginia Howard
2nd Storm Trooper ............................. Johnson Hayes
Ivanoff ........................................... Alexander Scourby
Bogrov ............................................ Norman Roland
Hrutsch ........................................... Robert Crozier
Albert ............................................ Daniel Polis
Luigi ............................................. Will Kuluva
Pablo ............................................. Henry Beckman
André ............................................ Geoffrey Barr
Barkeeper ......................................... Tony Ancona
Secretary ......................................... Lois Nettleton
President ......................................... Maurice Gosfield
```
Soldiers, Sailors, Judges and Jurors

Act I.—A prison; March, 1937. Act II.—The same; five weeks later. Act III.—The same; one week later.

Staged by Sidney Kingsley; associate producer, May Kirshner; settings by Frederick Fox; costumes by Kenn Barr.

See page 72.

FOUR TWELVES ARE 48

(2 performances)

Comedy in three acts by Joseph Kesselring, produced by Aldrich & Myers, Julius Fleischmann and Otto Preminger at the Forty-eighth Street Theatre, January 17, 1951.

Cast of characters—

```
Rose Bolton ...................................... Rosetta Le Noire
Dorothy Bawke ................................... Pat Crowley
Jerry ............................................. Billy James
Philippa Bawke ................................... Jane Du Frayne
Mischa Cogn ...................................... Joshua Shelley
Anton ............................................ Ludwig Donath
Mrs. Kelly ....................................... Mrs. Priestley Morrison
Uncle Snake Tooth ............................... Ernest Truex
Nellie Bawke ..................................... Anne Revere
Calendula Watkins ............................... Eulabelle Moore
Mary Bawke ....................................... Ruth Taylor
Philip Dupre ..................................... Hiram Sherman
Jane Dupre ....................................... Doro Merande
Joe Hungry Horse ................................ Royal Dano
"Dr." Berrystone ................................ Morton L. Stevens
```
The scene is the New York home of Nellie Bawke; early Spring. Act I.—Late afternoon. Act II.—Morning, next day. Act III.—The following morning.

Staged by Otto Preminger; set by Raymond Sovey; costumes by Peggy Morrison; stage manager, John Effrat.

Three generations of Osage females have begotten illegitimate children at the age of 12. Now the great-granddaughter of the first one imagines she is in an interesting condition. She isn't—and neither was Joseph Kesselring's comedy.

(Closed January 18, 1951)

ANGEL IN THE PAWNSHOP

(85 performances)

Comedy in two acts by A. B. Shiffrin, produced by Eddie Dowling and Anthony B. Farrell at the Booth Theatre, January 18, 1951.

Cast of characters—

Hilary	Eddie Dowling
Tom	John Farrell
Danny O'Keefe	Clark Williams
Lizzie Shaw	Joan McCracken
Drunk	John Farrell
Duke Jones	Willie Lewis
Timothy Spangle	Herbert Evers
Joe	Joseph Laurner
Young Man	Arthur Oshlag
Priscilla Nash	Elizabeth Kerr

The scene of the play is Hilary's pawnshop. Act I.—Scene 1—Monday. Scene 2—Tuesday. Scene 3—Wednesday. Act II.—Scene 1—Thursday. Scene 2—Friday. Scene 3—Sunday.

Staged by John Larson; incidental music by Will Irwin; set and costumes by John E. Blankenchip; stage manager, Paul M. Heller.

Into Hilary's pawnshop come such ordinary characters as hard-up writers, doctors and drunkards—and an odd girl named Lizzie Shaw. Lizzie has her own dream world, which is the Sixteenth Century, and by choosing from among Hilary's many pawned costumes she can pretend she is Queen Elizabeth or some other notable of the time. Hilary's problem, and the problem of Timothy Spangle, a struggling young writer, is to get Lizzie into the present long enough to marry Timothy.

(Closed March 31, 1951)

KING RICHARD II

(15 performances)

The Shakespeare history, produced by the New York City Theatre Company at the New York City Center of Music and Drama, January 24, 1951.

Cast of characters—

King Richard the Second	Maurice Evans
John of Gaunt, his uncle	Frederic Worlock
Henry Bolingbroke, Duke of Hereford, son of Gaunt; afterwards King Henry IV	Kent Smith
Thomas Mowbray, Duke of Norfolk	Bruce Gordon
The Duchess of Gloucester	Cavada Humphrey
Lord Marshall	Theodore Marcuse
The Duke of Aumerle, son to York, the King's cousin	George Roy Hill
Herald to Bolingbroke	Porter Van Zandt
Herald to Mowbray	Joseph Dooley
Green ⎫ Bagot ⎬ Servants to King Richard Bushy ⎭	John Kirchnak Everett Ripley Chester Stratton

```
Edmund Langley, Duke of York, the King's uncle ..Reynolds Evans
Queen to Richard ...................................Betsy Blair
The Earl of Northumberland ......................Louis Hector
Lord Ross .........................................John Straub
Lord Willoughby ...............................Chris Gampel
A Servant .....................................Tom Hughes Sand
Henry Percy, surnamed Hotspur, son of
     Northumberland ............................John Glennon
Captain of a Band of Welchmen ...................Clem Fowler
The Earl of Salisbury ⎫                    ⎧ Porter Van Zandt
The Bishop of Carlisle ⎬ adherents of Richard ⎨ Theodore Marcuse
Sir Stephen Scroop ⎭                       ⎩ Wendell Whitten
Ladies Attending the Queen ................ ⎧ June Prud'Homme
                                            ⎩ Patricia Jenkins
A Gardener ....................................Hamilton Mott
Second Gardener ...............................Joseph Dooley
Abbott of Westminster .........................Joseph Emmett
Sir Pierce of Exton ...........................Clem Fowler
Servant to Exton ..........................Porter Van Zandt
A Groom .......................................Joseph Dooley
A Keeper ......................................John Kirchnak
     Staged by Margaret Webster; Emmett Rogers, assistant director;
sets by Ben Edwards; incidental music by Herbert Manges; George
Schaefer, executive producer; stage manager, Thelma Chandler.
```

Maurice Evans first appeared in this Margaret Webster production of "King Richard II" in February, 1937, and gave 133 performances. In September, 1937, he returned for an additional 38 performances.

(Closed February 4, 1951)

PEER GYNT

(32 performances)

Play in two acts by Henrik Ibsen in a new version by Paul Green, produced by Cheryl Crawford and R. L. Stevens at the ANTA Playhouse, January 28, 1951.

Cast of characters—

```
Aase, a Peasant Widow ........................Mildred Dunnock
Peer Gynt, Her Son ...............................John Garfield
An Elderly Man ...................................Ray Gordon
An Elderly Woman ...............................Ann Boley
Aslak, a Smith ..................................John Randolph
Solveig ...........................................Pearl Lang
Her Father ....................................Joseph Anthony
Her Mother .......................................Anne Hegira
A Buttonmolder ..................................Karl Malden
Ingrid .........................................Rebecca Darke
Her Father ...................................Nehemia Persoff
Her Mother ....................................Peggy Meredith
Mads Moen .......................................Mahlon Naill
His Father ......................................Edward Binns
His Mother .......................................Lisa Baker
The Master Cook ................................Ray Gordon
1st Herd Girl ..................................Lucille Patton
2nd Herd Girl .................................Barbara Gaye
3rd Herd Girl ................................Beverlee Bozeman
```

A Greenclad Woman ....Sherry Britton
The Troll King ....Nehemia Persoff
The Ugly Brat ....Ed Horner
The Voice ....John Randolph
Kari ....Lisa Baker
Monsieur Ballon ....Joseph Anthony
Herr Von Eberkopf ....Edward Binns
Mr. Cotton ....Richard Purdy
Herr Trompetstraale ....John Randolph
The Flutist ....Hillel
A Thief ....Ray Gordon
A Healer ....Ed Horner
A Singer ....Aviva
Anitra ....Sono Osato
Anitra's Attendants ....Patricia Birsh, Barbara Gaye,
          Bob Emmett, Stuart Hodes
Dr. Begriffenfeldt ....Joseph Anthony
Hussein ....Richard Purdy
     Wedding Guests, Trolls, Inmates, Mourners: Lisa Baker, Patricia
Birsh, Ann Boley, Beverlee Bozeman, Rebecca Darke, Margaret
Feury, Barbara Gaye, Anne Hegira, Peggy Meredith, Lucille Patton,
Edward Binns, Irving Burton, Bob Emmett, Ray Gordon, Stuart
Hodes, Ed Horner, Mahlon Naill, Richard Purdy, John Randolph,
Lou Yetter.
     Dancers: Beverlee Bozeman, Patricia Birsh, Barbara Gaye, Lucille
Patton, Irving Burton, Bob Emmett, Stuart Hodes, Lou Yetter.
     Act I.—Scene 1—A hillside by Aase Gynt's mountain farm in
Norway. Scene 2—The yard of a neighboring farm. Scene 3—A
woods, high in the mountains. Scene 4—The Hall of the Troll
King. Scene 5—Peer's hut, high in the mountains. Scene 6—A
bedroom in Aase's house. Act II.—Scene 1—The coast of Morocco,
some years later. Scene 2—The Great Desert. Scene 3—A mental
hospital in Cairo. Scene 4—A churchyard in Norway. Scene 5—
In the Norway hills. Scene 6—The hut, high in the mountains.
     Staged by Lee Strasberg; choreography by Valerie Bettis; sets by
Donald Oenslager; costumes by Rose Bogdanoff; music by Lan
Adomian; Near East music by Hillel and Aviva.

(Closed February 24, 1951)

THE MIKADO

(8 performances)

The Gilbert and Sullivan operetta, produced by the D'Oyly Carte
Opera Company of London at the St. James Theatre, January 29,
1951.

Cast of characters—

The Mikado of Japan ....Darrell Fancourt
Nanki-Poo ....Neville Griffiths
Ko-Ko ....Martyn Green
Pooh-Bah ....Richard Watson
Pish-Tush ....Alan Styler
Go-To ....Donald Harris
Yum-Yum ....Margaret Mitchell
Pitti-Sing ....Joan Gillingham
Peep-Bo ....Joyce Wright
Katisha ....Ella Halman
     Sets and costumes by Charles Ricketts; orchestra directed by
Isidore Godfrey; stage director, Eleanor Evans.

After a tour in the U. S. and Canada, the D'Oyly Carte Company began a four-week engagement in New York before sailing home.

(Closed February 3, 1951)

WHERE'S CHARLEY?

(48 performances)

Musical comedy in two acts, based on Brandon Thomas' "Charley's Aunt," with book by George Abbott and songs by Frank Loesser; revived by Cy Feuer and Ernest H. Martin, in association with Gwen Rickard, at the Broadway Theatre, January 29, 1951.

Cast of characters—

Brassett	John Lynds
Jack Chesney	Robert Shackleton
Charley Wykeham	Ray Bolger
Kitty Verdun	Betty Oakes
Amy Spettigue	Allyn McLerie
Wilkinson	James Lane
Sir Francis Chesney	Paul England
Mr. Spettigue	Horace Cooper
Donna Lucia D'Alvadorez	Rose Inghram
Photographer	James Lane
Patricia	Irene Weston
Reggie	Ralph Lowe

This musical, starring Ray Bolger, ended a run of 792 performances on September 9, 1950, to allow its chief performer a rest. It resumed briefly in Boston and was brought to New York for a brief engagement prior to the star's making a Hollywood movie version.

(Closed March 10, 1951)

THE GREEN BAY TREE

(20 performances)

Play in three acts by Mordaunt Shairp, revived by Shepard Traube at the John Golden Theatre, February 1, 1951.

Cast of characters—

Trump	Francis Compton
Mr. Dulcimer	Joseph Schildkraut
Julian	Denholm Elliott
Leonora Yale	Anne Crawford
Mr. Owen	Mercer McLeod

Time, the present. Act I.—At Mr. Dulcimer's flat in Mayfair; Spring. Act II.—Scene 1—At Mr. Owen's house in Camden Town; August. Scene 2—At Mr. Dulcimer's; the same evening.

Act III.—Scene 1—At Mr. Dulcimer's; next morning.   Scene 2—
The same; three weeks later.
    Staged by Shepard Traube; sets by Raymond Sovey; stage man-
ager, Bill Ross.

The first New York production of "The Green Bay Tree" was
made by Jed Harris, October 20, 1933. The author, Mordaunt
Shairp, died in 1939.

(Closed February 17, 1951)

THE ROSE TATTOO

(133 performances)
(Continued)

Play in three acts by Tennessee Williams, produced by Cheryl
Crawford at the Martin Beck Theatre, February 3, 1951.

Cast of characters—

Salvatore	Salvatore Mineo
Vivi	Judy Ratner
Bruno	Salvatore Taormina
Assunta	Ludmilla Toretzka
Rosa delle Rose	Phyllis Love
Serafina delle Rose	Maureen Stapleton
Estelle Hohengarten	Sonia Sorel
The Strega	Daisy Belmore
Giuseppina	Rossana San Marco
Pepina	Augusta Merighi
Violetta	Vivian Nathan
Mariella	Penny Santon
Teresa	Nancy Franklin
Father de Leo	Robert Carricart
Doctor	Andrew Duggan
Miss Yorke	Dorrit Kelton
Flora	Jane Hoffman
Bessie	Florence Sundstrom
Jack Hunter	Don Murray
Salesman	Eddie Hyans
Alvar Mangiacavallo	Eli Wallach
Man	David Stewart
Man	Martin Balsam

    Time, today. The play is in three acts, during all of which the
curtain is dropped a number of times to denote the passage of time,
usually a few minutes or hours. Between the third and fourth scenes
of the first act, however, there is a three-year lapse.
    Staged by Daniel Mann; set by Boris Aronson; costumes by Rose
Bogdanoff; incidental music by David Diamond; production associate,
Bea Lawrence; stage manager, Ralph DeLauney.

See page 210.

TRIAL BY JURY and H.M.S. PINAFORE

(8 performances)

Gilbert and Sullivan double bill, presented by the D'Oyly Carte
Company of London at the St. James Theatre, February 5, 1951.

Cast of characters of "Trial by Jury"—

The Learned Judge.............................Richard Watson
Counsel for the Plaintiff.........................Alan Styler
Defendant.......................................Leonard Osborn
Foreman of the Jury............................Donald Harris
Usher..Radley Flynn
Associate...Ivor Emmanuel
The Plaintiff......................................Enid Walsh
First Bridesmaid.................................Joyce Wright

Cast of characters of "H.M.S. Pinafore"—

The Rt. Hon. Sir Joseph Porter, K.C.B..............Martyn Green
Capt. Corcoran...................................Eric Thornton
Ralph Rackstraw................................Neville Griffiths
Dick Deadeye..................................Darrell Fancourt
Bill Bobstay.......................................Donald Harris
Bob Beckett.....................................Radley Flynn
Josephine.......................................Muriel Harding
Hebe..Joan Gillingham
Little Buttercup..................................Ella Halman

(Closed February 10, 1951)

TI-COQ

(3 performances)

Comedy in two acts by Fridolin (Gratien Gélinas), produced by Fridolin Productions, in association with Lee and J. J. Shubert, at the Broadhurst Theatre, February 9, 1951.

Cast of characters—

Commanding Officer............................George Alexander
Padré..Jacques Auger
Jean-Paul.......................................Clement Latour
Ti-Coq   ....Fridolin
Papa Desilets.....................................Fred Barry
Mama Desilets..................................Amanda Alarie
Marie-Ange ....Huguette Oligny
Aunt Clara....................................Juliette Beliveau
Germaine.......................................Denise Pelletier
Rosie...Mary Barclay

Act I.—Scene 1—Padré's office in a military camp near Montreal; December, 1942.   Scene 2—Kitchen of the Desilets' home; two days later.   Scene 3—Padré's office; five days later.   Scene 4—Entrance of the house where Marie-Ange and Germaine live in Montreal; the following week.   Scene 5—Apartment of the two girls; four months later.   Scene 6—Aboard a troopship; June, 1943. Act II.—Scene 1 —Apartment of the two girls; November, 1943.   Scene 2—A military hospital in England; the following month.   Scene 3—Apartment of the two girls; a few weeks later.   Scene 4—A tavern near a repatriation camp in England; six months later.   Scene 5—At the door of Germaine's home; September, 1945.   Scene 6—Germaine's apartment; the following evening.

Staged by Fridolin; sets and costumes by Jean Fournier de Belleval; music by Maurice Blackburn; associate director, Fred Barry.

Ti-Coq (Little Rooster) is a French Canadian soldier who is sad because he is a bastard and an orphan. He falls in love with Marie-Ange, partly because she will give him a large collection of legitimate relatives. When he goes to war Marie-Ange tires of waiting and marries somebody else. In all his emotional crises, including the last one, Ti-Coq is advised and comforted by the Padré.

(Closed February 10, 1951)

BILLY BUDD

(105 performances)

Play in three acts by Louis O. Coxe and Robert Chapman, based on Herman Melville's novel of the same title, produced by Chandler Cowles and Anthony B. Farrell at the Biltmore Theatre, February 10, 1951.

Cast of characters—

Jenkins, Captain of the Maintop	Jeff Morrow
The Dansker, Mainmast Man	George Fells
Jackson, Maintopman	Bertram Tanswell
John Claggart, Master-at-Arms	Torin Thatcher
Talbot, Maintopman	James Daly
Butler, Maintopman	Leonard Yorr
Kincaid, Maintopman	Kenneth Paine
Payne, Maintopman	Judson Pratt
O'Daniel, Maintopman	Walter Burke
Messboy	Charles Hudson
Squeak, Master-at-Arms' Man	Bernard Kates
Duncan, Mate of the Main Deck	Robert McQueeney
Surgeon	Winston Ross
Gardiner, a Midshipman	Jack Manning
Billy Budd, Foretopman	Charles Nolte
Edward Fairfax Vere, Captain, Royal Navy	Dennis King
Hallam, a Marine	Lee Marvin
Rea, a Midshipman	Henry Garrard
Philip Michael Seymour, First Officer	Guy Spaull
John Ratcliffe, First Lieutenant	Preston Hanson
Bordman Wyatt, Sailing Master	Norman Ettlinger
Stoll, Helmsman	Charles Carshon
Byren, Relief Helmsman	Martin Brandt
Drummer	David Long
Sailor	Robert Dudley
2nd Marine	Bill Froelich

The action of the play takes place aboard H.M.S. *Indomitable* at sea in August, 1798—the year following the naval mutinies at Spithead and the Nore. Act I.—Scene 1—Crew's quarters; noon. Scene 2—Main deck; sunset. Scene 3—The same; several nights later. Act II.—Scene 1—Main deck; the following morning. Scene 2—The same; night. Scene 3—The same; two hours later. Act III.—Scene 1—Captain's cabin; later the same night. Scene 2—The same; 4 A.M. Scene 3—Main deck; sunrise.

Staged by Norris Houghton; sets by Paul Morrison; costumes by Ruth Morley; production associate, Benet Segal; general stage manager, Bob Margulies.

See page 100.

(Closed May 12, 1951)

THE BEST PLAYS OF 1950–1951

THE GONDOLIERS

(4 performances)

Gilbert and Sullivan operetta, presented by the D'Oyly Carte Company of London at the St. James Theatre, February 12, 1951.

Cast of characters—

The Duke of Plaza-Toro	Martyn Green.
Luiz	Henry Goodier
Don Alhambra del Bolero	Richard Watson
Marco Palmieri	Leonard Osborn
Giuseppe Palmieri	Alan Styler
Antonio	Peter Pratt
Francesco	Thomas Hancock
Giorgio	Radley Flynn
Annibale	Stanley Youngman
The Duchess of Plaza-Toro	Ella Halman
Casilda	Margaret Mitchell
Gianetta	Muriel Harding
Tessa	Joan Gillingham
Fiametta	Enid Walsh
Vittoria	Ceinwen Jones
Guilia	Joyce Wright
Inez	Caryl Fane

(Closed February 14, 1951)

NOT FOR CHILDREN

(7 performances)

Comedy in two acts by Elmer Rice, produced by the Playwrights' Company at the Coronet Theatre, February 13, 1951.

Cast of characters—

Elijah Silverhammer	Keene Crockett
Clarence Orth	Alexander Clark
Timothy Forrest	J. Edward Bromberg
Ambrose Atwater	Elliott Nugent
Theodora Effington	Betty Field
Irma Orth	Natalie Core
Prudence Dearborn	Ann Thomas
Evangeline Orth	Joan Copeland
Digby Walsh	Phil Arthur
Hugh McHugh	Fredd Wayne
Hitch Imborg	John Garstad
An Old Gentleman	Gar Moore
Pensacola Crawford	Frances Tannehill
Pianist	Budd Gregg

The action is continuous. The setting is a theatre stage and dressing rooms.

Staged by Elmer Rice; settings by John Root; songs by Robert Emmett Dolan; Miss Field's costumes by Main Bocher; stage manager, Scott Jackson.

Theodora Effington, a lecturer, and Ambrose Atwater, a professor, discuss a play while it is in the making and being performed on the stage. Characters in an impromptu series of events include a producer, a playwright, actors and actresses and a critic.

(Closed February 17, 1951)

IOLANTHE

(4 performances)

Gilbert and Sullivan operetta, presented by the D'Oyly Carte Company of London at the St. James Theatre, February 15, 1951.

Cast of characters—

The Lord Chancellor	Martyn Green
Earl of Mountararat	Eric Thornton
Earl Tolloller	Leonard Osborn
Private Willis	Richard Watson
Strephon	Alan Styler
Queen of the Fairies	Ella Halman
Iolanthe	Joan Gillingham
Celia	Enid Walsh
Lelia	Joyce Wright
Fleta	Henrietta Steytler
Phyllis	Margaret Mitchell

(Closed February 17, 1951)

THE SMALL HOURS

(20 performances)

Comedy in two acts by George S. Kaufman and Leueen MacGrath, produced by Max Gordon at the National Theatre, February 15, 1951.

Cast of characters—

Laura Mitchell	Dorothy Stickney
Henry Mitchell	Paul McGrath
Martin	Donald Keyes
Dorothy Mitchell	Joyce Lear
Peter Mitchell	Michael Wager
Carter Reynolds	Thomas Noyes
A Stranger	Carl Judd
Candice Barrett	Joan Wetmore
Pippa Shields	Leona Maricle
Lucy McLean	Polly Rowles
Philip Shields	Maurice Burke
Reed Armstrong	Paul Kirk Giles
John L. Barrett	Richard Barbee
A Maid	Vickie Marsden
Motorcycle Officer	Joseph Hardy
A Girl	Ludie Claire
Alice	Eileen Burns
Secretary	Bijou Fernandez
Bessie Palmer	Jean Casto
A Waiter	Ralph Longley
Mrs. Reynolds	Ruth Hammond
Mr. Reynolds	Donald McClelland

The Great Chesterton......................Heywood Hale Broun
Dunbar..John Marriott
Eddie...Oliver Grandi
Mrs. Carpenter...............................Kathleen Bolton
Doctor.......................................Wendell K. Phillips
Miss Murney..................................Vera Fuller Mellish
Florida Couples, Policemen, Nurse, Violinist, Trombonist, etc.
    The play begins and ends in the home of Mr. and Mrs. Henry
Mitchell, but frequently departs from it. There are twenty-six scenes.
    Staged by George S. Kaufman; sets by Donald Oenslager; costumes
by Alice Gibson; general stage manager, Joseph Olney.

Laura Mitchell, wife of Henry, a successful publisher, feels that
her husband has grown beyond her in his world of sophisticates.
She cannot compete with glittering celebrities and wits. But she
discovers that glittering celebrities and wits are as uncertain of
themselves as she is, and that her husband and children really
need her and rely upon her for strength and support.

(Closed March 3, 1951)

RAZZLE DAZZLE

(8 performances)

Revue in two acts; sketches and lyrics by Mike Stewart; music
by Leo Schumer, Shelley Mowell, James Reed Lawlor, Bernice
Kroll and Irma Jurist; dances by Nelle Fischer; production designed by William Riva; produced by David Heilweil and Derrick
Lynn-Thomas, in association with Madeline Capp and Greer Johnson, at the Arena, February 19, 1951.

Principal players—

James Jewell	Bob Hergert
Kate Friedlich	Barbara Hamilton
Dorothy Greener	James Harwood
Flori Warren	Lee Goodman
Frank Reynolds	Cris Goodyear
Jet MacDonald	Peter Conlow
Jean Sincere	Jane White
Christine Karner	

Staged by Edward Reveaux.

The principal sketch numbers in this revue involved a continuing
parody of the successful film, "All About Eve," with Dorothy
Greener as the would-be actress and Barbara Hamilton as the well-
established star. "Razzle Dazzle" was New York's first demonstration of what a musical show would look like in an arena-type, or
theatre-in-the-round, assembly hall.

(Closed February 24, 1951)

COX AND BOX and THE PIRATES OF PENZANCE

(8 performances)

Gilbert and Sullivan operettas, produced by the D'Oyly Carte Company of London at the St. James Theatre, February 19, 1951.

Cast of characters for "Cox and Box"—

Cox	Alan Styler
Box	Leonard Osborn
Bouncer	Eric Thornton

Cast of characters for "The Pirates of Penzance"—

Major-General Stanley	Martyn Green
The Pirate King	Darrell Fancourt
Samuel	Donald Harris
Frederic	Neville Griffiths
Sergeant of Police	Richard Watson
Mabel	Muriel Harding
Edith	Joan Gillingham
Kate	Joyce Wright
Isabel	Enid Walsh
Ruth	Ella Halman

(Closed February 24, 1951)

THE HIGH GROUND

(23 performances)

Play in three acts by Charlotte Hastings, produced by Alfred H. Rosen at the Forty-eighth Street Theatre, February 20, 1951.

Cast of characters—

Nurse Phillips	Marian Seldes
Nurse Brent	Patricia Hitchcock
Sister Josephine	Ruth McDevitt
Willy Pentridge	Logan Ramsey
Sister Mary Bonaventure	Margaret Webster
Dr. Jeffreys	Tom Helmore
The Mother Superior	Margery Maude
Melling	Neil Fitzgerald
Sarat Cairn	Leueen MacGrath
Miss Pierce	Mary Bell
Martha Pentridge	Jean Cameron

The action takes place in the hall of the Convent of Our Lady of Rheims in Denzil St. David, a village some miles from Norwich, England. The time is the present. Act I.—About 6 P.M. Act II.—Scene 1—Shortly after. Scene 2—The next morning. Act III.—Scene 1—Next afternoon. Scene 2—Three hours later.

Staged by Herman Shumlin; set and costumes by Peggy Clark; stage manager, Felix Jacoves.

Sarat Cairn, condemned for murder, is being taken to prison by a bailiff and a matron. A storm forces them to take refuge in a convent. One of the nuns, Sister Mary Bonaventure, instinctively believes in Sarat's innocence, and by re-examining the murder case as it was written up in the papers she unmasks the real criminal.

(Closed March 10, 1951)

THE KING OF FRIDAY'S MEN

(4 performances)

Comedy in three acts by Michael J. Molloy, produced by Michael Grace at the Playhouse, February 21, 1951.

Cast of characters—

Gaisceen	Ian Martin
Una Brehony	Maggie McNamara
Owen Fennigan	Mac McLeod
Maura Pender	Janet Ward
Boorla	Tudor Owen
Bartley Dowd	Walter Macken
Kitty	Peggy McCay
Rory Commons	Sean McClory
Biddy	Grania O'Malley
Murty	John Drew Devereaux
Caesar French	Frederic Tozere

The action takes place in the west of Ireland in 1787.   Act I.—The bedroom of Gaisceen's cottage; evening.   Act II.—Scene 1—Outside an abandoned hut across the river; 24 hours later. Scene 2—Two days later.   Act III.—Caesar French's house; evening of the same day.

No director was credited in the program with staging the production; sets and costumes by Stewart Chaney; stage manager, Windsor Lewis.

Bartley Dowd, a renowned fighter with the shillelagh, comes in search of new opponents to conquer. He falls in love with Una Brehony. Caesar French, landlord of the territory, also has his eye on Una. Bartley kills him—but the girl escapes with her own sweetheart, Owen Fennigan.

This comedy came from the Abbey Theatre, Dublin, and with it came Walter Macken, a leading Irish actor.

(Closed February 23, 1951)

SPRINGTIME FOLLY

(2 performances)

Comedy in three acts by Joseph Schulman, William H. Lieberson and Martin R. Lieberson, produced by United Producers at the John Golden Theatre, February 26, 1951.

Cast of characters—

Alec	Sam Jackson
Patsy	Betty Walker
Louis De Vito	Gilbert Mack

Miss Woods .... Michelle Condre
Mr. Small .... Ray Newcomer
Benjamin Tauber .... Jack Whiting
Martha Tauber .... Ann Sorg
Phil Gordon .... Philip Abbott
Winifred LaRue .... June St. Clair
George Baroff .... Jon Silo
Mrs. Anders .... Mabel Taliaferro
Miss Pomeroy .... Irene Dailey
Mr. Walters .... Maurice Fitzgerald
Mr. Kurlin .... Charles Mayer

The action takes place in the showroom of the Lullaby Dress Co., Inc., manufacturers of maternity dresses. Act I.—A Monday morning; Spring. Act II.—Scene 1—Fifteen minutes later. Scene 2—A half hour later. Act III.—Immediately after.

Staged by Leon Michel; setting by Louis Kennel; décor by Lawrence Mansfield; production supervisor, Leonard Altabell.

Manufacturers of a maternity dress called Springtime Folly get stuck with it because, through a mistake in design, the model has no sweep. Stuck with the play were the authors, the producers and the first night audience. There was only one more performance.

(Closed February 27, 1951)

MARY ROSE

(17 performances)

Play in three acts by J. M. Barrie, revived by Helen Hayes at the ANTA Playhouse, March 4, 1951.

Cast of characters—

Mrs. Otery .... Peg Mayo
Harry .... James Daly
Mr. Morland .... Leo G. Carroll
Mrs. Morland .... Patricia Collinge
Rev. George Amy .... Daniel Reed
Mary Rose .... Bethel Leslie
Cameron .... Oliver Thorndike

Act I.—A house in Sussex; 1919. Act II.—The island. Act III.—The house in Sussex.

Staged by John Stix; sets by Jack Landau; costumes by Aline Bernstein; production stage manager, Lucia Victor.

"Mary Rose" was first presented in New York December 22, 1920, with Ruth Chatterton in the title role. It had a run of 127 performances.

(Closed March 16, 1951)

THE AUTUMN GARDEN

(101 performances)

Comedy in three acts by Lillian Hellman, produced by Kermit Bloomgarden at the Coronet Theatre, March 7, 1951.

Cast of characters—

Rose Griggs ....Florence Eldridge
Mrs. Mary Ellis ....Ethel Griffies
General Benjamin Griggs ....Colin Keith-Johnston
Edward Crossman ....Kent Smith
Fredrick Ellis ....James Lipton
Carrie Ellis ....Margaret Barker
Sophie Tuckerman ....Joan Lorring
Leon ....Maxwell Glanville
Constance Tuckerman ....Carol Goodner
Nicholas Denery ....Fredric March
Nina Denery ....Jane Wyatt
Hilda ....Louise Holmes

The time is September, 1949. The place is the Tuckerman house in a Summer resort on the Gulf of Mexico, about 100 miles from New Orleans. Act I.—Monday night after dinner. Act II.—Scene 1—The following Sunday morning. Scene 2—That night. Act III.—Early the next morning.

Staged by Harold Clurman; set by Howard Bay; costumes by Anna Hill Johnstone; production supervisor, Del Hughes.

See page 125.

(Closed June 2, 1951)

THE MOON IS BLUE

(89 performances)
(Continued)

Comedy in three acts by F. Hugh Herbert, produced by Aldrich & Myers, with Julius Fleischmann, at Henry Miller's Theatre, March 8, 1951.

Cast of characters—

Patty O'Neill ....Barbara Bel Geddes
Donald Gresham ....Barry Nelson
David Slater ....Donald Cook
Michael O'Neill ....Ralph Dunn

Act I.—Scene 1—The observation tower of the Empire State Building; early evening. Scene 2—An apartment on East 49th Street; an hour later. Act II.—The same; two hours later. Act III.—Scene 1—The same; several hours later. Scene 2—The observation tower; the following afternoon.

Staged by Otto Preminger; sets by Stewart Chaney; stage manager, John Effrat.

Donald Gresham, young architect, picks up Patty O'Neill, young virgin, on the Empire State Building observation roof. He takes her to his apartment and the observation continues from there.

ROMEO AND JULIET

(49 performances)

Shakespeare's tragedy, arranged in two acts, produced by the late Dwight Deere Wiman and presented at the Broadhurst Theatre, March 10, 1951.

Cast of characters—

```
Escalus, Prince of Verona ..................... Gregory Morton
Paris ...................................................... Robert Duke
Montague ................................................. Herbert Ransom
Capulet ........................................................ Malcolm Keen
An Old Man of the Capulet Family ................. John McKee
Romeo ................................................... Douglas Watson
Mercutio .................................................... Jack Hawkins
Benvolio .................................................. Michael Higgins
Tybalt ..................................................... William Smithers
Friar Laurence ................................... James Hayter
Friar John .......................................... Carl Harbord
Balthasar ........................................................ Karl Light
Sampson ...................................................... Buck Kartalian
Gregory .......................................................... Rudy Bond
Peter ........................................................... Jack Fletcher
Abraham ........................................................ John Perkins
An Apothecary ................................................. Paul Genge
Page to Paris ................................................. Page Johnson
Lady Montague ................................... Dorothy Patten
Lady Capulet ..................................... Isobel Elsom
Juliet ...................................................... Olivia de Havilland
Nurse to Juliet ..................................... Evelyn Varden
```
   Citizens of Verona, Kinsfolk of Both Houses, Maskers, Guards, Watchmen and Attendants: Jo Rabb, Patricia Roe, Susan Svetlik, Evangeline Raleigh, Fran Benton, Robert Burr, Gerald Price, James Greene, Felice Orlandi, Alan Furlan, Marshall Flaum, Fred Vogel, Russell Gold, John Rallo and Dario Barri.
   Staged by Peter Glenville; sets and costumes by Oliver Messel; incidental music by David Diamond; stage manager, Arthur Marlowe.

(Closed April 14, 1951)

SPRINGTIME FOR HENRY

(53 performances)

Comedy in three acts by Benn W. Levy, revived by Harald Bromley and George Brandt, in association with Richard Doscher, at the John Golden Theatre, March 14, 1951.

Cast of characters—

```
Mr. Dewlip .............................. Edward Everett Horton
Mr. Jelliwell ................................. Hugh Wakefield
Mrs. Jelliwell .................................. Haila Stoddard
Miss Smith ................................... Ursula Howells
```
   Staged by Harald Bromley; set by H. A. Condell; costumes by David Ffolkes; stage manager, James Hagerman.

"Springtime for Henry" was first produced in New York December 19, 1931, with Leslie Banks, Nigel Bruce, Frieda Inescort and Helen Chandler in the cast. It ran for 199 performances. On May 1, 1933, it was revived for 16 performances with Mady Correll, Henry Hull, Gavin Muir and Edith Atwater in the cast. In 1932 Edward Everett Horton appeared in the comedy in California and for a part of each season since he has toured in it, playing most of the Summer theatres in the country, and has had more than 1,500 performances as Mr. Dewlip.

(Closed April 28, 1951)

THE GREEN PASTURES

(44 performances)

Play in two acts by Marc Connelly, based on Roark Bradford's stories of "Ol' Man Adam an' His Chillun," revived by the Wigreen Company (the estate of the late Dwight Deere Wiman) in association with Harry Fromkes at the Broadway Theatre, March 15, 1951.

Cast of characters—

Mr. Deshee, the Preacher	John Marriott
Myrtle	Joyce Gissentanner
First Boy	Philip Hepburn
Second Boy	Pierre Dillard
Randolph	Ernest Bloomfield
Carlisle	Philip Brinson
First Cook	William Veasey
A Voice	William McDaniel
Second Cook	Alma L. Hubbard
First Man Angel	Avon Long
First Mammy Angel	Ethel Purnello
A Stout Angel	Anna Mae Richardson
A Slender Angel	Margaret Williams
Archangel	William O. Davis
Teacher Angel	Courtenaye Olden
Gabriel	Ossie Davis
God	William Marshall
Choir Leader	Rodger Alford
Custard Maker	James Fuller
Adam	William Dillard
Eve	Milroy Ingram
Cain	Van Prince
Zeba	Vinie Burrows
Cain the Sixth	Van Prince
Boy Gambler	Philip Hepburn
Gamblers	James Fuller, George Hill, John Rainey, George Royston, Robert McFerrin
Voice in Shanty	Anna Mae Richardson
Noah	Alonzo Bosan
Noah's Wife	Alma L. Hubbard
Shem	Robert McFerrin
First Woman	Milroy Ingram
Second Woman	Anna Mae Richardson
Third Woman	Tina Marshall
First Man	John Bouie
Flatfoot	Randolph Sawyer
Ham	Avon Long
Japheth	James Fuller
First Cleaner	Margaret Williams
Second Cleaner	Anna Mae Richardson
Abraham	Alonzo Bosan
Isaac	Robert McFerrin
Jacob	John Bouie
Moses	John Marriott
Zipporah	Milroy Ingram
Aaron	William Veasey
A Candidate Magician	Rodger Alford
Pharaoh	John Bouie
A General	George O. Willis
A Concubine	Courtenaye Olden
A Manicurist	Tina Marshall
First Wizard	William O. Davis
Head Magician	Avon Long
Joshua	Van Prince
Scouts	Calvin Dash, George O. Willis, Rodger Alford

Master of Ceremonies ....Randolph Sawyer
King of Babylon ....Avon Long
The King's Favorites ....Hope Foye, Yvonne Jiggets,
 Jumel Jones, Milroy Ingram,
 Courtenaye Olden
Prophet ....William Veasey
High Priest ....John Bouie
His Guest ....Tina Marshall
Corporal ....Calvin Dash
Hezdrel ....William Dillard
Second Officer ....Robert McFerrin
  The Children: Patricia Bloomfield, Beatrice Edwards, Joyce Gis-
sentanner, Dierdre Greenway, Marcia Titus, Mary Young, Ernest
Bloomfield, Eugene Bloomfield, Philip Brinson, Jimmie Burton, Pierre
Dillard, Philip Hepburn, Robert Titus.
  The Choir (Hall Johnson, Director; Assistant Director, Louvinia
White): sopranos—Mabel Bergen, Maudine Brown, Miriam Burton,
Hope Foye, Louise Hawthorne, Alma L. Hubbard, Oci Johnson,
Madeline Preston, Louvinia White. altos—Alice Ajaye, Leona
Avery, Willie Mays, Louise Parker, Ethel Purnello. tenors—
Rodger Alford, Lawson Bates, Calvin Dash, William O. Davis,
Curtis Hawkins, William McDaniel, Robert McFerrin, George Roy-
ston. baritones—Alonzo Jones, John H. Rainey, Beecher Wilson.
bassos—Jack Carr, George Hill, William Veasey, George O. Willis.
  Act I.—The scenes are: The Sunday school, a fish fry, a garden,
outside the garden, a private office, a roadside and a house, a house,
a hillside, a mountain top. Act II.—The private office, the mouth
of a cave, a throne room, the foot of a mountain, a cabaret, the
private office, outside a temple, another fish fry.
  Musical program—Act I.—"Oh! Rise an' Shine," "When the
Saints Come Marchin' In," "Cert'n'y Lord My God Is So High,"
"Hallelujah!" "In Bright Mansions Above," "Don't You Let Nobody
Turn You Roun'," "Run, Sinner, Run," "Dere's No Hidin' Place
Down Dere," "Welcome Table," "I Want to Be Ready," "De Ole
Ark's a-Moverin'," "My Soul Is a Witness." Entr'-acte.—"City
Called Heaven." Act II.—"My Lord's a-Writin' All de Time,"
"Go Down, Moses," "Oh, Mary, Don't You Weep," "Lord, I Don't
Feel Noways Tired," "Joshua Fit de Battle of Jericho," "I Can't
Stay Away," "Hail de King of Babylon," "Death's Gointer Lay
His Cold Icy Hands on Me," "De Blin' Man Stood on de Road an'
Cried," "March On," "Oh! Rise an' Shine," "Hallelujah, King
Jesus!"
  Staged by Marc Connelly; production designed by Robert Edmond
Jones; choir under the musical direction of Hall Johnson; production
stage manager, Ben D. Kranz.

"The Green Pastures" was first presented in New York February
26, 1930, at the Mansfield Theatre, where it had a run of 640 performances. It was brought back to New York February 26, 1935,
for 73 performances. On the road and in New York the original
production totaled 1,642 performances.

(Closed April 21, 1951)

L'ECOLE DES FEMMES

(22 performances)

Comedy by Molière, arranged in two acts, produced by La
Compagnie Dramatique Française des Tournées at the ANTA Playhouse, March 18, 1951.

Cast of characters—

Horace .... Jean Richard
Arnolphe .... Louis Jouvet
Chrysalde .... Léo Lapara
Alain .... Fernand-Rene
Georgette .... Monique Melinand
Agnes .... Dominique Blanchar
The Notary .... Michel Etcheverry
The Notary's Clerk .... René Besson
Enrique .... Georges Riquier
Oronte .... Pierre Renoir
    The settings are the garden of Arnolphe's house and a street
scene outside the garden.
    Staged by Louis Jouvet; settings and costumes by Christian
Bérard; music by Vittorio Rieti; stage director, Marthe Herlin.

The noted French actor, Louis Jouvet, brought his company from
the Théatre de l'Athénée, Paris, to the ANTA Playhouse in celebration of International Theatre month.

(Closed April 3, 1951)

THE KING AND I

(69 performances)

(Continued)

Musical play in two acts; music by Richard Rodgers; book and
lyrics by Oscar Hammerstein 2d, based on Margaret Landon's
novel, "Anna and the King of Siam"; produced by Rodgers and
Hammerstein at the St. James Theatre, March 29, 1951.

Cast of characters—

Captain Orton .... Charles Francis
Louis Leonowens .... Sandy Kennedy
Anna Leonowens .... Gertrude Lawrence
The Interpreter .... Leonard Graves
The Kralahome .... John Juliano
The King .... Yul Brynner
Phra Alack .... Len Mence
Tuptim .... Doretta Morrow
Lady Thiang .... Dorothy Sarnoff
Prince Chulalongkorn .... Johnny Stewart
Princess Ying Yaowalak .... Baayork Lee
Lun Tha .... Larry Douglas
Sir Edward Ramsay .... Robin Craven
    Princesses and Princes: Cristanta Cornejo, Andrea Del Rosario,
Margie James, Barbara Luna, Nora Suarez, Corinne St. Dennis,
Bunny Warner, Rodolfo Cornejo, Robert Cortazal, Thomas Griffen,
Alfonso Maribo, James Maribo, Orlando Rodriguez.
    The Royal Dancers: Jamie Bauer, Lee Becker, Mary Burr, Gemze
DeLappe, Shellie Farrell, Marilyn Gennaro, Evelyn Giles, Ina Kur-
land, Nancy Lynch, Michiko, Helen Murrielle, Prue Ward, Dusty
Worrall and Yuriko.
    Wives, Amazons, Priests, Slaves.
    The action passes in and around the King's palace, Bangkok, Siam.
Time, the early 1860s.
    Staged by John van Druten; choreography by Jerome Robbins;
orchestrations by Robert Russell Bennett; ballet arrangements by

Trude Rittman; sets by Jo Mielziner; costumes by Irene Sharaff;
musical director, Frederick Dvonch; stage managers, Jerome Whyte,
John Cornell and Ruth Mitchell.

Principal musical numbers—

ACT I

"I Whistle a Happy Tune" ....Anna and Louis
"My Lord and Master" ....Tuptim
"Hello, Young Lovers!" ....Anna
"The Royal Siamese Children" ....Anna, The King, His Wives, and Children
"A Puzzlement" ....The King
"The Royal Bangkok Academy" ....Anna and Pupils
"Getting to Know You" ......Anna, Wives, Children and Michiko
"We Kiss in a Shadow" ....Tuptim and Lun Tha
"Shall I Tell You What I Think of You?" ....Anna
"Something Wonderful" ....Lady Thiang

ACT II

"Western People Funny" ....Lady Thiang and Wives
"I Have Dreamed" ....Tuptim and Lun Tha
Ballet—"The Small House of Uncle Thomas"
    Narrator ....Doretta Morrow
    Uncle Thomas ....Dusty Worrall
    Topsy ....Ina Kurland
    Little Eva ....Shellie Farrell
    Eliza ....Yuriko
    King Simon ....Gemze DeLappe
    Angel ....Michiko
    Royal Dancers ....Jamie Bauer, Lee Becker, Mary Burr,
        Marilyn Gennaro, Evelyn Giles, Margie James,
        Nancy Lynch, Helen Murielle, Prue Ward,
        Corrine St. Denis
    Musicians ....Doria Avila, Raul Celada, Beau Cunningham
    Drummer ....Tommy Gomez
"Shall We Dance?" ....Anna and The King

NIGHT MUSIC

(8 performances)

Play in two acts by Clifford Odets, revived by the Equity Library
Theatre at the ANTA Playhouse, April 8, 1951.

Cast of characters—

Lieutenant ....Mark Alan
Murph ....Paul Lambert
Steve Takis ....Leonard Barry
A. L. Rosenberger ....Rod Steiger
Fay Tucker ....Bette Grayson
Stagehand ....Paul Lambert
Beggar ....Michael V. Gazzo
A Girl ....Mildred Slavin
Gus ....Clarke Gordon
Sailor ....Joe Sargent
Mr. George ....Sidney Shertzel
Teddy ....Vincent Beck
Marty ....Stefan Gierasch
Dot ....Nance Robbins
Mr. Nichols ....Joe Balfior
Lily ....Joyce Barnett
Sleeping Man ....Michael V. Gazzo
Roy ....Herbert Gottlieb
Little Man ....Martin Greene
Al ....Michael Lewin
Mr. Tucker ....Hal Currier

Arnold ....Walter Landa
Blind Man ....Joe Balfior
    Act I.—Scene 1—A Police Station. Scene 2—Stage door at Dover
Theatre. Scene 3—Hotel Algiers Lobby. Scene 4—Rooms 212 and
214. Scene 5—Central Park. Act II.—Scene 1—Hotel Algiers
Lobby. Scene 2—The World's Fair. Scene 3—Rooms 212 and
214. Scene 4—The Police Station. Scene 5—The Airport.
    Staged by Peter Kass; sets by Richard Burns; costumes by Ruth
Morley.

"Night Music" was first produced by the Group Theatre February
22, 1940. It had 20 performances.

(Closed April 14, 1951)

ANGELS KISS ME

(2 performances)

Play in three acts by Scott Michel, produced by Trudi Michel at
the National Theatre, April 17, 1951.

Cast of characters—

Jimmy ....Dwight Foster
Charlie Corwin ....Allan Stevenson
Michael Bancroft ....Alan Manson
Helen Darcy ....Mary Best
Katherine Hobald ....Madeleine Clive
Myra Winters ....Maryanna Garé
Franklyn Winters ....Calvin Thomas
    Act I.—The living room of Mike Bancroft's apartment in New
York; a February night. Act II.—The same. An afternoon three
months later. Act III.—Living room and porch of Franklyn Win-
ter's home, a month later; early evening.
    Staged by Ramsey Burch; settings by Frederick Fox; costumes
by Kenn Barr; stage manager, Bill Ross.

Michael Bancroft, an up-from-nowhere newspaper distributor who
believes in his luck, marries Myra Winters, wealthy society girl.
He learns that Myra is suffering from manic-depressive insanity.
In the third act he prevents his pregnant bride from jumping in
a lake—or, as Lee Rogow, reviewer for the *Hollywood Reporter*
put it, from casting her brood upon the waters. It looked as though
Michael might be able to help Myra in her affliction—but he
couldn't help the play.

(Closed April 18, 1951)

MAKE A WISH

(50 performances)
(Continued)

Musical comedy in two acts, based on "The Good Fairy," by
Ferenc Molnar; book by Preston Sturges (with uncredited revisions

by Abe Burrows); music and lyrics by Hugh Martin; produced by Harry Rigby, Jule Styne and Alexander H. Cohen at the Winter Garden, April 18, 1951.

Cast of characters—

Dr. Didier .... Eda Heinemann
Dr. Francel .... Phil Leeds
Janette .... Nanette Fabray
Ricky .... Harold Lang
Poupette .... Helen Gallagher
Policeman .... Howard Wendell
Marius Frigo .... Melville Cooper
Paul Dumont .... Stephen Douglass
The Madam .... Mary Finney
Felix Labiche .... Le Roi Operti
Sales Manager .... Howard Wendell

Singers: Mary Harmon, Carol Hendricks, Anne Humphrey, Janie Janvier, Beverly McFadden, Ellen Martin, Claire Mitchell, Peggy O'Hara, Rica Owen, Dean Campbell, Robert Davis, Edward Gombos, David Huenergardt, Douglas Luther, Don McKay, Michael Mason, Robert Shaver, David Vogel.

Dancers: Aleen Buchanan, Lynn Joelson, Margaret Jeanne, Lida Koehring, Carol Lee, Charlotte Ray, Sue Scott, Thelma Tadlock, Norma Thornton, Gene Bayliss, Dick Crowley, Ray Dorian, John Laverty, Jack Purcell, Ernie Preston, Richard Reed, Kenneth Urmston, Ken Whelan.

Staged by John C. Wilson; dances and musical ensembles staged by Gower Champion; sets and costumes by Raoul Pène du Bois; orchestrations by Phil Lang and Allan Small; dance music arranged by Richard Pribor; musical director, Milton Rosenstock; production stage manager, Archie Thompson.

Principal musical numbers—

ACT I

"I Wanna Be Good 'n' Bad" .... Nanette Fabray and Girls
The Time Step .... Miss Fabray, Helen Gallagher and Harold Lang
"What I Was Warned About" .... Miss Fabray
"Who Gives a Sou?" .... Miss Fabray, Stephen Douglass,
                                        Miss Gallagher and Mr. Lang
"Tonight You Are in Paree" .... Miss Fabray, Girls and Boys
"When Does This Feeling Go Away?" .... Mr. Douglass
"Suits Me Fine" .... Miss Gallagher, Mr. Lang

ACT II

"That Face!" .... Miss Gallagher, Mr. Lang, Girls and Boys
"Make a Wish" .... Nanette Fabray
"I'll Never Make a Frenchman Out of You" .... Miss Gallagher
                                                   and Mr. Lang
"Over and Over" .... Miss Fabray and Boys
"Take Me Back to Texas with You" .... Miss Fabray,
                                        Miss Gallagher, Mr. Lang

A TREE GROWS IN BROOKLYN

(49 performances)
(Continued)

Musical in two acts; book by Betty Smith and George Abbott, based on Betty Smith's novel of the same title; music by Arthur Schwartz; lyrics by Dorothy Fields; produced by George Abbott, in association with Robert Fryer, at the Alvin Theatre, April 19, 1951.

Cast of characters—

Willie ....Billy Parsons
Allie ....Joe Calvan
Hildy ....Dody Heath
Della ....Beverly Purvin
Petey ....Lou Wills, Jr.
Katie ....Marcia Van Dyke
Aloysius ....Jordan Bentley
Johnny Nolan ....Johnny Johnston
Cissy ....Shirley Booth
Harry ....Nathaniel Frey
Max ....Bruno Wick
Mae ....Ruth Amos
Moriarty ....Roland Wood
Annie ....Claudia Campbell
Old Clothes Man ....Harland Dixon
Florence ....Janet Parker
Edgie ....Donald Duerr
Francie ....Nomi Mitty
Junior ....Howard Martin
Swanswine ....Albert Linville
Hick ....Alan Gilbert
Judge ....Harland Dixon
Salesman ....Art Carroll
Maudie ....Celine Flanagan
        The action takes place in Brooklyn around the turn of the century.
        Staged by George Abbott; sets by Jo Mielziner; choreography by Herbert Ross; musical supervision by Jay Blackton.

Principal musical numbers—

ACT I

"Payday" ....The Company
"Mine 'Til Monday" ....Johnny Johnston, Dody Heath and Company
"Make the Man Love Me" ..Marcia Van Dyke and Johnny Johnston
"I'm Like a New Broom" ....Johnny Johnston and Friends
"Look Who's Dancing" ....Marcia Van Dyke, Shirley Booth,
                    Johnny Johnston, Joe Calvan, Billy Parsons,
                              Lou Wills, Jr., and Doris Wright,
                                       Mary Statz, Dorothy Hill
"Love Is the Reason" ....Shirley Booth and Claudia Campbell,
                           Dody Heath, Beverly Purvin, Eleanor Williams
"If You Haven't Got a Sweetheart" ....Delbert Anderson
                                                 and Company
"I'll Buy You a Star" ....Johnny Johnston and Company

ACT II

"That's How It Goes" ....Harland Dixon, Patti Milligan,
                                   Janet Parker and Company
"He Had Refinement" ....Shirley Booth
"Growing Pains" ....Johnny Johnston, Nomi Mitty
"Is That My Prince?" ....Shirley Booth, Albert Linville
"Don't Be Afraid" ....Johnny Johnston

THE LONG DAYS

(3 performances)

Play in three acts by Davis Snow, produced by Tait-Buell at the Empire Theatre, April 20, 1951.

Cast of characters—

Ann Adams ....Neva Patterson
Charles Adams ....John O'Hare
Joe Adams ....Jeffrey Lynn
Marian Adams ....Frances Starr
Sylvia Adams ....Linda Mae Sirota
Frances Adams ....Susan Harris
Mary Adams ....Gale Ashworth
Samuel Adams ....Ralph Theadore
Paula Adams ....Katharine Bard

Act I.—Kitchen of the Adams family's New England farmhouse; late afternoon in early October of the present time. Act II.—The same; about midnight. Act III.—The same; about 3 P.M. the following day.

Staged by Edward Ludlum; scenery by Eldon Elder; costumes by Ruth Morley; stage manager, Gene Parlowin.

Marian Adams, an eighth-generation Adams from the same farmhouse, is a maniacal matriarch. Because of her loving interference, one son has run away from home, another son is drinking hard and would like to run away, a third son is in jail for drunkenness and a daughter-in-law is in a hospital for the insane. Mother Adams doesn't improve things any by accidentally shooting one of the sons dead.

(Closed April 21, 1951)

THE TAMING OF THE SHREW

(15 performances)

Shakespeare comedy arranged in two acts and an epilogue, produced by Margaret Webster for the New York City Theatre Company at the City Center of Drama and Music, April 25, 1951.

Cast of characters—

Christopher Sly ....Larry Gates
Hostess of the Tavern ....Nancy Marchand
A Tapster ....Frank Corsaro
A Lord ....Robert Pastene
A Huntsman ....Larry Hageman
Servants .... { Joseph Dooley
                                              Theodore Tenley
                                              Edmund Cambridge
Bartholomew ....John Glennon

A COMPANY OF TRAVELING PLAYERS

CHARACTERS IN THE PLAY

Lucentio ....Robert Quarry
Tranio ....David Lewis
Baptista ....John Straub
Gremio ....Thayer David
Hortensio ....George Roy Hill
Katherina, ...Claire Luce
Bianca, ...Susan Douglas
Biondello ....Herbert Coleman
Petruchio ....Ralph Clanton
Grumio ....Dion Allen
Curtis ....Nancy Marchand
A Pedant ....Don Somers

```
A Haberdasher ............................... Theodore Tenley
A Tailor .................................... Frederic Warriner
Vincentio .................................. Reynolds  Evans
An  Officer ................................ Edmund  Cambridge
Troilus .................................... Dooley  Horton-Hill
                                          ( Joseph  Dooley
Petruchio's Servants ...................... { Larry  Hageman
                                          ) Frank  Corsaro
                                          ( John  Glennon
A Widow ................................... Cavada  Humphrey
```
Staged by Margaret Webster; sets by Ben Edwards; costumes by
Emeline Roche; stage manager, Thelma Chandler.

(Closed May 6, 1951)

GRAMERCY GHOST

(45 performances)
(Continued)

Comedy in two acts by John Cecil Holm, produced by Roger
Clark, in association with Evan M. Frankel, at the Morosco
Theatre, April 26, 1951.

Cast of characters—

```
Margaret Collins ................................ Mabel Paige
Nancy Willard ................................. Sarah Churchill
Parker Burnett ................................. Robert Smith
Luther Ames ................................... Harry Sothern
Charley Stewart .............................. Robert Sterling
Nathaniel Coombes ........................... Richard Waring
Officer Morrison .............................. Kirk Brown
Irv ........................................... Harry Townes
Rocky ........................................ Mitchell Kowal
Ambulance Driver ............................. John Marley
Assistant  Driver ............................ Charles Boaz
```
The action takes place within 24 hours in the living room of Nancy
Willard's apartment in Gramercy Park, New York City. Act I.—
A Late afternoon in Spring. Act II.—Scene 1—After midnight.
Scene 2—A few hours later.
Staged by Reginald Denham; set by Raymond Sovey; production
stage manager, Hugh Rennie.

When the owner of her apartment house dies, Nancy Willard discovers that she has inherited the ghost of Nathaniel Coombes, a
Revolutionary War soldier who was killed nearby in 1776 and is
forced to haunt the environs until he completes a mission given him
by George Washington. The ghost falls in love with Nancy, who
already is faced with a choice between a live stockbroker and a
lively newspaperman. The newspaperman gets her.

THE LITTLE BLUE LIGHT

(16 performances)

Play in two acts by Edmund Wilson, produced by Quintus Productions (Peter Cookson, Hume Cronyn, Joe Magee, Martin Manulis

and the Brattle Theatre Company) at the ANTA Playhouse, April 29, 1951.

Cast of characters—

The Gardener	Martin Gabel
Judith	Arlene Francis
Gandersheim	Burgess Meredith
Frank	Melvyn Douglas
Ellis	Peter Cookson

The scene is a country house about an hour and a half from New York; time, the not-remote future. Act I.—Scene 1—The garden; early evening in mid-September. Scene 2—The workroom on the second floor; late afternoon in mid-October. Act II.—Scene 1—The same room; 11 A.M. early in December. Scene 2—The same room; Christmas Eve.

Staged by Albert Marre; sets by Lester Polakov; production stage manager, Paul A. Foley.

Frank, a magazine editor and publisher, is one of the few courageous men left in a country which now is ruled by pressure groups. The most sinister of the groups is, ostensibly, no more than an efficient employment bureau. When Frank defies the bureau's threats he is destroyed by a new secret weapon, leaving the gardener to admit that he is the Wandering Jew, still looking for some good in the world.

(Closed May 12, 1951)

GETTING MARRIED

(16 performances)

Comedy in one act by Bernard Shaw, revived by Marjorie and Sherman Ewing at the ANTA Playhouse, May 7, 1951.

Cast of characters—

Mrs. Bridgenorth	Margaret Bannerman
Collins	Bramwell Fletcher
Maid	Frances Greet
Maid	Michaele Myers
General Bridgenorth	Dennis Hoey
Lesbia Grantham	Edith Meiser
Reginald Bridgenorth	Arthur Treacher
Leo	Barbara Britton
Alfred Bridgenorth, Bishop of Chelsea	Guy Spaull
St. John Hotchkiss	John Buckmaster
Cecil Sykes	John Merivale
Edith	Dora Sayers
Soames	Frederic Warriner
The Beadle	Ronald Telfer
Mrs. George	Peggy Wood

The scene is the kitchen of a 12th Century Norman castle, now the palace of the Bishop of Chelsea. In this production, the single long act was divided into three. Time, a Spring morning in 1908.

Staged by Peter Frye; set and costumes by Paul Morrison; production stage manager, David M. Pardoll.

"Getting Married" was first produced in New York in 1916, with William Faversham as the Bishop and Henrietta Crosman as Mrs.

George.   It was revived by the Theatre Guild in 1931 with a cast
including Henry Travers, Ernest Cossart and Helen Westley.

(Closed May 20, 1951)

STALAG 17

(28 performances)

(Continued)

Comedy melodrama in three acts by Donald Bevan and Edmund
Trzcinski, produced by José Ferrer at the Forty-eighth Street
Theatre, May 8, 1951.

Cast of characters—

S.S. Guard	Curt Lowens
Stosh	Robert Strauss
Harry Shapiro	Harvey Lembeck
Price	Laurence Hugo
Herb Gordon	Robert Shawley
Hoffman	Frank Maxwell
Sefton	John Ericson
Duke	Arthur Walsh
McCarthy	Douglas Henderson
Horney	Frank Campanella
Marko	William Pierson
Corporal Shultz	Lothar Rewalt
Dunbar	Mark Roberts
Reed	Allan Melvin
Peterson	Jess Cain
Red-Dog	Garry Davis
Witherspoon	Richard Poston
McKay	Eric Fleming
German Captain	Otto Simanek
Geneva Man	Ludwig Roth
2nd Guard	Edwin Strome

Act I.—Scene 1—December 22, 1944; early morning.   Scene 2—
Later that evening.   Act II.—Scene 1—Afternoon the next day.
Scene 2—Later that night.   Scene 3—Christmas Eve; afternoon.
Act III.—That night.   The action takes place in a barrack of Stalag
17 somewhere in Germany.

Staged by José Ferrer; associate producer, Richard Condon; set
by John Robert Lloyd; costumes by Noel Taylor; production stage
manager, Buford Armitage.

A group of Americans, mostly captured airmen, are in a Nazi
prison camp.   Despite their having little food or clothing, they maintain their bounce and humor.   The one thing that worries them is
that, somewhere among them, is a spy for the Germans who tells
the enemy of their misdemeanors and their escape plots.   The spy
is unmasked, is forced to attempt an escape and is shot down by
the Nazis.

DREAM GIRL

(15 performances)

Comedy in two acts by Elmer Rice, revived by the New York City Theatre Company at the New York City Center of Drama and Music, May 9, 1951.

Cast of characters—

Georgina Allerton	Judy Holliday
Lucy Allerton	Ann Shoemaker
A Radio Announcer	William LeMassena
Dr. J. Gilmore Percival	William A. Lee
George Allerton	William A. Lee
Miriam Allerton Lucas	Marian Winters
The Obstetrician	William A. Lee
The Nurse	Ann Shoemaker
Jim Lucas	Walter Klavun
Claire Blakeley	Mary Welch
A Stout Woman	Sylvia Syms
A Doctor	Donald Symington
Clark Redfield	Don DeFore
A Policeman	J. English Smith
The Judge	William A. Lee
The District Attorney	William LeMassena
George Hand	Edmon Ryan
Bert	Donald Symington
A Mexican	Don DeFore
Two Other Mexicans	{ Joseph Dooley / Arny Freeman
A Waiter	J. English Smith
Arabella	Marian Winters
Luigi	Arny Freeman
An Usher	Sarah Marshall
Miss Delehanty	Adrienne Moore
Antonio	Donald Symington
Salarino	Theodore Tenley
A Theatre Manager	William A. Lee
A Headwaiter	William LeMassena
A Waiter	Theodore Tenley
Justice of the Peace Billings	William A. Lee
A Chauffeur	Joseph Dooley

The action takes place on a Spring day between 8 A.M. and 4 A.M. the next day.

Staged by Morton Da Costa; sets by Eldon Elder; costumes by Emeline Roche; music by William Brooks; musical director, Max Marlin; George Schaefer, executive producer; stage manager, Scott Jackson.

Chief interest in this revival of "Dream Girl" was the appearance of Judy Holliday in the role created by Betty Field. Miss Holliday had, not long before, won an "Oscar" for repeating on the screen her role of the dumb blonde in Garson Kanin's comedy, "Born Yesterday."

(Closed May 20, 1951)

FLAHOOLEY

(21 performances)

(Continued)

Musical comedy in two acts; book by E. Y. Harburg and Fred Saidy; music by Sammy Fain; lyrics by E. Y. Harburg; produced by Cheryl Crawford in association with Messrs. Harburg and Saidy at the Broadhurst Theatre, May 14, 1951.

Cast of characters—

A March of Time Voice ....Stanley Carlson
Clyde ....Bil Baird
Mirabelle ....Cora Baird
Sandy ....Barbara Cook
Sylvester ....Jerome Courtland
Griselda ....Fay DeWitt
Switchboard Operators ....Vicki Barrett, Jane Fischer,
        Laurel Shelby, Tafi Towers, Urylee Leonardos,
        Annaliese Widman
K. T. Pettigrew ....Edith Atwater
Board of Directors
    Quimsy ....Stanley Carlson
    Peabody ....Ted Thurston
    Evans ....Rowan Tudor
    Farquarson ....Richard Temple
    Lovingham ....Andrew Aprea
    Hastings ....Edgar Thompson
The Voice on the P.A. ....Tafi Towers
B. G. Bigelow ....Ernest Truex
Miss Buckley ....Marilyn Ross
Clayfoot Trowbridge ....Rowan Tudor
Fowzi (The Younger Arab) ....Nehemiah Persoff
El-Akbar (The Elder Arab) ....Louis Nye
Najla ....Yma Sumac
Buyers ....Lee Ballard, Ray Cook, Clifford Fearl,
        Franklin T. Syme, Laurel Shelby
Abou Ben Atom ....Irwin Corey
Elsa Bullinger ....Lulu Bates
Citizens of Capsulanti ....Norval Tormsen, Ray Cook,
        Clifford Fearl, Sheldon Ossosky
Arabs ....Stanley Carlson, Andrew Aprea,
        Ted Thurston, Anthony Tudor
Doctor Smith ....Frank T. Syme
Nurse ....Laurel Shelby
Flahooley ....Elizabeth Logue
A Radio Voice ....Edgar Thompson
    Singers: Vicki Barrett, Carol Donn, Urylee Leonardos, Laurel Shelby, Lois Shearer, Tafi Towers, Andrew Aprea, John Adnerson, Lewis Bolyard, Ray Cook, Clifford Fearl, Franklin T. Syme, Norval Tormsen, Edgar Thompson.
    Dancers: Sara Aman, Jane Fischer, Annaliese Widman, Normand Maxon, Joe Nash, Sheldon Ossosky, James M. Tarbutton.
    Marionette Operators: Bil Baird, Cora Baird, Carl Harms and Franz Fazakas.
    Puppet Singing Voices: Mirabelle, Cinderella, Poodle: Lois Shearer. Clyde, F.D.R.: John Anderson. Hen: Carl Donn. Rhino: Ted Thurston. Cat: Fay DeWitt. Lincoln: Stanley Carlson. Lion: Franz Fazakas. Tom Payne: Carl Harms.

Principal song numbers—

ACT I

"You Too Can Be a Puppet" .... Puppet Singers
"Here's to Your Illusions" .... Sung by Barbara Cook and
Jerome Courtland
"B. G. Bigelow, Inc." .... Sung by Executives and Personnel
"Najla's Song" .... Sung by Yma Sumac
"Who Says There Ain't No Santa Claus?" .... Sung by
Jerome Courtland, Barbara Cook,
Executives and Personnel
"Flahooley" .... Sung and danced by Fay DeWitt,
Marilyn Ross, Executives and Personnel
"The World Is Your Balloon" .... Sung by Barbara Cook,
Jerome Courtland and Puppet Singing Company
"He's Only Wonderful" .... Sung by Barbara Cook
and Jerome Courtland
"Arabian for 'Get Happy' " .... Sung by Yma Sumac

ACT II

"Spirit of Capsulanti" .... Sung and danced by Marilyn Ross
and Townspeople
"Happy Hunting" .... Sung by Lulu Bates, Marilyn Ross,
Fay DeWitt and Townspeople
"Enchantment" .... Sung by Yma Sumac
"Scheherezade" .... Sung by Arabs and Executives
"Come Back, Little Genie" .... Sung by Barbara Cook
"The Springtime Cometh .... Sung by Irwin Corey
Danced by Elizabeth Logue
Staged by E. Y. Harburg and Fred Saidy; dances staged by Helen
Tamiris; sets by Howard Bay; costumes by David Ffolkes; musical
director, Maurice Levine; orchestrations by Ted Royal; special ma-
terial for Yma Sumac written by Moises Vivanco; assistant to the
producers, Yola Miller.

IDIOT'S DELIGHT

(10 performances)
(Continued)

Play in three acts by Robert E. Sherwood, revived by the New
York City Theatre Company at the City Center of Music and
Drama, May 23, 1951.

Cast of characters—

Dumptsy .... John C. Becher
Donald Navadel .... Chester Stratton
Pittaluga .... Rock Rogers
Auguste .... Theodore Tenley
Captain Locicero .... Louis Borell
Dr. Waldersee .... Stefan Schnabel
Mr. Cherry .... Winston Ross
Mrs. Cherry .... Sybil Baker
Harry Van .... Lee Tracy
Shirley .... Irene Dailey
Beulah .... Gretchen Houser
Bebe .... Lillian Udvardy
Francine .... Rita Barry
Elaine .... Joanne Woodlock
Edna .... Nancy Pearson
Major .... Alan Furlan
First Officer .... Dan Rubinate
Second Officer .... Scott Fielding

```
Third  Officer  ....................................Felice  Orlandi
Fourth  Officer  ....................................Bruce  Jewell
Quillery .........................................Emmett  Rogers
Signor  Rossi  .....................................John  Weaver
Signora  Rossi  ................................Martine  Bartlett
Anna  ......................................... Sarah  Marshall
Achille  Weber  ..............................Stiano  Braggiotti
Irene  .........................................Ruth  Chatterton
```
    Musicians: Max Marlin, Michael DuChesne, Sidney Rich, Phil
Salomon.
    The scene is the cocktail lounge in the Hotel Monte Gabriele,
Italy, near the frontiers of Switzerland and Austria. Act I.—Afternoon of a Winter day. Act II.—Scene 1—Eight o'clock that evening. Scene 2—Eleven o'clock that evening. Scene 3—After midnight. Act III.—The following afternoon.
    Staged by George Schaefer; set by Eldon Elder; costumes by
Emeline Roche.

"Idiot's Delight" was first produced by the Theatre Guild March
24, 1936. It was awarded the Pulitzer prize for that season.

OKLAHOMA!

(4 performances)
(Continued)

Musical play in two acts, based on "Green Grow the Lilacs,"
by Lynn Riggs; music by Richard Rodgers; book and lyrics by
Oscar Hammerstein 2d; revived by the Theatre Guild at the Broadway Theatre, May 29, 1951.

Cast of characters—

```
Aunt  Eller  ......................................Mary  Marlo
Curly  ............................................Ridge  Bond
Laurey  .......................................Patricia  Northrop
Cord  Elam  ......................................Owen  Martin
Fred  ........................................Warren  Schmoll
Will  Parker  ...................................Walter  Donahue
Jess  .............................................Robert  Early
Jud  Fry  ........................................Henry  Clarke
Ado  Annie  Carnes  ...........................Jacqueline  Sundt
Ali  Hakim  .........................................Jerry  Mann
Gertie  Cummings  ..............................Patricia  Johnson
Kate  ...........................................Judy  Rawlings
Armina  .........................................Jeanne  Parsons
"Child  in  Pig  Tails"  ...........................Muriel  Ives
"Girl  Who  Falls  Down"  ........................Audree  Wilson
Andrew  Carnes  ..................................Dave  Mallen
"Laurey"  in  the  Ballet  ..........................Claire  Pasch
"Curly"  in  the  Ballet  .............................Roy  Milton
"Jud"  in  the  Ballet  ..........................Valentin  Froman
Slim  .............................................John  Addis
Mike  ...........................................Charles  Scott
```
    Staged originally by Rouben Mamoulian; production reproduced
by Jerome Whyte; sets by Lemuel Ayers; costumes by Miles White;
dances staged by Agnes de Mille; stage manager, David Sidney
Weinstein.

"Oklahoma!" was first produced March 31, 1943, by the Theatre
Guild. It set the long-run record for American musicals with 2,248
performances.

OFF BROADWAY

Theatre enthusiasm ran high, as always, off Broadway; higher, perhaps, than *on* Broadway, but not with any particularly notable results. Early in June, 1950, a new Little Theatre group, Repertory Theatre, Inc., made its bow in the Cherry Lane Theatre in Greenwich Village with Ibsen's "Master-Builder Solness." In Chinatown the Sun Sing Players were giving what was, perhaps, New York's most repertorial repertoire—a different play each day, in Chinese. On East 74th St. the Masque and Lyre Light Opera Company was working its indefatigable way through Gilbert & Sullivan, and at the Madison Street Playhouse another group was striving with Ibsen's drama about the master builder. Also in June, Studio 7 presented Wedekind's "Earth Spirit" at the Provincetown Playhouse.

In July the Interplayers presented "The Beggar's Opera," with music by Mark Bucci, at the Carnegie Hall Theatre; the Players' Company gave Pirandello's "Right You Are if You Think You Are" at the Y.M.H.A. on East 92d St.; the information service of the Belgian Government offered a Belgian fantasy by Paul Willems titled "The Fine Old Wine of Monsieur Nuche"; the Circle Theatre, on 36th St. near Ninth Ave., offered a theatre-in-the-round performance of "The Doctored Wife," a comedy by Norman Hall and Chris Jaffe based on Molière's "Physician in Spite of Himself." The Oxford University Players, who had been touring the country, gave performances of "King Lear" and "The Alchemist" at the Master Institute on Riverside Drive in August.

In September the Masque and Lyre Savoyards were still going strong; Studio 7 tried Pirandello's "Naked" at the Provincetown Playhouse, and an ill-regarded play, "The Mourner's Bench," was tried by Theatre Enterprises at the Master Institute Theatre. A new group, Originals Only, offered "Hidden House," by Dr. Robert Bachmann, at its playhouse at Ninth St. and Sixth Ave.—for free, or at least for no admission charge.

In October an organization calling itself the Laughing Stock Company presented T. S. Eliot's "Family Reunion" at the Master Institute Theatre; Equity Library Theatre began a series of week-end productions at the Lenox Hill Playhouse, on East 70th St., which included during the season "Broadway," "Misalliance," "Payment Deferred," "Hedda Gabler," "Missouri Legend" and "Electra."

The Blackfriars, Catholic group on West 57th St., presented a comedy by Ted Farah titled "Angel With Red Hair."

The principal off-Broadway event in November was the presentation at the Bleecker Street Playhouse of Shaw's "Mrs. Warren's Profession," with a cast including Estelle Winwood, John Loder and Louisa Horton. The Laughing Stock Company got around to Priestley's "Dangerous Corner," and the players of Fordham University had fun with the old musical, "A Trip to Chinatown."

December brought its usual spate of children's entertainments, including one titled "The Cat That Hated Christmas," sponsored by the Kitten-Cat Company, at a church. In the grown-up field there was "Nat Turner," drama by Paul Peters about a Negro slave who tried a revolt in Virginia in 1831. It was offered by People's Drama, Inc., on the East Side's Eldridge St. Erwin Piscator's Dramatic Workshop gave a German drama about war guilt, "A House in Berlin," by Max Frisch. An arena theatre on Sheridan Square strove with "Dark of the Moon," and at the Cherry Lane Theatre there was a new play by Rae Dalvin titled "Season in Hell."

January, 1951, found the Masque and Lyre players still doing Gilbert & Sullivan, and the Laughing Stock Company was doing Euripides' "Electra" in modern dress. A new group, the Journeymen, essayed a new newspaper comedy, "Sky High," by Powers Moulton, at the Provincetown Playhouse. The Fordham University Theatre tried "Colombyre," by Gabriel Marcel, a French existentialist, and the Equity Community Theatre offered "Missouri Legend" at a Bronx high school for a 90-cent top.

In February a band of hopefuls named the Globe Repertory Players offered Ibsen's "Pillars of Society" at the Cherry Lane Theatre and Modern Play Productions gave "The Merchant of Venice" at the Provincetown Playhouse. The annual production of the Snarks at the Amateur Comedy Club's theatre was "Miranda," an English comedy by Peter Blackmore. In the Bronx the Equity Library Players gave Shaw's "Major Barbara," and the Columbia University Players gave Eliot's "Murder in the Cathedral."

In March, Originals Only offered, for whatever contributions the freely admitted audience might give, a drama by Alvin Keller titled "Roots in the Wasteland," and the Brooklyn College Varsity Players presented the Chinese fantasy, "Lady Precious Stream." The Equity Library group tried its first musical, "Babes in Arms," at the Bronx Community Center. The one off-Broadway play of the season to reach Broadway was "Stalag 17," which was given by the Junior Lambs at the Lambs Club. Jose Ferrer subsequently produced this play, by Edmund Trszciuski and Don Bevan, on Broad-

way with considerable success. The Columbia University Opera
Workshop presented "Giants in the Earth," with a libretto by Arnold
Sundgaard (based on O. E. Rolvaag's novel) and music by Douglas
Moore, a Columbia music professor. This work won Mr. Moore the
Pulitzer prize in music. The Blue Hill Troupe, 27-year-old amateur
group, gave "The Pirates of Penzance" and "Trial by Jury" at the
Hunter College Playhouse, and the Equity Library Theatre wound
up its Bronx community season with "You Can't Take It with You."
The season, incidentally, netted a profit of nineteen cents after play-
ing to more than 11,000 paying patrons.

In April, the blind players of the Lighthouse gave "Goodbye, My
Fancy," and the Laughing Stock Company tried a revue, "You
Twisted My Arm." The off-Broadway novelty of the year was
"Dope," a dramatization of the narcotics problem by Maryat Lee,
which was played in various vacant lots in Harlem under the spon-
sorship of the East Harlem Protestant Parish. And, in May, the
Playhouse Theatre Company of the Henry Street Playhouse gave
the old melodrama, "The Streets of New York."

STATISTICAL SUMMARY

Plays	Number Performances	
Clutterbuck	218	(Closed June 10, 1950)
Death of a Salesman	742	(Closed November 18, 1950)
Lost in the Stars	273	(Closed July 1, 1950)
Mister Roberts	1,157	(Closed January 6, 1951)
Peter Pan	321	(Closed January 27, 1951)
Tickets, Please	245	(Closed November 25, 1950)
The Cocktail Party	409	(Closed January 13, 1951)
The Consul	269	(Closed November 4, 1950)
The Member of the Wedding	501	(Closed March 17, 1951)
The Wisteria Trees	165	(Closed September 16, 1950)
Where's Charley?	792	(Closed September 9, 1950)

LONG RUNS ON BROADWAY

To June 1, 1951

(Plays marked with asterisk were still playing June 1, 1951)

Plays	Number Performances	Plays	Number Performances
Life with Father	3,224	State of the Union	765
Tobacco Road	3,182	The First Year	760
Abie's Irish Rose	2,327	Death of a Salesman	742
Oklahoma!	2,248	Sons o' Fun	742
Harvey	1,775	The Man Who Came to	739
Born Yesterday	1,642	Dinner	739
The Voice of the Turtle	1,557	Call Me Mister	734
Arsenic and Old Lace	1,444	High Button Shoes	727
Hellzapoppin	1,404	Finian's Rainbow	725
Angel Street	1,295	Claudia	722
Lightnin'	1,291	The Gold Diggers	720
Mister Roberts	1,157	I Remember Mama	714
Annie Get Your Gun	1,147	Junior Miss	710
Pins and Needles	1,108	Seventh Heaven	704
*Kiss Me, Kate	1,010	Peg o' My Heart	692
Anna Lucasta	957	The Children's Hour	691
Kiss and Tell	956	Dead End	687
Carousel	890	The Lion and the Mouse	686
Hats Off to Ice	889	White Cargo	686
Follow the Girls	882	Dear Ruth	683
*South Pacific	873	East Is West	680
The Bat	867	The Doughgirls	671
My Sister Eileen	865	Irene	670
White Cargo	864	Boy Meets Girl	669
Song of Norway	860	Blithe Spirit	657
A Streetcar Named Desire	855	The Women	657
You Can't Take It with		A Trip to Chinatown	657
You	837	Bloomer Girl	654
Three Men on a Horse	835	Rain	648
Stars on Ice	830	Janie	642
Where's Charley?	792	The Green Pastures	640
The Ladder	789	Is Zat So?	618

Plays	Number Performances	Plays	Number Performances
Separate Rooms	613	Let's Face It	547
Star and Garter	609	Within the Law	541
The Student Prince	608	The Music Master	540
Broadway	603	What a Life	538
Adonis	603	The Red Mill	531
Street Scene	601	The Boomerang	522
Kiki	600	Rosalinda	521
A Society Circus	596	Chauve Souris	520
Blossom Time	592	Blackbirds	518
The Two Mrs. Carrolls	585	Sunny	517
Detective Story	581	Victoria Regina	517
Brigadoon	581	The Vagabond King	511
Brother Rat	577	The New Moon	509
Show Boat	572	Shuffle Along	504
The Show-Off	571	Up in Central Park	504
Sally	570	Carmen Jones	503
One Touch of Venus	567	The Member of the Wedding	501
Happy Birthday	564		
The Glass Menagerie	561	Personal Appearance	501
Rose Marie	557	Panama Hattie	501
Strictly Dishonorable	557	Bird in Hand	500
Ziegfeld Follies	553	Sailor, Beware!	500
Floradora	553	Room Service	500
Good News	551	Tomorrow the World	500

NEW YORK DRAMA CRITICS CIRCLE AWARDS

The Critics Circle's annual prize-giving on the first Tuesday of April, 1951, offered something of a surprise when "Billy Budd" showed unpredicted strength in the balloting. Sidney Kingsley's "Darkness at Noon" got the prize with ten votes, but "Billy Budd," by Louis O. Coxe and Robert Chapman, was very close with eight. An overwhelming choice for the best foreign play was "The Lady's Not for Burning," by Christopher Fry. When it came to voting on a musical, one member of the Circle found support for his suggestion that the citation be split between "Guys and Dolls" and the Rodgers-Hammerstein "The King and I." But the majority preferred to take one musical at a time, and the winner was "Guys and Dolls," by Jo Swerling, Abe Burrows and Frank Loesser.

Circle awards have been—

1935-36—Winterset, by Maxwell Anderson
1936-37—High Tor, by Maxwell Anderson
1937-38—Of Mice and Men, by John Steinbeck
1938-39—No award.
1939-40—The Time of Your Life, by William Saroyan
1940-41—Watch on the Rhine, by Lillian Hellman
1941-42—No award.
1942-43—The Patriots, by Sidney Kingsley
1943-44—No award.
1944-45—The Glass Menagerie, by Tennessee Williams
1945-46—No award.
1946-47—All My Sons, by Arthur Miller
1947-48—A Streetcar Named Desire, by Tennessee Williams
1948-49—Death of a Salesman, by Arthur Miller
1949-50—The Member of the Wedding, by Carson McCullers
1950-51—Darkness at Noon, by Sidney Kingsley

PULITZER PRIZE WINNERS

For the fifth time since the Pulitzer awards were established the Pulitzer drama judges announced that there would be no award for the 1950-51 season. As is customary, no explanation was offered. As also is customary, there were expressions of disappointment and dissatisfaction in theatrical circles.

Pulitzer awards have been—

1917-18—Why Marry?, by Jesse Lynch Williams
1918-19—No award.
1919-20—Beyond the Horizon, by Eugene O'Neill
1920-21—Miss Lulu Bett, by Zona Gale
1921-22—Anna Christie, by Eugene O'Neill
1922-23—Icebound, by Owen Davis
1923-24—Hell-bent fer Heaven, by Hatcher Hughes
1924-25—They Knew What They Wanted, by Sidney Howard
1925-26—Craig's Wife, by George Kelly
1926-27—In Abraham's Bosom, by Paul Green
1927-28—Strange Interlude, by Eugene O'Neill
1928-29—Street Scene, by Elmer Rice
1929-30—The Green Pastures, by Marc Connelly
1930-31—Alison's House, by Susan Glaspell
1931-32—Of Thee I Sing, by George S. Kaufman, Morrie Rys-
        kind, Ira and George Gershwin
1932-33—Both Your Houses, by Maxwell Anderson
1933-34—Men in White, by Sidney Kingsley
1934-35—The Old Maid, by Zoe Akins
1935-36—Idiot's Delight, by Robert E. Sherwood
1936-37—You Can't Take It with You, by Moss Hart and George
        S. Kaufman
1937-38—Our Town, by Thornton Wilder
1938-39—Abe Lincoln in Illinois, by Robert E. Sherwood
1939-40—The Time of Your Life, by William Saroyan
1940-41—There Shall Be No Night, by Robert E. Sherwood
1941-42—No award.
1942-43—The Skin of Our Teeth, by Thornton Wilder
1943-44—No award.
1944-45—Harvey, by Mary Coyle Chase

1945-46—State of the Union, by Howard Lindsay and Russel
          Crouse
1946-47—No award.
1947-48—A Streetcar Named Desire, by Tennessee Williams
1948-49—Death of a Salesman, by Arthur Miller
1949-50—South Pacific, by Richard Rodgers, Oscar Hammerstein
          II and Joshua Logan
1950-51—No award.

PREVIOUS VOLUMES OF BEST PLAYS

Plays chosen to represent the theatre seasons from 1899 to 1950 are as follows:

1899-1909

BARBARA FRIETCHIE, by Clyde Fitch. Life Publishing Co.
THE CLIMBERS, by Clyde Fitch. Macmillan.
IF I WERE KING, by Justin Huntly McCarthy. Samuel French.
THE DARLING OF THE GODS, by David Belasco. Little, Brown.
THE COUNTY CHAIRMAN, by George Ade. Samuel French.
LEAH KLESCHNA, by C. M. S. McLellan. Samuel French.
THE SQUAW MAN, by Edwin Milton Royle.
THE GREAT DIVIDE, by William Vaughn Moody. Samuel French.
THE WITCHING HOUR, by Augustus Thomas. Samuel French.
THE MAN FROM HOME, by Booth Tarkington and Harry Leon Wilson. Samuel French.

1909-1919

THE EASIEST WAY, by Eugene Walter. G. W. Dillingham and Houghton Mifflin.
MRS. BUMPSTEAD-LEIGH, by Harry James Smith. Samuel French.
DISRAELI, by Louis N. Parker. Dodd, Mead.
ROMANCE, by Edward Sheldon. Macmillan.
SEVEN KEYS TO BALDPATE, by George M. Cohan. Published by Bobbs-Merrill as a novel by Earl Derr Biggers; as a play by Samuel French.
ON TRIAL, by Elmer Reizenstein. Samuel French.
THE UNCHASTENED WOMAN, by Louis Kaufman Anspacher. Harcourt, Brace and Howe.
GOOD GRACIOUS ANNABELLE, by Clare Kummer. Samuel French.
WHY MARRY? by Jesse Lynch Williams. Scribner.
JOHN FERGUSON, by St. John Ervine. Macmillan.

1919-1920

ABRAHAM LINCOLN, by John Drinkwater. Houghton Mifflin.
CLARENCE, by Booth Tarkington. Samuel French.
BEYOND THE HORIZON, by Eugene G. O'Neill. Boni & Liveright.

DÉCLASSÉE, by Zoe Akins. Liveright, Inc.

THE FAMOUS MRS. FAIR, by James Forbes. Samuel French.

THE JEST, by Sem Benelli. (American adaptation by Edward Sheldon.)

JANE CLEGG, by St. John Ervine. Henry Holt.

MAMMA'S AFFAIR, by Rachel Barton Butler. Samuel French.

WEDDING BELLS, by Salisbury Field. Samuel French.

ADAM AND EVA, by George Middleton and Guy Bolton. Samuel French.

1920-1921

DEBURAU, adapted from the French of Sacha Guitry by H. Granville Barker. Putnam.

THE FIRST YEAR, by Frank Craven. Samuel French.

ENTER MADAME, by Gilda Varesi and Dolly Byrne. Putnam.

THE GREEN GODDESS, by William Archer. Knopf.

LILIOM, by Ferenc Molnar. Boni & Liveright.

MARY ROSE, by James M. Barrie. Scribner.

NICE PEOPLE, by Rachel Crothers. Scribner.

THE BAD MAN, by Porter Emerson Browne. Putnam.

THE EMPEROR JONES, by Eugene G. O'Neill. Boni & Liveright.

THE SKIN GAME, by John Galsworthy. Scribner.

1921-1922

ANNA CHRISTIE, by Eugene G. O'Neill. Boni & Liveright.

A BILL OF DIVORCEMENT, by Clemence Dane. Macmillan.

DULCY, by George S. Kaufman and Marc Connelly. Putnam.

HE WHO GETS SLAPPED, adapted from the Russian of Leonid Andreyev by Gregory Zilboorg. Brentano's.

SIX CYLINDER LOVE, by William Anthony McGuire.

THE HERO, by Gilbert Emery.

THE DOVER ROAD, by Alan Alexander Milne. Samuel French.

AMBUSH, by Arthur Richman.

THE CIRCLE, by William Somerset Maugham.

THE NEST, by Paul Geraldy and Grace George.

1922-1923

RAIN, by John Colton and Clemence Randolph. Liveright, Inc.

LOYALTIES, by John Galsworthy. Scribner.

ICEBOUND, by Owen Davis. Little, Brown.

YOU AND I, by Philip Barry. Brentano's.

THE FOOL, by Channing Pollock. Brentano's.

MERTON OF THE MOVIES, by George Kaufman and Marc Connelly, based on the novel of the same name by Harry Leon Wilson.
WHY NOT? by Jesse Lynch Williams. Walter H. Baker Co.
THE OLD SOAK, by Don Marquis. Doubleday, Page.
R.U.R., by Karel Capek. Translated by Paul Selver. Doubleday, Page.
MARY THE 3D, by Rachel Crothers. Brentano's.

1923-1924

THE SWAN, translated from the Hungarian of Ferenc Molnar by Melville Baker. Boni & Liveright.
OUTWARD BOUND, by Sutton Vane. Boni & Liveright.
THE SHOW-OFF, by George Kelly. Little, Brown.
THE CHANGELINGS, by Lee Wilson Dodd. Dutton.
CHICKEN FEED, by Guy Bolton. Samuel French.
SUN-UP, by Lula Vollmer. Brentano's.
BEGGAR ON HORSEBACK, by George Kaufman and Marc Connelly. Boni & Liveright.
TARNISH, by Gilbert Emery. Brentano's.
THE GOOSE HANGS HIGH, by Lewis Beach. Little, Brown.
HELL-BENT FER HEAVEN, by Hatcher Hughes. Harper.

1924-1925

WHAT PRICE GLORY? by Laurence Stallings and Maxwell Anderson. Harcourt, Brace.
THEY KNEW WHAT THEY WANTED, by Sidney Howard. Doubleday, Page.
DESIRE UNDER THE ELMS, by Eugene G. O'Neill. Boni & Liveright.
THE FIREBRAND, by Edwin Justus Mayer. Boni & Liveright.
DANCING MOTHERS, by Edgar Selwyn and Edmund Goulding.
MRS. PARTRIDGE PRESENTS, by Mary Kennedy and Ruth Warren. Samuel French.
THE FALL GUY, by James Gleason and George Abbott. Samuel French.
THE YOUNGEST, by Philip Barry. Samuel French.
MINICK, by Edna Ferber and George S. Kaufman. Doubleday, Page.
WILD BIRDS, by Dan Totheroh. Doubleday, Page.

1925-1926

CRAIG'S WIFE, by George Kelly. Little, Brown.
THE GREAT GOD BROWN, by Eugene G. O'Neill. Boni & Liveright.

THE GREEN HAT, by Michael Arlen.
THE DYBBUK, by S. Ansky, Henry G. Alsberg-Winifred Katzin
   translation. Boni & Liveright.
THE ENEMY, by Channing Pollock. Brentano's.
THE LAST OF MRS. CHEYNEY, by Frederick Lonsdale. Samuel
   French.
BRIDE OF THE LAMB, by William Hurlbut. Boni & Liveright.
THE WISDOM TOOTH, by Marc Connelly. George H. Doran.
THE BUTTER AND EGG MAN, by George Kaufman. Boni & Liveright.
YOUNG WOODLEY, by John Van Druten. Simon & Schuster.

1926-1927

BROADWAY, by Philip Dunning and George Abbott. George H.
   Doran.
SATURDAY'S CHILDREN, by Maxwell Anderson. Longmans, Green.
CHICAGO, by Maurine Watkins. Knopf.
THE CONSTANT WIFE, by William Somerset Maugham. George H.
   Doran.
THE PLAY'S THE THING, by Ferenc Molnar and P. G. Wodehouse.
   Brentano's.
THE ROAD TO ROME, by Robert Emmet Sherwood. Scribner.
THE SILVER CORD, by Sidney Howard. Scribner.
THE CRADLE SONG, translated from the Spanish of G. Martinez
   Sierra by John Garrett Underhill. Dutton.
DAISY MAYME, by George Kelly. Little, Brown.
IN ABRAHAM'S BOSOM, by Paul Green. McBride.

1927-1928

STRANGE INTERLUDE, by Eugene G. O'Neill. Boni & Liveright.
THE ROYAL FAMILY, by Edna Ferber and George Kaufman. Dou-
   bleday, Doran.
BURLESQUE, by George Manker Watters and Arthur Hopkins. Dou-
   bleday, Doran.
COQUETTE, by George Abbott and Ann Bridgers. Longmans, Green.
BEHOLD THE BRIDEGROOM, by George Kelly. Little, Brown.
PORGY, by DuBose Heyward. Doubleday, Doran.
PARIS BOUND, by Philip Barry. Samuel French.
ESCAPE, by John Galsworthy. Scribner.
THE RACKET, by Bartlett Cormack. Samuel French.
THE PLOUGH AND THE STARS, by Sean O'Casey. Macmillan.

1928-1929

STREET SCENE, by Elmer Rice. Samuel French.
JOURNEY'S END, by R. C. Sherriff. Brentano's.
WINGS OVER EUROPE, by Robert Nichols and Maurice Browne. Covici-Friede.
HOLIDAY, by Philip Barry. Samuel French.
THE FRONT PAGE, by Ben Hecht and Charles MacArthur. Covici-Friede.
LET US BE GAY, by Rachel Crothers. Samuel French.
MACHINAL, by Sophie Treadwell.
LITTLE ACCIDENT, by Floyd Dell and Thomas Mitchell.
GYPSY, by Maxwell Anderson.
THE KINGDOM OF GOD, by G. Martinez Sierra; English version by Helen and Harley Granville-Barker. Dutton.

1929-1930

THE GREEN PASTURES, by Marc Connelly (adapted from "Ol' Man Adam and His Chilllun," by Roark Bradford). Farrar & Rinehart.
THE CRIMINAL CODE, by Martin Flavin. Horace Liveright.
BERKELEY SQUARE, by John Balderston.
STRICTLY DISHONORABLE, by Preston Sturges. Horace Liveright.
THE FIRST MRS. FRASER, by St. John Ervine. Macmillan.
THE LAST MILE, by John Wexley. Samuel French.
JUNE MOON, by Ring W. Lardner and George S. Kaufman. Scribner.
MICHAEL AND MARY, by A. A. Milne. Chatto & Windus.
DEATH TAKES A HOLIDAY, by Walter Ferris (adapted from the Italian of Alberto Casella). Samuel French.
REBOUND, by Donald Ogden Stewart. Samuel French.

1930-1931

ELIZABETH THE QUEEN, by Maxwell Anderson. Longmans, Green.
TOMORROW AND TOMORROW, by Philip Barry. Samuel French.
ONCE IN A LIFETIME, by George S. Kaufman and Moss Hart. Farrar & Rinehart.
GREEN GROW THE LILACS, by Lynn Riggs. Samuel French.
AS HUSBANDS GO, by Rachel Crothers. Samuel French.
ALISON'S HOUSE, by Susan Glaspell. Samuel French.
FIVE-STAR FINAL, by Louis Weitzenkorn. Samuel French.
OVERTURE, by William Bolitho. Simon & Schuster.

THE BARRETTS OF WIMPOLE STREET, by Rudolf Besier. Little, Brown.

GRAND HOTEL, adapted from the German of Vicki Baum by W. A. Drake.

1931-1932

OF THEE I SING, by George S. Kaufman and Morrie Ryskind; music and lyrics by George and Ira Gershwin. Knopf.

MOURNING BECOMES ELECTRA, by Eugene G. O'Neill. Horace Liveright.

REUNION IN VIENNA, by Robert Emmet Sherwood. Scribner.

THE HOUSE OF CONNELLY, by Paul Green. Samuel French.

THE ANIMAL KINGDOM, by Philip Barry. Samuel French.

THE LEFT BANK, by Elmer Rice. Samuel French.

ANOTHER LANGUAGE, by Rose Franken. Samuel French.

BRIEF MOMENT, by S. N. Behrman. Farrar & Rinehart.

THE DEVIL PASSES, by Benn W. Levy. Martin Secker.

CYNARA, by H. M. Harwood and R. F. Gore-Browne. Samuel French.

1932-1933

BOTH YOUR HOUSES, by Maxwell Anderson. Samuel French.

DINNER AT EIGHT, by George S. Kaufman and Edna Ferber. Doubleday, Doran.

WHEN LADIES MEET, by Rachel Crothers. Samuel French.

DESIGN FOR LIVING, by Noel Coward. Doubleday, Doran.

BIOGRAPHY, by S. N. Behrman. Farrar & Rinehart.

ALIEN CORN, by Sidney Howard. Scribner.

THE LATE CHRISTOPHER BEAN, adapted from the French of René Fauchois by Sidney Howard. Samuel French.

WE, THE PEOPLE, by Elmer Rice. Coward-McCann.

PIGEONS AND PEOPLE, by George M. Cohan.

ONE SUNDAY AFTERNOON, by James Hagan. Samuel French.

1933-1934

MARY OF SCOTLAND, by Maxwell Anderson. Doubleday, Doran.

MEN IN WHITE, by Sidney Kingsley. Covici-Friede.

DODSWORTH, by Sinclair Lewis and Sidney Howard. Harcourt, Brace.

AH, WILDERNESS, by Eugene O'Neill. Random House.

THEY SHALL NOT DIE, by John Wexley. Knopf.

HER MASTER'S VOICE, by Clare Kummer. Samuel French.

NO MORE LADIES, by A. E. Thomas.

WEDNESDAY'S CHILD, by Leopold Atlas. Samuel French.
THE SHINING HOUR, by Keith Winter. Doubleday, Doran.
THE GREEN BAY TREE, by Mordaunt Shairp. Baker International
    Play Bureau.

1934-1935

THE CHILDREN'S HOUR, by Lillian Hellman. Knopf.
VALLEY FORGE, by Maxwell Anderson. Anderson House.
THE PETRIFIED FOREST, by Robert Sherwood. Scribner.
THE OLD MAID, by Zoe Akins. Appleton-Century.
ACCENT ON YOUTH, by Samson Raphaelson. Samuel French.
MERRILY WE ROLL ALONG, by George S. Kaufman and Moss Hart.
    Random House.
AWAKE AND SING, by Clifford Odets. Random House.
THE FARMER TAKES A WIFE, by Frank B. Elser and Marc Connelly.
LOST HORIZONS, by John Hayden.
THE DISTAFF SIDE, by John Van Druten. Knopf.

1935-1936

WINTERSET, by Maxwell Anderson. Anderson House.
IDIOT'S DELIGHT, by Robert Emmet Sherwood. Scribner.
END OF SUMMER, by S. N. Behrman. Random House.
FIRST LADY, by Katharine Dayton and George S. Kaufman. Ran-
    dom House.
VICTORIA REGINA, by Laurence Housman. Samuel French.
BOY MEETS GIRL, by Bella and Samuel Spewack. Random House.
DEAD END, by Sidney Kingsley. Random House.
CALL IT A DAY, by Dodie Smith. Samuel French.
ETHAN FROME, by Owen Davis and Donald Davis. Scribner.
PRIDE AND PREJUDICE, by Helen Jerome. Doubleday, Doran.

1936-1937

HIGH TOR, by Maxwell Anderson. Anderson House.
YOU CAN'T TAKE IT WITH YOU, by Moss Hart and George S. Kauf-
    man. Farrar & Rinehart.
JOHNNY JOHNSON, by Paul Green. Samuel French.
DAUGHTERS OF ATREUS, by Robert Turney. Knopf.
STAGE DOOR, by Edna Ferber and George S. Kaufman. Doubleday,
    Doran.
THE WOMEN, by Clare Boothe. Random House.
ST. HELENA, by R. C. Sherriff and Jeanne de Casalis. Samuel
    French.

YES, MY DARLING DAUGHTER, by Mark Reed. Samuel French.
EXCURSION, by Victor Wolfson. Random House.
TOVARICH, by Jacques Deval and Robert E. Sherwood. Random House.

1937-1938

OF MICE AND MEN, by John Steinbeck. Covici-Friede.
OUR TOWN, by Thornton Wilder. Coward-McCann.
SHADOW AND SUBSTANCE, by Paul Vincent Carroll. Random House.
ON BORROWED TIME, by Paul Osborn. Knopf.
THE STAR-WAGON, by Maxwell Anderson. Anderson House.
SUSAN AND GOD, by Rachel Crothers. Random House.
PROLOGUE TO GLORY, by E. P. Conkle. Random House.
AMPHITRYON 38, by S. N. Behrman. Random House.
GOLDEN BOY, by Clifford Odets. Random House.
WHAT A LIFE, by Clifford Goldsmith. Dramatists' Play Service.

1938-1939

ABE LINCOLN IN ILLINOIS, by Robert E. Sherwood. Scribner.
THE LITTLE FOXES, by Lillian Hellman. Random House.
ROCKET TO THE MOON, by Clifford Odets. Random House.
THE AMERICAN WAY, by George S. Kaufman and Moss Hart. Random House.
NO TIME FOR COMEDY, by S. N. Behrman. Random House.
THE PHILADELPHIA STORY, by Philip Barry. Coward-McCann.
THE WHITE STEED, by Paul Vincent Carroll. Random House.
HERE COME THE CLOWNS, by Philip Barry. Coward-McCann.
FAMILY PORTRAIT, by Lenore Coffee and William Joyce Cowen. Random House.
KISS THE BOYS GOOD-BYE, by Clare Boothe. Random House.

1939-1940

THERE SHALL BE NO NIGHT, by Robert E. Sherwood. Scribner.
KEY LARGO, by Maxwell Anderson. Anderson House.
THE WORLD WE MAKE, by Sidney Kingsley.
LIFE WITH FATHER, by Howard Lindsay and Russel Crouse. Knopf.
THE MAN WHO CAME TO DINNER, by George S. Kaufman and Moss Hart. Random House.
THE MALE ANIMAL, by James Thurber and Elliott Nugent. Random House, New York, and MacMillan Co., Canada.
THE TIME OF YOUR LIFE, by William Saroyan. Harcourt, Brace.
SKYLARK, by Samson Raphaelson. Random House.

MARGIN FOR ERROR, by Clare Boothe. Random House.
MORNING'S AT SEVEN, by Paul Osborn. Samuel French.

1940-1941

NATIVE SON, by Paul Green and Richard Wright. Harper.
WATCH ON THE RHINE, by Lillian Hellman. Random House.
THE CORN IS GREEN, by Emlyn Williams. Random House.
LADY IN THE DARK, by Moss Hart. Random House.
ARSENIC AND OLD LACE, by Joseph Kesselring. Random House.
MY SISTER EILEEN, by Joseph Fields and Jerome Chodorov. Random House.
FLIGHT TO THE WEST, by Elmer Rice. Coward-McCann.
CLAUDIA, by Rose Franken Meloney. Farrar & Rinehart.
MR. AND MRS. NORTH, by Owen Davis. Samuel French.
GEORGE WASHINGTON SLEPT HERE, by George S. Kaufman and Moss Hart. Random House.

1941-1942

IN TIME TO COME, by Howard Koch. Dramatists' Play Service.
THE MOON IS DOWN, by John Steinbeck. Viking.
BLITHE SPIRIT, by Noel Coward. Doubleday, Doran.
JUNIOR MISS, by Jerome Chodorov and Joseph Fields. Random House.
CANDLE IN THE WIND, by Maxwell Anderson. Anderson House.
LETTERS TO LUCERNE, by Fritz Rotter and Allen Vincent. Samuel French.
JASON, by Samson Raphaelson. Random House.
ANGEL STREET, by Patrick Hamilton. Constable & Co., under the title "Gaslight."
UNCLE HARRY, by Thomas Job. Samuel French.
HOPE FOR A HARVEST, by Sophie Treadwell. Samuel French.

1942-1943

THE PATRIOTS, by Sidney Kingsley. Random House.
THE EVE OF ST. MARK, by Maxwell Anderson. Anderson House.
THE SKIN OF OUR TEETH, by Thornton Wilder. Harper.
WINTER SOLDIERS, by Dan James.
TOMORROW THE WORLD, by James Gow and Arnaud d'Usseau. Scribner.
HARRIET, by Florence Ryerson and Colin Clements. Scribner.
THE DOUGHGIRLS, by Joseph Fields. Random House.

THE DAMASK CHEEK, by John Van Druten and Lloyd Morris. Random House.
KISS AND TELL, by F. Hugh Herbert. Coward-McCann.
OKLAHOMA!, by Oscar Hammerstein 2nd and Richard Rodgers. Random House.

1943-1944

WINGED VICTORY, by Moss Hart. Random House.
THE SEARCHING WIND, by Lillian Hellman. Viking.
THE VOICE OF THE TURTLE, by John Van Druten. Random House.
DECISION, by Edward Chodorov.
OVER 21, by Ruth Gordon. Random House.
OUTRAGEOUS FORTUNE, by Rose Franken. Samuel French.
JACOBOWSKY AND THE COLONEL, by S. N. Behrman. Random House.
STORM OPERATION, by Maxwell Anderson. Anderson House.
PICK-UP GIRL, by Elsa Shelley.
THE INNOCENT VOYAGE, by Paul Osborn.

1944-1945

A BELL FOR ADANO, by Paul Osborn. Knopf.
I REMEMBER MAMA, by John Van Druten. Harcourt, Brace.
THE HASTY HEART, by John Patrick. Random House.
THE GLASS MENAGERIE, by Tennessee Williams. Random House.
HARVEY, by Mary Chase.
THE LATE GEORGE APLEY, by John P. Marquand and George S. Kaufman.
SOLDIER'S WIFE, by Rose Franken. Samuel French.
ANNA LUCASTA, by Philip Yordan. Random House.
FOOLISH NOTION, by Philip Barry.
DEAR RUTH, by Norman Krasna. Random House.

1945-1946

STATE OF THE UNION, by Howard Lindsay and Russel Crouse. Random House.
HOME OF THE BRAVE, by Arthur Laurents. Random House.
DEEP ARE THE ROOTS, by Arnaud d'Usseau and James Gow. Scribner.
THE MAGNIFICENT YANKEE, by Emmet Lavery. Samuel French.
ANTIGONE, by Lewis Galantiere (from the French of Jean Anouilh). Random House.
O MISTRESS MINE, by Terence Rattigan. Published and revised by the author.

BORN YESTERDAY, by Garson Kanin. Viking.
DREAM GIRL, by Elmer Rice. Coward-McCann.
THE RUGGED PATH, by Robert E. Sherwood. Scribner.
LUTE SONG, by Will Irwin and Sidney Howard. Published version
by Will Irwin and Leopoldine Howard.

1946-1947

ALL MY SONS, by Arthur Miller. Reynal & Hitchcock.
THE ICEMAN COMETH, by Eugene G. O'Neill. Random House.
JOAN OF LORRAINE, by Maxwell Anderson. Published by Maxwell
Anderson.
ANOTHER PART OF THE FOREST, by Lillian Hellman. Viking.
YEARS AGO, by Ruth Gordon. Viking.
JOHN LOVES MARY, by Norman Krasna. Copyright by Norman
Krasna.
THE FATAL WEAKNESS, by George Kelly. Samuel French.
THE STORY OF MARY SURRATT, by John Patrick. Dramatists' Play
Service.
CHRISTOPHER BLAKE, by Moss Hart. Random House.
BRIGADOON, by Alan Jay Lerner and Frederick Loewe. Coward-
McCann.

1947-1948

A STREETCAR NAMED DESIRE, by Tennessee Williams. New Direc-
tions.
MISTER ROBERTS, by Thomas Heggen and Joshua Logan. Houghton
Mifflin.
COMMAND DECISION, by William Wister Haines. Random House.
THE WINSLOW BOY, by Terence Rattigan.
THE HEIRESS, by Ruth and Augustus Goetz.
ALLEGRO, by Richard Rodgers and Oscar Hammerstein 2d. Knopf.
Music published by Williamson Music, Inc.
EASTWARD IN EDEN, by Dorothy Gardner. Longmans, Green.
SKIPPER NEXT TO GOD, by Jan de Hartog.
AN INSPECTOR CALLS, by J. B. Priestley.
ME AND MOLLY, by Gertrude Berg.

1948-1949

DEATH OF A SALESMAN, by Arthur Miller. Viking.
ANNE OF THE THOUSAND DAYS, by Maxwell Anderson. Sloane.
THE MADWOMAN OF CHAILLOT, by Maurice Valency, adapted from
the French of Jean Giraudoux. Random House.
DETECTIVE STORY, by Sidney Kingsley. Random House.

EDWARD, MY SON, by Robert Morley and Noel Langley. Random House, New York, and Samuel French, London.

LIFE WITH MOTHER, by Howard Lindsay and Russel Crouse. Knopf.

LIGHT UP THE SKY, by Moss Hart. Random House.

THE SILVER WHISTLE, by Robert Edward McEnroe. Dramatists' Play Service.

TWO BLIND MICE, by Samuel Spewack. Dramatists' Play Service.

GOODBYE, MY FANCY, by Fay Kanin. Samuel French.

1949-1950

THE COCKTAIL PARTY, by T. S. Eliot. Harcourt, Brace.

THE MEMBER OF THE WEDDING, by Carson McCullers. Houghton Mifflin.

THE INNOCENTS, by William Archibald. Coward-McCann.

LOST IN THE STARS, by Maxwell Anderson and Kurt Weill. Sloane.

COME BACK, LITTLE SHEBA, by William Inge. Random House.

THE HAPPY TIME, by Samuel Taylor. Random House.

THE WISTERIA TREES, by Joshua Logan. Random House.

I KNOW MY LOVE, by S. N. Behrman. Random House.

THE ENCHANTED, by Maurice Valency, adapted from a play by Jean Giraudoux. Random House.

CLUTTERBUCK, by Benn W. Levy. Dramatists' Play Service.

WHERE AND WHEN THEY WERE BORN

(Compiled from the most authentic records available)

Abbott, George .... Forestville, N. Y. 1895
Abel, Walter .... St. Paul, Minn. 1898
Adams, Maude .... Salt Lake City, Utah 1872
Addy, Wesley .... Omaha, Neb. 1912
Aherne, Brian .... King's Norton, England 1902
Aldrich, Richard .... Boston 1902
Anders, Glenn .... Los Angeles, Cal. 1890
Anderson, Judith .... Australia 1898
Anderson, Maxwell .... Atlantic City, Pa. 1888
Andrews, A. G. .... Buffalo, N. Y. 1861
Arthur, Jean .... New York City 1905
Ashcroft, Peggy .... Croydon, Eng. 1907

Bainter, Fay .... Los Angeles, Cal. 1892
Bankhead, Tallulah .... Huntsville, Ala. 1902
Banks, Leslie .... West Derby, England 1890
Barrymore, Ethel .... Philadelphia, Pa. 1879
Barrymore, Lionel .... Philadelphia, Pa. 1878
Barton, James .... Gloucester, N. J. 1890
Behrman, S. N. .... Worcester, Mass. 1893
Bell, James .... Suffolk, Va. 1891
Bellamy, Ralph .... Chicago, Ill. 1905
Belmore, Bertha .... Manchester, England 1882
Bergman, Ingrid .... Stockholm 1917
Bergner, Elisabeth .... Vienna 1901
Berlin, Irving .... Russia 1888
Blackmer, Sidney .... Salisbury, N. C. 1898
Bolger, Ray .... Dorchester, Mass. 1906
Bondi, Beulah .... Chicago, Ill. 1892
Bourneuf, Philip .... Boston, Mass. 1912
Boyer, Charles .... Figeac, France 1899
Braham, Horace .... London, England 1896
Brent, Romney .... Saltillo, Mex. 1902
Brice, Fannie .... Brooklyn, N. Y. 1891
Bruce, Carol .... Great Neck, L. I. 1919
Bruce, Nigel .... San Diego, Cal. 1895

Burke, Billie .... Washington, D. C. 1885
Buckmaster, John .... Essex, Eng. 1915
Byington, Spring .... Colorado Springs, Colo. 1898

Cagney, James .... New York 1904
Cagney, Jeanne .... New York 1920
Calhern, Louis .... New York 1895
Cantor, Eddie .... New York 1894
Carlisle, Kitty .... New Orleans, La. 1912
Carnovsky, Morris .... St. Louis, Mo. 1898
Carradine, John .... New York City 1906
Carroll, Leo G. .... Weedon, England 1892
Carroll, Madeleine .... West Bromwich, England 1906
Catlett, Walter .... San Francisco, Cal. 1889
Caulfield, Joan .... New York City 1924
Chase, Ilka .... New York City 1905
Chatterton, Ruth .... New York 1893
Christians, Mady .... Vienna, Austria 1907
Claire, Ina .... Washington, D. C. 1892
Clark, Bobby .... Springfield, Ohio 1888
Clift, Montgomery .... Omaha, Neb. 1921
Clive, Colin .... St. Malo, France 1900
Coburn, Charles .... Macon, Ga. 1877
Collinge, Patricia .... Dublin 1894
Collins, Russell .... New Orleans, La. 1901
Colt, Ethel Barrymore ...... Mamaroneck, N. Y. 1911
Colt, John Drew .... New York 1914
Conroy, Frank .... London, England 1885
Cook, Donald .... Portland, Ore. 1902
Cook, Joe .... Evansville, Ind. 1890
Cooper, Melville .... Birmingham, England 1896
Corbett, Leonora .... London, England 1908
Cornell, Katharine .... Berlin, Germany 1898
Cossart, Ernest .... Cheltenham, England 1876
Coulouris, George .... Manchester, England 1906
Coward, Noel .... Teddington, England 1899
Cowl, Jane .... Boston, Mass 1887
Crothers, Rachel .... Bloomington, Ill. 1878
Cummings, Constance ...... Seattle, Wash. 1911

Dale, Margaret .... Philadelphia, Pa. 1880
Daniell, Henry .... London 1904
Davis, Owen .... Portland, Me. 1874
Derwent, Clarence .... London 1884

Dixon, Jean .... Waterbury, Conn. 1905
Douglas, Susan .... Prague, Czechoslovakia 1925
Dowling, Eddie .... Woonsocket, R. I. 1895
Drake, Alfred .... New York City 1914
Dressler, Eric .... Brooklyn, N. Y. 1900
Duncan, Augustin .... San Francisco 1873
Duncan, Todd .... Danville, Ky. 1900
Dunning, Philip .... Meriden, Conn. 1890
Durante, Jimmy .... New York City 1893

Eldridge, Florence .... Brooklyn, N. Y. 1901
Evans, Edith .... London, England 1888
Evans, Maurice .... Dorchester, England 1901
Evans, Wilbur .... Philadelphia, Pa. 1908
Evelyn, Judith .... Seneca, S. Dak. 1913
Ewell, Tom............... Owensboro, Ky. 1912

Fabray, Nanette .... New Orleans, La. 1921
Fay, Frank .... San Francisco 1897
Ferber, Edna .... Kalamazoo, Mich. 1887
Ferrer, Jose .... Puerto Rico 1912
Field, Betty .... Boston 1918
Field, Virginia .... London 1917
Fields, Gracie .... Rochdale, England 1890
Fitzgerald, Barry .... Dublin, Ireland 1888
Fitzgerald, Geraldine ...... Dublin, Ireland 1914
Flemyng, Robert .... Liverpool 1912
Fletcher, Bramwell .... Bradford, Yorkshire, Eng. ... 1904
Fonda, Henry .... Grand Island, Neb. 1905
Fontanne, Lynn .... London, England 1887
Forbes, Brenda .... London, England 1909
Forbes, Ralph .... London, England 1905
Foy, Eddie, Jr. .... New Rochelle, N. Y. 1907
Francis, Arlene .... Boston, Mass. 1908
Fraser, Elizabeth .... Brooklyn, N. Y. 1920

Gaxton, William .... San Francisco, Cal. 1893
Geddes, Barbara Bel .... New York 1922
Geddes, Norman Bel .... Adrian, Mich. 1893
George, Grace .... New York City 1879
Gershwin, Ira .... New York 1896
Gielgud, John .... London, England 1904
Gillmore, Margalo .... England 1901
Gilmore, Virginia .... El Monte, Cal. 1919

Gish, Dorothy .... Dayton, Ohio 1898
Gish, Lillian .... Springfield, Ohio 1896
Golden, John .... New York 1874
Goodner, Carol .... New York City 1904
Gordon, Ruth .... Wollaston, Mass. 1896
Gough, Lloyd .... New York City 1906
Greaza, Walter .... St. Paul, Minn. 1900
Green, Mitzi .... New York City 1920
Greenstreet, Sydney .... England 1880
Guinness, Alec .... London 1904
Gwenn, Edmund .... Glamorgan, Wales 1875

Hammerstein, Oscar, II ...... New York City 1895
Hampden, Walter .... Brooklyn, N. Y. 1879
Hannen, Nicholas .... London, England 1881
Hardie, Russell .... Griffin Mills, N. Y. 1906
Hardwicke, Sir Cedric .... Lye, Stourbridge, England 1893
Harris, Julie .... Grosse Point, Mich. 1936
Harrison, Rex .... Huyton, England 1908
Hart, Moss .... New York City 1904
Hart, Richard .... Providence, R. I. 1915
Havoc, June .... Seattle, Wash. 1916
Haydon, Julie .... Oak Park, Ill. 1910
Hayes, Helen .... Washington, D. C. 1900
Heflin, Frances .... Oklahoma City, Okla. 1924
Heineman, Eda .... Japan 1891
Henie, Sonja .... Oslo, Norway 1912
Hepburn, Katharine .... Hartford, Conn. 1907
Hiller, Wendy .... Bramhall, England 1902
Holliday, Judy .... New York City 1924
Holmes, Taylor .... Newark, N. J. 1872
Homolka, Oscar .... Vienna 1898
Hull, Josephine .... Newtonville, Mass. 1886
Hull, Henry .... Louisville, Ky. 1888
Hunt, Martita .... Argentine Republic 1900
Hussey, Ruth .... Providence, R. I. 1917

Inescort, Frieda .... Hitchin, Scotland 1905
Ives, Burl .... Hunt Township, Ill. 1909

Jolson, Al .... Washington, D. C. 1883
Johnson, Harold J. (Chic) ... Chicago, Ill. 1891
Joy, Nicholas .... Paris, France 1892

Kane, Whitford .... Larne, Ireland 1882
Kanin, Garson .... Rochester, N. Y. 1912
Karloff, Boris .... Dulwich, England 1887
Kaufman, George S. .... Pittsburgh, Pa. 1889
Kaye, Danny .... New York City ...¯.........1914
Kazan, Elia .... Constantinople 1909
Keith, Robert .... Fowler, Ind. 1898
Kilbride, Percy .... San Francisco, Cal. 1880
King, Dennis .... Coventry, England 1897
Kingsford, Walter .... England 1881
Kingsley, Sidney .... New York City 1906
Kirkland, Patricia .... New York 1927
Knox, Alexander .... Ontario 1907
Kruger, Otto .... Toledo, Ohio 1885

Lackland, Ben .... Waco, Texas 1901
Landis, Jessie Royce .... Chicago, Ill. 1904
Laughton, Charles .... Scarborough, England 1899
Lawrence, Gertrude .... London 1898
LeGallienne, Eva .... London 1899
Leighton, Margaret .... Barnt Green, England 1922
Lillie, Beatrice .... Toronto, Canada 1898
Lindsay, Howard .... Waterford, N. Y. 1899
Linn, Bambi .... Brooklyn, N. Y. 1926
Loeb, Philip .... Philadelphia, Pa. 1892
Lockhart, Gene .... Ontario 1892
Lonergan, Lenore .... Toledo, Ohio 1928
Lord, Pauline .... Hanford, Cal. 1890
Lunt, Alfred .... Milwaukee, Wis. 1893
Lytell, Bert .... New York City 1885

MacMahon, Aline .... McKeesport, Pa. 1899
Mamoulian, Rouben .... Tiflis 1898
Mantle, Burns .... Watertown, N. Y. 1873
March, Fredric .... Racine, Wis. 1897
Margetson, Arthur .... London, England 1897
Martin, Mary .... Weatherford, Texas 1913
Mason, James .... Huddersfield, England 1909
Massey, Raymond .... Toronto, Canada 1896
Matteson, Ruth .... San Jose, Cal... 1905
McClintic, Guthrie .... Seattle, Wash. 1893
McCormick, Myron .... Albany, Ind. 1907
McCracken, Joan .... Philadelphia, Pa. 1923

McGrath, Paul .... Chicago, Ill. 1900
McGuire, Dorothy .... Omaha, Neb. 1918
Menotti, Gian-Carlo .... Italy 1912
Meredith, Burgess .... Cleveland, Ohio 1908
Merman, Ethel .... Astoria, R. I. 1909
Middleton, Ray .... Chicago, Ill. 1907
Miller, Gilbert .... New York 1884
Mitchell, Thomas .... Elizabeth, N. J. 1892
Moore, Victor .... Hammondton, N. J. 1876
Morgan, Claudia .... New York 1912
Morley, Robert .... Semley, England 1908
Morris, McKay .... San Antonio, Texas 1890
Moss, Arnold .... Brooklyn, N. Y. 1910
Muni, Paul .... Lemberg, Austria 1895

Nagel, Conrad .... Keokuk, Iowa 1897
Natwick, Mildred .... Baltimore 1908
Nesbitt, Cathleen .... Cheshire, England 1889
Nugent, Elliott .... Dover, Ohio 1900

Odets, Clifford .... Philadelphia 1906
Oenslager, Donald .... Harrisburg, Pa. 1902
Olivier, Sir Laurence ...... Dorking, Surrey, England 1907
Olsen, John Siguard (Ole) ... Peru, Ind. 1892
O'Malley, Rex .... London, England 1906
O'Neal, Frederick .... Brookville, Miss. 1905
O'Neill, Eugene Gladstone ... New York 1888

Palmer, Lilli .... Austria 1904
Petina, Irra .... Leningrad, Russia 1900
Picon, Molly .... New York City 1898
Pinza, Ezio .... Rome, Italy 1895
Porter, Cole .... Peru, Indiana 1892
Price, Vincent .... St. Louis, Mo. 1914

Raitt, John .... Santa Ana, Cal. 1917
Rathbone, Basil .... Johannesburg, ... 1892
Redman, Joyce .... Newcastle, Ireland 1918
Reed, Florence .... Philadelphia, Pa. 1883
Rennie, James .... Toronto, Canada 1890
Richardson, Sir Ralph ...... Cheltenham, England 1902
Rice, Elmer .... New York City 1892
Roberts, Joan .... New York City 1918

Rodgers, Richard .... New York City 1902
Ross, Anthony .... New York 1906
Royle, Selena .... New York 1905

Sarnoff, Dorothy .... Brooklyn, N. Y. 1919
Scheff, Fritzi .... Vienna, Austria 1879
Scott, Martha .... Jamesport, Mo. 1914
Segal, Vivienne .... Philadelphia, Pa. 1897
Shaw, Bernard .... Dublin 1856
Sherman, Hiram .... Boston, Mass. 1908
Sherwood, Robert Emmet .... New Rochelle, N. Y. 1896
Shubert, Lee .... Syracuse, N. Y. 1875
Simms, Hilda .... Minneapolis, Minn. 1920
Skinner, Cornelia Otis .... Chicago 1902
Smith, Kent .... Smithfield, Me. 1910
Stickney, Dorothy .... Dickinson, N. D. 1903
Stoddard, Haila .... Great Falls, Mont. 1914
Stone, Carol .... New York 1917
Stone, Dorothy .... New York 1905
Stone, Ezra .... New Bedford, Mass. 1918
Stone, Fred .... Denver, Colo. 1873
Sullavan, Margaret .... Norfolk, Va. 1910
Sullivan, Francis L. .... London 1903

Tandy, Jessica .... London, Eng. 1909
Tetzel, Joan .... New York 1923
Thomas, John Charles .... Baltimore, Md. 1887
Tozere, Frederick .... Brookline, Mass. 1901
Tracy, Lee .... Atlanta 1898
Truex, Ernest .... Red Hill, Mo. 1890

Van Druten, John .... London, Eng. 1902
Van Patten, Dick .... New York 1929
Van Patten, Joyce .... New York City 1934
Varden, Evelyn .... Venita, Okla. 1893

Walker, Nancy .... Philadelphia, Pa. 1922
Walker, June .... New York 1904
Wanamaker, Sam .... Chicago, Ill. 1919
Ward, Penelope .... London, England 1914
Warfield, David .... San Francisco, Cal. 1866
Waring, Richard .... Buckinghamshire, England ... 1912
Waters, Ethel .... Chester, Pa. 1900

Watson, Lucile .... Quebec, Canada 1879
Watson, Minor .... Marianna, Ark. 1889
Webb, Clifton .... Indiana 1891
Webster, Margaret .... New York City 1905
Welles, Orson .... Kenosha, Wis. 1915
West, Mae .... Brooklyn, N. Y. 1892
Weston, Ruth .... Boston, Mass. 1911
Widmark, Richard .... Sunrise, Minn. 1914
Wilder, Thornton .... Madison, Wis. 1897
Willard, Catherine .... Dayton, Ohio 1895
Williams, Emlyn .... Wales 1905
Williams, Rhys .... Wales 1903
Wiman, Dwight Deere ...... Moline, Ill. 1895
Winwood, Estelle .... England 1883
Wood, Peggy .... Brooklyn, N. Y. 1894
Wyatt, Jane .... Campgaw, N. J. 1912
Wynn, Ed .... Philadelphia, Pa. 1886
Wynn, Keenan .... New York City 1917

Yurka, Blanche .... Bohemia 1893

NECROLOGY

Allgood, Sara, 66, actress. Made stage debut in London in 1904 with Irish National Players; had a long career with Abbey Players in Dublin; appeared in New York in a revival of "Juno and the Paycock" in 1940; appeared in many British and American films. Born Dublin; died Hollywood, September 13, 1950.

Anderson, Julia, 86, actress and playwright. An early David Belasco student at the American Academy of Dramatic Art; had a success in "A Wife's Secret" in 1888; wrote "The Day After," "Jack Cortney's Wife" and "Rainbow Follies of 1922." Born Holland; died New York, July 3, 1950.

Andrews, Albert G., 82, actor. Made first stage appearance in 1862 in "Masks and Faces" and his last one in 1944 as the servant in Eva Le Gallienne's revival of "The Cherry Orchard." He survived his wife, actress Winona Shannon, less than a month. Born London; died New York, November 26, 1950.

Armstrong, Harry, 72, songwriter. Wrote 300 songs, including "Sweet Adeline," "I Love My Wife but Oh You Kid" and "Can't You See I'm Lonely." Began as a prize fighter in Boston. Died New York, February 28, 1951.

Brentano, Lowell, 55, playwright, novelist, editor. Was co-author of "The Spider," "Zeppelin," "Great Lady" and other plays and librettos. Born New York; died New York, July 8, 1950.

Brice, Fanny, 59, actress. Won fame singing "My Man" in Ziegfeld "Follies," was "Follies" star from 1916 on; took her stage characterization of Baby Snooks into radio in 1938 and had an 11-year run. Born New York; died Hollywood, May 29, 1951.

Bridie, James, 63, playwright. Real name, Dr. Osborne Henry Mavor. First play, "The Sunlight Sonata," was a success in Glasgow in 1928; first London hit was "The Anatomist"; his last play, "Daphne Laureola," was produced on Broadway in 1950. Born Glasgow; died Edinburgh, January 29, 1951.

Carpenter, Edward Chids, 76, playwright and novelist. Was author or co-author of "The Dragon Fly," "The Challenge," "Bab," "The Bachelor Father," "Whistling in the Dark" and many other plays. Born Philadelphia; died Torrington, Conn., October 7, 1950.

Clayton, Lou, 63, singer. Was member of the night club and vaudeville team of Clayton, Jackson and Durante; became Jimmy Durante's manager when the latter left the stage for films and radio. Born New York; died Santa Monica, Calif., September 12, 1950.

Cochran, Sir Charles B., 78, producer. At age of 18 came to New York to be an actor, but with modest success, although he did tour with Joseph Jefferson in "Rip van Winkle." Was secretary to Richard Mansfield; became producer with "John Gabriel Borkman" in 1897 in New York; first London production was "Sporting Simpson" in 1902; first London success was "The Miracle" in 1911. Sir Charles developed such stars as Beatrice Lillie and Noel Coward. Born Sussex, England; died London, January 31, 1951.

Cossart, Ernest, 74, actor. Made debut in London in 1896; made New York debut in 1906 in "The Girls of Gottenberg"; played Shaw and Shakespeare with Granville Barker; was in many Theatre Guild plays, also in many films. Born Cheltenham, England; died New York, January 21, 1951.

Costello, Maurice, 73, actor. Began with amateur acting company in Pittsburgh. Played leading roles in New York and soon became a pioneer film actor with Edison and Vitagraph. Born Pittsburgh; died Hollywood, October 29, 1950.

Cowl, Jane, 65, actress, dramatist. Reached stardom in 1912 in "Within the Law." Successes included "Easy Virtue," "The Road to Rome," "Romeo and Juliet," "Lilac Time" and "Smilin' Through." With Jane Murfin wrote "Lilac Time," "Smilin' Through" and other plays. Born Boston; died Santa Monica, Calif., June 22, 1950.

Dean, John W. (Jack), 75, actor. Played on New York stage and in silent films; was married to Fannie Ward. Born Bridgeport, Conn.; died New York, June 23, 1950.

De Cordoba, Pedro, 68, actor. Made debut with E. H. Sothern in 1902; was with Sothern-Marlowe company and the New Theatre; was in "Candida," "See Naples and Die" and many other Broadway plays; often played the role of a priest in films. Born New York; died Hollywood, September 17, 1950.

De Sylva, B. G. (Buddy), 55; author and stage and screen producer. Wrote lyrics for "Sinbad" in 1918; hits included several George White "Scandals," "Sally," "Queen High," "Manhattan Mary," "Flying High" and "Follow Thru." Member of pro-

ducing firm of De Sylva, Brown & Henderson; was motion
picture producer during latter years. Born New York; died
Hollywood, July 11, 1950.

De Wolfe, Elsie, 84, actress. Played for Charles Frohman in the
1880s and 1890s; had a success in Sardou's "Thermidor" in
1891; when she was with John Drew his niece, Ethel Barrymore, was her understudy; retired from stage in early 1900s
and became an interior decorator; married Sir Charles Mendl,
British diplomat, in 1926. Born New York; died Versailles,
July 12, 1950.

Edney, Florence, 71, actress. Began New York career in 1906 at
the Garrick Theatre in "The Price of Money"; was in "To-
paze," "The School for Scandal," "A Widow in Green," "Water-
loo Bridge," "Barchester Towers" and "Ladies in Retirement."
Specialized in cockney character maid roles. Born London;
died New York, November 24, 1950.

Ellinger, Desiree, 57, actress. Won great publicity in New York
in 1925 by flying in an open-cockpit biplane from Boston to
replace the ailing Mary Ellis in "Rose Marie"; also appeared
in New York in "The Wild Rose," "Cherry Blossoms" and
"Kiss Me." Born Manchester, England; died London, April
30, 1951.

Elliott, Gertrude, 76, actress. Made stage debut in New York in
1894; two of her most famous parts were in "Caesar and Cleo-
patra" and "The Light That Failed"; was Ophelia to the Hamlet of her husband, Sir Johnston Forbes-Robertson. Was sister
of Maxine Elliott. Born Rockland, Me.; died Kent, England,
December 24, 1950.

Elliston, Grace, 72, actress. Began as chorus girl with Frank
Daniels' Opera Company; was in the companies of many stars,
including Henry Miller, Nat Goodwin, George Arliss, Ethel
Barrymore, Richard Bennett, William Farnum and Willie Col-
lier. Founded Theatre Workshop at Stockbridge, Mass. Born
Memphis; died Lenox, Mass., December 14, 1950.

Forbes, Ralph, 45, actor. Began career in silent films in London,
then switched to stage; made New York debut in "Havoc" and
appeared in "The Green Hat," "The Swan," "The Man with a
Load of Mischief" and many other plays; also appeared in
many films. Born London; died New York, March 31, 1951.

Gates, Eleanor, 75, playwright and novelist. Wrote "The Poor
Little Rich Girl," "Pa Hardy" and other plays, and helped her
husband, Richard Walton Tully, write "The Bird of Paradise."
Born Shakopee, Minn.; died Los Angeles, March 7, 1951.

Graham, Ronald, 38, actor. Appeared in "The Boys from Syracuse," "Du Barry Was a Lady," "By Jupiter" and other musicals; also appeared in movies and on radio. Born Scotland; died New York, July 4, 1950.

Greet, Maurice, 70, actor. Nephew of Sir Philip Ben Greet. Made stage debut in "Midsummer Night's Dream" at age of 5; came to U. S. with Ben Greet Players in 1904; last appearance in 1932 with Fay Bainter in "The Man Who Changed His Name." Since then, operated a drama school in Washington, D. C. Born England; died Washington, May 29, 1951.

Grunwald, Alfred, 67, librettist. In Austria wrote librettos of "Countess Maritza," "The Yankee Princess," "The Last Waltz," "The Duchess of Chicago" and other musical hits. Born Vienna; died New York, February 24, 1951.

Hart, Richard, 35, actor. In 1945 had first Broadway success in "Dark of the Moon"; also was in "The Happy Time"; made several films and played Ellery Queen on television. Born Providence, R. I.; died New York, January 2, 1951.

Herne, Chrystal, 67, actress. Daughter of famed actor James A. Herne; made debut at age of 16 in a role written for her by her father in "Griffith Davenport." She played in "Shore Acres" and "Sag Harbor" and was E. H. Sothern's Queen in "Hamlet" in 1902; played first American performances of Shaw plays with Arnold Daly; last appearance was in "A Room in Red and White" in 1936. Born Dorchester, Mass.; died New York, September 19, 1950.

Jolson, Al (Asa Yoelson), actor, 64. As a boy sang in Washington, D. C., cafés and as a youth sang in New York saloons; went into vaudeville, then with Dockstader's Minstrels; in March, 1911, appeared at the Winter Garden in "La Belle Paree" and became a star in other Winter Garden shows, including "The Whirl of Society" and "Robinson Crusoe, Jr."; in 1921 starred in "Bombo" at the Jolson Theatre; in 1927 made first sound movie, "The Jazz Singer"; made last appearance on New York stage in "Wonder Bar" in 1931. Born St. Petersburg; died San Francisco, October 24, 1950.

Jordan, Walter C., 74, play broker and producer. Handled stage rights to "The Merry Widow," "Floradora," "Seven Days Leave" and many other hits; built Broadway's National Theatre in 1921 and operated it for many years. Born New York; died New York, November 13, 1951.

Kahn, Florence, 74, actress. Was leading lady for Richard Mansfield and played Roxane to his Cyrano; married Sir Max

Beerbohm in 1908 and retired from the stage until 1931, when she appeared in London in Pirandello's "The Life I Gave You." Born Memphis; died Rapallo, Italy, January 13, 1951.

LeMaire, Rufus, 55, producer. Was associated with his brother, George, in producing "Broadway Brevities" in 1920 and later produced a variety hit, "LeMaire's Affairs"; in 1931 began Hollywood career as casting director. Born New York; died Hollywood, December 2, 1950.

Linley, Betty, 61, actress. Came to New York in 1917 to understudy Lenore Ulric in "Tiger Rose"; appeared in "Hay Fever," "The Dybbuk" and "Six Cylinder Love," and toured in "Life with Father." Born Malmesbury, England; died New York, May 10, 1951.

Lord, Pauline, 60, actress. Made debut in Belasco Stock Company, San Francisco, in "Are You a Mason?" in 1903; notable roles included leads in "Anna Christie," "They Knew What They Wanted," "The Late Christopher Bean," and "Ethan Frome." Born near San Francisco; died Alamogordo, New Mexico, October 11, 1950.

Madden, Richard, 71, play broker. Began as company manager for Cohan and Harris; in 1914 joined Elisabeth Marbury and John W. Rumsey in the American Play Company. His clients included Eugene O'Neill, Somerset Maugham, Sean O'Casey, T. S. Eliot, Owen Davis and Cole Porter. He was married to the musical star, Tessa Kosta. Born Poughkeepsie, N. Y.; died New York, May 8, 1951.

Marlowe, Julia, 85, actress. Female half of the great team of Sothern and Marlowe. Made New York debut in 1887 in "Ingomar"; subsequently played Shakespeare almost exclusively. Real name Sarah Frances Frost. Made stage debut in Cincinnati. Born Cumberlandshire, England; died New York November 12, 1950.

Maude, Cyril, 88, actor. Most famous for his "Grumpy." Made stage debut in Denver in "East Lynne" in 1884; in 1925 had a New York hit in "These Charming People." Born London; died Torquay, England, February 20, 1951.

Mayo, Margaret, 68, playwright and actress. Real name Lillian Slatten. Wrote "Baby Mine," "Under Two Flags," "The Wall Street Girl" (with her husband, Edgar Selwyn) and many other plays or adaptations. Acted in "Charley's Aunt" and "Arizona" at the turn of the century. Born Brownsville, Ill.; died Ossining, N. Y., February 9, 1951.

McGlynn, Frank, 84, actor. Best known for his performance of Lincoln in John Drinkwater's "Abraham Lincoln." Made New York debut in "The Gold Bug" in 1896; toured with many Charles Frohman companies; entered films in 1909; made his first appearance as Lincoln in 1919. Born San Francisco; died Newburgh, N. Y., May 18, 1951.

Mendelssohn, Eleonora, 51, actress. Was leading woman for Max Reinhardt in Germany before Hitler; appeared in New York in "The Madwoman of Chaillot" and other plays. Was great-granddaughter of Felix Mendelssohn, the composer. Born Germany; died New York, January 24, 1951.

Metaxa, Georges, 51, actor. Made stage debut in London in 1926; was in "Bitter Sweet"; had greatest stage success in New York in 1931 in "The Cat and the Fiddle." Born Bucharest; died Monroe, La., December 8, 1950.

Morgan, Charles S. Jr., 75, producer and director. Staged more than 30 Mask & Wig shows at the University of Pennsylvania, beginning in 1895. Also directed for Princeton Triangle Club and the University of Michigan Mimes. On Broadway was with firm of Werba and Luescher; was co-producer of "All for the Ladies" and Victor Herbert's "Sweethearts." Born Pennsylvania; died Philadelphia, November 28, 1950.

Mountford, Harry, 79, actor, dramatist and editor. Helped found the Associated Actors and Artistes of America; edited *Vanity Fair* in 1911-1912; wrote "My Uncle's Love," adapted "Tess of the D'Urbervilles." Born Dublin; died New York, June 4, 1950.

Nethersole, Olga, 80, actress. Made startling success in Clyde Fitch's "Sapho" in 1900. Police stopped the play, but suffragists came to its defense and it reopened. At outbreak of World War I retired from stage, became surgical nurse. Born London; died Bournemouth, England, January 9, 1951.

Nicander, Edwin, 74, actor. Real name Nicander Edwin Rau. Played in stock in the 1890s and was at the Murray Hill Theatre with Laura Hope Crews; later appeared with John Drew, Billie Burke and Henry Miller. Born New York; died New York, January 1, 1951.

Novello, Ivor, 57, actor, composer and producer. Wrote the song, "Keep the Home Fires Burning"; had most of his career in London, but appeared in New York in "The Truth Game" in 1930. Born Cardiff, Wales; died London, March 6, 1951.

Ober, Robert, 69, actor. Began as box office man in St. Louis; played in St. Louis stock; made first New York appearance opposite Fay Templeton in "Forty-five Minutes from Broadway"; starred in "Brewster's Millions," "Ready Money" and "The Humming Bird"—the last-named play by his actress wife, Maude Fulton. Born St. Louis; died New York, December 7, 1950.

Robins, Adolph, 64, clown. Known in vaudeville, musical comedy and circus as "the banana man" for his production of 300 bananas from his clothing. Was a feature of "Jumbo" at the Hippodrome. Born White Plains, N. Y.; died Bournemouth, England, December 18, 1950.

Shannon, Winona, 76, actress. Began touring as Eva in "Uncle Tom's Cabin" at age of 5; was in "Butterfly on the Wheel" and "The Bat." Was married to actor A. G. Andrews and sister of actress Effie Shannon. Born Boston; died New York, October 17, 1951.

Shaw, Bernard, 94, playwright. The most important, most influential and most successful dramatist of his time. Born Dublin; died London, November 2, 1950.

Strange, Michael, 60, author and actress. Wrote "Claire de Lune" and several volumes of poetry; only New York acting appearance was in title role of "L'Aiglon" in 1927; married John Barrymore in 1920, divorced him in 1928. Born New York; died Boston, November 5, 1950.

Tuerk, John, 59, producer. Presented "Within the Gates," "The Command to Love," "The Furies" and other plays. Began theatre career with William A. Brady in 1908. Born New York; died New York, May 25, 1951.

Van, Billy B., 72, actor. Real name William Webster Vandergrift. Made debut in Philadelphia at age of 9; was in "The Rainbow Girl," "Little Nemo" and other plays; toured in vaudeville with James J. Corbett. In 1915 founded Equity Motion Picture Company, the forerunner of Metro-Goldwyn-Mayer. Born Pottstown, Pa.; died Newport, N. H., November 16, 1950.

Vroom, Lodewick, 66, producer and press agent. Began as press agent with Chales Frohman; was general manager for Gilbert and Henry Miller; co-producer of "Rosalinda," producer of "That Old Devil," "Temper the Wind" and other plays. Born St. John, N. B.; died New York, July 5, 1950.

Wiman, Dwight Deere, 55, producer. Studied drama at Yale under Monty Woolley; joined William A. Brady, Jr., as producer of hits including "The Road to Rome," "The Command to Love" and "The Little Show." His own productions included "The Vinegar Tree," "The Gay Divorce," "On Your Toes," "On

Borrowed Time" and "I Married an Angel."   Born Moline, Ill.; died Hudson, N. Y., January 20, 1951.

Woods, A. H., 81, producer. Real name, Albert Herman. One of the most colorful American managers, whose first success was "The Bowery After Dark."   Early hits included "Bertha, the Sewing Machine Girl" and "Nellie the Beautiful Cloak Model."   His last production was "Try and Get It," in 1943. Born New York; died New York, April 4, 1951.

THE DECADES' TOLL

(Prominent Theatrical Figures Who Have Died in Recent Years)

	Born	*Died*
Arliss, George	1869	1946
Baker, George Pierce	1866	1935
Barrymore, John	1882	1942
Bates, Blanche	1873	1941
Belasco, David	1856	1931
Bennett, Richard	1873	1944
Carroll, Earl	1893	1948
Carte, Rupert D'Oyly	1876	1948
Cochran, Charles B.	1872	1951
Cohan, George M.	1878	1942
Collier, Willie	1866	1943
Cowl, Jane	1884	1950
Craven, Frank	1890	1945
Crews, Laura Hope	1880	1942
Crosman, Henrietta	1865	1944
Digges, Dudley	1879	1947
Elliott, Maxine	1871	1940
Eltinge, Julian	1883	1941
Faversham, William	1868	1940
Fields, Lew	1867	1941
Fields, W. C.	1879	1946
Fiske, Harrison Grey	1861	1942
Frohman, Daniel	1851	1940
Gaige, Crosby	1883	1949
Gershwin, George	1898	1937
Gest, Morris	1881	1941
Hart, Lorenz	1895	1943
Hart, William S.	1870	1946
Hooker, Brian	1881	1947
Howard, Willie	1883	1949
Jolson, Al.	1886	1950
Kern, Jerome D.	1885	1945
Lehar, Franz	1870	1948

	Born	*Died*
Leonard, Eddie	1871	1941
Loftus, Cecilia	1876	1943
Lord, Pauline	1890	1950
Mantle, Burns	1873	1948
Marlowe, Julia	1866	1950
Merivale, Philip	1886	1946
Moore, Grace	1901	1947
Morgan, Helen	1900	1941
Nazimova, Alla	1879	1945
Nethersole, Olga	1870	1951
Patterson, Joseph Medill	1879	1946
Perry, Antoinette	1888	1946
Powers, James T.	1862	1943
Reinhardt, Max	1873	1943
Royle, Edwin Milton	1862	1941
Selwyn, Edgar	1875	1944
Shaw, G. B.	1856	1950
Sheldon, Edward	1886	1946
Skinner, Otis	1858	1942
Tarkington, Booth	1869	1946
Tauber, Richard	1890	1948
Tyler, George C.	1867	1946
Weber, Joe	1867	1942
Webster, Ben	1864	1947
Whitty, Dame May	1865	1948
Woods, Al H.	1870	1951
Woollcott, Alexander	1887	1943
Youmans, Vincent	1899	1946

INDEX OF AUTHORS

Abbott, George, 3, 17, 19, 346, 363, 384, 385
Abel, Robert, 42
Ade, George, 382
Adomian, Lan, 345
Aeschylus, 8, 331
Akins, Zoe, 380, 383, 388
Alsberg, Henry G., 385
Anderson, Maxwell, 379, 380, 384, 385, 386, 387, 388, 389, 390, 391, 392, 393
Andreyev, Leonid, 383
Anouilh, Jean, 8, 18, 19, 329, 391
Ansky, S., 385
Anspacher, Louis Kaufman, 382
Archer, William, 383
Archibald, William, 393
Arlen, Michael, 384
Atlas, Leopold, 388
Auerbach, Arnold, 334
Aviva and Hillel, 345

Baker, Melville, 384
Balderston, John, 386
Barrie, James M., 11, 355, 383
Barry, Philip, 9, 19, 283, 307, 339, 383, 384, 385, 386, 387, 389, 391
Bassman, George, 330
Baum, Vicki, 387
Bax, Clifford, 328
Beach, Lewis, 384
Becque, Henri, 312
Behrman, S. N., 17, 387, 388, 389, 391, 393
Belasco, David, 382
Benelli, Sem, 383
Bennett, Robert Russell, 336, 360
Benson, Sally, 22
Berg, Gertrude, 392
Berlin, Irving, 6, 16, 319
Besier, Rudolf, 387
Bevan, Donald, 368
Bhumibol & Chakraband, 309
Biggers, Earl Derr, 382
Blackburn, Maurice, 348
Bolitho, William, 386

Bolton, Guy, 383, 384
Boothe, Clare, 388, 389, 390
Bradford, Roark, 358, 386
Brand, Millen, 305
Bridgers, Ann, 385
Bridgewater, Leslie, 328
Bridie, James, 314
Brighouse, Harold, 43
Britten, Benjamin, 8, 333
Brooks, William, 369
Browne, Maurice, 386
Browne, Porter Emerson, 383
Burrows, Abe, 12, 29, 45, 304, 329, 363, 379
Butler, Rachel Barton, 383
Byrne, Dolly, 383

Capek, Karel, 384
Carroll, Paul Vincent, 389
Casella, Alberto, 386
Chakraband, 309
Chapman, Robert, 100, 305, 349, 379
Chase, Mary Coyle, 380, 391
Chodorov, Edward, 391
Chodorov, Jerome, 390
Cibber, Colley, 328
Clark, Bobby, 309
Clements, Colin, 390
Coffee, Lenore, 389
Cohan, George M., 382, 387
Colton, John, 383
Conkle, E. P., 389
Connelly, Marc, 11, 358, 380, 383, 384, 385, 386, 388
Cormack, Bartlett, 385
Coward, Noel, 43, 387, 390
Cowen, William Joyce, 389
Coxe, Louis O., 100, 305, 349, 379
Crabtree, Paul, 326
Craven, Frank, 383
Crothers, Rachel, 383, 384, 386, 387, 389
Crouse, Russel, 6, 14, 16, 319, 381, 389, 391, 393

413

Crozier, Eric, 8, 333
Crump, Owen, 315

Dane, Clemence, 383
Davis, Donald, 388
Davis, Owen, 380, 383, 388, 390
Dayton, Katharine, 388
de Casalis, Jeanne, 388
de Hartog, Jan, 392
Dell, Floyd, 386
Deval, Jacques, 389
Diamond, David, 347, 357
Dinner, William, 18, 327
Dodd, Lee Wilson, 384
Dolan, Robert Emmett, 350
Drake, W. A., 387
Drinkwater, John, 382
Dukes, Ashley, 312
Dunning, Philip, 385
d'Usseau, Arnaud, 6, 318, 390, 391

Eliot, T. S., 393
Elser, Frank B., 388
Emery, Gilbert, 383, 384
Epstein, Philip G. and Julius J., 42
Ervine, St. John, 382, 383, 386
Evans, Ray, 42

Fain, Sammy, 12, 309, 370
Fauchois, René, 387
Fay, Frank, 36
Ferber, Edna, 9, 341, 384, 385, 387, 388
Ferris, Walter, 386
Field, Salisbury, 383
Fields, Dorothy, 363
Fields, Joseph, 390
Finklehoffe, Fred F., 36, 315
Fitch, Clyde, 382
Flavin, Martin, 386
Forbes, James, 383
Franken, Rose, 387, 390, 391
Fridolin, 10, 31, 348
Fry, Christopher, 7, 14, 18, 324, 329, 379

Galantiere, Lewis, 391
Gale, Zona, 380
Galsworthy, John, 383, 385
Gannon, Kim, 22
Gardner, Dorothy, 392
Gélinas, Gratien, 10, 348

George, Grace, 383
Geraldy, Paul, 383
Gershwin, George and Ira, 380, 387
Gibbs, Wolcott, 6, 14, 16, 237, 307, 317
Gilbert and Sullivan, 27, 33, 345, 347, 350, 351, 353
Gilbert, Clement Scott, 43
Giraudoux, Jean, 43, 308, 392, 393
Glaspell, Susan, 380, 386
Gleason, James, 384
Goetz, Ruth and Augustus, 392
Goldsmith, Clifford, 389
Goldsmith, Oliver, 41
Gordon, Ruth, 391, 392
Gore-Brown, R. F., 387
Goulding, Edmund, 384
Gow, James, 6, 318, 390, 391
Granville-Barker, H. and H., 383, 386
Green, Paul, 3, 10, 344, 380, 385, 387, 388, 390
Greene, Herbert, 330
Guitry, Sasha, 383

Hagan, James, 387
Haines, William Wister, 392
Hamilton, Patrick, 390
Hammerstein, Oscar, II, 3, 12, 14, 21, 32, 360, 372, 379, 381, 391, 392
Harburg, E. Y., 12, 370
Hart, Moss, 43, 380, 386, 388, 389, 390, 391, 392, 393
Harwood, H. M., 387
Hastings, Charlotte, 353
Hayden, John, 388
Hecht, Ben, 9, 337, 386
Heggen, Thomas, 392
Hellman, Lillian, 11, 43, 125, 306, 355, 379, 388, 389, 390, 391, 392
Herbert, F. Hugh, 11, 14, 21, 356, 391
Heyman, Edward, 317
Heyward, Du Bose, 385
Hillel and Aviva, 345
Hilliard, Bob, 309
Holm, John Cecil, 22, 366
Hopkins, Arthur, 385
Houseman, Laurence, 388
Howard, Sidney, 380, 384, 385, 387, 392
Hughes, Hatcher, 380, 384
Hughes, Langston, 7, 323
Hurlbut, William, 385
Huxley, Aldous, 6, 318

Ibsen, Henrik, 3, 9, 10, 312, 339, 344
Inge, William, 393
Irwin, Will, 343, 392

James, Dan, 390
Jeffers, Robinson, 8, 331
Jerome, Helen, 388
Job, Thomas, 390
Jurist, Irma, 352

Kanin, Fay, 393
Kanin, Garson, 5, 313, 369, 392
Katzin, Winifred, 385
Kaufman, George S., 9, 11, 341, 351,
   380, 383, 384, 385, 386, 387, 388, 389,
   390, 391
Kelly, George, 380, 384, 385, 392
Kennedy, Harold J., 40
Kennedy, Mary, 384
Kent, Walter, 22
Kesselring, Joseph, 9, 342, 390
King, Philip, 43
Kingsley, Sidney, 3, 74, 305, 341, 379,
   380, 387, 388, 389, 390, 392
Koch, Howard, 390
Koestler, Arthur, 3, 74, 305, 341
Krasna, Norman, 391, 392
Kroll, Bernice, 352
Kummer, Clare, 382, 387

Lacey, Franklin, 43
Landon, Margaret, 12, 360
Lang, Phil, 363
Langley, Noel, 393
Lardner, Ring W., 386
Laurents, Arthur, 391
Lavery, Emmet, 391
Lawler, James Reed, 352
Lawrence, Reginald, 336
Lerner, Alan Jay, 392
Levy, Benn W., 11, 357, 387, 393
Lewis, Sinclair, 387
Liberman, Leo, 36
Lieberson, Martin R., 354
Lieberson, William H., 354
Lidor, Alexander, 32
Lindsay, Howard, 6, 14, 16, 319, 381,
   389, 391, 393
Livingston, Jay, 42
Loesser, Frank, 45, 304, 329, 346, 379
Loewe, Frederick, 392
Logan, Joshua, 381, 392, 393
Lonsdale, Frederick, 17, 322, 385

Lorca, Federico Garcia, 340
Luhan, James Graham, 340

MacArthur, Charles, 9, 337, 386
MacGrath, Leueen, 11, 351
Magidson, Herb, 309
Malleson, Miles, 41
Manges, Herbert, 344
Marquand, John P., 391
Marquis, Don, 384
Martin, Hugh, 363
Maugham, William Somerset, 383, 385
Mayer, Edwin Justus, 384
McCarthy, Justin Huntly, 382
McCullers, Carson, 379, 393
McEnroe, Robert Edward, 393
McGuire, William Anthony, 383
McLellan, C. M. S., 382
Meloney, Rose Franken, see Franken,
   Rose
Melville, Herman, 10, 74, 100, 305, 349
Menotti, Gian-Carlo, 18, 311
Meyerowitz, Jan, 7, 323
Michel, Scott, 362
Middleton, George, 383
Milholland, Bruce, 337
Miller, Alice D. G., 43
Miller, Arthur, 3, 9, 19, 339, 379, 381,
   392
Milne, Alan Alexander, 383, 386
Mitchell, Thomas, 386
Molière, 11, 22, 23, 41, 359
Molloy, Michael J., 354
Molnar, Ferenc, 4, 12, 362, 383, 384,
   385
Moody, William Vaughn, 382
Morley, Robert, 393
Morris, Lloyd, 391
Morum, William, 18, 327
Mowell, Shelley, 352

Nichols, Robert, 386
Nugent, Elliott, 389

O'Casey, Sean, 385
O'Connell, Richard L., 340
Odets, Clifford, 7, 14, 18, 178, 306, 325,
   361, 388, 389
Olsen and Johnson, 317
O'Neal, James, 37
O'Neill, Eugene, 380, 382, 383, 384,
   385, 387, 392

Osborn, Paul, 389, 390, 391
Overton, Hall, 309

Parker, Louis N., 382
Patrick, John, 17, 321, 391, 392
Phillips, H. I., 309
Phillips, Irving, 43
Pinero, Arthur Wing, 23
Pirandello, 23
Pitot, Genevieve, 320, 336
Pollock, Channing, 383, 385
Porter, Cole, 15, 19, 28, 336
Poulenc, Francis, 329
Pribor, Richard, 363
Priestley, J. B., 392
Pruneau, Philip, 332

Randolph, Clemence, 383
Raphaelson, Samson, 7, 323, 388, 389, 390
Rattigan, Terence, 391, 392
Reed, Mark, 389
Reizenstein, Elmer, 382
Rice, Elmer, 11, 350, 369, 380, 386, 387, 390, 392
Richman, Arthur, 383
Rieti, Vittorio, 360
Riggs, Lynn, 313, 372, 386
Rittman, Trudi, 336
Roblès, Emmanuel, 306
Rodgers, Richard, 3, 12, 14, 21, 360, 372, 379, 381, 391, 392
Rome, Harold, 309, 334
Roos, William, 22, 309
Root, Lynn, 43
Rotter, Fritz, 390
Royal, Ted, 330, 371
Royle, Edwin Milton, 382
Runyon, Damon, 3, 45, 305, 329
Ryerson, Florence, 43, 390
Ryskind, Morrie, 380, 387

Saidy, Fred, 12, 370
Saroyan, William, 379, 380, 389
Sartre, Jean-Paul, 23
Schulman, Joseph, 354
Schumer, Leo, 352
Schwartz, Arthur, 363
Scott, Raymond, 309
Selver, Paul, 384
Selwyn, Edgar, 384
Shairp, Mordaunt, 346, 347, 388

Shakespeare, William, 21, 23, 40, 43, 309, 337, 343, 356, 365
Shapiro, Dan, 309
Shaw, George Bernard, 7, 11, 23, 37, 40, 41, 321, 338, 367
Sheldon, Edward, 382
Shelley, Elsa, 391
Sheridan, Richard Brinsley, 42
Sherriff, R. C., 386, 388
Sherwood, Robert E., 9, 19, 283, 307, 339, 371, 380, 385, 387, 388, 389, 392
Shiffrin, A. B., 343
Sierra, G. Martinez, 385, 386
Small, Allan, 363
Smith, Betty, 12, 363
Smith, Dodie, 388
Smith, Harry James, 382
Snow, Davis, 364
Spewack, Bella, 388
Spewack, Samuel, 28, 331, 388, 393
Stallings, Laurence, 384
Steinbeck, John, 6, 17, 320, 379, 389, 390
Stept, Sammy, 309
Stewart, Donald Ogden, 24, 386
Stewart, Mike, 352
Storm, Leslie, 5, 316
Sturges, Preston, 3, 12, 362, 386
Styne, Jule, 309
Swerling, Jo, 45, 304, 329, 379

Tarkington, Booth, 22, 382
Taylor, Dwight, 336
Taylor, Samuel, 35, 41, 393
Thomas, A. E., 387
Thomas, Augustus, 382
Thomas, Brandon, 346
Thurber, James, 389
Tiffault, Leighton, 326
Tors, Ivan, 42
Totheroh, Dan, 384
Treadwell, Sophie, 386, 390
Trzcinski, Edmund, 368
Turney, Robert, 388

Underhill, John Garrett, 385

Vajda, Ernest, 43
Valency, Maurice, 308, 392, 393
Vanbrugh, John, 8, 328
Van Druten, John, 7, 14, 18, 155, 306, 325, 385, 388, 391
Vane, Sutton, 384

Varesi, Gilda, 383
Verneuil, Louis, 5, 259, 307, 315
Vincent, Allen, 390
Vivanco, Moises, 371
Vollmer, Lula, 384

Walden, William, 43
Walker, Don, 320, 334
Walter, Eugene, 307, 382
Warren, Ruth, 384
Watkins, Maurine, 385
Watters, George Manker, 385
Weill, Kurt, 393
Weitzenkorn, Louis, 386
Wells, Billy K., 309
Wexley, John, 386, 387
Wilder, Thornton, 380, 389, 390

Williams, Emlyn, 390
Williams, Jesse Lynch, 380, 382
Williams, Tennessee, 10, 31, 40, 43,
    210, 306, 347, 379, 381, 391, 392
Wilson, Edmund, 12, 23, 366
Wilson, Harry Leon, 382, 384
Winter, Keith, 388
Wodehouse, P. G., 385
Wolfson, Victor, 326, 389
Wouk, Herman, 43
Wright, Richard, 390
Wycherley, William, 23

Yordan, Philip, 391
Young, Victor, 317

Zilboorg, Gregory, 383

INDEX OF PLAYS AND CASTS

Bold face page numbers refer to pages on which
Cast of Characters may be found.

Abe Lincoln in Illinois, 380, 389
Abie's Irish Rose, 377
Abraham Lincoln, 382
Accent on Youth, 388
Adam and Eva, 383
Adding Machine, The, 35
Adonis, 378
Affairs of State, 5, 27, 259, 307, **315**
Ah, Wilderness, 387
Alien Corn, 387
Alison's House, 380, 386
All My Sons, 379, 392
Allegro, 392
Ambush, 383
American Way, The, 389
Amphitryon 38, 389
Androcles and the Lion, 23
Angel in the Pawnshop, 9, 31, 33, **343**
Angel Street, 15, 377, 390
Angels Kiss Me, 12, 27, 30, **362**
Animal Kingdom, The, 387
Anna and the King of Siam, 3, 12, **360**
Anna Christie, 380, 383
Anna Lucasta, 377, 391
Anne of the Thousand Days, 43, 392
Annie Get Your Gun, 377
Another Language, 387
Another Part of the Forest, 306, 392
Antigone, 391
Apple of His Eye, The, 15, 40
Arms and the Man, 7, 23, **321**
Arsenic and Old Lace, 9, 43, 377, 390
As Husbands Go, 386
As You Like It, 27, 28, 36, 40
Autumn Garden, The, 11, 27, 29, 125, 306, **355**
Awake and Sing, 178, 306, 388

Bad Man, The, 383
Ballet Ballads, 42
Ballets de Paris, Les, 36, 40
Barbara Frietchie, 382
Barretts of Wimpole Street, The, 40, 387
Barrier, The, 7, **323**
Bat, The, 377
Beggar on Horseback, 384
Behold the Bridegroom, 385
Bell, Book and Candle, 7, 14, 18, 155, 306, **325**
Bell for Adano, A, 391
Berkeley Square, 386
Beyond the Horizon, 380, 382
Big Knife, The, 7, 178, 306
Bill of Divorcement, A, 383
Billy Budd, 10, 27, 29, 74, 100, 305, **349**, 379
Biography, 387
Bird in Hand, 378
Black Chiffon, 5, 14, 16, **316**
Blackbirds, 378
Blackouts, 39
Bless You All, 8, 26, 28, **334**
Blind Alley, 16
Blithe Spirit, 377, 390
Bloomer Girl, 377
Blossom Time, 19, 27, 29, 378
Boomerang, The, 378
Born Yesterday, 5, 42, 43, 369, 377, 392
Borned in Texas, **313**
Borscht Capades, 27, 30, 33
Both Your Houses, 380, 387
Bottom of the Pile, 43
Boy Meets Girl, 377, 388
Bride of the Lamb, 385
Brief Moment, 387
Brigadoon, 378, 392

Broadway, 378, 385
Brother Rat, 378
Burlesque, 385
Burning Bright, 6, 17, **320**
Butter and Egg Man, The, 385

Call It a Day, 388
Call Me Madam, 6, 14, 16, **319**
Call Me Mister, 377
Candida, 11
Candle in the Wind, 390
Captain Brassbound's Conversion, 9, **338**
Carmen Jones, 378
Carousel, 377
Cellar and the Well, The, 8, **332**
Changelings, The, 384
Charley's Aunt, 19, **346**
Chauve Souris, 378
Cherry Orchard, The, 41
Chicago, 385
Chicken Feed, 384
Children's Hour, The, 125, 306, 377, 388
Chocolate Soldier, The, 35
Christopher Blake, 392
Circle, The, 383
Clarence, 382
Claudia, 43, 377, 390
Climbers, The, 382
Clutterbuck, 43, 376, 393
Clytemnestra, 8
Cocktail Party, The, 31, 376, 393
Come Back, Little Sheba, 27, 29, 32, 36, 40, 393
Command Decision, 392
Constant Wife, The, 385
Consul, The, 18, 27, 29, 312, 376
Coquette, 385
Corn Is Green, The, 42, 390
Country Girl, The, 7, 14, 15, 18, 178, 306, **325**
Country Wife, The, 23
County Chairman, The, 382
Courtin' Time, 14, 22, 26, 30
Cox and Box, 17, **353**
Cradle Song, The, 385
Craig's Wife, 380, 384
Crimes and Crimes, 314
Criminal Code, The, 386
Curious Savage, The, 17, **321**
Cynara, 387

Daisy Mayme, 385
Damask Cheek, The, 306, 391
Dancing Mothers, 384
Daphne Laureola, 5, **314**
Darkness at Noon, 3, 27, 29, 74, 305, 341, 379
Darling of the Gods, The, 382
Daughters of Atreus, 388
Day After Tomorrow, The, 17, **322**
Days to Come, 306
Dead End, 305, 377, 388
Dear Brutus, 16
Dear Ruth, 377, 391
Death of a Salesman, 3, 19, 27, 28, 36, 40, 376, 377, 379, 381, 392
Deburau, 383
Decision, 391
Déclassée, 383
Deep Are the Roots, 391
Desert Song, The, 40
Design for Living, 387
Desire Under the Elms, 384
Detective Story, 38, 378, 392
Devil Passes, The, 387
Devil's Disciple, The, 36, 40
Diamond Lil, 32, 33, 36, 40
Dinner at Eight, 387
Disraeli, 382
Distaff Side, The, 306, 388
Dodsworth, 387
Don Juan in Hell, 37, 41
Doughgirls, The, 377, 390
Dover Road, The, 383
Dream Girl, **369**, 392
Druid Circle, The, 306
Drunkard, The, 44
Duet with Two Hands, 35
Dulcy, 383
Dybbuk, The, 3, 385

Easiest Way, The, 382
East Is West, 377
Eastward in Eden, 392
Ecole des Femmes, L', 11, 22, **359**
Edward, My Son, 393
Edwina Black, 18, 27, **327**
Elizabeth the Queen, 386
Emperor Jones, The, 383
Enchanted, The, 43, 393
End of Summer, 388
Enemy, The, 385
Enemy of the People, An, 3, 9, **339**
Enter Madame, 383

Escape, 385
Ethan Frome, 388
Eve of St. Mark, The, 390
Excursion, 389

Fall Guy, The, 384
Family Portrait, 389
Famous Mrs. Fair, The, 383
Farmer Takes a Wife, The, 388
Farmer's Wife, The, 22
Fatal Weakness, The, 392
Finian's Rainbow, 16, 39, 377
Firebrand, The, 384
First Lady, 388
First Mrs. Fraser, The, 386
First Year, The, 377, 383
Five-Star Final, 386
Flahooley, 12, 26, 30, **370**
Flight to the West, 390
Floradora, 378
Follow the Girls, 377
Fool, The, 383
Foolish Notion, 391
Four Twelves Are 48, 9, 29, **342**
Front Page, 43, 386

Gentlemen Prefer Blondes, 35, 40
George Washington Slept Here, 390
Getting Married, 41, **367**
Giaconda Smile, The, 6, **318**
Glass Menagerie, The, 3, 210, 306, 378, 379, 391
Gold Diggers, The, 377
Golden Boy, 178, 306, 389
Golden State, The, 27, 28, **331**
Gondoliers, The, 17, **350**
Good Fairy, The, 4, 12, **362**
Good Gracious, Annabelle, 382
Good News, 378
Goodbye Again, 43
Goodbye, My Fancy, 393
Goose Hangs High, The, 384
Gramercy Ghost, 22, 27, 30, **366**
Grand Hotel, 387
Great Divide, The, 382
Great God Brown, The, 384
Great Man, The, 42
Green Bay Tree, The, **346,** 388
Green Goddess, The, 383
Green Grow the Lilacs, **372,** 386
Green Hat, The, 385
Green Pastures, The, 11, 20, 21, 27, 29, **358,** 377, 380, 386

Guardsman, The, 27, 30
Guys and Dolls, 3, 8, 12, 26, 28, 31, 37, 45, 304, **329,** 379
Gypsy, 386

Happy Birthday, 378
Happy Time, The, 393
Harriet, 390
Harvey, 43, 377, 380, 391
Hasty Heart, The, 391
Hats Off to Ice, 377
Hay Fever, 23
He Who Gets Slapped, 383
Heaven Help the Angels, 43
Heiress, The, 392
Hell-bent fer Heaven, 380, 384
Hellzapoppin, 377
Henry IV, 23
Her Master's Voice, 387
Here Come the Clowns, 307, 389
Hero, The, 383
High and Dry, 42
High Button Shoes, 377
High Ground, The, **353**
High Tor, 379, 388
Hilda Crane, 7, 27, 28, **323**
H.M.S. Pinafore, 17, **347**
Holiday, 307, 386
Home of the Brave, 391
Hope for a Harvest, 390
Horace, 40
Hotel Universe, 307
House of Bernarda Alba, **340**
House of Connelly, The, 387

I Know My Love, 17, 27, 29, 32, 33, 393
I Love Lydia, 42
I Remember Mama, 306, 377, 391
Icebound, 380, 383
Iceman Cometh, The, 3, 392
Idiot's Delight, **371,** 380, 388
If I Were King, 382
If You Please, 36
Imaginary Invalid, The, 23
In Abraham's Bosom, 380, 385
In Time to Come, 390
Innocent Voyage, The, 391
Innocents, The, 20, 27, 29, 32, 33, 36, 40, 393
Inspector Calls, An, 392
Iolanthe, 17, **351**
Irene, 377

Is Zat So, 377
It's a Great Day, 33
It's About Time, 24

Jacobowsky and the Colonel, 391
Jane Clegg, 383
Janie, 377
Jason, 390
Jealousy, 307
Jest, The, 383
Joan of Lorraine, 40, 392
John Ferguson, 382
John Loves Mary, 392
Johnny Johnson, 388
Journey's End, 386
Julius Caesar, 7, 23, 309
June Moon, 386
Junior Miss, 377, 390

Key Largo, 389
Kibitzer, 305
Kidders, The, 24
Kiki, 378
King and I, The, 3, 12, 14, 21, 360, 379
King Lear, 9, 11, 337
King of Friday's Men, The, 20, 354
King Richard II, 10, 343
Kingdom of God, The, 386
Kiss and Tell, 377, 391
Kiss Me Kate, 15, 16, 27, 28, 36, 40, 377
Kiss the Boys Goodbye, 389
Kitty Doone, 43

Ladder, The, 377
Lady from Paris, The, 26, 28
Lady from the Sea, The, 312
Lady in the Dark, 390
Lady's Not for Burning, The, 7, 14, 18, 27, 30, 31, 324, 379
Last Mile, The, 386
Last of Mrs. Cheyney, The, 385
Last Shift, The, 328
Late Christopher Bean, The, 387
Late Edwina Black, The, 28
Late George Apley, The, 391
Leah Kleshna, 382
L'Ecole des Femmes, 359
Left Bank, The, 387
Legend of Sarah, 6, 27, 28, 318
Lend an Ear, 33, 35
Let Me Hear the Melody, 27, 29

Let Us Be Gay, 386
Let's Face It, 378
Let's Make an Opera, 8, 19, 333
Letters to Lucerne, 390
Life with Father, 377, 389
Life with Mother, 393
Light up the Sky, 43, 393
Lightnin', 377
Liliom, 383
Lion and the Mouse, The, 377
Little Accident, 386
Little Blue Light, The, 12, 23, 24, 366
Little Boy Blue, 42
Little Foxes, The, 306, 389
Little Scandal, 43
Live Wire, The, 5, 43, 313
Long Days, The, 364
Lost Horizons, 388
Lost in the Stars, 32, 33, 35, 39, 376, 393
Love's Labour's Lost, 24
Loyalties, 383
Lute Song, 392

Machinal, 386
Madwoman of Chaillot, The, 5, 38, 40, 308, 392
Magistrate, The, 23
Magnificent Yankee, The, 391
Make a Wish, 4, 12, 26, 29, 362
Male Animal, The, 389
Mamma's Affair, 383
Man, The, 42, 43
Man and Superman, 37, 40
Man from Home, The, 382
Man That Corrupted Hadleyburg, The, 27, 30
Man Who Came to Dinner, The, 377, 389
Margin for Error, 390
Mary of Scotland, 387
Mary Rose, 11, 355, 383
Mary the 3d, 384
Me and Molly, 392
Medium, The, 7, 36, 42, 311
Melody in My Heart, 26
Member of the Wedding, The, 22, 31, 74, 376, 378, 379, 393
Men in White, 305, 380, 387
Merrily We Roll Along, 388
Merry Widow, The, 36, 39
Merton of the Movies, 384
Michael and Mary, 386

Michael Todd's Peep Show, **309**
Mikado, The, 10, 17, **345**
Mike McCauley, 32, 33, 36
Minick, 384
Misalliance, 23
Miss Liberty, 40
Miss Lulu Bett, 380
Mission Play, 44
Mister Roberts, 15, 16, 27, 28, 33, 376, 377, 392
Montserrat, 125, 306
Moon Is Blue, The, 11, 14, 21, 31, 32, 33, **356**
Moon Is Down, The, 390
Morning's at Seven, 390
Mourning Becomes Electra, 387
Mr. Big Shot, 42
Mr. and Mrs. North, 390
Mrs. Bumpstead-Leigh, 382
Mrs. Partridge Presents, 384
Much Ado About Nothing, 43
Mulatto, 7, **324**
Music Master, The, 378
My French Wife, 16
My Sister Eileen, 377, 390

Native Son, 390
Nest, The, 383
New Moon, The, 378
New York Latin Quarter Review, 42
Nice People, 383
Night Music, **361**
No Exit, 23, 35
No More Ladies, 387
No Time for Comedy, 389
Not for Children, 11, **350**

O Mistress Mine, 391
Of Mice and Men, 321, 379, 389
Of Thee I Sing, 6, 380, 387
Oklahoma, 12, 17, 27, 30, 33, **372**, 377, 391
Ol' Man Adam an' His Chillun, **358**, 386
Old Acquaintance, 306
Old Maid, The, 380, 388
Old Soak, The, 384
On Borrowed Time, 389
On the Town, 15
On Trial, 382
Once in a Lifetime, 42, 386
One Foot in Heaven, 43
One Sunday Afternoon, 387

One Touch of Venus, 378
Our Town, 43, 380, 389
Out of This World, 8, 19, 26, 28, **336**
Outrageous Fortune, 391
Outward Bound, 384
Outward Room, The, 305
Over Twenty-one, 16, 391
Overture, 386

Pagan in the Parlor, 43
Panama Hattie, 378
Pardon Our French, 6, 16, **317**
Paris Bound, 306, 385
Parisienne, **312**
Patience, 17
Patriots, The, 305, 379, 390
Payment Deferred, 42
Peep Show, 3, 27, **309**
Peer Gynt, 3, 10, **344**
Peg o' My Heart, 377
Personal Appearance, 378
Peter Pan, 20, 27, 29, 33, 376
Petrified Forest, The, 388
Philadelphia Story, The, 307, 389
Pick-up Girl, 391
Pied Piper of Hamelin, The, 43
Pigeons and People, 387
Pilgrimage Play, 44
Pinafore, 17, **347**
Pins and Needles, 377
Pirates of Penzance, The, 17, **353**
Play's the Thing, The, 385
Plough and the Stars, The, 385
Porgy, 385
Present Laughter, 43
Pride and Prejudice, 388
Pride's Crossing, **326**
Prologue to Glory, 389
Punch for Judy, A, 307

Racket, The, 385
Rain, 23, 377, 383
Ramona, 44
Razzle Dazzle, 7, **352**
Rebound, 386
Red Mill, The, 378
Red, White and Blue, 32, 33, 42
Regina, 39
Relapse, The, 8, 24, 27, 28, **328**
Reunion in Vienna, 387
Ring Round the Moon, 8, 18, **329**
Rio Rita, 40
Rivals, The, 42

Road to Rome, The, 385
Roaring Girl, The, 24
Rocket to the Moon, 178, 389
Romance, 382
Romeo and Juliet, 11, 21, **356**
Room Service, 378
Rosalinda, 378
Rose Marie, 35, 39, 378
Rose Tattoo, The, 10, 31, 33, 210, 306,
347
Royal Family, The, 9, **341**, 385
R.U.R., 384
Rugged Path, The, 392

Sailor, Beware, 378
Saint Helena, 388
Sally, 378
Saturday's Children, 385
School for Scandal, The, 42
Searching Wind, The, 306, 391
Season in the Sun, 6, 14, 16, 237, 307,
317
Second Man, The, 15, 42
Second Threshold, 9, 19, 283, 307, **339**
See How They Run, 43
Separate Rooms, 378
Seven Keys to Baldpate, 382
Seventeen, 14, 22
Seventh Heaven, 377
Shadow and Substance, 389
She Stoops to Conquer, 41
Shining Hour, The, 388
Show Boat, 378
Show-Off, The, 378, 384
Shuffle Along, 378
Silver Cord, The, 385
Silver Whistle, The, 43, 393
Six Characters in Search of an Author,
23
Six Cylinder Love, 383
Skin Game, The, 383
Skin of Our Teeth, The, 380, 390
Skipper Next to God, 392
Skylark, 389
Small Hours, The, 11, **351**
Society Circus, A, 378
Soldier's Wife, 391
Song of Norway, 377
Sons o' Fun, 377
South Pacific, 5, 21, 31, 32, 33, 35, 39,
377, 381
Southern Exposure, **315**
Springboard to Nowhere, 32, 33

Springtime Folly, 11, **354**
Springtime for Henry, 11, 27, 29, **357**
Square Needle, The, 35, 41
Squaw Man, The, 382
Stage Door, 388
Stalag 17, 12, **368**
Star and Garter, 378
Star Wagon, The, 389
Stars on Ice, 377
State of the Union, 377, 381, 391
Storm Operation, 391
Story for a Sunday Evening, A, **326**
Story of Mary Surratt, The, 392
Strange Interlude, 380, 385
Street Scene, 378, 380, 386
Streetcar Named Desire, A, 19, 27, 28,
33, 210, 306, 377, 379, 381, 392
Strictly Dishonorable, 36, 40, 378, 386
Strictly Informal, 35
Student Prince, The, 378
Summer and Smoke, 40, 43, 210
Sunny, 378
Sun-Up, 384
Susan and God, 389
Swan, The, 384
Sweet and Low, 24

Taming of the Shrew, The, **365**
Tarnish, 384
Tartuffe, 23, 41
Telephone, The, 7, 36, 42, **311**
Ten Million Ghosts, 305
Texas, Li'l Darlin', 32, 33
There Shall Be No Night, 380, 389
There's Always Juliet, 306
They Knew What They Wanted, 380,
384
They Shall Not Die, 387
Three Men on a Horse, 377
Three Sisters, The, 23
Three Wishes for Jamie, 37
Ti-Coq, 10, 31, 33, **348**
Tickets, Please, 376
Till the Day I Die, 178
Time of Your Life, The, 379, 380, 389
Tobacco Road, 377
Tomorrow and Tomorrow, 386
Tomorrow the World, 6, 378, 390
Tovarich, 389
Tower Beyond Tragedy, The, 8, **331**
Tree Grows in Brooklyn, A, 3, 12, 26,
30, **363**
Trial by Jury, 17, **347**

Trio, 35
Trip to Chinatown, A, 377 .
Twelfth Night, 41
Twentieth Century, 9, **337**
Two Blind Mice, 33, 393
Two Mrs. Carrolls, The, 378
Two on the Aisle, 27

Unchastened Woman, The, 382
Uncle Harry, 390
Uniform of Flesh, 100
Up in Central Park, 378

Vagabond King, The, 42, 378
Valley Forge, 388
Verve Folle, La., 307
Victoria Regina, 378, 388
Virtue in Danger, 8, **328**
Voice of the Turtle, The, 306, 377, 391

Waiting for Lefty, 178, 306
Watch on the Rhine, 306, 379, 390
We, the People, 387
Wedding Bells, 383
Wednesday's Child, 388
What a Life, 378, 389
What Every Woman Knows, 42
What Price Glory, 384
When Ladies Meet, 387
Where's Charley, 10, 19, 36, 39, 304,
  346, 376, 377

White Cargo, 377
White Steed, The, 389
White Wings, 307
Why Marry, 380, 382
Why Not, 384
Wild Birds, 384
Wind Without Rain, 42
Winged Victory, 391
Wings over Europe, 386
Winslow Boy, The, 40, 392
Winter Soldiers, 390
Winterset, 379, 388
Wisdom Tooth, The, 385
Wisteria Trees, The, 376, 393
Witching Hour, The, 382
Within the Law, 378
Without Love, 307
Women, The, 377, 388
World We Make, The, 305, 389

Years Ago, 392
Yes, M' Lord, 23
Yes, My Darling Daughter, 389
You and I, 383
You Can't Take It with You, 42, 377,
  380, 388
Young Woodley, 306, 385
Youngest, The, 384

Ziegfeld Follies, 378
Zuleika Dobson, 237

INDEX OF PRODUCERS, DIRECTORS AND DESIGNERS

Abbott, George, 17, 320, 336, 363, 364
Actman, Irving, 330
Actors' Album, 41
Adams, Peter, 41
Adoue, Tad, 315
Aldrich & Myers, 342, 356
Alswang, Ralph, 309, 319, 327, 333, 338
Altabell, Leonard, 355
American Legion, 32, 42
American National Theatre and Academy, 4, 8, 9, 11, 12, 22, 24, 41, 331, 332, 337
Ames, Harriet, 312, 313, 323
Anderson, Judith, 332
Armitage, Buford, 326, 337, 368
Aronson, Boris, 325, 347
Association of Theatrical Press Agents and Managers, 4
Atlantis Productions, 324
Austin, Frances, 41
Ayers, Lemuel, 9, 336, 372

Band, Albert, 41
Barr, Kenn, 316, 342, 362
Barr, Richard, 321
Barry, Fred, 348
Barry, Philip, Jr., 327, 340
Bay, Howard, 311, 312, 313, 314, 323, 356, 371
Bérard, Christian, 360
Bernstein, Aline, 320, 333, 339, 355
Bettis, Valerie, 345
Bishop, Ward, 336
Blackton, Jay, 320, 364
Blankenchip, John E., 343
Blitstein, Marc, 333, 338
Bloomgarden, Kermit, 318, 355
Bogdanoff, Rose, 345, 347
Bolger, Ray, 19
Boroff, George, 42
Boston Summer Theatre, 15
Brandt, George, 357

Brattle Theatre Company, 22, 23, 24, 41, 329, 367
Breen, Robert, 331
Bromley, Harald, 357
Brown, Elmer, 315
Burch, Ramsey, 362
Burns, Richard, 362
Burr, Courtney, 237, 317

Callas, May, 313, 314
Capp, Al, 15
Capp, Madeline, 352
Cappy, Ted, 329
Carroll, Earl, 38
Castillo, 329, 332
Caubisens, Henri, 330
Chambers, William, 331
Champion, Gower, 363
Chandler, Thelma, 339, 344, 366
Chaney, Stewart, 340, 354, 356
Circle Players, 41
Clark, Bobby, 311
Clark, Peggy, 353
Clark, Roger, 366
Clurman, Harold, 356
Cohen, Alexander H., 337, 363
Coletti, Frank, 334
Collier, Constance, 41
Colt, Alvin, 330
Colvil, Alison, 324
Compagnie Dramatique Française des Tournées, 359
Condell, H. A., 324, 357
Condon, Richard, 337, 368
Connelly, Marc, 359
Cookson, Peter, 366
Cooper, Theodore, 326
Cornell, John, 361
Council of the Living Theatre, 4
Cowles, Chandler, 100, 311, 349
Crabtree, Paul, 326
Crawford, Cheryl, 331, 344, 347, 370

Cronyn, Hume, 323, 366
Crump, Owen, 42

Da Costa, Morton, 339, 369
Davenport, Pembroke, 336
de Belleval, Jean Fournier, 348
De Launey, Ralph, 347
de Liagre, Alfred, Jr., 155, 308, 339, 340
de Mille, Agnes, 336, 372
Del Mar, Norman, 8, 333
Denham, Reginald, 366
Doolittle, James A., 42
Doscher, Richard, 357
Dowling, Eddie, 31, 32, 343
D'Oyly Carte Opera Company, 10, 17, 27, 29, 33, 345, 346, 347, 350, 351, 353
du Bois, Raoul Pène, 320, 363
Dufy, Raoul, 329
du Pont, Paul, 312, 313, 314
Dvonch, Frederick, 361

Edwards, Ben, 319, 339, 341, 344, 366
Effrat, John, 342, 356
Eggleston, Larry, 316
Elder, Eldon, 365, 369, 372
Eley, Robert T., 35
Engel Lehman, 334
Equity Library Theatre, 361
Evans, Eleanor, 345
Evans, Maurice, 10, 36, 40, 339
Ewing, Marjorie and Sherman, 367
Experimental Theatre, 100

Falk, Lee, 15
Farrell, Anthony Brady, 100, 343, 349
Feder, 318, 332
Ferrer, José, 337, 368
Ferrer, Mel, 43
Festival Productions, 23
Feuer, Cy, and Ernest H. Martin, 329, 346
Ffolkes, David, 357, 371
Fields, Lew, 26
Fischer, Nelle, 352
Flamm, Donald, 327
Fleischmann, Julius, 342, 356
Foley, Paul A., 323, 367
Forsythe, Henderson, 332
Fox, Frederick, 75, 316, 342, 362
Frankel, Beulah, 309

Frankel, Evan M., 366
Frederick, Burry, 328
Freedley, George, 332
Freedley, Vinton, 26
Fridolin Productions, 348
Fromkes, Harry, 358
Frye, Peter, 367
Fryer, Robert, 364
Furse, Roger, 314

Gibson, Alice, 352
Gibson, Chloe, 327
Gielgud, John, 324
Gilbert, Edward, 322
Glenville, Peter, 322, 357
Godfrey, Isidore, 345
Goldman, William, 28
Good, Kip, 313
Gordon, Max, 26, 351
Grace, Michael, 354
Gregory, Paul, 41
Griffith, Robert, 320
Group Theatre, 306, 362
Gurian, Manning, 315

Habib, George, 312, 313
Hagerman, James, 357
Haggott, John, 315
Halpern, Mortimer, 333
Hambleton, T. Edward, 326
Hammerstein, Oscar, II, 320, 360
Hammerstein, Ted, 311
Harburg, E. Y., 370, 371
Hardwicke, Cedric, 41
Harris, Jed, 341, 347
Hastings, Philippa, 316
Hayden, Terese, 312, 313
Hayes, Helen, 11, 355
Hayward, Leland, 15, 17, 314, 319
Heilweil, David, 6, 309, 311, 321, 352
Heller, Paul M., 343
Herlin, Marthe, 360
Hickman, Charles, 316
Hollywood Actors' Company, 41
Holm, Hanya, 336
Houghton, Norris, 349
Houseman, John, 338
Houston, Grace, 331
Hover, Herman D., 38
Hughes, Del, 356
Humphrey, Doris, 324
Hunter, Mary, 24

Jackson, Scott, 350, 369
Jacoves, Felix, 353
James, Morgan O'Brien, 309
James, Spencer, 316
Jenkins, Dorothy, 315, 338
Jenkins, George, 322, 326
Johnson, Albert, 317
Johnson, Greer, 352
Johnson, Hall, 359
Johnson, William, 341
Johnstone, Anna Hill, 322, 325, 326, 356
Jones, Margo, 315, 316
Jones, Robert Edmond, 359
Joseph, Robert L., 337
Jouvet, Louis, 11, 22, 360

Kanin, Garson, 313
Kaplan, Saul, 20
Kass, Peter, 362
Kaufman, George S., 45, 330, 352
Kennedy, Harold J., 38, 39, 40, 41
Kennel, Louis, 355
Kerz, Leo, 327
Kidd, Michael, 330
King, Clinton, 321
Kingsley, Sidney, 342
Kirshner, May, 342
Krakeur, Richard W., 315
Kranz, Ben D., 329, 359

La Jolla Playhouse, Inc., 43
Landau, Jack, 355
Larson, John, 343
Laughton, Charles, 41
Lawrence, Bea, 347
Lawrence, Lawrence Shubert, 28, 30
Lawrence, Peter, 333
League of New York Theatres, 4
Lee, Auriol, 156
Leontovich, Leonie, 41
Lester, Edwin, 36
Levin, Dan, 309
Levin, Herman, 334
Levine, Maurice, 371
Levy, Benn W., 319
Lewis & Young, 321
Lewis, Robert, 339
Lewis, Windsor, 320, 354
Lloyd, John Robert, 368
Lonsdale, Frederick, 322
Los Angeles Light Opera Association, 34, 39

Ludlum, Edward, 365
Lynn-Thomas, Derrick, 6, 309, 311, 321, 352

MacDonald, Jeanette, 30
Macdonald, Murray, 314
Magee, Joe, 366
Main Bocher, 320, 350
Maley, Edward G., 35
Mamoulian, Rouben, 39, 372
Mann, Daniel, 347
Mann, Gene, 39, 42
Mansfield, Lawrence, 355
Manulis, Martin, 327, 366
Margulies, Bob, 349
Marlin, Max, 369
Marlowe, Arthur, 357
Marre, Albert, 328, 367
Martin, Ernest H., 329, 346
McClintic, Guthrie, 320
McDermott, William, 312
McGuire, Dorothy, 43
McHugh, Edward, 322, 338
Meeker, Jesse, 320
Menotti, Gian-Carlo, 312
Messel, Oliver, 324, 357
Michel, Leon, 355
Michel, Trudi, 362
Mielziner, Jo, 320, 330, 361, 364
Miller, Gilbert, 329
Miller, Yola, 371
Mitchell, Ruth, 361
Montgomery, Patricia, 326
Morgan, Miles, 328
Morley, Ruth, 332, 349, 362, 365
Morrison, Paul, 315, 321, 332, 349, 367
Morrison, Peggy, 342
Mosser, Jack, 317
Murray, Dennis, 317
Myerberg, Michael, 323

New York City Center of Music and Drama, 5, 9, 10
New York City Theatre Company, 338, 341, 343, 365, 369, 371
Nichols, Dudley, 42
Nordenson, Lars, 339

Odets, Clifford, 325
Oenslager, Donald, 313, 340, 345, 352
O'Hearn, Robert, 328
Olney, Joseph, 352

Olsen and Johnson, 6, 16, 317
Owen, Terence, 314

Pardoll, David M., 312, 367
Parlowin, Gene, 365
Pasadena Playhouse, 43
Patrick, Leonard, 319
Paul, John, 324
Pearson, Malcolm, 317
Peck, Gregory, 43
Peter Dabney Productions, Ltd., 327
Phillips, Thomas, 328
Playwrights Company, 11, 341, 350
Polakov, Lester, 331, 367
Preminger, Otto, 342, 356
Prinz, Le Roy, 42

Quayle, Anthony, 328
Quintus Productions, 366

Ramsdell, Roger, 314
Rennie, Hugh, 327, 366
Reveaux, Edward, 352
Rice, Elmer, 350
Rickard, Gwen, 346
Ricketts, Charles, 345
Rigby, Harry, 363
Ritchard, Cyril, 328
Rittman, Trude, 361
Riva, William, 312, 352
Robbins, Jerome, 320, 360
Roche, Emeline, 341, 366, 369, 372
Rodgers, Richard, 320, 360
Rogers, Emmett, 344
Root, John, 350
Rosen, Alfred H., 353
Rosenstock, Milton, 363
Ross, Bill, 318, 347, 362
Ross, Herbert, 364
Ross, Robert, 332
Roth, Wolfgang, 332, 337

Sadler's Wells Ballet, 20, 33, 42
Saidy, Fred, 370, 371
Samrock, Victor, 323
San Francisco Light Opera Association, 34
San Francisco Repertory Company, 35
Sater, William, Jr., 312, 313
Schaefer, George, 339, 341, 344, 369, 372
Schwab and Mandel, 26
Schwartz, Arthur, 323

Segal, Benet, 349
Selznick, Irene Mayer, 155, 325
Sharaf, Irene, 311, 361
Sherwood, Robert E., 4
Short, Hassard, 311
Show-of-the-Month Club, 333
Shubert, Lee and J. J., 13, 322, 348
Shumlin, Herman, 10, 100, 314, 353
Simon, Robert F., 339
Sloane, Mike, 42
Smith, Hardy William, 322
Smith, Oliver, 334
Sola, John E., 325
Sovey, Raymond, 329, 342, 347, 366
Spector, Joel, 323
Spewack, Bella and Samuel, 331
Starbuck, James, 311
Stevens, R. L., 332, 344
Stix, John, 314, 355
Stone, Paula, 42
Strasberg, Lee, 345
Sturges, Preston, 42
Styne, Jule, 363
Subber, Saint, 336
Sukman, Harry, 317
Sutherland, Mildred, 327

Tait-Buell, 364
Tamiris, Helen, 334, 371
Taylor, Noel, 368
Tennent Productions, Ltd., 324
Thayer, Forrest, 313
Theatre Guild, 17, 24, 28, 31, 32, 34, 306, 321, 324, 328, 368, 372
Thomas, Milo, 1st, 326
Thompson, Archie, 363
Todd, Michael, 5, 27, 309, 313
Traube, Shepard, 318, 346, 347
Trio Productions, 326
Tumarin, Boris, 340
Turner, Lily, 340

United Producers, 354

Valentina, 326
Van Druten, John, 326, 360
Vega, José, 326
Verneuil, Louis, 259, 307, 315
Victor, Lucia, 355
Von Kantzow, Elfi, 327

Wakhevitch, Georges, 8, 329
Walker, Natalie Barth, 316
Wanamaker, Sam, 312, 313, 314

Warnick, Clay, 311
Webster, Margaret, 10, 344, 365, 366
Weidman, Charles, 324
Weinstein, David Sidney, 372
Welles, Orson, 309
Whale, James, 43
White, Miles, 334, 372
Whitehead, Robert, 24
Whorf, Richard, 341

Whyte, Jerome, 361, 372
Wigreen Company, 358
Wildberg, John C., 316
Wilson, John C., 324, 334, 363
Wiman, Dwight Deere, 20, 325, 356, 358

Ziegfeld, Florenz, 26
Zipper, Herbert, 324